DISCARDED

D0221438

DISCARDED

IMMIGRATION

IMMIGRATION

A Documentary and Reference Guide

Edited by *Thomas Cieslik, David Felsen,*
and Akis Kalaitzidis

Greenwood Press

Westport, Connecticut • London

Library of Congress Cataloging-in-Publication Data

Cieslik, Thomas, 1972–
    Immigration : a documentary and reference guide / edited by Thomas Cieslik, David
Felsen, and Akis Kalaitzidis.
        p. cm.
    Includes bibliographical references and index.
    ISBN 978-0-313-34910-2 (alk. paper)
    1. United States—Emigration and immigration. 2. United States—Politics and
government. I. Felsen, David. II. Kalaitzidis, Akis, 1969- III. Title.
JV6465.C54 2009
325.73—dc22   2008029139

British Library Cataloguing in Publication Data is available.

Copyright © 2009 by Thomas Cieslik, David Felsen, and Akis Kalaitzidis

All rights reserved. No portion of this book may be
reproduced, by any process or technique, without the
express written consent of the publisher.

Library of Congress Catalog Card Number: 2008029139
ISBN: 978-0-313-34910-2

First published in 2009

Greenwood Press, 88 Post Road West, Westport, CT 06881
An imprint of Greenwood Publishing Group, Inc.
www.greenwood.com

Printed in the United States of America

The paper used in this book complies with the
Permanent Paper Standard issued by the National
Information Standards Organization (Z39.48–1984).

10 9 8 7 6 5 4 3 2 1

Contents

Reader's Guide to Documents and Sidebars

Note: Many documents appear in more than one category. Documents and sidebars are listed within each category in the order in which they appear.

Addresses and Statements

Legal Status and Citizenship

Mexico and Central and South America

Nativism

Political Platforms and Positions

Preferences

Pro-Immigration Commentary

Quotas

Acknowledgments

The authors thank Sandy Towers and her colleagues at Greenwood Press for their encouragement and hard work in helping us complete this project. Thanks also to Hilary Claggett for her initial encouragement and assistance in the early development of this book.

In addition, we recognize the tremendous support of our colleagues at our respective institutions. Dr. Thomas Cieslik thanks Dr. Claus Gramckow and the other staff at the Friedrich Naumann Foundations of Mexico City and Washington, D.C., for their support. Dr. David Felsen thanks his colleagues at the Marshall Goldsmith School of Management, Alliant International University for their encouragement and support of his research activity, especially Dr. Louise Kelly, Associate Dean Fred Phillips, and Dean Jim Goodrich. Dr. Akis Kalaitzidis thanks colleagues Jim Staab, Shari Bax, Gregory Streich, Darlene Bud, and Henry Wambuii of the Department of Political Science at the University of Central Missouri for their support and enthusiasm for his project.

We also recognize the enormous efforts of our research assistants and thank them for their diligence and hard work, notably Evgenia Lobkova, Elisabeth Maigler, Sara Santarelli, Wilbur Liverly, Scott Keiffer, David Bock, Orlando Diaz, Ming Fong, and Mariya Petrosyan. A special thanks also to Bruce Harley, librarian at San Diego State University, for his very helpful assistance with materials. In addition, we thank Dr. Tom Gold, Dr. Michael Hait, Dr. Gregory Streich, and Ray Guerrero for taking the time to read and comment on parts of the manuscript.

Last, but not least, we acknowledge our families' unwavering patience, love, and support during this undertaking. Dr. Cieslik thanks his wife, Denisse, and his new daughter, Charlotte. Dr. Felsen thanks his wife, Rosa Maria, and his son, Emilio. Dr. Kalaitzidis thanks his wife, Peggy, and his sons Miltos, Alex, and Jason. We dedicate this work to them.

Introduction

David Felsen

In the past few years the debate over immigration to the United States has become more shrill and has ignited a great deal of passion. At the same time, the issues involved have become more complex than ever. The controversy today focuses on the presence of the millions of undocumented workers in the country who live and work in the shadow economy, the divisive discussion of the potential security risk posed by uncontrolled and unchecked immigration, and by what some view as a cultural threat posed by foreigners who resist integration into mainstream American culture.

Since the events of September 11, 2001, immigration has become inextricably tied to the question of U.S. national security. Following the terrorist attacks, Americans consistently have demanded that the federal government plug the holes in U.S. border security. The presence in the country of a large number of undocumented workers who have crossed without proper papers reminds citizens of just how vulnerable the American borders remain. If so many millions of undocumented workers from Mexico and elsewhere can cross into the United States undetected, the government and citizens alike fear terrorist elements planning harm to the country can do the same. In short, the insecurity of Americans and the greater challenges that law enforcement faces in monitoring the borders have fanned the flames of anti-immigrant sentiment.

One unfortunate consequence of the rising collective preoccupation with security and immigration is the perceptible growth in racism and intolerance toward minority groups. In a 2005 study by the Council on American-Islamic Relations in Washington, D.C., it was reported that, since 9/11, Americans of the Muslim faith have experienced an increase in racial attacks and have felt less at home in the United States (Parry 2005). On the evidence of a 2007 Federal Bureau of Investigation annual survey on hate crimes, Latinos, who now comprise the largest minority group inside the country, have also experienced a rise in racist attacks. Unfortunately, this comes as no surprise, because the greatest number of undocumented workers come from Mexico and other Latin American countries. The resultant rise of intolerance, however, has adversely impacted not only these undocumented workers but also permanent residents and U.S.-born Mexican Americans.

The immigration issue has the potential of giving rise in the longer term to more difficult relations among the many groups that make up the fabric of U.S. society. Political leaders from the two major political parties, the Republicans and the Democrats, remain uncertain about how to position themselves on the immigration debate. Early in his first administration, before September 11, President George W. Bush actively sought to work with his Mexican counterpart, Vicente Fox, on immigration initiatives such as a guest worker program. A former "border governor" (of Texas), President Bush appeared to grasp U.S.-Mexican relations better than most. Moreover, the Bush campaign of 2000 managed to make significant inroads among Hispanic voters. A sympathetic view concerning the immigration issue was shared by Democrats, too.

By the beginning of the 2008 presidential campaign, the leading Republican candidates had largely turned their backs on Hispanics and their attention to addressing the fears of angry voters. The candidates brandished their tough credentials on border security and promised not to be "soft" on immigration. Even John McCain, the senator who had just cosponsored comprehensive reform legislation that would have included a temporary worker program and a path to legalization (legislation that eventually failed), touted his strong stance on border security. The Republican Party candidates pursued this tack despite warnings from strategists inside the party to avoid pandering to radical anti-immigrant grassroots activists and to focus on courting Hispanics for the sake of the party's future, given that the Hispanic population is growing and that they share the same family-oriented views as Republicans (Rutenberg 2007).

Inside the Democratic Party, considered the more inclusive of the two major American political parties, the mood is also not overwhelmingly supportive of immigration. Trade union activists inside the party have demanded curbs on illegal crossings into the country because of the downward pressure placed on wages by undocumented workers. Rank and file workers and various minority groups inside the party have also come out against both legal and undocumented immigrants. Many Democrats also seek to better protect American workers from skilled foreign workers, allowed into the United States on nonresident work visas, arguing that these jobs should go to Americans. In the wake of the current economic downturn, immigration has become a more pressing economic issue, with candidates making promises not only to control immigration to the United States but also to revisit trade treaties such as the North American Free Trade Agreement (NAFTA). When asked directly about immigration by their constituents, leading Democrats were wary of taking positions that would show sympathy for undocumented workers. When then-Governor Eliot Spitzer of New York proposed allowing undocumented workers to obtain driver's licenses in 2007, he was forced to beat a hasty retreat, facing opposition from congressional Democratic leaders.

In contrast, business leaders continue to push the government to admit more nonresident skilled workers into the country. Firms are becoming increasingly worried about filling jobs that require engineering degrees, computer skills, and specialized scientific and technical training. These are areas in which American colleges are not producing sufficient graduates, and high-tech companies increasingly depend on skilled workers with specialized visas to fill the gaps. Yet these visas, argue business leaders, have been reduced just when the United States requires more of them. Microsoft Chairman Bill Gates repeatedly has warned that the government needs to grant more highly skilled visas or risk losing its status as a global leader in technological innovation (Romano 2008).

Local state governments have also been taking matters into their own hands since the failure of comprehensive immigration reform. Hazleton and Escondidco attempted to pass ordinances forbidding landlords from renting to individuals who cannot produce social security numbers. Other laws aim to deny health care benefits, education, and other benefits to undocumented workers. Local ordinances have been successfully challenged by the American Civil Liberties Union (Spagat 2006). These actions are symptomatic both of Americans' growing intolerance of individuals who seem to have been able to evade American border controls and laws with such ease, and the frustration at the federal government's inability to find solutions.

At the time of writing, the rhetoric is hardening on both sides. Both "pro-immigrant" and "anti-immigrant" groups remain mobilized. Right-wing talk radio is awash with warnings against the granting of any sort of "amnesty" to "illegal immigrants," while right-wing militias, most notably the Minute Men, offer their services to the border patrol to help guard the frontiers. This strong anti-immigration sentiment manifests itself in anti-Hispanic vitriol and has prompted reaction in support of and in defense of these workers. Pro-immigrant groups have staged mass demonstrations in the country's largest cities to show support for legislation that offers a path to citizenship. The debate has become heated, intense, and racially infused. Time will tell if the rhetoric and tensions surrounding the immigration issue will dissipate or worsen.

This documentary and reference guide presents material to help the reader understand the historical context of the immigration debate in the United States, the cyclical nature of the debate, and the different sides of the immigration issue in this country. This text does not try to offer policy prescriptions, nor does it attempt to answer all of the questions concerning immigration. Instead, this book will present, for the most part, primary sources that will assist in shedding light on the historical, social, political, legal, economic, and cultural aspects of the immigration discussion in the United States.

Each chapter will present documents that help elucidate a particular historical period or current theme and provide a brief analysis of the documentation and its context. The chapters also provide some suggested references, readings, and Internet materials for readers.

The chapters of Part I follow a chronological pattern. Chapters 1, 2, and 3 offer historical immigration documents and a historical discussion of immigration from the colonial period to the early 1900s and World War I. The chapters highlight the various cyclical episodes of anti-immigrant sentiment that have occurred during U.S. history. Chapters 4 and 5 examine the immigration debate during the post-World War I period, the Great Depression, and during the early post-World War II era. Particular attention is paid to how immigration policy changes were reflected in the economic circumstances confronting the United States in the first half of the twentieth century.

Chapter 6 looks at documents surrounding the landmark changes to immigration policy in the 1960s that did away with the quota system and introduced a preference-based system. Chapter 7 examines documents that deal with the heated immigration debate environment of the 1980s and 1990s, a period that witnessed an amnesty on undocumented workers during the Reagan years as well as significantly increased immigration flows in the 1990s.

Chapter 8 includes documents pertaining to the immigration debate following the September 11 attacks. It looks at the securitization of immigration debate and specifically the linkage between immigration and American border security.

The chapters of Part II take up specific aspects of the contemporary immigration debate. Chapter 9 looks specifically at the debate over Mexican immigration, since Mexicans constitute the single largest immigrant group arriving in the United States. Chapter 10 looks at documents that pertain to growing U.S. border security in recent years. Chapters 11 and 12, respectively, present documents that help elucidate the judicial and economic aspects of immigration to the United States. Finally, Chapter 13 examines how immigration has figured as a political issue in the 2008 presidential campaign in the United States.

PART I

CHAPTER 1

Immigration from Colonial Times to the Revolution

David Felsen

During the colonial period, a disparate array of settlers representing different religions, nationalities, and linguistic groups came to the New World. In contrast to other continental European powers, notably Spain and France, the British permitted both British and non-British immigrants and members of different faiths to settle. With fewer restrictions barring immigration to British North America, British colonial economies developed faster than other colonies, and self-governing colonial institutions emerged more rapidly.

EARLY IMMIGRATION TO BRITISH NORTH AMERICA

Spain's exploitation of the territories and peoples of the New World proceeded quickly following the 1492 voyage of Christopher Columbus. By 1521 Cortes had successfully laid siege to Tenochtitlan and had subdued the Aztec Empire. A decade later, in 1531, Francisco Pizarro had conquered the Inca Empire of Peru. Together, the Spanish Crown, the powerful Roman Catholic Church, and the ambitious Spanish aristocracy pursued a policy of repressing the indigenous inhabitants and forcibly converting them to Catholicism. The mining of gold and silver for enrichment and the conversion of the indigenous population became the main thrust of Spanish colonial policy throughout the 1500s and 1600s. The establishment of permanent settlements was of secondary importance, and those who were admitted to settle the New World needed to profess loyalty to the Catholic faith.

To protect colonial interests, Spain eschewed foreign trade for fear of enabling others to accrue wealth that ought, to go to the Spanish Crown. Hence, Spanish colonial policy did not encourage immigration but rather guaranteed that political and social structures of its colonies would remain centralized and hierarchical, and ensured that Spain's territories would remain closed and dependent on the Crown.

Similarly, French colonial policy was not geared toward large-scale immigration, and non-Catholics were unwelcome in New France. While famous explorers such as Giovanni da

TABLE 1.1 Ethno-Linguistic Backgrounds of United States Free Citizens, 1790

	E	S	I	G	D	F	Sw	Other	Total
Maine	60.0	4.5	11.7	1.3	0.1	1.3	–	21.1	100.0
New Hamp.	61.0	6.2	7.5	0.4	0.1	0.7	–	24.1	100.0
Vermont	76.0	5.1	5.1	0.2	0.6	0.4	–	12.6	100.0
Mass.	82.0	4.4	3.9	0.2	0.6	0.4	–	8.4	100.0
Rhode Island	71.0	5.8	2.8	0.5	0.4	0.8	0.1	18.6	100.0
Connecticut	67.0	2.2	2.9	0.3	0.3	0.9	–	26.4	100.0
New York	52.0	7.0	8.1	8.2	17.5	3.8	0.5	2.9	100.0
New Jersey	47.0	7.7	9.5	9.2	16.6	2.4	3.9	3.7	100.0
Pennsylvania	35.3	8.6	14.5	33.3	1.8	1.8	0.8	3.9	100.0
Delaware	60.0	8.0	11.7	1.1	4.3	1.6	8.9	4.1	100.0
Maryland/DC	64.5	7.6	12.3	11.7	0.5	1.2	0.5	1.7	100.0
Virginia/West	68.5	10.2	11.7	6.3	0.3	1.5	0.6	0.9	100.0
North Carolina	66.0	14.8	11.1	4.7	0.3	1.7	0.2	1.2	100.0
South Carolina	60.2	15.1	13.8	5.0	0.4	3.9	0.2	1.4	100.0
Georgia	57.4	15.5	15.3	7.6	0.2	2.3	0.6	1.1	100.0
Total US	60.1	8.1	9.5	8.6	3.1	2.3	0.7	7.6	100.0

Source: Roger Daniels, *Coming to America: A History of Immigration and Ethnicity in American Life,* 2nd ed. (New York: Perennial/Harper Collins, 2002), 67–68.

Key: E = English; S = Scotch; I = Irish; G = German; D = Dutch; F = French; Sw = Swedish.

Verrazano, who traveled from Florida north to Newfoundland in 1524, and Jacques Cartier, who sailed up the St. Lawrence River in 1534, flew under the flag of France and received the financial support of the French Crown, most early French subjects who came to the New World as fur traders were principally interested in selling their goods back in France and elsewhere on the continent. There were also representatives of the Church, notably the Jesuits, who came to French North America to set up outposts to convert indigenous peoples. It was as late as 1663 that New France (Quebec) only became a royal colony, well over one hundred years after the first explorations. By 1760, on the eve of the American Revolution, New France had only 85,000 colonists against the well over two million colonists who were present in the thirteen colonies.

British North American colonies grew more quickly because they demonstrated greater tolerance toward religious difference. The enlightened colonial policy toward religion was due in large part to the fact that the Church of England earlier had broken with the Catholic Church in Rome. Although that did not mean that British North America was free of religious tensions, it very early experienced religious pluralism, and demonstrated respect for freedom of worship. In addition, there was a great degree of encouragement on the part of Britain of colonial settlement and economic development.

Throughout the 1600s and 1700s, British colonial policy continued to reflect economic pragmatism. Different religious, linguistic, and ethnic groups were attracted to British North America for its openness. Many persecuted religious groups and repressed minorities found a haven in the New World. French Protestants, the Huguenots, found refuge during France's anti-Protestant backlash. British Puritans, pacifist Quakers from Europe, Catholics, and Jews all came to British North America without being hindered by British authorities. For instance, Plymouth colony was founded in 1620 by Anglican dissidents; Massachusetts, Connecticut, and Rhode Island were founded by other Puritan groups. Pennsylvania was founded by the Quaker William Penn. Maryland was founded by a Catholic aristocrat, Lord Baltimore, who wanted the territory to be open to all faiths and a model for healing religious strife (Proper 1900, 57–59).

This greater toleration for religious pluralism gave rise to an important document in American colonial history, the Maryland Toleration Act of 1649. (See Document 1.) This forward-looking document, passed by the Maryland Assembly, was enacted just four decades after the first settlement was established in British North America. Both Lord Baltimore and the Maryland assembly wanted to further religious toleration and foster a stable political environment that would be conducive to economic growth and development. The act explicitly links good government to religious toleration by stating in the second-to-last paragraph that "the enforcing of the conscience in matters of Religion hath frequently fallen out to be of dangerous Consequence in those commonwealths where it hath been practiced."

The act sanctions strong penalties for "whatsoever person or persons shall from henceforth use or utter any reproachful words or Speeches concerning the blessed Virgin Mary the Mother of our Savior or the holy Apostles or Evangelists or any of them," a warning to those who would publicly display anti-Catholic attitudes. The document cautions colonists to be respectful to a host of other minorities living in Maryland, stating that persons who seek "to wrong, disturb, trouble, or molest any person whatsoever within this Province professing to believe in Jesus Christ for or in respect of his or her religion or the free exercise thereof" will be punished.

Because Maryland's openness was not shared by other colonial authorities, this act stands out as a remarkable document for its era and espouses a position of tolerance for religious pluralism that was ahead of its age, auguring well for America's future openness to religious pluralism and a country open to different peoples from around the globe.

COLONIAL ERA IMMIGRATION IN THE 1700s

Colonial America witnessed settlement by different religious and cultural groups. During the 1700s there was a significant increase in immigration by many non-Protestant and non-English speaking groups to British North America. In this period, just under of one million people settled in the American colonies. A large proportion of these were Scottish, Irish, German, and French Protestants. Many of the settlers brought with them traditional attitudes. For instance, the Protestant Scots-Irish immigrants from war-ravaged Ulster were extremely anti-Catholic. Many set sail for the New World between 1688 and 1691, during the Williamite War between Protestant supporters of William of Orange and Catholics. Toward the middle of the century, anti-Catholicism began to rise with the arrival of these radicalized Protestant immigrants. As historian Emberson Proper notes, "The colonial archives of the period are filled with laws placing restrictions in the way of Catholic settlers." (See Document 2.)

Of much concern to American colonial leaders of the prerevolutionary period was also the arrival of immigrants with cultures and languages that did not appear to integrate well with British culture. In particular, large numbers of Germans were settling in the colonies, and they constituted the single largest group of settlers after the British at the time of the Revolution. In William Penn's colony, which had been for so long a symbol of religious toleration, the arrival of so many non-English speakers gave rise to a backlash. In 1729 a tax, aimed at German settlers, was placed on foreigners coming to the colony, which "marked the first (albeit modest) wave of anti-immigrant sentiment in the New World" (Muller 1993, 18). Even Benjamin Franklin expressed concern about the growing German cultural presence in the colonies. In one essay he asks, "Why should the Palatine Boors be suffered to swarm into our settlements, and by herding together establish their language and manners to the exclusion of ours?" (See Document 3.)

THE REVOLUTION AND THE NATURALIZATION ACTS OF THE 1790s

On the eve of the American Revolution, American colonial leaders' anger over the British attempt to regulate and limit immigration to the colonies was just one of many grievances that the colonists had with the British Crown. The American colonial leaders wanted more immigrants because the colonies were growing fast, while the British Crown was becoming wary of the colonists' independence of mind. The American Revolution divided British families, but it did not stop the influx of Europeans to the Americas.

Soon after the adoption of the U.S. Constitution in 1789, the United States faced the question of how American citizenship should be acquired. How does an individual become a "naturalized" American? This was an important question of how the country would define itself. The first attempt by the American Congress to address the issue occurred in 1790. The Naturalization Act of 1790 created a rather open and relaxed immigration policy, requiring only that an individual reside within the boundaries of the United States for two years to become a naturalized citizen of the country. It stipulates "that any alien, being a free white person, who shall have resided within the limits and under the jurisdiction of the United States for the term of two years, may be admitted to become a citizen thereof...." (See Document 4.)

The American Congress introduced the two-year residency requirement so that immigrants could become acquainted with American ideals of freedom and democracy. The new naturalization policy did not, however, apply to "non-white" races or to those who were "non-free." Slavery was still practiced in the United States, and racism was still acceptable during the period of the founding of the Republic.

THE NATURALIZATION LAW OF 1795

In the mid-1790s, with war raging in Europe between France and Britain, the new American republic wanted to maintain its neutrality in the conflict. Yet many revolutionary radicals from France and elsewhere in Europe were arriving in the United States, threatening peace and order. Congress, in an attempt to prevent extremists from coming to settle, passed the 1795 Naturalization Act. Congress asked that immigrants show loyalty to the United States and made naturalization more difficult. The Act specifically stated that the immigrant "will support the Constitution of the United States; and that he does absolutely and entirely renounce and abjure all allegiance and fidelity to any foreign prince, potentate, state, or sovereignty whatever and particularly by name the prince, potentate, state, or sovereignty whereof he was before a citizen or subject." This statement was directed equally to French revolutionaries and to British immigrants who might profess loyalty to the Crown. (See Document 5.)

The Act went on to ban British subjects who fought against America from becoming Americans, stating that "no person heretofore proscribed by any state, or who has been legally convicted of having joined the army of Great Britain during the late war, shall be admitted as foresaid without the consent of the legislature of the state in which such person was proscribed." Finally, it raised the number of years of required residency to five years. Through these provisions, Congress hoped that immigrants would come with a sincere commitment to stay in America and leave European loyalties and Old World ideas behind.

NEUTRALITY, NATURALIZATION, AND THE ALIEN AND SEDITION ACTS OF 1798

Concern over the possibility of European interference in the new Republic's affairs did not diminish, but, rather, increased in the closing years of the 1790s. In fact, in his final official address, published in the *Philadelphia Daily American Advertiser* on Sept. 17, 1796, President George Washington emphasized the need for the United States to isolate itself from European wars and foreign alliances (LeMay 2006:34). In response, the U.S. Congress passed four tough measures, which collectively became know as the Alien and Sedition Acts of 1798, to ensure that the new republic would not be drawn into European intrigue. Nevertheless, they were subsequently used to have newspaper publishers who supported Thomas Jefferson arrested, illustrating how overtly political the laws were (Jones 1995, 87).

The third Naturalization Act of 1798 was the first of these four laws. (See Document 6.) It states that aliens were required to, "Declare and prove, to the satisfaction of the court having jurisdiction in the case, that he has resided within the United States *fourteen years*, at least." Apart from an unreasonable fourteen-year residency requirement, for the first time, immigrant aliens were required to register their presence inside the United States and would pay a fine or even serve jail time if they did not do so. The law stipulated that "it be further enacted that every alien who shall continue to reside or who shall arrive, as aforesaid, of whom a report is required as aforesaid, who shall refuse or neglect to make such report, and to receive a certificate thereof, shall forfeit and pay the sum of two dollars.... and in failure of such surety, such alien shall and may be committed to the common gaol."

Other laws, such as the Alien Enemies Act, the Alien Act, and the Sedition Act, were directed at immigrants as well. The legislation approved draconian wartime measures such as making it easier to arrest, imprison, and deport foreign nationals and forbidding the publication of scandalous and malicious writings, which was punishable by fines or imprisonment. The Alien Enemies Act states that "all natives, citizens, denizens, or subjects of the hostile nation or government, being males of the age of fourteen years and upwards, who shall be within the United States, and not actually naturalized, shall be liable to be apprehended, restrained, secured and removed, as alien enemies." (See Document 7.)

Ostensibly, the Alien and Sedition Acts were meant to give immigrants time (fourteen years!) to acquire proper American values and to prevent radical aliens from spreading seditious ideas in the United States. In effect, however, the acts were a blow struck by John Adams's Federalists, who dominated Congress in those years, against the Jeffersonians, because many of the newly arrived immigrants who became naturalized tended to support Jefferson and his ideals for less centralized government. Opposition leaders such as Jefferson and James Madison condemned the acts as infringing upon states' rights. Federalists defended the measures, citing the real possibility of war with France, and linked the measures to national security (Jones 1995, 87).

In the end, because these laws violated the freedoms of Americans and the Bill of Rights to such a great extent, the backlash against them that was immense. In 1800 Jefferson took office as president and had most of the measures repealed, with the residency requirement once again being brought from fourteen down to five years. What is clear, however, is that in the first full decade that followed American independence, Congress had already begun wrestling with the issue of how to best regulate the process of immigrating to America.

DOCUMENTS

Document 1: The Maryland Toleration Act

Significance: Early document displaying tolerance for different religious groups in America.

"An Act Concerning Religion"

Forasmuch as in a well governed and Christian Common Wealth matters concerning Religion and the honor of God ought in the first place to bee taken, into serious consideration and endeavoured to bee settled, Be it therefore ordered and enacted by the Right Honourable

DID YOU KNOW?

Capitalism and Colonization of the Americas

Spanish colonization of the Americas had become profitable during the 1500s. As a result, there was growing interest by other European powers—above all on the part of Spain's chief rival, England—to share in these New World resources and begin establishing their own settlements. During the era of Queen Elizabeth I (1558–1603) famous explorers and adventurers such as Sir Humphrey Gilbert and Sir Francis Drake carried out expeditions to the New World. Yet venture capitalists for much of that period found it a better return on their investments, and more expedient, to finance expeditions that merely attacked Spanish fleets bearing gold and silver mined in Mexico and Peru returning to Spain. Only in the post-Elizabethan era, in 1607, was British America's first colony, Jamestown, founded (Samuel Eliot Morison, *The Oxford History of the American People* [New York: Oxford University Press, 1965], 43–45).

Cecilius Lord Baron of Baltimore absolute Lord and Proprietary of this Province with the advise and consent of this Generall Assembly:

That whatsoever person or persons within this Province and the Islands thereunto belonging shall from henceforth blaspheme God, that is Curse him, or deny our Saviour Jesus Christ to bee the son of God, or shall deny the holy Trinity the father son and holy Ghost, or the Godhead of any of the said Three persons of the Trinity or the Unity of the Godhead, or shall use or utter any reproachful Speeches, words or language concerning the said Holy Trinity, or any of the said three persons thereof, shall be punished with death and confiscation or forfeiture of all his or her lands and goods to the Lord Proprietary and his heiress.

And bee it also Enacted by the Authority and with the advise and assent aforesaid, That whatsoever person or persons shall from henceforth use or utter any reproachful words or Speeches concerning the blessed Virgin Mary the Mother of our Saviour or the holy Apostles or Evangelists or any of them shall in such case for the first offence forfeit to the said Lord Proprietary and his heirs Lords and Proprietaries of this Province the sum of five pound Sterling or the value thereof to be Levied on the goods and chattels of every such person so offending, but in case such Offender or Offenders, shall not then have goods and chattels sufficient for the satisfying of such forfeiture, or that the same bee not otherwise speedily satisfied that then such Offender or Offenders shall be publicly whipped and bee imprisoned during the pleasure of the Lord Proprietary or the Lieutenant or chief Governor of this Province for the time being. And that every such Offender or Offenders for every second offence shall forfeit ten pound sterling or the value thereof to bee levied as aforesaid, or in case such offender or Offenders shall not then have goods and chattels within this Province sufficient for that purpose then to bee publicly and severely whipped and imprisoned as before is expressed. And that every person or persons before mentioned offending herein the third time, shall for such third Offence forfeit all his lands and Goods and bee for ever banished and expelled out of this Province.

And be it also further Enacted by the same authority advise and assent that whatsoever person or persons shall from henceforth upon any occasion of Offence or otherwise in a reproachful manner or Way declare call or denominate any person or persons whatsoever inhabiting, residing, trafficking, trading or comerceing within this Province or within any the Ports, Harbors, Creeks or Havens to the same belonging an heritick, Scismatick, Idolator, Puritan, Independent, Prespiterian, Popish priest, Jesuit, Jesuited papist, Lutheran, Calvinist, Anabaptist, Brownist, Antinomian, Barrowist, Roundhead, Separatist, or any other name or term in a reproachful manner relating to matter of Religion shall for every such Offence forfeit and loose the sum of ten shillings sterling or the value thereof to bee levied on the goods and chattels of every such Offender and Offenders, the one half thereof to be forfeited and paid unto the person and persons of whom such reproachful words are or shall be spoken or uttered, and the other half thereof to the Lord Proprietary and his heirs Lords and Proprietaries of this Province. But if such prson or persons who shall at any time utter or speak any such reproachful words or Language shall not have Goods or Chattels sufficient and overt within this Province to bee taken to satisfy the penalty aforesaid or that the same bee not otherwise speedily satisfied, that then the person or persons so offending shall be publicly whipped, and shall suffer imprisonment without bail or maineprise until he, she or they respectively shall satisfy the party so offended or grieved by such reproachful Language by asking him or her respectively forgiveness publicly for such his Offence before the Magistrate of cheif Officer or Officers of the Towne or place where such Offence shall be given.

And be it further likewise Enacted by the Authority and consent aforesaid That every person and persons within this Province that shall at any time hereafter profane the Sabbath or Lords day called Sunday by frequent swearing, drunkenness or by any uncivil or disorderly recreation, or by working on that day when absolute necessity doth not require it shall for every such first offence forfeit 2s 6d sterling or the value thereof, and for the second offence 5s sterling or the value thereof, and for the third offence and so for every time he shall offend in like manner afterwards 10s sterling or the value thereof. And in case such offender and offenders shall not have sufficient goods or chattels within this Province to satisfy any of the said Penalties respectively hereby imposed for profaning the Sabbath or Lords day called Sunday as aforesaid, That in Every such case the party so offending shall for the first and second offence in that kind be imprisoned till he or she shall publicly in open Court before the chief Commander Judge or Magistrate, of that County Towne or precinct where such offence shall be committed acknowledge the Scandal and

DID YOU KNOW?

William Penn's "Holy Experiment"

The Society of Friends, also known as the Quakers, was founded during the era of Puritan England and spread throughout the country in the seventeenth century. William Penn, who in 1667 converted to this strongly pacifist sect, was the son of a highly decorated war hero, Admiral William Penn. The admiral at first did not approve of his son's pacifism but was later reconciled to it. Through the Penn family's connections with the English Crown, William Penn obtained a slice of the Duke of York's territory in the colonies, Pennsylvania, as payment for a previous debt owed to his father. Penn set about to create an experiment in political and religious liberty that would be open to all forms of worship. He called it his "Holy Experiment." Pennsylvania and its capital, Philadelphia, attracted people from all over the world. Philadelphia emerged as the most important center of commerce in the United States by 1700 (Samuel Eliot Morison, et al., *The Growth of the American Republic, vol. 1* [New York: Oxford University Press, 1980], 73–75).

offence he hath in that respect given against God and the good and civil Government of this Province, And for the third offence and for every time after shall also bee publicly whipped.

And whereas the enforcing of the conscience in matters of Religion hath frequently fallen out to be of dangerous Consequence in those commonwealths where it hath been practiced, And for the more quiet and peaceable government of this Province, and the better to preserve mutual Love and amity amongst the Inhabitants thereof, Be it Therefore also by the Lord Proprietary with the advise and consent of this Assembly Ordained and enacted (except as in this present Act is before Declared and set forth) that no person or persons whatsoever within this Province, or the Islands, Ports, Harbors, Creeks, or havens thereunto belonging professing to believe in Jesus Christ, shall from henceforth be any ways troubled, Molested or discountenanced for or in respect of his or her religion nor in the free exercise thereof within this Province or the Islands thereunto belonging nor any way compelled to the belief or exercise of any other Religion against his or her consent, so as they be not unfaithful to the Lord Proprietary, or molest or conspire against the civil Government established or to bee established in this Province under him or his heirs. And that all and every person and persons that shall presume Contrary to this Act and the true intent and meaning thereof directly or indirectly either in person or estate willfully to wrong disturb trouble or molest any person whatsoever within this Province professing to believe in Jesus Christ for or in respect of his or her religion or the free exercise thereof within this Province other than is provided for in this Act that such person or persons so offending, shall be compelled to pay trebble damages to the party so wronged or molested, and for every such offence shall also forfeit 20s sterling in money or the value thereof, half thereof for the use of the Lord Proprietary, and his heirs Lords and Proprietaries of this Province, and the other half for the use of the party so wronged or molested as aforesaid, Or if the party so offending as aforesaid shall refuse or bee unable to recompense the party so wronged, or to satisfy such fine or forfeiture, then such Offender shall be severely punished by public whipping and imprisonment during the pleasure of the Lord Proprietary, or his Lieutenant or chief Governor of this Province for the time being without bail or mainprise.

And be it further also Enacted by the authority and consent aforesaid That the Sheriff or other Officer or Officers from time to time to be appointed and authorized for that purpose, of the County Towne or precinct where every particular offence in this present Act contained shall happen at any time to bee committed and whereupon there is hereby a forfeiture fine or penalty imposed shall from time to time distraine and seize the goods and estate of every such person so offending as aforesaid against this present Act or any part thereof, and sell the same or any part thereof for the full satisfaction of such forfeiture, fine, or penalty as aforesaid, Restoring unto the party so offending the Remainder or overplus of the said goods or estate after such satisfaction sot made as aforesaid.

The freemen have assented.

Document 2: Excerpt from Emberson Edward Proper, *Colonial Immigration Laws: A Study of the Regulation of Immigration by the English Colonies in America.* New York: Columbia University Press, 1900.

Significance: Early anti-Catholic sentiment in the American colonies.

"As might naturally be supposed, the anti-immigration laws passed by the American colonists were few in number, and very limited in their application..."

...Although most of the settlements were made by Englishmen, they nevertheless differed fundamentally in character and purpose, and pursued, in some instances, widely varying policies in the admission of new settlers. Massachusetts discouraged the coming of all who did not agree with her policy of ecclesiastical domination. Virginia, whose founders were avowed Episcopalians, wanted no Non-Conformists, and took active measures to enforce this policy.

The fact that England undertook the colonization of this country made it certain that Protestantism was to be the dominating religion of the colonies; and the records of their legislation show a general tendency to restrict the immigration of Catholic settlers. These statutes vary in purpose from absolute prohibition, in the Puritan colonies, to petty regulations and annoyances, as practiced in some of the middle colonies.

Many of the early charters expressly, or impliedly, forbade admission of Catholics, and during the first part of the seventeenth century the immigration of this sect was so unimportant that no especial attention was given to them outside a few of the colonies. But with the final commitment of England to the cause of Protestantism there were severe parliamentary statutes passed against the Catholics, which were soon, either wholly or partially, embodied in colonial legislation. The colonial archives of the period are filled with laws placing restrictions in the way of Catholic settlers. These took the form of a duty on Irish Catholic servants; a positive prohibition of the Roman worship; a double tax on their lands; and the "Abjuration Oath," which practically excluded members of this faith, unless they chose to break their vows."

(Proper 1900:17–18)

Document 3: Excerpt from Benjamin Franklin's "Observations Concerning the Increase in Mankind, Peopling of Countries, Etc." (1751). Reprinted in Tarrytown, NY: W. Abbott, 1918.

Significance: Benjamin Franklin's views on immigration in pre-revolutionary America.

"21. The Importation of Foreigners into a Country that has as many Inhabitants as the present Employments and Provisions for Subsistence will bear; will be in the End no Increase of People; unless the New Comers have more Industry and Frugality than the Natives, and then they will provide more Subsistence, and increase in the Country; but they will gradually eat the Natives out. Nor is it necessary to bring in Foreigners to fill up any occasional Vacancy in a Country; for such Vacancy (if the Laws are good, (Symbol omitted) 14,16) will soon be filled by natural Generation. Who can now find the Vacancy made in *Sweden*, *France* or other Warlike Nations, by the Plague of Heroism 40 Years ago; in *France*, by the Expulsion of the Protestants; in *England*, by the Settlement of her Colonies; or in *Guinea*, by 100 Years Exportation of Slaves, that has blackened half *America?* The thinness of Inhabitants in *Spain*, is owing to National Pride and Idleness, and other Causes, rather than to the Expulsion of the *Moors*, or to the making of new Settlements.

23. In fine, A Nation well regulated is like a Polypus; take away a Limb, its Place is soon supply'd; cut it in two, and each deficient Part shall speedily grow out of the Part remaining. Thus if you have Room and Subsistence enough, as you may by dividing, make ten Polypes out of one, you may of one make ten Nations, equally populous and powerful; or rather, increase a Nation ten fold in Numbers and Strength. And since Detachments of *English* from *Britain* sent to *America*, will have their Places at Home so soon supply'd and increase so largely here; why should the *Palatine Boors* be suffered to swarm into our Settlements, and by herding together establish their Language and Manners to the Exclusion of ours? Why should *Pennsylvania*, founded by the *English*, become a Colony of *Aliens*, who will shortly be so numerous as to Germanize us instead of our Anglifying them, and will never adopt our Language or Customs, any more than they can acquire our Complexion."

Document 4: Naturalization Act of 1790

Significance: The first immigration legislation of the Republic.

"An Act to Establish an Uniform Rule of Naturalization"

Section 1. *Be it enacted by the Senate and House of Representatives of the United States of America in Congress assembled*, That any alien, being a free white person, who shall have resided within the limits and under the jurisdiction of the United States for the term of two years, may be admitted to become a citizen thereof, on application to any common law court of record, in any one of the states wherein he shall have resided for the term of one year at least, and making proof to the satisfaction of such court, that he is a person of good character, and taking the oath or affirmation prescribed by law, to support the constitution of the United States, which oath or affirmation such court shall administer; and the clerk of such court shall record such application, and the proceedings thereon; and thereupon such person shall be considered as a citizen of the United States. And the children of such persons so naturalized, dwelling within the United States, being under the age of twenty-one years at the time of such naturalization, shall also be considered as citizens of the United States. And the children of citizens of the United States, that may be born beyond sea, or out of the limits of the United States, shall be considered as natural born citizens: *Provided*, That the right of citizenship shall not descend to persons whose fathers have never been resident in the United States: *Provided also*, That no person heretofore proscribed by any state, shall be admitted a citizen aforesaid, except by an act of the legislature of the state in which such person was proscribed.

Approved, March 26, 1790.

Document 5: Naturalization Act of 1795

Significance: The strengthening of rules concerning naturalization.

"An Act to Establish an Uniform Rule of Naturalization; and to Repeal the Act Heretofore Passed on That Subject; For carrying into complete effect, the power given by the constitution, to establish an uniform rule of naturalization throughout the United States"

SECTION 1. Be it enacted by the Senate and House of Representatives of the United States of America, in Congress assembled, that any alien, being a free white person, may be admitted to become a citizen of the United States, or any of them, on the following conditions, and not otherwise. First, he shall have declared, on oath or affirmation, before the Supreme, Superior, District, or Circuit Court of some one of the states, or of the territories northwest or south of the Ohio River, or a Circuit or District Court of the United States, three years at least before his admission, that it was, bona fide, his intention to become a citizen of the United States, and to renounce forever all allegiance and fidelity to any foreign prince, potentate, state, or sovereignty whereof such alien may at that time be a citizen or subject. Secondly. He shall, at the time of his application to be admitted, declare on oath or affirmation before some one of the courts aforesaid that he has resided within the United States five years at least, and within the state or territory where such court is at the time held, one year at least; that he will support the Constitution of the United States; and that he does absolutely and entirely renounce and abjure all allegiance and fidelity to any foreign prince, potentate, state, or sovereignty whatever and particularly by name the prince, potentate, state, or sovereignty whereof he was before a citizen or subject; which proceedings shall be recorded by the clerk of the court. Thirdly. The court admitting such alien shall be satisfied that he has resided within the limits and under the jurisdiction of the United States five years. It shall further appear to their satisfaction that during that time he has behaved as a man of a good moral character, attached to the principles of the Constitution of the United States, and well-disposed to the good order and happiness of the same. Fourthly. In case the alien applying to be admitted to citizenship shall have borne any hereditary title, or been of any of the orders of nobility, in the kingdom or state from which he came, he shall, in addition to the above requisites, make an express renunciation of his title or order of nobility in the court to which his application shall be made; which renunciation shall be recorded in the said court.

SEC. 2. Provided always, and be it further enacted, That any alien now residing within the limits and under the jurisdiction of the United States may be admitted to become a citizen on his declaring, on oath or affirmation, in some one of the courts aforesaid, that he has resided two years, at least, within and under the jurisdiction of the same, and one year, at least, within the state or territory where such court is at the time held; that he will support the Constitution of the United States; and that he does absolutely and entirely renounce and abjure all allegiance and fidelity to any foreign prince, potentate, state, or sovereignty whatever, and particularly by name the prince, potentate, state, or sovereignty whereof he was before a citizen or subject. Moreover, on its appearing to the satisfaction of the court that, during the said term of two years, he has behaved as a man of good moral character, attached to the Constitution of the United States, and well-disposed to the good order and happiness of the same; and when the alien applying for admission to citizenship shall have borne any hereditary title, or been of any of the orders of nobility in the kingdom or state from which he came, on his, moreover, making in the court an express renunciation of his title or order of nobility, before he shall be entitled to such admission; all of which proceedings, required in this proviso to be performed in the court, shall be recorded by the clerk thereof.

SEC. 3. And be it further enacted, that the children of persons duly naturalized, dwelling within the United States, and being under the age of twenty-one years at the time of such naturalization, and the children of citizens of the United States born out of the limits and jurisdiction of the United States, shall be considered as citizens of the United States. Provided, that the right of citizenship shall not descend on persons whose fathers have never been resident of the United States. No person heretofore proscribed by any state, or who has been legally convicted of having joined the army of Great Britain during the late war, shall be admitted as foresaid, without the consent of the legislature of the state in which such person was proscribed.

SEC. 4. And be it further enacted, that the Act, intituled, "An act to establish an uniform rule of naturalization," passed the twenty-sixth day of March, one thousand seven hundred and ninety, be, and the same is hereby repealed.

APPROVED, January the 29th, 1795.

Document 6: Naturalization Act of 1798

"Chap. LIV – An Act supplementary to and to amend the act, intituled "An act to establish an uniform rule of naturalization; and to repeal the act heretofore passed on that subject"

Section 1. *Be it enacted by the Senate and House of Representatives of the United States of America in Congress assembled*, That no alien shall be admitted to become a citizen of the United States, or of any state, unless in the manner prescribed by the act, intituled, "An act to establish an uniform rule of naturalization; and to repeal the act heretofore passed on that subject," he shall have declared his intention to become a citizen of the United States, five years, at least, before his admission, and shall, at the time of his application to be admitted, declare and prove, to the satisfaction of the court having jurisdiction in the case, that he has resided within the United States fourteen years, at least, and within the state or territory where, or for which such court is at the time held, five years, at least, besides conforming to the other declarations, renunciations and proofs, by the said act required, anything therein to the contrary hereof notwithstanding: *Provided*, that any alien, who was residing within the limits, and under the jurisdiction of the United States, before the twenty-ninth day of January, one thousand seven hundred and ninety-five, may, within one year after the passing of this act – and any alien who shall have made the declaration of his intention to become a citizen of the United States, in conformity to the provisions of the act, intituled, "An act to establish an uniform rule of naturalization, and to repeal the act heretofore passed on the subject," may, within four years after having made the declaration aforesaid, be admitted to become a citizen, in the manner prescribed by the said act, upon his making proof that he has resided five years, at least, within the limits, and under the jurisdiction of the United States; *And provided also*, that no alien, who shall be a native, citizen, denizen or subject of any nation or state with whom the United States shall be at war, at the time of his application, shall be then admitted to become a citizen of the United States.

Section 2. And be it further enacted, that it shall be the duty of the clerk, or other recording officer of the court before whom a declaration has been, or shall be made, by any alien, of his intention to become a citizen of the United States, to certify and transmit to the office of the Secretary of State of the United States, to be there filed and recorded, an abstract of such declaration, in which, when hereafter made, shall be a suitable description of the name, age, nation, residence and occupation, for the time being, of the alien; such certificate to be made in all cases, where the deceleration has been or shall be made, before the passing of this act, within three months thereafter; and in all other cases, within two months after the declaration shall be received by the court. And in all cases hereafter arising, there shall be paid to the clerk, or recording officer as aforesaid, to defray the expense of such abstract and certificate, a fee of two dollars; and the clerk or officer to whom such fee shall be paid or tendered, who shall refuse or neglect to make and certify an abstract, as aforesaid, shall forfeit and pay the sum of ten dollars.

Section 3. And it be further enacted that in all cases of naturalization heretofore permitted or which shall be permitted, under the laws of the United States, a certificate shall be made to, and filed in the office of the Secretary of State, containing a copy of the record respecting the alien, and the decree or order of admission by the court before whom the proceedings thereto have been, or shall be had: And it shall be the duty of the clerk or other recording officer of such court, to make and transmit such certificate, in all cases which have already occurred, within three months after passing of this act; and in all future cases, within two months from and after naturalization of an alien shall be granted by any court competent thereto: And in future cases, there shall be paid to such clerk or recording officer the sum of two dollars, as a fee for such certificate, before the naturalization prayed for, shall be allowed. And the clerk or recording officer, whose duty it shall be, to make and transmit the certificate aforesaid, who shall be convicted of a willful neglect therein, shall forfeit and pay the sum of ten dollars, for each and every offence.

Section 4. And be it further enacted that all white persons, aliens, (accredited foreign ministers, consuls, or agents, their families and domestics, excepted) who, after the passing of this act, shall continue to reside, or who shall arrive, or come to reside in any port or place within the territory of the United States, shall be reported, if free, and of the age of twenty-one years, by themselves, or being under the age of twenty-one years, or holden of service, by their parent, guardian, master or mistress in whose care they shall be, to the clerk of the district court of the district, if living within ten miles of the port or place, in which their residence or arrival shall be, and otherwise, to the collector of such port or place, or some officer or other person there, or nearest thereto, who shall be authorized by the President of the United States to register aliens: And report, as aforesaid, shall be made in all cases of residence, within six months from and after passing of this act, and in all after cases, within forty-eight hours after the first arrival or coming into the territory of the United States, and shall ascertain the sex, place of birth, age, nation, place of allegiance or citizenship, condition of occupation, and place of actual or intended residence within the United States, of the alien or aliens reported, and by whom the report is made...]

Section 5. And it be further enacted that every alien who shall continue to reside or who shall arrive, as aforesaid, of whom a report is required as aforesaid, who shall refuse or neglect to make such report, and to receive a certificate thereof, shall forfeit and pay the sum of two dollars; and any justice of the peace, or other civil magistrate, who has authority to require surety of the peace, shall and may, on complaint to him made thereof, cause such alien to be brought before him, there to give surety of the peace and good behavior during his residence within the United States, as for such term as the justice or other magistrate shall deem reasonable, and until a report and registry of such alien shall be made, and a certificate thereof, received as aforesaid; and in failure of such surety, such alien shall and may be committed to the common gaol, and shall be there held, until the order which the justice or magistrate shall and may reasonably make, in the premises, shall be performed. And every person, whether alien, or other, having the care of any alien or aliens, under the age of twenty-one years, or of any white alien holden in service, who shall refuse and neglect to make report thereof, as aforesaid, shall forfeit the sum of two dollars, for each and every such minor or servant, monthly, and every month, until a report and registry, and a certificate thereof, shall be had, as aforesaid.

Section 6. And be it further enacted that in respect to every alien, who shall come to reside within the United States after the passing of this act, the time of the registry of such alien shall be taken to be the time when the term of residence within the limits, and under the jurisdiction of the United States, shall have commenced, in case of an application by such alien, to be admitted a citizen of the United States; and a certificate of such registry shall be required, in proof of the term of residence, by the court to whom such application shall and may be made.

Section 7. And be it further enacted that all and singular the penalties established by this act, shall and may be recovered in the name, and to the use of any person, who will inform and sue for the same, before any judge, justice, or court, having jurisdiction in such case, and to the amount of such penalty, respectively.

Approved, June 18, 1798.

Document 7: The Alien Enemies Act

"The Alien Enemies Act: An Act Respecting Alien Enemies"

SECTION 1. Be it enacted by the Senate and House of Representatives of the United States of America, in Congress assembled, That whenever there shall be a declared war between the United States and any foreign nation or government, or any invasion or predatory incursion shall be perpetrated, attempted, or threatened against the territory of the United States, by any foreign nation or government, and the President of the United States shall make public proclamation of the event, all natives, citizens, denizens, or subjects of the hostile nation or government, being males of the age of fourteen years and upwards, who shall be within the United States, and not actually naturalized, shall be liable to be apprehended, restrained, secured and removed, as alien enemies. And the President of the United States shall be, and he is hereby authorized, in any event, as aforesaid, by his proclamation thereof, or other public act, to direct the conduct to be observed, on the part of the United States, towards the aliens who shall become liable, as aforesaid; the manner and degree of the restraint to which they shall be subject, and in what cases, and upon what security their residence shall be permitted, and to provide for the removal of those, who, not being permitted to reside within the United States, shall refuse or neglect to depart therefrom; and to establish any other regulations which shall be found necessary in the premises and for the public safety: Provided, that aliens resident within the United States, who shall become liable as enemies, in the manner aforesaid, and who shall not be chargeable with actual hostility, or other crime against the public safety, shall be allowed, for the recovery, disposal, and removal of their goods and effects, and for their departure, the full time which is, or shall be stipulated by any treaty, where any shall have been between the United States, and the hostile nation or government, of which they shall be natives, citizens, denizens or subjects: and where no such treaty shall have existed, the President of the United States may ascertain and declare such reasonable time as may be consistent with the public safety, and according to the dictates of humanity and national hospitality.

SEC. 2. And be it further enacted, That after any proclamation shall be made as aforesaid, it shall be the duty of the several courts of the United States, and of each state, having criminal jurisdiction, and of the several judges and justices of the courts of the United States, and they shall be, and are hereby respectively, authorized upon complaint, against any alien or alien enemies, as aforesaid, who shall be resident and at large within such jurisdiction or district, to the danger of the public peace or safety, and contrary to the tenor or intent of such proclamation, or other regulations which the President of the United States shall and may establish in the premises, to cause such alien or aliens to be duly apprehended and convened before such court, judge or justice; and after a full examination and hearing on such complaint, and sufficient cause therefor appearing, shall and may order such alien or aliens to be removed out of the territory of the United States, or to give sureties of their good behaviour, or to be otherwise restrained, conformably to the proclamation or regulations which shall and may be established as aforesaid, and may imprison, or otherwise secure such alien or aliens, until the order which shall and may be made, as aforesaid, shall be performed.

SEC. 3. And be it further enacted, That it shall be the duty of the marshal of the district in which any alien enemy shall be apprehended, who by the President of the United States, or by order of any court, judge or justice, as aforesaid, shall be required to depart, and to be removed, as aforesaid, to provide therefor, and to execute such order, by himself or his deputy, or other discreet person or persons to be employed by him, by causing a removal of such alien out of the territory of the United States; and for such removal the marshal shall have the warrant of the President of the United States, or of the court, judge or justice ordering the same, as the case may be.

APPROVED, July 6, 1798.

FURTHER READINGS

Carey, Patrick. *Catholics in America: A History*. Westport, Conn.: Praeger, 2004.

Daniels, Roger. *Coming to America: A History of Immigration and Ethnicity in American Life*, 2nd ed. New York: Perennial/Harper Collins, 2002.

Dickson, R. J. *Ulster Emigration to Colonial America, 1718–1775*. Belfast: Ulster Historical Foundation, 1988.

Franklin, Benjamin. "Observations Concerning the Increase in Mankind, Peopling of Countries, Etc." (1751). Reprinted in Tarrytown, NY: W. Abbott, 1918.

Franklin, Frank. *The Legislative History of Naturalization in the United States*. New York: Arno Press, 1969.

Griffith, R. Marie, ed. *American Religions: A Documentary History*. New York: Oxford University Press, 2008.

Hansen, Marcus Less. *Atlantic Migration, 1601–1860*. New York: Harper Torchbooks, 1961.

Jones, Maldwyn A. *The Limits of Liberty: American History, 1607–1992*, 2nd ed. New York: Oxford University Press, 1995.

Krugler, John D. *English and Catholic: The Lords Baltimore in the Seventeenth Century*. Baltimore: Johns Hopkins University Press, 2004.

LeMay, Michael. *Guarding the Gates: Immigration and National Security*. Westport, Conn.: Praeger Security International, 2006.

Muller, Thomas. *Immigrants and the American City*. New York: New York University Press, 1993.

Noll, Mark A. and Luke E. Harlow, eds. *Religion and American Politics: From the Colonial Period to the Present*, 2nd ed. New York: Oxford University Press, 2007.

Phelan, Thomas Patrick, *Catholics in Colonial Days*. Ann Arbor: Gryphon Books, 1971.

Proper, Emberson E. *Colonial Immigration Laws: A Study of the Regulation of Immigration by the English Colonies in America*. New York: Columbia University Press, 1900.

Sewell, Thomas. *Ethnic America: A History*. New York: Basic Books, 1981.

Smith, James M. *Freedom's Fetters: Alien and Sedition Laws*. Ithaca: Cornell University Press, 1956.

Vickers, Daniel, ed. *A Companion to Colonial America*. Malden, Mass.: Blackwell, 2003.

Wald, Kenneth D., and Allison Calhoun-Brown. *Religion and Politics in the United States*, 5th ed. Lanham, Md.: Rowman and Littlefield, 2007.

Wilson, John F., and Donald L. Drakeman, eds. *Church and State in American History: Key Documents, Decisions and Commentary from the Past Three Centuries*, 3rd ed. (expanded and updated). Boulder, Colo.: Westview, 2003.

INTERNET RESOURCES

Library of Congress American Memory Project. http://memory.loc.gov/ammem/today/archive.html

National Museum of American History (Smithsonian). http://americanhistory.si.edu/

Smithsonian Institute–History and Culture. http://www.si.edu/Encyclopedia_SI/History_and_Culture/default.htm

CHAPTER 2

Immigration and America's Expansion in the 1800s

David Felsen

In the early 1800s, immigration to the United States was not a central policy focus and consisted principally of Protestant groups from the British isles. In post-Jefferson America, moreover, naturalization policy was more relaxed than it had been during the 1790s. By 1840, however, immigration to the United States picked up substantially, as did anti-immigrant sentiment. The rise of immigration coincided with population pressures in European countries—not least from the Great Famine in Ireland and political and social instability in Central European German States, which brought an influx of newcomers to America.

EUROPEAN IMMIGRATION IN THE 1800s

The early part of the 1800s was a period of increasing American self-confidence and territorial expansion. Still wary of European interference, the United States moved to consolidate its position on the continent. In 1803 Jefferson purchased Louisiana from France. General Andrew Jackson seized Florida in a campaign against the Spanish. President James Monroe issued the Monroe Doctrine of 1823 to warn European powers away from the Americas. Under President James K. Polk, the United States annexed Texas in 1845, bought the Oregon territory, and purchased much of the southwestern United States at the end of the Mexican-American war.

The U.S. authorities realized that they had to encourage settlement of its newly acquired territories. At the same time, in Europe, many people sought to escape poverty, famine, political strife, and religious persecution. Among the key groups to immigrate to the United States at mid-century were the Irish, followed by German-speaking groups, such as Mennonites and Lutherans, as well as Calvinists. In the 1830s approximately 50,000 immigrants came to the United States per year. This figure rose to 100,000 per year during the 1840s and to over 300,000 immigrants per year in the 1850s (Jones 1995, 129).

TABLE 2.1 Immigration by Region of Last Residence, 1820–1920

	1820–1860	1861–1900	1900–1920
Northwest Europe	95%	68%	41%
Southeast Europe	—	22%	44%
North America	3%	7%	6%
Asia	—	2%	4%
Latin America	—	—	4%
Other	2%	1%	1%

Source: Roger Daniels, *Coming to America: A History of Immigration and Ethnicity in American Life*, 2nd ed. (New York: Perennial/Harper Collins, 2002), 122.

TABLE 2.2 Immigration to the United States, 1820–1880

1820–30	151,824
1831–40	599,125
1841–50	1,713,251
1851–60	2,598,214
1861–70	2,314,824
1871–80	2,812,191

Source: Roger Daniels, *Coming to America: A History of Immigration and Ethnicity in American Life*, 2nd ed. (New York: Perennial/Harper Collins, 2002), 124.

TABLE 2.3 Immigration by Countries of Last Residence, 1820–1870

France	244,049
Germany	2,333,944
Ireland	3,392,335
Italy	25,518
Norway-Sweden	145,427
United Kingdom	1,401,213
China	105,744
Canada	271,020
Unspecified	203,149

Source: Immigration statistics data taken from Ines M. Miyares and Christopher A. Airriess, "Creating Contemporary Ethnic Geographies—A Review of Immigration Law," in *Contemporary Ethnic Geographies in America*, ed. Ines M. Miyares and Christopher A. Airriess (Lanham, Md.: Rowman and Littlefield, 2007), 30–32.

The Irish constituted the largest group to immigrate. In the 1830s, about 44 percent of all immigrants were Irish, and in the 1840s about half of all immigrants came from Ireland. (Morison 2002, 227). Irish immigration peaked at over 200,000 a year by the early 1850s. These Irish immigrants had to endure a difficult voyage, sailing under horrendous conditions with ships arriving on shore in the Americas with perhaps half the passengers having died of disease. These overcrowded "coffin ships" followed few to no sanitation procedures. Once the ships arrived at the St. Lawrence River, the passengers often had to wait months to get off. When they finally disembarked, they often brought epidemics (Document 1).

Most of the destitute Irish came to the eastern seaboard and settled in cities such as New York, Philadelphia, Boston, or Chicago. By 1860 New York had 200,000 Irish immigrants, Philadelphia had 95,000, and Boston 70,000 (Jones 1995, 131). Although they arrived at an opportune time when labor was desperately needed in the growing cities, the Irish soon provoked anti-Catholic sentiment as their numbers increased. As a group, the Irish

TABLE 2.4 Irish and German Immigration to the United States in 1800s

	Irish	% of Total Immigration	German	% of Total Immigration
1830–40	207,381	34.6	124,726	23.2
1840–50	780,719	45.6	385,434	27.0
1850–60	914,119	35.2	976,072	34.7
1860–70	435,778	18.8	723,734	34.8
1870–80	436,871	15.5	751,769	27.4
1880–90	655,482	12.5	1,445,181	27.5
1890–1900	388,416	10.5	579,072	15.7

Source: Combined data from Roger Daniels, *Coming to America: A History of Immigration and Ethnicity in American Life*, 2nd ed. (New York: Perennial/Harper Collins, 2002), 129, and Don Heinrich Tolzmann, *The German-American Experience* (New York: Humanity Books, 2000), 447. Note that Daniels compiled data by decade from 1831 to 1900 and Tolzmann from 1830 to 1899.

experienced strong discrimination in their search for employment. The phrase "No Irish Need Apply" was observed frequently in the large coastal cities in which they settled.

German immigration to the United States also increased significantly during the 1800s. Many came out of economic need, because agricultural changes in Europe forced many off their lands. Others were enticed by hearing about America through letters from family and friends living in the New World. Still others came as political exiles after the failed 1848 democratic revolutions that swept Europe or to avoid mandatory conscription to fight in the German wars of unification in the 1860s. While the Irish congregated in the eastern cities, the new midwestern cities of Milwaukee, Cincinnati, and St. Louis attracted numerous German settlers. The German settlers pursued both agriculture and industry.

Another significant immigrant group was from the Scandinavian countries. This group settled Minnesota, Wisconsin, Iowa, and the Dakotas. In addition, older immigrant groups—the Dutch, Scottish and Scots-Irish—continued to arrive in considerable numbers. The Ulster Scots, who continued to arrive in large numbers, with their brand of anti-Catholicism, blended to oppose the growth in well with homegrown American anti-Catholicism that emerged after the 1840s, in the number of Roman Catholics in the country.

ANTI-IMMIGRANT SENTIMENT AND ANTI-CATHOLICISM

Before 1830 immigration to the United States consisted of predominantly Protestants from Britain. During the next three decades, Catholic immigration changed the demographics of the country. By 1860 there were over three million Roman Catholics making up about 10 percent of the population of the country (Jones 1995, 132). Despite restrictions placed on Irish immigrants that made it harder to come to America, the 1840s and 1850s continued to see a rise in Catholic immigration. The rapid growth of the Catholic population provoked a backlash. There were riots and mob violence in urban centers and a rise of new nativist movements at the local and national levels. One of the most notable events was a riot that erupted in 1844 in Philadelphia, which resulted in several Catholic churches being set ablaze and numerous Catholics being killed or injured (Morrison 1994, 230-31).

Secretive anti-Catholic social orders and political parties proliferated. These included the Secret Order of the Star Spangled Banner, founded in 1849 as a secret anti-Catholic society, and the American Party, which contested the federal elections in 1854. These organizations were part of the "Know-Nothing Movement," named as such because their members were expected to tell people, when asked, that they knew nothing about these organizations.

This 1852 broadside announcing the publication of the *American Patriot*, a short-lived Boston nativist newspaper, exemplifies the explicitly anti-Catholic character of mid-19th century nativist polemics. The paper opposes "Papal Aggression & Roman Catholicism. Foreigners holding office. Raising Foreign Military Companies in the United States. Nunneries and the Jesuits. To being taxed for the support of Foreign paupers millions of dollars yearly. To secret Foreign Orders in the U.S." Library of Congress, Prints and Photographs Division, LC-DIG-ppmsca-07575.

The anti-Catholic and anti-immigrant Know-Nothing movement involved obscure organizational structures and regulations.

Politicians linked to the Know-Nothing movement won mayoral elections in Boston and Chicago, and the Know-Nothing-linked American Party won a stunning victory in the Massachusetts gubernatorial race in 1854. In that same year, the American Party surpassed the Whigs to become the second-largest party in the U.S. House of Representatives, contributing in no small part to the collapse of the old Whigs and the rise of the new Republican Party. (From the 1820s to the 1850s, the dominant parties in the two-party system were the Whigs and the Democrats; the Republicans emerged in the 1850s with the demise of the Whigs [McPherson 1988, 135–36].)

In the gubernatorial election campaign in Virginia of 1855—a contest between Democratic candidate Henry A. Wise and the Know-Nothings in which Wise emerged victoriousa—a secret Know-Nothing "constitution" was circulated to illustrate the secretive nature of the Know-Nothings (Document 2). The Know-Nothing text addresses the perceived threat to America of Catholicism.

The reaction of many German immigrants, particularly German Catholics, to the rise of the anti-immigrant Know-Nothings in the 1850s is captured in Document 3. In the text one German community leaders states, alarmingly, that in the United States, "people are not content with a mere hate against immigrants; no, they are proceeding to measures which should only be applied in a land of despotism, not in a free land" and that "the crowd of poor laboring men and shopkeepers, who have recently arrived, are imbued with these sentiments; and some are already looking on the American people as a tyrant, only second to the

Government they left behind." The writer urges Germans to unite to defend themselves from xenophobic Know-Nothing hostility.

Immigrants, Catholics, and progressive Protestants were alarmed by the rise of the Know-Nothings. Frequent brawling occurred in New York, New Jersey, and elsewhere between anti-Catholics and Catholic workers. As Catholic immigration began to wane in the 1860s, the Know-Nothings and the American Party gradually disappeared. Yet, the 1850s are remembered for pervasive and intense anti-foreigner, anti-immigrant and anti-Catholic sentiment in the growing urban centers of the United States.

IMMIGRATION AND THE CIVIL WAR

The Know-Nothing movement and the American Party eventually fizzled out and, in 1856, a new two-party system already had begun to consolidate. The new Republican Party of the mid-1800s remained open to immigration as industrializing and growing cities were in need of laborers. The Republicans were supported by progressive, business-oriented firms from the Northeast, wealthy farmers, and others who benefited from the process of industrialization and the construction of railroads. The Democrats, who had emerged some thirty years

On the cover of its Jan. 20, 1866, issue, Frank Leslie's *Illustrated Newspaper* depicted a purportedly raucous and emotional occasion, "Irish Emigrants Leaving Their Home for America—The Mail Coach from Cahirciveen, County Kerry, Ireland." In 1866, according to the U.S. Department of the Treasury, 116,000 German immigrants and 131,000 British or Irish immigrants came to the United States—some three-quarters of the total who arrived that year, continuing pre–Civil War immigration patterns. Library of Congress, Prints and Photographs Division, LC-USZ62-2022.

earlier under Andrew Jackson, represented by the 1850s many less well off and close-minded whites, who supported slavery, disliked foreigners, and remained anti-Catholic. They wanted to defend what they viewed as traditional American culture and values.

By the Civil War, Lincoln's Republicans dominated the United States Congress and sought to encourage immigration to the country and specifically to the territories in which slavery was not permitted. By way of the Homestead Act of 1862, immigrants were offered extremely cheap land of up to 160 acres to settle on in exchange for a five-year commitment to stay on the land and become citizens (Document 4).

There were also additional government incentives offered to attract laborers to build railroads during this period to offset a labor shortage that emerged because of the war (McPherson 1988, 606). In 1864 the U.S. government passed "An Act to Encourage Immigration" (Document 5). Unlike the Homestead Act, this legislation was meant to entice immigrants to move to urban centers and work in industry. Prospective immigrants were offered binding work contracts even before arriving in the United States. Moreover, the act created the new post of Commissioner for Immigration, to be responsible to the Secretary of State and an immigration office in New York City, by then America's largest urban center. Article 3 of the act further stipulates that "no emigrant to the United States who shall arrive after the passage of this act shall be compulsively enrolled for military service during the existing insurrection," allaying concern that would-be immigrants could be conscripted to fight in the Civil War.

THE EXCLUSION OF CHINESE IMMIGRANTS

As anti-Catholicism diminished, and the influence of the Know-Nothings subsided, anti-foreigner sentiment became directed toward a new group: Chinese immigrants who came to work from midcentury onward on the railroads and in the mines. In particular, the California Gold Rush of 1848 and the development of the steam engine led to the development of rail and the expansion of mining, bringing many Chinese laborers to the state.

Chinese immigrants very quickly became a large part of the population of the southwestern United States. By 1860, they made up over 25 percent of the California workforce (LeMay 2000). It was not surprising that it was in California that a strong anti-Chinese backlash took hold. The first anti-Chinese legislation came into force in 1862 (Document 6), in the very year that the federal government passed the Homestead Act to encourage European immigration. With the legislation, a Chinese Poll Tax was created, "hereby levied on each person, male and female, of the Mongolian race, of the age of eighteen years and upwards, residing in this State, except such as shall, under laws now existing, or which may hereafter be enacted, take out licenses to work in the mines, or to prosecute some kind of business, a monthly capitation tax of two dollars and fifty cents." The burden to pay the tax was placed on the businesses who hired them, making hiring Chinese workers less attractive to companies.

By the 1870s, anti-Chinese sentiment spread all the way to Washington, D.C. A global economic depression hit the United States and Europe after 1873, igniting strong anti-Chinese feeling across the country. The Chinese came to be referred to as the "Yellow Menace." Verbal and physical attacks against Chinese immigrants rose, and anti-Chinese discrimination worsened with the deepening of the economic downturn, culminating in the passage of the Chinese Exclusion Act of 1882 by the U.S. Congress (Document 7).

The anti-Chinese racism was propagated by groups such as the Chinese Exclusion League and the Order of Caucasians, in addition to organized labor groups who did not want Chinese workers to compete with them. Public opinion and Congress were swayed by these grassroots organizations. The Act of 1882 moved to completely stop Chinese migrants from entering the United States. The law stipulated that "the coming of Chinese laborers to the United States be, and the same is hereby, suspended; and during such suspension it shall not be lawful for any Chinese laborer to come, or having so come after the expiration of said ninety days to remain within the United States."

The ban on Chinese laborers under the legislation was renewed in 1892 for another ten years. Moreover, other measures were introduced. In 1884 the U.S. Congress issued the requirement for all Chinese permanent residents to obtain a "re-entry certificate" before traveling back to China. In 1888 the U.S. Congress passed legislation to prevent Chinese nationals who had traveled back to China from returning to their work, revoking their re-entry certificates (LeMay 2006, 94). Under this measure, no matter how long a Chinese national had been living in the country, he could be barred from returning to the United States if he ever left the country.

CONCLUSION

The 1800s began as a period of relatively open immigration policy. Yet, the growing number of non-Protestant immigrants helped stoke anti-foreigner reaction. This anti-foreigner feeling was strongest in the 1850s against the Catholics and in the 1880s against the Chinese. But the United States was yet to experience its largest immigration influx. After 1880 millions of Southern and Eastern Europeans arrived at its shores and changed the face of the country forever.

DOCUMENTS

Document 1: Account of Voyage of Robert Whyte on a "Coffin Ship" in 1847

Significance: The difficulties of mass Irish immigration to America.

June 15, 1847: The reports this morning were very afflicting, and I felt much that I was unable to render any assistance to my poor fellow passengers. The captain desired the Mistress to give them everything out of his own stores that she considered to be of service to any of them. He felt much alarmed; nor was it to be wondered at that contagious fever – which under the most advantageous circumstances and under the watchful eyes of the most skilful physicians requires the greatest ability – should terrify one having the charge of so many human beings, likely to fall prey to the unchecked progress of the dreadful disease. For once having shown itself in the unventilated hold of a small brig, containing 110 living creatures, how could it possibly be stayed without suitable medicines, medical skill and pure water to slake the patients' burning thirst. The prospect before us was indeed an awful one, and there was no hope for us but in the mercy of God.

June 16: The past night was very rough, and I enjoyed little rest. No additional cases of sickness were reported, but there were signs of insubordination amongst the healthy men who complained of starvation and want of water for their sick wives and children. A deputation came aft to acquaint the

DID YOU KNOW?

Anti-Catholic Riots in the 1840s

One of the ugliest anti-immigrant riots took place in Philadelphia in 1844. In 1843 the Philadelphia school board acceded to the Catholic bishop's request that Catholic students be able to use the Catholic Douay version of the Bible and be exempt from other Protestant religious rituals. It led to a strong anti-Irish and anti-Catholic campaign in the city, prompting an Irish Catholic reaction. In the spring 1844 municipal election, Protestant "American Republican" voters were assaulted and prevented from voting in Irish districts. This provoked further reprisals on the part of Protestants. On May 1 anti-Catholics carrying arms burned down thirty houses as well as St. Michael's and St. Augustine's Catholic churches. The militia had to restore order in the city. A subsequent riot resulted in the burning of another church; 30 were killed and 150 were wounded from these two riots (Samuel Eliot Morison, *The Oxford History of the American People* [New York: Oxford University Press, 1965], 482).

DID YOU KNOW?

Immigrants and the California Gold Rush of 1849

The California Gold Rush of 1849 that lasted throughout the middle of the nineteenth century received national and world attention and galvanized both economic growth and immigration. Astoundingly, in the years 1851–1855, California produced 45 percent of the world's entire gold output. The gold rush meant a lot for the country, because it helped the United States solve its shortages in gold specie and develop its capital markets, contributing to the rapid pace of U.S. expansion in the second half of the nineteenth century. Before the first gold strike, the non-native population was 14,000, but by 1852 the population topped 250,000. The state attracted a great number of immigrant workers and adventurers from all over the world who came to settle in California and Nevada. In 1852 Nevada County counted 12,500 white males but 4,000 migrant Chinese cooks. The gold rush also helped promote America's reputation as a land of opportunity (Paul Johnson, *A History of the American People* [New York: Harper Collins, 1997], 385–386).

DID YOU KNOW?

Tammany Hall

Tammany Hall, or Tammany Society, started as a patriotic social club in New York at the time of the Revolutionary War and transformed itself into the foremost political patronage machine of the nineteenth century. It managed to attract the swelling immigrant population of New York from the 1840s onward. It sided with many issues popular with the new immigrants, including the abolition of the property requirement for voting, the repeal of the debtors' prison law, and standing with immigrants in opposition to the Know-Nothings. The organization, led for much of its heyday by Boss Tweed, particularly helped Irish immigrants advance through patronage appointments, placing many Irish leaders in prominent positions in local politics. It became the most convenient means by which immigrants could connect to the power structures of America of the nineteenth century (Kenneth D. Ackerman, *Boss Tweed: The Rise and Fall of the Corrupt Pol Who Conceived the Soul of Modern New York* [New York: Carroll and Graf, 2005], 21).

captain with their grievances, but he ordered them away, and would not listen to a word from them. When he went below the ring leaders threatened that they would break into the provision store... In order to make a deeper impression on their minds, be brought out the old blunderbuss from which he fired a shot, the report of which was equal to the report of a small cannon. The deputation slunk away muttering complaints. If they were resolute they could easily have seized upon the provisions. In fact, I was surprised how famished men could so easily bear with their own and their starved children's sufferings. The captain would willingly have listened if it were in his power to relieve their distress...

August 1: Of the passengers I never afterwards saw any but two, both of them young men who got employment upon the Lachine Canal. The rest wandered over the country, carrying nothing with them but disease, and that but few of them survived the severity of the succeeding winter (ruined as their constitutions were) I am quite confident.

(Source: Robert Whyte, *The Ocean Plague: A Voyage to Quebec in an Irish Immigrant Vessel*, 1848—reprinted on pp. 144–146 of Peter Gray, *The Irish Famine* [New York: Harry N. Abrams, 1995])

Document 2: Know-Nothing Constitution, Excerpt

Significance: Purported to be the secret rituals and rules of the Know-Nothing movement.

The Know-Nothing Ritual Exposed

The Know-Nothing Ritual or "Constitution of the Grand Council of the United States of North America—Adopted Unanimously, June 17, 1854—The Anniversary of the Battle of Bunker Hill"

Article I
This organization shall be known by the name and title *The Grand council of the United States of North America*, and its jurisdiction and power shall extend to all the states, districts, and territories of the United States of North America.

Article II
A person to become a member of any subordinate council must be twenty-one years of age; he must believe in the existence of a Supreme Being as the Creator and Preserver of the Universe; he must be a native born citizen; a Protestant, born of Protestant parents, reared under Protestant influence, and not united in marriage with a Roman

Catholic; Provided, nevertheless, that in this last respect, the state, district, or territorial council shall be authorized to so construct their respective constitutions as shall best promote the interest of the American cause in their several jurisdictions; And provided, moreover, that no member who may have a Roman Catholic wife shall be eligible to any office in this order.

Article III

Sec. 1. The object of this organization shall be to resist the insidious policy of the Church of Rome, and other foreign influence against the institutions of our country by placing in all offices in the gift of the people, or by appointment, none but native born Protestant citizens.

Sec. 2. The Grand Council shall hold its annual meeting on the first Tuesday in the month of June, at such place as shall be designated by the Grand Council at the previous annual meeting, and it may adjourn from time to time. Special meetings shall be called by the President on the written request of five delegations representing five State Councils; Provided, that sixty days' notice shall be given to the State Councils previous to said meeting.

SEC. 3. The Grand Council shall be composed of thirteen delegates, from each state, to be chosen by the State Councils; and each district, or territory where a District or Territorial Council shall exist, shall be entitled to send five delegates, to be chosen from said Councils; and when no District or Territorial Council shall exist, such district or territory shall be entitled to send five delegates, if five or more Subordinate Councils shall exist in such district or territory; Provided, that in the nomination of candidates for President and Vice President of the United States, each state shall be entitled to the same number of votes as they shall have member in both houses of Congress, In all sessions of the Grand Council, thirty-two delegates, representing thirteen states, territories, or districts, shall constitute a quorum for the transaction of business,

Sec. 4. The Grand Council shall be vested with the following powers and privileges:

It shall be the head of the organization for the United States of North America, and shall fix and establish all signs, grips, passwords, and such other secret work as may seem to it necessary.

It shall have power to decide upon all matters appertaining to national politics.

It shall have the power to exact from the State Councils quarterly or annual statements as to the number of members under their jurisdictions and in relation to all other matters necessary for its information.

It shall have the power to form state, territorial or district councils, and to grant dispensations for the formation of such bodies when five subordinate councils shall have been put in operation in any state, territory or district, and application made.

It shall have the power to determine upon a mode of punishment in case of any dereliction of duty on the part of its members or officers.

It shall have the power to adopt cabalistic characters for the purpose of writing or telegraphing – said characters to be communicated to the presidents of the State Councils, and by them to the presidents of the Subordinate Council.

It shall have the power to adopt any and every measure it may deem necessary to secure the success of the organization; provided, that nothing shall be done by the said Grand Council in violation of the Constitution; and provided, further, that in all political matters, its members may be instructed by the State Councils, and if so instructed, shall carry out such instructions of the State Councils which they represent until overruled by a majority of the Grand Council.

(Source: James Hambleton, A Biographical Sketch of Henry Wise. Virginia: John Nowlan, 1856)

Document 3: "The Germans and the Know-Nothings" (1855)

Significance: Immigrants confront the anti-immigrant and xenophobic nativists.

"We observe in our various German exchanges at the present time, a feeling arising, which we very much regret to see. The Know-Nothing movement is considered to be especially directed against the Germans, and these are everywhere soon moved to unite against their oppressors, and to form a separate body on the American soil: The *Abend Zeitung* of this City estimates the decrease of German immigration, owing to this hostility to foreigners, as nearly 120,000 for this year alone. In the *Staats Zeitung* of Wednesday, is an important address from a German Association in Ohio to one in New Haven, in which these passages occur:

'This is the land in which they are beginning to nourish a universal hatred of strangers that has already spread itself with its poisonous roots over the Union. People are not content with a mere hate against immigrants; no, they are proceeding to measures which should only be applied in a land of despotism, not in a free land. Let any one read the laws lately considered in the Legislature of Massachusetts against immigrants, and he will find how far the hate of strangers goes, for they have attempted to put us lower than the slaves—to rob us of our right of franchise.' To meet these efforts, 'no other proceeding can be recommended but a union of all Germans and a thorough enlightenment as to what stands before us.'

It is then proposed that these two Associations unite, and that everywhere similar efforts should be made to form societies and bring up the Germans in a mass against the plans of the Know-Nothings.

We are not surprised at such projects and such expressions of feeling on the part of the Germans, much as we may regret them. The whole Know-Nothing movement seems to them dictated by narrow-minded hatred of strangers, and to have for its great object the disenfranchising of Germans. Accordingly, as is most natural, the leaders are stimulating the masses to unite against this tyranny. An intense, bitter feeling is springing up among them, against what they think the universal opinion, rather than the mere prejudice of a party. The crowd of poor laboring men and shopkeepers, who have recently arrived, are imbued with these sentiments; and some are already looking on the American people as a tyrant, only second to the Government they left behind. Demagogues and windy editors foment the excitement; and now the German and official papers at home, who desire to lessen emigration, are exaggerating the troubles which await the stranger in America, and are frightening back the immigrant. All this is very bad. The diminution of 120,000 immigrants would probably be a loss to New York alone, of one and a half million dollars, in money expended to them, beside the loss of so many profitable consumers and industrious workers. The German immigration—even the Know-Nothings must confess—has been generally a useful one to the country..."

(Source: "The Germans and Know-Nothings," *New York Times*, June 16, 1855, 4)

Document 4: The Homestead Act of 1862

Significance: This legislation was intended to attract settlers to America.

"An Act to Secure Homestead to Actual Settlers on Public Domains

Section 1. *Be It enacted by the Senate and House of Representatives of the United States of America in Congress assembled,* That any person who is the head of a family, or who has arrived at the age of twenty-one years, and is a citizen of the United States, or who shall have filed his declaration intention to become such, as required by the naturalization laws of the United States, and who has never borne arms against the United States Government or given aid and comfort to its enemies, shall, from and after the first January, eighteen hundred and sixty-three, be entitled to enter one quarter section or a less quantity of unappropriated public lands, upon which said person may have filed a preëmption claim, or which may, at the time the application is made, be subject to preëmption at one dollar and twenty-five cents, or less, per acre; or eighty acres or less of such unappropriated lands, at two dollars and fifty cents per acre, to be located in a body, in conformity to the legal subdivision of the public lands, and after the same shall have been surveyed: Provided, That any person owning and residing on land may, under the provisions of this act, enter other land lying contiguous to his or her said land, which shall not, with the land so already owned and occupied, exceed in the aggregate one hundred and sixty acres.

Section 2. *And be it further enacted,* That the person applying for the benefit of this act shall, upon application to the register of the land office in which he or she is about to make such entry, make affidavit before the said register or receiver that he or she is the head of a family, or is twenty-one year or more of age, or shall have performed service in the army or navy of the United States, and that he has never borne arms against the Government of the United States or given aid and comfort to its enemies, and that such application is made for his or her exclusive use and benefit, and that said entry is made for the purpose of actual settlement and cultivation, and not either directly or indirectly for the use or benefit of any other person or person whomever; and upon filing the said affidavit with register or receiver, and on payment of ten dollars, he or she shall thereupon be permitted to enter the quantity of land specified: *Provided, however,* That no certificate shall be given or patent issued therefor until the expiration of five years from the date of such entry; and if, at the expiration of such time, or at any time within two years thereafter; the person making such entry; or, if he be dead, his widow; or in case of her death, his heirs or devisee; or in case of a widow making such entry, her heirs or devisee, in case of her death; shall prove by two credible witnesses that he, she, or they have resided upon or cultivated the same for the term of five years immediately succeeding the time of filing the affidavit aforesaid, and shall make affidavit that no part of said land has been alienated, and that he has borne true allegiance to the Government of the United States; then, in such case, he, she, or they, if at that time a citizen of the United States, shall be entitled to a patent, as in other cases provided for by law; *And provided further,* That in case of the death of both father and mother, leaving an infant child or children, under twenty-one years of age, the right and fee shall enure to the benefit of said infant child or children; and the executor, administrator or guardian may, at any time within two years after the death of the surviving parent, and in accordance with the laws of the State in which such children for the time being have their domicil, sell said land for the benefit of said infants, but for no other purpose; and the purchaser shall acquire the absolute title by the purchase, and be entitled to a patent from the United States, on payment of the office fees and sum of money herein specified.

Section 3. *And be it further enacted,* That the register of the land office shall note all such applications on the tract books and plats of his office, and keep a register of all such entries, and make return thereof to the General Land Office, together with the proof upon which they have been founded.

Section 4. *And be it further enacted,* That no lands acquired under the provisions of this act shall in any event become liable to the satisfaction of any debt of debts contracted prior to the issuing of the patent therefore.

Section 5. *And be it further enacted,* That if, at any time after the filing of the affidavit, as required in the second section of this act, and before the expiration of the five years aforesaid, it shall be proven, after due notice to the settler, to the satisfaction of the register of the land office, that the person having filed such affidavit shall have actually changed his or her residence or abandoned the said land for more than six months at any time, then and in that event the land so entered shall revert to the government.

Section 6. *And be it further enacted,* That no individual shall be permitted to acquire title to more than one quarter section under the provision of this act; and that the Commissioner of the General Land Office is hereby required to prepare and issue such rules and regulations, consistent with this act, as shall be necessary and proper to carry its provision into effect; and that the registers and receivers of the several land offices shall be entitled to receive the same compensation for any lands entered under the provision of this act that they are now entitled to receive when the same quantity of land is entered with money, one half to be paid by the person making the application at the time of so doing, and the other half on the issue of the certificate by the person to whom it may be issued; but this shall not be construed to enlarge the maximum of compensation now prescribed by law for any register or receiver; *Provided,* That nothing contained in this act shall be so construed as to impair or interfere in any manner whatever with existing pre-emption rights. *And provided, further,* That all persons who may have filed their applications for a pre-emption right prior to the passage of this act, shall be entitled to all privileges of this act: Provided, further, That no person who has served, or may hereafter serve, for a period of not less than fourteen days in the army or navy of the United States, either regular or volunteer, under the laws thereof, during the existence of an actual war, domestic or foreign, shall be deprived of the benefits of this act on account of not having attained the age of twenty-one years.

Section 7. *And be it further enacted,* That the fifth section of the act entitled "An act in addition to an act more effectually to provide for the punishment of certain crimes against the United States, and for other purposes," approved the third of March, in the year eighteen hundred and fifty-seven, shall extend to all oaths, affirmations, and affidavits, required or authorized by this act.

Section 8. *And be it further enacted,* That nothing in this act shall be so construed as to prevent any person who has availed him or herself of the benefits of the first section of this act, from paying the minimum price, or the price to which the same may have graduated, for the quantity of land so entered at any time before the expiration of the five years, and obtaining a patent therefor from the government, as in other cases provided by law, on making proof of settlement and cultivation as provided by existing laws granting pre-emption rights.

Approved May 20, 1862.

Document 5: Act to Encourage Immigration of 1864

Significance: Setting up the office of the Commissioner of Immigration to bolster immigration numbers. Immigrants were offered contracts even before arriving in the United States.

"An Act to Encourage Immigration"

Be it enacted by the Senate and House of Representatives of the United States of America in Congress assembled, that the President of the United States is hereby authorized, by and with the advice and consent of the Senate, to appoint a commissioner of immigration, who shall be subject to the direction of the Department of State, shall hold his office for four years, and shall receive a salary at the rate of two thousand five hundred dollars a year. The said commissioner may employ not more than three clerks, of such grade as the Secretary of State shall designate, to be appointed by him, with the approval of the Secretary of State, and to hold their offices at his pleasure.

Section 2. And be it further enacted that all contracts that shall be made by emigrants to the United States in foreign countries, in conformity to regulations that may be established by the said commissioner, whereby emigrants shall pledge the wages of their labor for a term not exceeding twelve months, to repay the expenses of their emigration, shall be held to be valid in law, and may be enforced in the courts of the United States, or of the several states and territories; and such advances, if so stipulated in the contract, and the contract be recorded in the recorder's office in the county where the emigrant shall settle, shall operate as a lien upon any land thereafter acquired by the emigrant, whether under the homestead law when the title is consummated, or on property otherwise acquired until liquidated by the emigrant; but nothing herein contained shall be deemed to authorize any contract contravening the Constitution of the United States, or creating in any way the relation of slavery or servitude.

Section 3. And be it further enacted that no emigrant to the United States who shall arrive after the passage of this act shall be compulsively enrolled for military service during the existing insurrection, unless such emigrant shall voluntarily renounce under oath his allegiance to the country of his birth, and declare his intention to become a citizen of the United States.

Section 4. And be it further enacted that there shall be established in the city of New York an office to be known as the United States Emigrant Office; and there shall be appointed, by and with the advice and consent of the Senate, an officer for said city, to be known as superintendent of immigration, at an annual salary of two thousand dollars; and the said superintendent shall employ a clerk of the first class; and such superintendent shall, under direction of the commissioner of immigration, make contracts with the different railroads and transportation companies of the United States for transportation tickets, to be furnished to such immigrants, and to be paid for by them, and shall under such rules as may be prescribed by the commissioner of immigration, protect such immigrants from imposition and fraud, and shall furnish them such information and facilities as will enable them to proceed in the cheapest and most expeditious manner to the place of their destination. And such superintendent of immigration shall perform such other duties as may be prescribed by the commissioner of immigration: Provided that the duties hereby imposed upon the superintendent in the city of New York shall not be held to effect the powers and duties of the commissioner of immigration of the State of New York; and it shall be the duty of said superintendent in the city of New York to see that the provisions of the act commonly known as the passenger act are strictly complied with, and all breaches thereof punished according to law.

Section 5. And be it further enacted that no person shall be qualified to fill any office under this act who shall be directly or indirectly interested in any corporation having lands for sale to immigrants, or in the carrying or transportation of immigrants, either from foreign countries to the United States and its territories, or to any part thereof, or who shall receive any fee or reward, or the promise thereof, for any service performed, or any benefit rendered, to any person or persons in the line of his duty under this act. And if any officer provided for by this act shall receive from any person or company any fee or reward, or promise thereof, for any services performed or any benefit rendered to any person or persons in the line of his duty under the act, he shall upon conviction, be fined one thousand dollars, or be imprisoned, not to exceed three years, at the discretion of a court of competent jurisdiction, and forever after be ineligible to hold any office of honor, trust, or profit in the United States.

Section 7. And be it further enacted that said commissioner of immigration shall, at the commencement of each annual meeting of Congress, submit a detailed report of the foreign immigration during the proceeding year, and a detailed account of all expenditures under this act.

Section 8. And be it further enacted that the sum of twenty-five thousand dollars, or so much thereof as may be necessary, in the judgment of the President, is hereby appropriated, out of any money in the treasury not otherwise appropriated, for the purpose of carrying the provisions of this act into effect.

Approved July 4, 1864.

Document 6: Anti-Chinese Act, State of California (1862)

Significance: Anti-Chinese legislation in California, an early example of anti-Catholic laws in America.

An Act to Protect Free White Labor Against Competition With Chinese Coolie Labor, and to Discourage The Immigration of The Chinese into the State of California April 26, 1862

The People of the State of California, represented in Senate and Assembly, do enact as follows:

SECTION 1. There is hereby levied on each person, male and female, of the Mongolian race, of the age of eighteen years and upwards, residing in this State, except such as shall, under laws now existing, or which may hereafter be enacted, take out licenses to work in the mines, or to prosecute some kind of business, a monthly capitation tax of two dollars and fifty cents, which tax shall be known as the Chinese Police Tax; provided, That all Mongolians exclusively engaged in the production and manufacture of the following articles shall be exempt from the provisions of this Act, viz: sugar, rice, coffee, tea....

SECTION 4. The Collector shall collect the Chinese police tax, provided for in this Act, from all persons refusing to pay such tax, and sell the same at public auction, by giving notice by proclamation one hour previous to such sale; and shall deliver the property, together with a bill of sale thereof, to the person agreeing to pay, and paying, the highest thereof, which delivery and bill of sale shall transfer to such person a good and sufficient title to the property. And after deducting the tax and necessary expenses incurred by reason of such refusal, seizure, and sale of property, the Collector shall return the surplus of the proceeds of the sale, if any, to the person whose property was sold; provided, That should any person, liable to pay the tax imposed in this Act, in any county in this State, escape into any other County, with the intention to evade the payment of such tax, then, and in that event, it shall be lawful for the Collector, when he shall collect Chinese police taxes, as provided for in this section, shall deliver to each of the persons paying such taxes a police tax receipt, with the blanks properly filled; provided, further, That any Mongolian, or Mongolians, may pay the above named tax to the County Treasurer, who is hereby authorized to receipt for the same in the same manner as the Collector. And any Mongolian, so paying said tax to the Treasurer of the County, if paid monthly, shall be entitled to a reduction of twenty percent of said tax. And if paid in advance for the year next ensuing, such Mongolian, or Mongolians, shall be entitled to a reduction of thirty-three and one third percent on said tax. But in all cases where the County Treasurer receipts for said tax yearly in advance, he shall do it by issuing for each month separately; and any Mongolian who shall exhibit a County Treasurer's receipt, as above provided, to the Collector for the month for which said receipt was given.

SECTION 5. Any person charged with the collection of Chinese police taxes, who shall give any receipt other than the one prescribed in this Act, or receive money for such taxes without giving the necessary receipt therefor, or who shall insert more than one name in any receipt, shall be guilty of a felony, and, upon conviction thereof, shall be fined in a sum not exceeding one thousand dollars, and be imprisoned in the State Prison for a period not exceeding one year.

SECTION 6. Any Tax Collector who shall sell, or cause to be sold, any police tax receipt, with the date of the sale left blank, or which shall not be dated and signed, and blanks filled with ink, by the Controller, Auditor, and Tax Collector, and any person who shall make any alteration, or cause the same to be made, in any police tax receipt, shall be deemed guilty of a felony, and, on conviction thereof, shall be fined in a sum not exceeding one thousand dollars, and imprisoned in the State prison for a period not exceeding 2 years; and the police tax receipt so sold, with blank date, or which shall not be signed and dated, and blanks filled with ink, as aforesaid, or which shall have been altered, shall be received in evidence in any Court of competent jurisdiction.

SECTION 7. Any person or company who shall hire persons liable to pay the Chinese police tax shall be held responsible for the payment of the tax due from each person so hired; and no employer shall be released from this liability on the ground that the employee is indebted to him (the employer), and the Collector may proceed against any such employer in the same manner as he might against the original party owing the taxes. The Collector shall have power to require any person or company believed to be indebted to, or to have any money, gold dust, or property of any kind, belonging to any person liable for police taxes, or in which such person is interested, in his or their possession, or under his or their control, to answer, under oath, as to such indebtedness, or the possession of such money, gold dust, or other property. In case a party is indebted, or has possession or control of any moneys, gold dust, or other property, as aforesaid, of such person liable for police taxes, he may collect from such party the amount of such taxes, and may require the delivery of such money, gold dust, or other property, as aforesaid; and in all cases the receipt of the Collector to said party shall be a complete bar to any demand made against said party, or his legal representatives, for the amounts of money, gold dust, or property, embraced therein.

SECTION 8. The Collector shall receive for his service, in collecting police taxes, twenty percent of all moneys which he shall collect from persons owing such taxes. All of the residue, after deducting the percentage of the Collector, forty percent shall be paid into the County Treasury, for the use of the State, forty percent into the general County Fund, for the use of the County, and the remaining twenty percent into the School Fund, for the benefit of schools within the County; provided, That in counties where the Tax Collector receives a specific salary, he shall not be required to pay the percentage allowed for collecting the police tax into the County Treasury, but shall be allowed to retain the same for his own use and benefit; provided, That where he shall collect the police tax by Deputy, the percentage shall go to the Deputy...

SECTION 10. It is hereby made the duty of the various officers charged with the execution of the provisions of this Act, to carry out said provisions by themselves of Deputies; and for the faithful performance of their said duties in the premises, they shall be liable on their official bonds, respectively. The Treasurer of the respective counties shall make their statements and settlements under this Act with the Controller of State, at the same time and in the same manner they make their settlements under the general Revenue Act.

SECTION 11. This Act shall be take effect and be in force from and after the first day of May, next ensuing.

Document 7: Chinese Exclusion Act of 1882

Significance: This famous piece of legislation, motivated by racism in America, banned Chinese workers from the country.

"An Act to execute certain treaty stipulations relating to Chinese."

Whereas in the opinion of the Government of the United States the coming of Chinese laborers to this country endangers the good order of certain localities within the territory thereof: Therefore,

Be it enacted by the Senate and House of Representatives of the United States of America in Congress assembled, That from and after the expiration of ninety days next after the passage of this act, and until the expiration of ten years next after the passage of this act, the coming of Chinese laborers to the United States be, and the same is hereby, suspended; and during such suspension it shall not be lawful for any Chinese laborer to come, or having so come after the expiration of said ninety days to remain within the United States.

SEC. 2. That the master of any vessel who shall knowingly bring within the United States on such vessel, and land or permit to be landed, any Chinese laborer, from any foreign port or place, shall be deemed guilty of a misdemeanor, and on conviction thereof shall be punished by a fine of not more than five hundred dollars for each and every such Chinese laborer so brought, and maybe also imprisoned for a term not exceeding one year.

SEC. 3. That the two foregoing sections shall not apply to Chinese laborers who were in the United States on the seventeenth day of November, eighteen hundred and eighty, or who shall have come into the same before the expiration of ninety days next after the passage of this act, and who shall produce to such master before going on board such vessel, and shall produce to the collector of the port in the United States at which such vessel shall arrive, the evidence hereinafter in this act required of his being one of the laborers in this section mentioned; nor shall the two foregoing sections apply to the case of any master whose vessel, being bound to a port not within the United States, shall come within the jurisdiction of the United States by reason of being in distress or in stress of weather, or touching at any port of the United States on its voyage to any foreign port or place: Provided, That all Chinese laborers brought on such vessel shall depart with the vessel on leaving port.

SEC. 4. That for the purpose of properly identifying Chinese laborers who were in the United States on the seventeenth day of November eighteen hundred and eighty, or who shall have come into the same before the expiration of ninety days next after the passage of this act, and in order to furnish them with the proper evidence of their right to go from and come to the United States of their free will and accord, as provided by the treaty between the United States and China dated November seventeenth, eighteen hundred and eighty, the collector of customs of the district from which any such Chinese laborer shall depart from the United States shall, in person or by deputy, go on board each vessel having on board any such Chinese laborers and cleared or about to sail from his district for a foreign port, and on such vessel make a list of all such Chinese laborers, which shall be entered in registry-books to be kept for that purpose, in which shall be stated the name, age, occupation, last place of residence, physical marks of peculiarities, and all facts necessary for the identification of each of such Chinese laborers, which books shall be safely kept in the custom-house.; and every such Chinese laborer so departing from the United States shall be entitled to, and shall receive, free of any charge or cost upon application therefore, from the collector or his deputy, at the time such list is taken, a certificate, signed by the collector or his deputy and attested by his seal of office, in such form as the Secretary of the Treasury shall prescribe, which certificate shall contain a statement of the name, age, occupation, last place of residence, persona description, and facts of identification of the Chinese laborer to whom the certificate is issued, corresponding with the said list and registry in all particulars. In case any Chinese laborer after having received such certificate shall leave such vessel before her departure he shall deliver his certificate to the master of the vessel, and if such Chinese laborer shall fail to return to such vessel before her departure from port the certificate shall be delivered by the master to the collector of customs for cancellation. The certificate herein provided for shall entitle the Chinese laborer to whom the same is issued to return to and re-enter the United States upon producing and delivering the same to the collector of customs of the district at which such Chinese laborer shall seek to re-enter; and upon delivery of such certificate by such Chinese laborer to the collector of customs at the time of re-entry in the United States said collector shall cause the same to be filed in the custom-house anti duly canceled.

SEC. 5. That any Chinese laborer mentioned in section four of this act being in the United States, and desiring to depart from the United States by land, shall have the right to demand and receive, free of charge or cost, a certificate of identification similar to that provided for in section four of this act to be issued to such Chinese laborers as may desire to leave the United States by water; and it is hereby made the duty of the collector of customs of the district next adjoining the foreign country to which said Chinese laborer desires to go to issue such certificate, free of charge or cost, upon application by such Chinese laborer, and to enter the same upon registry-books to be kept by him for the purpose, as provided for in section four of this act.

SEC. 6. That in order to the faithful execution of articles one and two of the treaty in this act before mentioned, every Chinese person other than a laborer who may be entitled by said treaty and this act to come within the United States, and who shall be about to come to the United States, shall be identified as so entitled by the Chinese Government in each case, such identity to be evidenced by a certificate issued under the authority of said government, which certificate shall be in the English language or (if not in the English language) accompanied by a translation into English, stating such right to come, and which certificate shall state the name, title or official rank, if any, the age, height, and all physical peculiarities, former and present occupation or profession, and place of residence in China of the person to whom the certificate is issued and that such person is entitled, conformably to the treaty in this act mentioned to come within the United States. Such certificate shall be prima-facie evidence of the fact set forth therein, and shall be produced to the collector of customs, or his deputy, of the port in the district in the United States at which the person named therein shall arrive.

SEC. 7. That any person who shall knowingly and falsely alter or substitute any name for the name written in such certificate or forge any such certificate, or knowingly utter any forged or fraudulent certificate, or falsely personate any person named in any such certificate, shall be deemed guilty of a misdemeanor; and upon conviction thereof shall be fined in a sum not exceeding one thousand dollars, and imprisoned in a penitentiary for a term of not more than five years.

SEC. 8. That the master of any vessel arriving in the United States from any foreign port or place shall, at the same time he delivers a manifest of the cargo, and if there be no cargo, then at the time of making a report of the entry of the vessel pursuant to law, in addition to the other matter required to be reported, and before landing, or permitting to land, any Chinese passengers, deliver and report to the collector of customs of the district in which such vessels shall have arrived a separate list of all Chinese passengers taken on board his vessel at any foreign port or place, and all such passengers on board the vessel at that time. Such list shall show the names of such passengers (and if accredited officers of the Chinese Government traveling on the business of that government, or their servants, with a note of such facts), and the names and other particulars, as shown by their respective certificates; and such list shall be sworn to by the master in the manner required by law in relation to the manifest of the cargo. Any willful refusal or neglect of any such master to comply with the provisions of this section shall incur the same penalties and forfeiture as are provided for a refusal or neglect to report and deliver a manifest of the cargo.

SEC. 9. That before any Chinese passengers are landed from any such line vessel, the collector, or his deputy, shall proceed to examine such passenger, comparing the certificate with the list and with the passengers; and no passenger shall be allowed to land in the United States from such vessel in violation of law.

SEC. 10. That every vessel whose master shall knowingly violate any of the provisions of this act shall be deemed forfeited to the United States, and shall be liable to seizure and condemnation in any district of the United States into which such vessel may enter or in which she may be found.

SEC. 11. That any person who shall knowingly bring into or cause to be brought into the United States by land, or who shall knowingly aid or abet the same, or aid or abet the landing in the United States from any vessel of any Chinese person not lawfully entitled to enter the United States, shall be deemed guilty of a misdemeanor, and shall, on conviction thereof, be fined in a sum not exceeding one thousand dollars, and imprisoned for a term not exceeding one year.

SEC. 12. That no Chinese person shall be permitted to enter the United States by land without producing to the proper officer of customs the certificate in this act required of Chinese persons seeking to land from a vessel. And any Chinese person found unlawfully within the United States shall be caused to be removed therefrom to the country from whence he came, by direction of the President of the United States, and at the cost of the United States, after being brought before some justice, judge, or commissioner of a court of the United States and found to be one not lawfully entitled to be or remain in the United States.

SEC. 13. That this act shall not apply to diplomatic and other officers of the Chinese Government traveling upon the business of that government, whose credentials shall be taken as equivalent to the certificate in this act mentioned, and shall exempt them and their body and house-hold servants from the provisions of this act as to other Chinese persons.

SEC. 14. That hereafter no State court or court of the United States shall admit Chinese to citizenship; and all laws in conflict with this act are hereby repealed.

SEC. 15. That the words "Chinese laborers," wherever used in this act shall be construed to mean both skilled and unskilled laborers and Chinese employed in mining.

Approved, May 6, 1882.

FURTHER READINGS

Billington, Ray. *The Origins of Nativism in the United States, 1800-1844.* New York: Arno Press, 1974.

Clarke, Duncan. *A New World: A History of Immigration into the United States.* San Diego: Thunder Bay Press, 2000.

Daniels, Roger. *Coming to America: A History of Immigration and Ethnicity in American Life,* 2nd ed. New York: Perennial/HarperCollins, 2002.

Gellinek, Christian. *Going Dutch, Gone American: Germans Settling in North America.* Munster: Aschendorff, 2003.

Jones, Maldwyn A. *The Limits of Liberty: American History, 1607–1992,* 2nd ed. New York: Oxford University Press, 1995.

Kamphoefner, Walter D., Wolfgang Helbich, and Ulrike Sommer, eds. *News from the Land of Freedom: German Immigrants Write Home.* Ithaca: Cornell University Press, 1991.

Kenny, Kevin. *The American Irish: A History.* New York: Longman, 2000.

Laxton, Edward. *The Famine Ships: The Irish Exodus to America, 1846–1851.* London: Bloomsbury, 1996.

Lee, Erika. *At America's Gates: Chinese Immigration during the Exclusion Era, 1882–1943.* Chapel Hill: University of North Carolina Press, 2003.

Mahin, Dean. *The Blessed Place of Freedom: Europeans in Civil War America.* Washington, D.C.: Brassey's, 2002.

McPherson, James M. *Battle Cry of Freedom: The Civil War Era.* New York: Oxford University Press, 1988.

Miyares, Ines M. and Christopher A. Airriess, eds. *Contemporary Ethnic Geographies in America.* Lanham, Md.: Rowman and Littlefield, 2007.

Moran, Gerard P. *Sending Out Ireland's Poor: Assisted Emigration to North America in the Nineteenth Century.* Dublin: Four Courts Press, 2004.

Morison, Samuel Eliot. *The Oxford History of the American People: 1789 through Reconstruction,* vol. 2 of *The Oxford History of the American People,* 3 vols. 1972; reprint, New York: Meridian, 1994.

Roy, Jody. *Rhetorical Campaigns of the 19th Century Anti-Catholics and Catholics in America.* Lewiston, N.Y.: Edwin Mellen Press, 1990.

Tolzmann, Don Heinrich. *The German-American Experience.* New York: Humanity Books, 2000.

Tong, Benson. *The Chinese Americans.* Boulder: University of Colorado Press, 2003.

CHAPTER 3

The Great Wave of Immigration from 1880 to 1920

David Felsen

A great wave of immigration to America took place from 1880 until 1920. It brought about 23 million immigrants to the country, predominantly from Southern and Eastern Europe. The decade of the 1880s brought over 5 million immigrants, the 1890s saw just under 4 million immigrants arrive. In the 1900s, a staggering 9 million immigrants came, and in the 1910s about 5.5 million immigrants reached America. Most were non-Protestant, overwhelmingly Catholics from Italy, Eastern Orthodox from Russia and elsewhere in Eastern and Southern Europe, and Jews from Central and Eastern Europe. Over 5 million immigrants came from the newly unified Italy alone, whereas 4 million came from the disintegrating Austro-Hungarian Empire in Central Europe, and approximately the same number came from the Russian Empire. In 1910 the foreign-born segment of the U.S. population stood as high as 14.8 percent.

This wave of immigrants contributed to the rapid growth of American cities and changed American society and culture. By 1910 one-third of the population of the twelve largest cities of the United States was born abroad, and another one-third were the children of immigrants (Jones 1995, 321).

Immigration increased both as a result of advances in technology—mostly notably the development of the steamship—that made it easier to cross from Europe and because of the economic attractiveness of the New World. The earliest and most notable group to emigrate en masse to the United States from their native country came from Italy. Over 5 million Italians, mostly from the poor southern part of the country, came to America. This was part of an approximately 9–10 million people who left the newly unified Italian state. In addition to the United States, many settled in South America and elsewhere in Europe. The *Risorgimento* in Italy that brought about statehood in the 1870s left the economic and political power in the hands of the very few, while the vast majority of Italians carried on in poverty.

TABLE 3.1 Immigration to the United States from Selected Countries, 1871–1920

	1871–80	1881–90	1891–1900	1901–10	1911–20
Germany	718,182	1,452,970	505,152	341,498	143,945
Ireland	436,871	655,540	388,416	339,065	146,199
England	548,043	807,357	271,538	525,950	341,408
Scandinavia	242,934	655,494	371,512	505,324	203,452
Italy	55,795	307,309	651,873	2,045,877	1,209,524
Austro-Hun	72,969	362,719	574,069	2,145,266	901,656
Russia/Baltic	39,287	213,282	505,281	1,597,308	921,957
Total Immi.	2,812,191	5,246,613	3,687,564	8,795,386	5,735,811

Source: Leonard Dinnerstein and David M. Reimers, *Ethnic Americans: A History of Immigration and Assimilation* (New York: Dodd, Mead and Company, 1975), 11.

TABLE 3.2 Foreign Born as a Percentage of Population, 1850–1920

1850	9.7
1860	13.2
1870	14.0
1880	13.3
1890	14.7
1900	13.6
1910	14.7
1920	13.3

Source: Taken from Roger Daniels, *Coming to America: A History of Immigration and Ethnicity in American Life*, 2nd ed. (New York: Perennial/Harper Collins, 2002), 125.

TABLE 3.3 Immigration by Country of Last Residence, 1871–1920

Austria	1,644,986
Hungary	1,570,133
France	288,716
Germany	3,161,747
Greece	370,217
Ireland	1,966,015
Italy	4,170,362
Sweden	1,078,572
Russia/USSR	3,276,363
United Kingdom	2,494,296
China	241,594
Japan	241,995
Turkey	326,046
Canada	1,701,666
Mexico	276,692

Source: Immigration statistics data taken from Ines M. Miyares and Christopher A. Airriess, "Creating Contemporary Ethnic Geographies—A Review of Immigration Law," in *Contemporary Ethnic Geographies in America*, ed. Ines M. Miyares and Christopher A. Airriess (Lanham, Md.: Rowman & Littlefield, 2007), 30–32.

Poor growing conditions, agricultural disease, and weak food prices in these years heightened the plight of Italian peasants. Hence, the 1880s and 1890s witnessed a surge of Italians coming to the United States fleeing economic hardship and social exclusion.

A second group to arrive in large numbers in the United States were Jews fleeing persecution in Eastern Europe. About 2 million Jews left the Russian Empire at the turn of the century because of unrest and instability and resultant to state-sponsored anti-Semitic persecution. Jews were subjected to restrictions under the Russian Empire, and became scapegoats for the Russian Czars during times of political and economic crisis. The violent pogroms—government-orchestrated murder, looting, and pillaging—throughout Russia from the final years of the nineteenth century and onward forced many Jews to make the voyage to America. Following the infamous Kishinev pogrom of 1903, there was a spike in emigration of Jews from Russia to the United States.

Emigration from the dying Austro-Hungarian Empire also increased as the empire was coming under strain due to the growing force of ethnic nationalism within its boundaries. About 2 million immigrants of different ethnic groups arrived in the United States; many of them were Slavic or Jewish. About 1 million Polish nationals also came to the United States, as did about 350,000 Greeks fleeing Ottoman rule. Political uncertainty, the repression of ethnic minorities in Europe, encouragement by relatives already in America, and better transportation in that era caused millions to make the voyage to America.

The attention given to immigration in these years is captured in an article that appeared in *The New York Times* in 1902 (Document 1). The early 1900s were a period in which the idea of the American dream was conceived, where, according to the document, "No proclamations made by the press of lynching bees, and miners' strikes, and the bad treatment of immigrants in New York can offset the hope to better their condition." The piece further adds that Americans "feel anxiety lest the assimilative powers of the Great Republic shall not be equal to the task of weaving all these threads of diverse races into a homogeneous whole." However, all in all, the writer notes that America holds a a good opinion of the mass of immigrants, concluding that, "So far it cannot be said that the immigration offers any very serious drawbacks, although many bad elements enter with the good. Our population is now so large that it may be depended upon to neutralize even so tremendous a foreign element, broken as it is into so many unconnected parts, separated yet further by diversity of language."

Almost half of all Americans trace their heritage to this wave of immigration. The Statue of Liberty, which was just given to the United States in this period, and Ellis Island, which became the first point of entry for most European immigrants at this time, fittingly have become national monuments that are part of America's collective memory.

RESPONSES TO THE INCREASE IN IMMIGRATION IN THE 1880s AND 1890s

The arrival of millions of immigrants over a short period invariably sparked anti-immigrant and xenophobic sentiment. Once again, nativist groups flourished at the end of the nineteenth century. Violent anti-immigration actions were unleashed in major cities, such as the Haymarket Riot in Chicago in 1886, and there was a rise in anti-immigrant.

Furthermore, concern over the need to impose controls over immigration grew in the U.S. Congress. The Immigration Act of August 1882 was passed only months after the Chinese Exclusion Act. The new law specified who should be banned from getting into the United States, making inadmissable those with "moral turpitude," people who were mentally handicapped, convicts, and anyone who could not take care of himself or herself that would become a public charge (Document 2).

As a result of the 1882 Immigration Law and subsequent measures introduced by Congress in the 1880s to restrict American companies from offering employment contracts to European would-be immigrants, immigration fell substantially in the decade from 1890 to 1900. Although 5.2 million or so immigrated to the United States in the 1880–1890 period, only 3.7 million came in the 1890–1900 period.

Growing xenophobia also played a role in reducing immigrant numbers. The 1880s and 1890s saw the rise of social Darwinist ideas about racial purity and the superiority of certain racial groups over others. Politics spoke about the "new immigrants" being less intelligent and less easy to integrate than the "old immigrants." Congressional leaders, such as Senator Henry Cabot Lodge, were linked to anti-immigrant positions and groups such as the Immigration Restriction League. In this period, Congress also proposed imposing literacy tests as a means to bar immigrants. By the end of the nineteenth century, the United States was gaining a reputation for being an unwelcome and hostile climate to immigrants.

THE DAWN OF THE TWENTIETH CENTURY AND THE RENEWED PROMISE OF AMERICA

With renewed economic growth in the early twentieth century, the first decade of the twentieth century saw the largest number of immigrants arriving in the United States. Nine million people immigrated during the first ten years of the century. This owed to deteriorating political conditions as the Russian and Austro-Hungarian Empires grew more unstable, forcing large numbers to emigrate to the New World. Inside the United States a loose coalition of pro-immigrant interests, including American economic leaders from the North, Southern senators who sought cheaper labor from abroad, and progressive and ethnic representative organizations, such as the National Liberal Immigration League, the Hebrew Immigrant Aid Society, and the German-American Alliance, all helped exert influence on Congress to maintain a more open immigration policy. Both political parties were sensitive to the pro-immigrant pressure (Jones 1995, 261–262).

Edwin Levick's December 1906 photograph of immigrants on the deck of the S.S. *Patricia*, a German-built commercial steamer on the Hamburg-America line, demonstrates that while conditions had improved since the terrible days of the "coffin ships," immigrants traveling in steerage still faced uncomfortable conditions on crowded Atlantic liners. In 1906 the *Patricia* accommodated 162 first-class passengers, 184 second-class passengers, and 2,143 third-class passengers. Library of Congress, Prints and Photographs Division, LC-USZ62-11202.

Yet, within a few years, the pro-immigration coalition began to disintegrate, southern states began expressing worries that immigrants were taking jobs away, while the American Federation of Labor came out strongly against immigration that resulted in cheap labor. In the wake of the economic crisis of 1907, Congress passed a new, more restrictrive, Immigration Act. It raised the head tax imposed on immigrants, it broadened the powers of the commissioner of immigration and tightened grounds for inadmissibility to the country. Most notably, the legislation established a commission of inquiry to study all aspects of immigration (Document 3). This commission stated that it "shall make full inquiry; examination, and investigation by subcommittee or otherwise into the subject of immigration. For the purpose of said inquiry; examination; and investigation; said commission is authorized to send for persons and papers; make all necessary travel; either in the United States or any foreign country, and, through the chairman of the commission or any member thereof to administer oaths and to examine witnesses and papers respecting all matters pertaining to the subject; and to employ necessary clerical and other assistance." The commission became known as the Dillingham Commission.

THE DILLINGHAM COMMISSION RECOMMENDATIONS OF 1911 AND THE IMMIGRATION ACT OF 1917

The Dillingham Commission studied many of the most salient immigration questions of the time over the course of four years from 1907 to 1911, producing a forty-two-volume study for Congress and the public. The commissioners themselves held strongly anti-immigrant and social Darwinist prejudices. Racist language pervades the Dillingham Report. In short, the report asserted that the "old immigration" of taller, blonder, white, predominantly Protestant, British, Scandinavian, and German immigrants were somehow easier to integrate and

Newly arrived immigrants report to the rebuilt Ellis Island immigration center for processing, 1907. The original 1892 building burned down in 1897, and the design of the expanded new facility, completed in 1900, expedited the medical screening and other inspections given to immigrants on arrival. Those determined to be paupers or "imbeciles" or to have infectious diseases were returned to their point of departure at the expense of the shipping line that brought them. Library of Congress, George Grantham Bain Collection.

more desirable than the more recently arrived Eastern European, Mediterranean, Chinese, and Jewish immigration. The report covered a whole range of subjects, including general immigration statistics; conditions in Europe that motivated immigration; immigrant workers involved in manufacturing, mining, tobacco, and agriculture; immigrants' social conditions in cities; immigrant children in American schools; immigration and crime; a comparative analysis of immigration with other countries; and a volume entitled "Changes in bodily form of descendents of immigrants." In its discussion of the inquiry's scope, the text states:

> The new immigration as a class is far less intelligent than the old, approximately one-third of all those over 14 years of age when admitted being illiterate. Racially they are for the most part essentially unlike the British, German, and other peoples who came during the period prior to 1880, and generally speaking they are actuated in coming, by different ideals, for the old immigration came to be a part of the country, while the new, in a large measure, comes with the intention of profiting, in a pecuniary way, by the superior advantages of the new world and then returning to the old country.

The recommendations of the report are also telling of the prejudiced attitudes of the time. The commission recommended greater selectivity in who should be allowed to come to the United States, penalties on immigrants who try to "prevent" the Americanization of other immigrants through helping them keep their ties with their original countries, new quotas on immigrant numbers by ethnic or racial group, the continued ban on Chinese immigrants, the banning of immigrants who came without their families, and, most controversially, the need to implement a literacy test of some form for all immigrants.

The immediate response to the report to Congress in 1911 was an attempt by Congress to pass a literacy test with a view to dramatically curtailing immigration, which was vetoed by President Taft in 1913. In the end, however, with the outbreak of World War I, immigration numbers did fall without additional legislation. In 1915 immigration fell to 300,000, down from 1.2 million the previous year.

Subsequently, American worry over the Bolshevik Revolution in Russia of 1917 led to new immigration legislation to restrict immigration from Europe, to better Americanize the millions of European immigrants, and to protect Americans from radical ideas from the European continent. Furthermore, the Immigration Act of 1917 implemented a number of provisions recommended by the Dillingham Report (Document 5).

The most important provision—a clear challenge by congressional leaders to President Woodrow Wilson—was the successful insertion of a mandatory literacy test. The legislation states that "for the purpose of ascertaining whether aliens can read the immigrant inspectors shall be furnished with slips of uniform size, prepared under the direction of the Secretary of Labor, each containing not less than thirty nor more than forty words in ordinary use, printed in plainly legible type in some one of the various languages or dialects of immigrants. Each alien may designate the particular language or dialect in which he desires the examination to be made, and shall be required to read the words printed on the slip in such language or dialect." The bill was vetoed by the president but was then taken up by Congress again and eventually passed despite President Wilson's objections.

CONCLUSION

At the end of World War I, the great wave of immigration came to an end. By the end of the global conflict, the U.S. congressional leadership and American citizens were signaling a desire to remain isolationist, to refrain from getting involved in European affairs, and to limit European immigrants from coming to America's shores. The immigration policies in the decades that followed clearly continued to reflect this mood.

DOCUMENTS

Document 1: The Rush to America (May 4, 1902)

Significance: The *New York Times* article discusses the remarkable impact of mass immigration on turn-of-the-century America.

"So far the year 1902 has broken the record of the past decade for immigrants landing at this port. January and February showed a large increase on the figures for the same months last year.

This March showed 23,000 more than March 1901, and during the first two weeks of April there entered 40,000 souls, as against 28,000 in the same fortnight a year ago. For the rest of April the proportions are as large if not larger, and May bids fair to outdo April. None too soon have the new quarters of the Emigrant Palace on Ellis Island been made ready.

The flood of immigration which subsided a little after the lean years of the nineties, is rising to unprecedented heights during the fat years which bear a rotund O auspiciously in the place of their penultimate numeral.

Rules that immigrants must have money in their pouch, that they must be healthy, and free from suspicion of crime, have no deterrent effect. The Spanish war, the advance of American manufactures into Europe, the outcry of European papers against the American bugbear, and the evidence of their own senses, which show them how North America has become the land above all others which feeds Europe, have impressed the dullest and least imaginative.

No proclamations made by the press of lynching bees, and miners' strikes, and the bad treatment of immigrants in New York can offset the hope to better their condition. Would-be colonial kingdoms and empires spread their lures in vain. Russia is losing her most stalwart and trustworthy soldiers by the exodus from Finland. Hungary and Galicia pour their thousands through the German ports of Hamburg and Bremen. Germany herself, having for a term of years marked with complacency the great industrial advances and how the empire was absorbing her laboring men, is grown anxious again, now that things financial and commercial in the Fatherland are less propitious. Irish immigration is not so great, only because the population has already sunk so low by previous outgoings to America and the British colonies.

It is particularly Italy that sends a stream of immigrants, breaking for the peninsula all previous records. Next are the Poles and Slovaks of Austria, with Greeks and denizens of Turkey and the Balkans to swell the flood; South Russians, too, and a small but constant contingent of Irish, Scotch, English, and Germans.

The old bogy of illiteracy among the immigrants has lost much of its former force, since other nations are paying attention to education, although they have not attained that low percentage of illiterates we find in Scandinavia, Switzerland, and Northern Germany. Strange to say, it is this improvement in popular education which has done much to cause the rush to the land of dollars, since a reading people has the press and cheap mails to aid them in deciding where their chances of a livelihood are best. The situation is a serious one not only for the European nations who live in a constant state of menace of war, but for us, who may fairly feel anxiety lest the assimilative powers of the Great Republic shall not be equal to the task of weaving all these threads of diverse races into a homogeneous whole.

DID YOU KNOW?

Chicago and the Great Wave of Immigration (1880–1920)

While the eastern cities of Boston, New York, and Philadelphia had already become established well before the revolution, the rise of America's second-largest city, Chicago, and of midwestern cities more broadly, is a direct result of the Great Wave of immigration of the 1880–1920 period. In 1880 the population of Chicago stood at half a million, but grew to more than a million by 1890, becoming the second-largest city in the country. While one-quarter of Philadelphians and one-third of Bostonians were born abroad in 1890, Chicago had as many people residing in the city who were born abroad in 1890 as native-born Americans. One journalist observed that only Berlin and Hamburg had a larger German population than Chicago, only Christiana and Bergen had more Norwegians than Chicago, and only Stockholm and Gotenborg had more Swedes than Chicago (Arthur Meier Schlesinger, "The Rise of the City, 1878-1898." Reprinted in Andrew S. Bersky and James P. Shenton, eds., *The Historians' History of the United States*, vol. II [New York: G.P. Putnam's and Sons, 1966], 909).

DID YOU KNOW?

Muckrakers

The terrible working conditions of the millions of immigrants who came to America's shores gave rise to critiques of American capitalism in the late nineteenth and early twentieth centuries. Prominent writers, such as Upton Sinclair and Jack London, wrote about difficult conditions for immigrants and about the travails of the lower classes. Sinclair's *The Jungle* was published in 1906 and exposed the horrid conditions for workers at U.S. meatpacking plants in Chicago through the story of an immigrant laborer, Jurgis Rudkus. Similarly, journalistic pieces by Ida Tarbell, who exposed Standard Oil Company, and Lincoln Steffen, who wrote about corruption in big cities, and others, earned these journalists the title "muckrakers" for raking up muck on American capitalism (Howard Zinn, *A People's History of the United States, 1492–Present* [New York: Harper Collins, 1999], 322–323).

In the large cities the Germans are being driven out of the barbers' shops by Italians and the Irish out of rude laboring employments. Germans take to shopkeeping, beer selling, and other better-paying occupations. Irishmen turn to salaried places as janitors or through their singularly keen political sense obtain offices under municipal government in the great cities. The South Russian immigrants go largely to the West as farmers, and the Turkish subjects become peddlers of fruit and cheap Oriental goods, which are being made here in great quantities. Englishmen take to factory work and shopkeeping. The Italian immigrants are doing so well that they now import their families and settle down, generally in the large cities, instead of returning to Italy as they were formerly wont to do. The Slavs of Austria find employment in the mines.

So far it cannot be said that the immigration offers any very serious drawbacks, although many bad elements enter with the good. Our population is now so large that it may be depended upon to neutralize even so tremendous a foreign element, broken as it is into so many unconnected parts, separated yet further by diversity of language. Whether in the coming years we shall be forced to render immigration more difficult in order to winnow more thoroughly the desirable from the

Italian immigrants sell bread from a cart on Mulberry Street in New York City, circa 1900, in this image recorded by an unidentified photographer for the Byron Company, a commercial studio that flourished in the city from 1892 to 1942. "Mulberry Bend," at Mulberry Street's southern end, was New York City's most densely populated Italian slum. Library of Congress, Prints and Photographs Division, LC-D401-13585.

undesirable parts remains to be seen. A singular feature is the fact that, with the exception of certain lines of rough labor, this exodus of working people has not seriously affected the labor market. This perhaps is to be expected so long as prosperity reigns."

(Source: "The Rush to America," *New York Times*, May 4, 1902, 6)

Document 2: Immigration Act of 1882

Significance: A reaction to the beginnings of mass immigration.

Be it enacted by the Senate and House of Representatives of the United States of America in Congress assembled that there shall be levied, collected and paid a duty of fifty cents for each and every passenger not a citizen of the United States who shall come by steam or sail vessel from a foreign port to any port within the United States. The said duty shall be paid to the collector of customs of the port to which such passenger shall come, or if there be no collector at such port, then to the collector of customs nearest thereto, by the master, owner, agent, or consignee of every such vessel, within twenty-four hours after the entry thereof into such port. The money thus collected shall be paid into the United States Treasury, and shall constitute a fund to be called the immigrant fund, and shall be used, under the direction of the Secretary of the Treasury, to defray the expense of regulating immigration under this act, and for the care of immigrants arriving in the United States, for the relief of such as are in distress, and for the general purposes and expenses of carrying this act into effect. The duty imposed by this section shall be a lien upon the vessels which shall bring such passengers into the United States, and shall be a debt in favor of the United States against the owner or owners by any legal or equitable remedy. Provided, that no greater sum shall be expected for the purposes hereinbefore mentioned, at any port, than shall have been collected as such port.

Sec. 2. That the Secretary of the Treasury is hereby charged with the duty of executing the provisions of this act and with the supervision over the business of immigration to the United States, and for that purpose he shall have the power to enter into contracts with such State commission, board, or officers as may be designated for that purpose by the governor of any State to take charge of the local affairs of immigration in the ports within said State, and to provide for the support and relief of such immigrants therein landing as may fall into distress or need public aid, under the rules and regulations to be prescribed by said Secretary; and it shall be the duty of such State commission, board, or officers so designated to examine into the condition of passengers arriving at the ports within such State in any ship or vessel, and for that purpose all or any of such commissioners or officers, or such other person or persons as they shall appoint, shall be authorized to go on board of and through any such ship or vessel; and if on such examination there shall be found among such passengers any convict, lunatic, idiot, or any person unable to take care of himself or herself without becoming a public charge, they shall report the same in writing to the collector of such port, and such persons shall not be permitted to land.

Sec. 3. That the Secretary of the Treasury shall establish such regulations and rules and issue from time to time such instructions not inconsistent with law as he shall deem best calculated to protect the United States and immigrants into the United States from fraud and loss, and for carrying out the provisions of this act and the immigration laws of the United States; and he shall prescribe all forms of bonds, entries, and other papers to be used under and in the enforcement of the various provisions of this act.

Sec. 4. That all foreign convicts except those convicted of political offenses, upon arrival, shall be sent back to the nations to which they belong and from whence they came. The Secretary of the Treasury may designate the State board of charities of any State in which such board shall exist by law, or any commission in any State, or any person or persons in any State whose duty it shall be to execute the provisions of this section without compensation. The Secretary of the Treasury shall prescribe regulations for the return of the aforesaid persons to the countries from whence they came, and shall furnish instructions to the board, commission, or persons charged with the execution of the provisions of this section as to the mode of procedure in respect thereto, and may change such instructions from time to time. The expense of such return of the aforesaid persons not permitted to land shall be borne by the owners of the vessels in which they came.

Sec. 5. That this act shall take effect immediately.

Approved August 3, 1882.

Document 3: Immigration Act of 1907

Significance: A further attempt to stem immigration flows by widening criteria of ineligibility.

CHAP. 1134.—An Act to regulate the immigration of aliens into the United States.

Be it enacted by the Senate and House of Representatives of the United States of America in Congress, That there shall be levied, collected, and paid a tax of four dollars for every alien entering the United States. The said tax shall he paid to the collector of customs of the port or customs district to which said alien shall come, or, if there be no collector at such port or district, then to the collector nearest thereto, by the master, agent, owner, or consignee of the vessel, transportation line, or other conveyance or vehicle bringing such alien to the United States. The money thus collected, together with all fines and rentals collected under the laws regulating the immigration of aliens into the United States, shall be paid into the Treasury of the United States, and shall constitute a permanent appropriation to be called the "immigrant fund," to be used under the direction of the Secretary of Commerce and Labor to defray the expense of regulating the immigration of aliens into the United States under said laws, including the contract labor laws, the cost of reports of decisions of the Federal courts, and digest thereof, for the use of the Commissioner-General of Immigration, and the salaries and expenses of all officers, clerks, and employees appointed to enforce said laws. The tax imposed by this section shall be a lien upon the vessel, or other vehicle of carriage or transportation bringing such aliens to the United States, and shall be a debt in favor of the United States against the owner or owners of such vessel, or other vehicle, and the payment of such tax may be enforced by any legal or equitable remedy. That the said tax shall not be levied upon aliens who shall enter the United States after an uninterrupted residence of at least one year, immediately preceding such entrance, in the Dominion of Canada, Newfoundland, the Republic of Cuba, or the Republic of Mexico, nor upon otherwise admissible residents of any possession of the United States, nor upon aliens in transit through the United States, nor upon aliens who have been lawfully admitted to the United States and who later shall go in transit from one part of the United States to another through foreign contiguous territory: *Provided,* That the Commissioner-General of Immigration, under the direction or with the approval of the Secretary of Commerce and Labor, by agreement: with transportation lines, as provided in section thirty-two of this Act, may arrange in some other manner for the payment of the tax imposed by this section upon any or all aliens seeking admission from foreign contiguous territory: *Provided further,* That if in any fiscal year the amount of money collected under the provisions of this section shall exceed two million five hundred-thousand dollars, the excess above that amount shall not be added to the "immigrant fund:" *Provided further,* That the provisions of this section shall not apply to aliens arriving in Guam, Puerto Rico, or Hawaii; but if any such alien, not having become a citizen of the United States, shall later arrive at any port or place of the United States on the North American Continent the provisions of this section shall apply: *Provided further,* That whenever the President shall be satisfied that passports issued by ally foreign government to its citizens to go to any country other than the United States or to any insular possession of the

Thomas Nast's cartoon in the Harper's Weekly issue of March 25, 1882, drew a connection between the nativist movement's success in excluding the Chinese and an underlying threat to all immigrants—including the Germans and Irish, who by this time had long since begun to assimilate into the American mainstream. Library of Congress, Prints and Photographs Division, LC-USZ61-2195.

United States or to the Canal Zone are being used for the purpose of enabling the holders to come to the continental territory of the United States to the detriment of labor conditions therein, the President may refuse to permit such citizens of the country issuing such passports to enter the continental territory of the United States from such other country or from such insular possessions or from the Canal Zone.

Sec. 2. That the following classes of aliens shall be excluded from admission into the United States: All idiots, imbeciles, feeble-minded persons, epileptics, insane persons, and persons who have been insane within five years previous; persons who have had two or more attacks of insanity at any tine previously: paupers; persons likely to become a public charge; professional beggars; persons afflicted with tuberculosis or with a loathsome or dangerous contagious disease; persons not comprehended within any of the foregoing excluded classes who are found to be and are certified by the examining surgeon as being mentally or physically defective, such mental or physical defect being of a nature which may affect the ability of such alien to earn a living; persons who have been convicted of or admit having committed a felony or other crime or misdemeanor involving moral turpitude; polygamists, or persons who admit their belief in the practice of polygamy, anarchists, or persons who believe in or advocate the overthrow by force or violence of the Government of the United States, or of all government, or of all forms of law, or the assassination of public officials; prostitutes, or women or girls coming into the United States for the purpose of prostitution or for any other immoral purpose; persons who procure or attempt to bring in prostitutes or women or girls for the purpose of prostitution or for any other immoral purpose; persons hereinafter called contract laborers, who have been induced or solicited to migrate to this country by offers or promises of employment or in consequence of agreements, oral, written or printed, express or implied, to perform labor in this country of any kind, skilled or unskilled; those who have been, within one year from the date of application for admission to the United States, deported as having been induced or solicited to migrate as above described; any person whose ticket or passage is paid for with the money of another, or who is assisted by others to come, unless it is affirmatively and satisfactorily shown that such person does not belong to one of the foregoing excluded classes, and that said ticket or passage was not paid for by any corporation, association, society, municipality, or foreign government, either directly or indirectly; all children under sixteen years of age, unaccompanied by one or both of their parents, at the discretion of the Secretary of Commerce and Labor or under such regulations as lie may from time to time prescribe: *Provided*, That nothing in this Act shall exclude, if otherwise admissible, persons convicted of an offense purely political, not involving moral turpitude: *Provided further*, That the provisions of this section relating to the payments for tickets or passage by any corporation, association, society, municipality, or foreign government shall not apply to the tickets or passage of aliens in immediate and continuous transit through the United States to foreign contiguous territory: *And provided further*, That skilled labor may be imported if labor of like kind unemployed can not be found in this country: And provided further, That the provisions of this law applicable to contract labor shall not be held to exclude professional actors, artists, lecturers, singers, ministers of any religious denomination, professors for colleges or seminaries, persons belonging to any recognized learned profession, or persons employed strictly as personal or domestic servants.

SEC. 22. That the Commissioner-General of Immigration; in addition to such other duties as may by law be assigned to him; shall; under the direction of the Secretary of Commerce and Labor, have charge of the administration of all laws relating to the immigration of aliens into the United States, and shall have the control; direction; and supervision of all officers; clerks; and employees appointed thereunder. He shall establish such rules and regulations, prescribe such forms of bond; reports; entries; and other papers; and shall issue from time to time such instructions; not inconsistent with law; as he shall deem best calculated for carrying out the provisions of this Act and for protecting the United States and aliens migrating thereto from fraud and loss; and shall have authority to enter into contract for the support and relief of such aliens as may fall into distress or need public aid; all under the direction or with the approval of the Secretary of Commerce and Labor. And it shall be the duty of the Commissioner-General of Immigration to detail officers of the immigration service from time to time as may be necessary; in his judgment; to secure information as to the number of aliens detained in the penal; reformatory; and charitable institutions (public and private) of the several States and Territories, the District of Columbia, and other territory of the United States and to inform the officers of such institutions of the provisions of law in relation to the deportation of aliens who have become public charges: *Provided*; That the Commissioner-General of Immigration may, with the approval of the Secretary of Commerce and Labor; whenever in his judgment such action may be necessary to accomplish the purposes of this Act; detail immigration officers; and also surgeons; in accordance with the provisions of section seventeen; for service in foreign countries.

SEC. 39. That a commission is hereby created; consisting of three Senators; to be appointed by the President of the Senate, and three members of the House of Representatives; to be appointed by the Speaker of the House of Representatives; and three persons; to be appointed by the President of the United States. Said commission shall make full inquiry; examination, and investigation by sub-committee or otherwise into the subject of immigration. For the purpose of said inquiry; examination; and investigation; said commission is authorized to send for persons and papers; make all necessary travel; either in the United States or any foreign country, and, through the chairman of the commission or any member thereof to administer oaths and to examine witnesses and papers respecting all matters pertaining to the subject; and to employ necessary clerical and other assistance. Said commission shall report to the Congress the conclusions reached by it and make such recommendations as in its judgment may seem proper.

SEC. 40. The authority is hereby given the Commissioner-General of Immigration to establish; under the direction and control of the Secretary of Commerce and Labor; a division of information in the Bureau of Immigration and Naturalization; and the Secretary of Commerce and Labor shall provide such clerical assistance as may be necessary. It shall lie the duty of said division to promote a beneficial distribution of aliens admitted into the United States among the several States and Territories desiring immigration. Correspondence shall be had with the proper officials of the States and Territories; and said division shall gather from all available sources useful information regarding the resources; products; and physical characteristics of each State and Territory; and shall publish such information in different languages and distribute the publications among all admitted aliens who may ask for such information at the immigrant stations of the United States and to such other persons as may desire the same. When any State or Territory appoints and maintains an agent or agents to represent it at any of the immigrant stations of the United States; such agents shall; under regulations prescribed by the Commissioner-General of Immigration; subject to the approval of the Secretary of Commerce and Labor, have access to aliens who have been admitted to the United States for the purpose of presenting; either orally or in writing; the special inducements offered by such State or Territory to aliens to settle therein. While on duty at any immigrant station such agents shall be subject to all the regulations prescribed by the Commissioner-General of Immigration; who; with the approval of the Secretary of Commerce and Labor, may; for violation of any such regulations; deny to the agent guilty of such violation any of the privileges herein granted.

Document 4: Excerpts from the Dillingham Commission Report (1911)

Significance: The largest and most extensive commission established to that point in U.S. history to study the impact of immigration. The commission was biased in favor of Anglo-Saxon immigrants and against the "new" immigrants of Southern and Eastern Europe.

Introductory

The complete report of the Immigration Commission consists of 42 volumes. In volume 1 there is presented a brief history of the organization and work of the Commission, together with its conclusions and recommendations, but this volume, as well as volume 2, consists for the most part of abstracts of the more extended reports of the Commission upon various phases of the subject under consideration. In preparing these abstracts it was the purpose of the Commission to present in a condensed form some of the more essential results of its investigations, and while the various abstracts lack the great mass of important statistical and other data contained in the reports upon which they are based, it is believed that they are sufficiently exhaustive to meet the requirements of the average student of the immigration problem.

Included in the two volumes are the complete reports of the Commission on various subjects, and also the present United States immigration laws and regulations, the treaty, laws, and regulations governing the admission of Chinese, and the United States naturalization laws and regulations.

Purpose of the Inquiry

As previously stated, the act creating the Commission directed that it should "make full inquiry, examination, and investigation, by subcommittee or otherwise, into the subject of immigration," and the Commission has followed this instruction. In the beginning two plans of work were considered. One plan contemplated bringing together in a new form already existing data; conducting an inquiry into the effectiveness of the existing immigration law and its administration, and by means of hearings securing information and expressions of opinion from persons interested in various phases of the subject under consideration. By the second plan it was proposed to utilize such existing data as might be considered of value, but also to make an original inquiry into fundamental phases of the subject which had previously been considered only in a superficial manner, or not at all. After due consideration the Commission reached the conclusion that the first-mentioned plan, no matter haw carefully it might be carried out, would yield very little new information that would be of value to Congress in a serious consideration of the Government's immigration policy. Consequently it was discarded in favor of an original investigation which, it perfectly apparent, would necessarily be more far reaching and involve more work than any inquiry of a similar nature, except the census alone, that had ever been undertaken by the Government.

Plan and Scope of the Inquiry

Briefly stated, the plan of work adopted by the Commission included a study of the sources of recent immigration in Europe, the general character of incoming immigrants, the methods employed here and abroad to prevent the immigration of persons classed as undesirable in the United States immigration law, and finally a thorough investigation into the general status of the more recent immigrants as residents of the United States, and the effect of such immigration upon the institutions, industries, and people of this country. As above suggested, the chief basis of the Commission's work was the changed character of the immigration movement to the United States during the past twenty-five years.

During the fiscal year 1907, in which the Commission was created, a total of 1,285,349 immigrants were admitted to the United States. Of this number 1,207,619 were from Europe, including Turkey in Asia, and of these 979,661, or 81 percent, came from the southern and eastern countries, comprising Austria-Hungary, Bulgaria, Greece, Italy, Montenegro, Poland, Portugal, Roumania, Russia, Servia, Spain, Turkey in Europe, and Turkey in Asia.

Twenty-five years earlier, in the fiscal year 1882, 648,186 European immigrants came to the United States, and of these only 84,973, or 13.1 per cent, came from the countries above enumerated, while 663,213, or 86.9 per cent, were from Belgium, Great Britain and Ireland, France, Germany, the Netherlands, Scandinavia, and Switzerland, which countries furnished about 95 per cent of the immigration movement from Europe to the United States between 1819 and 1883.

During the entire period for which statistics are available—July 1, 1819, to June 30, 1910—a total of 25,528,410 European immigrants, including 106,481 from Turkey in Asia, were admitted to the United States. Of these, 16,052,900, or 62.9 per cent, came from the northern and western countries enumerated, and 9,475,510, or 37.1 per cent, from southern and eastern Europe and Turkey in Asia. For convenience the former movement will be referred to in the Commission's reports as the "old immigration" and the latter as the "new immigration." The old and the new immigration differ in many essentials. The former was, from the beginning, largely a movement of settlers who came from the most progressive sections of Europe for the purpose of making for themselves homes in the New World. They entered practically every line of activity in nearly every part of the country. Coming during a period of agricultural development, many of them entered agricultural pursuits, sometimes as independent farmers, but more often as farm laborers, who nevertheless, as a rule soon became landowners. They formed an important part of the great movement toward the West, during the last century, and as pioneers were most potent factors in the development of the territory between the Allegheny Mountains and the Pacific coast. They mingled freely with the native Americans and were quickly assimilated, although a large proportion of them,

Strong anti-Chinese feeling across the United States, especially in the West, was stoked during periods of economic depression, culminating in the passage of the Chinese Exclusion Act in 1882. Then and later, the irony of the United States, champion of freedom and opportunity, discriminating against Asians was not lost on observers at home or abroad, as shown in this cartoon by L. M. Glackens published in the Jan. 3, 1912, *Puck* magazine. Library of Congress, Prints and Photographs Division, LC-USZC2-1043.

particularly in later years, belonged to non-English-speaking races. This natural bar to assimilation, however, was soon overcome by them, while the racial identity of their children was almost entirely lost and forgotten.

On the other hand, the new immigration has been largely a movement of unskilled laboring men who have come, in large part temporarily, from the less progressive and advanced countries of Europe in response to the call for industrial workers in the eastern and middle western States. They have almost entirely avoided agricultural pursuits, and in cities and industrial communities have congregated together in sections apart from native Americans and the older immigrants to such an extent that assimilation has been slow as compared to that of the earlier non-English-speaking races.

The new immigration as a class is far less intelligent than the old, approximately one-third of all those over 14 years of age when admitted being illiterate. Racially they are for the most part essentially unlike the British, German, and other peoples who came during the period prior to 1880, and generally speaking they are actuated in coming, by different ideals, for the old immigration came to be a part of the country, while the new, in a large measure, comes with the intention of profiting, in a pecuniary way, by the superior advantages of the new world and then returning to the old country.

The old immigration movement, which in earlier days was the subject of much discussion and the cause of no little apprehension among the people of the country, long ago became thoroughly merged into the population, and the old sources have contributed a comparatively small part, of the recent immigrant tide. Consequently the Commission paid but little attention to the foreign-born element of the old immigrant class and directed its efforts almost entirely to an inquiry relative to the general status of the newer immigrants as residents of the United States.

In pursuance of this policy the Commission began its study of the subject in the countries of Europe which are the chief sources of the new immigration, and followed the emigration movement to ports of embarkation, across the ocean in the steerage, and finally to every part of the United States and into practically every line of activity in which the new immigrants were to be found.

The general plan and scope of the Commission's work are briefly stated in the pages following...

Conclusions

While it has been no part of the work of the Commission to enforce the provisions of the immigration laws, it has been thought best to furnish from time to time to the proper authorities such information acquired in the course of the investigation as could further good administration and the enforcement of the law. City, state, and federal officials have officially recognized such assistance in their attempts to control the so-called "white slave traffic," in the proper regulation of the immigrant societies and homes, in securing evidence and penal certificates to accomplish the deportation of criminals, and in the administration of the Chinese-exclusion act. In some instances such information has led to local reorganization of the immigrant service. While mention is made of this matter the real work of the Commission has consisted in the collection and preparation of new material, largely statistical in nature, which might form a basis on which to frame legislation. A very condensed summary of the results on some of the principal questions investigated follows.

Sources of Immigration and Character of Immigrants

From 1820 to June 30, 1910, 27,918,992 immigrants were admitted to the United States. Of this number 92.3 per cent came from European countries, which countries are the source of about 93.7 per cent of the present immigration movement. From 1820 to 1883 more than 95 per cent of the total immigration from Europe originated in the United Kingdom, Germany, Scandinavia, the Netherlands, Belgium, France, and Switzerland. In what follows the movement from these countries will be referred to as the "old immigration." Following 1883 there was a rapid change in the ethnical character of European immigration, and in recent years more than 70 per cent of the movement has originated in southern and eastern Europe. The change geographically, however, has been somewhat greater than the change in the racial character of the immigration, this being due very largely to the number of Germans who have come from Austria-Hungary and Russia. The movement from southern and eastern Europe will be referred to as the "new immigration." In a single generation Austria-Hungary, Italy, and Russia have succeeded the United Kingdom and Germany as the chief sources of immigration. In fact, each of the three countries first named furnished more immigrants to the United States in 1907 than came in the same year from the United Kingdom, Germany, Scandinavia, France, the Netherlands, Belgium, and Switzerland combined.

The old immigration movement in recent years has rapidly declined, both numerically and relatively, and under present conditions there are no indications that it will materially increase. The new immigration movement is very large, and there are few, if any, indications of its natural abatement. The new immigration, coming in such large numbers, has provoked a widespread feeling of apprehension as to its effect on the economic and social welfare of the country. Because of this the Commission's investigations have been mainly directed toward a study of its general status as part of the population of the country.

The old immigration movement was essentially one of permanent settlers. The new immigration is very largely one of individuals, a considerable proportion of whom apparently have no intention of permanently changing their residence, their only purpose in coming to America being to temporarily take advantage of the greater wages paid for industrial labor in this country. This, of course, is not true of all the new immigrants, but the practice is sufficiently common to warrant referring to it as a characteristic of them as a class. From all data that are available it appears that nearly 40 per cent of the new immigration movement returns to Europe and that about two-thirds of those who go remain there. This does not mean that all of these immigrants have acquired a competence and returned to live on it. Among the immigrants who return permanently are those who have failed, as well as those who have succeeded. Thousands of those returning have, under unusual conditions of climate, work, and food, contracted tuberculosis and other diseases; others are injured in our industries; still others are the widows and children of aliens dying here. These, with the aged and temperamentally unfit, make up a large part of the aliens who return to their former homes to remain.

The old immigration came to the United States during a period of general development and was an important factor in that development, while the new immigration has come during a period of great industrial expansion and has furnished a practically unlimited supply of labor to meet expansion.

As a class the new immigrants are largely unskilled laborers coming from countries where their highest wage is small compared with the lowest wage in the United States. Nearly 75 per cent of them are males. About 83 per cent are between the ages of 14 and 45 years, and consequently are producers rather than dependents. They bring little money into the country and send or take a considerable part or their earnings out. More than 35 per cent are illiterate, as compared with less than 3 per cent of the old immigrant class. Immigration prior to 1882 was practically unregulated, and consequently many were not self-supporting, so that the care of alien paupers in several States was a serious problem. The new immigration has for the most part been carefully regulated so far as health and likelihood of pauperism are concerned, and, although drawn from low in the economic scale, the new immigrants as a rule are the strongest, the most enterprising, and the best of their class.

Recommendations

As a result of the investigation the Commission is unanimously of the opinion that in framing legislation emphasis should be laid upon the following principles:

1. While the American people, as in the past, welcome the oppressed of other lands, care should be taken that immigration be such both in quality and quantity as not to make too difficult the process of assimilation.

2. Since the existing law and further special legislation recommended in this report deal with the physically and morally unfit, further general legislation concerning the admission of aliens should be based primarily upon economic or business considerations touching the prosperity and economic well-being of our people.

3. The measure of the rational, healthy development of a country is not the extent of its investment of capital, its output of products, or its exports and imports, unless there is a corresponding economic opportunity afforded to the citizen dependent upon employment for his material, mental, and moral development.

4. The development of business may be brought about by means which lower the standard of living of the wage earners. A slow expansion of industry which would permit the adaptation and assimilation of the incoming labor supply is preferable to a very rapid industrial expansion which results in the immigration of laborers of low standards and efficiency, who imperil the American standard of wages and conditions of employment.

The Commission agrees that:

1. To protect the United States more effectively against the immigration of criminal and certain other debarred classes

(a) Aliens convicted of serious crimes within a period of five years after admission should be deported in accordance with the provisions of House bill 20980, Sixty-first Congress, second session.

(b) Under the provisions of section 39 of the immigration act of February 20, 1907, the President should appoint commissioners to make arrangements with such countries as have adequate police records to supply emigrants with copies of such records, and that thereafter immigrants from such countries should be admitted to the United States only upon the production of proper certificates showing an absence of convictions for excludable crimes.

(c) So far as practicable the immigration laws should be so amended as to be made applicable to alien seamen.

(d) Any alien who becomes a public charge within three years after his arrival in this country should be subject to deportation in the discretion of the Secretary of Commerce and Labor.

2. Sufficient appropriation should be regularly made to enforce vigorously the provisions of the laws previously recommended by the Commission and enacted by Congress regarding the importation of women for immoral purposes.

3. As the new statute relative to steerage conditions took effect so recently as January 1, 1909, and as the most modern steerage fully complies with all that is demanded under the law, the Commission's only recommendation in this connection is that a statute be immediately enacted providing for the placing of Government officials, both men and women, on vessels carrying third-class or steerage passengers for the enforcement of the law and the protection of the immigrant. The system inaugurated by the Commission of sending investigators in the steerage in the guise of immigrants should be continued at intervals by the Bureau of Immigration.

4. To strengthen the certainty of just and humane decisions of doubtful cases at ports of entry it is recommended—

That section 25 of the immigration act of 1907 be amended to provide that boards of special inquiry should be appointed by the Secretary of Commerce and Labor, and that they should be composed of men whose ability and training qualify them for the performance of judicial functions; that the provisions compelling their hearings to be separate and apart from the public should be repealed, and that the office of an additional Assistant Secretary of Commerce and Labor to assist in reviewing such appeals be created.

5. To protect the immigrant against exploitation; to discourage sending savings abroad; to encourage permanent residence and naturalization; and to secure better distribution of alien immigrants throughout the country—

(a) The States should enact laws strictly regulating immigrant banks.

(b) Proper State legislation should be enacted for the regulation of employment agencies.

(c) Since numerous aliens make it their business to keep immigrants from influences that may tend toward their assimilation and naturalization as American citizens with the purpose of using their funds, and of encouraging investment of their savings abroad and their return to their home land, aliens who attempt to persuade immigrants not to become American citizens should be made subject to deportation.

(d) Since the distribution of the thrifty immigrant to sections of the country where he may secure a permanent residence to the best advantage, and especially where he may invest his savings in farms or engage in agricultural pursuits, is most desirable, the Division of Information, in the Bureau of Immigration and Naturalization, should be so conducted as to cooperate with States desiring immigrant settlers; and information concerning the opportunities for settlement should be brought to the attention of immigrants in industrial centers who have been here for some time and who might be thus induced to invest their savings in this country and become permanent agricultural settlers. The division might also secure and furnish to all laborers alike information showing opportunities for permanent employment in various sections of the country, together with the economic conditions in such places.

6. One of the provisions of section 2 of the act of 1907 reacts as follows:

And provided further, That skilled labor may be imported if labor of like kind unemployed can not be found, in this country. Instances occasionally arise, especially in the establishment of new industries in the United States, where labor of the kind desired, unemployed, can not be found in this country and it becomes necessary to import such labor. Under the law the Secretary of Commerce and Labor has no authority to determine the question of the necessity for importing such labor in advance of the importation, and it is recommended that an amendment to the law be adopted by adding to the clause cited above a provision to the effect that the question of the necessity of importing such skilled labor in any particular instance may be determined by the Secretary of Commerce and Labor upon the application of any person interested prior to any action in that direction by such person; such determination: by the Secretary of Commerce and Labor to be reached after a full hearing and an investigation into the facts of the case.

7. The general policy adopted by Congress in 1882 of excluding Chinese laborers should be continued.

The question of Japanese and Korean immigration should be permitted to stand without further legislation so long as the present method of restriction proves to be effective.

An understanding should be reached with the British Government whereby East Indian laborers would be effectively prevented from coming to the United States.

8. The investigations of the Commission show an oversupply of unskilled labor in basic industries to an extent which indicates an oversupply of unskilled labor in the industries of the country as a whole, a condition which demands legislation restricting the further admission of such unskilled labor.

It is desirable in making the restriction that—

(a) A sufficient number be debarred to produce a marked effect upon the present supply of unskilled labor.

(b) As far as possible, the aliens excluded should be those who come to this country with no intention to become American citizens or even to maintain a permanent residence here, but merely to save enough, by the adoption, if necessary, of low standards of living, to return permanently to their home country. Such persons are usually men unaccompanied by wives or children.

(c) As far as possible the aliens excluded should also be those who, by reason of their personal qualities or habits, would least readily be assimilated or would make the least desirable citizens.

The following methods of restricting immigration have been suggested:

(a) The exclusion of those unable to read or write in some language.

(b) The limitation of the number of each race arriving each year to a certain percentage of the average of that race arriving during a given period of years.

(c) The exclusion of unskilled laborers unaccompanied by wives or families.

(d) The limitation of the number of immigrants arriving annually at any port,

(e) The material increase in the amount of money required to be in the possession of the immigrant at the port of arrival.

(f) The material increase of the head tax.

(g) The levy of the head tax so as to make a marked discrimination in favor of men with families.

All these methods would be effective in one way or another in seeming restrictions in a greater or less degree. A majority of the Commission favor the reading and writing test as the most feasible single method of restricting undesirable immigration.

The Commission as a whole recommends restriction as demanded by economic, moral, and social considerations, furnishes in its report reasons for such restriction, and points out methods by which Congress can attain the desired result if its judgment coincides with that of the Commission.

Document 5: Immigration Act of 1917

Significance: An act to restrict immigration, incorporating suggestions of the Dillingham Commission, including literacy testing.

CHAP. 29—An Act to regulate the immigration of aliens to, and the residence of aliens in, the United States.

Be it enacted By the Senate and House of Representatives of the United States of America in Congress assembled, That the word "alien" wherever used in this Act shall include any person not a native-born or naturalized citizen of the United States; but this definition shall not be held to include Indians of the United States not taxed or citizens of the islands under the jurisdiction of the United States. That the term "United States" as used in the title as well as in the various sections of this Act shall be construed to mean the United States, and any waters, territory, or other place subject to the jurisdiction thereof, except the Isthmian Canal Zone; but if any alien shall leave the Canal Zone or any insular possession of the United States and attempt to enter any other place under the jurisdiction of the United States, nothing contained in this Act shall be construed as permitting him to enter under any other conditions than those applicable to all aliens. That the term "seaman" as used in this Act shall include every person signed on the ship's articles and employed in any capacity on board any vessel arriving in the United States from any foreign port or place....

SEC. 2. That there shall be levied, collected, and paid a tax of $8 for every alien, including alien seamen regularly admitted as provided in this Act, entering the United States: *Provided,* That children under sixteen years of age who accompany their father or their mother shall not be subject to said tax. The said tax shall be paid to the collector of customs of the port or customs district to which said alien shall come, or, if there be no collector at such port or district, then to the collector nearest thereto, by the master, agent, owner, or consignee of the vessel, transportation line, or other conveyance or vehicle bringing such alien to the United States, or by the alien himself if he does not come by a vessel, transportation line, or other conveyance or vehicle or when collection from the master, agent, owner, or consignee of the vessel, transportation line, or other conveyance, or vehicle bringing such alien to the United States is impracticable. The tax imposed by this section shall be a lien upon the vessel or other vehicle of carriage or transportation bringing such aliens to the United States, and shall be a debt in favor of the United States against the owner or owners of such vessel or other vehicle, and the payment of such tax may be enforced by any legal or equitable remedy. That the said tax shall not be levied on account of aliens who enter the United States after an uninterrupted residence of at least one year immediately preceding such entrance in the Dominion of Canada, Newfoundland, the Republic of Cuba, or the Republic of Mexico, for a temporary stay, nor on account of otherwise admissible residents or citizens of any possession of the United States, nor on account of aliens in transit through the United States, nor upon aliens who have been lawfully admitted to the United States and who later shall go in transit from one part of the United States to another through foreign contiguous territory, and the Commissioner General of Immigration with the approval of the Secretary of Labor shall issue rules and regulations and prescribe the conditions necessary to prevent abuse of these exceptions: *Provided,* That the Commissioner General of Immigration, under the direction or with the approval of the Secretary of Labor, by ageement with transportation lines, as provided in section twenty-three of this Act, may arrange in some other manner for the payment of the tax imposed by this section upon any or all aliens seeking admission from foreign contiguous territory: *Provided further,* That said tax, when levied upon aliens entering the Philippine Islands shall be paid into the treasury of said islands, to be expended for the benefit of such islands: *Provided further,* That in the cases of aliens applying from foreign contiguous territory and rejected, the head tax collected shall upon application, upon a blank which shall be furnished and explained to him, be refunded to the alien.

SEC. 3. That the following classes of aliens shall be excluded from admission into the United States: All idiots, imbeciles, feeble-minded persons, epileptics, insane persons; persons who have had one or more attacks of insanity at any time previously; persons of constitutional psychopathic inferiority; persons with chronic alcoholism; paupers; professional beggars; vagrants; persons afflicted with tuberculosis in any form or with a loathsome or dangerous contagious disease; persons not comprehended within any of the foregoing excluded classes who are found to be and are certified by the examining surgeon as being mentally or physically defective, such physical defect being of a nature which may affect the ability of such alien to earn a living; persons who have been convicted of or admit having committed a felony or other crime or misdemeanor involving moral turpitude; polygamists, or persons who practice polygamy or believe in or advocate the practice of polygamy; anarchists, or persons who believe in or advocate the overthrow by force or violence of the Government of the United States, or of all forms of law, or who disbelieve in or are opposed to organized government, or who advocate the assassination of public officials, or who advocate or teach the unlawful destruction of property; persons who are members of or affiliated with any organization entertaining and teaching disbelief in or opposition to organized government, or who advocate or teach the duty, necessity, or propriety of the unlawful assaulting or killing of any officer or officers, either of specific individuals or of officers generally, of the Government of the United States or of any other organized government, because of his or their official character, or who advocate or teach the unlawful destruction of property; prostitutes, or persons coming into the United States for the purpose of prostitution or for any other immoral purpose; persons who directly or indirectly procure or attempt to procure or import prostitutes or persons for the purpose of prostitution or for any other immoral purpose; persons who are supported by or receive in whole or in part the proceeds of prostitution; persons hereinafter called contract laborers, who have been induced, assisted, encouraged, or solicited to migrate to this country by offers or promises of employment whether such offers or promises are true or false, or in consequence of agreements, oral, written or printed, express or implied, to perform labor in this country of any kind, skilled or unskilled; persons who have come in consequence of advertisements for laborers printed, published, or distributed in a foreign country; persons likely to become a public charge; persons who have been deported under any of the provisions of this Act, and who may again seek admission within one year from the date of such deportation, unless prior to their reembarkation at a foreign port or their attempt to be admitted from foreign contiguous territory the Secretary of Labor shall have consented to their reapplying for admission; persons whose tickets or passage is paid for with the money of another, or who are assisted by others to come, unless it is affirmatively and satisfactorily shown that such persons do not belong to one of the foregoing excluded classes; persons whose ticket or passage is paid for by any corporation, association, society, municipality, or foreign Government, either directly or indirectly; stowaways, except that any such stowaway, if otherwise admissible, may be admitted in the discretion of the Secretary of Labor; all children under sixteen years of age, unaccompanied by or not coming to one or both of their parents, except that any such children may, in the discretion of the Secretary of Labor, be admitted if in his opinion they are not likely to become a public charge and are otherwise eligible; unless otherwise provided for by existing treaties, persons who are natives of islands not possessed by the United States adjacent to the Continent of Asia, situated south of the twentieth parallel latitude north, west of the one hundred and sixtieth meridian of longitude east from Greenwich, and north of the tenth parallel of latitude south, or who are natives of any country, province, or dependency situated on the Continent of Asia west of the one hundred and tenth meridian of longitude east from Greenwich and east of the fiftieth meridian of longitude, east from Greenwich and south of the fiftieth parallel of latitude north, except that portion of said territory situated between the fiftieth and the sixty-fourth meridians of longitude east from Greenwich and the twenty-fourth and thirty-eighth parallels of latitude north, and no alien now in any way excluded from, or prevented from entering, the United States shall be admitted to the United States. The provision next foregoing, however, shall not apply to persons of the following status or occupations: Government officers, ministers or religious teachers, missionaries, lawyers, physicians, chemists, civil engineers, teachers, students, authors, artists, merchants, and travelers for curiosity or pleasure, nor to their legal wives or their children under sixteen years of age who shall accompany them or who subsequently may apply for admission to the United States, but such persons or their legal wives or foreign-born children who fail to maintain in the United States a status or occupation placing them within the excepted classes shall be deemed to be in the United States contrary to law, and shall be subject to deportation as provided in section nineteen of this Act.

That after three months from the passage of this Act, in addition to the aliens who are by law now excluded from admission into the United States, the following persons shall also be excluded from admission thereto, to wit:

All aliens over sixteen years of age, physically capable of reading, who can not read the English language, or some other language or dialect, including Hebrew or Yiddish: *Provided*, That any admissible alien, or any alien heretofore or hereafter legally admitted, or any citizen of the United States, may bring in or send for his father or grandfather over fifty-five years of age, his wife, his mother, his grandmother, or his unmarried or widowed daughter, if otherwise admissible, whether such relative can read or not; and such relative shall be permitted to enter. That for the purpose of ascertaining whether aliens can read the immigrant inspectors shall be furnished with slips of uniform size, prepared under the direction of the Secretary of Labor, each containing not less than thirty nor more than forty words in ordinary use, printed in plainly legible type in some one of the various languages or dialects of immigrants. Each alien may designate the particular language or dialect in which he desires the examination to be made, and shall be required to read the words printed on the slip in such language or dialect. That the following classes of persons shall be exempt from the operation of the illiteracy test, to wit: All aliens who shall prove to the satisfaction of the proper immigration officer or to the Secretary of Labor that they are seeking admission to the United States to avoid religious persecution in the country of their last permanent residence, whether such persecution be evidenced by overt acts or by laws or governmental regulations that discriminate against the alien or the race to which he belongs because of his religious faith; all aliens who have been lawfully admitted to the United States and who have resided therein continuously for five years, and who return to the United States within six months from the date of their departure therefrom; all aliens in transit through the United States; all aliens who have been lawfully admitted to the United States and who later shall go in transit from one part of the United States to another through foreign contiguous territory: *Provided*, That nothing in this Act shall exclude, if otherwise admissible, persons convicted, or who admit the commission, or who teach or advocate the commission, of an offense purely political: *Provided further*, That the provisions of this Act, relating to the payments for tickets or passage by any corporation, association, society, municipality, or foreign Government shall not apply to the tickets or passage of aliens in immediate and continuous transit through the United States to foreign contiguous territory: *Provided further*, That skilled labor, if otherwise admissible, may be imported if labor of like kind unemployed can not be found in this country, and the question of the necessity of importing such skilled labor in any particular instance may be determined by the Secretary of Labor upon the application of any person interested, such application to be made before such importation, and such determination by the Secretary of Labor to be reached after a full hearing and an investigation into the facts of the case: *Provided further*, That the provisions of this law applicable to contract labor shall not be held to exclude professional actors, artists, lecturers, singers, nurses, ministers of any religious denomination, professors for colleges or seminaries, persons belonging to any recognised learned profession, or persons employed as domestic servants: *Provided further*, That whenever the President shall be satisfied that passports issued by any foreign Government to its citizens or subjects to go to any country other than the United States, or to any insular possession of the United States or to the Canal Zone, are being used for the purpose of enabling the holder to come to the continental territory of the United States to the detriment of labor conditions therein, the President shall refuse to permit such citizens or subjects of the country issuing such passports to enter the continental territory of the United States from such other country or from such insular possession or from the Canal Zone: *Provided further,* That aliens returning after a temporary absence to an unrelinquished United States domicile of seven consecutive years may be admitted in the discretion of the Secretary of Labor, and under such conditions as he may prescribe: *Provided further,* That nothing in the contract-labor or reading-test provisions of this Act shall be construed to prevent, hinder, or restrict any alien exhibitor, or holder of concession or privilege for any fair or exposition authorized by Act of Congress, from bringing into the United States, under contract, such otherwise admissible alien mechanics, artisans, agents, or other employees, natives of his country as may be necessary for installing or conducting his exhibit or for preparing for installing or conducting any business authorized or permitted under any concession or privilege which may have been or may be granted by any such fair or exposition in connection therewith, under such rules and regulations as the Commissioner General of Immigration, with the approval of the Secretary of Labor, may prescribe both as to the admission and return of such persons: *Provided further,* That the Commissioner General of Immigration with the approval of the Secretary of Labor shall issue rules and prescribe conditions, including exaction of such bonds as may be necessary, to control and regulate the admission and return of otherwise inadmissible aliens applying for temporary admission: *Provided further,* That nothing in this Act shall be construed to apply to accredited officials of foreign Governments, nor to their suites, families, or guests.

SEC. 4. That the importation into the United States of any alien for the purpose of prostitution, or for any other immoral purpose, is hereby forbidden; and whoever shall, directly or indirectly, import, or attempt to import into the United States any alien for the purpose of prostitution or for any other immoral purpose, or shall hold or attempt to hold any alien for any such purpose in pursuance of such illegal importation, or shall keep, maintain, control, support, employ, or harbor in any house or other place, for the purpose of prostitution or for any other immoral purpose, any alien, in pursuance of such illegal importation, shall in every such case be deemed guilty of a felony, and on conviction thereof shall be punished by imprisonment for a term of not more than ten years and by a fine of not more than $5,000. Jurisdiction for the trial and punishment of the felonies hereinbefore set forth shall be in any district to or into which said alien is brought in pursuance of said importation by the person or persons accused, or in any district in which a violation of any of the foregoing provisions of this section occurs. That any alien who shall, after he has been excluded and deported or arrested and deported in pursuance of the provisions of this Act which relate to prostitutes, procurers, or other like immoral persons, attempt thereafter to return to or to enter the United States shall be deemed....

FURTHER READINGS

Cosco, Joseph P. *Imagining Italians: The Clash of Romance and Race in American Perceptions, 1880–1910.* Albany, N.Y.: SUNY, 2003.

Daniels, Roger. *A History of Immigration and Ethnicity in American Life,* 2nd ed. New York: HarperCollins, 2002.

Dinnerstein, Leonard, and David M. Reimers. *Ethnic Americans: A History of Immigration and Assimilation,* 2nd ed. New York: Harper & Row, 1982.

Graham, Otis L. *Unguarded Gates: A History of America's Immigration Crisis.* Lanham, Md.: Rowman & Littlefield, 2006.

Greene, Victor R. *A Singing Ambivalence: American Immigrants between Old World and New, 1830–1930.* Kent, Ohio: Kent State University Press, 2004.

Hoerder, Dirk, ed. *American Labor and Immigration History: 1877–1920.* Urbana, Ill.: University of Illinois Press, 1982.

Jones, Maldwyn A. *The Limits of Liberty: American History, 1607–1992,* 2nd ed. New York: Oxford University Press, 1995.

Rockaway, Robert. *Words of the Uprooted: Jewish Immigrants in Early Twentieth-Century America*. Ithaca, N.Y.: Cornell University Press, 1998.

Sterba, Christopher. *Good Americans: Italian and Jewish Immigrants during the First World War*. New York: Oxford University Press, 2003.

Walch, Timothy. *Immigrant America: European Ethnicity in the United States*. New York: Garland, 1994.

CHAPTER 4

Immigration to the United States during the 1920s and 1930s

Akis Kalaitzidis

Immigration policy before the turn of the twentieth century was haphazard and subject to state wishes, as we have seen in the previous chapters. Starting in the 1920s, however, we see a change in the nature of immigration policy that can be traced to the cultural and political debates of the day. Two issues that had the greatest effect on immigration policy in the era between the World Wars were American nativism and racism. As Roger Daniel (1991) suggests, American nativism was present from the first day of the founding of United States, but it becomes politically viable or even politically expedient in the eyes of U.S. politicians and other leaders in the 1920s. Historian Michael LeMay (2006) calls this era "the pet door cycle," suggesting that there are consistent policies aimed at restricting immigration to the United States, which went from "the open door policy" to "the door ajar" and to the infinitely smaller "pet door policy." This is certainly corroborated by the documents presented in this chapter, which suggest that immigration to the United States was dramatically restricted in the 1920s.

The decade of the 1920s was also a time of great political and social upheaval in the United States on many fronts. The 1920s was an era of economic prosperity and optimism for the United States, and the decade is often called the "Roaring Twenties" for this reason. Anyone who has read the literary works of the age, such as F. Scott Fitzgerald's *The Great Gatsby* (1925), understands this characterization. The Communist Party and other left-wing groups rose to relative prominence after the Soviet Union's October Revolution of 1917. The decade also saw the apex of the Ku Klux Klan's political activity, its racist and anti-immigrant message finding acceptance among an alarming proportion of the country's population. The era also witnessed social and theological upheavals with the racially motivated Scopes Trial (1925), otherwise known as the "Monkey Trial," in Tennessee. Immigration policy, however, was most affected by the resurgence of political racism, and the corresponding groups that peddled such ideas.

Nativism became an umbrella idea for all the disaffected peoples of the United States who tended to view the immigrants as undesirable and socially disruptive. It is little wonder that this era has been characterized as the tribal twenties by John Higham. It was the era of fending for one's own kind and the era of exclusion based on ethnicity, religion, and ideology. It is evident, however, that lawmakers who passed immigration laws in the 1920s were influenced by more than mere fleeting social disruption. Racism had become rationalized and validated in scientific discourse, and the "science" of racism informed the debate throughout the decade. Eugenics was an expression of such racism. On the basis of hereditary socio-biological research of the time, politicians and the public separated the races into pure and strong stock. In this chapter's documents section, Elliot Durant Smith argues that immigration to the United States should be shut down because of the effects that immigration from southern Europe and other areas had on the U.S. "pure stock." White Anglo-Saxon Protestantism in America sought to prevent unwanted races from entering the country in order to preserve the biological lineage of the race. In other words, immigrants were difficult to assimilate because of cultural differences. Most importantly, these non–white Anglo-Saxon Protestant (non-WASP) immigrants were considered racially inferior and should not be allowed in the country to begin with.

The interesting fact about this racially motivated debate is that both supporters and detractors of immigration used it. Supporters of immigration used racial science to validate the need for specific races. M. Lynne Getz (2001) argues that racial statements were commonplace among supporters of immigrant groups and quotes Fred Roberts, president of the South Texas Cotton Growers Association, "There never was a more docile animal in the world than the Mexican." Getz also cites an exchange between congressional representatives Addison Smith (R-Idaho) and Adolph Sabath (D-Illinois), who agreed that in the case of

A group of Mexican women with a child enter the United States at the U.S. immigration station in El Paso, Texas, in June 1938. The photograph was taken by Dorothea Lange, whose many images of Depression-era immigrants in the American West provide a poignant record of the difficult conditions they faced. Library of Congress, Farm Security Administration, Office of War Information Photograph Collection, LC-USF34-018215-E.

weeding beets, Mexicans "not only can …do it better than anybody else, but there is scarcely any other work they can do successfully." Peter Quinn highlights the importance of eugenics for the National Socialist Party's agenda in Germany and points out the fact that the 1924 immigration law was applauded by Adolf Hitler in his book *Mein Kampf* (2 vols., 1925, 1927). Later, the Nazis would model German national laws on the U.S. laws. In fact, Nancy Ordover explains the persistence of these biological theories as part of the larger will of the state to regulate those who could not regulate themselves, including those who were handicapped or disabled. A deep racial overtone is evident in the political environment of the time, and one example of this was immigration policy.

Following the passage of the Immigration Act of 1917, the cultural tide swung toward the Americanization of all immigrants and the restriction of any further immigration into the country. Non-Protestant constituencies became targets, including Catholics, Jews, Greeks, and Armenians. Public hysteria against the immigrants, especially Eastern Europeans, was fueled by national security concerns. At the height of the October Revolution, the Bolsheviks were present in the United States. The United States frantically tried to stop what was perceived as "fifth column" infiltration of the United States by the Bolsheviks. It took strong action against Americans who embraced or supported socialism, as evident from the famous U.S. Supreme Court cases *Schenk* v. *United States* and *Gitlow* v. *New York*. Eugenics and political and ideological fear turned the public stage against immigration. The Emergency Quota Act of 1921, otherwise known as the Johnson Quota Act of 1921, after Senator Albert Johnson (R-Washington), was defended by the author as follows: "It is no wonder, therefore, that the myth of the melting pot has been discredited.… The United States is our land.… We intend to maintain it so. The day of unallowed welcome to all peoples, the day of indiscriminate acceptance of all races, has definitely ended" (Daniels 1991, 284).

In the 1921 act (see Document 1), immigration was restricted annually to 3 percent of the total number of each immigrant group already residing in the United States, as determined by the 1910 census, and the total number of immigrants allowed in the United States under this law would be 357,802 immigrants. This law also consists of quotas from different regions of the world. Under the law, most could come from North and West Europe, and the remainder from Eastern and Southeastern Europe. No immigrants could come in from Asia. It was passed by Congress in 1921 with a solid majority and signed into law by President Warren G. Harding.

Three years later, the Immigration Act of 1924, which included the National Origins Act and the Asian Exclusion Act (otherwise known as the Johnson Reed Act) further restricted immigration. This act reduced the percentage of allowable immigrants into the country to 2 percent from 3 percent. Table 4.1 shows that the number of immigrants coming to the United States does not fall immediately due to delays in implementation. However, under this law nonquota immigrants could be allowed in for employment specific reasons (e.g., for people with needed expertise for the United States) as well as family members of existing legal immigrants.

TABLE 4.1 Immigration in the United States during the 1920s

Year	Immigration	Emigration	Net Immigration
1921	805,228	247,718	557,510
1922	309,556	198,712	110,844
1923	522,919	81,450	441,469
1924	706,896	76,789	630,107
1925	294,314	92,728	201,586
1926	304,488	76,992	227,496
1927	335,175	73,336	261,839
1928	307,255	77,457	229,798
1929	279,678	69,203	210,475
1930	241,700	50,661	191,039
Total	4,107,209	1,045,046	3,062,163

Source: Daniels 1991: 288.

TABLE 4.2 Immigration to the United States, 1921–1945, by period and region

Period	Number of Immigrants	Europe	%	Americas	%	Other	%
1921–24	2,344,599	1,541,008	65.7	720,393	30.7	83,198	3.6
1925–30	1,762,610	936,845	53.2	796,323	45.2	29,442	1.7
1931–45	669,283	401,355	57.4	269,751	38.8	28,177	4.0
Total	4,806,492	2,879,208	59.9	1786,467	37.2	140,808	2.9

The result of immigration legislation in the 1920s was the favoring of white, Prostestant, North European immigrants. Hutchinson (1949) argues that the real intended result of the quotas was to preserve the racial purity of the United States. He notes, "During the seventeen years of operation of the national quota system up to 1946, northern and western European used on the average only 18.3 percent of its annual quota of 125,853." Asians faced a complete ban, as we saw in the previous chapters, which continued until World War II. Table 4.2 shows that between 1921 and 1945 U.S. patterns of immigration remained the same.

DID YOU KNOW?

Nativism

Nativism is a movement in U.S. politics opposing immigration to the United States. The term *nativism* separates people into two groups: native-born and "others." Anti-immigrant groups can be nativist or non-nativist depending on their interests, and not all anti-immigrant groups are nativist.

In the United States along historical lines, anti-Irish and anti-Catholic nativist sentiment existed from the founding of the Republic until the 1900s. Anti-Irish and anti-Catholic nativism was the first and probably most persistent expression of nativism in the United States. Early in the life of the American republic, anti-Catholic sentiment produced riots in places such as New York City. Nativism in the 1800s also contributed to the Mexican-American War (Pinheiro 2001).

Anti-Asian nativist feeling was prominent in mid-nineteenth and twentieth centuries. In 1882 Congress passed the Chinese Exclusion Act, which excluded Chinese laborers from coming to the United States. The law was repealed in 1943. Anti-Asian nativism culminated with Japanese internment during World War II.

Anti-Mexican nativism is present today among many groups in the United States. Mexicans are viewed with suspicion both on racial terms (being non-Anglo-Saxon) and religious terms (being non-Protestant) (Carrigan 2003).

DOCUMENTS

Document 1: The Quota Act of 1921

When: Approved May 26, 1924

Significance: The establishment of quotas for immigration to the United States

Emergency Quota Act of 1921

United States Statutes at Large (57th Cong., Sess. I, Chp. 8, p. 5–7)

An Act

To limit the immigration of aliens into the United States.

Be it enacted by the Senate and House of Representatives of the United States of America in Congress assembled, That as used in this Act—

The term "United States" means the United States, and any waters, territory, or other place subject to the jurisdiction thereof except the Canal Zone and the Philippine Islands; but if any alien leaves the Canal Zone or any insular possession of the United States and attempts to enter any other place under the jurisdiction of the United States nothing contained in this Act shall be construed as permitting him to enter under any other conditions than those applicable to all aliens.

The word "alien" includes any person not a native-born or naturalized citizen of the United States, but this definition shall not be held to include Indians of the United States not taxed nor citizens of the islands under the jurisdiction of the United States.

The term "Immigration Act" means the Act of February 5, 1917, entitled "An Act to regulate the immigration of aliens to, and the residence of aliens in, the United States"; and the term "immigration laws" includes such Act and all laws, conventions, and treaties of the United States relating to the immigration, exclusion, or expulsion of aliens.

Sec. 2. (a) That the number of aliens of any nationality who may be admitted under the immigration laws to the United States in any fiscal year shall be limited to 3 per centum of the number of foreign born persons of such nationality resident in the United States as determined by the United States census of 1910. This provision shall not apply to the following, and they shall not be counted in reckoning any of the percentage limits provided in this Act: (1) Government officials, their families, attendants, servants, and employees; (2) aliens in continuous transit through the United States; (3) aliens lawfully admitted to the United States who later go in transit from one part of the United States to another through foreign contiguous territory; (4) aliens visiting the United States as tourists or temporarily for business or pleasure; (5) aliens from countries immigration from which is regulated in accordance with treaties or agreements relating solely to immigration; (6) aliens from the so-called Asiatic barred zone, as described in section 3 of the Immigration Act; (7) aliens who have resided continuously for at least one year immediately preceding the time of their admission to the United States in the Dominion of Canada, Newfoundland, the Republic of Cuba, the Republic of Mexico, countries of Central or South America, or adjacent islands; or (8) aliens under the age of eighteen who are children of citizens of the United States.

(b) For the purposes of this Act nationality shall be determined by country of birth, treating as separate countries the colonies or dependencies for which separate enumeration was made in the United States census of 1910.

(c) The Secretary of State, the Secretary of Commerce, and the Secretary of Labor, jointly, shall, as soon as feasible after the enactment of this Act, prepare a statement showing the number of persons of the various nationalities resident in the United States as determined by the United States census of 1910, which statement shall be the population basis for the purposes of this Act. In case of changes in political boundaries in foreign countries occurring subsequent to 1910 and resulting (1) in the creation of new countries, the Governments of which are recognized by the United States, or (2) in the transfer of territory from one country to another, such transfer being recognized by the United States, such officials, jointly, shall estimate the number of persons resident in the United States in 1910 who were born within the area included in such new countries or in such territory so transferred, and revise the population basis as to each country involved in such change of political boundary. For the purpose of such revision and for the purposes of this Act generally aliens born in the area included in any such new country shall be considered as having been born in such country, and aliens born in any territory so transferred shall be considered as having been born in the country to which such territory was transferred.

(d) When the maximum number of aliens of any nationality who may be admitted in any fiscal year under this Act shall have been admitted all other aliens of such nationality, except as otherwise provided in this Act, who may apply for admission during the same fiscal year

---

DID YOU KNOW?

Ku Klux Klan

The Ku Klux Klan (KKK), a secret racist organization of the deep South, was formed right after the end of the Civil War by Confederate veterans from Pulaski, Tennessee. The organization's name comes from the Greek word *Kyklos* ("circle") and the word *clan*. The KKK was opposed to the enfranchisement of the African-American population and promoted the notion of white supremacy, nativism, and opposition to immigration.

The organizational structure of the group is as follows: Supreme head of the order was the "Grand Wizard," the ruler of a "Realm" is a "Grand Dragon," that of a "Dominion" a "Grand Titan," that of a "Province" a "Grand Giant," and that of a "Den" a "Grand Cyclops." This organizational structure has survived to this day. In the early 1920s the Klan was reportedly as powerful as 1.5 million members.

The Ku Klux Klan has spawned a political party (Knights Party) that advocates white people's rights. Their political platform also includes recognition of the United States as a white Christian nation, repeal of the North Amercian Free Trade Agreement (NAFTA), cessation of foreign aid, abolition of affirmative action programs, drug testing for welfare recipients, and repeal of the Federal Reserve Act. According to the Anti-Defamation League, today the KKK is resurfacing with immigration as its main focus.

shall be excluded: Provided, That the number of aliens of any nationality who may be admitted in any month shall not exceed 20 per centum of the total number of aliens of such nationality who are admissible in that fiscal year: Provided further, That aliens returning from a temporary visit abroad, aliens who are professional actors, artists, lecturers, singers, nurses, ministers of any religious denomination, professors for colleges or seminaries, aliens belonging to any recognized learned profession, or aliens employed as domestic servants, may, if otherwise admissible, be admitted notwithstanding the maximum number of aliens of the same nationality admissible in the same month or fiscal year, as the case may be, shall have entered the United States; but aliens of the classes included in this proviso who enter the United States before such maximum number shall have entered shall (unless excluded by subdivision (a) from being counted) be counted in reckoning the percentage limits provided in this Act: Provided further, That in the enforcement of this Act preference shall be given so far as possible to the wives, parents, brothers, sisters, children under eighteen years of age, and fiancees, (1) of citizens of the United States, (2) of aliens now in the United States who have applied for citizenship in the manner provided by law, or (3) of persons eligible to United States citizenship who served in the military or naval forces of the United States at any time between April 6, 1917, and November 11, 1918, both dates inclusive, and have been separated from such forces under honorable conditions.

Sec. 3. That the Commissioner General of Immigration, with the approval of the Secretary of Labor, shall, as soon as feasible after the enactment of this Act, and from time to time thereafter, prescribe rules and regulations necessary to carry the provisions of this Act into effect. He shall, as soon as feasible after the enactment of this Act, publish a statement showing the number of aliens of the various nationalities who may be admitted to the United States between the date this Act becomes effective and the end of the current fiscal year, and on June 30 thereafter he shall publish a statement showing the number of aliens of the various nationalities who may be admitted during the ensuing fiscal year. He shall also publish monthly statements during the time this Act remains in force showing the number of aliens of each nationality already admitted during the then current fiscal year and the number who may be admitted under the provisions of this Act during the remainder of such year, but when 75 per centum of the maximum number of any nationality admissible during the fiscal year shall have been admitted such statements shall be issued weekly thereafter. All statements shall be made available for general publication and shall be mailed to all transportation companies bringing aliens to the United States who shall request the same and shall file with the Department of Labor the address to which such statements shall be sent. The Secretary of Labor shall also submit such statements to the Secretary of State, who shall transmit the information contained therein to the proper diplomatic and consular officials of the United States, which officials shall make the same available to persons intending to emigrate to the United States and to others who may apply.

Sec. 4. That the provisions of this Act are in addition to and not in substitution for the provisions of the immigration laws.

Sec. 5. That this Act shall take effect and be enforced 15 days after its enactment (except sections 1 and 3 and subdivisions (b) and (c) of section 2, which shall take effect immediately upon the enactment of this Act), and shall continue in force until June 30, 1922, and the number of aliens of any nationality who may be admitted during the remaining period of the current fiscal year, from the date when this Act becomes effective to June 30, shall be limited in proportion to the number admissible during the fiscal year 1922.

Document 2: The Immigration Act of 1924, Excerpt

Date: Approved, May 26, 1924

Significance: The restriction of immigration to the United States by reducing the quotas and using the national origins of peoples as justification for whether or not they are welcome to the United States.

Immigration Act of 1924

United States Statutes at Large (68th Cong., Sess. I, Chp. 190, pp. 153–169)

An Act

To limit the immigration of aliens into the United States, and for other purposes.

Be it enacted by the Senate and House of Representatives of the United States of America in Congress assembled, That this Act may be cited as the "Immigration Act of 1924."

Immigration Visas.

Sec. 2. (a) A consular officer upon the application of any immigrant (as defined in section 3) may (under the conditions hereinafter prescribed and subject to the limitations prescribed in this Act or regulations made thereunder as to the number of immigration visas which may be issued by such officer) issue to such immigrant an immigration visa which shall consist of one copy of the application provided for in section 7, visaed by such consular officer. Such visa shall specify (1) the nationality of the immigrant; (2) whether he is a quota immigrant (as defined in section 5) or a non-quota immigrant (as defined in section 4); (3) the date on which the validity of the immigration visa shall expire; and (4) such additional information necessary to the proper enforcement of the immigration laws and the naturalization laws as may be by regulations prescribed.

(b) The immigrant shall furnish two copies of his photograph to the consular officer. One copy shall be permanently attached by the consular officer to the immigration visa and the other copy shall be disposed of as may be by regulations prescribed.

(c) The validity of an immigration visa shall expire at the end of such period, specified in the immigration visa, not exceeding four months, as shall be by regulations prescribed. In the case of an immigrant arriving in the United States by water, or arriving by water in foreign contiguous territory on a continuous voyage to the United States, if the vessel, before the expiration of the validity of his immigration visa, departed from the last port outside the United States and outside foreign contiguous territory at which the immigrant embarked, and if the immigrant proceeds on a continuous voyage to the United States, then, regardless of the time of his arrival in the United States, the validity of his immigration visa shall not be considered to have expired.

(d) If an immigrant is required by any law, or regulations or orders made pursuant to law, to secure the visa of his passport by a consular officer before being permitted to enter the United States, such immigrant shall not be required to secure any other visa of his passport than the immigration visa issued under this Act, but a record of the number and date of his immigration visa shall be noted on his passport without charge therefore. This subdivision shall not apply to an immigrant who is relieved, under subdivision (b) of section 13, from obtaining an immigration visa.

(e) The manifest or list of passengers required by the immigration laws shall contain a place for entering thereon the date, place of issuance, and number of the immigration visa of each immigrant. The immigrant shall surrender his immigration visa to the immigration officer at the port of inspection, who shall at the time of inspection indorse on the immigration visa the date, the port of entry, and the name of the vessel, if any, on which the immigrant arrived. The immigration visa shall be transmitted forthwith by the immigration officer in charge at the port of inspection to the Department of Labor under regulations prescribed by the Secretary of Labor.

(f) No immigration visa shall be issued to an immigrant if it appears to the consular officer, from statements in the application, or in the papers submitted therewith, that the immigrant is inadmissible to the United States under the immigration laws, nor shall such immigration visa be issued if the application fails to comply with the provisions of this Act, nor shall such immigration visa be issued if the consular officer knows or has reason to believe that the immigrant is inadmissible to the United States under the immigration laws.

(g) Nothing in this Act shall be construed to entitle an immigrant, to whom an immigration visa has been issued, to enter the United States, if, upon arrival in the United States, he is found to be inadmissible to the United States under the immigration laws. The substance of this subdivision shall be printed conspicuously upon every immigration visa.

(h) A fee of $9 shall be charged for the issuance of each immigration visa, which shall be covered into the Treasury as miscellaneous receipts.

Definition of "Immigrant."

Sec. 3. When used in this Act the term "immigrant" means any alien departing from any place outside the United States destined for the United States, except (1) a government official, his family, attendants, servants and employees, (2) an alien visiting the United States temporarily as a tourist or temporarily for business or pleasure, (3) an alien in continuous transit through the United States, (4) an alien lawfully admitted to the United States who later goes in transit from one part of the United States to another through foreign contiguous territory, (5) a bona fide alien seaman serving as such on a vessel arriving at a port of the United States and seeking to enter temporarily the United States solely in the pursuit of his calling as a seaman, and (6) an alien entitled to enter the United States solely to carry on trade under and in pursuance of the provisions of a present existing treaty of commerce and navigation.

Non-Quota Immigrants.

Sec. 4. When used in this Act the term "non-quota immigrant" means—

(a) An immigrant who is the unmarried child under 18 years of age, or the wife, of a citizen of the United States who resides therein at the time of the filing of a petition under section 9;

(b) An immigrant previously lawfully admitted to the United States, who is returning from a temporary visit abroad;

(c) An immigrant who was born in the Dominion of Canada, Newfoundland, the Republic of Mexico, the Republic of Cuba, the Republic of Haiti, the Dominican Republic, the

Virtually from the beginning, California's expanding agriculture industry relied on the labor of immigrant workers, including children. In 1937 Dorothea Lange captured several images of a crew of 55 Filipino boys working in the lettuce fields in California's Imperial Valley. Library of Congress, Farm Security Administration, Office of War Information Photograph Collection.

Canal Zone, or an independent country of Central or South America, and his wife, and his unmarried children under 18 years of age, if accompanying or following to join him;

(d) An immigrant who continuously for at least two years immediately preceding the time of his application for admission to the United States has been, and who seeks to enter the United States solely for the purpose of, carrying on the vocation of minister of any religious denomination, or professor of a college, academy, seminary, or university; and his wife, and his unmarried children under 18 years of age; if accompanying or following to join him; or

(e) An immigrant who is a bona fide student at least 15 years of age and who seeks to enter the United States solely for the purpose of study at an accredited school, college, academy, seminary, or university, particularly designated by him and approved by the Secretary of Labor, which shall have agreed to report to the Secretary of Labor the termination of attendance of each immigrant student, and if any such institution of learning fails to make such reports promptly the approval shall be withdrawn.

Quota Immigrants.

Sec. 5. When used in this Act the term "quota immigrant" means any immigrant who is not a non-quota immigrant. An alien who is not particularly specified in this Act as a non-quota immigrant or a non-immigrant shall not be admitted as a non-quota immigrant or a non-immigrant by reason of relationship to any individual who is so specified or by reason of being excepted from the operation of any other law regulating or forbidding immigration.

Preferences within Quotas.

Sec. 6. (a) In the issuance of immigration visas to quota immigrants preference shall be given—

(1) To a quota immigrant who is the unmarried child under 21 years of age, the father, the mother, the husband, or the wife, of a citizen of the United States who is 21 years of age or over; and

(2) To a quota immigrant who is skilled in agriculture, and his wife, and his dependent children under the age of 16 years, if accompanying or following to join him. The preference provided in this paragraph shall not apply to immigrants of any nationality the annual quota for which is less than 300.

(b) The preference provided in subdivision (a) shall not in the case of quota immigrants of any nationality exceed 50 per centum of the annual quota for such nationality. Nothing in this section shall be construed to grant to the class of immigrants specified in paragraph (1) of subdivision (a) a priority in preference over the class specified in paragraph (2).

(c) The preference provided in this section shall, in the case of quota immigrants of any nationality, be given in the calendar month in which the right to preference is established, if the number of immigration visas which may be issued in such month to quota immigrants of such nationality has not already been issued; otherwise in the next calendar month.

....

Numerical Limitations.

Sec. 11. (a) The annual quota of any nationality shall be 2 per centum of the number of foreign-born individuals of such nationality resident in continental United States as determined by the United States census of 1890, but the minimum quota of any nationality shall be 100.

(b) The annual quota of any nationality for the fiscal year beginning July 1, 1927, and for each fiscal year thereafter, shall be a number which bears the same ratio to 150,000 as the number of inhabitants in continental United States in 1920 having that national origin (ascertained as hereinafter provided in this section) bears to the number of inhabitants in continental United States in 1920, but the minimum quota of any nationality shall be 100.

(c) For the purpose of subdivision (b) national origin shall be ascertained by determining as nearly as may be, in respect of each geographical area which under section 12 is to be treated as a separate country (except the geographical areas specified in subdivision (c) of section 4) the number of inhabitants in continental United States in 1920 whose origin by birth or ancestry is attributable to such geographical area. Such determination shall not be made by tracing the ancestors or descendants of particular individuals, but shall be based upon statistics of immigration and emigration, together with rates of increase of population as shown by successive decennial United States censuses, and such other data as may be found to be reliable.

(d) For the purpose of subdivisions (b) and (c) the term "inhabitants in continental United States in 1920" does not include (1) immigrants from the geographical areas specified in subdivision (c) of section 4 or their descendants, (2) aliens ineligible to citizenship or their descendants, (3) the descendants of slave immigrants, or (4) the descendants of American aborigines.

(e) The determination provided for in subdivision (c) of this section shall be made by the Secretary of State, the Secretary of Commerce, and the Secretary of Labor, jointly. In making such determination such officials may call for information and expert assistance from the Bureau of the Census. Such officials shall, jointly, report to the President the quota of each nationality, determined as provided in subdivision (b), and the President shall proclaim and make known the quotas so reported. Such proclamation shall be made on or before April 1, 1927. If the proclamation is not made on or before such date, quotas proclaimed therein shall not be in effect for any fiscal year beginning before the expiration of 90 days after the date of the proclamation. After the making of a proclamation under this subdivision the quotas proclaimed therein shall continue with the same effect as if specifically stated herein, and shall be final and conclusive for every purpose except (1) in so far as it is made to appear to the satisfaction of such officials and proclaimed by the President, that an error of fact has occurred in such determination or in such proclamation, or (2) in the case provided for in subdivision (c) of section 12. If for any reason quotas proclaimed under this subdivision are not in effect for any fiscal year, quotas for such year shall be determined under subdivision (a) of this section.

(f) There shall be issued to quota immigrants of any nationality (1) no more immigration visas in any fiscal year than the quota for such nationality, and (2) in any calendar month of any fiscal year no more immigration visas than 10 per centum of the quota for such nationality, except that if such quota is less than 300 the number to be issued in any calendar month shall be prescribed by the Commissioner General, with the approval of the Secretary of Labor, but the total number to be issued during the fiscal year shall not be in excess of the quota for such nationality.

(g) Nothing in this Act shall prevent the issuance (without increasing the total number of immigration visas which may be issued) of an immigration visa to an immigrant as a quota immigrant even though he is a non-quota immigrant.

Nationality.

Sec. 12. (a) For the purposes of this Act nationality shall be determined by country of birth, treating as separate countries the colonies, dependencies, or self-governing dominions, for which separate enumeration was made in the United States census of 1890; except that (1) the nationality of a child under twenty-one years of age not born in the United States, accompanied by its alien parent not born in the United States, shall be determined by the country of birth of such parent if such parent is entitled to an immigration visa, and the nationality of a child under twenty-one years of age not born in the United States, accompanied by both alien parents not born in the United States, shall be determined by the country of birth of the father if the father is entitled to an immigration visa; and (2) if a wife is of a different nationality from her alien husband and the entire number of immigration visas which may be issued to quota immigrants of her nationality for the calendar month has already been issued, her nationality may be determined by the country of birth of her husband if she is accompanying him and he is entitled to an immigration visa, unless the total number of immigration visas which may be issued to quota immigrants of the nationality of the husband for the calendar month has already been issued. An immigrant born in the United States who has lost his United States citizenship shall be considered as having been born in the country of which he is citizen or subject, or if he is not a citizen or subject of any country, then in the country from which he comes.

(b) The Secretary of State, the Secretary of Commerce, and the Secretary of Labor, jointly, shall, as soon as feasible after the enactment of this Act, prepare a statement showing the number of individuals of the various nationalities resident in continental United States as determined by the United States census of 1890, which statement shall be the population basis for the purposes of subdivision (a) of section 11. In the case of a country recognized by the United States, but for which a separate enumeration was not made in the census of 1890, the number of individuals born in such country and resident in continental United States in 1890, as estimated by such officials jointly, shall be considered for the purposes of subdivision (a) of section 11 as having been determined by the United States census of 1890. In the case of a colony or dependency existing before 1890, but for which a separate enumeration was not made in the census of 1890 and which was not included in the enumeration for the country to which such colony or dependency belonged, or in the case of territory administered under a protectorate, the number of individuals born in such colony, dependency, or territory, and resident in continental United States in 1890, as estimated by such officials jointly, shall be considered for the purposes of subdivision (a) of section 11 as having been determined by the United States census of 1890 to have been born in the country to which such colony or dependency belonged or which administers such protectorate.

(c) In case of changes in political boundaries in foreign countries occurring subsequent to 1890 and resulting in the creation of new countries, the Governments of which are recognized by the United States, or in the establishment of self-governing dominions, or in the transfer of territory from one country to another, such transfer being recognized by the United States, or in the surrender by one country of territory, the transfer of which to another country has not been recognized by the United States, or in the administration of territories under mandates, (1) such officials, jointly, shall estimate the number of individuals resident in continental United States in 1890 who where born within the area included in such new countries or self-governing dominions or in such territory so transferred or surrendered or administered under a mandate, and revise (for the purposes of subdivision (a) of section 11) the population basis as to each country involved in such change of political boundary, and (2) if such changes in political boundaries occur after the determination provided for in subdivision (c) of section 11 has been proclaimed, such officials, jointly, shall revise such determination, but only so far as necessary to allot the quotas among the countries involved in such change of political boundary. For the purpose of such revision and for the purpose of determining the nationality of an immigrant, (A) aliens born in the area included in any such new country or self-governing dominion shall be considered as having been born in such country or dominion, and aliens born in any territory so transferred shall be considered as having been born in the country to which such territory was transferred, and (B) territory so surrendered or administered under mandate shall be treated as a separate country. Such treatment of territory administered under a mandate shall not constitute consent by the United States to the proposed mandate where the United States has not consented in a treaty to the administration of the territory by a mandatory power.

(d) The statements, estimates, and revisions provided in this section shall be made annually, but for any fiscal year for which quotas are in effect as proclaimed under subdivision (e) of section 11, shall be made only (1) for the purpose of determining the nationality of immigrants seeking admission to the United States during such year, or (2) for the purposes of clause (2) of subdivision (c) of this section.

(e) Such officials shall, jointly, report annually to the President the quota of each nationality under subdivision (a) of section 11, together with the statements, estimates, and revisions provided for in this section. The President shall proclaim and make known the quotas so reported and thereafter such quotas shall continue, with the same effect as if specifically stated herein, for all fiscal year except those years for which quotas are in effect as proclaimed under subdivision (e) of section 11, and shall be final and conclusive for every purpose.

A Filipino boy working as a member of a "labor gang" pauses for a moment in a cauliflower field near Santa Maria, California. This photograph was taken by Dorothea Lange in March 1937. Library of Congress, Farm Security Administration, Office of War Information Photograph Collection, LC-USF34-016200-E.

Exclusion from United States.

Sec. 13. (a) No immigrant shall be admitted to the United States unless he (1) has an unexpired immigration visa or was born subsequent to the issuance of the immigration visa of the accompanying parent, (2) is of the nationality specified in the visa in the immigration visa, (3) is a non-quota immigrant if specified in the visa in the immigration visa as such, and (4) is otherwise admissible under the immigration laws.

(b) In such classes of cases and under such conditions as may be by regulations prescribed immigrants who have been legally admitted to the United States and who depart therefrom temporarily may be admitted to the United States without being required to obtain an immigration visa.

(c) No alien ineligible to citizenship shall be admitted to the United States unless such alien (1) is admissible as a non-quota immigrant under the provisions of subdivision (b), (d), or (e) of section 4, or (2) is the wife, or the unmarried child under 18 years of age, of an immigrant admissible under such subdivision (d), and is accompanying or following to join him, or (3) is not an immigrant as defined in section 3.

(d) The Secretary of Labor may admit to the United States any otherwise admissible immigrant not admissible under clause (2) or (3) of subdivision (a) of this section, if satisfied that such in admissibility was not known to, and could not have been ascertained by the exercise of reasonable diligence by, such immigrant prior to the departure of the vessel from the last port outside the United States and outside foreign contiguous territory, or, in the case of an immigrant coming from foreign contiguous territory, prior to the application of the immigrant for admission.

(e) No quota immigrant shall be admitted under subdivision (d) if the entire number of immigration visas which may be issued to quota immigrants of the same nationality for the fiscal year has already been issued. If such entire number of immigration visas has not been issued, then the Secretary of State, upon the admission of a quota immigrant under subdivision (d), shall reduce by one the number of immigration visas which may be issued to quota immigrants of the same nationality during the fiscal year in which such immigrant is admitted; but if the Secretary of State finds that it will not be practicable to make such reduction before the end of such fiscal year, then such immigrant shall not be admitted.

(f) Nothing in this section shall authorize the remission or refunding of a fine, liability to which has accrued under section 16.

Deportation.

Sec. 14. Any alien who at any time after entering the United States is found to have been at the time of entry not entitled under this Act to enter the United States, or to have remained therein for a longer time than permitted under this Act or regulations made thereunder, shall be taken into custody and deported in the same manner as provided for in sections 19 and 20 of the Immigration Act of 1917: Provided, That the Secretary of Labor may, under such conditions and restrictions as to support and care as he may deem necessary, permit permanently to remain in the United States, any alien child who, when under sixteen years of age was heretofore temporarily admitted to the United States and who is now within the United States and either of whose parents is a citizen of the United States.

Maintenance of Exempt Status.

Sec. 15. The admission to the United States of an alien excepted from the class of immigrants by clause (2), (3), (4), (5), or (6) of section 3, or declared to be a non-quota immigrant by subdivision (e) of section 4, shall be for such time as may be by regulations prescribed, and under such conditions as may be by regulations prescribed (including, when deemed necessary for the classes mentioned in clauses (2), (3), (4), or (6) of section 3, the giving of bond with sufficient surety, in such sum and containing such conditions as may be by regulations prescribed) to insure that, at the expiration of such time or upon failure to maintain the status under which admitted, he will depart from the United States.

Penalty for Illegal Transportation.

Sec. 16. (a) It shall be unlawful for any person, including any transportation company, or the owner, master, agent, charter, or consignee of any vessel, to bring to the United States by water from any place outside thereof (other than foreign contiguous territory) (1) any immigrant who does not have an unexpired immigration visa, or (2) any quota immigrant having an immigration visa the visa in which specifies him as a non-quota immigrant.

(b) If it appears to the satisfaction of the Secretary of Labor that any immigrant has been so brought, such person, or transportation company, or the master, agent, owner, charterer, or consignee of any such vessel, shall pay to the collector of customs of the customs district in which the port of arrival is located the sum of $1,000 for each immigrant so brought, and in addition a sum equal to that paid by such immigrant for his transportation from the initial point of departure, indicated in his ticket, to the port of arrival, such latter sum to be delivered by the collector of customs to the immigrant on whose account assessed. No vessel shall be granted clearance pending the determination of the liability to the payment of such sums, or while such sums remain unpaid, except that clearance may be granted prior to the determination of such question upon the deposit of an amount sufficient to cover such sums, or of a bond with sufficient surety to secure the payment thereof approved by the collector of customs.

(c) Such sums shall not be remitted or refunded, unless it appears to the satisfaction of the Secretary of Labor that such person, and the owner, master, agent, charterer, and consignee of the vessel, prior to the departure of the vessel from the last port outside the United States, did not know, and could not have ascertained by the exercise of reasonable diligence, (1) that the individual transported was an immigrant, if the fine was imposed for bringing an immigrant without an unexpired immigration visa, or (2) that the individual transported was a quota immigrant, if the fine was imposed for bringing a quota immigrant the visa in whose immigration visa specified him as being a non-quota immigrant.

Entry from Foreign Contiguous Territory.

Sec. 17. The Commissioner General, with the approval of the Secretary of Labor, shall have power to enter into contracts with transportation lines for the entry and inspection of aliens coming to the United States from or through foreign contiguous territory. In prescribing rules and regulations and making contracts for the entry and inspection of aliens applying for admission from or through foreign contiguous territory due care shall be exercised to avoid any discriminatory action in favor of transportation companies transporting to such territory aliens destined to the United States, and all such transportation companies shall be required, as a condition precedent to the inspection or examination under such rules and contracts at the ports of such contiguous territory of aliens brought thereto by them, to submit to and comply with all the requirements of this Act which would apply were they bringing such aliens directly to ports of the United States. After this section takes effect no alien applying for admission from or through foreign contiguous territory (except an alien previously lawfully admitted to the United States who is returning from a temporary visit to such territory) shall be permitted to enter the United States unless upon proving that he was brought to such territory by a transportation company which had submitted to and complied with all the requirements of this Act, or that he entered, or has resided in, such territory more than two years prior to the time of his application for admission to the United States.

Unused Immigration Visas.

Sec. 18. If a quota immigrant of any nationality having an immigration visa is excluded from admission to the United States under the immigration laws and deported, or does not apply for admission to the United States before the expiration of the validity of the immigration visa, or if an alien of any nationality having an immigration visa issued to him as a quota immigrant is found not to be a quota immigrant, no additional immigration visa shall be issued in lieu thereof to any other immigrant.

Alien Seamen.

Sec. 19. No alien seaman excluded from admission into the United States under the immigration laws and employed on board any vessel arriving in the United States from any place outside thereof, shall be permitted to land in the United States, except temporarily for medical treatment, or pursuant to such regulations as the Secretary of Labor may prescribe for the ultimate departure, removal, or deportation of such alien from the United States.

Sec. 20. (a) The owner, charterer, agent, consignee, or master of any vessel arriving in the United States from any place outside thereof who fails to detain on board any alien seaman employed on such vessel until the immigration officer in charge at the port of arrival has inspected such seaman (which inspection in all cases shall include a personal physical examination by the medical examiners), or who fails to detain such seaman on board after such inspection or to deport such seaman if required by such immigration officer or the Secretary of Labor to do so, shall pay to the collector of customs of the customs district in which the port of arrival is located the sum of $1,000 for each alien seaman in respect of whom such failure occurs. No vessel shall be granted clearance pending the determination of the liability to the payment of such fine, or while the fine remains unpaid, except that clearance may be granted prior to the determination of such question upon the deposit of a sum sufficient to cover such fine, or of a bond with sufficient surety to secure the payment thereof approved by the collector of customs.

(b) Proof that an alien seaman did not appear upon the outgoing manifest of the vessel on which he arrived in the United States from any place outside thereof, or that he was reported by the master of such vessel as a deserter, shall be prima facie evidence of a failure to detain or deport after requirement by the immigration officer or the Secretary of Labor.

(c) If the Secretary of Labor finds that deportation of the alien seaman on the vessel on which he arrived would cause undue hardship to such seaman he may cause him to be deported on another vessel at the expense of the vessel on which he arrived, and such vessel shall not be granted clearance until such expense has been paid or its payment guaranteed to the satisfaction of the Secretary of Labor.

(d) Section 32 of the Immigration Act of 1917 is repealed, but shall remain in force as to all vessels, their owners, agents, consignees, and masters, and as to all seamen, arriving in the United States prior to the enactment of this Act.

Preparation of Documents.

Sec. 21. (a) Permits issued under section 10 shall be printed on distinctive safety paper and shall be prepared and issued under regulations prescribed under this Act.

(b) The Public Printer is authorized to print for sale to the public by the Superintendent of Public Documents, upon prepayment, additional copies of blank forms of manifests and crew lists to be prescribed by the Secretary of Labor pursuant to the provisions of sections 12, 13, 14, and 36 of the Immigration Act of 1917.

Offenses in Connection with Documents.

Sec. 22. (a) Any person who knowingly (1) forges, counterfeits, alters, or falsely makes any immigration visa or permit, or (2) utters, uses, attempts to use, possesses, obtains, accepts, or receives any immigration visa or permit, knowing it to be forged, counterfeited, altered, or falsely made, or to have been procured by means of any false claim or statement, or to have been otherwise procured by fraud or unlawfully obtained; or who, except under direction of the Secretary of Labor or other proper officer, knowingly (3) possesses any blank permit, (4) engraves, sells, brings into the United States, or has in his control or possession any plate in the likeness of a plate designed for the printing of permits, (5) makes any print, photograph, or impression in the likeness of any immigration visa or permit, or (6) has in his possession a distinctive paper which has been adopted by the Secretary of Labor for the printing of immigration visas or permits, shall, upon conviction thereof, be fined not more than $10,000, or imprisoned for not more than five years, or both.

(b) Any individual who (1) when applying for an immigration visa or permit, or for admission to the United States, personates another, or falsely appears in the name of a deceased individual, or evades or attempts to evade the immigration laws by appearing under an assumed or fictitious name, or (2) sells or otherwise disposes of, or offers to sell or otherwise dispose of, or utters, an immigration visa or permit, to any person not authorized by law to receive such document, shall, upon conviction thereof, be fined not more than $10,000, or imprisoned for not more than five years, or both.

(c) Whoever knowingly makes under oath any false statement in any application, affidavit, or other document required by the immigration laws or regulations prescribed thereunder, shall, upon conviction thereof, be fined not more than $10,000, or imprisoned for not more than five years, or both.

Burden of Proof.

Sec. 23. Whenever any alien attempts to enter the United States the burden of proof shall be upon such alien to establish that he is not subject to exclusion under any provision of the immigration laws; and in any deportation proceeding against any alien the burden of proof shall be upon such alien to show that he entered the United States lawfully, and the time, place, and manner of such entry into the United States, but in presenting such proof he shall be entitled to the production of his immigration visa, if any, or of other documents concerning such entry, in the custody of the Department of Labor.

. . . .

Sec. 27. Section 10 of the Immigration Act of 1917 is amended to read as follows:

"Sec. 10. (a) That it shall be the duty of every person, including owners, masters, officers, and agents of vessels of transportation lines, or international bridges or toll roads, other than railway lines which may enter into a contract as provided in section 23, bringing an alien to, or providing a means for an alien to come to, the United States, to prevent the landing of such alien in the United States at any time or place other than as designated by the immigration officers. Any such person, owner, master, officer, or agent who fails to comply with the foregoing requirements shall be guilty of a misdemeanor and on conviction thereof shall be punished by a fine in each case of not less than $200 nor more than $1,000, or by imprisonment for a term not exceeding one year, or by both such fine and imprisonment; or, if in the opinion of the Secretary of Labor, it is impracticable or inconvenient to prosecute the person, owner, master, officer, or agent of any such vessel, such person, owner, master, officer, or agent shall be liable to a penalty of $1,000, which shall be a lien upon the vessel whose owner, master, officer, or agent violates the provisions of this section, and such vessel shall be libeled therefor in the appropriate United States court.

"(b) Proof that the alien failed to present himself at the time and place designated by the immigration officers shall be prima facie evidence that such alien has landed in the United States at a time or place other than as designated by the immigration officers."

....

Authorization of Appropriation.

Sec. 29. The appropriation of such sums as may be necessary for the enforcement of this Act is hereby authorized.

Act of May 19, 1921.

Sec. 30. The Act entitled "An Act to limit the immigration of aliens into the United States," approved May 19, 1921, as amended and extended, shall, notwithstanding its expiration on June 30, 1924, remain in force thereafter for the imposition, collection, and enforcement of all penalties that may have accrued thereunder, and any alien who prior to July 1, 1924, may have entered the United States in violation of such Act or regulations made thereunder may be deported in the same manner as if such Act had not expired.

Time of Taking Effect.

Sec. 31. (a) Sections 2, 8, 13, 14, 15, and 16, and subdivision (f) of section 11, shall take effect on July 1, 1924, except that immigration visas and permits may be issued prior to that date, which shall not be valid for admission to the United States before July 1, 1924. In the case of quota immigrants of any nationality, the number of immigration visas to be issued prior to July 1, 1924, shall not be in excess of 10 per centum of the quota for such nationality, and the number of immigration visas so issued shall be deducted from the number which may be issued during the month of July 1, 1924. In the case of immigration visas issued before July 1, 1924, the four-month period referred to in subdivision (c) of section 2 shall begin to run on July 1, 1924, instead of at the time of the issuance of the immigration visa.

(b) The remainder of this Act shall take effect upon its enactment.

(c) If any alien arrives in the United States before July 1, 1924, his right to admission shall be determined without regard to the provisions of this Act, except section 23.

....

Document 3: Speech by Rep. Robert H. Clancy (D-Mich.) to the U.S. House of Representatives

When: April 8, 1924

Significance: Clancy outlines the arguments for the immigrant side, especially highlighting the fact that every American has foreign roots. Clancy argued against the Immigration Act of 1924, praising the virtues of his multinational district and highlighting the benefits it received from such a diverse ethnolinguistic and religious background.

Document

Since the foundations of the American commonwealth were laid in colonial times over 300 years ago, vigorous complaint and more or less bitter persecution have been aimed at newcomers to our shores. Also the congressional reports of about 1840 are full of abuse of English, Scotch, Welsh immigrants as paupers, criminals, and so forth.

Old citizens in Detroit of Irish and German descent have told me of the fierce tirades and propaganda directed against the great waves of Irish and Germans who came over from 1840 on for a few decades to escape civil, racial, and religious persecution in their native lands.

The "Know-Nothings," lineal ancestors of the Ku-Klux Klan, bitterly denounced the Irish and Germans as mongrels, scum, foreigners, and a menace to our institutions, much as other great branches of the Caucasian race of glorious history and antecedents are berated to-day. All are riff-raff, unassimilables, "foreign devils," swine not fit to associate with the great chosen people—a form of national pride and hallucination as old as the division of races and nations.

But to-day it is the Italians, Spanish, Poles, Jews, Greeks, Russians, Balkanians, and so forth, who are the racial lepers. And it is eminently fitting and proper that so many Members of this House with names as Irish as Paddy's pig, are taking the floor these days to attack once more as their kind has attacked for seven bloody centuries the fearful fallacy of chosen peoples and inferior peoples. The fearful fallacy is that one is made to rule and the other to be abominated....

In this bill [Immigration Act 1924] we find racial discrimination at its worst—a deliberate attempt to go back 84 years in our census taken every 10 years so that a blow may be aimed at peoples of eastern and southern Europe, particularly at our recent allies in the Great War—Poland and Italy.

Jews in Detroit Are Good Citizens

Of course the Jews too are aimed at, not directly, because they have no country in Europe they can call their own, but they are set down among the inferior peoples. Much of the animus against Poland and Russia, old and new, with the countries that have arisen from the ruins of the dead Czar's European dominions, is directed against the Jew.

We have many American citizens of Jewish descent in Detroit, tens of thousands of them—active in every profession and every walk of life. They are particularly active in charities and merchandising. One of our greatest judges, if not the greatest, is a Jew. Surely no fair-minded person with a knowledge of the facts can say the Jews of Detroit are a menace to the city's or the country's well-being....

Forty or fifty thousand Italian-Americans live in my district in Detroit. They are found in all walks and classes of life—common hard labor, the trades, business, law, medicine, dentistry, art, literature, banking, and so forth.

They rapidly become Americanized, build homes, and make themselves into good citizens. They brought hardihood, physique, hope, and good humor with them from their outdoor life in Sunny Italy, and they bear up under the terrific strain of life and work in busy Detroit.

One finds them by thousands digging streets, sewers, and building foundations, and in the automobile and iron and steel fabric factories of various sorts. They do the hard work that the native-born American dislikes. Rapidly they rise in life and join the so-called middle and upper classes....

The Italian-Americans of Detroit played a glorious part in the Great War. They showed themselves as patriotic as the native born in offering the supreme sacrifice.

In all, I am informed, over 300,000 Italian-speaking soldiers enlisted in the American Army, almost 10 percent of our total fighting force. Italians formed about 4 percent of the population of the United States and they formed 10 percent of the American military force. Their casualties were 12 percent....

Detroit Satisfied with the Poles

I wish to take the liberty of informing the House that from my personal knowledge and observation of tens of thousands of Polish-Americans living in my district in Detroit that their Americanism and patriotism are unassailable from any fair or just standpoint.

The Polish-Americans are as industrious and as frugal and as loyal to our institutions as any class of people who have come to the shores of this country in the past 300 years. They are essentially home builders, and they have come to this country to stay. They learn the English language as quickly as possible, and take pride in the rapidity with which they become assimilated and adopt our institutions.

Figures available to all show that in Detroit in the World War the proportion of American volunteers of Polish blood was greater than the proportion of Americans of any other racial descent....

Polish-Americans do not merit slander nor defamation. If not granted charitable or sympathetic judgment, they are at least entitled to justice and to the high place they have won in American and European history and citizenship.

The force behind the Johnson bill and some of its champions in Congress charge that opposition to the racial discrimination feature of the 1800 quota basis arises from "foreign blocs." They would give the impression that 100 percent Americans are for it and that the sympathies of its opponents are of the "foreign-bloc" variety, and bear stigma of being "hyphenates." I meet that challenge willingly. I feel my Americanism will stand any test.

Every American Has Foreign Ancestors

The foreign born of my district writhe under the charge of being called "hyphenates." The people of my own family were all hyphenates—English-Americans, German-Americans, Irish-Americans. They began to come in the first ship or so after the *Mayflower*. But they did not come too early to miss the charge of anti-Americanism. Roger Williams was driven out of the Puritan colony of Salem to die in the wilderness because he objected "violently" to blue laws and the burning or hanging of rheumatic old women on witchcraft charges. He would not "assimilate" and was "a grave menace to American Institutions and democratic government."

My family put 11 men and boys into the Revolutionary War, and I am sure they and their women and children did not suffer so bitterly and sacrifice until it hurt to establish the autocracy of bigotry and intolerance which exists in many quarters to-day in this country. Some of these men and boys shed their blood and left their bodies to rot on American battlefields. To me real Americanism and the American flag are the product of the blood of men and of the tears of women and children of a different type than the rampant "Americanizers" of to-day.

My mother's father fought in the Civil War, leaving his six small children in Detroit when he marched away to the southern battle fields to fight against racial distinctions and protect his country.

My mother's little brother, about 14 years old, and the eldest child, fired by the traditions of his family, plodded off to the battlefields to do his bit. He aspired to be a drummer boy and inspire the men in battle, but he was found too small to carry a drum and was put at the ignominious task of driving army mules, hauling cannons and wagons.

I learned more of the spirit of American history at my mother's knee than I ever learned in my four years of high school study of American history and in my five and a half years of study at the great University of Michigan.

All that study convinces me that the racial discriminations of this bill are un-American....

It must never be forgotten also that the Johnson bill, although it claims to favor the northern and western European peoples only, does so on a basis of comparison with the southern and western European peoples. The Johnson bill cuts down materially the number of immigrants allowed to come from northern and western Europe, the so-called Nordic peoples....

Then I would be true to the principles for which my forefathers fought and true to the real spirit of the magnificent United States of to-day. I can not stultify myself by voting for the present bill and overwhelm my country with racial hatreds and racial lines and antagonisms drawn even tighter than they are to-day. [Applause.]

Source: Speech by Robert H. Clancy, April 8, 1924, *Congressional Record*, 68th Congress, 1st Session (Washington D.C.: Government Printing Office, 1924), vol. 65, 5929–5932.

Also found at: http://historymatters.gmu.edu/d/5079

Document 4: Speech by U.S. Senator Ellison DuRant Smith (D-South Carolina)

When: April 9, 1924

Significance: Durant's speech makes reference to Malthusian arguments of depravation which leads to war, the cultural, linguistic, ethnicity, and identity concerns prevalent to the restrictionists of the day but most importantly makes reference to the biological "eugenics" reasons why the U.S. should shut the door and breed an American race on its own.

Document

It seems to me the point as to this measure—and I have been so impressed for several years—is that the time has arrived when we should shut the door. We have been called the melting pot of the world. We had an experience just a few years ago, during the great World War, when it looked as though we had allowed influences to enter our borders that were about to melt the pot in place of us being the melting pot.

I think that we have sufficient stock in America now for us to shut the door, Americanize what we have, and save the resources of America for the natural increase of our population. We all know that one of the most prolific causes of war is the desire for increased land ownership for the overflow of a congested population. We are increasing at such a rate that in the natural course of things in a comparatively few years the landed resources, the natural resources of the country, shall be taken up by the natural increase of our population. It seems to me the part of wisdom now that we have throughout the length and breadth of continental America a population which is beginning to encroach upon the reserve and virgin resources of the country to keep it in trust for the multiplying population of the country.

I do not believe that political reasons should enter into the discussion of this very vital question. It is of greater concern to us to maintain the institutions of America, to maintain the principles upon which this Government is founded, than to develop and exploit the underdeveloped resources of the country. There are some things that are dearer to us, fraught with more benefit to us, than the immediate development of the undeveloped resources of the country. I believe that our particular ideas, social, moral, religious, and political, have demonstrated, by virtue of the progress we have made and the character of people that we are, that we have the highest ideals of any member of the human family or any nation. We have demonstrated the fact that the human family, certainty the predominant breed in America, can govern themselves by a direct government of the people. If this Government shall fail, it shall fail by virtue of the terrible law of inherited tendency. Those who come from the nations which from time immemorial have been under the dictation of a master fall more easily by the law of inheritance and the inertia of habit into a condition of political servitude than the descendants of those who cleared the forests, conquered the savage, stood at arms and won their liberty from their mother country, England.

I think we now have sufficient population in our country for us to shut the door and to breed up a pure, unadulterated American citizenship. I recognize that there is a dangerous lack of distinction between people of a certain nationality and the breed of the dog. Who is an

American? Is he an immigrant from Italy? Is he an immigrant from Germany? If you were to go abroad and some one were to meet you and say, "I met a typical American," what would flash into your mind as a typical American, the typical representative of that new Nation? Would it be the son of an Italian immigrant, the son of a German immigrant, the son of any of the breeds from the Orient, the son of the denizens of Africa? We must not get our ethnological distinctions mixed up with out anthropological distinctions. It is the breed of the dog in which I am interested. I would like for the Members of the Senate to read that book just recently published by Madison Grant, *The Passing of a Great Race*. Thank God we have in America perhaps the largest percentage of any country in the world of the pure, unadulterated Anglo-Saxon stock; certainly the greatest of any nation in the Nordic breed. It is for the preservation of that splendid stock that has characterized us that I would make this not an asylum for the oppressed of all countries, but a country to assimilate and perfect that splendid type of manhood that has made America the foremost Nation in her progress and in her power, and yet the youngest of all the nations. I myself believe that the preservation of her institutions depends upon us now taking counsel with our condition and our experience during the last World War.

Without offense, but with regard to the salvation of our own, let us shut the door and assimilate what we have, and let us breed pure American citizens and develop our own American resources. I am more in favor of that than I am of our quota proposition. Of course, it may not meet the approbation of the Senate that we shall shut the door—which I unqualifiedly and unreservedly believe to be our duty—and develop what we have, assimilate and digest what we have into pure Americans, with American aspirations, and thoroughly familiar with the love of American institutions, rather than the importation of any number of men from other countries. If we may not have that, then I am in favor of putting the quota down to the lowest possible point, with every selective element in it that may be.

The great desideratum of modern times has been education not alone book knowledge, but that education which enables men to think right, to think logically, to think truthfully, men equipped with power to appreciate the rapidly developing conditions that are all about us, that have converted the world in the last 50 years into a brand-new world and made us masters of forces that are revolutionizing production. We want men not like dumb, driven cattle from those nations where the progressive thought of the times has scarcely made a beginning and where they see men as mere machines; we want men who have an appreciation of the responsibility brought about by the manifestation of the power of that individual. We have not that in this country to-day. We have men here to-day who are selfishly utilizing the enormous forces discovered by genius, and if we are not careful as statesmen, if we are not careful in our legislation, these very masters of the tremendous forces that have been made available to us will bring us under their domination and control by virtue of the power they have in multiplying their wealth.

We are struggling to-day against the organized forces of man's brain multiplied a million times by materialized thought in the form of steam and electricity as applied in the everyday affairs of man. We have enough in this country to engage the brain of every lover of his country in solving the problems of a democratic government in the midst of the imperial power that genius is discovering and placing in the hands of man. We have population enough to-day without throwing wide our doors and jeopardizing the interests of this country by pouring into it men who willingly become the slaves of those who employ them in manipulating these forces of nature, and they few reap the enormous benefits that accrue therefrom.

We ought to Americanize not only our population but our forces. We ought to Americanize our factories and our vast material resources, so that we can make each contribute to the other and have an abundance for us under the form of the government laid down by our fathers.

The Senator from Georgia [Mr. Harris] has introduced an amendment to shut the door. It is not a question of politics. It is a question of maintaining that which has made you and me the beneficiaries of the greatest hope that ever burned in the human breast for the most splendid future that ever stood before mankind, where the boy in the gutter can look with confidence to the seat of the Presidency of the United States; where the boy in the gutter can look forward to the time when, paying the price of a proper citizen, he may fill a seat in this hall; where the boy to-day poverty-stricken, standing in the midst of all the splendid opportunities of America, should have and, please God, if we do our duty, will have an opportunity to enjoy the marvelous wealth that the genius and brain of our country is making possible for us all.

We do not want to tangle the skein of America's progress by those who imperfectly understand the genius of our Government and the opportunities that lie about us. Let up keep what we have, protect what we have, make what we have the realization of the dream of those who wrote the Constitution.

I am more concerned about that than I am about whether a new railroad shall be built or whether there shall be diversified farming next year or whether a certain coal mine shall be mined. I would rather see American citizenship refined to the last degree in all that makes America what we hope it will be than to develop the resources of America at the expense of the citizenship of our country. The time has come when we should shut the door and keep what we have for what we hope our own people to be.

Source: Speech by Ellison DuRant Smith, April 9, 1924, *Congressional Record*, 68th Congress, 1st Session (Washington D.C.: Government Printing Office, 1924), vol. 65, 5961–5962.

Also found at: http://historymatters.gmu.edu/d/5080

FURTHER READINGS

Books

Daniels, Roger. *Coming to America: A History of Immigration and Ethnicity in American Life.* New York: Harper Perennial, 1991.

LeMay, Michael. *Guarding the Gates: Immigration and National Security.* Westport, Conn.: Praeger Security International, 2006.

McCaffrey Paul, ed. *Hispanic Americans.* Bronx, N.Y.: H. W. Wilson, 2007.

Ordover, Nancy. *American Eugenics: Race, Queer Anatomy, and the Science of Nationalism.* Minneapolis: University of Minnesota Press, 2003.

Rips, Gladys Nadler. *Coming to America: Immigrants from Southern Europe.* New York: Delacorte Press, 1981.

Robbins, Albert. *Coming to America: Immigrants from Northern Europe.* New York: Delacorte Press, 1981.

Articles

Carrigan, William. "The Lynching of Persons of Mexican Descent in the United States, 1948–1928." *Journal of Social History* (Winter 2003).

Crane, F. Lucius. "The Nationality of Married Women." *Journal of Comparative Legislation and International Law* (7:1, 1925), 53–60.

Dickinson, D. Edwin. "The Meaning of Nationality in the Recent Immigration Acts." *The American Journal of International Law* (19:2, April 1925), 344–347.

Getz, M. Lynne. "Biological Determinism in the Making of Immigration Policy in the 1920s." *International Science Review* (70:1&2, 2001), 26–33.

Hutsinson, R. Edward. "Immigration Policy Since World War I." *Annals of American Academy of Political and Social Science* (Vol. 262, March 1949), 15–21.

Pinheiro, John. "Extending the Light and Blessing of Our Purer Faith: Anti-Catholic Sentiment among American Soldiers in the Mexican-American War." *Journal of Popular Culture* (Fall 2001).

Quinn, Peter. "Closets Full of Bones." *America* (00027049, 2/18/1995), 172:5.

CHA5TER

Immigration in the Early Postwar Period

Akis Kalaitzidis

After World War II the United States immigration debate centered on how to deal with (1) refugees displaced from the war, (2) the persecuted peoples who were languishing in camps across Germany Austria, and Poland, (3) persons of national interests such as former Nazi officials with important knowledge for the government, and (4) people from the new enemy states who wished to emigrate to the United States.

In 1948 the U.S. Congress attempted to deal with the issue of displaced persons. These included people who entered Germany, Austria, or Italy as of January 1948 or Czechoslovakians fleeing persecution. The Displaced Persons Act of 1948 sought to solve the huge postwar problem of displaced persons, who numbered 8 million, of whom 1 million were still in camps (LeMay 2006). Internationally, the pressure for the United States, the new global hegemon, was great to deal with the displaced persons issue. American opinion, however, was ambivalent about an influx of refugees into the country. Race, religion, and ethnic identity were salient issues. Displaced Jewish concentration camp survivors believed that they would be welcome in the United States. However, under the preference provisions of the Displaced Persons Act (Daniels 1991), just as many Nazi sympathizers and beneficiaries entered the United States as did victims of the Nazi campaign. Preference was given to individuals who possessed skills and experience that were specifically important to the United Statess such as agriculture, construction, education, science, and technology. It was easy for people such as Albert Einstein and Thomas Mann to get into the United States, but for the majority of displaced persons, things were not easy. In total, only about 450,000 displaced persons were finally admitted to the United States, an average of 60,000 a year in the postwar period. The total number of Jews allowed into the country during that time was only 140,000 (Dinnerstein 1982).

Moreover, the 1948 Act did not enjoy full presidential support. Owing to its unfairness, President Harry S. Truman opposed it, stating that "It is with great reluctance that I have signed S. 2242, the Displaced Persons Act of 1948." The bill displays "a pattern of discrimination and intolerance wholly inconsistent with the American sense of Justice.... The bill discriminates in callous fashion against displaced persons of the Jewish faith.... The bill also excludes many displaced persons of the Catholic faith who deserve admission.... I know what a bitter disappointment this bill is—to the many displaced victims of persecution who looked to the United States for hope."

For the sake of political compromise, displaced persons were allowed to emigrate to the United States in greater numbers than their national quota, and the overage was to be deducted from future national immigration quotas. The objections of then Senator John F. Kennedy highlight the severity of the immigration inequity imposed upon nationalities that were already discriminated against in the National Origins Formula. The senator points out that, according to the 1948 bill, Poland's immigration debt would be paid out by 1999, Greece's by 2013, Lithuania's by 2087, and Latvia's by 2274.

Unfortunately for those from Eastern Europe of all faiths and colors, an "Iron Curtain" soon descended upon that region of the world. With much of Eastern Europe on the "wrong side" of the Iron Curtain, U.S. immigration policy became dominated by anti-Communist ideology between 1950 and 1952. The "friendly Asians vs. enemy Asians" debate of World War II was replaced with "friendly immigrants vs. Communist immigrants" (Campi 2004). Ideology replaced race in Congress as a criteria to regulate immigration. Congress denied people with subversive ideologies the right to come in the United States. President Truman had established a commission to study the case of immigration; however, it was ignored during the presidency of Dwight Eisenhower, and the nativist or restrictionist forces, led by representative Francis Walter and Senator Patrick McCarran, dominated the immigration agenda. McCarran even denounced the Truman commission's report as being communist-inspired (Daniels 1991, 333).

In 1952 Walter and McCarran proposed an omnibus bill in the U.S. Congress to overhaul the existing immigration legislations of the country. Walter and McCarran made the existing National Origins Formula obsolete by giving presidential agencies, more specifically the attorney general's office, authority to overrule the quotas that were established for each nation. Furthermore, the McCarran-Walter Act made positive changes in the overall immigration system in the United States by eliminating race and sex as determinants of immigration. It ended the blanket ban on immigration from the Asia-Pacific trianglet. However, the quotas established for the Asia-Pacific triangle peoples were still as low as smaller regions in Eastern and Southern Europe. Favorable treatment of Northern Europeans over all other potential immigrants continued. Marion Bennett argues that the due process of law was also greatly enhanced by the act because it strengthened the enforcement of security provisions against subversives, incorporated judicial interpretation of immigration policies, safeguarded against unfair administrative practices, and revised the laws concerning citizenship (Bennett 1966).

The McCarran-Walter Act's reach extended further than simply restricting immigration from ideologically undesirable countries. The McCarran-Walter Act became a vehicle by which the U.S. government excluded unwanted persons, sometimes very famous persons, purely for ideological reasons. With the McCarran-Walter Act, the U.S. government was able to restrict the public debate in the United States by excluding persons such as Nobel Laureates Gabriel García Márquez and Octavio Paz as well as other famous personalities such as Jorge Luis Borges and Julio Cortázar for their political stands on issues (Shapiro 1987, 930). These exclusions hardly represented the spirit of the McCarran-Walter Act, which was supposed to protect the country from enemies—communists and anarchists and the spread of their ideas (Shapiro 1987).

Many of those excluded hardly fit the profile of subversives, ready to do harm once inside the country. Yet, the government held all the cards in the case of the McCarran-Walter Act, especially since it could trump due process by denying entrance to anyone without having to show proof of any action that can be perceived to have violated the law. In the case of Fouad Rafeedie, a resident of Cleveland and married to a U.S. citizen for more than a decade, the U.S. government charged that he was connected to the Palestinian Liberation Organization (PLO), which was at the time designated a terrorist organization. After Mr. Rafeedie denied the charges, the U.S. government, citing McCarran-Walter, did not have to show proof of the charges and denied him entry on the basis of confidential information (*The Nation* 1988, 737). Similarly, Gerry Adams, the leader of the Irish political party Sinn Fein, and members of Parliament in Northern Ireland were denied visas in March of 1988 for their connection to the IRA. The U.S. Supreme Court finally ruled that the U.S. government had exceeded its authority by denying visas to further foreign policy goals. As we will see later, these types of issues resurfaced once again after the terrorist attacks on the World Trade Center in New York on September 11, 2001.

The U.S. immigration debate in the United States produced a variety of other laws, in tune with the new world order that emerged after World War II, in which the United States was pitted against the Soviet Union for global influence. In this struggle the first victim was the free exchange of ideas, according to Albert Einstein. In October 1952, he wrote, "The free, unhampered exchange of ideas and scientific conclusions is necessary for the sound development of science as it is in all spheres of cultural life. In my opinion, there can be no doubt that the intervention of political authorities of this country in the free exchange of knowledge between individuals has already had damaging effects.... The intrusion of the political authorities into the scientific life of our country is especially evident in the obstruction of the travels of American scientists and scholars abroad and foreign scientists seeking to come to this country" (reprinted in *Bulletin of Atomic Scientists*, 1987, 2).

Several other less significant pieces of immigration legislation were passed during the early post-war years. The Chinese Exclusion Repeal Act of 1943 (Magnuson Act), the Luce Cellar Act of 1942, and the War Brides Act of 1945 were all passed in these years. In 1953, Congress passed the Refugee Relief Act. Under the Refugee Relief Act, signed by President Eisenhower into law on August 7, 1953, up to 214,000 refugees, escapees, and expellees could stay in the United States as nonquota immigrants. In his words, "This emergency legislation is, at once, a significant humanitarian act and an important contribution toward greater understanding and cooperation among the free nations of the world." Eisenhower signed this bill into law even though it contradicted the McCarran-Walter Act allowing the U.S. government to admit people from a number of countries over their allotted quota.

DOCUMENTS

Document 1: Displaced Persons Act of 1948

When: June 25, 1948

Significance: It allows for some refugees from war-torn Europe to enter the United States but clearly it still discriminates on the basis of ethnicity and religion, leaving the vast majority of people who needed help out of the country.

Displaced Persons Act of 1948, U.S. Statutes at Large, 80th Cong., Sess. II, Chp. 647, pp. 1009-1014

An Act

To authorize for a limited period of time the admission into the United States of certain European

---

DID YOU KNOW?

John Lennon

The famous "Beatle" John Lennon had immigration problems until 1975, when he was finally given his green card by the United States Immigration office. In their documentary film *The US vs. John Lennon,* David Leaf and John Scheinfeld trace the famous artist's troubles with the Nixon administration. His antiwar (Vietnam) stance, his friendships with U.S. radicals such as Abbie Hoffman and Bobby Seale, and his promotion of anti-establishment political ideas attracted the ire of Strom Thurmond, Senator from South Carolina, who suggested to the White House on February 9, 1972, that John Lennon be deported. President Nixon, facing a campaign in which for the first time 11 million new voters (the eighteen-year-old bloc) would be voting because of the Twenty-sixth Amendment, made John Lennon's influence on the election very important. On February 29, 1972, the Immigration and Naturalization Service sent a notice of deportation to John Lennon and Yoko Ono. Lennon appealed, and on October 9, 1975, his birthday, his appeal was successful. His son was born, all on the same day.

DID YOU KNOW?

Famous immigrants include:

Hakeem Olajuwon – NBA Star, Nigeria

Patrick Ewing – NBA Star, Jamaica

Sammy Sosa – MBL Star, Dominican Republic

Isabelle Allende – Author, Chile

Charlie Chaplin – Actor, UK

Arnold Schwarzenegger – Actor, Governor of California, Austria

Michael J. Fox – Actor, Canada

Ang Lee – Director, Taiwan

Henry Kissinger – NSA and Secretary of State, Germany

Madeline Albright – Secretary of State, Czech Republic

Tom Lantos – U.S. Congressman, Hungary

Albert Einstein – Scientist, Nobel Prize Winner, Germany

Joseph Pulitzer – Journalist, Hungary

Felix Frankfurter – U.S. Supreme Court Justice, Austria

Elie Wiesel – Author, Political Activist, Nobel Prize Winner, Romania

Enrico Fermi – Scientist, Nobel Prize Winner, Italy

The *Washington Post* reported on October 12, 2007, that more than a third of U.S. Nobel Laureates in the past 15 years were immigrants.

displaced persons for permanent residence, and for other purposes. Be it enacted by the Senate and House of Representatives of the United States of America in Congress assembled, That this Act may be cited as the Displaced Persons Act of 1948.

Sec. 2. When used in this Act the term—....

(c) "Eligible displaced person" means a displaced person as defined in subsection (b) above, (1) who on or after September 1, 1939, and on or before December 22, 1945, entered Germany, Austria, or Italy and who on January 1, 1948, was in Italy or the American sector, the British sector, or the French sector of either Berlin or Vienna or the American zone, the British zone, or the French zone of either Germany or Austria; or a person who, having resided in Germany or Austria, was a victim of persecution by the Nazi government and was detained in, or was obliged to flee from such persecution and was subsequently returned to, one of these countries as a result of enemy action, or of war circumstances, and on January 1, 1948, had not been firmly resettled therein, and (2) who is qualified under the immigration laws of the United States for admission into the United States for permanent residence, and (3) for whom assurances in accordance with the regulations of the Commission have been given that such person, if admitted into the United States, will be suitably employed without displacing some other person from employment and that such person, and the members of such person's family who shall accompany such person and who propose to live with such person, shall not become public charges and will have safe and sanitary housing without displacing some other person from such housing. The spouse and unmarried dependent child or children under twenty-one years of age of such an eligible displaced person shall, if otherwise qualified for admission into the United States for permanent residence, also be deemed eligible displaced persons.

(d) "Eligible displaced person" shall also mean a native of Czechoslovakia who has fled as a direct result of persecution or fear of persecution from that country since January 1, 1948, and (1) who is on the effective date of this Act in Italy or the American sector, the British sector, or the French sector of either Berlin or Vienna, or the American zone, the British zone, or the French zone of either Germany or Austria, and (2) who is qualified under the immigration laws of the United States for admission into the United States for permanent residence, and (3) for whom assurances in accordance with the regulations of the Commission have been given that such person, if admitted into the United States, will be suitably employed without displacing some other person from employment and that such person, and the members of such person's family who shall accompany such person and who propose to live with such person, shall not become public charges and will have safe and sanitary housing without displacing some other person from such housing. The spouse and unmarried dependent child or children under twenty-one years of age of such an eligible displaced person shall, if otherwise qualified for admission into the United States for permanent residence, also be deemed eligible displaced persons.

(e) "Eligible displaced orphan" means a displaced person (1) who is under the age of sixteen years, and (2) who is qualified under the immigration laws of the United States for admission into the United States for permanent residence, and (3) who is an orphan because of the death or disappearance of both parents, and (4) who, on or before the effective date of this Act, was in Italy or in the American sector, the British sector, or the French sector of either Berlin or Vienna or the American zone, the British zone or the French zone of either Germany or Austria, and (5) for whom satisfactory assurances in accordance with the regulations of the Commission have been given that such person, if admitted into the United States, will be cared for properly.

Sec. 3 (a) During the two fiscal years following the passage of this Act a number of immigration visas not to exceed two hundred and two thousand may be issued without regard to quota limitations for those years to eligible displaced persons as quota immigrants, as provided in subsection (b) of this section: Provided, That not less than 40 per centum of the visas issued pursuant to this Act shall be available exclusively to eligible displaced persons whose place of origin or country of nationality has been de facto annexed by a foreign power: Provided further, That not more than two thousand visas shall be issued to eligible displaced persons as defined in subsection (d) of section 2 of this Act.

....

Sec. 4. (a) Any alien who (1) entered the United States prior to April 1, 1948, and (2) is otherwise admissible under the immigration laws, and (3) is a displaced person residing in the United States as defined in this section may apply to the Attorney General for an adjustment of his immigration status. If the Attorney General shall, upon consideration of all the facts and circumstances of the case, determine that such alien is qualified under the provisions of this section, the Attorney General shall report to the Congress all of the pertinent facts in the case. If during the session of the Congress at which a case is reported, or prior to the end of the session of the Congress next following the session at which a case is reported, the Congress passes a concurrent resolution stating in substance that it favors the granting of the status of permanent residence to such alien the Attorney General is authorized, upon receipt of a fee of $18.00, which shall be deposited in the Treasury of the United States to the account of miscellaneous receipts, to record the admission of the alien for permanent residence as of the date of the alien's last entry into the United States. If prior to the end of the session of the Congress next following the session at which a case is reported, the Congress does not pass such resolution, the Attorney General shall thereupon deport such alien in the manner provided by law: Provided, That the number of displaced persons who shall be granted the status of permanent residence pursuant to this section shall not exceed 15,000. Upon the grant of status of permanent residence to such alien as provided for in this section, the Secretary of State shall, if the alien was a quota immigrant at the time of entry, reduce by one the immigration quota of the country of the alien's nationality as defined in Section 12 of the Immigration Act of May 26, 1924, for the fiscal year then current or the next succeeding fiscal year in which a quota number is available, but not more than 50 per centum of any quota shall be used for this purpose in any given fiscal year: Provided further, That quota deductions provided for in this section shall be made within the 50 per centum limitations contained in section 3(b) of this Act.

(b) When used in this section the term "Displaced Person residing in the United States" means a person who establishes that he lawfully entered the United States as a non-immigrant under section 3 or as a nonquota immigrant student under subdivision (e) of Section 4 of the Immigration Act of May 26, 1924, as amended, and that he is a person displaced from the country of his birth, or nationality, or of his last residence as a result of events subsequent to the out-break of World War II; and that he cannot return to any of such countries because of persecution or fear of persecution on account of race, religion or political opinions.

....

Sec. 6. The preferences provided within the quotas by Section 6 of the Immigration Act of 1924 (43 Stat. 155-156; 47 Stat. 656; 45 Stat. 1009; 8 U.S.C. 206), shall not be applicable in the case of any eligible displaced person receiving an immigration visa under this Act, but in lieu of such preferences the following preferences, without priority in time of issuance of visas as between such preferences, shall be granted to eligible displaced persons and their family dependents who are the spouse or the unmarried dependent child or children under twenty-one years of age, in the consideration of visa applications:

(a) First. Eligible displaced persons who have been previously engaged in agricultural pursuits and who will be employed in the United States in agricultural pursuits: Provided, That not less than 30 per centum of the visas issued pursuant to this Act shall be made available exclusively to such persons; and Provided further, That the wife, and unmarried dependent child or children under twenty-one years of age, of such persons may, in accordance with the regulations of the Commission, be deemed to be of that class of persons who have been previously engaged in agricultural pursuits and who will be employed in the United States in agricultural pursuits.

(b) Second. Eligible displaced persons who are household, construction, clothing, and garment workers, and other workers needed in the locality in the United States in which such persons propose to reside; or eligible displaced persons possessing special educational, scientific, technological or professional qualifications.

(c) Third. Eligible displaced persons who are the blood relatives of citizens or lawfully admitted alien residents of the United States, such relationship in either case being within the third degree of consanguinity computed according to the rules of the common law.

Sec. 7. Within the preferences provided in section 6, priority in the issuance of visas shall be given first to eligible displaced persons who during World War II bore arms against the enemies of the United States and are unable or unwilling to return to the countries of which they are nationals because of persecution or fear of persecution on account of race, religion or political opinions and second, to eligible displaced persons who, on January 1, 1948, were located in displaced persons camps and centers, but in exceptional cases visas may be issued to those eligible displaced persons located outside of displaced persons camps and centers upon a showing, in accordance with the regulations of the Commission, of special circumstances which would justify such issuance.

....

Sec. 10. No eligible displaced person shall be admitted into the United States unless there shall have first been a thorough investigation and written report made and prepared by such agency of the Government of the United States as the President shall designate, regarding such person's character, history, and eligibility under this Act. The burden of proof shall be upon the person who seeks to establish his eligibility under this Act. Any person who shall willfully make a misrepresentation for the purpose of gaining admission into the United States as an eligible displaced person shall thereafter not be admissible into the United States. No eligible displaced orphan or eligible displaced person shall be admitted into the United States under the provisions of this Act except in pursuance of the regulations of the Commission, but, except as otherwise expressly provided in this Act, the administration of this Act, under the provisions of this Act and the regulations of the Commission as herein provided, shall be by the officials who administer the other immigration laws of the United States. Except as otherwise authorized in this Act, all immigration laws, including deportation laws, shall be applicable to eligible displaced orphans and eligible displaced persons who apply to be or who are admitted into the United States pursuant to this Act.

Sec. 11. After June 30, 1948, no preference or priority shall be given to any person because of his status as a displaced person, or his status as an eligible displaced person, in the issuance of visas under the other immigration laws of the United States.

Sec. 12. The Secretary of State is hereby authorized and directed to immediately resume general consular activities in Germany and Austria to the end that the German and Austrian quotas shall be available for applicants for immigration visas pursuant to the immigration laws. From and after June 30, 1948 and until July 1, 1950, notwithstanding the provisions of section 12 of the Immigration Act of May 26, 1924, as amended, 50 per centum of the German and Austrian quotas shall be available exclusively to persons of German ethnic origin who were born in Poland, Czechoslovakia, Hungary, Romania or Yugoslavia and who, on the effective date of this Act, reside in Germany or Austria.

Sec. 13. No visas shall be issued under the provisions of this Act to any person who is or has been a member of, or participated in, any movement which is or has been hostile to the United States or the form of government of the United States.

Sec. 14. Any person or persons who knowingly violate or conspire to violate any provision of this Act, except section 9, shall be guilty of a felony, and upon conviction thereof shall be fined not less than $500 nor more than $10,000, or shall be imprisoned not less than two or more than ten years, or both.

Approved June 25, 1948.

Document 2: The Immigration and Nationality Act (INA), Excerpt

When: June 27, 1952

Significance: The most significant piece of legislation in its era, this law spawned several thousand pages. This law attempted to overhaul the previous regime by focusing on denying entry to immigrants with noncompatible ideology.

United States Statutes at Large, 1952, Vol. 66, 82nd Cong., pp. 163–282

Document: McCarran-Walter Act of 1952

An Act

To revise the laws relating to immigration, naturalization, and nationality; and for other purposes.

Be it enacted by the Senate and House of Representatives of the United States of America in Congress assembled, That this Act, divided into titles, chapters, and sections according to the following table of contents, may be cited as the "Immigration and Nationality Act."

Table of Contents

Title I-General

Definitions

(27) The term "nonquota immigrant" means-

(A) an immigrant who is the child or the spouse of a citizen of the United States;

(B) an immigrant, lawfully admitted for permanent residence, who is returning from a temporary visit abroad;

(C) an immigrant who was born in Canada, the Republic of Mexico, the Republic of Cuba, the Republic of Haiti, the Dominican Republic, the Canal Zone, or an independent country of Central or South America, and the spouse or the child of any such immigrant, if accompanying or following to join him;

....

(f) For the purposes of this Act-

No person shall be regarded as, or found to be, a person of good moral character who, during the period for which good moral character is required to be established, is, or was-

(1) a habitual drunkard;

(2) one who during such period has committed adultery;

(3) a member of one or more of the classes of persons, whether excludable or not, described in paragraphs (11), (12), and (31) of section 212 (a) of this Act; or paragraphs (9), (10), and (23) of section 212 (a), if the offense described therein, for which such person was convicted or of which he admits the commission, was committed during such period;

(4) one whose income is derived principally from illegal gambling activities;

(5) one who has been convicted of two or more gambling offenses committed during such period;

(6) one who has given false testimony for the purpose of obtaining any benefits under this Act;

(7) one who during such period has been confined, as a result of conviction, to a penal institution for an aggregate period of one hundred and eighty days or more, regardless of whether the offense, or offenses, for which he has been confined were committed within or without such period;

(8) one who at any time has been convicted of the crime of murder.

The fact that any person is not within any of the foregoing classes shall not preclude a finding that for other reasons such person is or was not of good moral character. (g) For the purposes of this Act any alien ordered deported (whether before or after the enactment of this Act) who has left the United States, shall be considered to have been deported in pursuance of law, irrespective of the source from which the expenses of his transportation were defrayed or of the place to which he departed.

Title II-Immigration

Chapter 1-Quota System

Numerical Limitations; Annual Quota Based upon National Origin; Minimum Quotas

Sec. 201. (a) The annual quota of any quota area shall be one-sixth of 1 per centum of the number of inhabitants in the continental United States in 1920, which number, except for the purpose of computing quotas for quota areas within the Asia-Pacific triangle, shall be the

Sen. Patrick A. McCarran looks on as crew members aboard a liner newly arrived in New York City are screened by U.S. immigration officers, on Dec. 24, 1952. Senator McCarran's immigration stance was directly linked to his obsessive anti-Communism; he was the chief sponsor of the McCarran Internal Security Act (1950) as well as cosponsor of the McCarran-Walter Act (1952). Wide World / Library of Congress, Prints and Photographs Division, LC-USZ62-67903.

same number heretofore determined under the provisions of section 11 of the Immigration Act of 1924, attributable by national origin to such quota area: Provided, That the quota existing for Chinese persons prior to the date of enactment of this Act shall be continued, and, except as otherwise provided in section 202 (e), the minimum quota for any quota area shall be one hundred.

(b) The determination of the annual quota of any quota area shall be made by the Secretary of State, the Secretary of Commerce, and the Attorney General, jointly. Such officials shall, jointly, report to the President the quota of each quota area, and the President shall proclaim and make known the quotas so reported. Such determination and report shall be made and such proclamation shall be issued as soon as practicable after the date of enactment of this Act. Quotas proclaimed therein shall take effect on the first day of the fiscal year, or the next fiscal half year, next following the expiration of six months after the date of the proclamation, and until such date the existing quotas proclaimed under the Immigration Act of 1924 shall remain in effect. After the making of a proclamation under this subsection the quotas proclaimed therein shall continue with the same effect as if specifically stated herein and shall be final and conclusive for every purpose, except (1) insofar as it is made to appear to the satisfaction of such officials and proclaimed by the President, that an error of fact has occurred in such determination or in such proclamation, or (2) in the case provided for in section 202 (e).

(e) The quota numbers available under the annual quotas of each quota area proclaimed under this Act shall be reduced by the number of quota numbers which have been ordered to be deducted from the annual quotas authorized prior to the effective date of the annual quotas proclaimed under this Act.

(1) section 19 (c) of the Immigration Act of 1917, as amended;

(2) the Displaced Persons Act of 1948, as amended; and

(3) any other Act of Congress enacted prior to the effective date of the quotas proclaimed under this Act.

....

Determination of Quota to which an Immigrant is Chargeable

Sec. 202. (a) Each independent country, self-governing dominion, mandated territory, and territory under the international trusteeship system of the United Nations, other than the United States and its outlying possessions and the countries specified in section 101(a) (27) (C), shall be treated as a separate quota area when approved by the Secretary of State. All other inhabited lands shall be attributed to a quota area specified by the Secretary of State. For the purposes of this Act, the annual quota to which an immigrant is chargeable shall be determined by birth within a quota area, except that-

(1) an alien child, when accompanied by his alien parent or parents may be charged to the quota of the accompanying parent or of either accompanying parent if such parent has received or would be qualified for an immigrant visa, if necessary to prevent the separation of the child from the accompanying parent or parents, and if the quota to which such parent has been or would be chargeable is not exhausted for that fiscal year;

(2) if an alien is chargeable to a different quota from that of his accompanying spouse, the quota to which such alien is chargeable may, if necessary to prevent the separation of husband and wife, be determined by the quota of the accompanying spouse, if such spouse has received or would be qualified for an immigrant visa and if the quota to which such spouse has been or would be chargeable is not exhausted for that fiscal year;

(3) an alien born in the United States shall be considered as having been born in the country of which he is a citizen or subject, or if he is not a citizen or subject of any country then in the last foreign country in which he had his residence as determined by the consular officer;

(4) an alien born within any quota area in which neither of his parents was born and in which neither of his parents had a residence at the time of such alien's birth may be charged to the quota area of either parent;

(5) notwithstanding the provisions of paragraphs (2), (3), and (4) of this subsection, any alien who is attributable by as much as one-half of his ancestry to a people or peoples indigenous to the Asia-Pacific triangle defined in subsection (b) of this section, unless such alien is entitled to a nonquota immigrant status under paragraph (27) (A), (27) (B), (27) (D), (27) (E), (27) (F), or (27) (G) of section 101 (a), shall be chargeable to a quota as specified in subsection (b) of this section: Provided, That the child of an alien defined in section 101 (a) (27) (C), if accompanying or following to join him, shall be classified under section 101 (a) (27) (C), notwithstanding the provisions of subsection (b) of this section.

(b) With reference to determination of the quota to which shall be chargeable an immigrant who is attributable by as much as one-half of his ancestry to a people or peoples indigenous to the Asia-Pacific triangle comprising all quota areas and all colonies and other dependent areas situate wholly east of the meridian sixty degrees east of Greenwich, wholly west of the meridian one hundred and sixty-five degrees west, and wholly north of the parallel twenty-five degrees south latitude-

(1) there is hereby established, in addition to quotas for separate quota areas comprising independent countries, self-governing dominions, and territories under the international trusteeship system of the United Nations situated wholly within said Asia-Pacific triangle, an Asia-Pacific quota of one hundred annually, which quota shall not be subject to the provisions of subsection (e);

(e) After the determination of quotas has been made as provided in section 201, revision of the quotas shall be made by the Secretary of State, the Secretary of Commerce, and the Attorney General, jointly, whenever necessary, to provide for any change of boundaries resulting in transfer of territory from one sovereignty to another, a change of administrative arrangements of a colony or other dependent area, or any other political change, requiring a change in the list of quota areas or of the territorial limits thereof, but any increase in the number of minimum quota areas above twenty within the Asia-Pacific triangle shall result in a proportionate decrease in each minimum quota of such area in order that the sum total of all minimum quotas within the Asia-Pacific triangle shall not exceed two thousand. In the case of any change in the territorial limits of quota areas, not requiring a change in the quotas for such areas, the Secretary of State shall, upon recognition of such change, issue appropriate instructions to all consular offices concerning the change in the territorial limits of the quota area involved.

Sec. 203. (a) Immigrant visas to quota immigrants shall be allotted in each fiscal year as follows:

(1) The first 50 per centum of the quota of each quota area for such year, plus any portion of such quota not required for the issuance of immigrant visas to the classes specified in paragraphs (2) and (3), shall be made available for the issuance of immigrant visas (A) to qualified quota immigrants whose services are determined by the Attorney General to be needed urgently in the United States because of the high education, technical training, specialized experience, or exceptional ability of such immigrants and to be substantially beneficial prospectively to the national economy, cultural interests, or welfare of the United States, and (B) to qualified quota immigrants who are the spouse or children of any immigrant described in clause (A) if accompanying him.

(2) The next 30 per centum of the quota for each quota area for such year, plus any portion of such quota not required for the issuance of immigrant visas to the classes specified in paragraphs (1) and (3), shall be made available for the issuance of immigrant visas to qualified quota immigrants who are the parents of citizens of the United States, such citizens being at least twenty-one years of age.

(3) The remaining 20 per centum of the quota for each quota area for such year, plus any portion of such quota not required for the issuance of immigrant visas to the classes specified in paragraphs (1) and (2), shall be made available for the issuance of immigrant visas to qualified quota immigrants who are the spouses or the children of aliens lawfully admitted for permanent residence.

....

Sec. 212. (a) Except as otherwise provided in this Act, the following classes of aliens shall be ineligible to receive visas and shall be excluded from admission into the United States:

(1) Aliens who are feeble-minded;

(2) Aliens who are insane;

(3) Aliens who have had one or more attacks of insanity;

(4) Aliens afflicted with psychopathic personality, epilepsy, or a mental defect;

(5) Aliens who are narcotic drug addicts or chronic alcoholics;

(6) Aliens who are afflicted with tuberculosis in any form, or with leprosy, or any dangerous contagious disease;

(7) Aliens not comprehended within any of the foregoing classes who are certified by the examining surgeon as having a physical defect, disease, or disability, when determined by the consular or immigration officer to be of such a nature that it may affect the ability of the alien to earn a living, unless the alien affirmatively establishes that he will not have to earn a living;

(8) Aliens who are paupers, professional beggars, or vagrants;

(9) Aliens who have been convicted of a crime involving moral turpitude (other than a purely political offense), or aliens who admit having committed such a crime, or aliens who admit committing acts which constitute the essential elements of such a crime; except that aliens who have committed only one such crime while under the age of eighteen years may be granted a visa and admitted if the crime was committed more than five years prior to the date of the application for a visa or other documentation, and more than five years prior to date of application for admission to the United States, unless the crime resulted confinement in a prison or correctional institution, in which case such alien must have been released from

such confinement more than five years prior to the date of the application for a visa or other documentation, and for admission, to the United States;

(10) Aliens who have been convicted of two or more offenses (other than purely political offenses), regardless of whether the conviction was in a single trial or whether the offenses arose from a single scheme of misconduct and regardless of whether the offenses involved moral turpitude, for which the aggregate sentences to confinement actually imposed were five years or more;

(11) Aliens who are polygamists or who practice polygamy or advocate the practice of polygamy;

(12) Aliens who are prostitutes or who have engaged in prostitution, or aliens coming to the United States solely, principally, or incidentally to engage in prostitution; aliens who directly or indirectly procure or attempt to procure, or who have procured or attempted to procure or to import, prostitutes or persons for the purpose of prostitution or for any other immoral purpose; and aliens who are or have been supported by, or receive or have received, in whole or in part, the proceeds of prostitution or aliens coming to the United States to engage in any other unlawful commercialized vice, whether or not related to prostitution;

(14) Aliens seeking to enter the United States for the purpose of performing skilled or unskilled labor, if the Secretary of Labor has determined and certified to the Secretary of State and to the Attorney General that (A) sufficient workers in the United States who are able, willing, and qualified are available at the time (of application for a visa and for admission to the United States) and place (to which the alien is destined) to perform such skilled or unskilled labor, or (B) the employment of such aliens will adversely affect the wages and working conditions of the workers in the United States similarly employed. The exclusion of aliens under this paragraph shall apply only to the following classes: (i) those aliens described in the nonpreference category of section 203 (a) (4), (ii) those aliens described in section 101 (a) (27) (C), (27) (D), or (27) (E) (other than the parents, spouses, or children of United States citizens or of aliens lawfully admitted to the United State for permanent residence), unless their services are determined by the Attorney General to be needed urgently in the United States because of the high education, technical training, specialized experience, or exceptional ability of such immigrants and to be substantially beneficial prospectively to the national economy, cultural interest or welfare of the United States;

(15) Aliens who, in the opinion of the consular officer at the time of application for a visa, or in the opinion of the Attorney General at the time of application for admission, are likely at any time to become public charges;

(19) Any alien who seeks to procure, or has sought to procure, or has procured a visa or other documentation, or seeks to enter the United States, by fraud, or by willfully misrepresenting a material fact.

....

Sec. 212. (a) (28) Aliens who are, or at any time have been, a member of any of the following classes:

(A) Aliens who are anarchists;

(B) Aliens who advocate or teach, or who are members of or affiliated with any organization that advocates or teaches, opposition to all organized government;

(C) Aliens who are members of or affiliated with (i) the Communist Party of the United States, (ii) any other totalitarian party of the United States, (iii) the Communist Political Association, (iv) the Communist or any other totalitarian party of any State of the United States, of any foreign state, or of any political or geographical subdivision of any foreign state, (v) any section, subsidiary, branch, affiliate, or subdivision of any such association or party, regardless of what name such group may adopt: Provided, That nothing in this paragraph, or in any other provision of this Act, shall be construed as declaring that the Communist Party does not advocate the overthrow of the Government of the United States by force, violence, or other unconstitutional means;

(D) Aliens not within any of the other provisions of this paragraph who advocate the economic, international, and governmental doctrines of world communism or the establishment in the United States of a totalitarian dictatorship, or who are members of or affiliated with any organization that advocates the economic, international, and governmental doctrines of world communism or the establishment in the United States of a totalitarian dictatorship, either through its own utterances or through any written or printed publications issued or published by or with the permission or consent of or under the authority of such organization or paid for by the funds of, or funds furnished by, such organization;

(G) Aliens who write or publish, or cause to be written or published, or who knowingly circulate, distribute, print, or display, or knowingly cause to be circulated, distributed, printed, published or displayed, or who knowingly have in their possession for the purpose of circulation, publication, distribution, or display any written or printed matter, advocating or teaching opposition to all organized government, or advocating or teaching (i) the overthrow by force, violence, or other unconstitutional means of the Government of the United States or of all forms of law; or (ii) the duty, necessity, or propriety of the unlawful assaulting or killing of any officer or officers (either of specific individuals or of officers generally) of the Government of the United States or of any other organized government, because of his or their official character; or (iii) the unlawful damage, injury, or destruction of property; or (iv) sabotage; or (v) the economic, international, and governmental doctrines of world communism or the establishment in the United States of a totalitarian dictatorship.

. . . .

Immigration Officers and Employees

Sec. 287. (a) Any officer or employee of the Service authorized under regulation prescribed by the Attorney General shall have power without warrant –

(1) to interrogate any alien or person believed to be an alien as to his right to be or to remain in the United States;

(2) to arrest any alien who in his presence or view is entering or attempting to enter the United States in violation of any law or regulation made in pursuance of law regulating the admission, exclusion, or expulsion of aliens, or to arrest any alien in the United States, if he has reason to believe that the alien so arrested is in the United States in violation of any such law or regulation and is likely to escape before a warrant can be obtained for his arrest, but the alien arrested shall be taken without unnecessary delay for examination before an officer of the Service having authority to examine aliens as to their right to enter or remain in the United States.

(3) within a reasonable distance from any external boundary of the United States, to board and search for aliens on any vessel within the territorial waters of the United States and any railway car, aircraft, conveyance, or vehicle, and within a distance of twenty-five miles from any such external boundary to have access to private lands, but not dwellings, for the purpose of patrolling the border to prevent the illegal entry of aliens into the United States;

(4) to make arrests for felonies which have been committed and which are cognizable under any law of the United States regulating the admission, exclusion, or expulsion of aliens, if he has reason to believe that the person so arrested is guilty of such felony and if there is likelihood of the person escaping before a warrant can be obtained for his arrest, but the person arrested shall be taken without unnecessary delay before the nearest available officer empowered to commit persons charged with offenses also have the power to execute any warrant or other process issued by any officer under any law regulating the admission, exclusion, or expulsion of aliens.

(c) Any officer or employee of the Service authorized and designated under regulations prescribed by the Attorney General, whether individually or as one of a class, shall have power to conduct a search, without warrant, of the person, and of the personal effects in the possession of any person seeking admission to the United States, concerning whom such officer or employee may have reasonable cause to suspect that grounds exist for exclusion from the United States under this Act which would be disclosed by such search.

Title III – Nationality and Naturalization

Eligibility for Naturalization

Sec. 311. The right of a person to become a naturalized citizen of the United States shall not be denied or abridged because of race or sex or because such person is married. Notwithstanding section 405 (b), this section shall apply to any person whose petition for naturalization shall hereafter be filed, or shall have been pending on the effective date of this Act.

....

Title IV-Miscellaneous

Sec. 402. (h) (1) The first sentence of subsection (c) of section 3 of the Act of June 25, 1948, as amended (62 Stat. 1009; 64 Stat. 219), is amended by deleting therefrom the language "from the immigration quota for the country of the alien's nationality as defined in section 12 of the Immigration Act of May 26, 1924 (8 U.S.C. 212)" and by substituting therefor the language "from the annual quota to which an immigrant is chargeable as provided in section 202 of the Immigration and Nationality Act."

(2) The second proviso to subsection (c) of section 3 of the Act of June 25, 1948, as amended (62 Stat. 1009; 64 Stat. 219), is amended by deleting the language "as defined in section 6 of the Act of May 26, 1924, as amended (8 U.S.C. 206)," and by substituting therefor "as provided in section 203 (a) (4) of the Immigration and Nationality Act."

(3) The proviso to section 4 (a) of the Act of June 25, 1948, as amended, is amended by deleting the language "the immigration quota of the country of the alien's nationality as defined in section 12 of the Immigration Act of May 26, 1924," and by substituting therefor the language "the annual quota to which an immigrant is chargeable as provided in section 202 of the Immigration and Nationality Act."

(4) Section 5 of the Act of June 25, 1948, as amended (62 Stat. 1009; Public Law 60, Eighty-second Congress), is amended to read as follows:

"Sec. 5. The quota to which an alien is chargeable for the purposes of this Act shall be determined in accordance with the provisions of section 202 of the Immigration and Nationality Act and no eligible displaced person shall be issued an immigrant visa if he is known or believed by the consular officer to be subject to exclusion from the United States under any provision of the immigration laws, with the exception of section 212 (a) (14) of the Immigration and Nationality Act; and all eligible displaced persons, eligible displaced orphans and orphans under section 2 (f) shall be exempt from paying visa fees and head taxes."

(5) Section 6 of the Act of June 25, 1948, as amended (62 Stat. 1009; 64 Stat. 219), is further amended by deleting the language "section 6 of the Immigration Act of 1924, as amended (8 U.S.C. 206)," and by substituting therefor the language "section 203 of the Immigration and Nationality Act." The last sentence of section 6 of the Act of June 25, 1948, is amended by deleting the language "sections 19 and 20 of the Immigration Act of February 5, 1917, as amended" and by substituting therefor the language "sections 241, 242, and 243 of the Immigration and Nationality Act."

(6) The first sentence of subsection (a) of section 12 of the Act of June 25, 1948, as amended (62 Stat. 1009; 64 Stat. 219), is amended by deleting the language "section 12 of the Act of May 26, 1924, as amended," and by substituting therefor the language "section 202 of the Immigration and Nationality Act." Subsection (b) of section 12 of the Act of June 25, 1948, as amended (62 Stat. 1009; 64 Stat. 219), is amended by deleting the language "section 11 (f) of the Immigration Act of May 26, 1924 (8 U.S.C. 211)," and by substituting therefor the language "section 201 of the Immigration and Nationality Act." Subsection (b) of section 12 of the Act of June 25, 1948, as amended, is amended by deleting the language "from the immigration quota of the country of nationality of the person who receives the visa as defined in section 12 of the Immigration Act of May 26, 1924 (8 U.S.C. 212)" and by substituting therefor the language "from the annual quota to which the person

who receives the visa is chargeable as provided in section 202 of the Immigration and Nationality Act." The last sentence of subsection (c) of section 12 of the Act of June 25, 1948, as amended, is further amended to read as follows:

"Those provisions of section 5 of this Act which relate to section 212 (a) (14) of the Immigration and Nationality Act shall be applicable to persons whose admission is authorized under the provisions of this section."

Sec. 403. (a) The following Acts and all amendments thereto and parts of Acts and all amendments thereto are repealed:

(13) Act of February 5, 1917 (39 Stat. 874);

(23) Act of May 26, 1924 (43 Stat. 153);

Effective Date

Sec. 407. Except as provided in subsection (k) of section 401, this Act shall take effect at 12:01 ante meridian United States Eastern Standard Time on the one hundred eightieth day immediately following the date of its enactment.

In the House of Representatives, U.S. June 26, 1952.

Resolved, That the said bill pass, two-thirds of the House of Representatives agreeing to pass the same.

Attest: Ralph R Roberts Clerk.

In the Senate of the United States, June 27, 1952.

Resolved, That the said bill pass, two-thirds of the Senators present having voted in the affirmative. Attest:

Leslie L Biffle Secretary.

Document 3: Speech of Honorable Pat McCarran (D-Nev.) on the McCarran-Walter Act

When: 1953

Significance: These testimonies from the Congressional Record are especially illuminating when it comes to the restrictionist and anti-restrictionist debate in the U.S. Senate. This article highlights the restrictionist view.

The Honorable Pat McCarran (Senator D-Nevada):

"Recognizing the need for a comprehensive evaluation of our immigration laws, the 80th congress, in 1947 empowered the Senate Committee of the judiciary to make a full and complete investigation of our entire immigration system.

....

"The subcommittee studies not only the history of the immigration policy of the United States, but the immigration policies of other countries. We delved into the history of and development of international migrations and the problems of population and natural resources. We studied the characteristics of the population of the United States, insofar as they were related to our immigration and naturalization system."

....

"We learned that 60 percent of the total world immigration from early in the nineteenth century to 1930 has come to the United States. Canada, which has ranked next to the United States, has received 11.5 percent of total world immigration, or less than one-fifth as much as the United States. Argentina has received about 10 percent of total immigration, while Brazil has been the place of destination for 7 percent to 8 percent of world immigration. Australia, New Zealand, and South Africa have received most of the remainder. So it is not an idle boast that we have the most liberal immigration policies in the Western Hemisphere.

"Today, as never before, a sound immigration and naturalization system is essential to the preservation of our way of life, because that system is a conduit through which a stream of humanity flows into the fabric of our society. If that stream is healthy, the impact on our society is salutary; but if that stream is polluted, our institutions and our way of life become infected."

....

"We have retained the national origins quota system as the basis for our quantitative restriction of immigration to this country. This formula for computing quotas is that the quota for each quota area shall be one-sixth of 1 percent of the number of inhabitants in the continental United States in the 1920 attributable by national origin to such quota area. In addition, several countries which previously had no quotas are allotted minimum quotas of 100. The national origins quota system has been integral part of our establishment in 1929, and, while it has been frequently criticized and attacked, no one as yet has come forward with an acceptable substitute.

"Congress had two purposes in mind when it adopted the national origins formula. The first was to provide a basis for determining quotas for numerical restriction of the flow of immigrants to this country. The second, and broader purpose, was to preserve the composition of population of the United States on the basis of the proportionate contribution made by various nationality groups....

"Although the flow of immigration has not followed the pattern contemplated under the national origins formula, it has provided a fixed and easily determinable method of controlling immigration which is not subject to the whims and caprice of administrative interpretation, and which is automatically resistant to the pressures for special treatment.... The national origins formula was and is a rational and logical method of numerically restricting immigration in such a manner as to preserve best the sociological and cultural balance in the population of the United States. It is eminently fair and sound for visas to be allocated in a ratio which will be more readily assimilable because of the similarity of their cultural background to that of the principal components of our population."

....

"It was urged by some that we pool unused quotas and apportion them to low quota countries. Let me point out, however, that the pooling of unused quotas would be in direct conflict with the national origins quota principle, which is the foundation of our protective immigration system, and which seeks to maintain the relative composition of our population. The effect of pooling unused quotas would be not only to increase substantially the number of aliens coming to the United States for permanent residence but would in the course of a generation or so, tend to change the ethnic composition of our nation....

"Another significant change made by the new act is the removal of discriminations based on sex. Certain of its provisions would permit American women citizens to bring their alien husbands to this country as non-quota immigrants, and enable alien husbands of resident women aliens to come in under a quota in a preferred status....

"One of the most significant changes made by the new act is the introduction of a principle of selectivity into a quota system. Under this provision, 50 percent of each quota is allocated to aliens whose services are needed in this country because of their special knowledge or skills.

"This new act also revises those provisions of law relating to the qualitative grounds for exclusion of aliens so that the criminal and immoral classes, the subversives and other undesirables can be excluded from admission into this country."

....

"Never before have our nationality and naturalization laws been integrated with our immigration laws, as if the case in this new act. Race is eliminated as a bar to naturalization. No one who has been lawfully admitted to this country for permanent residence will be denied the privilege of citizenship solely because of race.

"Other significant provisions of the naturalization part of this act broaden and refine the exceptions to expatriation by residence abroad of a naturalized citizen....

"It has been suggested that we treat the Communists too harshly in the new Immigration Act. Frankly, they are accorded the type of treatment deserved by traitors to this country, which is what they are. If anyone in this land of ours still doubts that the Communist Party of the United States is part and parcel of the international Communist conspiracy, he has only to read the Federal Bureau of Investigation's Documentary proof on the subject. Nurtured by the Soviet Union, it strives incessantly to make the United States of a Soviet America. Does anyone still have a doubt? Should they be handled with kid gloves?

"I believe that this nation is the last hope of western civilization and if this oasis of the world shall be overrun, perverted, contaminated, or destroyed, then the last flickering of light of humanity will be extinguished. I take no issue with those who would praise the contributions which have been made to our society by people of many races, of varied creeds and colors. America is indeed a joining together of many streams which go to form a mighty river which we call the American way. However, we have in the United States today hard core indigestible blocs who have not become integrated into the American way of life but which, on the contrary, are its deadly enemies. Today as never before untold millions are storming our gates for admission and those gates are cracking under the strain. The solution to the problems of Europe and Asia will not come through a transplanting of those problems en masse to the United States. A solution remains possible only if American is maintained strong and free; only if our institutions, our way of life, are preserved by those who are part and parcel of that way of life so that America may lead the world in a way dedicated to the worth and dignity of the human soul. I do not intend to be prophetic, but if the enemies of this legislation succeed in riddling it to pieces, or in amending it beyond recognition, they will have contributed more to promote this nation's downfall than any other group since we achieved our independence as a nation."

(Source: Article published in the February 1953 issue of USA, magazine of American Affairs, reprinted in the congressional record, March 2, 1953)

Document 4: Hon. John F. Kennedy (D-Mass.) to Senate Judiciary Subcommittee on the McCarran-Walter Act

When: November 21, 1955

Significance: These testimonies from the Congressional Record are especially illuminating when it comes to the restrictionist and anti-restrictionist debate in the U.S. Senate. This article highlights the anti-restrictionist view.

The Honorable John F. Kennedy (Senator D-Massachusetts):

"Many evils and discriminations unfortunately, and to this nation's embarrassment, have characterized our immigration policy since 1921.

"For years the United States has taken pride in its reputation as the world's melting pot; our strength has been due in large part to the wide diversity of the cultural and ethnic backgrounds of our citizens. It is amazing that against this background, our national policy since 1921, as enacted by Congress has repudiated these principles and ignored the rich rewards of our past experience.

"The obvious weakness and discriminatory features most recently adopted by Congress in the passage of the McCarran-Walter Act in 1952 cry out for correction with a voice which cannot be ignored.

"First: Perhaps the most blatant piece of discrimination in our nation's history is the so-called National Origins formula first enacted in 1921 and included in our present immigration law. Regarded as an affront to the entire world by leaders of every major religious group, this formula disregards one of the fundamental propositions upon which this nation is founded – all men are created equal. The National Origins formula, basing the number of immigrants who can be admitted to this nation from any country in a single year upon the ratio which the number of immigrants residing in the United States in 1920 from that country have to all resident immigrants in that year, is in direct conflict with the Declaration of Independence, the principles set forth in the Constitution of the United States and our traditional standards of common decency and justice.

"It is not difficult to demonstrate that this formula has worked a hardship upon many deserving individuals who might now be useful citizens of the United States. Between 1900 and 1910, 2,045,877 immigrants from Italy entered the United States, an average of over 200,000 per year. The Act of 1921 decreased the amount to 42,000 per year and under the National Origins formula of the McCarran-Walter Act this figure was further reduced to less than 6,000. During the 1900-10 period over 167,000 Greeks migrated to this country, an average of over 16,000 a year; under McCarran-Walter 308 Greeks are entitled to enter the United States each year. It is apparent to every observer of the Greek and Italian situations that significant increases in the number of people who migrate from countries – in the case of Italy as many as 200,000 per year for a ten-year period – are essential if they are to continue their economic recovery and to take their proper places in the countries of the Free World.

"Another example of the effect of additional restrictions placed upon the initial National Origins formula is the further decrease in the Polish immigrant quota from 31,000 in 1921 to 6,488 under the McCarran-Walter Act. These figures are not unusual ones specially selected, but unfortunately they portray accurately the effect of the national origins system which by design discriminates against southern and eastern European nationals and the so-called Asiatic-Pacific triangle. On the other hand, the quotas established for the northern and western European countries have been far in excess of the actual needs and desires of those countries as evidenced by the fact that 44 percent of the total quota since the adoption of the National Origins formula has remained unused, the unused portion being almost completely composed of northern European quotas. It should be noted that the quota for Great Britain under the McCarran-Walter Act is 65,721 or approximately 40 percent of the total of about 153,000 admissible in any single year.

"In short the McCarran-Walter Act permits immigration to this country by those who do not wish to do so while it denies that right to those who have both the need and desire to relocate in the United States.

"Second: The McCarran-Walter Act, unfortunately, continues the requirement of the Displaced Persons Act that the number of displaced persons admitted to this country under that act be charged to the present and future normal immigration quotas of the countries from which these unfortunate persons originated. For some countries this has produced such 'mortgages' against their future quotas that they will be permitted to send to the United States only 50 percent of an already shockingly low 'National Origins' quota for many years to come. For example, Poland will not have repaid its 'immigration debt' until 1999; Greece until the year 2013, Lithuania until 2087, and Latvia 2274.

"Third: a further aspect of our immigration and naturalization policy which demands remedial action is the difference in the status of our citizens. Once we have accepted an individual for citizenship he should have the same rights, privileges, obligations, and duties and burdens as all other citizens – special tests and standards should not be applied.

"Fourth: The present manner in which our immigration policies are administered also requires substantial revision. With two independent departments of the Government – State and Justice – dividing the responsibilities and administrative functions there has been confusion, inefficiency, duplication, and financial waste. Since immigration and naturalization are quite far removed from the primary functions and responsibilities of each of the two departments involved, there has been little in a way of effective leadership by any official with cabinet or agency head status. Divided and ineffective administration in such an important field cannot continue. Perhaps the most glaring deficiency in the administrative procedure in the immigration field is the absence of any right of appeal from the initial decision of the United States consul as to the admissibility of the applicant for a vise. Moreover, the alien who reaches this country has inadequate and limited rights of appeal from decisions which may be rendered concerning his entrance into the United States. This obviously does not meet the standards of fair play and due process which characterize our general attitude toward administrative and judicial determinations.

....

(Source: Statement submitted to the Senate Judiciary Subcommittee on Immigration and Naturalization on November 21, 1955)

FURTHER READINGS

Books

Blumenthal, Shirley. *Coming to America: Immigrants from Eastern Europe.* New York: Delacorte Press, 1981.

Daniels, Roger. *Coming to America: A History of Immigration and Ethnicity in American Life.* New York: Harper Perennial, 1991.

Dinnerstein, Leonard, and David M. Reimers. *Ethnic Americans*, 2nd ed. New York: Harper & Row, 1982.

Johnson, Kevin. *The "Huddled Masses" Myth: Immigration and Civil Rights.* Philadelphia: Temple University Press, 2003.

Kanstroom, Daniel. *Deportation Nation: Outsiders in American History.* Cambridge, Mass.: Harvard University Press, 2007.

Ong Hing, Bill. *Defining America Through Immigration Policy.* Philadelphia: Temple University Press, 2004.

Articles

Bennett, Marion. "Immigration and Nationality (McCarran-Walter) Act of 1952, as Amended to 1965." *Annals of the American Academy of Political Science*, Vol. 367, The New Immigration (September 1966), 127–136.

Campi, Alicia. "The McCarran-Walter Act: A Contradictory Legacy on Race, Quotas, and Ideology." Immigration Policy Brief, Immigration Policy Center (June 2004).

Center for Migration Studies. "The Immigration and Nationality Act of 1952 as Amended through 1961." *International Migration Digest*, Vol. 1, No. 1 (Spring 1964), 34–46.

Cole, David. "9/11 and the LA 8." *The Nation* (October 27, 2003), 56.

Helton, Arthur. "Alien Exclusion." *The Nation* (May 28, 1988), 737–738.

Kulischer, Eugene. "Displaced Persons in the Modern World." *Annals of the Academy of Political and Social Science*, Vol. 262, Reappraising our Immigration Policy (March 1949), 166–177.

Shapiro, Steven. "Ideological Exclusions: Closing the Border to Political Dissidents." *Harvard Law Review*, Vol. 100 (1987), 930–945.

CHAPTER 6

From the Quota System
to the Preference System

Akis Kalaitzidis

The year 1965 was a watershed for immigration legislation in the United States. The Immigration and Nationality Act amended the 1952 McCarran-Walter Act by completely dismantling the quota system and replacing it with a preference system. To understand the magnitude of the change and how it was achieved, we must understand the sociocultural context in which it was undertaken.

The turbulent 1960s saw some of the most radical changes in American politics and society. Some of the most important were as follows: (1) the Civil Rights movement, which reached its apogee with a massive march on Washington, D.C., and an eloquent plea for equality; (2) the Black Nationalist movement, which was a response to racism and repression; (3) an antiwar movement showing its full strength and costing the Democrats the presidency, a blow from which the party did not recover until the 1990s; (4) women's liberation, the sexual revolution, and feminism. Though no one event can be seen as the progenitor of the sweeping changes in immigration law in the 1960s, one can safely argue that the 1965 Immigration and Nationality Act (INA) measures were enacted in the spirit of these changing times and very much with the civil rights movement in mind.

The national origins formula seemed out of place at a time when the United States was attempting to eliminate racial barriers at home. The national origins formula had many political enemies, notably President Harry Truman, whose veto power was overridden in order for the McCarran-Walters Act to pass, and later Presidents Kennedy and Johnson, who made it clear they would attempt to change it. Kennedy strongly opposed the national origins formula; as witnessed by his statements presented in the previous chapter. In his book, *A Nation of Immigrants* (1959), his views on the immigration subject were against quotas. His brother, Edward Kennedy, Massachusetts senator and chairman of the subcommittee on immigration, took charge of the issue, in committee.

What did the 1965 measures change? Most importantly, the quota system was replaced with a preference system of immigrant visa allocation. It eliminated origin, race, gender, and ancestry as a determinant of immigration to the United States. The new law established an immigration cap of 20,000 persons per country. The preference system listed the following seven preferences in order of importance: (1) unmarried children of U.S. citizens; (2) spouses and unmarried children of permanent residents; (3) professionals of exceptional ability; (4) married children of U.S. citizens; (5) siblings of U.S. citizens; (6) skilled and unskilled workers in short supply; and (7) refugees. Moreover, the amendments established two categories of immigrants that would not be subject to numerical restrictions: (1) immediate relatives of U.S. citizens and (2) special immigrants, such as certain ministers of religions, and former U.S. government employees.

The new system established a limit of 170,000 for the Eastern Hemisphere and a limit of 120,000 for the Western Hemisphere, which up to that point was unrestricted. In addition, the national limitation of 20,000 per country did not apply to the Western Hemisphere nations. The amendments also attempted to address a traditional grievance of labor unions and restrictionists in the United States, who claimed that immigrants took away jobs from U.S. citizens. Under the new laws, aliens seeking employment in the United States would have to show that they would not replace an American worker or adversely affect the working conditions and wages of Americans. This placed the onus of proof upon the U.S. business community by imposing restrictions on the hiring process such as adequate advertising time. Any business wishing to hire an immigrant to fill a position must advertise the job for 90 days and make a case why the immigrant is the best fit from the pool of applicants.

What Congress hoped to do was to eliminate race, origin, and gender as a means by which an immigrant was admitted to the United States. In reality, however, identifiers such as race and gender are very hard to eliminate. Research shows that women refugees are less likely to have their claims processed and that Haitian immigrants had a harder time getting their immigration status processed (Kelly 1993; Jacobson 2006). More worryisome, research reveals the development of immigration code words to deal with such identifiers (Omi and Winant 1993). The development of a new immigration narrative that stresses the lack of attention to race or gender of its own policy only adds to the racial and gender-loaded discourse (Luibhéid 1997). Even though the new law failed to eliminate race, origin, and gender as an identifier in the immigration procedures, it did succeed in giving new immigration opportunities to immigrants from countries underrepresented in the past centuries.

The 1965 changes opened the door to a new wave of immigration to the United States. Within a decade of its passage, the new immigration laws succeeded in increasing immigration by 60 percent, with immigration from many Asian countries predictably reaching an increase in several thousand percentage points (LeMay 2006, 157). Table 6.1 shows the calculated increase and change in composition after the law was enacted by region:

TABLE 6.1 Annual Average Immigration (in thousands) by Region of Origin

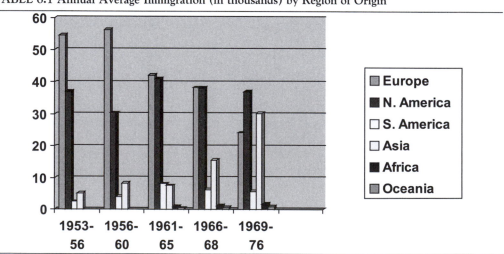

Source: Author's own calculations from Keely 1971 and Keely 2001.

It is obvious that the major beneficiaries of this legislation a decade later were Asian immigrants. Also, while the law intended to streamline integration according to national need, immigration rose significantly overall due to this legislation. It led to a resurgence of nativist or restrictionist forces in the political arena, particularly after the amnesty offered by President Ronald Reagan in the 1980s.

During the 1970s, other legislation made immigration to the United States easier for special immigrants by changing some of the requirements in special immigration categories. For example, in 1970, finances and intracompany transfers were addressed, and new rules on permanent residency were introduced. In 1972 the U.S. Congress reduced the residency requirement for acquiring U.S. citizenship. In 1974 the "coolie trade" legislation of 1862 was repealed although by then most laws targeting Asians had been repealed anyway. Another significant change, in 1976, concerned the status of refugees. Many of these refugees in the 1970s came from Southeast Asia, most notably from Cambodia, Vietnam, and Laos. The government created a special category of immigrants for those who helped the United States during its presence in the region, and immigrants who faced reprisals or danger from their compatriots when the U.S. forces were withdrawn. Examples of such immigrant groups are the Hmong or highland Laotian tribes, who were allowed into the United States legally after it became clear they would be persecuted by the Laotian army after the withdrawal of the U.S. forces. Persecution continues to this day; there is film footage of atrocities as recently as 2004 (BBC; May 13, 2004). Between the 1960s and 1970s, the refugee asylum seekers from Southeast Asia arrived en masse to the United States (i.e., 340,000 from Vietnam, 110,000 from Laos, approximately 70,000 from Cambodia, in addition to the refugees from the former Soviet Union and other communist bloc countries that provided a steady number or asylum seekers every year) (LeMay 2006, 164).

The most important piece of legislation from the U.S. Congress regarding immigration in this period was passed in October 1976, titled Immigration and Nationality Act Amendments, which modified the previous changes to the INA. These amendments set the same limits on countries of the Western Hemisphere as to those of the East, making it harder for immigrants from the Americas to come to the United States while keeping the overall hemispheric immigration levels the same (170,000 for the Western Hemispher and 120,000 for the Eastern Hemisphere). It also raised the number of visa allocations for colonies and other dependent areas, from 200 annually to 600, while demanding that allocations both be deducted from the country ceiling of 20,000 as well as the hemispheric ceiling. The rules set up a triggering mechanism whereby once the ceiling of 20,000 was reached for a specific country, the hemispheric allotment for various preference categories became applicable. The amendments made Cuban refugees exempt from any numerical limitation provided that they reached the United States. These amendments began the national debate about refugee policy in the United States, starting with the Mariel Boatlift of Cuban refugees in 1980. It continues today with thousands of Haitian refugees attempting to cross the treacherous Caribbean Sea to Florida. Given these desparate boat crossings, for the first time, the government of the United States was forced to consider an immigration policy on humanitarian grounds.

DOCUMENTS

Document 1: Immigration and Nationality Act of 1965

When: October 3, 1965

Significance: The very first immigration law to move away from the national origins formula into a preference system.

Public Law 89–236

DID YOU KNOW?

The Mariel Boatlift

Immortalized by Hollywood in the famous 1983 Brian De Palma movie *Scarface*, the Mariel Boatlift happened between April 15 and October 31, 1980. The boatlift takes its name from the town of Mariel in northwest Cuba from where most of the boats originated. The Mariel boatlift led to approximately 125,000 Cubans coming to the United States by using 1,700 boats.

The so-called "Marielitos" refugees were put in refugee camps throughout the country, including Fort Chaffee, which previously housed Vietnamese refugees. In Fort Chafee, riots among the Cuban refugees got out of hand and cost then Arkansas Governor Bill Clinton his reelection bid. Famous "Marielitos" include journalist Mirta Ojito, who won a Pulitzer Prize in 2000 for her series "How Race is Lived in America."

An Act

To amend the Immigration and Nationality Act, and for other purposes. [H. R. 2580]

Be it enacted by the Senate and House of Representatives of the United States of America in Congress assembled, That section 201 of immigration and the Immigration and Nationality Act (66 Stat. 175; 8 U.S.C. 1151) be amended to read as follows:

"SEC. 201. (a) Exclusive of special immigrants defined in section 101 (a) (27), and of the immediate relatives of United States citizens specified in subsection (b) of this section, the number of aliens who may be issued immigrant visas or who may otherwise acquire the status of an alien lawfully admitted to the United States for permanent residence, or who may, pursuant to section 203(a) (7) enter conditionally, (i) shall not in any of the first three quarters of any fiscal year exceed a total of 45,000 and (ii) shall not in any fiscal year exceed a total of 170,000.

"(b) The 'immediate relatives' referred to in subsection (a) of this section shall mean the children, spouse, and parents of a citizen of the United States: Provided, That in the case of parents, such citizen must be at least twenty-one years of age. The immediate relatives specified in this subsection who are otherwise qualified for admission as immigrants shall be admitted as such, without regard to the numerical limitations in this Act.

"(c) During the period from July 1, 1965, through June 30, 1968, the annual quota of any quota area shall be the same as that which existed for that area on June 30, 1965. The Secretary of State shall, not later than on the sixtieth day immediately following the date of enactment of this subsection and again on or before September 1, 1966, and September 1, 1967, determine and proclaim the amount of quota numbers which remain unused at the end of the fiscal year ending on June 30, 1965, June 30, 1966, and June 30, 1967, respectively, and are available for distribution pursuant to subsection (d) of this section.

"(d) Quota numbers not issued or otherwise used during the previous fiscal year, as determined in accordance with subsection (c) hereof, shall be transferred to an immigration pool. Allocation of numbers from the pool and from national quotas shall not together exceed in any fiscal year the numerical limitations in subsection (a) of this section. The immigration pool shall be made available to immigrants otherwise admissible under the provisions of this Act who are unable to obtain prompt issuance of a preference visa due to oversubscription of their quotas, or subquotas as determined by the Secretary of State. Visas and conditional entries shall be allocated from the immigration pool within the percentage limitations and in the order of priority specified in section 203 without regard to the quota to which the alien is chargeable.

"(e) The immigration pool and the quotas of quota areas shall terminate June 30, 1968. Thereafter immigrants admissible under the provisions of this Act who are subject to the numerical limitations of subsection (a) of this section shall be admitted in accordance with the percentage limitations and in the order of priority specified in section 203."

SEC. 2. Section 202 of the Immigration and Nationality Act (66 Foreign states. Stat. 175; 8 U.S.C. 1152) is amended to read as follows:

"(a) No person shall receive any preference or priority or be discriminated against in the issuance of an immigrant visa because of his race, sex, nationality, place of birth, or place of residence, except as specifically provided in section 101(a) (27), section 201 (b), and section

203: Provided, That the total number of immigrant visas and the number of conditional entries made available to natives of any single foreign state under paragraphs (1) through (8) of section 203(a) shall not exceed 20,000 in any fiscal year: Provided further, That the foregoing proviso shall not operate to reduce the number of immigrants who may be admitted under the quota of any quota area before June 30,1968.

"(b) Each independent country, self-governing dominion, mandated territory, and territory under the international trusteeship system of the United Nations, other than the United States and its outlying possessions shall be treated as a separate foreign state for the purposes of the numerical limitation set forth in the proviso to sub section (a) of this section when approved by the Secretary of State. All other inhabited lands shall be attributed to a foreign state specified by the Secretary of State. For the purposes of this Act the foreign state to which an immigrant is chargeable shall be determined by birth within such foreign state except that (1) an alien child, when accompanied by his alien parent or parents, may be charged to the same foreign state as the accompanying parent or of either accompanying parent if such parent has received or would be qualified for an immigrant visa, if necessary to prevent the separation of the child from the accompanying parent or parents, and if the foreign state to which such parent has been or would be chargeable has not exceeded the numerical limitation set forth in the proviso to subsection (a) of this section for that fiscal year; (2) if an alien is chargeable to a different foreign state from that of his accompanying spouse, the foreign state to which such alien is chargeable may, if necessary to prevent the separation of husband and wife, be determined by the foreign state of the accompanying spouse, if such spouse has received or would be qualified for an immigrant visa and the foreign state to which such spouse has been or would be chargeable has not exceeded the numerical limitation set forth in the proviso to subsection (a) of this section for that fiscal year; (3) an alien born in the United States shall be considered as having been born in the country of which he is a citizen or subject, or if he is not a citizen or subject of any country then in the last foreign country in which he had his residence as determined by the consular officer; (4) an alien born within any foreign state in which neither of his parents was born and in which neither of his parents had a residence at the time of such alien's birth may be charged to the foreign state of either parent.

"(c) Any immigrant born in a colony or other component or dependent area of a foreign state unless a special immigrant as provided in section 101 (a) (27) or an immediate relative of a United States citizen as specified in section 201 (b), shall be chargeable, for the purpose of limitation set forth in section 202(a), to the foreign state, except that the number of persons born in any such colony or other component or dependent area overseas from the foreign state chargeable to the foreign state in any one fiscal year shall not exceed 1 per centum of the maximum number of immigrant visas available to such foreign state.

"(d) In the case of any change in the territorial limits of foreign states, the Secretary of State shall, upon recognition of such change, issue appropriate instructions to all diplomatic and consular offices."

DID YOU KNOW?

The Southeast Asian Refugees

America's involvement in the Vietnam War from 1965 to April 30, 1975, produced a large number of refugees from Vietnam, Laos, and Cambodia.

The Degar, otherwise known as Montagnards or mountain people by the French Colonists, are indigenous people of Vietnam. Approximately 40,000 Degar people fought along the Americans against the Communists in Vietnam and became a major part of the refugee movement to the United States after the American withdrawal in 1975.

Another group of Southeastern refugees to come to the United States were the Hmong people of Laos. Initially, they fought against the French in a revolt between 1919 and 1921, called the "War of the Flowering of the Law" (in Hmong it is Roj Paj Cai, which was named after the leader of the revolt Paj Cai, whom the French had assassinated in 1921 to bring an end to the revolt). Later they took part as special guerrilla units against the North Vietnamese using Laos and the Ho Chi Minh Trail to reach South Vietnam and the Pathet Lao (the Laotian Army). About 260,000 Laotian Hmong have resettled in the United States since the 1970s.

Another group of refugees are the Cambodian peoples who came to the United States following the collapse of the U.S. forces. Approximately 147,000 came to the United States after the end of the war in Vietnam; following the Khmer Rouge seizure of power, which saw the mass murder of millions of people and the creation of what the world knows as "the killing fields." These groups are still being persecuted today for their activities of more than thirty years ago.

SEC. 3. Section 203 of the Immigration and Nationality Act (66 Stat. 175; 8 U.S.C. 1153) is amended to read as follows:

"SEC. 203. (a) Aliens who are subject to the numerical limitations specified in section 201(a) shall be allotted visas or their conditional entry authorized, as the case may be, as follows:

"(1) Visas shall be first made available, in a number not to exceed 20 per centum of the number specified in section 201 (a) (ii), to qualified immigrants who are the unmarried sons or daughters of citizens of the United States.

"(2) Visas shall next be made available, in a number not to exceed 20 per centum of the number specified in section 201 (a) (ii), plus any visas not required for the classes specified in paragraph (1), to qualified immigrants who are the spouses, unmarried sons or unmarried daughters of an alien lawfully admitted for permanent residence.

"(3) Visas shall next be made available, in a number not to exceed 10 per centum of the number specified in section 201 (a) (ii), to qualified immigrants who are members of the professions, or who because of their exceptional ability in the sciences or the arts will substantially benefit prospectively the national economy, cultural interests, or welfare of the United States.

"(4) Visas shall next be made available, in a number not to exceed 10 per centum of the number specified in section 201 (a) (ii), plus any visas not required for the classes specified in paragraphs (1) through (3), to qualified immigrants who are the married sons or the married daughters of citizens of the United States.

"(5) Visas shall next be made available, in a number not to exceed 24 per centum of the number specified in section 201 (a) (ii), plus any visas not required for the classes specified in paragraphs (1) through (4), to qualified immigrants who are the brothers or sisters of citizens of the United States.

"(6) Visas shall next be made available, in a number not to exceed 10 per centum of the number specified in section 201 (a) (ii), to qualified immigrants who are capable of performing specified skilled or unskilled labor, not of a temporary or seasonal nature, for which a shortage of employable and willing persons exists in the United States.

"(7) Conditional entries shall next be made available by the Attorney General, pursuant to such regulations as he may prescribe and in entries-a number not to exceed 6 per centum of the number specified in section 201 (a) (ii), to aliens who satisfy an Immigration and Naturalization Service officer at an examination in any non-Communist or non-Communist-dominated country, (A) that (i) because of persecution or fear of persecution on account of race, religion, or political opinion they have fled (I) from any Communist or Communist-dominated country or area, or (II) from any country within the general area of the Middle East, and (ii) are unable or unwilling to return to such country or area on account of race, religion, or political opinion, and (iii) are not nationals of the countries or areas in which their application for conditional entry is made; or (B) that they are persons uprooted by catastrophic natural calamity as defined by the President who are unable to return to their usual place of abode. For the purpose of the foregoing the term 'general area of the Middle East' means the area between and including (1) Libya on the west, (2) Turkey on the north, (3) Pakistan on the east, and (4) Saudi Arabia and Ethiopia on the south: Provided, That immigrant visas in a number not exceeding one-half the number specified in this paragraph may be made available, in lieu of conditional entries of a like number, to such aliens who have been continuously physically present in the United States for a period of at least two years prior to application for adjustment of status.

"(8) Visas authorized in any fiscal year, less those required for issuance to the classes specified in paragraphs (1) through (6) and less the number of conditional entries and visas made available pursuant to paragraph (7), shall be made available to other qualified immigrants strictly in the chronological order in which they qualify. Waiting lists of applicants shall be maintained in accordance with regulations prescribed by the Secretary of State. No immigrant visa shall be issued to a nonpreference immigrant under this paragraph, or to an immigrant with a preference under paragraph (3) or (6) of this subsection, until the consular officer is in receipt of a determination made by the Secretary of Labor pursuant to the provisions of section 212(a)(14).

"(9) A spouse or child as defined in section 101(b)(l) (A). (B), (C), (D), or (E) shall otherwise entitled to an immigrant status and the immediate issuance of a visa or to conditional entry under paragraphs (1) through (8), be entitled to the same status, and the same order of consideration provided in subsection (b), if accompanying, or following to join, his spouse or parent.

"(b) In considering applications for immigrant visas under subsection (a) consideration shall be given to applicants in the order in which the classes of which they are members are listed in subsection (a).

"(c) Immigrant visas issued pursuant to paragraphs (1) through (6) of subsection (a) shall be issued to eligible immigrants in the order in which a petition in behalf of each such immigrant is filed with the Attorney General as provided in section 204.

"(d) Every immigrant shall be presumed to be a nonpreference immigrant until he establishes to the satisfaction of the consular officer and the immigration officer that he is entitled to a preference status under paragraphs (1) through (7) of subsection (a), or to a special immigrant status under section 101 (a) (27), or that he is an immediate relative of a United States citizen as specified in section 201 (b). In the case of any alien claiming in his application for an immigrant visa to be an immediate relative of a United States citizen as specified in section 201 (b) or to be entitled to preference immigrant status under paragraphs (1) through (6) of subsection (a), the consular officer shall not grant such status until he has been authorized to do so as provided by section 204.

"(e) For the purposes of carrying out his responsibilities in the orderly administration of this section, the Secretary of State is authorized to make reasonable estimates of the anticipated numbers of visas to be issued during any quarter of any fiscal year within each of the categories of subsection (a), and to rely upon such estimates in authorizing the issuance of such visas. The Secretary of State, in his discretion, may terminate the registration on a waiting list of any alien who fails to evidence his continued intention to apply for a visa in such manner as may be by regulation prescribed.

"(f) The Attorney General shall submit to the Congress a report containing complete and detailed statement of facts in the case of each alien who conditionally entered the United States pursuant to subsection (a) (7) of this section. Such reports shall be submitted on or before January 15 and June 15 of each year.

"(g) Any alien who conditionally entered the United States as a refugee, pursuant to subsection (a) (7) of this section, whose conditional entry has not been terminated by the Attorney General pursuant to such regulations as he may prescribe, who has been in the United States for at least two years, and who has not acquired permanent residence, shall forthwith return or be returned to the custody of the Immigration and Naturalization Service and shall thereupon be inspected and examined for admission into the United States, and his case dealt with in accordance with the provisions of sections 235, 236, 1225 and 237 of this Act.

"(h) Any alien who, pursuant to subsection (g) of this section, is found, upon inspection by the immigration officer or after hearing before a special inquiry officer, to be admissible as an immigrant under this Act at the time of his inspection and examination, except for the fact that he was not and is not in possession of the documents required by section 212(a) (20), shall be regarded as lawfully admitted to the United States for permanent residence as of the date of his arrival."

sec. 4. Section 204 of the Immigration and Nationality Act (66 Stat. 176; 8 U.S.C. 1154) is amended to read as follows:

"sec. 204. (a) Any citizen of the United States claiming that an alien is entitled to a preference status by reason of the relationships described in paragraphs (1), (4), or (5) of section 203(a), or to an immediate relative status under section 201 (b), or any alien lawfully admitted for permanent residence claiming that an alien is entitled to a preference status by reason of the relationship described in section 203(a) (2), or any alien desiring to be classified as a preference immigrant under section 203(a) (3) (or any person on behalf of such an alien), or any person desiring and intending to employ within the United States an alien entitled to classification as a preference immigrant under section 203(a) (6), may file a petition with the Attorney General for such classification. The petition shall be in such form as the Attorney General may by regulations prescribe and shall contain such information and be supported by such documentary evidence as the Attorney General may require. The petition shall be made under oath administered by any individual having authority to administer oaths, if executed in the United States, but, if executed outside the United States, administered by a consular officer or an immigration officer.

"(b) After an investigation of the facts in each case, and after consultation with the Secretary of Labor with respect to petitions to accord a status under section 203(a) (3) or (6), the Attorney General shall, if he determines that the facts stated in the petition are true and that the alien in behalf of whom the petition is made is an immediate relative specified in section 201 (b) or is eligible for a preference status under section 203(a), approve the petition and forward one copy thereof to the Department of State. The Secretary of State shall then authorize the consular officer concerned to grant the preference status.

"(c) Notwithstanding the provisions of subsection (b) no more than two petitions may be approved for one petitioner in behalf of a child as defined in section 101 (b) (1) (E) or (F) unless necessary to prevent the separation of brothers and sisters and no petition shall be approved if the alien has previously been accorded a nonquota or preference status as the spouse of a citizen of the United States or the spouse of an alien lawfully admitted for permanent residence, by reason of a marriage determined by the Attorney General to have been entered into for the purpose of evading the immigration laws.

"(d) The Attorney General shall forward to the Congress a report on each approved petition for immigrant status under sections 203(a)(3) or 203(a)(6) stating the basis for his approval and such facts as were by him deemed to be pertinent in establishing the beneficiary's qualifications for the preferential status. Such reports shall be submitted to the Congress on the first and fifteenth day of each calendar month in which the Congress is in session.

"(e) Nothing in this section shall be construed to entitle an immigrant, in behalf of whom a petition under this section is approved, to enter the United States as a preference immigrant under section 203(a) or as an immediate relative under section 201 (b) if upon his arrival at a port of entry in the United States he is found not to be entitled to such classification."

sec. 5. Section 205 of the Immigration and Nationality Act (66 Stat. 176; 8 U.S.C. 1155) is amended to read as follows:

"sec. 205, The Attorney General may, at any time, for what he deems to be good and sufficient cause, revoke the approval of any petition approved by him under section 204. Such revocation shall be effective as of the date of approval of any such petition. In no case, however, shall such revocation have effect unless there is mailed to the petitioner's last known address a notice of the revocation and unless notice of the revocation is communicated through the Secretary of State to the beneficiary of the petition before such beneficiary commences his journey to the United States. If notice of revocation is not so given, and the beneficiary applies for admission to the United States, his admissibility shall be determined in the manner provided for by sections 235 and 236."

"sec. 6. Section 206 of the Immigration and Nationality Act is amended to read as follows:

"sec. 206. If an immigrant having an immigrant visa is excluded from admission to the United States and deported, or does not apply for admission before the expiration of the validity of his visa, or if an alien having an immigrant visa issued to him as a preference immigrant is found not to be a preference immigrant, an immigrant visa or a preference immigrant visa, as the case may be, may be issued in lieu thereof to another qualified alien."

"sec. 7. Section 207 of the Immigration and Nationality Act (66 Stat. 181; 8 U.S.C. 1157) is stricken.

"sec. 8. Section 101 of the Immigration and Nationality Act (66 Stat. 166; 8 U.S.C. 1101) is amended as follows:

(a) Paragraph (27) of subsection (a) is amended to read as follows: "(27) The term 'special immigrant' means—

"(A) an immigrant who was born in any independent foreign country of the Western Hemisphere or in the Canal Zone and the spouse and children of any such immigrant, if accompanying, or following to join him: Provided, That no immigrant visa shall be issued pursuant to this clause until the consular officer is in receipt of a determination made by the Secretary of Labor pursuant to the provisions of section 212(a) (14);

"(B) an immigrant, lawfully admitted for permanent residence, who is returning from a temporary visit abroad;

"(C) an immigrant who was a citizen of the United States and may, under section 324(a) or 327 of title III, apply for reacquisition of citizenship;

"(D) (i) an immigrant who continuously for at least two years immediately preceding the time of his application for admission to the United States has been, and who seeks to enter the United States solely for the purpose of carrying on the vocation of minister of a religious denomination, and whose services are needed by such religious denomination having a bona fide organization in the United States; and (ii) the spouse or the child of any such immigrant, if accompanying or following to join him; or

"(E) an immigrant who is an employee, or an honorably retired former employee, of the United States Government abroad, and who has performed faithful service for a total of fifteen years, or more, and his accompanying spouse and children: Provided, That the principal officer of a Foreign Service establishment, in his discretion, shall have recommended the granting of special immigrant status to such alien in exceptional circumstances and the Secretary of State approves such recommendation and finds that it is in the national interest to grant such status."

....

(c) Subparagraph (1) (F) of subsection (b) is amended as follows:

"(F) a child, under the age of fourteen at the time a petition is filed in his behalf to accord a classification as an immediate relative under section 201(b), who is an orphan because of the death or disappearance of, abandonment or desertion by, or separation or loss from, both parents, or for whom the sole or surviving parent is incapable of providing proper care which will be provided the child if admitted to the United States and who has in writing irrevocably released the child for emigration and adoption; who has been adopted abroad by the United States citizen and his spouse who personally saw and observed the child prior to or during the adoption proceedings; or who is coming to the United States for adoption by a United States citizen and if any, of the child's proposed residence: Provided, that no natural parent or prior adoptive parent of any such child shall thereafter, by virtue of such parentage, be accorded any right, privilege, or status under this Act."

SEC. 9. section 211 of the Immigration and Nationality Act (66 Stat. 181; 8 U.S.C.1181) is amended to read as follows:

"SEC. 211. (a) Except as provided in subsection (b) no immigrant shall be admitted into the United States unless at the time of application for admission he (1) has a valid unexpired immigrant visa or was born subsequent to the issuance of such visa of the accompanying parent, and (2) presents a valid unexpired passport or other suitable travel document, or document of identity and nationality, if such document is required under the regulations issued by the Attorney General. With respect to immigrants to be admitted under the quotas of quota areas prior to June 30, 1968, no immigrant visa shall be deemed valid unless the immigrant is properly chargeable to the quota are a under the quota of which the visa is issued.

"(b) Notwithstanding the provisions of section 212 (a) (20) of this Act is such cases or in such cases of cases and under such conditions as may be by regulations prescribed, returning resident immigrants, defined in section 101 (a) (27) (B), who are otherwise admissible may be readmitted to the United States by the Attorney general in his direction without being required to obtain a passport, immigrant visa, reentry permit or documentation."

SEC. 10 Section 212 (a) of the Immigration and Nationality Act (66 stat. 182; 8 U.S.C. 1182) is amended as follows:

Paragraph (14) is amended to read as follows:

"Aliens seeking to enter the United States, for the purpose of performing skilled or unskilled labor, unless the Secretary of Labor has determined and certified to the Secretary of State and to the Attorney General that (A) there not sufficient workers in the United States who are able, willing, qualified and available at the time of application for a visa and admission to the United States and at the place to which the alien is destined to perform such skilled or unskilled labor, and (B) the employment of such aliens will not adversely affect the wages and working conditions of the workers in the United States similarly employed. The exclusion of aliens under this paragraph shall apply to special immigrants defined in section 101 (a) (27) (A) (other than the parents, spouses, or children of United States citizens or of aliens lawfully admitted to the United States for permanent residence), to preference immigrant aliens described in section 203 (a) (3) and (6), and to nonpreference immigrant aliens described in section 203 (a) (8);"

....

SEC. 12. Section 244 of the Immigration and Nationality Act (66 Stat. 214; 8 U.S.C. 1254) is amended as follows:

Subsection (d) is amended to read:

"(d) upon the cancellation of deportation in the case of any alien under this section, the attorney general shall record the alien's lawful admission for permanent residence as of the date of cancellation of deportation of such aliens is made, and unless the alien is entitled to a special immigrant classification under section 101 (a) (27) (A), or is an immediate relative within the meaning of section 201 (b) the Secretary of State shall reduce by one the number of nonprefernce immigrant visas authorized to be issued under section 203 (a) (8) for the fiscal year then current."

....

(c) Sections 212 (f), (g) and (h) of the Immigration and Nationality Act of September 26, 1961 (75 stat. 654, 655; 8 U.S.C. 1182), are hereby redesignated sections 212 (g), (h), and (i), respectively, and section 212 (g) as so redesignated is amended by inserting before the words "afflicted by tuberculosis in any form" the following: "who is excludable from the United States under paragraph (1) of subsection (a) of this section, or any alien" and by adding at the end of such subsection the following sentence: "by adding at the end of such subsection the following sentence: "Any alien excludable under paragraph (3) of subsection (a) of this section conditions because of past history of mental illness who has one of the same family relationships as are prescribed in this subsection for aliens afflicted with tuberculosis and whom the Surgeon General of the United States Public Health Service finds to have been free of such mental illness for a period of time sufficient in the light of such history to demonstrate recovery shall be eligible for a visa in accordance with the terms of this subsection."

....

sec. 18. So much of section 272(a) of the Immigration and Nationality Act (66 Stat. 226; 8 U.S.C. 1322(a)) as precedes the words "shall pay to the collector of customs" is amended to read as follows:

"SEC. 272. (a) Any person who shall bring to the United States an alien (other than an alien crewman) who is (1) mentally retarded, (2) insane, (3) afflicted with psychopathic personality, or with sexual deviation, (4) a chronic alcoholic, (5) afflicted with any dangerous contagious disease, or (6) a. narcotic drug addict."

sec. 19. Section 249 of the Immigration and Nationality Act (66 Stat. 219; 8 U.S.C. 1259) is amended by striking out "June 28, 1940" in clause (a) of such section and inserting in lieu thereof "June 30, 1948."

sec. 20. This Act shall become effective on the first day of the first month after the expiration of thirty days following the date of its enactment except as provided herein.

sec. 21. (a) There is hereby established a Select Commission on Western Hemisphere Immigration (hereinafter referred to as the "Commission") to be composed of fifteen members. The President shall appoint the Chairman of the Commission and four other members thereof. The President of the Senate, with the approval of the majority and minority leaders of the Senate, shall appoint five members from the membership of the Senate. The Speaker of the House of Representatives, with the approval of the majority and minority leaders of the House, shall appoint five members from the membership of the House. Not more than three members appointed by the President of the Senate and the Speaker of the House of Representatives, respectively, shall be members of the same political party. A vacancy in the membership of the Commission shall be filled in the same manner as the original designation and appointment.

(b) The Commission shall study the following matters:

Prevailing and projected demographic, technological, and economic trends, particularly as they pertain to Western Hemisphere nations;

Present and projected unemployment in the United States, by occupations, industries, geographic areas and other factors, in relation to immigration from the Western Hemisphere;

The interrelationships between immigration, present and future, and existing and contemplated national and international programs and projects of Western Hemisphere nations, including programs and projects for economic and social development;

The operation of the immigration laws of the United States as they pertain to Western Hemisphere nations, including the adjustment of status for Cuban refugees, with emphasis on the adequacy of such laws from the standpoint of fairness and from the standpoint of the impact of such laws on employment and working conditions within the United States;

The implications of the foregoing with respect to the security and international relations of Western Hemisphere nations; and any other matters which the Commission believes to be germane to the purposes for which it was established.

(c) On or before July 1, 1967, the Commission shall make a first report to the President and the Congress, and on or before January 15, 1968; the Commission shall make a final report to the President and the Congress. Such reports shall include the recommendation of the Commission as to what changes, if any, are needed in the immigration laws in the light of its study. The Commission's recommendations shall include, but shall not be limited to, recommendations as to whether, and if so how, numerical limitations should be imposed upon immigration to the United States from the nations of the Western Hemisphere. In formulating its recommendations on the latter subject, the Commission shall give particular attention to the impact of such immigration on employment and working conditions within the United States and to the necessity of preserving the special relationship of the United States with its sister Republics of the Western Hemisphere.

(d) The life of the Commission shall expire upon the filing of its final report, except that the Commission may continue to function for up to sixty days thereafter for the purpose of winding up its affairs.

(e) Unless legislation inconsistent herewith is enacted on or before June 30, 1968, in response to recommendations of the Commission or otherwise, the number of special immigrants within the meaning of section 101 (a) (27) (A) of the Immigration and Nationality Act, as amended, exclusive of special immigrants who are immediate relatives of United States citizens as described in section 201(b) of that Act, shall not, in the fiscal year beginning July 1, 1968, or in any fiscal year thereafter, exceed a total of 120,000.

(f) All Federal agencies shall cooperate fully with the Commission to the end that it may effectively carry out its duties.

(g) Each member of the Commission who is not otherwise in the service of the Government of the United States shall receive the sum of $100 for each day spent in the work of the Commission, shall be paid actual travel expenses, and per diem in lieu of subsistence expenses, when away from his usual place of residence, in accordance with section 5 of the Administrative Expenses Act of 1946, as amended. Each member of the Commission who is otherwise in the service of the Government of the United States shall serve without compensation in addition to that received for such other service, but while engaged in the work of the Commission shall be paid actual travel expenses, when away from his usual place of residence, in accordance with the Administrative Expenses Act of 1946, as amended.

(h) There is authorized to be appropriated, out of any money in the Treasury not otherwise appropriated, so much as may be necessary to carry out the provisions of this section.

....

Approved October 3, 1965, 3:25 P.M.

Document 2: Public Law 94–571, 94th Congress Amendments to INA

When: October 29, 1976

Significance: These amendments are important in that for the first time the United States imposes numerical restrictions in Western Hemispheric immigration. The issues relating to immigration from Mexico and South America are becoming apparent.

An Act

To amend the immigration and Nationality Act, and for other purposes.

Be it enacted by the Senate and House of Representatives of the United States of America in Congress assembled, That this Act may be cited as the "Immigration and Nationality Act Amendments of 1976."

Sec. 2. Section 201 of the Immigration and Nationality Act (8 U.S.C. 1151) is amended–

(1) by striking out subsection (a) and inserting in lieu thereof the following:

SEC. 201. (a) Exclusive of special immigrants defined in section 101 (a) (27), and immediate relatives of United States citizens as specified in subsection (b) of this section, (1) the number of aliens born in any foreign state or dependent area located in the Eastern Hemisphere who may be issued immigrant visas or who may otherwise acquire the status of an alien lawfully admitted to the United States for permanent residence, or who may, pursuant to section 203 (a) (7), enter conditionally, shall not in any of the first three quarters of any fiscal year exceed a total of 45,000 and shall not in any fiscal year exceed a total of 170,000; and (2) the number of aliens born in any foreign state of the Western Hemisphere or in the Canal Zone, or in a dependent area located in the Western Hemisphere, who may be issued immigrant visas or who may otherwise acquire the status of an alien lawfully admitted to the United States for permanent residence, or who may, pursuant to section 203 (a) (7), enter conditionally shall not in any of the first three quarters of the fiscal year exceed a total of 32,000 and shall not in any fiscal year exceed a total of 120,000."; and

(2) by striking out subsections (c), (d), and (e).

SEC.3. Section 202 of the Immigration and Nationality Act (8 U.S.C. 1152) is amended—

(1) by striking out the last proviso in subsection (a);

(2) by striking out subsection (c) and inserting in lieu thereof the following:

"(c) Any immigrant born in a colony or other component or dependent area of a foreign state overseas from the foreign state, other than a special immigrant, as defined in section 201 (b), shall be chargeable for the purpose of the limitations set forth in sections 201 (a) and 202 (a), to the hemisphere in which such colony or other component or dependent area is located, and to the foreign state, respetively, and the number of immigrant visas available to each such colony or other component or dependent area shall not exceed 600 in any fiscal year."; and

(3) by inserting at the end thereof the following subsection:

"(e) Whenever the maximum number of visas or conditional entries have been made available under section 202 to natives of any single foreign state as defined in subsection (b) of this section or any dependent area as defined in subsection (c) of this section in any fiscal year, in the next following fiscal year a number of visas and conditional entries, not to exceed 20,000, in the case of a foreign state or 600 in the case of a dependent area, shall be made available and allocated as follows:

"(1) Visas shall first be made available, in a number not to exceed 20 per centum of the number specified in this subsection, to qualified immigrants who are the unmarried sons or daughters of citizens of the United States.

"(2) Visas shall next be made available, in a number not to exceed 20 per centum of the number specified in this subsection, plus any visas not required for the classes specified in paragraph (1), to qualified immigrants who are the spouses, unmarried sons, or unmarried daughters of an alien Lawfully admitted for permanent residence.

"(3) Visas shall next be made available, in a number not to exceed 10 per centum of the number specified in this subsection, to qualified immigrants who are members of the professions, or who because of their exceptional ability in the sciences or the arts will substantially benefit prospectively the national economy, cultural interests, or welfare of the United States, and whose services in the professions, sciences, or arts are sought by an employer in the United States.

"(4) Visas shall next be made available, in a number not to exceed 10 per centum of the number specified in this subsection, plus any visas not required for the classes specified in paragraphs (1) through (3), to qualified immigrants who are the married sons or the married daughters of citizens of the United States.

"(5) Visas shall next be made available, in a number not to exceed 24 per centum of the number specified in this subsection, plus any visas not required for the classes specified in paragraphs (1) through (4), to qualified immigrants who are the brothers or sisters of citizens of the United States, provided such citizens are at least twenty-one years of age.

"(6) Visas shall next be made available, in a number not to exceed 10 per centum of the number specified in this subsection, to qualified immigrants capable of performing specified skilled or unskilled labor, not of a temporary or seasonal nature, for which a shortage of employable and willing persons exists in the United States.

"(7) Conditional entries shall next be made available by the Attorney General, pursuant to such regulations as he may prescribe, in a number not to exceed 6 per centum of the number specified in this subsection, to aliens who satisfy an Immigration and Naturalization Service officer at an examination in any non-Communist or non-Communist-dominated country, (A) that (i) because of persecution or fear of persecution on account of race, religion, or political opinion they have fled (I) from any Communist or Communist-dominated country or area, or (II) from any country within the general area of the Middle East, and (ii) are unable or unwilling to return to such country or area on account of race, religion, or political opinion, and (iii) are not nationals of the countries or areas in which their application for conditional entry is made; or (B) that they are persons uprooted by catastrophic natural calamity as defined by the President who are unable to return to their usual place of abode. For the purpose of the foregoing the term 'general area of the Middle East' means the area between and including (1) Libya on the west, (2) Turkey on the north, (3) Pakistan on the east, and (4) Saudi Arabia and Ethiopia on the south: Provided, That immigrant visas in a number not exceeding one-half the number specified in this paragraph may be made available, in lieu of conditional entries of a like number, to such aliens who have been continuously physically present in the United States for a period of at least two years prior to application for adjustment of status.

"(8) Visas so allocated but not required for the classes specified in paragraphs (1) through (7) shall be made available to other qualified immigrants strictly in the chronological order in which they qualify."

SEC. 4. Section 203 of the Immigration and Nationality Act (8 U.S.C. 1153) is amended—

(1) by striking out "201 (a) (ii)" each place it appears in paragraphs (1) through (7) of subsection (a) and inserting in lieu thereof in each such place "201 (a) (1) or (2)'"; by striking out the period at the end of paragraph (3) of subsection (a) and inserting in lieu thereof a comma and the following: "and whose services in the professions, sciences, or arts are sought by an employer in the United States."; by striking out the period at the end of paragraph (5) of subsection (a) and inserting in lieu thereof a comma and the following: "provided such citizens are at least twenty-one years of age."; and by striking out the second sentence of subsection (e) and inserting in lieu thereof the following: "The Secretary of State shall terminate the registration of any alien who fails to apply for an immigrant visa within one year following notification to him of the availability of such visa, but the Secretary shall reinstate the registration of any such alien who establishes within two years following notification of the availability of such visa that such failure to apply was due to circumstances beyond his control. Upon such termination the approval of any petition approved pursuant to section 204(b) shall be automatically revoked."

SEC. 5. Section 212(a)(14) of such Act (8 U.S.C, 1182(a)(14)) is amended to read as follows:

"(14) Aliens seeking to enter the United States, for the purpose of performing skilled or unskilled labor, unless the Secretary of Labor has determined and certified to the Secretary of State and the Attorney General that (A) there are not sufficient workers who are able, willing, qualified (or equally qualified in the case of aliens who are members of the teaching profession or who have exceptional ability in the sciences or the arts), and available at the time of application for a visa and admission to the United States and at the place where the alien is to perform such skilled or unskilled labor, and (B) the employment of such aliens will not adversely affect the wages and working conditions of the workers in the United States similarly employed. The exclusion of aliens under this paragraph shall apply to preference immigrant aliens described in section 203(a) (3) and (6), and to non-preference immigrant aliens described in section 203(a) (8)."

SEC. 6. Section 245 of the Immigration and Nationality Act (8 U.S.C. 1255) is amended to read as follows:

"SEC. 245. (a) The status of an alien who was inspected and admitted or paroled into the United States may be adjusted by the Attorney General, in his discretion and under such regulations as he may prescribe, to that of an alien lawfully admitted for permanent residence if (1) the alien makes an application for such adjustment, (2) the alien is eligible to receive an immigrant visa and is admissible to the United States for permanent residence, and (3) an immigrant visa is immediately available to him at the time his application is filed.

"(b) Upon the approval of an application for adjustment made under subsection (a), the Attorney General shall record the alien's lawful admission for permanent residence as of the date the order of the Attorney General approving the application for the adjustment of status is made, and the Secretary of State shall reduce by one the number of the preference or non-preference visas authorized to be issued under sections 202 (e) or 203 (a) within the class to which the alien is chargeable for the fiscal year then current.

. . . .

SEC. 8. The Act entitled "An Act to adjust the status of Cuban refugees to that of lawful permanent residents of the United States, and for other purposes to read," approved

November 2, 1966 (8 U.S.C. 1255, note), is amended by adding at the end thereof the following new section:

"SEC. 5. The approval of an application for adjustment of status to that of lawful permanent resident of the United States pursuant to the provisions of section 1 of this Act shall not require the Secretary of State to reduce tho number of visas authorized to be issued in any class in the case of any alien who is physically present in the United States on or before the effective date of the Immigration and Nationality Act Amendments of 1976."

SEC. 9. (a) The amendments made by this Act shall not operate to affect the entitlement to immigrant status or the order of consideration for issuance of an immigrant visa of an alien entitled to a preference status, under section 203(a) of the Immigration and Nationality Act, as in effect on the day before the effective date of this Act, on the basis of a petition filed with the Attorney General prior to such effective date.

(b) An alien chargeable to the numerical limitation contained in section 21 (e) of the Act of October 3, 1965 (79 Stat. 921), who established a priority date at a consular office on the basis of entitlement to immigrant status under statutory or regulatory provisions in existence on the day before the effective date of this Act shall be deemed to be entitled to immigrant status under section 203(a) (8) of the Immigration and Nationality Act and shall be accorded the priority date previously established by him. Nothing in this section shall be construed to preclude the acquisition by such an alien of a preference status under section 203 (a) of the Immigration and Nationality Act, as amended by section 4 of this Act. Any petition filed by, or in behalf of, such an alien to accord him a preference status under section 203 (a) shall, upon approval, be deemed to have been filed as of the priority date previously established by such alien. The numerical limitation to which such an alien shall be chargeable shall be determined as provided in sections 201 and 202 of the Immigration and Nationality Act, as amended by this Act.

SEC. 10. The foregoing provisions of this Act, including the amendments made by such provisions, shall become effective on the first day of the first month which begins more than sixty days after the date of enactment of this Act.

Approved October 20, 1976.

Document 3: Congressional Record of the U.S. Senate

When: October 5, 1965

Significance: The congressional record provides a highlight of some of the problems with immigration legislation as well as the debate climate of the times.

The Immigration and Nationality Act of 1965

Mr. INOUYE. Mr. President, it is especially fitting to say a few words about one of this year's most significant legislative accomplishments, the reform of our immigration laws. We all have an interest in this subject if only because, in the phrase of President Kennedy, we are all, except for the Indians, a nation of immigrants or their descendants. But for 40 years, and despite the urging of four presidents, our immigration laws contained the discriminatory national origins formula, emphasizing birthplace in choosing our immigrants rather than personal merit or family ties.

The results were grotesque, a much-needed scientific or medical research specialist would be kept out because he was born in a disfavored country, while an unskilled laborer from northern Europe would be welcomed. The laborer would also be favored ahead of the mother of an American citizen born in the wrong place, who might have to wait for years before her son could bring her to join him. Such a system, which presumes that some people are inferior to others solely because of their birthplace, was intolerable on principle alone.

Perhaps the single most discriminatory aspect of the law was the so-called Asian-Pacific triangle provision. This clause required persons of 50 percent or more Asian ancestry to be assigned to national quotas not by their own place of birth, but according to that of their Asian forebears.

There was the case of a young South American in the Republic of Colombia, who was eligible and fully qualified to come here. His wife was also a native and a citizen of Colombia. But she was the daughter of a Chinese father. As a result, this young woman had to be considered half-Chinese and thus admissible only under the quota for Chinese persons of 105. This meant that if her husband chose to come ahead to the United States, he would have to wait for his wife until the year 2048 if he did not become a citizen. If he did become a citizen, however, he and his wife could be reunited in a mere 5 years.

To end the injustice and the costs which the national origins system needlessly inflicted, President Johnson last January called on Congress, in a special message, to pass the administration's immigration reform bill and to do so promptly. The new law which he signed on October 3, at the Statue of Liberty, selects immigrants within an overall unit of 170,000 on the basis not of birth place or ancestry but rather by a system of preferences based on family relation ships to our people and special skills that will be of real benefit to our country.

The new law means fairer, better selection of immigrants within the limits we are willing to accept. The law does not open the floodgates to an excessive amount of immigration. Moreover, all the present safeguards against subversives, criminals, illiterates, potential public charges, and other undesirables are retained. The safeguards against immigrants who might cause unemployment are actually strengthened. The overall result is an immigration law that is far more just, humane, and beneficial to the Nation.

Signing of the Immigration Act by President Johnson

Mr. CHURCH. Mr. President, on October 3, President Johnson, standing before the Statue of Liberty in New York Harbor, signed into law a most important act of Congress to improve our immigration laws. This legislation, which he recommended to Congress in a special message earlier this year, has abolished the national origins quota system of immigration. As the President observed in his special message, this system reflected "neither good government nor good sense."

For a good many years, thousands upon thousands of people in excess of the numbers we can reasonably admit have desired to come to this country. As a result, the basic problem for our national immigration policy is to maintain a fair system of selection among the applicants for admission.

For over 40 years we have made our choice by means of the national origins system, under which quotas were assigned to each country on the basis of the national origins of the population of the United States in 1920.

The new law has abolished that system and the injustices it has produced. Now we have turned away from an irrational concern with the place of birth of an immigrant—or of his ancestors—and have committed ourselves to a meaningful concern with the contribution he can make or the need for reuniting him with his family.

There were many objections to the system we have discarded. First of all, it did not even do what it proposed. It assumed that each country would use its quota in full. But the countries with the largest quotas—England and Ireland included—fell 50,000 short of their total each year. Since the law did not allow transfers of unused quota numbers between nations, these 50,000 numbers were denied to countries with waiting lists. In short, the numbers were lost. The new law, by doing away with quotas and establishing a first-come, first-served arrangement, prevents this wastage.

I might add that the new law does not significantly increase the total immigration per year. It allows for an increase about equal to these 50,000 numbers unused under the quota system.

A second objection to our prior policy was that it failed to serve the national interest. No matter how skilled or badly needed a man might be, if he was born in the wrong country, he had to wait— perhaps beyond his life expectancy—while others less qualified than he could enter the United States at will. That situation has been corrected, and a man with qualifications or skills we need will be considered equally with others in his position.

A third aspect of the policy we have changed is perhaps the most compelling. That aspect was its frequent cruelty. One of the fundamental objectives of our society is unity and integrity of the family. Unfortunately, the old system often kept parent from child and brother from brother for years—and sometimes for decades. It separated families arbitrarily and without rational purpose.

Now we have insured that parent need not be kept apart from son or daughter and have given adequate recognition to family relationships generally. Best of all, we have ended the possibility that families may remain broken simply because of differing places of birth.

A fourth point to make is that we have removed from our statute books an affront to most of the nations of the world. No longer need we be defensive about a scheme that blatantly proclaimed as a matter of national policy that some peoples are not as worthy of consideration for American citizenship as others. As all our Presidents beginning with President Truman have pointed out, the national origins law was a constant irritant to amicable relations around the globe.

Finally, the national origins system contradicted our fundamental national ideals and basic values. It denied recognition to the individual and treated him as one of a mass. It judged a man not on the basis of his worth or ability to contribute to our society, but on his place of birth—or, worse yet, in some cases, on the place of birth of his ancestors.

We have now rid ourselves of these distortions of our true principles and have returned to our early practice of viewing all men for admission to our land without regard to their origins, or the origins of their forebears. The act of Congress that the President signed before the "Grand Old Lady" on Liberty Island does the Nation proud.

Document 4: Congressional Record, House of Representatives

When: September 29, 1976

Significance: The congressional record provides a highlight of some of the problems with immigration legislation as well as the debate climate of the times. Here the implication of the differences in Eastern and Western Hemispheric immigration rules are considered.

Amending the Immigration and Nationality Act

Mr. EILBERG. Mr. Speaker, this is the Western Hemisphere preference bill. The gentleman will remember that there is presently a ceiling of 170,000 per year for the Eastern Hemisphere and 120,000 per year for the Western Hemisphere.

As for the Eastern Hemisphere, there is an inordinate preference system whereby the policies of our Government to unite families and to bring people here are clearly denned preference by preference.

There is no preference system for the Western Hemisphere. We simply have the total ceiling of 120,000. It is first-come, first-served, so that presently we have a backlog of about 300,000 people who wish to enter the United States from Canada to the north or from any of the countries to the south. It may be that a neighbor in Canada is waiting in line behind a neighbor in South America or it may be that a relative outside of the United States, in the Hemisphere, is waiting to enter the country and must wait for the approximate $2\frac{1}{2}$ years that it would take to enter this country once the application has been filed.

Mr. Speaker, this is a badly needed bill. It is strongly supported by the administration and by many groups and organizations.

I urge that the bill be accepted.

Mr. WYLIE. Does the bill increase the immigration quota?

Mr. EILBERG. It does not increase the quota at all.

Mr. WYLIE. It just is a reallocation of the quota; is that correct?

Mr. EILBERG. It provides for orderly reallocations in a preference system identical to that of the Eastern Hemisphere.

Mr. Speaker, this legislation is not new to the Members of this body. In fact, in the last Congress the full House by a vote of 336–30, approved similar legislation. Regrettably, the Senate did not act on this legislation.

In this Congress, the bill was unanimously approved by the full Judiciary Committee after being approved and cosponsored by all the members of the Immigration Subcommittee and the distinguished chairman of the full committee.

The primary purpose of this bill is to establish an orderly system of immigration for natives of the Western Hemisphere.

With two minor exceptions, the preference system which currently regulates immigration from the Eastern Hemisphere is extended to the Western Hemisphere. The preference system in the Eastern Hemisphere has been working satisfactorily, and except for two countries visas are currently available in all of the relative preference categories in the Eastern Hemisphere.

Contrast that with the current situation in the Western Hemisphere. No emphasis is placed on family reunification—other than the immediate family—and intending immigrants from the Western Hemisphere who do qualify are currently experiencing a 29-month delay in receiving their visas.

This unfortunate situation has resulted in numerous—and in my opinion—unnecessary hardships for potential Western Hemisphere immigrants, and these inequities must be eliminated. Therefore, in order to facilitate consideration of this urgently needed legislation, the subcommittee restricted the scope of the provisions of this bill to those areas most urgently in need of reform.

As I have noted, this legislation is primarily designed to equalize the treatment accorded to the Eastern and Western Hemisphere for immigration purposes, and I will now attempt to briefly summarize some of the major provisions in the bill.

First of all, the numerical limitations of 170,000 visas for the Eastern Hemisphere and 120,000 visas for the Western Hemisphere are retained, and a limit of 20,000 is established for all countries in the world. At the same time because of the heavy oversubscription in the dependent areas, most of which are located in the Caribbean, the numerical limit for these areas is increased from 200 to 600. Second, the bill would propose a formula which would provide that visas be distributed throughout the preference categories in those cases where a country has reached its 20,000 limit for visa issuance. This is designed to prevent one preference category from continuously utilizing a disproportionate share of visas by providing for the allocation of visas to all of the relative and labor preference categories in certain years. This distribution formula is extremely necessary if we are to insure that the goal of family reunification is achieved for all countries in the world.

The subcommittee made only two changes in the existing preference system. One is the requirement of a job offer for all aliens who are being admitted under the labor preference categories—in effect this would require third preference applicants, namely professionals, to have prearranged employment in order to be able to immigrate. The other is a requirement that U.S. citizens who are filing immigration petitions for their brothers and sisters be at least 21 years of age—the same age currently required in order for a U.S. citizen to file for his parent as an immediate relative.

Another provision contained in this legislation would address the serious problem that has confronted a large number of colleges and universities in this country. That provision—contained in an amendment to the labor certification section of the Immigrant and Nationality Act (section 212(a) (14)) — would require the Secretary of Labor to determine that "equally qualified" American teachers are available in order to deny a labor certification application. The purpose of this provision is to overcome the rigid interpretation given by the Department of Labor to the labor certification provision as it pertains to applications submitted by foreign scholars who possess unique qualifications or who are of exceptional merit and ability. Just this week, I received a letter from the American Association of Universities representing 48 major U.S. universities strongly supporting this legislation and stating that current law "denies the institutions and students the benefit of the teaching and research talents of foreign scholars and frustrates the search for excellence. The number of individuals involved is small, but the consequences for teaching and research are important."

Third, the subcommittee has also included a provision which authorizes the adjustment of status—from nonimmigrant to permanent resident alien—of natives of the Western Hemisphere. Another important provision of the bill would remove Cuban adjustments—that is, Cuban refugees who adjust their status to permanent resident aliens—from the Western Hemisphere numerical ceiling.

Mr. Speaker, as I have noted, this is a noncontroversial bill which is strongly supported by the administration, organized labor, and the voluntary agencies traditionally concerned with immigration matters. As a matter of fact, during the 13 days of hearings on this legislation in the past two Congresses, we heard no opposition to its enactment from any source.

It is a good bill, which will provide uniform treatment for all intending immigrants, and it is a major step forward in advancing the primary objective of our immigration law—the reunification of families.

I urge my colleagues' support of this meritorious, remedial legislation.

Mr. WYLIE. Mr. Speaker, I withdraw my reservation of objection.

Mr. FISH. Mr. Speaker, reserving the right to object, and of course, I shall not object, I am happy to join with my colleague from Pennsylvania, Mr. Eilberg, in support of the bill, H.R. 14535. The main purpose of this bill, as Mr. Eilberg indicated, is to establish a preference system for immigration by natives of the Western Hemisphere. Such a system now exists, but only for natives of the Eastern Hemisphere, and no one has been heard to defend the lack of such orderly system of immigration for natives of the Western Hemisphere. The committee will recall that in 1965, the last major revision of the Immigration and Nationality Act was passed. In order to obtain approval by the other body, a ceiling on Western Hemisphere immigration which was theretofore unrestricted, was accepted as the political price this House had to pay to obtain passage of our broad amendments which did away with the national origins quota system dating back to the 1920s. However, no preference system was established for Western Hemisphere immigration.

At the present time, persons seeking to immigrate to this country are treated vastly different depending solely on the country of their birth. If they are natives of the Eastern Hemisphere, they are entitled to a visa through a preference system and can come to this country to rejoin members of their family. If they have no such relatives, but have skills needed in the U.S. labor market, they may immigrate to this country through the labor certification procedure. On the other hand, if one is a native of the Western Hemisphere, unless they qualify as an immediate relative—parent, spouse or child, of a U.S. citizen, there is no preference based on relationship and one must obtain a labor certification which results in a wait for approximately 27 months to immigrate to this country. The system has often operated to keep families separated for several years which is a result opposite to one main objective of our immigration system, that of reuniting families.

Our subcommittee heard 6 days of testimony on the establishment of such a preference system and we heard no one defend the present system as fair or equitable.

During the 93rd Congress, our committee reported H.R. 981 which was a similar, but more extensive bill. But its main purpose—establishment of a Western Hemisphere preference system—was the same as our bill. However, the other body failed to act on that bill during the last Congress. This year, the Senate Judiciary Committee has considered immigration legislation—and we hope during the present Congress, they can concur with this bill to cure a serious inequity in the present immigration law. The bill we report today is not as extensive as the bill we reported during the last Congress, only because the subcommittee felt that a bill such as H.R. 14535, which does not contain any of the more controversial provisions of H.R. 981, would have a better chance of ultimate passage this year. Therefore, our bill merely establishes a preference system for the Western Hemisphere with a per country ceiling of 20,000, the same as applies in the Eastern Hemisphere; and a yearly Western Hemisphere ceiling of 120,000, the same as it is at present. It makes other changes which are for the most part more technical in nature to provide for better functioning for our system of immigration.

The administration supports establishment of a preference system for Western Hemisphere natives, and, as I have said, no opposition has been heard. The Committee on the Judiciary reported this bill by unanimous voice vote.

This bill is a well-considered piece of legislation and I urge my colleagues to vote favorably to suspend the rules and pass H.R. 14535.

Mr. Speaker, I withdraw my reservation of objection.

The SPEAKER. Is there objection to the request of the gentleman from Pennsylvania? There was no objection.

FURTHER READINGS

Books

Bennett, David. *The Party of Fear: From Nativist Movements to the New Right in American History*. Chapel Hill, N.C.: University of North Carolina Press, 1988.

Kennedy, John Fitzgerald. *A Nation of Immigrants*, updated and enlarged ed. New York: Harper Perennial, 2008. (First edition, 1959)

Omi, Michael, and Howard Winant. *Racial Formation in the United States*. New York: Routledge, 1986.

Articles

Fragomen, Austin T. Jr. "1976 Amendments to Immigration and Nationality Act." *International Migration Review*, vol. 11, no 1 (Spring 1977), 95–100.

Fragomen, Austin T. Jr. "The Immigration and Nationality Act Part I–International Personnel." *International Migration Review*, vol. 14, no. 1 (1980), 116–123.

Graham, Otis L. Jr. "A Vast Social Experiment: The Immigration Act of 1965." http://www.npg.org/forum_series/socialexp.html

Keely, Charles B. "Effects of the Immigration Act of 1965 on the Selected Population Characteristics of Immigrants to the United States." *Demography*, vol. 8, no. 2 (May 1971), 157–169.

Keely, Charles B. "The Development of U.S. Immigration Policy since 1965." *Journal of International Affairs*, vol. 33, no. 2 (Fall/Winter 1979), 249–264.

Kelly, Nancy. "Gender-Related Persecution: Assessing the Asylum Claims of Women." *Cornell International Law Journal*, vol. 26 (1993), 626–627.

Kennedy, Edward M. "The Immigration Act of 1965." *Annals of the American Academy of Political and Social Science*, vol. 367, The New Immigration (September 1966), 137–149.

Luibhéid, Eithne. "The 1965 Immigration and Nationality Act: An 'End' to Exclusion?" *Positions*, vol. 5, no. 2 (Fall 1997), 501–522.

CHAPTER 7

The Growing Immigration Debate in the 1980s and 1990s

Akis Kalaitzidis

The 1965 Immigration and Nationality Act led to an upsurge in immigration and, by the 1980s, domestic policymakers were under pressure to stem the flow of immigration due to rising numbers and a slowing economy. Politicians faced several tough issues, beginning with the nature of immigration to the United States. Not all immigrants were economic immigrants, which created a bifurcated policy, one for economic immigrants and one for refugees. The U.S. Congress addressed this issue of past refugee admissions with the 1980 Refugee Act, which decided what types of people were considered refugees and who were invited to the United States, as well as how to deal with them when they got here. The act established a 5,000-person limit to be admitted as refugees and to become resident aliens (Keely 1994). However, the refugee problem did not go away. Even as Congress tried to alleviate the pressures from the Mariel Boatlift, more people clearly needed political asylum. Asylum seekers came from Central America (due to civil war and political persecution) and from the former Soviet and Eastern European region, where people fled the numerous local conflicts and civil wars spurred by the collapse of the Soviet Union.

The numbers of undocumented economic immigrants mainly from the Western Hemisphere increased throughout the 1970s and 1980s. Suzan Gonzales Baker notes, "In the mid-1970s, the INS began issuing estimates of resident illegal immigrant populations on the order of 12 million. By the time the 1980 census figures substituted these estimates with more reasonable alternatives of 2 million to 4 million, the social construction of a nation losing control of its borders was well entrenched in the public sentiment, making border control a popular policy theme and amnesty a very hard political sell" (Gonzales Baker 1997). Despite the public opposition and political pressures, the numbers of undocumented immigrants remained great, and the problem needed to be addressed.

In 1986 the U.S. Congress considered a comprehensive immigration reform bill—the Immigration Reform and Control Act (IRCA), the first of its kind in twenty years. This bill offered amnesty to the existing unauthorized aliens in the country and allowed for more legal immigration based on occupational criteria (special immigrants) while increasing the funding

A human smuggler rafts illegal Mexican immigrants across the Rio Grande at El Paso, Texas, in the early morning hours of July 5, 1987. AP Photo.

for border enforcement. More specifically, the law gave an opportunity to people who had entered the United States illegally before 1982 to adjust their status and become legal. It also gave the opportunity for those who worked as agricultural workers for ninety days, between May 1, 1985, and May 1, 1986, to gain legal status. In addition, the law criminalized the hiring of illegal workers, established penalties for such practices, and created the I-9 form, which employers used to ensure workers are in the United States legally.

The law had several provisions to protect domestic workers against unfair labor practices and discrimination. It made it illegal to bypass the legal immigrant employment requirement by subcontracting jobs to other companies; something several U.S. corporations were found guilty of, including Wal-Mart. In addition, the law revised the legal action for the transportation of undocumented aliens into the United States and established a $35 million fund for improving border enforcement. The law included, upon California's request, a temporary worker authorization system mainly for agricultural workers and increases in the quota for U.S. territories from 600 to 5,000 persons. The law addressed the issue of immigration costs, especially costs associated with incarceration of undocumented immigrants convicted of felonies, and made provisions for the deportation of such violent offenders.

The law divided the political and economic forces in the country at several levels. Once again, it caused debate about race, coupled with a debate on the impact of the amnesty on the economy. Opponents of the bill feared that the immigration policy would fail and give undocumented immigrants a "free pass," establishing a precedent that would encourage future undocumented immigrants to wait for the next amnesty. (Such a view is also held by many these days, as the U.S. Congress is considering immigration proposals.) The IRCA was generally opposed by unions; the National Association of Colored People (NAACP), which feared loss of jobs for the African American community to immigrants; and by citizen groups and states that are net recipients of immigration, such as Arizona and Texas. Senator Pete Wilson, who led California's demands for guest workers and later became governor and prime advocate of restricting illegal immigrants' social services supported the IRCA. The business community demanded even more changes to immigration laws and received a special agricultural workers provision.

Studies done on the impact of IRCA on immigration to the United States indicate that IRCA did little to stem the flow of immigration (Donato, Durand, and Massey 1992; Woodrow and Passel 1990). However, some studies using INS apprehensions data indicate that, following the passing of IRCA, immigration to the United States seems to have abated for the short term. During the filing period, apprehensions remained low, which would indicate that there was no attempt at fraud by illegal immigrants (Bean et al. 1990; White, Bean, and Espenshade 1990; Orrenius and Zavodny 2003). Nonetheless, the Unites States finds itself facing a similar situation today with much larger numbers of illegal immigrants. In Table 7.1 one can clearly see this trend.

In 1990, the U.S. Congress passed a new immigration act (IMMACT). The major provision of this law was to move away from hemispheric immigration to a total flexible cap of 675,000 immigrants per year, 480,000 of whom would be family related, 140,000 employment-based immigrants, and 55,000 diversity immigrants. This law also changed the status of undocumented nationals from "hot spot" countries such as Nicaragua and El Salvador. Susan Cutin says that when Salvadorans applied for political asylum in this country, they were rejected at a rate of 90 percent while at the same time Eastern Europeans and Middle Easterners were approved at rates ranging from 32 percent to 60 percent (2004). The reasons were clearly related to U.S. foreign policy in Central America and Eastern Europe in the late 1980s and early 1990s. The law attempted to redress this.

The U.S.-backed El Salvador government was extremely brutal, so Congress responded to the widespread condemnation of the Salvadoran government by including in the legislation an 18-month temporary protected status to about 187,000 Salvadorans who had come to the United States. The law also reorganized the bureaucracy dealing with naturalizations by placing the authority with the U.S. attorney general instead of the courts. It also revised the categories of non-immigrant visas and amended the requirements for naturalization. Congress also included new guidelines and new personnel for border enforcement and a whole new list of criteria for exclusion and deportation. The law created nine categories for exclusion, which included thirty-two specific grounds. It also broadened the definition of aggravated felony, which made immigrants eligible for deportation. The new law also added at least 1,000 additional border guards and upped the sanction on the violators of the provisions of IRCA.

The new law failed to slow the immigrant waves to the U.S., so Congress passed another two immigration measures in 1996 in reaction to the public's concern over the issue. Previously,

DID YOU KNOW?

The U.S. Minutemen

Historically, the Minutemen were the militia organized in colonial America to defend against the British and other external threats.

Today, the term has been appropriated by two distinct groups of political activists whose main purpose is to guard the U.S. border with Mexico against illegal crossings.

The Minuteman Civil Defense group is led by Chris Simcox, and the Minuteman Project Inc. is led by Jim Gilchrist. The two groups used to be together but split because of differences between the two leaders. The groups position themselves at the U.S. border with Mexico. Most members are armed. Their activities have been derided as a new version of American nativist vigilantism by Vicente Fox, former president of Mexico, and organizations such as the Southern Poverty Law Center. The Anti-Defamation League has observed that white supremacist and Neo-Nazi groups have campaigned for the Minuteman Project.

TABLE 7.1 Immigration by Application Type (numbers in thousands)

Year/Type	1989	1990	1991	1992	1993
Family Related	341.6	446.2	453.2	500.9	530.5
Employment Based	52.8	56.7	58.0	119.8	149.2
Humanitarian	179.5	186.4	168.1	220.8	246.9
Refugees	107.2	122.3	112.8	132.1	119.5
Asylees	81.3	58.9	49.6	83.2	120.3
Cubans	11.0	5.2	5.7	5.5	7.1
Total Legal Immigration	603.0	731.3	711.8	883.1	971.9
Illegal Immigration	250.0	250.0	300.0	300.0	300.0
Total Immigration	853.0	981.3	1,011.8	1,183.1	1,271.9

Source: Allen Greenblatt. "History of Immigration Policy." *Congressional Quarterly Weekly Report.* April 15, 1995, 53:15; 1067.

states that received the bulk of immigrants, such as California, Texas, and Florida, sued the federal government to recover funds spent on undocumented immigrants for social services, incarceration, hearings, and deportations. Moreover, in California, the issue became part of the electoral agenda, and the state attempted to legislate denial of social services to undocumented immigrants in that state. In its famous Proposition 187, California attempted to restrict all social provisions to these aliens, including attending public schools, and to raise the penalties for violating the immigration laws in what was termed the "Save our state" initiative.

Senator Pete Wilson, who supported IRCA in 1986, rode the anti-immigration wave to the governor's mansion. Proposition 187 was passed with 59 percent of the vote on November 8, 1994, but it was blocked by a federal court on November 11, 1994, and effectively died when Wilson's successor, Governor Gray Davis, dropped the appeals process in the courts. California's actions impacted the halls of the U.S. Congress who took up some of the main points that the California proposition included. In two legislative actions, one on August 22, 1996, and another the following month (September 30, 1996), the U.S. Congress passed most of the provisions of Proposition 187 (LeMay 2006). The first measure stipulated the provisions that immigrants can receive once inside the United States, while the second law dealt mainly with the enforcement side of immigration.

The Personal Responsibility and Work Opportunity Reconciliation Act of 1996 restricted most social provisions for unauthorized immigrants, such as federal grants, loans, licenses, and all benefits (e.g., retirement unemployment). The federal law prohibited all states from providing any of these benefits themselves with the exception of public school lunches. Furthermore, the law restricted the ability of legal residents from receiving any state or federal benefits for five years, with the exception of refugees and asylees.

The Illegal Immigration Reform and Immigrant Responsibility Act authorized the doubling of border agents and an additional 900 INS agents to investigate smuggling, harboring, and employing illegal immigrants. It gave them additional wiretapping and other enforcement powers. The law authorized construction of a border fence between the United States and Mexico.

Both laws did not impact stem the flow of immigration to United States. By the end of the 1990s, the United States had by all accounts a large number of undocumented immigrants. Even with the changes that followed September 11, 2001, to be discussed in a later chapter, the problem of illegal immigration in the United States is still very much unsolved.

DID YOU KNOW?

The Story of Ricardo Gomez Garcia

In a report by Claudio Sanchez of National Public Radio (NPR), in September of 2007 the Immigration and Naturalization Service raided the defense contracting company Michael Bianco Inc. in New Bedford, Massachusetts. Michael Bianco Inc., which holds a $230 million U.S. government contract, has been given several fines by OSHA for serious workplace health violations in health hazards and poor working conditions. The company makes vests and backpacks for U.S. troops in Iraq and Afghanistan. The "successful" raid in New Bedford netted 361 unauthorized immigrants, among them several parents of infants and other very young U.S. citizens. The immigrants were transported to a detention facility in El Paso, Texas.

According to Sanchez's follow-up story on November 12, 2007, one of the unauthorized workers, Ricardo Gomez Garcia, was deported to Guatemala on August 30. There his mother sold her house to obtain the necessary $5,000 for Ricardo's return to his family in the United States, where they had been left without the means to support themselves. After a long and arduous trip across the Mexico-Arizona border all the way to Massachusetts, Ricardo Gomez Garcia made it back home on October 28, 2007, where he died from an airway blockage in the arms of his wife. "He looked sick when he came in the door," said his wife, but he did not want to risk going to the emergency room because he was an undocumented immigrant.

Ricardo Gomez Garcia's son Mauricio is autistic and requires special schooling and therapy sessions in Boston. The couple has another four children in Guatemala with their maternal grandmother.

This is only one of many such stories.

DOCUMENTS

Document 1: The Immigration Reform and Control Act (IRCA)

When: November 6, 1986

Significance: This legislation offered legalization to approximately 3 million previously illegal immigrants and made it a crime to transport/hire illegal immigrants in the hopes of stemming further illegal immigration.

An Act to amend the Immigration and Nationality Act to revise and reform the immigration laws, and for other purposes.

Be it enacted by the Senate and House of Representatives of the United States of America in Congress assembled,

SECTION 1. SHORT TITLE; REFERENCES IN ACT.

(a) SHORT TITLE.—This Act may be cited as the "Immigration Reform and Control Act of 1986." "8 USC 1101 note"

(b) AMENDMENTS TO IMMIGRATION AND NATIONALITY ACT.—Except as otherwise specifically provided in this Act, whenever in this Act an amendment or repeal is expressed as an amendment to, or repeal of, a provision, the reference shall be deemed to be made to the Immigration and Nationality Act.

....

"SEC. 274A. (a) 8 USC 1324a MAKING EMPLOYMENT OF UNAUTHORIZED ALIENS UNLAWFUL. —

"(1) IN GENERAL.—It is unlawful for a person or other entity to hire, or to recruit or refer for a fee, for employment in the United States—

"(A) an alien knowing the alien is an unauthorized alien (as defined in subsection (h)(3)) with respect to such employment, or

"(B) an individual without complying with the requirements of subsection (b).

"(2) CONTINUING EMPLOYMENT.—It is unlawful for a person or other entity, after hiring an alien for employment in accordance with paragraph (1), to continue to employ the alien in the United States knowing the alien is (or has become) an unauthorized alien with respect to such employment.

"(3) DEFENSE.—A person or entity that establishes that it has complied in good faith with the requirements of subsection (b) with respect to the hiring, recruiting, or referral for employment of an alien in the United States has established an affirmative defense that the person or entity has not violated paragraph (1)(A) with respect to such hiring, recruiting, or referral.

"(4) USE OF LABOR THROUGH CONTRACT.—For purposes of this section, a person or other entity who uses a contract, subcontract, or exchange, entered into, renegotiated, or extended after the date of the enactment of this section, to obtain the labor of an alien in the United States knowing that the alien is an unauthorized alien (as defined in subsection (h)(3)) with respect to performing such labor, shall be considered to have hired the alien for employment in the United States in violation of paragraph (1)(A).

"(5) USE OF STATE EMPLOYMENT AGENCY DOCUMENTATION.—For purposes of paragraphs (1)(B) and (3), a person or entity shall be deemed to have complied with the requirements of subsection (b) with respect to the hiring of an individual who was referred for such employment by a State employment agency (as defined by the Attorney General), if the person or entity has and retains (for the period and in the manner described in subsection (b)(3)) appropriate documentation of such referral by that agency, which documentation certifies that the agency has complied with the procedures specified in subsection (b) with respect to the individual's referral.

"(b) EMPLOYMENT VERIFICATION SYSTEM.—The requirements referred to in paragraphs (1)(B) and (3) of subsection (a) are, in the case of a person or other entity hiring, recruiting, or referring an individual for employment in the United States, the requirements specified in the following three paragraphs:

....

"(4) CEASE AND DESIST ORDER WITH CIVIL MONEY PENALTY FOR HIRING, RECRUITING, AND REFERRAL VIOLATIONS.—With respect to a violation of subsection (a)(1)(A) or (a)(2), the order under this subsection—

"(A) shall require the person or entity to cease and desist from such violations and to pay a civil penalty in an amount of—

"(i) not less than $250 and not more than $2,000 for each unauthorized alien with respect to whom a violation of either such subsection occurred,

"(ii) not less than $2,000 and not more than $5,000 for each such alien in the case of a person or entity previously subject to one order under this subparagraph, or

"(iii) not less than $3,000 and not more than $10,000 for each such alien in the case of a person or entity previously subject to more than one order under this subparagraph; and

"(B) may require the person or entity—

"(i) to comply with the requirements of subsection (b) (or subsection (d) if applicable) with respect to individuals hired (or recruited or referred for employment for a fee) during a period of up to three years, and

"(ii) to take such other remedial action as is appropriate.

"In applying this subsection in the case of a person or entity composed of distinct, physically separate subdivisions each of which provides separately for the hiring, recruiting, or referring for employment, without reference to the practices of, and not under the control of or common control with, another subdivision, each such subdivision shall be considered a separate person or entity.

"(5) ORDER FOR CIVIL MONEY PENALTY FOR PAPERWORK VIOLATIONS.—With respect to a violation of subsection (a)(1)(B), the order under this subsection shall require the person or entity to pay a civil penalty in an amount of not less than $100 and not more than $1,000 for each individual with respect to whom such violation occurred. In determining the amount of the penalty, due consideration shall be given to the size of the business of the employer being charged, the good faith of the employer, the seriousness of the violation, whether or not the individual was an unauthorized alien, and the history of previous violations."

....

SEC. 112. UNLAWFUL TRANSPORTATION OF ALIENS TO THE UNITED STATES.

(a) CRIMINAL PENALTIES.—Subsection (a) of Section 274 (8 U.S.C. 1324) is amended to read as follows:

"(a) CRIMINAL PENALTIES.—(1) Any person who—

"(A) knowing that a person is an alien, brings to or attempts to bring to the United States in any manner whatsoever such person at a place other than a designated port of entry or place other than as designated by the Commission, regardless of whether such alien has received prior official authorization to come to, enter, or reside in the United States and regardless of any future official action which may be taken with respect to such alien;

"(B) knowing or in reckless disregard of the fact that an alien has come to, entered, or remains in the United States in violation of law, transports, or moves or attempts to transport or move such alien within the United States by means of transportation or otherwise, in furtherance of such violation of law;

"(C) knowing or in reckless disregard of the fact that an alien has come to, entered, or remains in the United States in violation of law, conceals, harbors, or shields from detection, or attempts to conceal, harbor, or shield from detection, such alien in any place, including any building or any means of transportation; or

"(D) encourages or induces an alien to come to, enter, or reside in the United States, knowing or in reckless disregard of the fact that such coming to, entry, or residence is or will be in violation of law, shall be fined in accordance with title 18, United States Code, imprisoned not more than five years, or both, for each alien in respect to whom any violation of this subsection occurs.

"(2) Any person who, knowing or in reckless disregard of the fact that an alien has not received prior official authorization to come to, enter, or reside in the United States, brings to or attempts to bring to the United States in any manner whatsoever, such alien, regardless of any official action which may later be taken with respect to such alien shall, for each transaction constituting a violation of this paragraph, regardless of the number of aliens involved—

"(A) be fined in accordance with title 18, United States Code, or imprisoned not more than one year, or both; or

"(B) in the case of—

"(i) a second or subsequent offense,

"(ii) an offense done for the purpose of commercial advantage or private financial gain, or

"(iii) an offense in which the alien is not upon arrival immediately brought and presented to an appropriate immigration officer at a designated port of entry, be fined in accordance with title 18, United States Code, or imprisoned not more than five years, or both."

TITLE II—LEGALIZATION

SEC. 201. LEGALIZATION OF STATUS.

(a) PROVIDING FOR LEGALIZATION PROGRAM.—(1) Chapter 5 of title II is amended by inserting after section 245 (8 U.S.C. 1255) the following new section: for ADJUSTMENT OF STATUS OF CERTAIN ENTRANTS BEFORE JANUARY 1, 1982, TO THAT OF PERSON ADMITTED FOR LAWFUL RESIDENCE

"SEC. 245A. (8 U.S.C. 1255a) (a) TEMPORARY RESIDENT STATUS.—The Attorney General shall adjust the status of an alien to that of an alien lawfully admitted for temporary residence if the alien meets the following requirements:

"(1) TIMELY APPLICATION.—

"(A) DURING APPLICATION PERIOD.—Except as provided in subparagraph (B), the alien must apply for such adjustment during the 12-month period beginning on a date (not later than 180 days after the date of enactment of this section) designated by the Attorney General.

"(B) APPLICATION WITHIN 30 DAYS OF SHOW-CAUSE ORDER.—An alien who, at any time during the first 11 months of the 12-month period described in subparagraph (A), is the subject of an order to show cause issued under section 242, "8 USC 1252" must make application under this section not later than the end of the 30-day period beginning either on the first day of such 18-month period or on the date of the issuance of such order, whichever day is later.

"(C) INFORMATION INCLUDED IN APPLICATION.—Each application under this subsection shall contain such information as the Attorney General may require, including information on living relatives of the applicant with respect to whom a petition for preference or other status may be filed by the applicant at any later date under section 204(a). "8 USC 1154"

"(2) CONTINUOUS UNLAWFUL RESIDENCE SINCE 1982.—

"(A) IN GENERAL.—The alien must establish that he entered the United States before January 1, 1982, and that he has resided continuously in the United States in an unlawful status since such date and through the date the application is filed under this subsection.

"(B) NONIMMIGRANTS.—In the case of an alien who entered the United States as a nonimmigrant before January 1, 1982, the alien must establish that the alien's period of authorized stay as a nonimmigrant expired before such date through the passage of time or the alien's unlawful status was known to the Government as of such date.

"(C) EXCHANGE VISITORS.—If the alien was at any time a nonimmigrant exchange alien (as defined in section 101(a)(15)(J)), "8 USC 1101" the alien must establish that the alien was not subject to the two-year foreign residence requirement of section 212(e) "8 USC 1182" or has fulfilled that requirement or received a waiver thereof.

"(3) CONTINUOUS PHYSICAL PRESENCE SINCE ENACTMENT.—

A U.S. Border Patrol officer apprehended four illegal immigrants in the Yuha Desert near El Centro, California, in August 1997. Despite 116°F heat, the men were attempting to enter the United States through this exceptionally hot portion of the Sonoran Desert but were spotted in the brush by a Border Patrol helicopter. AP Photo/Lenny Ignelzi.

"(A) IN GENERAL.—The alien must establish that the alien has been continuously physically present in the United States since the date of the enactment of this section.

"(B) TREATMENT OF BRIEF, CASUAL, AND INNOCENT ABSENCES.—An alien shall not be considered to have failed to maintain continuous physical presence in the United States for purposes of subparagraph (A) by virtue of brief, casual, and innocent absences from the United States.

"(C) ADMISSIONS.—Nothing in this section shall be construed as authorizing an alien to apply for admission to, or to be admitted to, the United States in order to apply for adjustment of status under this subsection.

"(4) ADMISSIBLE AS IMMIGRANT.—The alien must establish that he—

"(A) is admissible to the United States as an immigrant, except as otherwise provided under subsection (d)(2),

"(B) has not been convicted of any felony or of three or more misdemeanors committed in the United States,

"(C) has not assisted in the persecution of any person or persons on account of race, religion, nationality, membership in a particular social group, or political opinion, and

"(D) is registered or registering under the Military Selective Service Act, "50 USC app. 451" if the alien is required to be so registered under that Act.

For purposes of this subsection, an alien in the status of a Cuban and Haitian entrant described in paragraph (1) or (2)(A) of section 501(e) of Public Law 96-422 "8 USC 1522 note" shall be considered to have entered the United States and to be in an unlawful status in the United States.

"(b) SUBSEQUENT ADJUSTMENT TO PERMANENT RESIDENCE AND NATURE OF TEMPORARY RESIDENT STATUS.—

"(1) ADJUSTMENT TO PERMANENT RESIDENCE.—The Attorney General shall adjust the status of any alien provided lawful temporary resident status under subsection (a) to that of an alien lawfully admitted for permanent residence if the alien meets the following requirements:

"(A) TIMELY APPLICATION AFTER ONE YEAR'S RESIDENCE.—The alien must apply for such adjustment during the one-year period beginning with the nineteenth month that begins after the date the alien was granted such temporary resident status.

"(B) CONTINUOUS RESIDENCE.—

"(i) IN GENERAL.—The alien must establish that he has continuously resided in the United States since the date the alien was granted such temporary resident status.

"(ii) TREATMENT OF CERTAIN ABSENCES.—An alien shall not be considered to have lost the continuous residence referred to in clause (i) by reason of an absence from the United States permitted under paragraph (3)(A).

"(C) ADMISSIBLE AS IMMIGRANT.—The alien must establish that he—

"(i) is admissible to the United States as an immigrant, except as otherwise provided under subsection (d)(2), and

"(ii) has not been convicted of any felony or three or more misdemeanors committed in the United States.

"(D) BASIC CITIZENSHIP SKILLS.—

"(i) IN GENERAL.—The alien must demonstrate that he either—

"(I) meets the requirements of section 312 "8 USC 1423" (relating to minimal understanding of ordinary English and a knowledge and understanding of the history and government of the United States), or

"(II) is satisfactorily pursuing a course of study (recognized by the Attorney General) to achieve such an understanding of English and such a knowledge and understanding of the history and government of the United States.

"(ii) EXCEPTION FOR ELDERLY INDIVIDUALS.—The Attorney General may, in his discretion, waive all or part of the requirements of clause (i) in the case of an alien who is 65 years of age or older.

"(iii) RELATION TO NATURALIZATION EXAMINATION.—In accordance with regulations of the Attorney General, an alien who has demonstrated under clause (i)(I) that the alien meets the requirements of section 312 may be considered to have satisfied the requirements of that section "8 USC 1401" for purposes of becoming naturalized as a citizen of the United States under title III.

"(2) TERMINATION OF TEMPORARY RESIDENCE.—The Attorney General shall provide for termination of temporary resident status granted an alien under subsection (a)—

"(A) if it appears to the Attorney General that the alien was in fact not eligible for such status;

"(B) if the alien commits an act that (i) makes the alien inadmissible to the United States as an immigrant, except as otherwise provided under subsection (d)(2), or (ii) is convicted of any felony or three or more misdemeanors committed in the United States; or

"(C) at the end of the thirty-first month beginning after the date the alien is granted such status, unless the alien has filed an application for adjustment of such status pursuant to paragraph (1) and such application has not been denied.

"(3) AUTHORIZED TRAVEL AND EMPLOYMENT DURING TEMPORARY RESIDENCE.—During the period an alien is in lawful temporary resident status granted under subsection (a)—

"(A) AUTHORIZATION OF TRAVEL ABROAD.—The Attorney General shall, in accordance with regulations, permit the alien to return to the United States after such brief and casual trips abroad as reflect an intention on the part of the alien to adjust to lawful permanent resident status under paragraph (1) and after brief temporary trips abroad occasioned by a family obligation involving an occurrence such as the illness or death of a close relative or other family need.

"(B) AUTHORIZATION OF EMPLOYMENT.—The Attorney General shall grant the alien authorization to engage in employment in the United States and provide to that alien an 'employment authorized' endorsement or other appropriate work permit.

....

TITLE III—REFORM OF LEGAL IMMIGRATION
PART A—TEMPORARY AGRICULTURAL WORKERS
SEC. 301. H-2A AGRICULTURAL WORKERS.
(a) PROVIDING NEW "H-2A" NONIMMIGRANT CLASSIFICATION FOR TEMPO-
RARY AGRICULTURAL LABOR.—Paragraph (15)(H) of section 101(a) (8 U.S.C.
1101(a)) is amended by striking out "to perform temporary services or labor," in clause (ii)
and inserting in lieu thereof "(a) to perform agricultural labor or services, as defined by the
Secretary of Labor in regulations and including agricultural labor defined in section 3121(g)
"26 USC 3121" of the Internal Revenue Code of 1954 and agriculture as defined in section
3(f) of the Fair Labor Standards Act of 1938 (29 U. S.C. 203(f)), of a temporary or seasonal
nature, or (b) to perform other temporary service or labor."

....

"SEC. 216. (a) CONDITIONS FOR APPROVAL OF H-2A PETITIONS. "8 USC
1186"—(1) A petition to import an alien as an H-2A worker (as defined in subsection
(i)(2)) may not be approved by the Attorney General unless the petitioner has applied to
the Secretary of Labor for a certification that—

"(A) there are not sufficient workers who are able, willing, and qualified, and who will be
available at the time and place needed, to perform the labor or services involved in the petition, and

"(B) the employment of the alien in such labor or services will not adversely affect the
wages and working conditions of workers in the United States similarly employed.

"(2) The Secretary of Labor may require by regulation, as a condition of issuing the certification, the payment of a fee to recover the reasonable costs of processing applications for
certification.

"(b) CONDITIONS FOR DENIAL OF LABOR CERTIFICATION.—The Secretary of
Labor may not issue a certification under subsection (a) with respect to an employer if the conditions described in that subsection are not met or if any of the following conditions are met:

"(1) There is a strike or lockout in the course of a labor dispute which, under the regulations, precludes such certification.

"(2)(A) The employer during the previous two-year period employed H-2A workers and the
Secretary of Labor has determined, after notice and opportunity for a hearing, that the employer
at any time during that period substantially violated a material term or condition of the labor
certification with respect to the employment of domestic or nonimmigrant workers.

"(B) No employer may be denied certification under subparagraph (A) for more than
three years for any violation described in such subparagraph.

"(3) The employer has not provided the Secretary with satisfactory assurances that if the
employment for which the certification is sought is not covered by State workers' compensation law, the employer will provide, at no cost to the worker, insurance covering injury and
disease arising out of and in the course of the worker's employment which will provide benefits at least equal to those provided under the State workers' compensation law for comparable employment.

"(4) The Secretary determines that the employer has not made positive recruitment
efforts within a multi-state region of traditional or expected labor supply where the Secretary
finds that there are a significant number of qualified United States workers, who, if recruited,
would be willing to make themselves available for work at the time and place needed. Positive recruitment under this paragraph is in addition to, and shall be conducted within the
same time period as, the circulation through the interstate employment service system of the
employer's job offer. The obligation to engage in positive recruitment under this paragraph
shall terminate on the date the H-2A workers depart for the employer's place of
employment.

....

"(f) VIOLATORS DISQUALIFIED FOR 5 YEARS.—An alien may not be admitted to the United States as a temporary agricultural worker if the alien was admitted to the United States as such a worker within the previous five-year period and the alien during that period violated a term or condition of such previous admission.

．．．．．．．．．．．．．．．．．．．．

"(7) PENALTIES FOR FALSE STATEMENTS IN APPLICATIONS.—
"(A) CRIMINAL PENALTY.—Whoever—
"(i) files an application for adjustment of status under this section and knowingly and will-fully falsifies, conceals, or covers up a material fact or makes any false, fictitious, or fraudulent statements or representations, or makes or uses any false writing or document knowing the same to contain any false, fictitious, or fraudulent statement or entry, or
"(ii) creates or supplies a false writing or document for use in making such an application, shall be fined in accordance with title 18, United States Code, or imprisoned not more than five years, or both.

．．．．．．．．．．．．．．．．．．．．

"(f) TEMPORARY DISQUALIFICATION OF NEWLY LEGALIZED ALIENS FROM RECEIVING AID TO FAMILIES WITH DEPENDENT CHILDREN.—During the five-year period beginning on the date an alien was granted lawful temporary resident status under subsection (a), and notwithstanding any other provision of law, the alien is not eligible for aid under a State plan approved under part A of title IV of the Social Security Act. "42 USC 601" Notwithstanding the previous sentence, in the case of an alien who would be eligible for aid under a State plan approved under part A of title IV of the Social Security Act but for the previous sentence, the provisions of paragraph (3) of section 245A(h) shall apply in the same manner as they apply with respect to paragraph (1) of such section and, for this purpose, any reference in section 245A(h)(3) to paragraph (1) is deemed a reference to the previous sentence."

．．．．．．．．．．．．．．．．．．．．

Document 2: IMMACT, 1990

When: November 29, 1990

Significance: The IMMACT of 1990 is significant because it moves the U.S. immigration from hemispheric quotas to one total flexible cap of 675,000 immigrants per year.

Immigration Act of 1990

AN ACT to amend the Immigration and Nationality Act to change the level, and preference system for admission, of immigrants to the United States, and to provide for administrative naturalization, and for other purposes.

Be it enacted by the Senate and House of Representatives of the United States of America in Congress assembled,

SECTION 1. SHORT TITLE; REFERENCES IN ACT; TABLE OF CONTENTS.

(a) SHORT TITLE.—This Act may be cited as the "Immigration Act of 1990."

(b) REFERENCES IN ACT.—Except as specifically provided in this Act, whenever in this Act an amendment or repeal is expressed as an amendment to or repeal of a provision, the reference shall be deemed to be made to the Immigration and Nationality Act.

U.S. Immigration and Customs Enforcement officers escort employees from the Michael Bianco, Inc. leather factory in New Bedford, Mass., following an immigration raid conducted in March 2007 by some 300 officers of the U.S. Department of Homeland Security. More than 350 workers, mostly women, were sent to distant detention centers, devastating the families and community left behind. AP Photo/*The New Bedford Standard Times*, Peter Pereira.

(c) TABLE OF CONTENTS.—The table of contents of this Act is as follows:
Sec. 1. Short title; references in Act; table of contents.

TITLE I—IMMIGRANTS
Subtitle A—Worldwide and Per Country Levels
Sec. 101. Worldwide levels.
Sec. 102. Per country levels.
Sec. 103. Treatment of Hong Kong under per country levels.
Sec. 104. Asylee adjustments.
Subtitle B—Preference System

PART 1—FAMILY-SPONSORED IMMIGRANTS
Sec. 111. Family-sponsored immigrants.
Sec. 112. Transition for spouses and minor children of legalized aliens.

PART 2—EMPLOYMENT-BASED IMMIGRANTS
Sec. 121. Employment-based immigrants.
Sec. 122. Changes in labor certification process.
Sec. 123. Definitions of managerial capacity and executive capacity.
Sec. 124. Transition for employees of certain United States businesses operating in Hong Kong.

Sec. 403. Waiver of English language requirement for naturalization.
Sec. 404. Treatment of service in armed forces of a foreign country.
Sec. 405. Naturalization of natives of the Philippines through certain active-duty service during World War II.
Sec. 406. Public education regarding naturalization benefits.
Sec. 407. Conforming amendments.
Sec. 408. Effective dates and savings provisions.

TITLE V—ENFORCEMENT
Subtitle A—Criminal Aliens
Sec. 501. Aggravated felony definition.
Sec. 502. Shortening period to request judicial review.
Sec. 503. Enhancing enforcement authority of INS officers.
Sec. 504. Custody pending determination of deportability and excludability.
Sec. 505. Elimination of judicial recommendations against deportation.
Sec. 506. Clarification respecting discretionary authority in deportation proceedings for incarcerated aliens.
Sec. 507. Requiring coordination plan with INS as a condition for receipt of drug control and system improvement grants under the Omnibus Crime Control and Safe Streets Act of 1968.
Sec. 508. Deportation for attempted violations of controlled substances laws.
Sec. 509. Good moral character definition.
Sec. 510. Report on criminal aliens.
Sec. 511. Limitation on waiver of exclusion for returning permanent residents convicted of an aggravated felony.
Sec. 512. Authorization of additional immigration judges for deportation proceedings involving criminal aliens.
Sec. 513. Effect of filing petition for review.
Sec. 514. Extending bar on reentry of aliens convicted of aggravated felonies.
Sec. 515. Asylum in the case of aliens convicted of aggravated felonies.
Subtitle B—Provision Relating to Employer Sanctions
Sec. 521. Elimination of paperwork requirement for recruiters and referrers.
Subtitle C—Provisions Relating to Anti-Discrimination
Sec. 531. Dissemination of information concerning anti-discrimination protections under IRCA and title VII of the Civil Rights Act of 1964.
Sec. 532. Inclusion of certain seasonal agricultural workers within scope of antidiscrimination protections.
Sec. 533. Elimination of requirement that aliens file a declaration of intending to become a citizen in order to file anti-discrimination complaint.
Sec. 534. Anti-retaliation protections.
Sec. 535. Treatment of certain actions as discrimination.
Sec. 536. Conforming civil money penalties for anti-discrimination violations to those for employer sanctions.
Sec. 537. Period for filing of complaints.
Sec. 538. Special Counsel access to employment eligibility verification forms.
Sec. 539. Additional relief in orders.
Subtitle D—General Enforcement
Sec. 541. Authorizing increase by 1,000 in border patrol personnel.
Sec. 542. Application of increase in penalties to enhance enforcement activities.
Sec. 543. Increase in fine levels; authority of the INS to collect fines.
Sec. 544. Civil penalties for document fraud.
Sec. 545. Deportation procedures; required notice of deportation hearing; limitation on discretionary relief.

TITLE VI—EXCLUSION AND DEPORTATION
Sec. 601. Revision of grounds for exclusion.

....

"(c) WORLDWIDE LEVEL OF FAMILY-SPONSORED IMMIGRANTS.—(1)(A) The worldwide level of family-sponsored immigrants under this subsection for a fiscal year is, subject to subparagraph (B), equal to—

"(i) 480,000, minus

"(ii) the number computed under paragraph (2), plus

"(iii) the number (if any) computed under paragraph (3).

"(B)(i) For each of fiscal years 1992, 1993, and 1994, 465,000 shall be substituted for 480,000 in subparagraph (A)(i).

"(ii) In no case shall the number computed under subparagraph (A) be less than 226,000.

....

"(d) WORLDWIDE LEVEL OF EMPLOYMENT-BASED IMMIGRANTS.—(1) The worldwide level of employment-based immigrants under this subsection for a fiscal year is equal to—

"(A) 140,000, plus

"(B) the number computed under paragraph (2).

"(2) The number computed under this paragraph for a fiscal year is the difference (if any) between the maximum number of visas which may be issued under section 203(a) (relating to family-sponsored immigrants) during the previous fiscal year and the number of visas issued under that section during that year.

"(e) WORLDWIDE LEVEL OF DIVERSITY IMMIGRANTS.—The worldwide level of diversity immigrants is equal to 55,000 for each fiscal year."

....

"(4) SPECIAL RULES FOR SPOUSES AND CHILDREN OF LAWFUL PERMANENT RESIDENT ALIENS.—

"(A) 75 PERCENT OF MINIMUM 2ND PREFERENCE SET-ASIDE FOR SPOUSES AND CHILDREN NOT SUBJECT TO PER COUNTRY LIMITATION.—

....

SEC. 104. ASYLEE ADJUSTMENTS.

(a) INCREASE IN NUMERICAL LIMITATION ON ADJUSTMENT OF ASYLEES.—

(1) IN GENERAL.—Section 209(b) (8 U.S.C. 1159(b)) is amended by striking "five thousand" and inserting "10,000."

....

PART 1—FAMILY-SPONSORED IMMIGRANTS
SEC. 111. FAMILY-SPONSORED IMMIGRANTS.
Section 203 (8 U.S.C. 1153) is amended—
(1) by redesignating subsections (b) through (e) as subsections (d) through (g), respectively, and (2) by striking subsection (a) and inserting the following:
"(a) PREFERENCE ALLOCATION FOR FAMILY-SPONSORED IMMIGRANTS.— Aliens subject to the worldwide level specified in section 201(c) for family-sponsored immigrants shall be allotted visas as follows:
"(1) UNMARRIED SONS AND DAUGHTERS OF CITIZENS.—Qualified immigrants who are the unmarried sons or daughters of citizens of the United States shall be allocated visas in a number not to exceed 23,400, plus any visas not required for the class specified in paragraph (4).
"(2) SPOUSES AND UNMARRIED SONS AND UNMARRIED DAUGHTERS OF PERMANENT RESIDENT ALIENS.—Qualified immigrants—
"(A) who are the spouses or children of an alien lawfully admitted for permanent residence, or
"(B) who are the unmarried sons or unmarried daughters (but are not the children) of an alien lawfully admitted for permanent residence, shall be allocated visas in a number not to exceed 114,200, plus the number (if any) by which such worldwide level exceeds 226,000, plus any visas not required for the class specified in paragraph (1); except that not less than 77 percent of such visa numbers shall be allocated to aliens described in subparagraph (A).
"(3) MARRIED SONS AND MARRIED DAUGHTERS OF CITIZENS.—Qualified immigrants who are the married sons or married daughters of citizens of the United States shall be allocated visas in a number not to exceed 23,400, plus any visas not required for the classes specified in paragraphs (1) and (2).
"(4) BROTHERS AND SISTERS OF CITIZENS.—Qualified immigrants who are the brothers or sisters of citizens of the United States, if such citizens are at least 21 years of age, shall be allocated visas in a number not to exceed 65,000, plus any visas not required for the classes specified in paragraphs (1) through (3)."

....

PART 2—EMPLOYMENT-BASED IMMIGRANTS
SEC. 121. EMPLOYMENT-BASED IMMIGRANTS. (a) IN GENERAL.—Section 203 (8 U.S.C. 1153) is amended by inserting after subsection (a), as inserted by section 111, the following new subsection:
"(b) PREFERENCE ALLOCATION FOR EMPLOYMENT-BASED IMMIGRANTS.— Aliens subject to the worldwide level specified in section 201(d) for employment-based immigrants in a fiscal year shall be allotted visas as follows:
"(1) PRIORITY WORKERS.—Visas shall first be made available in a number not to exceed 40,000, plus any visas not required for the classes specified in paragraphs (4) and (5), to qualified immigrants who are aliens described in any of the following subparagraphs (A) through (C):
"(A) ALIENS WITH EXTRAORDINARY ABILITY.—An alien is described in this subparagraph if—
"(i) the alien has extraordinary ability in the sciences, arts, education, business, or athletics which has been demonstrated by sustained national or international acclaim and whose achievements have been recognized in the field through extensive documentation,
"(ii) the alien seeks to enter the United States to continue work in the area of extraordinary ability, and
"(iii) the alien's entry into the United States will substantially benefit prospectively the United States."

....

"(3) SKILLED WORKERS, PROFESSIONALS, AND OTHER WORKERS.—
"(A) IN GENERAL.—Visas shall be made available, in a number not to exceed 40,000, plus any visas not required for the classes specified in paragraphs (1) and (2), to the following classes of aliens who are not described in paragraph (2):

"(i) SKILLED WORKERS.—Qualified immigrants who are capable, at the time of petitioning for classification under this paragraph, of performing skilled labor (requiring at least 2 years training or experience), not of a temporary or seasonal nature, for which qualified workers are not available in the United States.

"(ii) PROFESSIONALS.—Qualified immigrants who hold baccalaureate degrees and who are members of the professions.

"(iii) OTHER WORKERS.—Other qualified immigrants who are capable, at the time of petitioning for classification under this paragraph, of performing unskilled labor, not of a temporary or seasonal nature, for which qualified workers are not available in the United States.

"(B) LIMITATION ON OTHER WORKERS.—Not more than 10,000 of the visas made available under this paragraph in any fiscal year may be available for qualified immigrants described in subparagraph (A)(iii).

"(C) LABOR CERTIFICATION REQUIRED.—An immigrant visa may not be issued to an immigrant under subparagraph (A) until the consular officer is in receipt of a determination made by the Secretary of Labor pursuant to the provisions of section 212(a)(5)(A).

"(4) CERTAIN SPECIAL IMMIGRANTS.—Visas shall be made available, in a number not to exceed 10,000, to qualified special immigrants described in section 101(a)(27) (other than those described in subparagraph (A) or (B) thereof), of which not more than 5,000 may be made available in any fiscal year to special immigrants described in subclause (II) or (III) of section 101(a)(27)(C)(ii)."

....

"(c) DIVERSITY IMMIGRANTS.—

"(B) IDENTIFICATION OF HIGH-ADMISSION AND LOW-ADMISSION REGIONS AND HIGH-ADMISSION AND LOW-ADMISSION STATES.—The Attorney General—

"(i) shall identify—

"(I) each region (each in this paragraph referred to as a 'high-admission region') for which the total of the numbers determined under subparagraph (A) for states in the region is greater than 1/6 of the total of all such numbers, and

"(II) each other region (each in this paragraph referred to as a 'low-admission region'); and

"(ii) shall identify—

"(I) each foreign state for which the number determined under subparagraph (A) is greater than 50,000 (each such state in this paragraph referred to as a 'high-admission state'), and

"(II) each other foreign state (each such state in this paragraph referred to as a 'low-admission state')."

....

SEC. 132. DIVERSITY TRANSITION FOR ALIENS WHO ARE NATIVES OF CERTAIN ADVERSELY AFFECTED FOREIGN STATES.

(a) IN GENERAL.—Notwithstanding the numerical limitations in sections 201 and 202 of the Immigration and Nationality Act, there shall be made available to qualified immigrants described in subsection (b) 40,000 immigrant visas in each of fiscal years 1992, 1993, and 1994.

(b) QUALIFIED ALIEN DESCRIBED.—An alien described in this subsection is an alien who—

(1) is a native of a foreign state that is not contiguous to the United States and that was identified as an adversely affected foreign state for purposes of section 314 of the Immigration Reform and Control Act of 1986,

(2) has a firm commitment for employment in the United States for a period of at least 1 year (beginning on the date of admission under this section), and

(3) except as provided in subsection (c), is admissible as an immigrant.

....

SEC. 141. COMMISSION ON LEGAL IMMIGRATION REFORM.

(a) ESTABLISHMENT AND COMPOSITION OF COMMISSION.—(1) Effective October 1, 1991, there is established a Commission on Legal Immigration Reform (in this section referred to as the "Commission") which shall be composed of 9 members to be appointed as follows:

(A) One member who shall serve as Chairman, to be appointed by the President.

(B) Two members to be appointed by the Speaker of the House of Representatives who shall select such members from a list of nominees provided by the Chairman of the Subcommittee on Immigration, Refugees, and International Law of the Committee on the Judiciary of the House of Representatives.

(C) Two members to be appointed by the Minority Leader of the House of Representatives who shall select such members from a list of nominees provided by the ranking minority member of the Subcommittee on Immigration, Refugees, and International Law of the Committee on the Judiciary of the House of Representatives.

(D) Two members to be appointed by the Majority Leader of the Senate who shall select such members from a list of nominees provided by the Chairman of the Subcommittee on Immigration and Refugee Affairs of the Committee on the Judiciary of the Senate.

(E) Two members to be appointed by the Minority Leader of the Senate who shall select such members from a list of nominees provided by the ranking minority member of the Subcommittee on Immigration and Refugee Affairs of the Committee on the Judiciary of the Senate.

(2) Initial appointments to the Commission shall be made during the 45-day period beginning on October 1, 1991. A vacancy in the Commission shall be filled in the same manner in which the original appointment was made.

(3) Members shall be appointed to serve for the life of the Commission, except that the term of the member described in paragraph (1)(A) shall expire at noon on January 20, 1993, and the President shall appoint an individual to serve for the remaining life of the Commission.

(b) FUNCTIONS OF COMMISSION.—The Commission shall—

(1) review and evaluate the impact of this Act and the amendments made by this Act, in accordance with subsection (c); and

(2) transmit to the Congress—

(A) not later than September 30, 1994, a first report describing the progress made in carrying out paragraph (1), and

(B) not later than September 30, 1997, a final report setting forth the Commission's findings and recommendations, including such recommendations for additional changes that should be made with respect to legal immigration into the United States as the Commission deems appropriate.

....

SEC. 303. SPECIAL TEMPORARY PROTECTED STATUS FOR SALVADORANS.

(a) DESIGNATION.—

(1) IN GENERAL.—El Salvador is hereby designated under section 244A(b) of the Immigration and Nationality Act, subject to the provisions of this section.

(2) PERIOD OF DESIGNATION.—Such designation shall take effect on the date of the enactment of this section and shall remain in effect until the end of the 18-month period beginning January 1, 1991.

(b) ALIENS ELIGIBLE.—

(1) IN GENERAL.—In applying section 244A of the Immigration and Nationality Act pursuant to the designation under this section, subject to section 244A(c)(3) of such Act, an alien who is a national of El Salvador meets the requirements of section 244A(c)(1) of such Act only if—

(A) the alien has been continuously physically present in the United States since September 19, 1990;

(B) the alien is admissible as an immigrant, except as otherwise provided under section 244A(c)(2)(A) of such Act, and is not ineligible for temporary protected status under section 244A(c)(2)(B) of such Act; and

(C) in a manner which the Attorney General shall establish, the alien registers for temporary protected status under this section during the registration period beginning January 1, 1991, and ending June 30, 1991.

．．．．．．．．．．．．．．．．．．．．．

TITLE IV—NATURALIZATION
SEC. 401. ADMINISTRATIVE NATURALIZATION.

(a) NATURALIZATION AUTHORITY.—Section 310 (8 U.S.C. 1421) is amended to read as follows:

"NATURALIZATION AUTHORITY

"SEC. 310. (a) AUTHORITY IN ATTORNEY GENERAL.—The sole authority to naturalize persons as citizens of the United States is conferred upon the Attorney General.

"(b) ADMINISTRATION OF OATHS.—An applicant for naturalization may choose to have the oath of allegiance under section 337(a) administered by the Attorney General or by any District Court of the United States for any State or by any court of record in any State having a seal, a clerk, and jurisdiction in actions in law or equity, or law and equity, in which the amount in controversy is unlimited. The jurisdiction of all courts in this subsection specified to administer the oath of allegiance shall extend only to persons resident within the respective jurisdiction of such courts."

．．．．．．．．．．．．．．．．．．．．．

SEC. 403. WAIVER OF ENGLISH LANGUAGE REQUIREMENT FOR NATURALIZATION.

Section 312(1) (8 U.S.C. 1423(1)) is amended by striking "is over fifty years of age and has been living in the United States for periods totaling at least twenty years subsequent to a lawful admission for permanent residence" and inserting "either (A) is over 50 years of age and has been living in the United States for periods totaling at least 20 years subsequent to a lawful admission for permanent residence, or (B) is over 55 years of age and has been living in the United States for periods totaling at least 15 years subsequent to a lawful admission for permanent residence."

．．．．．．．．．．．．．．．．．．．．．

TITLE V—ENFORCEMENT
Subtitle A—Criminal Aliens
SEC. 501. AGGRAVATED FELONY DEFINITION.

(a) IN GENERAL.—Paragraph (43) of section 101(a) (8 U.S.C. 1101(a)) is amended—

(1) by aligning its left margin with the left margin of paragraph (42),

(2) by inserting "any illicit trafficking in any controlled substance (as defined in section 102 of the Controlled Substances Act), including" after "murder,"

(3) by inserting after "such title," the following: "any offense described in section 1956 of title 18, United States Code (relating to laundering of monetary instruments), or any crime of violence (as defined in section 16 of title 18, United States Code, not including a purely political offense) for which the term of imprisonment imposed (regardless of any suspension of such imprisonment) is at least 5 years,"

(4) by striking "committed within the United States",

(5) by adding at the end the following: "Such term applies to offenses described in the previous sentence whether in violation of Federal or State law", and

(6) by inserting before the period of the sentence added by paragraph (5) the following: "and also applies to offenses described in the previous sentence in violation of foreign law for which the term of imprisonment was completed within the previous 15 years."

(b) EFFECTIVE DATE.—The amendments made by subsection (a) shall apply to offenses committed on or after the date of the enactment of this Act, except that the amendments made by paragraphs (2) and (5) of subsection (a) shall be effective as if included in the enactment of section 7342 of the Anti-Drug Abuse Act of 1988.

SEC. 502. SHORTENING PERIOD TO REQUEST JUDICIAL REVIEW.

(a) IN GENERAL.—Section 106(a)(1) (8 U.S.C. 1152a(a)(1)) is amended by striking "60 days" and inserting "30 days."

(b) EFFECTIVE DATE.—The amendment made by subsection (a) shall apply to final deportation orders issued on or after January 1, 1991.

SEC. 503. ENHANCING ENFORCEMENT AUTHORITY OF INS OFFICERS.

(a) BROADENING AUTHORITY.—Section 287(a) (8 U.S.C. 1357(a)) is amended—

(1) by striking "and" at the end of paragraph (3), and

(2) in paragraph (4), by striking "United States" the second place it appears and all that follows and inserting the following:

"United States, and

"(5) to make arrests—

"(A) for any offense against the United States, if the offense is committed in the officer's or employee's presence, or

"(B) for any felony cognizable under the laws of the United States, if the officer or employee has reasonable grounds to believe that the person to be arrested has committed or is committing such a felony, if the officer or employee is performing duties relating to the enforcement of the immigration laws at the time of the arrest and if there is a likelihood of the person escaping before a warrant can be obtained for his arrest.

"Under regulations prescribed by the Attorney General, an officer or employee of the Service may carry a firearm and may execute and serve any order, warrant, subpoena, summons, or other process issued under the authority of the United States. The authority to make arrests under paragraph (5)(B) shall only be effective on and after the date on which the Attorney General publishes final regulations which (i) prescribe the categories of officers and employees of the Service who may use force (including deadly force) and the circumstances under which such force may be used,

"(ii) establish standards with respect to enforcement activities of the Service,

"(iii) require that any officer or employee of the Service is not authorized to make arrests under paragraph (5)(B) unless the officer or employee has received certification as having completed a training program which covers such arrests and standards described in clause (ii), and (iv) establish an expedited, internal review process for violations of such standards, which process is consistent with standard agency procedure regarding confidentiality of matters related to internal investigations."

....

SEC. 504. CUSTODY PENDING DETERMINATION OF DEPORTABILITY AND EXCLUDABILITY.

(a) DEPORTABILITY.—Section 242(a)(2) (8 U.S.C. 1252(a)(2)) is amended—

(1) in the first sentence, by striking "upon completion of the alien's sentence for such conviction" and inserting "upon release of the alien (regardless of whether or not such release is on parole, supervised release, or probation, and regardless of the possibility of rearrest or further confinement in respect of the same offense)",

....

"(B) The Attorney General shall release from custody an alien who is lawfully admitted for permanent residence on bond or such other conditions as the Attorney General may prescribe if the Attorney General determines that the alien is not a threat to the community and that the alien is likely to appear before any scheduled hearings."

(b) EXCLUDABILITY.—Section 236 (8 U.S.C. 1226) is amended by adding at the end the following new subsection:

"(e)(1) Pending a determination of excludability, the Attorney General shall take into custody any alien convicted of an aggravated felony upon completion of the alien's sentence for such conviction.

"(2) Notwithstanding any other provision of this section, the Attorney General shall not release such felon from custody unless the Attorney General determines that the alien may not be deported because the condition described in section 243(g) exists.

"(3) If the determination described in paragraph (2) has been made, the Attorney General may release such alien only after—

"(A) a procedure for review of each request for relief under this subsection has been established,

"(B) such procedure includes consideration of the severity of the felony committed by the alien, and

"(C) the review concludes that the alien will not pose a danger to the safety of other persons or to property."

....

Subtitle D—General Enforcement

SEC. 541. AUTHORIZING INCREASE BY 1,000 IN BORDER PATROL PERSONNEL.

There are authorized to be appropriated for fiscal year 1991 such additional sums as may be necessary to provide for an increase of 1,000 in the authorized personnel level of the border patrol of the Immigration and Naturalization Service, above the authorized level of the patrol as of September 30, 1990.

SEC. 542. APPLICATION OF INCREASE IN PENALTIES TO ENHANCE ENFORCEMENT ACTIVITIES.

(a) IN GENERAL.—Section 280 (8 U.S.C. 1330) is amended—

(1) by inserting "(a)" after "280," and

(2) by adding at the end the following new subsection:

"(b) Notwithstanding section 3302 of title 31, United States Code, the increase in penalties collected resulting from the amendments made by sections 203(b), 543(a), and 544 of the Immigration Act of 1990 shall be credited to the appropriation—

"(1) for the Immigration and Naturalization Service for activities that enhance enforcement of provisions of this title, including—

"(A) the identification, investigation, and apprehension of criminal aliens,

"(B) the implementation of the system described in section 242(a)(3)(A), and

"(C) for the repair, maintenance, or construction on the United States border, in areas experiencing high levels of apprehensions of illegal aliens, of structures to deter illegal entry into the United States; and

"(2) for the Executive Office for Immigration Review in the Department of Justice for the purpose of removing the backlogs in the preparation of transcripts of deportation proceedings conducted under section 242."

....

SEC. 543. INCREASE IN FINE LEVELS; AUTHORITY OF THE INS TO COLLECT FINES.

....

(8) DUTY TO PREVENT UNAUTHORIZED ENTRIES.—Section 271(a) (8 U.S.C. 1321) is amended by striking "$1,000" and inserting "$3,000."

(9) BRINGING IN CERTAIN ALIENS.—Section 272 (8 U.S.C. 1322) is amended—

(A) in subsection (a)—

(i) by striking "collector of customs of the customs district in which the place of arrival is located" and inserting "Commissioner", and

(ii) by striking "$1,000" and inserting "$3,000";

(B) in subsection (b)—

(i) by striking "collector of customs of the customs district in which the place of arrival is located" and inserting "Commissioner", and

(ii) by striking "$250" and inserting "$3,000"; and

....

(2) CONCEALMENT OF ALIENS.—Section 275 (8 U.S.C. 1325) is amended—

(A) by inserting "or attempts to enter" after "(1) enters",

(B) by inserting "attempts to enter or" after "or (3)", and

(C) by striking "shall, for the first commission", and all that follows through "$1,000" and inserting "shall, for the first commission of any such offense, be fined not more than $2,000 (or, if greater, the amount provided under title 18, United States Code) or imprisoned not more than 6 months, or both, and, for a subsequent commission of any such offense, be fined under title 18, United States Code, or imprisoned not more than 2 years."

....

SEC. 545. DEPORTATION PROCEDURES; REQUIRED NOTICE OF DEPORTATION HEARING; LIMITATION ON DISCRETIONARY RELIEF.

(a) IN GENERAL.—Chapter 5 of title II is amended by inserting after section 242A the following new section:

"DEPORTATION PROCEDURES

"SEC. 242B.(a) NOTICES.—

"(1) ORDER TO SHOW CAUSE.—In deportation proceedings under section 242, written notice (in this section referred to as an 'order to show cause') shall be given in person to the alien (or, if personal service is not practicable, such notice shall be given by certified mail to the alien or to the alien's counsel of record, if any) specifying the following:

"(A) The nature of the proceedings against the alien.

"(B) The legal authority under which the proceedings are conducted.

"(C) The acts or conduct alleged to be in violation of law.

"(D) The charges against the alien and the statutory provisions alleged to have been violated.

"(E) The alien may be represented by counsel and, upon request, the alien will be provided a list of counsel prepared under subsection (b)(2).

"(F)(i) The requirement that the alien must immediately provide (or have provided) the Attorney General with a written record of an address and telephone number (if any) at which the alien may be contacted respecting proceedings under section 242.

"(ii) The requirement that the alien must provide the Attorney General immediately with a written record of any change of the alien's address or telephone number.

"(iii) The consequences under subsection (c)(2) of failure to provide address and telephone information pursuant to this subparagraph."

....

TITLE VI—EXCLUSION AND DEPORTATION

SEC. 601. REVISION OF GROUNDS FOR EXCLUSION.

(a) REVISED GROUNDS FOR EXCLUSION.—Subsection (a) of section 212 (8 U.S.C. 1182) is amended to read as follows:

"(a) CLASSES OF EXCLUDABLE ALIENS.—Except as otherwise provided in this Act, the following describes classes of excludable aliens who are ineligible to receive visas and who shall be excluded from admission into the United States:

"(1) HEALTH-RELATED GROUNDS.—
"(2) CRIMINAL AND RELATED GROUNDS.—
"(A) CONVICTION OF CERTAIN CRIMES.—
"(B) MULTIPLE CRIMINAL CONVICTIONS
"(C) CONTROLLED SUBSTANCE TRAFFICKERS
"(D) PROSTITUTION AND COMMERCIALIZED VICE
"(E) CERTAIN ALIENS INVOLVED IN SERIOUS CRIMINAL ACTIVITY WHO HAVE ASSERTED IMMUNITY FROM PROSECUTION
"(F) WAIVER AUTHORIZED
"(3) SECURITY AND RELATED GROUNDS
"(B) TERRORIST ACTIVITIES.—
"(C) FOREIGN POLICY.—
"(ii) EXCEPTION FOR OFFICIALS.—An alien who is an official of a foreign government or a purported government, or who is a candidate for election to a foreign government office during the period immediately preceding the election for that office, shall not be excludable or subject to restrictions or conditions on entry into the United States under clause (i) solely because of the alien's past, current, or expected beliefs, statements, or associations, if such beliefs, statements, or associations would be lawful within the United States.
"(D) IMMIGRANT MEMBERSHIP IN TOTALITARIAN PARTY.—
"(ii) EXCEPTION FOR INVOLUNTARY MEMBERSHIP
"(iii) EXCEPTION FOR PAST MEMBERSHIP
"(E) PARTICIPANTS IN NAZI PERSECUTIONS OR GENOCIDE.—
"(i) PARTICIPATION IN NAZI PERSECUTIONS
"(ii) PARTICIPATION IN GENOCIDE
"(4) PUBLIC CHARGE"

....

(c) REVIEW OF EXCLUSION LISTS.—The Attorney General and the Secretary of State shall develop protocols and guidelines for updating lookout books and the automated visa lookout system and similar mechanisms for the screening of aliens applying for visas for admission, or for admission, to the United States. Such protocols and guidelines shall be developed in a manner that ensures that in the case of an alien-

(1) whose name is in such system, and

(2) who either (A) applies for entry after the effective date of the amendments made by this section, or (B) requests (in writing to a local consular office after such date) a review, without seeking admission, of the alien's continued excludability under the Immigration and Nationality Act, if the alien is no longer excludable because of an amendment made by this section the alien's name shall be removed from such books and system and the alien shall be informed of such removal and if the alien continues to be excludable the alien shall be informed of such determination.

....

Document 3: Proposition 187: Text of Proposed Law, State of California (1994)

What: California State Law passed in 1994

When: November 8, 1994

Significance: This is an example of how U.S. border states are begging to deal with immigration. The law aims to restrict the use of social services, health care, and public education by illegal immigrants in California. It was overturned by a federal court on November 20, 1995.

Proposition 187: Text of Proposed Law

1994 - California

This initiative measure is submitted to the people in accordance with the provisions of Article II, Section 8 of the Constitution.

This initiative measure adds sections to various codes; therefore, new provisions proposed to be added are printed in {+ *italic type* +} to indicate that they are new.

PROPOSED LAW

SECTION 1. Findings and Declaration.

The People of California find and declare as follows:

That they have suffered and are suffering economic hardship caused by the presence of illegal aliens in this state.

That they have suffered and are suffering personal injury and damage caused by the criminal conduct of illegal aliens in this state.

That they have a right to the protection of their government from any person or persons entering this country unlawfully.

Therefore, the People of California declare their intention to provide for cooperation between their agencies of state and local government with the federal government, and to establish a system of required notification by and between such agencies to prevent illegal aliens in the United States from receiving benefits or public services in the State of California.

SECTION 2. Manufacture, Distribution or Sale of False Citizenship or Resident Alien Documents: Crime and Punishment.

Section 113 is added to the Penal Code, to read:

{+ *113. Any person who manufactures, distributes or sells false documents to conceal the true citizenship or resident alien status of another person is guilty of a felony, and shall be punished by imprisonment in the state prison for five years or by a fine of seventy-five thousand dollars ($75,000).* +}

SECTION 3. Use of False Citizenship or Resident Alien Documents: Crime and Punishment.

Section 114 is added to the Penal Code, to read:

{+ *114. Any person who uses false documents to conceal his or her true citizenship or resident alien status is guilty of a felony, and shall be punished by imprisonment in the state prison for five years or by a fine of twenty-five thousand dollars ($25,000).* +}

SECTION 4. Law Enforcement Cooperation with INS.

Section 834b is added to the Penal Code, to read:

{+ *834b. (a) Every law enforcement agency in California shall fully cooperate with the United States Immigration and Naturalization Service regarding any person who is arrested if he or she is suspected of being present in the United States in violation of federal immigration laws.* +}

{+ *(b) With respect to any such person who is arrested, and suspected of being present in the United States in violation of federal immigration laws, every law enforcement agency shall do the following:* +}

{+ *(1) Attempt to verify the legal status of such person as a citizen of the United States, an alien lawfully admitted as a permanent resident, an alien lawfully admitted for a temporary period of time or as an alien who is present in the United States in violation of immigration laws. The verification process may include, but shall not be limited to, questioning the person regarding his or her date and place of birth, and entry into the United States, and demanding documentation to indicate his or her legal status.* +}

{+ *(2) Notify the person of his or her apparent status as an alien who is present in the United States in violation of federal immigration laws and inform him or her that, apart from any criminal justice proceedings, he or she must either obtain legal status or leave the United States.* +}

{+ *(3) Notify the Attorney General of California and the United States Immigration and Naturalization Service of the apparent illegal status and provide any additional information that may be requested by any other public entity.* +}

{+ *(c) Any legislative, administrative, or other action by a city, county, or other legally authorized local governmental entity with jurisdictional boundaries, or by a law enforcement agency, to prevent or limit the cooperation required by subdivision (a) is expressly prohibited.* +}

SECTION 5. Exclusion of Illegal Aliens from Public Social Services.

Section 10001.5 is added to the Welfare and Institutions Code, to read:

{+ *10001.5. (a) In order to carry out the intention of the People of California that only citizens of the United States and aliens lawfully admitted to the United States may receive the benefits of* +}

public social services and to ensure that all persons employed in the providing of those services shall diligently protect public funds from misuse, the provisions of this section are adopted. +}

{+ (b) A person shall not receive any public social services to which he or she may be otherwise entitled until the legal status of that person has been verified as one of the following: +}

{+ (1) A citizen of the United States. +}

{+ (2) An alien lawfully admitted as a permanent resident. +}

{+ (3) An alien lawfully admitted for a temporary period of time. +}

{+ (c) If any public entity in this state to whom a person has applied for public social services determines or reasonably suspects, based upon the information provided to it, that the person is an alien in the United States in violation of federal law, the following procedures shall be followed by the public entity: +}

{+ (1) The entity shall not provide the person with benefits or services. +}

{+ (2) The entity shall, in writing, notify the person of his or her apparent illegal immigration status, and that the person must either obtain legal status or leave the United States. +}

{+ (3) The entity shall also notify the State Director of Social Services, the Attorney General of California, and the United States Immigration and Naturalization Service of the apparent illegal status, and shall provide any additional information that may be requested by any other public entity. +}

SECTION 6. Exclusion of Illegal Aliens from Publicly Funded Health Care.

Chapter 1.3 (commencing with Section 130) is added to Part 1 of Division 1 of the Health and Safety Code, to read:

{+ Chapter 1.3. Publicly-Funded Health Care Services +}

{+ 130. (a) In order to carry out the intention of the People of California that, excepting emergency medical care as required by federal law, only citizens of the United States and aliens lawfully admitted to the United States may receive the benefits of publicly-funded health care, and to ensure that all persons employed in the providing of those services shall diligently protect public funds from misuse, the provisions of this section are adopted. +}

{+ (b) A person shall not receive any health care services from a publicly-funded health care facility, to which he or she is otherwise entitled until the legal status of that person has been verified as one of the following: +}

{+ (1) A citizen of the United States. +}

{+ (2) An alien lawfully admitted as a permanent resident. +}

{+ (3) An alien lawfully admitted for a temporary period of time. +}

{+ (c) If any publicly-funded health care facility in this state from whom a person seeks health care services, other than emergency medical care as required by federal law, determines or reasonably suspects, based upon the information provided to it, that the person is an alien in the United States in violation of federal law, the following procedures shall be followed by the facility: +}

{+ (1) The facility shall not provide the person with services. +}

{+ (2) The facility shall, in writing, notify the person of his or her apparent illegal immigration status, and that the person must either obtain legal status or leave the United States. +}

{+ (3) The facility shall also notify the State Director of Health Services, the Attorney General of California, and the United States Immigration and Naturalization Service of the apparent illegal status, and shall provide any additional information that may be requested by any other public entity. +}

{+ (d) For purposes of this section "publicly-funded health care facility" shall be defined as specified in Sections 1200 and 1250 of this code as of January 1, 1993. +}

SECTION 7. Exclusion of Illegal Aliens from Public Elementary and Secondary Schools.

Section 48215 is added to the Education Code, to read:

{+ 48215. (a) No public elementary or secondary school shall admit, or permit the attendance of, any child who is not a citizen of the United States, an alien lawfully admitted as a permanent resident, or a person who is otherwise authorized under federal law to be present in the United States. +}

{+ (b) Commencing January 1, 1995, each school district shall verify the legal status of each child enrolling in the school district for the first time in order to ensure the enrollment or attendance only of citizens, aliens lawfully admitted as permanent residents, or persons who are otherwise authorized to be present in the United States. +}

{+ (c) By January 1, 1996, each school district shall have verified the legal status of each child already enrolled and in attendance in the school district in order to ensure the enrollment or attendance only of citizens, aliens lawfully admitted as permanent residents, or persons who are otherwise authorized under federal law to be present in the United States. +}

{+ (d) By January 1, 1996, each school district shall also have verified the legal status of each parent or guardian of each child referred to in subdivisions (b) and (c), to determine whether such parent or guardian is one of the following: +}

{+ (1) A citizen of the United States. +}

{+ (2) An alien lawfully admitted as a permanent resident. +}

{+ (3) An alien admitted lawfully for a temporary period of time. +}

{+ (e) Each school district shall provide information to the State Superintendent of Public Instruction, the Attorney General of California, and the United States Immigration and Naturalization Service regarding any enrollee or pupil, or parent or guardian, attending a public elementary or secondary school in the school district determined or reasonably suspected to be in violation of federal immigration laws within forty-five days after becoming aware of an apparent violation. The notice shall also be provided to the parent or legal guardian of the enrollee or pupil, and shall state that an existing pupil may not continue to attend the school after ninety calendar days from the date of the notice, unless legal status is established. +}

{+ (f) For each child who cannot establish legal status in the United States, each school district shall continue to provide education for a period of ninety days from the date of the notice. Such ninety day period shall be utilized to accomplish an orderly transition to a school in the child's country of origin. Each school district shall fully cooperate in this transition effort to ensure that the educational needs of the child are best served for that period of time. +}

SECTION 8. Exclusion of Illegal Aliens from Public Postsecondary Educational Institutions.

Section 66010.8 is added to the Education Code, to read:

{+ 66010.8. (a) No public institution of postsecondary education shall admit, enroll, or permit the attendance of any person who is not a citizen of the United States, an alien lawfully admitted as a permanent resident in the United States, or a person who is otherwise authorized under federal law to be present in the United States. +}

{+ (b) Commencing with the first term or semester that begins after January 1, 1995, and at the commencement of each term or semester thereafter, each public postsecondary educational institution shall verify the status of each person enrolled or in attendance at that institution in order to ensure the enrollment or attendance only of United States citizens, aliens lawfully admitted as permanent residents in the United States, and persons who are otherwise authorized under federal law to be present in the United States. +}

{+ (c) No later than 45 days after the admissions officer of a public postsecondary educational institution becomes aware of the application, enrollment, or attendance of a person determined to be, or who is under reasonable suspicion of being, in the United States in violation of federal immigration laws, that officer shall provide that information to the State Superintendent of Public Instruction, the Attorney General of California, and the United States Immigration and Naturalization Service. The information shall also be provided to the applicant, enrollee, or person admitted. +}

SECTION 9. Attorney General Cooperation with the INS.

Section 53069.65 is added to the Government Code, to read:

{+ 53069.65. Whenever the state or a city, or a county, or any other legally authorized local governmental entity with jurisdictional boundaries reports the presence of a person who is suspected of being present in the United States in violation of federal immigration laws to the Attorney General of California, that report shall be transmitted to the United States Immigration and Naturalization Service. The Attorney General shall be responsible for maintaining on-going and accurate records of such reports, and shall provide any additional information that may be requested by any other government entity. +}

SECTION 10. Amendment and Severability.

The statutory provisions contained in this measure may not be amended by the Legislature except to further its purposes by statute passed in each house by rollcall vote entered in the journal, two-thirds of the membership concurring, or by a statute that becomes effective only when approved by the voters.

In the event that any portion of this act or the application thereof to any person or circumstance is held invalid, that invalidity shall not affect any other provision or application of the act, which can be given effect without the invalid provision or application, and to that end the provisions of this act are severable.

FURTHER READINGS

Books

Edmonston, Barry, ed. *Statistics on U.S. Immigration: An Assessment of Data Needs For Future Research*. Washington, D.C.: National Academy Press, 1996.

Papademetriou, Demetrios and Mark Miller, eds. *The Unavoidable Issue: US Immigration Policy in the 1980s*. Philadelphia: Institute for the Study of Human Issues, 1983.

Articles

Bean, F. D., T. J. Espenshade, M. J. White, and R. F. Dymowski. "Post-IRCA Changes in the Volume and Composition of Undocumented Migration to the United States." In *Undocumented Migration to the United States*, edited by F. D. Bean, B. Edmonston, and J. S. Passel. Santa Monica: RAND, 1990.

Carlson, Alvar W. "America's New Immigration: Characteristics, Destinations, and Impact, 1970-1989." *Social Science Journal*, vol. 31, no. 3 (1994).

Donato, K. M., and R.S. Carter. "Mexico and U.S. Policy on Illegal Immigration: A Fifty-Year Retrospective." In *Illegal Immigration in America*, edited by D.W. Haines and K.E. Rosenblum. Westport, Conn.: Greenwood Press, 1999.

Gonzales Baker, Susan. "The Amnesty Aftermath: Current Policy Issues Stemming from the Legalization Programs of the 1986 Immigration Reform and Control Act." *International Migration Review*, vol. 31, no. 1 (Spring 1997), 5–27.

Keely, Charles. The Challenge of Mass Asylum, Research Paper, *U.S. Commission on Immigration Reform* (January 1994).

Orrenius, Pia, and Madeline Zavodny. "Do Amnesty Programs Reduce Undocumented Immigration? Evidence from IRCA." *Demography*, vol. 40, no. 3 (August 2003), 437–450.

White, M. J., F. D. Bean, and T. J. Espenshade. "The U.S. 1986 Immigration Reform and Control Act and Undocumented Immigration to the United States." *Population Research and Policy Review*, vol. 9 (1990), 93–116.

CHA**8**TER

The Response to Immigration after September 11, 2001

David Felsen

In the aftermath of the September 11 attacks, immigration became a front-and-center issue in the United States. The immigration question became inexorably linked to America's security. Never before had Americans felt as vulnerable as they did when hijacked planes crashed into the Twin Towers in New York and into the Pentagon in Washington, D.C. It was the largest and most devastating terrorist attack on United States soil in its history. Moreover, the hijackers were not American; all were foreigners from Middle Eastern countries who were present in the United States on student visas. The attacks invariably led to questions over how visitors and students from abroad can be better monitored, how entry visas are to be issued, and how America's borders can be better protected. Moreover, the attacks have forced a reexamination of America's values, institutions, and ideals.

THE IMMEDIATE AFTERMATH: THE USA PATRIOT ACT OF 2001

Immediately after the attacks there was palpable pressure on the Bush administration and the United States Congress to address American insecurities and vulnerabilities. There was also a groundswell of anger in the country against the organizers of the attack and a desire to punish the perpetrators, Al Qaeda, and its leader Osama Bin Laden. The military response of the United States came in October 2001 when the United States went to war against Afghanistan's Taliban government, which had hosted Al Qaeda's leadership and terrorist training camps. In the invasion, the United States was joined by a dozen allies, including Britain, Germany, Canada, and Australia.

The domestic response was equally as rapid and dramatic, but controversial. Although Congress wanted to give the president tools to fight terrorism and passed the legislation by an overwhelming 357-66 vote in the House of Representatives and 98-1 vote in the Senate,

The September 11, 2001, terrorist attacks on the World Trade Center in New York City—as well as on the Pentagon in Washington, D.C., and aboard a San Francisco-bound plane over Pennsylvania—riveted public attention on national security and bound border security issues to the already contentious immigration debate. AP Photo/Amy Sancetta.

the USA PATRIOT Act of 2001 (PL 107-56) attracted the concern of civil liberties groups because of the far-reaching nature of the bill. The bill was signed into law by President Bush October 26, 2001, a mere six weeks after the terrorist attacks.

The PATRIOT Act expands funding dramatically for counterterrorism agency abilities, enhances law enforcement powers, and grants new powers to the Treasury to track terrorist-related money laundering. It updates the existing legal framework dealing with terrorism, surveillance, immigration, and law enforcement matters. One of the most controversial parts of the act, section 215, makes it easier for domestic agencies such as the FBI to look into financial, library, and medical records and to monitor Internet activity. New provisions enable law enforcement to investigate terrorism with few restrictions, allowing police to more easily use wiretaps, searches, seizures, and interrogations with little oversight.

Title IV of the PATRIOT Act makes several important changes directly related to border and immigration issues (Document 1). The definition of terrorism was expanded significantly to include association and support of terrorist groups. Anybody accused of association of any kind with terrorist organizations would be barred from entering or remaining in the country. Association was loosely defined as "any alien who the Secretary of State, after consultation with the Attorney General, or the Attorney General, after consultation with the Secretary of State, determines has been associated with a terrorist organization and intends while in the United States to engage solely, principally or incidentally in activities that could endanger the welfare, safety, or security of the United States is inadmissible."

Section 416 enhanced monitoring of foreign students studying in the United States—of particular concern for law enforcement given the profiles of the 9/11 terrorists. This part of the act calls for a "full implementation and expansion of foreign student visa monitoring program." The PATRIOT Act also gives more investigative powers directly to the attorney general's office, and it gave the Department of State and INS more access to criminal background information databases of other departments.

The PATRIOT Act was criticized not only by civil liberties groups but also by many state and local governments. Hundreds of governments across the country passed "Anti-PATRIOT Act" resolutions to protect civil liberties when no evidence of wrongdoing by a person exists (Burns and Peterson 2005, 177).

THE DEPARTMENT OF HOMELAND SECURITY UNVEILED IN 2002

The terrorist attacks also prompted American policy makers to think about how to more effectively organize and coordinate all immigration, intelligence, and law enforcement agencies of the executive branch. The United States Congress put together legislation to carry out the largest reorganization to the federal bureaucracy in over half a century. President George W. Bush signed the Homeland Security Act of 2002, Public Law 107-26, on November 25, 2002. Governor Tom Ridge became the first secretary of the Department of Homeland Security (DHS), a cabinet-level position. DHS began to operate January 1, 2003.

The creation of DHS meant the amalgamation of twenty-two government agencies and 180,000 people. President Bush noted in his remarks upon signing the bill that the reorganization was, among other things, to eliminate duplication of law enforcement functions, to bring about better cooperation among federal, state, and local law enforcement, and to coordinate better border protection (Document 2). President Bush remarked, "The Homeland Security Act of 2002 takes the next critical steps in defending our country. The continuing threat of terrorism, the threat of mass murder on our own soil, will be met with a unified, effective response. Dozens of agencies charged with homeland security will now be located within one Cabinet Department with the mandate and legal authority to protect our people."

The immigration and border controls were completely overhauled. Immigration and Naturalization Services (INS) and the United States Customs Service were replaced by new agencies: the U.S. Customs and Border Protection (CBP), the Citizenship and Immigration Services (CIS), and the Immigration and Customs Enforcement (ICE). Another agency created to help protect air travel was the Transportation Security Administration (TSA). Homeland Security also incorporated the Federal Emergency Management Agency (FEMA) and the Coast Guard. While there was talk of bringing the FBI and CIA into DHS, it was decided that these intelligence agencies should stay outside the new department. Nevertheless, close coordination was expected, as President Bush signaled in his speech: "When the Department of Homeland Security is fully operational it will enhance the safety of our people in very practical ways. First, this new Department will analyze intelligence information on terror threats collected by the CIA, the FBI, the National Security Agency, and others."

DHS has launched programs that use new technologies to monitor entry of aliens into the country, including the US-Visit program, begun in 2004, requiring non-U.S. citizens or residents entering the country to give eye scans and fingerprints that will be fed into a DHS database. Another initiative is the no-fly list to prevent potential terrorists from boarding flights. The programs are meant to prevent entry of people who may pose security risks into the United States, but they have attracted criticism because they have also ensnared innocent individuals on occasion.

At a July 2006 anti-immigration rally held at Ground Zero in New York City, pro-immigration demonstrators outnumbered Minuteman Project supporters and other marchers. AP Photo/Seth Wenig.

ENHANCED BORDER SECURITY AND FAILED IMMIGRATION REFORM

As American policy became more security-conscious, Washington began to debate how to deal with the estimated 12 million undocumented workers living in the United States. Finding a solution to undocumented workers was a priority of President Bush in his first months in office, but any talk of immigration was put on hold after the attacks. There were other immigration questions that had to be addressed in the post-September 11 environment, notably how to deal with student visas and visas for highly skilled foreign workers so that the United States could protect itself without harming its ability to attract the best and the brightest from around the world. There was a significant drop-off in the number of visas granted to highly skilled workers who were needed by the United States.

The post-9/11 atmosphere made comprehensive immigration reform difficult to achieve. Early in his second term, President Bush asked Congress to send him something to solve the situation of undocumented workers by creating a temporary employment program (see Document 1 in Chapter 10).

The bipartisan McCain-Kennedy bill initially enjoyed considerable support in 2005. It included a guest worker program with H-5A visas and offered a path to legalization of undocumented workers. Anti-immigrant critics seized upon the provision in the bill that would offer a path to legalization for undocumented workers and called it "amnesty." They further

Soldiers of Stryker Brigade at Fort Lewis, Washington, are sworn in as citizens of the United States in November 2005. President George W. Bush signed an executive order in 2002 permitting immigrants on active duty in the U.S. Military after Sept. 11, 2001, to apply immediately for citizenship. AP Photo/Ted S. Warren.

argued that granting amnesty to these workers would encourage millions of others to come and weaken, not strengthen, American border security.

In President Bush's second term, pro-immigrant and anti-immigrant groups mobilized over immigration reform both in Congress and in the streets. In the House of Representatives, a strongly worded anti-immigrant measure was passed, which offered no guest worker program, no path to legalization, and extra money to complete a fence on the U.S.-Mexican border. Anti-immigrant talk radio hosts blasted proposals that would include "amnesty." The Minute Men, the militia group that offered their "help" to the border patrol, became more visible and gained recruits. On the other side, pro-immigrant civil groups engaged in mass demonstrations and rallies to show their support for a bill that would create a path to legalization. The White House repeatedly tried to explain why the legislation was not amnesty.

A May 2006 compromise between Republicans and Democrats was reached to adopt a "legalization plus enforcement" approach to strike a balance to include measures to beef up border security in addition to provisions that offered a path to citizenship—albeit difficult one—for undocumented workers. The new temporary work program was kept in the bill, and a process was adopted whereby undocumented workers would pay fines and return to their countries of origin for a time before reentering the United States. Yet the House refused to consider a bill that was viewed as an amnesty for undocumented workers. Senate and House leaders could not find a compromise, and the immigration bill died in the Senate. In the end, no new legislation is scheduled for consideration before the new Congress takes office in 2009.

THE RESPONSE OF STATES TO IMMIGRATION ENFORCEMENT

The perceived federal government inaction over immigration angered many states who felt overwhelmed by the demands placed by undocumented workers on their social services.

States argued that they were compelled to take action against what they see as the abuse of their health, education, and welfare services by individuals who are illegally in the country.

A number of towns, counties, and states adopted laws to prevent access of these immigrants to health and education, to ban landlords from renting apartments to individuals without social security numbers, and even to heavily penalize businesses, as in the case of the new Arizona law, for employing illegal immigrants. The new Arizona law, the "Legal Arizona Workers Act," survived a court challenge and went into effect in January 2008. The legislation threatens stiff penalties against companies that continue to hire illegal workers.

The Arizona law stipulates that the first-time offender will lose one's business license for ten days, but "for a second violation of subsection 'A' during the period of probation, the court shall order the appropriate agencies to permanently revoke all licenses that are held by the employer and that are necessary to operate the employer's business at the employer's business location where the unauthorized alien performed work" (Document 4). Other states are watching with interest the economic consequences of Arizona's tough legislation.

THE RESPONSE OF AMERICAN BUSINESS TO POST 9/11 IMMIGRATION ISSUES

American business leaders are concerned that the new focus on border security has dissuaded the world's most talented workers from wanting to come to the United States to study, work, and engage in scientific and technological conferences and research. There is evidence that, after 9/11, a sharp drop occurred in the number of business, scientific, and student applications for entry to the United States, particularly from China and India, countries that had sent tens of thousands of their brightest to do business and engage in research in the country.

Richard Florida, in an article in *Harvard Business Review*, writes that the number of applications for student visas fell dramatically. He noted that in a report by the Council of Graduate Schools, it was found that the number of Chinese and Indian students who applied to American schools fell by 76 percent and 58 percent, respectively, between the years 2001 and 2003. The number of GRE test-takers fell in this same period by 50 percent in China and 37 percent in India. The rejection rate for highly skilled worker visas—the "H-1B" class of visas—rose from 9.5 percent to 17.8 percent from 2001 to 2003. In short, there has been a significant reduction in the intellectual capital flowing into the United States (Florida 2004).

The question of highly skilled H-1B visas was addressed by Bill Gates in testimony before a Senate committee with the theme of strengthening American competitiveness (Document 5). Gates argued that leading companies like Microsoft, Apple, and others need more engineers and computer scientists than ever before, but the Bush administration permitted the H-1B visa cap to fall to 1990 levels. Gates notes in his testimony, "Unfortunately, our immigration policies are driving away the world's best and brightest precisely when we need them most. The fact is that the terrible shortfall in the visa supply for highly skilled scientists and engineers stems from visa policies that have not been updated in more than 15 years. We live in a different economy now, and it makes no sense to tell well-trained, highly skilled individuals—many of whom are educated at our top universities—that they are not welcome here."

CONCLUSION

In the post-September 11 climate, immigration remains a prominent issue in American politics. As one recent poll noted, "17 percent of likely Republican voters in New Hampshire's first-in-the-nation presidential primary named illegal immigration as the one issue they want to hear candidates talk about, making it second only to Iraq. In Iowa, where caucuses kick off the presidential nominating season, immigration was the leading issue for 18 percent of Republicans, ahead of Iraq." (Ramer, 2007). Not only are Americans worried about the recent economic turmoil caused by the housing downturn and credit crunch in 2007-8 has made Americans feel economically insecure. Although many Americans are indeed sympathetic to the plight of these laborers who work in the shadows, many more citizens do not want to grant them a path to legalization until Americans are more confident about their own economic and personal security.

DOCUMENTS

Document 1: Uniting and Strengthening America by Providing Appropriate Tools Required to Intercept and Obstruct Terrorism Act of 2001 (USA-PATRIOT ACT) – PL 107-56 (115 STAT 345), Excerpt

When: October 26, 2001

Significance: First and far-reaching legislative response to tighten security in wake of 9/11 attacks.

Subtitle B—Enhanced Immigration Provisions

Sec. 411. Definitions Relating To Terrorism.

(a) GROUNDS OF INADMISSIBILITY.—Section 212(a)(3) of the Immigration and Nationality Act (8 U.S.C. 1182(a)(3)) is amended—

(1) in subparagraph (B)—

(A) in clause (i)—

(i) by amending subclause (IV) to read as follows:

"(IV) is a representative (as defined in clause (v)) of—

"(aa) a foreign terrorist organization, as designated by the Secretary of State under section 219, or

"(bb) a political, social or other similar group whose public endorsement of acts of terrorist activity the Secretary of State has determined undermines United States efforts to reduce or eliminate terrorist activities,";

(ii) in subclause (V), by inserting "or" after "section 219,"; and

(iii) by adding at the end the following new subclauses:

"(VI) has used the alien's position of prominence within any country to endorse or espouse terrorist activity, or to persuade others to support terrorist activity or a terrorist organization, in a way that the Secretary of State has determined undermines United States efforts to reduce or eliminate terrorist activities, or

"(VII) is the spouse or child of an alien who is inadmissible under this section, if the activity causing the alien to be found inadmissible occurred within the last 5 years,";

DID YOU KNOW?

Visas and the Visa Waiver Program

Most visitors to the United States for the purpose of tourism and business must obtain visas at U.S. consulates in their home countries. The United States' Visa Waiver Program, established in 1986, permits nationals from twenty-seven different countries to come to the United States for business or tourism without obtaining a visa. The countries are Andorra, Australia, Austria, Belgium, Brunei, Denmark, Finland, France, Germany, Iceland, Ireland, Italy, Japan, Liechtenstein, Luxembourg, Monaco, Netherlands, New Zealand, Norway, Portugal, San Marino, Singapore, Slovenia, Spain, Sweden, Switzerland, and United Kingdom. In addition, other immigration provisions also exempt Canada and Bermuda from visas in most cases of travel and business (U.S. Department of State website).

DID YOU KNOW?

Tourism Post–September 11, 2001

Tourism to the United States has declined considerably since the 9/11 terrorist attacks. The number of visits from countries other than Canada and Mexico to the United States in 2006 totaled 21.7 million. This was a full 17 percent below the peak of 26 million tourist visits reached in 2000. Yet total cross-border travel in this period around the world actually rose by 20 percent, meaning that the United States' share of global tourism has declined significantly. Among the six countries that provide the most tourists—Britain, Germany, Japan, France, South Korea, and Australia—there has been a 15 percent drop in tourist traffic into the United States between 2000 and 2006, but a 39 percent rise in tourist visits from these six countries to other countries. This has cost the United States around $100 billion in lost tourist spending and $16 billion in lost tax revenue (Jim Abrams, "Congress Looks to Boost U.S. Tourism," *Washington Post* [July 5, 2007]).

(B) by redesignating clauses (ii), (iii), and (iv) as clauses (iii), (iv), and (v), respectively;

(C) in clause (i)(II), by striking "clause (iii)" and inserting "clause (iv)";

(D) by inserting after clause (i) the following:

"(ii) EXCEPTION.—Subclause (VII) of clause (i) does not apply to a spouse or child—

"(I) who did not know or should not reasonably have known of the activity causing the alien to be found inadmissible under this section; or

"(II) whom the consular officer or Attorney General has reasonable grounds to believe has renounced the activity causing the alien to be found inadmissible under this section.";

(E) in clause (iii) (as redesignated by subparagraph (B))—

(i) by inserting "it had been" before "committed in the United States"; and

(ii) in subclause (V)(b), by striking "or firearm" and inserting, "firearm, or other weapon or dangerous device";

(F) by amending clause (iv) (as redesignated by subparagraph (B)) to read as follows:

"(iv) ENGAGE IN TERRORIST ACTIVITY DEFINED.—

As used in this chapter, the term "engage in terrorist activity" means, in an individual capacity or as a member of an organization—

"(I) to commit or to incite to commit, under circumstances indicating an intention to cause death or serious bodily injury, a terrorist activity;

"(II) to prepare or plan a terrorist activity;

"(III) to gather information on potential targets for terrorist activity;

"(IV) to solicit funds or other things of value for—

"(aa) a terrorist activity;

"(bb) a terrorist organization described in clause (vi)(I) or (vi)(II); or

"(cc) a terrorist organization described in clause (vi)(III), unless the solicitor can demonstrate that he did not know, and should not reasonably have known, that the solicitation would further the organization's terrorist activity;

"(V) to solicit any individual—

"(aa) to engage in conduct otherwise described in this clause;

"(bb) for membership in a terrorist organization described in clause (vi)(I) or (vi)(II); or

"(cc) for membership in a terrorist organization described in clause (vi)(III), unless the solicitor can demonstrate that he did not know, and should not reasonably have known, that the solicitation would further the organization's terrorist activity; or

"(VI) to commit an act that the actor knows, or reasonably should know, affords material support, including a safe house, transportation, communications, funds, transfer of funds or other material financial benefit, false documentation or identification, weapons (including chemical, biological, or radiological weapons), explosives, or training—

"(aa) for the commission of a terrorist activity;

"(bb) to any individual who the actor knows, or reasonably should know, has committed or plans to commit a terrorist activity;

"(cc) to a terrorist organization described in clause (vi)(I) or (vi)(II); or

"(dd) to a terrorist organization described in clause (vi)(III), unless the actor can demonstrate that he did not know, and should not reasonably have known, that the act would further the organization's terrorist activity. This clause shall not apply to any material support the alien afforded to an organization or individual that has committed terrorist activity, if the Secretary of State, after consultation with the Attorney General, or the Attorney General, after consultation with the Secretary of State, concludes in his sole unreviewable discretion, that this clause should not apply."; and

(G) by adding at the end the following new clause:

"(vi) TERRORIST ORGANIZATION DEFINED.— As used in clause (i)(VI) and clause (iv), the term "terrorist organization" means an organization—

"(I) designated under section 219;

"(II) otherwise designated, upon publication in the Federal Register, by the Secretary of State in consultation with or upon the request of the Attorney General, as a terrorist organization, after finding that the organization engages in the activities described in subclause (I), (II), or (III) of clause (iv), or that the organization provides material support to further terrorist activity; or

"(III) that is a group of two or more individuals, whether organized or not, which engages in the activities described in subclause (I), (II), or (III) of clause (iv)."; and

(2) by adding at the end the following new subparagraph:

"(F) ASSOCIATION WITH TERRORIST ORGANIZATIONS.—

Any alien who the Secretary of State, after consultation with the Attorney General, or the Attorney General, after consultation with the Secretary of State, determines has been associated with a terrorist organization and intends while in the United States to engage solely, principally, or incidentally in activities that could endanger the welfare, safety, or security of the United States is inadmissible."

(b) CONFORMING AMENDMENTS.—

(1) Section 237(a)(4)(B) of the Immigration and Nationality Act (8 U.S.C. 1227(a)(4)(B)) is amended by striking "section 212(a)(3)(B)(iii)" and inserting "section 212(a)(3)(B)(iv)."

(2) Section 208(b)(2)(A)(v) of the Immigration and Nationality Act (8 U.S.C. 1158(b)(2)(A)(v)) is amended by striking "or (IV)" and inserting "(IV), or (VI)."

(c) RETROACTIVE APPLICATION OF AMENDMENTS.—

(1) IN GENERAL.—Except as otherwise provided in this subsection, the amendments made by this section shall take effect on the date of the enactment of this Act and shall apply to—

(A) actions taken by an alien before, on, or after such date; and

(B) all aliens, without regard to the date of entry or attempted entry into the United States—

(i) in removal proceedings on or after such date (except for proceedings in which there has been a final administrative decision before such date); or

(ii) seeking admission to the United States on or after such date.

(2) SPECIAL RULE FOR ALIENS IN EXCLUSION OR DEPORTATION PROCEEDINGS.—Notwithstanding any other provision of law, sections 212(a)(3)(B) and 237(a)(4)(B) of the Immigration and Nationality Act, as amended by this Act, shall apply to all aliens in exclusion or deportation proceedings on or after the date of the enactment of this Act (except for proceedings in which there has been a final administrative decision before such date) as if such proceedings were removal proceedings.

(3) SPECIAL RULE FOR SECTION 219 ORGANIZATIONS AND ORGANIZATIONS DESIGNATED UNDER SECTION 212(a)(3)(B)(vi)(II).—

(A) IN GENERAL.—Notwithstanding paragraphs (1) and (2), no alien shall be considered inadmissible under section 212(a)(3) of the Immigration and Nationality Act (8 U.S.C.

DID YOU KNOW?

Foreign-Born Individuals Residing in the United States

It is estimated there are approximately 50 million foreigners living in the United States today. Foreign-born individuals residing in the United States fall into various categories. In 2005 11.5 million, or 31 percent of the total, were naturalized citizens; 10.5 million, or 28 percent of the total, were legal permanent residents; 1.3 million, or 3 percent of the total, were temporary legal residents; 2.6 million, or 7 percent of the total, were refugee arrivals; 11.1 million (estimate), or 30 percent of the total, were undocumented workers. In other words, there were more undocumented workers than legal "green card" holders estimated in 2005 (Jeffrey S. Passel, "The Size and Characteristics of the Unauthorized Migrant Population in the US: Estimates Based on the March 2005 Current Population Survey," Pew Hispanic Center [March 7, 2006], 9).

1182(a)(3)), or deportable under section 237(a)(4)(B) of such Act (8 U.S.C. 1227(a)(4)(B)), by reason of the amendments made by subsection (a), on the ground that the alien engaged in a terrorist activity described in subclause (IV)(bb), (V)(bb), or (VI)(cc) of section 212(a)(3)(B)(iv) of such Act (as so amended) with respect to a group at any time when the group was not a terrorist organization designated by the Secretary of State under section 219 of such Act (8 U.S.C. 1189) or otherwise designated under section 212(a)(3)(B)(vi)(II) of such Act (as so amended).

(B) STATUTORY CONSTRUCTION.—Subparagraph (A) shall not be construed to prevent an alien from being considered inadmissible or deportable for having engaged in a terrorist activity—

(i) described in subclause (IV)(bb), (V)(bb), or (VI)(cc) of section 212(a)(3)(B)(iv) of such Act (as so amended) with respect to a terrorist organization at any time when such organization was designated by the Secretary of State under section 219 of such Act or otherwise designated under section 212(a)(3)(B)(vi)(II) of such Act (as so amended); or

(ii) described in subclause (IV)(cc), (V)(cc), or (VI)(dd) of section 212(a)(3)(B)(iv) of such Act (as so amended) with respect to a terrorist organization described in section 212(a)(3)(B)(vi)(III) of such Act (as so amended).

(4) EXCEPTION.—The Secretary of State, in consultation with the Attorney General, may determine that the amendments made by this section shall not apply with respect to actions by an alien taken outside the United States before the date of the enactment of this Act upon the recommendation of a consular officer who has concluded that there is not reasonable ground to believe that the alien knew or reasonably should have known that the actions would further a terrorist activity.

(c) DESIGNATION OF FOREIGN TERRORIST ORGANIZATIONS.—Section 219(a) of the Immigration and Nationality Act (8 U.S.C. 1189(a)) is amended—

(1) in paragraph (1)(B), by inserting "or terrorism (as defined in section 140(d)(2) of the Foreign Relations Authorization Act, Fiscal Years 1988 and 1989 (22 U.S.C. 2656f(d)(2)), or retains the capability and intent to engage in terrorist activity or terrorism" after "212(a)(3)(B)";

(2) in paragraph (1)(C), by inserting "or terrorism" after "terrorist activity";

(3) by amending paragraph (2)(A) to read as follows:

"(A) NOTICE.—

"(i) TO CONGRESSIONAL LEADERS.—Seven days before making a designation under this subsection, the Secretary shall, by classified communication, notify the Speaker and Minority Leader of the House of Representatives, the President pro tempore, Majority Leader, and Minority Leader of the Senate, and the members of the relevant committees of the House of Representatives and the Senate, in writing, of the intent to designate an organization under this subsection, together with the findings made under paragraph

(1) with respect to that organization, and the factual basis therefor.

"(ii) PUBLICATION IN FEDERAL REGISTER.—The Secretary shall publish the designation in the Federal Register seven days after providing the notification under clause (i).";

(4) in paragraph (2)(B)(i), by striking "subparagraph (A)" and inserting "subparagraph (A)(ii)";

(5) in paragraph (2)(C), by striking "paragraph (2)" and inserting "paragraph (2)(A)(i)";

(6) in paragraph (3)(B), by striking "subsection (c)" and inserting "subsection (b)";

(7) in paragraph (4)(B), by inserting after the first sentence the following: "The Secretary also may redesignate such organization at the end of any 2-year redesignation period (but not sooner than 60 days prior to the termination of such period) for an additional 2-year period upon a finding that the relevant circumstances described in paragraph (1) still exist. Any redesignation shall be effective immediately following the end of the prior 2-year designation or redesignation period unless a different effective date is provided in such redesignation.";

(8) in paragraph (6)(A)—

(A) by inserting "or a redesignation made under paragraph (4)(B)" after "paragraph (1)";

(B) in clause (i)—

(i) by inserting "or redesignation" after "designation" the first place it appears; and

(ii) by striking "of the designation"; and (C) in clause (ii), by striking "of the designation";

(9) in paragraph (6)(B)—

(A) by striking "through (4)" and inserting "and (3)"; and

(B) by inserting at the end the following new sentence:

"Any revocation shall take effect on the date specified in the revocation or upon publication in the Federal Register if no effective date is specified.";

(10) in paragraph (7), by inserting "or the revocation of a redesignation under paragraph (6)," after "paragraph (5) or (6)"; and

(11) in paragraph (8)—

(A) by striking "paragraph (1)(B)" and inserting "paragraph (2)(B), or if a redesignation under this subsection has become effective under paragraph (4)(B)";

(B) by inserting "or an alien in a removal proceeding" after "criminal action"; and

(C) by inserting "or redesignation" before "as a defense."

Sec. 416. *Foreign Student Monitoring Program.*

(a) FULL IMPLEMENTATION AND EXPANSION OF FOREIGN STUDENT VISA MONITORING PROGRAM REQUIRED.—The Attorney General, in consultation with the Secretary of State, shall fully implement and expand the program established by section 641(a) of the Illegal Immigration Reform and Immigrant Responsibility Act of 1996 (8 U.S.C. 1372(a)).

(b) INTEGRATION WITH PORT OF ENTRY INFORMATION.—For each alien with respect to whom information is collected under section 641 of the Illegal Immigration Reform and Immigrant Responsibility Act of 1996 (8 U.S.C. 1372), the Attorney General, in consultation with the Secretary of State, shall include information on the date of entry and port of entry.

(c) EXPANSION OF SYSTEM TO INCLUDE OTHER APPROVED EDUCATIONAL INSTITUTIONS.—Section 641 of the Illegal Immigration Reform and Immigrant Responsibility Act of 1996 (8 U.S.C.1372) is amended—

(1) in subsection (a)(1), subsection (c)(4)(A), and subsection (d)(1) (in the text above subparagraph (A)), by inserting "other approved educational institutions," after "higher education" each place it appears;

(2) in subsections (c)(1)(C), (c)(1)(D), and (d)(1)(A), by inserting "or other approved educational institution," after "higher education" each place it appears;

(3) in subsections (d)(2), (e)(1), and (e)(2), by inserting "other approved educational institution," after "higher education" each place it appears; and

(4) in subsection (h), by adding at the end the following new paragraph:

"(3) OTHER APPROVED EDUCATIONAL INSTITUTION.—The term 'other approved educational institution' includes any air flight school, language training school, or vocational school, approved by the Attorney General, in consultation with the Secretary of Education and the Secretary of State, under subparagraph (F), (J), or (M) of section 101(a)(15) of the Immigration and Nationality Act."

(d) AUTHORIZATION OF APPROPRIATIONS.—There is authorized to be appropriated to the Department of Justice $36,800,000 for the period beginning on the date of enactment of this Act and ending on January 1, 2003, to fully implement and expand prior to January 1, 2003, the program established by section 641(a) of the Illegal Immigration Reform and Immigrant Responsibility Act of 1996 (8 U.S.C. 1372(a)).

Document 2: President George W. Bush, Remarks on Signing the Homeland Security Act of 2002

When: November 25, 2002

Significance: President Bush explained the key changes of the Homeland Security Act of 2002.

Thanks for coming. Thanks for the warm welcome, and welcome to the White House.

Today we are taking historic action to defend the United States and protect our citizens against the dangers of a new era. With my signature, this act of Congress will create a new Department of Homeland Security, ensuring that our efforts to defend this country are comprehensive and united.

The new Department will analyze threats, will guard our borders and airports, protect our critical infrastructure, and coordinate the response of our Nation to future emergencies. The Department of Homeland Security will focus the full resources of the American Government on the safety of the American people. This essential reform was carefully considered by Congress and enacted with strong bipartisan majorities.

I want to thank Tom Ridge, the Homeland Security Adviser, for his hard work on this initiative. I want to thank all the members of my Cabinet who are here for their work. I want to thank the Members of Congress who are with us today, particularly those Members of Congress who were essential to the passage, many of whom stand up here on the stage with me. One Member not with us is our mutual friend from Texas, Phil Gramm. I appreciate his hard work. I thank the work of Senator Fred Thompson and Senator Joe Lieberman. I appreciate Zell Miller and Don Nickles' hard work as well. We've got a lot of Members from the House here, and I want to thank you all for coming. I particularly want to pay homage to Dick Armey, who shepherded the bill to the floor of the House of Representatives. I'll miss him. I'm not so sure everybody will. [Laughter] But I appreciate your time here. I thank Tom DeLay for making sure the bill got passed. I thank Rob Portman for his hard work. And I want to thank Ellen Tauscher as well for her leadership on this issue.

I appreciate Kay James of the Office of Personnel Management, who worked so hard to make sure this effort was understood by everybody in our Government. And I want to thank the other administration officials who are here, many of whom are going to be responsible for seeing to it this new Department functions well.

I want to thank all the local and State officials who are here with us today–I see Governors and county judges, mayors–for coming. My own mayor, the Mayor of Washington, DC, I appreciate you coming, Mr. Mayor. I want to thank the local and State law enforcement officials who are here, the chiefs of police and fire chiefs who are with us today. I see the chief of my city now is here as well. Thank you, Mr. Chief, for coming.

I want to thank the union representatives who are here. We look forward to working with you to make sure that your people are treated fairly in this new Department. I want to thank the Federal workers who are here. You're charged with being on the front line of protecting America. I understand your job. We look forward to working with you to make sure you get your job done. I want to thank the President's Homeland Security Advisory Council as well, and thank you all for coming.

From the morning of September the 11th, 2001, to this hour, America has been engaged in an unprecedented effort to defend our freedom and our security. We're fighting a war against terror with all our resources, and we're determined to win.

With the help of many nations, with the help of 90 nations, we're tracking terrorist activity; we're freezing terrorist finances; we're disrupting terrorist plots; we're shutting down terrorist camps; we're on the hunt one person at a time. Many terrorists are now being interrogated. Many terrorists have been killed. We've liberated a country.

We recognize our greatest security is found in the relentless pursuit of these cold-blooded killers. Yet, because terrorists are targeting America, the front of the new war is here in America. Our life changed and changed in dramatic fashion on September the 11th, 2001.

In the last 14 months, every level of our Government has taken steps to be better prepared against a terrorist attack. We understand the nature of the enemy. We understand they hate us because of what we love. We're doing everything we can to enhance security at our airports and power plants and border crossings. We've deployed detection equipment to look for weapons of mass destruction. We've given law enforcement better tools to detect and disrupt terrorist cells which might be hiding in our own country.

And through separate legislation I signed earlier today, we will strengthen security at our nation's 361 seaports, adding port security agents, requiring ships to provide more information about the cargo, crew, and passengers they carry. And I want to thank the Members of Congress for working hard on this important piece of legislation as well.

The Homeland Security Act of 2002 takes the next critical steps in defending our country. The continuing threat of terrorism, the threat of mass murder on our own soil, will be met with a unified, effective response. Dozens of agencies charged with homeland security will now be located within one Cabinet Department with the mandate and legal authority to protect our people. America will be better able to respond to any future attacks, to reduce our vulnerability and, most important, prevent the terrorists from taking innocent American lives.

The Department of Homeland Security will have nearly 170,000 employees, dedicated professionals who will wake up each morning with the overriding duty of protecting their fellow citizens. As Federal workers, they have rights, and those rights will be fully protected. And I'm grateful that the Congress listened to my concerns and retained the authority of the President to put the right people in the right place at the right time in the defense of our country.

I've great confidence in the men and women who will serve in this Department and in the man I've asked to lead it. As I prepare to sign this bill into law, I am pleased to announce that I will nominate Governor Tom Ridge as our nation's first Secretary of Homeland Security. Americans know Tom as an experienced public servant and as the leader of our homeland security efforts since last year. Tom accepted that assignment in urgent circumstances, resigning as the Governor of Pennsylvania to organize the White House Office of Homeland Security and to develop a comprehensive strategy to protect the American people. He's done a superb job. He's the right man for this new and great responsibility.

We're going to put together a fine team to work with Tom. The Secretary of the Navy, Gordon England, will be nominated for the post of Deputy Secretary. And Asa Hutchinson of Arkansas, now the Administrator of the Drug Enforcement Administration, will be nominated to serve as Under Secretary for Border and Transportation Security.

The Secretary-designate and his team have an immense task ahead of them. Setting up the Department of Homeland Security will involve the most extensive reorganization of the Federal Government since Harry Truman signed the National Security Act. To succeed in their mission, leaders of the new Department must change the culture of many diverse agencies, directing all of them toward the principal objective of protecting the American people. The effort will take time and focus and steady resolve. It will also require full support from both the administration and the Congress. Adjustments will be needed along the way. Yet this is pressing business, and the hard work of building a new Department begins today.

When the Department of Homeland Security is fully operational, it will enhance the safety of our people in very practical ways. First, this new Department will analyze intelligence information on terror threats collected by the CIA, the FBI, the National Security Agency, and others. The Department will match this intelligence against the Nation's vulnerabilities and work with other agencies and the private sector and State and local governments to harden America's defenses against terror.

Second, the Department will gather and focus all our efforts to face the challenge of cyber-terrorism and the even worse danger of nuclear, chemical, and biological terrorism. This Department will be charged with encouraging research on new technologies that can detect these threats in time to prevent an attack.

Third, state and local governments will be able to turn for help and information to one Federal domestic security agency, instead of more than 20 agencies that currently divide these responsibilities. This will help our local governments work in concert with the Federal Government for the sake of all the people of America.

Fourth, the new Department will bring together the agencies responsible for border, coastline, and transportation security. There will be a coordinated effort to safeguard our transportation systems and to secure the border so that we're better able to protect our citizens and welcome our friends.

Fifth, the Department will work with state and local officials to prepare our response to any future terrorist attack that may come. We have found that the first hours and even the first minutes after the attack can be crucial in saving lives, and our first-responders need the carefully planned and drilled strategies that will make their work effective.

The Department of Homeland Security will also end a great deal of duplication and overlapping responsibilities. Our objective is to spend less on administrators in offices and more on working agents in the field, less on overhead and more on protecting our neighborhoods and borders and waters and skies from terrorists.

With a vast nation to defend, we can neither predict nor prevent every conceivable attack. And in a free and open society, no Department of Government can completely guarantee our safety against ruthless killers who move and plot in shadows. Yet our government will take every possible measure to safeguard our country and our people.

We're fighting a new kind of war against determined enemies. And public servants long into the future will bear the responsibility to defend Americans against terror. This administration and this Congress have the duty of putting that system into place. We will fulfill that duty. With the Homeland Security Act, we're doing everything we can to protect America. We're showing the resolve of this great nation to defend our freedom, our security, and our way of life.

It's now my privilege to sign the Homeland Security Act of 2002.

Document 3: Proposed McCain-Kennedy Legislation: "Secure America and Orderly Immigration Act" (S 1033/HR 2330), Excerpt

When: 2005

Significance: A bipartisan attempt at comprehensive immigration reform that failed to gain approval.

Titles III and VII (pertaining to new temporary visas and regularization process)

Title III–Essential Worker Visa Program

SEC. 302. ADMISSION OF ESSENTIAL WORKERS.

(a) In General- Chapter 2 of title II of the Immigration and Nationality Act (8 U.S.C. 1181 et seq.) is amended by inserting after section 218 the following:

"ADMISSION OF TEMPORARY H-5A WORKERS

"SEC. 218A. (a) The Secretary of State may grant a temporary visa to a nonimmigrant described in section 101(a)(15)(H)(v)(a) who demonstrates an intent to perform labor or services in the United States (other than those occupational classifications covered under the provisions of clause (i)(b) or (ii)(a) of section 101(a)(15)(H) or subparagraph (L), (O), (P), or (R)) of section 101(a)(15).

"(b) Requirements for Admission- In order to be eligible for nonimmigrant status under section 101(a)(15)(H)(v)(a), an alien shall meet the following requirements:

"(1) ELIGIBILITY TO WORK- The alien shall establish that the alien is capable of performing the labor or services required for an occupation under section 101(a)(15)(H)(v).

"(2) EVIDENCE OF EMPLOYMENT- The alien's evidence of employment shall be provided through the Employment Eligibility Confirmation System established under section 274E or in accordance with requirements issued by the Secretary of State, in consultation with the Secretary of Homeland Security. In carrying out this paragraph, the Secretary may consider evidence from employers, employer associations, and labor representatives.

"(3) FEE- The alien shall pay a $500 application fee to apply for the visa in addition to the cost of processing and adjudicating such application. Nothing in this paragraph shall be construed to affect consular procedures for charging reciprocal fees.

"(4) MEDICAL EXAMINATION- The alien shall undergo a medical examination (including a determination of immunization status) at the alien's expense, that conforms to generally accepted standards of medical practice.

"(c) Grounds of Inadmissibility-

"(1) IN GENERAL- In determining an alien's admissibility as a nonimmigrant under section 101(a)(15)(H)(v)(a)–

'(A) paragraphs (5), (6) (except for subparagraph (E)), (7), (9), and (10)(B) of section 212(a) may be waived for conduct that occurred before the date on which the Secure America and Orderly Immigration Act was introduced;

"(B) the Secretary of Homeland Security may not waive—

"(i) subparagraph (A), (B), (C), (E), (G), (H), or (I) of section 212(a)(2) (relating to criminals);

'(ii) section 212(a)(3) (relating to security and related grounds); or

"(iii) subparagraph (A) or (C) of section 212(a)(10) (relating to polygamists and child abductors);

"(C) for conduct that occurred before the date on which the Secure America and Orderly Immigration Act was introduced, the Secretary of Homeland Security may waive the application of any provision of section 212(a) not listed in subparagraph (B) on behalf of an individual alien for humanitarian purposes, to ensure family unity, or when such waiver is otherwise in the public interest; and

"(D) nothing in this paragraph shall be construed as affecting the authority of the Secretary of Homeland Security to waive the provisions of section 212(a).

"(2) WAIVER FINE- An alien who is granted a waiver under subparagraph (1) shall pay a $1,500 fine upon approval of the alien's visa application.

"(3) APPLICABILITY OF OTHER PROVISIONS- Sections 240B(d) and 241(a)(5) shall not apply to an alien who initially seeks admission as a nonimmigrant under section 101(a)(15)(H)(v)(a).

"(4) RENEWAL OF AUTHORIZED ADMISSION AND SUBSEQUENT ADMISSIONS- An alien seeking renewal of authorized admission or subsequent admission as a nonimmigrant under section 101(a)(15)(H)(v)(a) shall establish that the alien is not inadmissible under section 212(a).

"(d) Period of Authorized Admission-

"(1) INITIAL PERIOD- The initial period of authorized admission as a nonimmigrant described in section 101(a)(15)(H)(v)(a) shall be 3 years.

"(2) RENEWALS- The alien may seek an extension of the period described in paragraph (1) for 1 additional 3-year period.

"(3) LOSS OF EMPLOYMENT-

"(A) IN GENERAL- Subject to subsection (c), the period of authorized admission of a nonimmigrant alien under section 101(a)(15)(H)(v)(a) shall terminate if the nonimmigrant is unemployed for 45 or more consecutive days.

"(B) RETURN TO FOREIGN RESIDENCE- Any alien whose period of authorized admission terminates under subparagraph (A) shall be required to return to the country of the alien's nationality or last residence.

"(C) PERIOD OF VISA VALIDITY- Any alien, whose period of authorized admission terminates under subparagraph (A), who returns to the country of the alien's nationality or last residence under subparagraph (B), may reenter the United States on the basis of the same visa to work for an employer, if the alien has complied with the requirements of subsection (b)(1).

"(4) VISITS OUTSIDE UNITED STATES-

"(A) IN GENERAL- Under regulations established by the Secretary of Homeland Security, a nonimmigrant alien under section 101(a)(15)(H)(v)(a)—

"(i) may travel outside of the United States; and

"(ii) may be readmitted without having to obtain a new visa if the period of authorized admission has not expired.

"(B) EFFECT ON PERIOD OF AUTHORIZED ADMISSION- Time spent outside the United States under subparagraph (A) shall not extend the period of authorized admission in the United States.

"(e) Portability- A nonimmigrant alien described in this section, who was previously issued a visa or otherwise provided nonimmigrant status under section 101(a)(15)(H)(v)(a), may accept new employment with a subsequent employer.

"(f) Waiver of Rights Prohibited- A nonimmigrant alien described in section 101(a)(15)(H)(v)(a) may not be required to waive any rights or protections under the Secure America and Orderly Immigration Act.

"(g) Change of Address- An alien having nonimmigrant status described in section 101(a)(15)(H)(v)(a) shall comply by either electronic or paper notification with the change of address reporting requirements under section 265.

"(h) Bar to Future Visas for Violations-

"(1) IN GENERAL- Any alien having the nonimmigrant status described in section 101(a)(15)(H)(v)(a) shall not be eligible to renew such nonimmigrant status if the alien willfully violates any material term or condition of such status.

"(2) WAIVER- The alien may apply for a waiver of the application of subparagraph (A) for technical violations, inadvertent errors, or violations for which the alien was not at fault.

"(i) Collection of Fees- All fees collected under this section shall be deposited in the Treasury in accordance with section 286(w)."

(b) Conforming Amendment Regarding Presumption of Nonimmigrant Status- Section 214(b) of the Immigration and Nationality Act (8 U.S.C. 1184(b)) is amended by inserting "(H)(v)(a)," after "(H)(i).

(c) Clerical Amendment- The table of contents for the Immigration and Nationality Act (8 U.S.C. 1101 et seq.) is amended by inserting after the item relating to section 218 the following:

"Sec. 218A. Admission of temporary H-5A workers.'"

SEC. 305. MARKET-BASED NUMERICAL LIMITATIONS.

Section 214(g) of the Immigration and Nationality Act (8 U.S.C. 1184(g)) is amended–

(1) in paragraph (1)–

(A) by striking "(beginning with fiscal year 1992)";

(B) in subparagraph (B), by striking the period at the end and inserting "; and"; and

(C) by adding at the end the following:

"(C) under section 101(a)(15)(H)(v)(a), may not exceed—

"(i) 400,000 for the first fiscal year in which the program is implemented...]"

SEC. 306. ADJUSTMENT TO LAWFUL PERMANENT RESIDENT STATUS.

Section 245 of the Immigration and Nationality Act (8 U.S.C. 1255) is amended by adding at the end the following:

"(n)(1) For purposes of adjustment of status under subsection (a), employment-based immigrant visas shall be made available to an alien having nonimmigrant status described in section 101(a)(15)(H)(v)(a) upon the filing of a petition for such a visa—

"(A) by the alien's employer; or

"(B) by the alien, if the alien has maintained such nonimmigrant status in the United States for a cumulative total of 4 years.

"(2) An alien having nonimmigrant status described in section 101(a)(15)(H)(v)(a) may not apply for adjustment of status under this section unless the alien—

"(A) is physically present in the United States; and

"(B) the alien establishes that the alien—

"(i) meets the requirements of section 312; or

"(ii) is satisfactorily pursuing a course of study to achieve such an understanding of English and knowledge and understanding of the history and government of the United States.

"(3) An alien who demonstrates that the alien meets the requirements of section 312 may be considered to have satisfied the requirements of that section for purposes of becoming naturalized as a citizen of the United States under title III.

"(4) Filing a petition under paragraph (1) on behalf of an alien or otherwise seeking permanent residence in the United States for such alien shall not constitute evidence of the alien's ineligibility for nonimmigrant status under section 101(a)(15)(H)(v)(a).

"(5) The limitation under section 302(d) regarding the period of authorized stay shall not apply to any alien having nonimmigrant status under section 101(a)(15)(H)(v)(a) if—

"(A) a labor certification petition filed under section 203(b) on behalf of such alien is pending; or

"(B) an immigrant visa petition filed under section 204(b) on behalf of such alien is pending.

"(6) The Secretary of Homeland Security shall extend the stay of an alien who qualifies for an exemption under paragraph (5) in 1-year increments until a final decision is made on the alien's lawful permanent residence.

"(7) Nothing in this subsection shall be construed to prevent an alien having nonimmigrant status described in section 101(a)(15)(H)(v)(a) from filing an application for adjustment of status under this section in accordance with any other provision of law."

Title VII–H-5B Nonimmigrants

SEC. 701. H-5B NONIMMIGRANTS.

(a) In General- Chapter 5 of title II of the Immigration and Nationality Act (8 U.S.C. 1255 et seq.) is amended by adding after section 250 the following:

"H-5B NONIMMIGRANTS

"SEC. 250A. (a) In General- The Secretary of Homeland Security shall adjust the status of an alien to that of a nonimmigrant under section 101(a)(15)(H)(v)(b) if the alien—

"(1) submits an application for such adjustment; and

"(2) meets the requirements of this section.

"(b) Presence in the United States- The alien shall establish that the alien—

"(1) was present in the United States before the date on which the Secure America and Orderly Immigration Act was introduced, and has been continuously in the United States since such date; and

"(2) was not legally present in the United States on the date on which the Secure America and Orderly Immigration Act was introduced under any classification set forth in section 101(a)(15).

"(c) Spouses and Children- Notwithstanding any other provision of law, the Secretary of Homeland Security shall, if the person is otherwise eligible under subsection (b)—

"(1) adjust the status to that of a nonimmigrant under section 101(a)(15)(H)(v)(b) for, or provide a nonimmigrant visa to, the spouse or child of an alien who is provided nonimmigrant status under section 101(a)(15)(H)(v)(b); or

"(2) adjust the status to that of a nonimmigrant under section 101(a)(15)(H)(v)(b) for an alien who, before the date on which the Secure America and Orderly Immigration Act was introduced in Congress, was the spouse or child of an alien who is provided nonimmigrant status under section 101(a)(15)(H)(v)(b), or is eligible for such status, if—

"(A) the termination of the qualifying relationship was connected to domestic violence; and

"(B) the spouse or child has been battered or subjected to extreme cruelty by the spouse or parent alien who is provided nonimmigrant status under section 101(a)(15)(H)(v)(b).

"(d) Other Criteria-

"(1) IN GENERAL- An alien may be granted nonimmigrant status under section 101(a)(15)(H)(v)(b), or granted status as the spouse or child of an alien eligible for such status under subsection (c), if the alien establishes that the alien–

"(A) is not inadmissible to the United States under section 212(a), except as provided in paragraph (2); or

"(B) has not ordered, incited, assisted, or otherwise participated in the persecution of any person on account of race, religion, nationality, membership in a particular social group, or political opinion…"

SEC. 702. ADJUSTMENT OF STATUS FOR H-5B NONIMMIGRANTS.

(a) In General- Chapter 5 of title II of the Immigration and Nationality Act (8 U.S.C. 1255 et seq.) is amended by inserting after section 245A the following:

"ADJUSTMENT OF STATUS OF FORMER H-5B NONIMMIGRANT TO THAT OF PERSON ADMITTED FOR LAWFUL PERMANENT RESIDENCE

"SEC. 245B. (a) Requirements- The Secretary shall adjust the status of an alien from non-immigrant status under section 101(a)(15)(H)(v)(b) to that of an alien lawfully admitted for permanent residence under this section if the alien satisfies the following requirements:

"(1) COMPLETION OF EMPLOYMENT OR EDUCATION REQUIREMENT- The alien establishes that the alien has been employed in the United States, either full time, part time, seasonally, or self-employed, or has met the education requirements of subsection (f) or (g) of section 250A during the period required by section 250A(e).

"(2) RULEMAKING- The Secretary shall establish regulations for the timely filing and processing of applications for adjustment of status for nonimmigrants under section 101(a)(15)(H)(v)(b).

"(3) APPLICATION AND FEE- The alien who applies for adjustment of status under this section shall pay the following:

"(A) APPLICATION FEE- An alien who files an application under section 245B of the Immigration and Nationality Act, shall pay an application fee, set by the Secretary.

"(B) ADDITIONAL FINE- Before the adjudication of an application for adjustment of status filed under this section, an alien who is at least 21 years of age shall pay a fine of $1,000.

"(4) ADMISSIBLE UNDER IMMIGRATION LAWS- The alien establishes that the alien is not inadmissible under section 212(a), except for any provision of that section that is not applicable or waived under section 250A(d)(2).

"(5) MEDICAL EXAMINATION- The alien shall undergo, at the alien's expense, an appropriate medical examination (including a determination of immunization status) that conforms to generally accepted professional standards of medical practice.

"(6) PAYMENT OF INCOME TAXES-

"(A) IN GENERAL- Not later than the date on which status is adjusted under this section, the alien shall establish the payment of all Federal income taxes owed for employment during the period of employment required by section 250A(e) by establishing that—

"(i) no such tax liability exists;

"(ii) all outstanding liabilities have been met; or

"(iii) the alien has entered into an agreement for payment of all outstanding liabilities with the Internal Revenue Service.

"(B) IRS COOPERATION- The Commissioner of Internal Revenue shall provide documentation to an alien upon request to establish the payment of all income taxes required by this paragraph.

"(7) BASIC CITIZENSHIP SKILLS-

'(A) IN GENERAL- Except as provided in subparagraph (B), the alien shall establish that the alien—

"(i) meets the requirements of section 312; or

"(ii) is satisfactorily pursuing a course of study to achieve such an understanding of English and knowledge and understanding of the history and government of the United States.

"(B) RELATION TO NATURALIZATION EXAMINATION- An alien who demonstrates that the alien meets the requirements of section 312 may be considered to have satisfied the requirements of that section for purposes of becoming naturalized as a citizen of the United States under title III.

"(8) SECURITY AND LAW ENFORCEMENT BACKGROUND CHECKS- The Secretary shall conduct a security and law enforcement background check in accordance with procedures described in section 250A(h).

"(9) MILITARY SELECTIVE SERVICE- The alien shall establish that if the alien is within the age period required under the Military Selective Service Act (50 U.S.C. App. 451 et seq.), that such alien has registered under that Act.

"(b) Treatment of Spouses and Children-

"(1) ADJUSTMENT OF STATUS- Notwithstanding any other provision of law, the Secretary of Homeland Security shall—

"(A) adjust the status to that of a lawful permanent resident under this section, or provide an immigrant visa to the spouse or child of an alien who adjusts status to that of a permanent resident under this section; or

"(B) adjust the status to that of a lawful permanent resident under this section for an alien who was the spouse or child of an alien who adjusts status or is eligible to adjust status to that of a permanent resident under section 245B in accordance with subsection (a), if–

"(i) the termination of the qualifying relationship was connected to domestic violence; and

"(ii) the spouse or child has been battered or subjected to extreme cruelty by the spouse or parent who adjusts status to that of a permanent resident under this section.

"(2) APPLICATION OF OTHER LAW- In acting on applications filed under this subsection with respect to aliens who have been battered or subjected to extreme cruelty, the Secretary of Homeland Security shall apply the provisions of section 204(a)(1)(J) and the protections, prohibitions, and penalties under section 384 of the Illegal Immigration Reform and Immigrant Responsibility Act of 1996 (8 U.S.C. 1367).

"(c) Judicial Review; Confidentiality; Penalties- Subsections (n), (o), and (p) of section 250A shall apply to this section."

(b) Clerical Amendment- The table of contents for the Immigration and Nationality Act (8 U.S.C. 1101 et seq.) is amended by inserting after the item relating to section 245A the following:

"Sec. 245B. Adjustment of status of former H-5B nonimmigrant to that of person admitted for lawful permanent residence."

Document 4: Legal Arizona Workers Act of 2007 (House Bill 2779 version, State of Arizona), Excerpt

Significance: State reaction to perceived inaction of federal government on immigration issue.

House Bill 2779 - AN ACT

AMENDING SECTION 13-2009, ARIZONA REVISED STATUTES; AMENDING TITLE 23, CHAPTER 2, ARIZONA REVISED STATUTES, BY ADDING ARTICLE 2; MAKING APPROPRIATIONS; RELATING TO EMPLOYMENT. (TEXT OF BILL BEGINS ON NEXT PAGE)

H.B. 2779

-1-

Be it enacted by the Legislature of the State of Arizona:

Section 1. Section 13-2009, Arizona Revised Statutes, is amended to read:

13-2009. Aggravated taking identity of another person or entity; classification

A. A person commits aggravated taking the identity of another person or entity if the person knowingly takes, purchases, manufactures, records, possesses or uses any personal identifying information or entity identifying information of either:

1. Five THREE or more other persons or entities, including real or fictitious persons or entities, without the consent of the other persons or entities, with the intent to obtain or use the other persons' or entities' identities for any unlawful purpose or to cause loss to the persons or entities whether or not the persons or entities actually suffer any economic loss.

2. Another person or entity, including a real or fictitious person or entity, without the consent of that other person or entity, with the intent to obtain or use the other person's or entity's identity for any unlawful purpose and causes another person or entity to suffer an economic loss of three thousand dollars or more.

3. ANOTHER PERSON, INCLUDING A REAL OR FICTITIOUS PERSON, WITH THE INTENT TO OBTAIN EMPLOYMENT.

B. In an action for aggravated taking the identity of another person or entity under subsection A, paragraph 1 of this section, proof of possession out of the regular course of business of the personal identifying information or entity identifying information of five THREE or more other persons or entities may give rise to an inference that the personal identifying information or entity identifying information of the five THREE or more other persons or entities was possessed for an unlawful purpose.

C. This section does not apply to a violation of section 4-241 by a person who is under twenty-one years of age.

D. Aggravated taking the identity of another person or entity is a class 3 felony.

Sec. 2. Title 23, chapter 2, Arizona Revised Statutes, is amended by adding article 2, to read:

ARTICLE 2. EMPLOYMENT OF UNAUTHORIZED ALIENS

23-211. Definitions

IN THIS ARTICLE, UNLESS THE CONTEXT OTHERWISE REQUIRES:

1. "AGENCY" MEANS ANY AGENCY, DEPARTMENT, BOARD OR COMMISSION OF THIS STATE OR A COUNTY, CITY OR TOWN THAT ISSUES A LICENSE FOR PURPOSES OF OPERATING A BUSINESS IN THIS STATE.

2. "BASIC PILOT PROGRAM" MEANS THE BASIC EMPLOYMENT VERIFICATION PILOT PROGRAM AS JOINTLY ADMINISTERED BY THE UNITED STATES DEPARTMENT OF HOMELAND SECURITY AND THE SOCIAL SECURITY ADMINISTRATION OR ITS SUCCESSOR PROGRAM.

H.B. 2779

"EMPLOYEE" MEANS ANY PERSON WHO PERFORMS EMPLOYMENT SERVICES FOR AN EMPLOYER PURSUANT TO AN EMPLOYMENT RELATIONSHIP BETWEEN THE EMPLOYEE AND EMPLOYER.

4. "EMPLOYER" MEANS ANY INDIVIDUAL OR TYPE OF ORGANIZATION THAT TRANSACTS BUSINESS IN THIS STATE, THAT HAS A LICENSE ISSUED BY AN AGENCY IN THIS STATE AND THAT EMPLOYS ONE OR MORE INDIVIDUALS WHO PERFORM EMPLOYMENT SERVICES IN THIS STATE. EMPLOYER INCLUDES THIS STATE, ANY POLITICAL SUBDIVISION OF THIS STATE AND SELF-EMPLOYED PERSONS.

5. "INTENTIONALLY" HAS THE SAME MEANING PRESCRIBED IN SECTION 13-105.

6. "KNOWINGLY EMPLOY AN UNAUTHORIZED ALIEN" MEANS THE ACTIONS DESCRIBED IN 8 UNITED STATES CODE SECTION 1324A. THIS TERM SHALL BE INTERPRETED CONSISTENTLY WITH 8 UNITED STATES CODE SECTION 1324A AND ANY APPLICABLE FEDERAL RULES AND REGULATIONS.

7. "LICENSE":

(a) MEANS ANY AGENCY PERMIT, CERTIFICATE, APPROVAL, REGISTRATION, CHARTER OR SIMILAR FORM OF AUTHORIZATION THAT IS REQUIRED BY LAW AND THAT IS ISSUED BY ANY AGENCY FOR THE PURPOSES OF OPERATING A BUSINESS IN THIS STATE.

(b) INCLUDES:

(i) ARTICLES OF INCORPORATION UNDER TITLE 10.

(ii) A CERTIFICATE OF PARTNERSHIP, A PARTNERSHIP REGISTRATION OR ARTICLES OF ORGANIZATION UNDER TITLE 29.

(iii) A GRANT OF AUTHORITY ISSUED UNDER TITLE 10, CHAPTER 15.

(iv) ANY TRANSACTION PRIVILEGE TAX LICENSE.

(c) DOES NOT INCLUDE:

(i) ANY LICENSE ISSUED PURSUANT TO TITLE 45 OR 49 OR RULES ADOPTED PURSUANT TO THOSE TITLES.

(ii) ANY PROFESSIONAL LICENSE.

8. "UNAUTHORIZED ALIEN" MEANS AN ALIEN WHO DOES NOT HAVE THE LEGAL RIGHT OR AUTHORIZATION UNDER FEDERAL LAW TO WORK IN THE UNITED STATES AS DESCRIBED IN 8 UNITED STATES CODE SECTION 1324a(h)(3).

23-212. Employment of unauthorized aliens; prohibition; false and frivolous complaints; violation; classification; license suspension and revocation

A. AN EMPLOYER SHALL NOT INTENTIONALLY EMPLOY AN UNAUTHOR-IZED ALIEN OR KNOWINGLY EMPLOY AN UNAUTHORIZED ALIEN.

B. ON RECEIPT OF A COMPLAINT THAT AN EMPLOYER ALLEGEDLY INTEN-TIONALLY EMPLOYS AN UNAUTHORIZED ALIEN OR KNOWINGLY EMPLOYS AN UNAUTHORIZED ALIEN, THE ATTORNEY GENERAL OR COUNTY ATTORNEY SHALL INVESTIGATE WHETHER THE EMPLOYER HAS VIOLATED SUBSECTION A. WHEN INVESTIGATING A COMPLAINT, THE ATTORNEY GENERAL OR COUNTY ATTORNEY SHALL VERIFY THE WORK AUTHORIZATION OF THE ALLEGED UNAUTHORIZED ALIEN WITH THE FEDERAL GOVERNMENT PURSUANT TO 8 UNITED STATES CODE SECTION 1373(c). A STATE, COUNTY OR LOCAL OFFICIAL SHALL NOT ATTEMPT TO INDEPENDENTLY MAKE A FINAL DETERMINATION ON WHETHER AN ALIEN IS AUTHORIZED TO WORK IN THE UNITED STATES. AN ALIEN's IMMIGRATION STATUS OR WORK

H.B. 2779

AUTHORIZATION STATUS 1 SHALL BE VERIFIED WITH THE FEDERAL GOV-ERNMENT PURSUANT TO 8 UNITED STATES CODE SECTION 1373(c). A PERSON WHO KNOWINGLY FILES A FALSE AND FRIVOLOUS COMPLAINT UNDER THIS SUBSECTION IS GUILTY OF A CLASS 3 MISDEMEANOR.

C. IF, AFTER AN INVESTIGATION, THE ATTORNEY GENERAL OR COUNTY ATTORNEY DETERMINES THAT THE COMPLAINT IS NOT FRIVOLOUS:

1. THE ATTORNEY GENERAL OR COUNTY ATTORNEY SHALL NOTIFY THE UNITED STATES IMMIGRATION AND CUSTOMS ENFORCEMENT OF THE UNAUTHORIZED ALIEN.

2. THE ATTORNEY GENERAL OR COUNTY ATTORNEY SHALL NOTIFY THE LOCAL LAW ENFORCEMENT AGENCY OF THE UNAUTHORIZED ALIEN.

3. THE ATTORNEY GENERAL SHALL NOTIFY THE APPROPRIATE COUNTY ATTORNEY TO BRING AN ACTION PURSUANT TO SUBSECTION D IF THE COMPLAINT WAS ORIGINALLY FILED WITH THE ATTORNEY GENERAL.

D. AN ACTION FOR A VIOLATION OF SUBSECTION A SHALL BE BROUGHT AGAINST THE EMPLOYER BY THE COUNTY ATTORNEY IN THE COUNTY WHERE THE UNAUTHORIZED ALIEN EMPLOYEE IS EMPLOYED. THE COUNTY ATTORNEY SHALL NOT BRING AN ACTION AGAINST ANY EMPLOYER FOR ANY VIOLATION OF SUBSECTION A THAT OCCURS BEFORE JANUARY 1, 2008. A SECOND VIOLATION OF THIS SECTION SHALL BE BASED ONLY ON AN UNAUTHORIZED ALIEN WHO IS EMPLOYED BY THE EMPLOYER AFTER AN ACTION HAS BEEN BROUGHT FOR A VIOLATION OF SUBSECTION A.

E. FOR ANY ACTION IN SUPERIOR COURT UNDER THIS SECTION, THE COURT SHALL EXPEDITE THE ACTION, INCLUDING ASSIGNING THE HEARING AT THE EARLIEST PRACTICABLE DATE.

F. ON A FINDING OF A VIOLATION OF SUBSECTION A:

1. FOR A FIRST VIOLATION DURING A THREE YEAR PERIOD THAT IS A KNOWING VIOLATION OF SUBSECTION A, THE COURT:

(a) SHALL ORDER THE EMPLOYER TO TERMINATE THE EMPLOYMENT OF ALL UNAUTHORIZED ALIENS.

(b) SHALL ORDER THE EMPLOYER TO BE SUBJECT TO A THREE YEAR PROBA-TIONARY PERIOD. DURING THE PROBATIONARY PERIOD THE EMPLOYER SHALL FILE QUARTERLY REPORTS WITH THE COUNTY ATTORNEY OF EACH NEW EMPLOYEE WHO IS HIRED BY THE EMPLOYER AT THE SPECIFIC LOCA-TION WHERE THE UNAUTHORIZED ALIEN PERFORMED WORK.

(c) SHALL ORDER THE EMPLOYER TO FILE A SIGNED SWORN AFFIDAVIT WITH THE COUNTY ATTORNEY WITHIN THREE BUSINESS DAYS AFTER THE ORDER IS ISSUED. THE AFFIDAVIT SHALL STATE THAT THE EMPLOYER HAS TERMINATED THE EMPLOYMENT OF ALL UNAUTHORIZED ALIENS AND THAT THE EMPLOYER WILL NOT INTENTIONALLY OR KNOWINGLY EMPLOY AN

UNAUTHORIZED ALIEN. THE COURT SHALL ORDER THE APPROPRIATE AGENCIES TO SUSPEND ALL LICENSES SUBJECT TO THIS SUBDIVISION THAT ARE HELD BY THE EMPLOYER IF THE EMPLOYER FAILS TO FILE A SIGNED SWORN AFFIDAVIT WITH THE COUNTY ATTORNEY WITHIN THREE BUSINESS DAYS AFTER THE ORDER IS ISSUED. ALL LICENSES THAT ARE SUSPENDED UNDER THIS SUBDIVISION SHALL REMAIN SUSPENDED UNTIL THE EMPLOYER FILES A SIGNED SWORN AFFIDAVIT WITH THE COUNTY ATTORNEY. NOTWITHSTANDING ANY OTHER LAW, ON FILING OF THE AFFIDAVIT THE SUSPENDED LICENSES SHALL BE REINSTATED IMMEDIATELY BY THE APPROPRIATE AGENCIES FOR THE PURPOSES OF THIS SUBDIVISION, THE LICENSES THAT ARE SUBJECT TO SUSPENSION UNDER THIS SUBDIVISION ARE ALL LICENSES THAT ARE HELD BY THE EMPLOYER AND THAT ARE NECESSARY TO OPERATE THE EMPLOYER'S BUSINESS AT THE EMPLOYER's BUSINESS LOCATION WHERE THE UNAUTHORIZED ALIEN PERFORMED WORK. IF A LICENSE IS NOT NECESSARY TO OPERATE THE EMPLOYER'S BUSINESS AT THE SPECIFIC LOCATION WHERE THE UNAUTHORIZED ALIEN PERFORMED WORK, BUT A LICENSE IS NECESSARY TO OPERATE THE EMPLOYER'S BUSINESS IN GENERAL, THE LICENSES THAT ARE SUBJECT TO SUSPENSION UNDER THIS SUBDIVISION ARE ALL LICENSES THAT ARE HELD BY THE EMPLOYER AT THE EMPLOYER'S PRIMARY PLACE OF BUSINESS. ON RECEIPT OF THE COURT'S ORDER AND NOTWITHSTANDING ANY OTHER LAW, THE APPROPRIATE AGENCIES SHALL SUSPEND THE LICENSES ACCORDING TO THE COURT'S ORDER. THE COURT SHALL SEND A COPY OF THE COURT'S ORDER TO THE ATTORNEY GENERAL AND THE ATTORNEY GENERAL SHALL MAINTAIN THE COPY PURSUANT TO SUBSECTION G.

(d) MAY ORDER THE APPROPRIATE AGENCIES TO SUSPEND ALL LICENSES DESCRIBED IN SUBDIVISION (c) OF THIS PARAGRAPH THAT ARE HELD BY THE EMPLOYER FOR NOT TO EXCEED TEN BUSINESS DAYS. THE COURT SHALL BASE ITS DECISION TO SUSPEND UNDER THIS SUBDIVISION ON ANY EVIDENCE OR INFORMATION SUBMITTED TO IT DURING THE ACTION FOR A VIOLATION OF THIS SUBSECTION AND SHALL CONSIDER THE FOLLOWING FACTORS, IF RELEVANT:

(i) THE NUMBER OF UNAUTHORIZED ALIENS EMPLOYED BY THE EMPLOYER.

(ii) ANY PRIOR MISCONDUCT BY THE EMPLOYER.

(iii) THE DEGREE OF HARM RESULTING FROM THE VIOLATION.

(iv) WHETHER THE EMPLOYER MADE GOOD FAITH EFFORTS TO COMPLY WITH ANY APPLICABLE REQUIREMENTS.

(v) THE DURATION OF THE VIOLATION.

(vi) THE ROLE OF THE DIRECTORS, OFFICERS OR PRINCIPALS OF THE EMPLOYER IN THE VIOLATION.

(vii) ANY OTHER FACTORS THE COURT DEEMS APPROPRIATE.

2. FOR A FIRST VIOLATION DURING A FIVE YEAR PERIOD THAT IS AN INTENTIONAL VIOLATION OF SUBSECTION A, THE COURT SHALL:

(a) ORDER THE EMPLOYER TO TERMINATE THE EMPLOYMENT OF ALL UNAUTHORIZED ALIENS.

(b) ORDER THE EMPLOYER TO BE SUBJECT TO A FIVE YEAR PROBATIONARY PERIOD. DURING THE PROBATIONARY PERIOD THE EMPLOYER SHALL FILE QUARTERLY REPORTS WITH THE COUNTY ATTORNEY OF EACH NEW EMPLOYEE WHO IS HIRED BY THE EMPLOYER AT THE SPECIFIC LOCATION WHERE THE UNAUTHORIZED ALIEN PERFORMED WORK.

(c) ORDER THE APPROPRIATE AGENCIES TO SUSPEND ALL LICENSES, DESCRIBED IN SUBDIVISION (d) OF THIS PARAGRAPH THAT ARE HELD BY THE EMPLOYER FOR A MINIMUM OF TEN DAYS. THE COURT SHALL BASE ITS DECISION ON THE LENGTH OF THE SUSPENSION UNDER THIS SUBDIVISION ON

ANY EVIDENCE OR INFORMATION SUBMITTED TO IT DURING THE ACTION FOR A VIOLATION OF THIS SUBSECTION AND SHALL CONSIDER THE FOLLOWING FACTORS, IF RELEVANT:

i) THE NUMBER OF UNAUTHORIZED ALIENS EMPLOYED BY THE EMPLOYER.

(ii) ANY PRIOR MISCONDUCT BY THE EMPLOYER.

(iii) THE DEGREE OF HARM RESULTING FROM THE VIOLATION.

(iv) WHETHER THE EMPLOYER MADE GOOD FAITH EFFORTS TO COMPLY WITH ANY APPLICABLE REQUIREMENTS.

(v) THE DURATION OF THE VIOLATION.

(vi) THE ROLE OF THE DIRECTORS, OFFICERS OR PRINCIPALS OF THE EMPLOYER IN THE VIOLATION.

(vii) ANY OTHER FACTORS THE COURT DEEMS APPROPRIATE.

(d) ORDER THE EMPLOYER TO FILE A SIGNED SWORN AFFIDAVIT WITH THE COUNTY ATTORNEY. THE AFFIDAVIT SHALL STATE THAT THE EMPLOYER HAS TERMINATED THE EMPLOYMENT OF ALL UNAUTHORIZED ALIENS AND THAT THE EMPLOYER WILL NOT INTENTIONALLY OR KNOWINGLY EMPLOY AN UNAUTHORIZED ALIEN. ALL LICENSES THAT ARE SUSPENDED UNDER THIS SUBDIVISION SHALL REMAIN SUSPENDED UNTIL THE EMPLOYER FILES A SIGNED SWORN AFFIDAVIT WITH THE COUNTY ATTORNEY. FOR THE PURPOSES OF THIS SUBDIVISION, THE LICENSES THAT ARE SUBJECT TO SUSPENSION UNDER THIS SUBDIVISION ARE ALL LICENSES THAT ARE HELD BY THE EMPLOYER AND THAT ARE NECESSARY TO OPERATE THE EMPLOYER'S BUSINESS AT THE EMPLOYER's BUSINESS LOCATION WHERE THE UNAUTHORIZED ALIEN PERFORMED WORK. IF A LICENSE IS NOT NECESSARY TO OPERATE THE EMPLOYER'S BUSINESS AT THE SPECIFIC LOCATION WHERE THE UNAUTHORIZED ALIEN PERFORMED WORK, BUT A LICENSE IS NECESSARY TO OPERATE THE EMPLOYER'S BUSINESS IN GENERAL, THE LICENSES THAT ARE SUBJECT TO SUSPENSION UNDER THIS SUBDIVISION ARE ALL LICENSES THAT ARE HELD BY THE EMPLOYER AT THE EMPLOYER'S PRIMARY PLACE OF BUSINESS. ON RECEIPT OF THE COURT'S ORDER AND NOTWITHSTANDING ANY OTHER LAW, THE APPROPRIATE AGENCIES SHALL SUSPEND THE LICENSES ACCORDING TO THE COURT'S ORDER. THE COURT SHALL SEND A COPY OF THE COURT'S ORDER TO THE ATTORNEY GENERAL AND THE ATTORNEY GENERAL SHALL MAINTAIN THE COPY PURSUANT TO SUBSECTION G.

3. FOR A SECOND VIOLATION OF SUBSECTION A DURING THE PERIOD OF PROBATION, THE COURT SHALL ORDER THE APPROPRIATE AGENCIES TO PERMANENTLY REVOKE ALL LICENSES THAT ARE HELD BY THE EMPLOYER AND THAT ARE NECESSARY TO OPERATE THE EMPLOYER'S BUSINESS AT THE EMPLOYER'S BUSINESS LOCATION WHERE THE UNAUTHORIZED ALIEN PERFORMED WORK. IF A LICENSE IS NOT NECESSARY TO OPERATE THE EMPLOYER'S BUSINESS AT THE SPECIFIC LOCATION WHERE THE UNAUTHORIZED ALIEN PERFORMED WORK, BUT A LICENSE IS NECESSARY TO OPERATE THE EMPLOYER's BUSINESS IN GENERAL, THE COURT SHALL ORDER THE APPROPRIATE AGENCIES TO PERMANENTLYREVOKE ALL LICENSES THAT ARE HELD BY THE EMPLOYER AT THE EMPLOYER'S PRIMARY PLACE OF BUSINESS. ON RECEIPT OF THE ORDER AND NOTWITHSTANDING ANY OTHER LAW, THE APPROPRIATE AGENCIES SHALL IMMEDIATELY REVOKE THE LICENSES.

G. THE ATTORNEY GENERAL SHALL MAINTAIN COPIES OF COURT ORDERS THAT ARE RECEIVED PURSUANT TO SUBSECTION F AND SHALL MAINTAIN A DATABASE OF THE EMPLOYERS WHO HAVE A FIRST VIOLATION OF SUBSECTION A AND MAKE THE COURT ORDERS AVAILABLE ON THE ATTORNEY GENERAL'S WEBSITE.

H. ON DETERMINING WHETHER AN EMPLOYEE IS AN UNAUTHORIZED ALIEN, THE COURT SHALL CONSIDER ONLY THE FEDERAL GOVERNMENT'S

DETERMINATION PURSUANT TO 8 UNITED STATES CODE SECTION 1373(c). THE FEDERAL GOVERNMENT'S DETERMINATION CREATES A REBUTTABLE PRESUMPTION OF THE EMPLOYEE's LAWFUL STATUS. THE COURT MAY TAKE JUDICIAL NOTICE OF THE FEDERAL GOVERNMENT's DETERMINATION AND MAY REQUEST THE FEDERAL GOVERNMENT TO PROVIDE AUTOMATED OR TESTIMONIAL VERIFICATION PURSUANT TO 8 UNITED STATES CODE SECTION 1373(c).

I. FOR THE PURPOSES OF THIS SECTION, PROOF OF VERIFYING THE EMPLOYMENT AUTHORIZATION OF AN EMPLOYEE THROUGH THE BASIC PILOT PROGRAM CREATES A REBUTTABLE PRESUMPTION THAT AN EMPLOYER DID NOT INTENTIONALLY EMPLOY AN UNAUTHORIZED ALIEN OR KNOWINGLY EMPLOY AN UNAUTHORIZED ALIEN.

J. FOR THE PURPOSES OF THIS SECTION, AN EMPLOYER WHO ESTABLISHES THAT IT HAS COMPLIED IN GOOD FAITH WITH THE REQUIREMENTS OF 8 UNITED STATES CODE SECTION 1324b ESTABLISHES AN AFFIRMATIVE DEFENSE THAT THE EMPLOYER DID NOT INTENTIONALLY OR KNOWINGLY EMPLOY AN UNAUTHORIZED ALIEN.

23-213. Employer actions; federal or state law compliance

THIS ARTICLE SHALL NOT BE CONSTRUED TO REQUIRE AN EMPLOYER TO TAKE ANY ACTION THAT THE EMPLOYER BELIEVES IN GOOD FAITH WOULD VIOLATE FEDERAL OR STATE LAW.

23-214. Verification of employment eligibility; basic pilot program

AFTER DECEMBER 31, 2007, EVERY EMPLOYER, AFTER HIRING AN EMPLOYEE, SHALL VERIFY THE EMPLOYMENT ELIGIBILITY OF THE EMPLOYEE THROUGH THE BASIC PILOT PROGRAM.

Sec. 3. Employer notice

On or before October 1, 2007, the department of revenue shall provide a notice to every employer that is required to withhold tax pursuant to title 43, chapter 4, Arizona Revised Statutes. The notice shall explain the requirements of title 23, chapter 2, article 2, Arizona Revised Statutes, as added by this act, including the following:

1. A new state law prohibits employers from intentionally employing an unauthorized alien or knowingly employing an unauthorized alien.

2. For a first violation of this new state law during a three year period that is a knowing violation, the court will order the appropriate licensing agencies to suspend all licenses held by the employer unless the employer files a signed sworn affidavit with the county attorney within three business days. The filed affidavit must state that the employer has terminated the employment of all unauthorized aliens and that the employer will not intentionally or knowingly employ an unauthorized alien. A license that is suspended will remain suspended until the employer files a signed sworn affidavit with the county attorney. A copy of the court order will be made available on the attorney general's website.

3. For a first violation of this new state law during a five year period that is an intentional violation, the court will order the appropriate licensing agencies to suspend all licenses held by the employer for a minimum of ten days. The employer must file a signed sworn affidavit with the county attorney. The filed affidavit must state that the employer has terminated the employment of all unauthorized aliens and that the employer will not intentionally or knowingly employ an unauthorized alien. A license that is suspended will remain suspended until the employer files a signed sworn affidavit with the county attorney. A copy of the court order will be made available on the attorney general's website.

4. For a second violation of this new state law, the court will order the appropriate licensing agencies to permanently revoke all licenses that are held by the employer.

5. Proof of verifying the employment authorization of an employee through the basic pilot program, as defined in section 23-211, Arizona Revised Statutes, as added by this act, will create a rebuttable presumption that an employer did not violate the new state law.

6. After December 31, 2007, every employer, after hiring an employee, is required to verify the employment eligibility of the employee through the basic pilot program, as defined in section 23-211, Arizona Revised Statutes, as added by this act.

7. Instructions for the employer on how to enroll in the basic pilot program, as defined in section 23-211, Arizona Revised Statutes, as added by this act.

Sec. 6. Short title

This act shall be known as and may be cited as the "Legal Arizona Workers Act."

(http://www.azca.com/html/pdf/hb2779c.pdf)

Document 5: Transcript of Oral Testimony of Bill Gates, Chairman of Microsoft Corporation, at the U.S. Senate Committee on Health, Education, Labor and Pensions on "Strengthening American Competitiveness for the 21st Century"

When: March 7, 2007

Significance: Business leaders are increasingly worried about America's ability to bring in skilled workers needed by U.S. companies.

SEN. EDWARD KENNEDY (D-Mass.): [In progress...] I'd ask Senator Enzi if he would say a word, we'll go to Patty Murray, and then move on to your comments.

SEN. MICHAEL B. ENZI (R-Wyo.): Mr. Chairman, I thank you for holding this hearing. I think it's at a particularly critical time, and Mr. Gates is an outstanding person to present.

This year marks 50 years since Sputnik went up, and that's the last time that we really had a huge turmoil in this country worrying about engineering. It had a drastic effect on our system of education. It inspired people to be the best....

SEN. KENNEDY: All statements will be part of the record.

Mr. Gates, if Senator Murray doesn't give you a good introduction, we'll make sure we find someone up here that will. (Laughter.) But we're confident that she will. As you well know, she's been one of the great voices in this institution and in our country in terms of supporting innovativeness and creativity and competitiveness. Senator Murray, we're so glad to have you here....

[...BILL GATES: Thank you.

Well, thank you, Senator Murray, for that kind introduction and for your leadership on education and so many other issues that are important to Washington state and the nation.

Chairman Kennedy, Ranking Member Enzi, members of the Committee, I'm Bill Gates and I am the chairman of Microsoft Corporation. I am also a co-chair, with my wife, Melinda, of the Bill & Melinda Gates Foundation. It is an honor for me to appear before you today, and to share my thoughts on the future of American competitiveness. Any discussion of competitiveness in the 21st century must begin by recognizing the central role that technology and innovation play in today's economy. The United States has a great deal to be proud of in this respect. Many of the most important advances in computing, healthcare, telecommunications, manufacturing, and many other fields have originated here in the United States.

Yet when I reflect on the state of American competitiveness, my feeling of pride is mixed with deep anxiety. Too often, it seems we're content to live off the investments previous generations made, and that we are failing to live up to our obligation to make the investments needed to make sure the U.S. remains competitive in the future. We know we must change course, but we have yet to take the necessary action. In my view, our economic future is in peril unless we take three important steps:

First, we must equip America's students and workers with the knowledge and skills they need to succeed in today's knowledge economy.

Second, we need to reform our immigration policies for high skilled workers so that we can be sure our workforce includes the world's most talented people.

And third, we need to provide a foundation for future innovation by investing in new ideas and providing a framework for capturing their value.

Today, I would like to address these three priorities.

First, and foremost, the U.S. cannot maintain its economic leadership unless our workforce consists of people who have the knowledge and skills needed to drive innovation. The problem starts in our schools, with a great failure taking place in our high schools. Consider the following facts:

The U.S. has one of the lowest high school graduation rates in the industrialized world. Three out of 10 ninth-graders do not graduate on time. Nearly half of all African-American and Hispanic ninth graders do not graduate within four years. Of those who do graduate and continue on to college, nearly half have to take remedial courses on material they should have learned in high school.

Unless we transform the American high school, we'll limit the economic opportunities for millions of Americans. As a nation, we should start with the goal of every child in the United States graduating from high school....]

The second major area, and one I want to particularly underscore today, is the need to attract top science and engineering talent from around the globe to study, live and work in the United States.

America has always done its best when we bring the best minds to our shores. Scientists like Albert Einstein were born abroad but did great work here because we welcomed them. The contributions of such powerful intellects [have] been vital to many of the great breakthroughs made here in America.

Now we a face a critical shortage of scientific talent and there is only one way to solve that crisis today: Open our doors to highly talented scientists and engineers who want to live, work, and pay taxes here.

I cannot overstate the importance of overhauling our high-skilled immigration system. We have to welcome the great minds in this world, not shut them out of our country. Unfortunately, our immigration policies are driving away the world's best and brightest precisely when we need them most. The fact is that the terrible shortfall in the visa supply for highly skilled scientists and engineers stems from visa policies that have not been updated in more than 15 years. We live in a different economy now, and it makes no sense to tell well-trained, highly skilled individuals – many of whom are educated at our top universities – that they are not welcome here.

I see the negative effects of these policies every day at Microsoft. In my written testimony, I discuss some of the shortfalls of the current system. For 2007, the supply of H-1B visas ran out four months before the fiscal year even began. For 2008, they will run out even earlier, well before degreed candidates graduate. So, for the first time ever, we will not be able to seek H-1Bs for this year's graduating students. The wait times for green cards routinely reach five years, and are even longer for scientists and engineers from India and China, key recruiting grounds for skilled technical professionals.

The question we must ask is: "How do we create an immigration system that supports the innovation that drives American growth, economic opportunity and prosperity?" Congress can answer that question by acting immediately in two significant ways:

First, we need to encourage the best students from abroad to enroll in our colleges and universities, and to remain here when they finish their studies. Today, we take exactly the opposite approach.

Second, we should expedite the path into our workforce and into Permanent Resident status for highly skilled workers. These employees are vital to U.S. competitiveness, and we should encourage them to become permanent U.S. residents so they can drive innovation and economic growth alongside America's native born talent.

Finally, maintaining American competitiveness requires that we invest in research and reward innovation. Our nation's current economic leadership is a direct result of investments that previous generations made in scientific research, especially through public funding of projects in government and university research laboratories.

American companies have capitalized on these innovations, thanks to our world-class universities, innovative policies on technology transfer, and pro-investment tax rules. These policies have driven a surge in private sector research and development

While private sector research and development is important, federal research funding is vital. Unfortunately, while other countries and regions, such as China and the European Union, are increasing their public investment in R&D, federal research spending in the United States is not keeping pace. To address this problem, I urge Congress to take action.

The Federal Government should increase funding for basic scientific research. Recent expansion of the research budgets at the Department of Energy and the National Science Foundation is commendable, but more must be done. We should also increase funding for basic research by 10 percent annually for the next seven years. Second, Congress should increase and make permanent private sector tax credits for R&D. The United States ranks 17th among OECD nations in the tax treatment of R&D. Without a renewed commitment to R&D tax credits, we may drive innovative companies to locate their R&D operations outside U.S. borders.

We must also reward innovators. This means ensuring that inventors can obtain intellectual property protection for their innovations and enforce those rights in the marketplace. America is fortunate that our leaders recognize the importance of intellectual property protection at home and abroad. I know I join many other Americans in thanking this Congress and this Administration for their tireless efforts to promote such protection. The challenges confronting America's competitiveness and technological leadership are among the greatest we have faced in our lifetime. I recognize that conquering these challenges will not be easy, but I firmly believe that if we succeed, our efforts will pay rich dividends for all Americans. We have had the amazing good fortune to live through a period of incredible innovation and prosperity. The question before us today is: "Do we have the will to ensure that the generation that follows will also enjoy the benefits that come with economic leadership?" We must not squander this opportunity to secure America's continued competitiveness and prosperity. Thank you again for this opportunity to testify. I welcome your questions on these topics....]

[......]....SEN. JUDD GREGG (R-N.H.): Thank you.

Let me join my colleagues in thanking you for your efforts in putting your dollars behind your language, on the issue of education especially. And I agree with you that the issue is at the high school level. And when Senator Kennedy and I were putting together the No Child Left Behind, we focused on math and science because it was a quantitative event, but we didn't get into the high school, because the federal government really doesn't have a role in high school, we don't fund high schools.

The one place we do have a role is in this area of immigration, which you've mentioned. And I'm also in total agreement with your view, which I would characterize, maybe inappropriately, as going around the world and picking the best and the brightest, and having them come to the United States. And that's what we've done as a culture, and we've been very successful.

So, I guess my first question to you is, do you have a number that you think we need relative to the H-1B visa program? Today it's statutorily set at about 65,000, but we're up to 520,000. Do you think that number should be raised to 200,000, 300,000? What would make America—give us the capacity to get the people we need to come here to take advantage of our society, and we take advantage of their abilities?

BILL GATES: Well, my basic view is that an infinite number of people coming, who are taking jobs that pay over $100,000 a year, they're going to pay taxes, we create lots of other jobs around those people, my basic view is that the country should welcome as many of those people as we can get, because people with those great talents, particularly in engineering areas, the jobs are going to exist somewhere, and the jobs around them are going to be created wherever those uniquely talented people are.

So, even though it may not be realistic, I don't think there should be any limit. Other countries have systems where based on your education, your employability, you're scored for immigration, and so these people would not have difficulty getting into other rich countries.

In fact, countries like Canada and Australia have been beneficiaries of our system discouraging these people with both the limits and the long waits and what the process feels like as they go through the security checks.

There are some suggestions about if we could, say, in the green card system not have to count the family members. If you somewhat more than doubled that, you could start to clear the backlog and not have that be a problem.

Likewise, with H-1B, if you had a few categories, like people who are educated here in this country, that you gave an exemption outside of the quota, that somewhat more than doubling would get us what we need.

But to some degree that's sort of like a centrally managed economy, so we'll—

SEN. GREGG: Unfortunately, because my time is going to be up, unfortunately that's what we have here. I agree 100-percent that we shouldn't have a limit on highly skilled people coming into the country, but we do have a centrally managed economy, and right now it's not being managed well.

So, I would presume that if we were to double the number, say, to 300,000, you wouldn't have any problem with that, since you're willing to go to infinity?

BILL GATES: Well, it would be a fantastic improvement. And I do think that there's a draft bill that has provisions that would largely take care of this problem.

SEN. GREGG: We also have something called a lottery system, which allows 50,000 people in the country, simply because they win a lottery, and they could be a truck driver from the Ukraine. And last year I offered an amendment, which would have taken that system and required 60 percent of those to be people with advanced degrees in order to participate in the lottery, so you'd have to be a physicist from the Ukraine before you could win the lottery. Do you think that would be a better approach maybe?

BILL GATES: Well, I don't—I'm not an expert on the various categories that exist, and I don't actually know that lottery system. I know the engineers at Microsoft, nobody comes up to me and says, "Hey, I won this lottery."

SEN. GREGG: Well, that's the problem.

BILL GATES: But there's a lot of different categories in there, and I'm not sure how they should all be handled. But I do know in the case of the engineering situation, we should specifically have that be dramatically increased.

SEN. GREGG: Thank you.

Source http://www.microsoft.com/Presspass/exec/billg/speeches/2007/03-07Senate.mspx

FURTHER READINGS

Burns, Vincent, and Kate Dempsey Peterson. *Terrorism: A Documentary and Reference Guide.* Westport, Conn.: Greenwood Press, 2005.

Clarke, Richard. *Against All Enemies: Inside America's War on Terror.* New York: Free Press, 2004.

Fernandes, Deepa. *Targeted: Homeland Security and the Business of Immigration.* New York: Seven Stories Press, 2007.

Florida, Richard. "America's Looming Creativity Crisis." *Harvard Business Review* (October 2004), 122–136.

Hayworth, J.D. *Whatever it Takes: Illegal Immigration, Border Security, and the War on Terror.* Washington, D.C.: Regnery, 2006.

Lansford, Tom, Robert Pauly, Jr., and Jack Covarrubias. *To Protect and Defend: US Homeland Security Policy.* Aldershot: Ashgate, 2006.

Ramer, Holly. "Immigration a Big Issue to NH, Iowa GOP." Associated Press, December 17, 2007.

Swain, Carol, ed. *Debating Immigration.* New York: Cambridge University Press, 2007.

Torr, James D., ed. *Homeland Security.* San Diego: Greenhaven Press, 2004.

Varma, Roli. *Harbingers of Global Change: India's Techno-Immigrants in the United States.* Lanham, Md.: Lexington Books, 2006.

PART II

CHAPTER 9

Mexico and the U.S. Immigration Debate

David Felsen

In recent decades, the immigration debate has became more racially charged and increasingly viewed as a Mexican issue, largely because Mexicans account for over half of the undocumented workers inside the United States. There is now widespread support for the completion of a border fence between the United States and Mexico, which has caused tension in the bilateral relations between the two countries. Moreover, a key legislative initiative to create a new temporary workers program and a path to legalization recently failed. Meanwhile, state and local governments reacted to perceived federal inaction with ordinances and laws of their own. These have been enforced almost entirely against Mexican workers. Nevertheless, Mexico, in fact, has a long and complex history of immigration to the United States.

MEXICAN MIGRATION TO THE UNITED STATES IN THE EARLY TWENTIETH CENTURY

Large-scale immigration to the United States has generally aroused hostile reactions throughout American history. As we have seen elsewhere, this was the case for the Irish, Germans, Chinese, Italians, Jews, and Slavs who arrived in earlier times. Distinctions are always made between recent immigrants and earlier immigrants who always appear to have integrated more easily. Lost in the immigration debate is the fact that Mexican workers have come to the United States for generations. Mexicans, usually living along the U.S. border, always came to the United States to engage in agriculture and other jobs to make up for U.S. labor shortages.

Furthermore, there was not always such a large influx of Mexican immigrants to the United States. At the turn of the twentieth century, Mexico enjoyed political stability because of the order imposed by Mexico's dictator, Porfirio Diaz, who ruled from 1884 to 1910. This era of relative calm, the so-called *Porfiriato*, stood in marked contrast to the previous years of political upheaval in Mexico. The Porfiriato was an era of rapid industrialization and economic

TABLE 9.1 Immigration by Regions and Selected Countries of Last Residence after World War II

	1951–70	1971–80	1981–90	1991–2002
Europe (total)	2,449,219	800,368	761,550	1,917,403
Asia (total)	580,891	1,588,178	2,738,157	4,990,772
China (incl. Taiwan)	44,421	125,326	346,747	577,868
Philippines	117,683	354,987	548,764	1,003,295
India	29,162	164,134	250,786	547,700
North America (total)	2,713,318	1,982,735	3,615,225	6,550,088
Canada	791,262	169,939	156,938	384,379
Mexico	753,748	640,294	1,655,843	2,718,299
Central America	146,081	134,640	468,088	742,311
South America	349,568	295,741	461,847	899,267
Africa	43,046	80,779	176,893	364,016
Oceania	38,098	41,242	45,205	100,236

Source: Immigration statistics data taken from Ines M. Miyares and Christopher A. Airriess, "Creating Contemporary Ethnic Geographies—A Review of Immigration Law," in *Contemporary Ethnic Geographies in America*, eds. Ines M. Miyares and Christopher A. Airriess (Lanham, Md.: Rowman & Littlefield, 2007), 30–32.

development in Mexico—albeit at the cost of political freedoms and social inclusion of Mexico's ever more marginalized poor and indigenous groups. Yet, for the United States, the lengthy rule of Porfirio Diaz provided security at the southern border, created an economic climate that invited American and European investment, and permitted both countries to get over the mutual antagonism that followed the hostilities of the mid-1800s, most notably the annexation of Texas and the territorial issues from the U.S.-Mexican War.

Nevertheless, President Diaz became increasingly unpopular When opposition mounted after a rigged election in 1910, he soon went into exile in Paris. Thus began the bloody Mexican Revolution, which lasted for a decade, coming a century after the Mexican War of Independence from Spain (1810–1821). The violence produced refugees who came across the

American agriculture's need for low-salaried immigrant migrant workers to harvest crops prompted the massive guest-worker Bracero programs of the 1940s through the 1960s. AP Historic Image.

border into the United States. However, the migration flow was not overwhelming and for the most part not permanent.

Most Mexican refugees and migrants returned home when the political landscape calmed down in the 1920s. The United States, far from expressing hostility to Mexicans arriving, was eager to facilitate and increase the flow of migrants from and cross-border activity with Mexico when the political unrest had ended (Document 1). In 1921 the United States proposed a treaty to open up the border with Mexico and to establish a forty-mile zone on either side where citizens of both countries could freely cross without the need for documentation. The message sent from the U.S. State Department states that:

> Department has under consideration advisability abolishing all passport requirements with respect to residents of 40-mile zones on border, so that persons who have resided in the 40-mile zone on either side of the Mexican border for more than a year prior to entrance into this country, except Russians and hostile aliens, upon satisfying United States authorities at ports of entry of such residence, may enter American border zone without passports or border cards, provided they are otherwise admissible. Proposed plan will be put into effect provided Mexican authorities along border are given corresponding instructions with respect to *bona fide* residents in 40-mile zone who may wish to cross into Mexican zone. No visas will be required under this arrangement.

THE BRACERO PROGRAM

Twenty years later, during the second world war, the United States once again sought an agreement with Mexico to bring Mexican workers into the United States through what became

TABLE 9.2 Braceros in the United States under Contract, 1942–64

1942	4,203
1943	52,098
1944	62,170
1945	49,454
1946	32,043
1947	19,632
1948	35,345
1949	107,000
1950	67,500
1951	192,000
1952	197,100
1953	201,388
1954	309,033
1955	398,650
1956	445,197
1957	436,049
1958	432,857
1959	437,643
1960	315,846
1961	291,420
1962	194,978
1963	186,865
1964	177,736

Source: Taken from Leonard Dinnerstein and David M. Reimers, *Ethnic Americans: A History of Immigration and Assimilation* (New York: Dodd, Mead and Company, 1975), 100.

known as the "*Bracero* Program" (Document 2). The United States sought temporary laborers to work in agriculture, because there was a shortage of workers in the country owing to the war. The agreement was formalized on July 23, 1942. The following year, the agreement was expanded beyond agriculture to allow Mexicans to take on jobs in manufacturing, because the U.S. labor shortage had spread throughout the economy.

One of the interesting points of discussion—especially in the light of today's immigration debate—is the concern that too many Mexicans migrating to the United States might hurt the Mexican economy. The agreement states, "As it is impossible to determine at this time the number of workers who may be needed in the United States for agricultural labor employment, the employer shall advise the Mexican Government from time to time as to the number needed. The Government of Mexico shall determine in each case the number of workers who may leave the country without detriment to its national economy."

The Bracero program was in place until the 1960s and resulted in many thousands of Mexicans coming to the United States—most on a temporary and seasonal basis but some on a permanent basis. Although Mexican migrants, like other minority groups present in the United States, did experience racism during the first half of the twentieth century, overall the American public's perception of Mexican immigrants was not negative. For much of the twentieth century, Mexican labor was viewed as useful manpower for agriculture and industry and not as a threat to border security or to the economic welfare of the country. Indeed, unrestricted Mexican immigration to the United States was supported by an alliance of congressional leaders and business interests—so much so that when the National Origins Plan was established in 1929 to set quotas of immigrants for different countries of the world, Mexico was excluded from the new quota system. (See chapter 6 for a discussion of this subject.)

IMMIGRATION REFORM IN THE 1980s

By the 1960s, most of the immigrants coming to the United States came from the Western Hemisphere—Latin America and Canada. The Immigration Act of 1965 abolished the National Origins system and placed a cap on immigration coming from the Western Hemisphere, including Mexico. But immigration from Latin America, and Mexico in particular, continued to increase. In the 1970s a congressional amendment to limit immigration according to country of origin—with a cap of 20,000—was meant to curb hemispheric immigration, specifically Mexican immigration (LeMay 2006).

The severity of the problem of illegal crossings into the United States from Mexico forced President Reagan and the U.S. Congress to address the issue. Public opinion increasingly felt that undocumented immigration needed to be curbed and that the United States had lost control of its borders. The number of unauthorized aliens living in the United States had grown from hundreds of thousands in the early 1970s to almost 6 million in the 1980s, mostly from Mexico. One of the causes of this rise in the 1980s was the onset of the Mexican financial crisis of 1982, which impoverished millions of Mexicans and encouraged people who had nothing to lose to make the treacherous journey across to the United States.

With the support of President Reagan, in 1986 Congress passed the Immigration Reform and Control Act (IRCA) to improve border controls and cut these crossings. IRCA established a undocumented worker program, and offered a path to legalized status to most of those illegal workers in the country—an estimated 3.5 million people. Business groups largely supported the legislation, although labor groups and anti-immigrant organizations opposed the law (Document 3).

PROPOSITION 187 IN CALIFORNIA

The influx of undocumented workers from Mexico continued to increase in the 1990s. This placed a great burden on social services delivered particularly by the largest states along the southern border. California was by far the most important destination for undocumented workers, and its education and health services were stretched beyond capacity.

It is no surprise then that California was the first state to see an initiative to combat the trend in immigration. "Proposition 187" was put on the ballot for the midterm elections of 1994 (Document 4). It proposed making undocumented workers ineligible for social services, health care (other than emergency services), and public school education. It also required state and local agencies to report people suspected of being unauthorized workers to the California attorney general's office and the federal INS. It also made it a felony to make, distribute, or sell false citizenship and residence documents. There were strong arguments for and against the proposition, while the tensions surrounding the proposition created a spike in anti-Hispanic and anti-Mexican rhetoric. The proposition received 60 percent of the vote and the support of Governor Pete Wilson, but it was overturned by the federal courts because it was considered an encroachment on the federal government's jurisdiction over immigration policy.

Nevertheless, the Clinton administration took note and responded to the growing impatience of states over the issue. The president, helped by the Republican-led Congress, passed the Illegal Immigration Reform and Immigrant Responsibility Act of 1996 (IIRIRA) (PL 104-208). Restrictive provisions not dissimilar to those proposed by Proposition 187 were included in the 1996 act—a curtailment of federal benefits to undocumented immigrants, denial of welfare, Medicaid, social service grants, as well as penalties for fraudulent production and use of U.S. documents, in addition to more border patrol agents and the construction of a border fence along the U.S.-Mexican border at San Diego.

MEXICAN IMMIGRATION IN A POST-9/11 WORLD

In his first months in office, President Bush showed an interest in Mexico and the immigration issue. The president had been governor of Texas, and as a border governor, he appeared to understand well the U.S.-Mexican border and the complexities surrounding the

In the spring of 2006, large but peaceful rallies against punitive immigration legislation took place nationwide, including this march affirming immigrants' commitment to the United States, held in Washington, D.C., in April. AP Photo/Mannie García.

undocumented workers matter. He also developed a good personal rapport with Mexican President Vicente Fox. Within a month of being in office, Presidents Bush joined President Fox in issueing a joint statement in which "the two presidents agreed to instruct appropriate officials 'to engage, at the earliest opportunity, in formal high level negotiations aimed at achieving short and long-term agreements that will allow us to constructively address migration and labor issues between our two countries.'" (Document 5)

Nevertheless, the attacks of September 11 irreversibly altered the focus of U.S. policy. Attempts to find a solution to the 12 million undocumented workers living in the United States were replaced by concerns over border security. Among Republicans and large segments of the American public, opposition grew to any notion of granting an "amnesty" to undocumented workers. The comprehensive reform legislation, proposed during President Bush's second term, called for a guest worker program and a path to legalization. It did not receive the support needed in the Senate to proceed. The House of Representatives passed a bill calling for more enforcement without even considering the situation of undocumented workers. Despite large-scale demonstrations by the Latino community in 2006 and 2007 to support comprehensive reform on immigration, efforts to move forward on the issue failed.

Caught up in this fight was another piece of legislation that had been under consideration in different forms well before the consideration of comprehensive immigration reform. This bill would have helped hundreds of thousands of individuals who had come to the United States from Mexico as children, with no legal status. The proposed United States Development, Relief, and Education for Alien Minors Act (US DREAM ACT) (Document 6) would offer permanent residence to those who had been under 16 years old when they arrived, if they possessed high school diplomas or the equivalent and demonstrated good moral character. As the debate over immigration became more acrimonious, however, support in Congress for this bill waned. Right-wing opponents called the proposal another form of amnesty, and proponents failed to reach the required Senate approval to proceed with the legislation.

Furthermore, following the mid-term election of 2006, states and local authorities stepped into the immigration issue. The actions of many local authorities were not merely anti-immigrant, but anti-Hispanic and anti-Mexican as well. The recent debate has led to a rise in negative sentiment toward all Hispanics—undocumented aliens, legal aliens, and American citizens of Hispanic origin as well. The recent Arizona law and city ordinances discussed in the previous chapter seem directed toward Latinos. There are even cases in which Spanish language and culture have been attacked. In one example of targeting of Hispanics by a local public institution in late 2007, Marshall County Memorial Library in Lewisburg, Tennessee, a library employee named Nellie Rivera proposed holding a bilingual story time where children could hear stories in Spanish. Local townspeople began raising a fuss about the Spanish language reading session and demanded that library books be purchased in English only and that any book donated could be accepted only in English. Nevertheless, other citizens of Lewisburg opposed this racist sentiment and got together and began writing checks earmarked specifically for Spanish-language books (Navarrette 2007).

In another example, the records of the California attorney general's office show that between 2005 and 2006, a period in which the debates and protests over immigration were in evidence, there was a 16 percent rise in hate crimes directed toward Hispanics in California, while in San Diego the number of hate crimes against Hispanics tripled in that period (Carless 2008). The situation clearly has not been helped by the rise in such anti-immigrant militias as the Minute Men and other grassroots protest groups that create a climate that is less conducive to finding solutions to the immigration issue.

CONCLUSION

In 2009 when the new president and Congress begin their mandates, immigration reform will remain a salient matter. Given the number of undocumented workers who now reside in the country, America's concern over border security and worries over the economy, the immigration debate will not go away. Moreover, the centrality of Mexican undocumented workers to the general immigration debate will remain, because over half of all undocumented workers are from our southern neighbor. While a comprehensive reform should be in the interest of all Americans, for both security and economic reasons, it remains to be seen if such reform is politically feasible.

DOCUMENTS

Document 1: Relaxation of Regulations Governing Travel Between the United States and Mexico for Residents in a Forty-Mile Zone on Either Side of the Frontier

When: May 19, 1921–July 4, 1921

Significance: The establishment of a border zone with Mexico following the Mexican Revolution.

811.111/33680: Telegram
The Secretary of State to the Charge in Mexico (Hanna)

WASHINGTON, *May 19, 1921* – 6 P.M.

67. Department has under consideration advisability abolishing all passport requirements with respect to residents of 40-mile zones on border, so that persons who have resided in the 40-mile zone on either side of the Mexican border for more than a year prior to entrance into this country, except Russians and hostile aliens, upon satisfying United States authorities at ports of entry of such residence, may enter American border zone without passports or border cards, provided they are otherwise admissible. Proposed plan will be put into effect provided Mexican authorities along border are given corresponding instructions with respect to *bona fide* residents in 40-mile zone who may wish to cross into Mexican zone. No visas will be required under this arrangement.

Please take up informally with appropriate authorities, pointing out benefit that will result to border business intercourse, and request that the matter be given immediate consideration. Report results.

Hughes

MEXICO
811.111/33709: Telegram

The Charge in Mexico (Hanna) to the Secretary of State

MEXICO, *May 26, 1921* – noon.
[Received 9:45 P.M.]

107. Department's telegram 31 [67], May 19, 6 P.M. Foreign Office states that it agrees to plan in reference and will give instructions "to the end that persons desiring to cross into the Mexican zone shall only be required to sign a document issued by any municipal authority of the 40-mile zone on the American side in

---

DID YOU KNOW?

Unauthorized Workers

It is estimated that about 6.2 million, or 56 percent, of the undocumented workers in the United States are from Mexico, whereas 1.4 million, or 22 percent, are from the rest of Latin America. That means that a total of 78 percent of undocumented workers hail from Latin America. The next largest group of unauthorized workers is from South and East Asia, and they also account for 22 percent of the total—about the same as non-Mexican Latin Americans. Undocumented workers as a whole account for about 4.9 percent of the total civilian labor force. Almost 31 percent of undocumented workers work in the service sector. About 15 percent of the unauthorized workers are employed in production, installation, and repair jobs; 19 percent are in the construction and extractive jobs. Another 8 percent are involved in transportation and material moving. Finally, about 4 percent are involved in farming or farming-related occupations (Jeffrey S. Passel, "The Size and Characteristics of the Unauthorized Migrant Population in the US: Estimates based on the March 2005 Current Population Survey," Pew Hispanic Center [March 7, 2006]).

DID YOU KNOW?

Children of Undocumented Immigrants

The participation in American society by the children of undocumented immigrants is becoming a much more salient issue as a new generation of children grows up without legal status. This is being played out on community college campuses across the nation. Recently, in a widely watched move, the governor of North Carolina, Mike Easley, said on May 8, 2008, that he would encourage community colleges to go ahead and continue admitting the children of undocumented immigrants that meet admission requirements, given that there are no final federal rules on the issue. This contradicts the advice offered by North Carolina's Attorney General Roy Cooper. The difference in opinion between the state governor and the state's top attorney underscores the continuing challenge taking place across states in coming to terms with the growing population of children of undocumented immigrants coming of age and wanting to participate as full members of the society. The failed DREAM Act was meant to solve issues such as these (Gary Robertson, "Easley: Community Colleges Should Admit Illegal Immigrants," *Charlotte Observer* [May 8, 2008]).

which it is stated the bearer has resided within the zone mentioned for at least 1 year prior to his entry into Mexico. Likewise persons residing within the 40-mile zone on the Mexican side shall in the same manner prove their residence before the American authorities."

The Foreign Office requests that it be given ample notice so that the plan may be inaugurated simultaneously in both countries.

HANNA

811.111/33709: Telegram

The Secretary of State to the Charge in Mexico (Hanna)

WASHINGTON, *May 28, 1921 – 6* P.M.
74. Your 107.

Mexican authorities appear to have misinterpreted Department's proposal, which eliminates all documentation with respect to persons who have resided in 40-mile zones for more than a year (except Russians and hostile aliens desiring to enter United States), it being necessary only for such residents, provided they are otherwise admissible, to satisfy port authorities of residence requirement prior to their passage from one zone to the other.

Take matter up again informally with appropriate authorities, and request them to consent to plan as originally presented, to be put into effect beginning June 15, pointing out that American municipal authorities on border are now issuing identifying documents, but that this practice is unsatisfactory.

HUGHES

811.111/33796: Telegram

The Secretary of State to the Charge in Mexico (Summerlin)

WASHINGTON, *June 28,1921 – 1* P.M.
95. Your 137, June 11.

Department is submitting to President for signature Executive Order reading in part as follows:

"On and after July 1, 1921, citizens of Mexico desiring to enter the United States through Mexican Border ports, may do so without presenting to the Control Officers at Border ports any travel document whatsoever, provided such persons have been residents of the forty mile border zone for a period of one year or more and are otherwise admissible; and that such persons are known to the United States Immigration Officials. If such persons are unknown to the United States Immigration Inspectors they will be required to present proof, satisfactory to the Immigration Officers, that they are *bona fide* residents of the forty mile zone."

Order also provides that any alien domiciled in this country who visits 40 mile Border zone of Mexico, may return to this country within 6 months without passport. All other aliens, as well as Mexicans residing without Border zone required to present visaed passports.

Advised Foreign Office informally that it is proposed to put above order into effect as soon as this Government receives definite assurances of reciprocal action by Mexico. Please report by telegraph.

HUGHES

812.111/142

Executive Decree of July 4, 1921, Abolishing Passport Requirements in the Forty-Mile Zone on Either Side of the United States-Mexican Border

ALVARO OBREGON, Constitutional President of the United Mexican States, to its inhabitants make known:

That by virtue of faculties conferred upon me by Fraction one of Article 89 of the Federal Constitution, and

CONSIDERING; – That if the Government of the United States of America is courteously disposed to facilitate the entrance into its territory of Mexican citizens who desire to enter, without the necessity of presenting any form of documents for this purpose, provided that the Mexican citizens have resided for the period of a year or more in a forty mile zone along the frostier, it is just and international reciprocity demands that the Government of Mexico should extend equal facilities to the residents of the United States of America who desire in turn to enter the national territory, except only pernicious foreigners, and, therefore, I have seen fit to decree the following;–

ARTICLE 1. – After July 16 of the present year, citizens of the United States of America who desire to enter the United Mexican States through frontier cities, may do so without presenting to the Immigration Authorities any form of travel documents, provided that such persons have resided for a period of one year or more in a forty mile zone along the frontier, and are otherwise admissible, and moreover, that such persons are known to the immigration officials of the United Mexican States. Foreigners under the same circumstances, with the exception of pernicious foreigners, shall have the same privilege.

ARTICLE 2. – If the persons who desire to enter the national territory through frontier are unknown to the immigration inspectors of the United Mexican States, they will be required to present satisfactory proofs to the immigration authorities mentioned that they are *bona fide* residents of the forty mile zone along the frontier.

ARTICLE 3. – Any foreigner domiciled in the United Mexican States who visits the forty mile zone in the territory of the United States of America may return to Mexico without the necessity of a passport, provided that he does so within six months.

ARTICLE 4. – All other foreigners, as well as citizens of the United States of America, who reside outside of the zone mentioned, are required to present a passport duly visaed.

ARTICLE 5. – Articles 35, 36, 37, 38 and other similar provisions of the immigration inspection regulations, dated February 25, 1918, remain in force.

ACCORDINGLY, I order that this be printed, published, distributed and given due compliance.

Done in the National Palace of Mexico on the fourth day of the month of July of 1921.

(Source: Department of State, "Papers Related to the Foreign Relations of the United States," Papers, 1921, Vol. II, Government Printing Office, 522–827.)

Document 2: Bracero Program and Mexican Workers

When: August 4, 1942

Significance: Mexican workers were needed in the United States during World War II to make up for labor shortages.

Exchange of notes at Mexico, August 4, 1942, with recommendations signed at Mexico, July 23, 1942
Entered into force August 4, 1942
Replaced by agreement of April 26, 1943

56 Stat 1759; Executive Agreement Series 278

The Minister of Foreign Affairs to the American Ambassador
[TRANSLATION]
DEPARTMENT OF FOREIGN RELATIONS
UNITED MEXICAN STATES
MEXICO CITY

No 312 MEXICO, D.F., *August 4, 1942*
MR. AMBASSADOR:

I have the honor to refer to the matter presented by the Embassy worthily in Your Excellency's charge regarding the possibility that the Government of Mexico authorize the departure of Mexican workers for the United States and the conditions under which such emigration can be effected.

This Department considers itself under the obligation, first of all, of pointing out the importance for the country at the present moment of conserving intact its human material, indispensable for the development of the program of continental defense to which the Government of Mexico is jointly obligated and in which, by very urgent recommendation of the Head of the Executive Power, the intensification of activities and especially agricultural production take first rank. Nevertheless, the need for workers which exists in some parts of the United States having been laid before the President of the Republic himself, and the First Magistrate, being desirous of not scanting the cooperation which he has been offering to the Government worthily represented by Your Excellency in the measure that the Nation's resources permit, has been pleased to decide that no obstacles be placed in the way of the departure of such nationals as desire to emigrate, temporarily, for the performance of the tasks in which their services may be required and that no other essential conditions be fixed than those which are required by circumstances and those established by legal provisions in force in the two countries.

For the purpose of determining the scope of this matter it was agreed, as Your Excellency is aware, to treat it as a matter between States, and in order to examine it in all its aspects, it was deemed necessary to hold a meeting of Mexican and American experts, who have just completed their task, having already submitted the recommendations which they formulated and which, duly signed, are sent enclosed with this communication.

The conclusions in reference have been examined with all care, and the Government of Mexico gives them its full approval. I beg Your Excellency to be good enough to take steps that the Government of the United States of America may, if it sees fit, do likewise, in order that this matter may be concluded and that the proper instructions may be issued, consequently, to the various official agencies which are to intervene therein, and in this way the arrangement which has been happily arrived at may be immediately effective.

I avail myself of the opportunity to renew to Your Excellency the assurances of my highest and most distinguished consideration.

E. PADILLA

His Excellency

GEORGE S. MESSERSMITH,

Ambassador Extraordinary and Plenipotentiary of the United States of America, City

The American Ambassador to the Minister of Foreign Affairs

EMBASSY OF THE

UNITED STATES OF AMERICA

No. 503   MEXICO, *August 4, 1942*

EXCELLENCY:

I have the honor to acknowledge the receipt of Your Excellency's Note

No. 312 of August 4, 1942, regarding the temporary migration of Mexican workers to the United States to engage in agricultural work, the subject matter of which was presented by the Embassy some days ago.

Due note has been taken of the considerations expressed in Your Excellency's Note under acknowledgment with respect to the maintenance of indispensable labor within the Republic of Mexico for the development of the Continental Defense Program, especially agricultural production, to which the Government of Mexico is committed. My Government is fully conscious of these commitments and at the same time is deeply appreciative of the attitude of His Excellency President Manuel Avila Camacho for the sincere and helpful manner in which he has extended the cooperation of the Government of Mexico within the resources of the nation to permit Mexican nationals temporarily to emigrate to the United States for the purpose of aiding in our own agricultural production.

In order to determine the scope of the conditions under which Mexican labor might proceed to the United States for the purpose set forth above, it was agreed that the negotiations should be between our two Governments, and Your Excellency was kind enough to arrange for the meeting of Mexican and American representatives to submit recommendations which they have duly completed. Your Excellency was good enough to enclose a copy of these recommendations in Spanish with your Note under reference.

My Government accepts these recommendations as a satisfactory arrangement, and I am authorized to inform Your Excellency that my Government will place this arrangement in effect immediately, and in confirmation thereof I attach hereto the English text of the arrangement as agreed upon.

Accept, Excellency, the renewed assurances of my highest and most distinguished consideration.

GEORGE S. MESSERSMITH
Enclosure
His Excellency
Senor Lie. EZEQUIEL PADILLA
Minister for Foreign Affairs,
Mexico.

[ENCLOSURE]

In order to effect a satisfactory arrangement whereby Mexican agricultural labor may be made available for use in the United States and at the same time provide means whereby this labor will be adequately protected while out of Mexico, the following general provisions are suggested:

1) It is understood that Mexicans contracting to work in the United States shall not be engaged in any military service.

2) Mexicans entering the United States as a result of this understanding shall not suffer discriminatory acts of any kind in accordance with the Executive Order No. 8802 issued at the White House June 25, 1941.

3) Mexicans entering the United States under this understanding shall enjoy the guarantees of transportation, living expenses and repatriation established in Article 29 of the Mexican Labor Law.

4) Mexicans entering the United States under this understanding shall not be employed to displace other workers, or for the purpose of reducing rates of pay previously established.

In order to implement the application of the general principles mentioned above the following specific clauses are established.

(When the word "employer" is used hereinafter it shall be understood to mean the Farm Security Administration of the Department of Agriculture of the United States of America; the word "sub-employer" shall mean the owner or operator of the farm or farms in the United States on which the Mexican will be employed; the word "worker" hereinafter used shall refer to the Mexican farm laborer entering the United States under this understanding.)

CONTRACTS
a. Contracts will be made between the employer and the worker under the supervision of the Mexican Government. (Contracts must be written in Spanish.)
b. The employer shall enter into a contract with the sub-employer, with a view to proper observance of the principles embodied in this understanding.

ADMISSION
a. The Mexican health authorities will, at the place whence the worker comes, see that he meets the necessary physical conditions.

TRANSPORTATION

a. All transportation and living expenses from the place of origin to destination, and return, as well as expenses incurred in the fulfillment of any requirements of a migratory nature shall be met by the employer.

b. Personal belongings of the workers up to a maximum of 35 kilos per person shall be transported at the expense of the employer.

c. In accord with the intent of Article 29 of the Mexican Federal Labor Law, it is expected that the employer will collect all or part of the cost accruing under (a) and (b) of transportation from the sub-employer.

WAGES AND EMPLOYMENT

a. (1) Wages to be paid the worker shall be the same as those paid for similar work to other agricultural laborers in the respective regions of destination; but in no case shall this wage be less than 30 cents per hour (U.S. currency); piece rates shall be so set as to enable the worker of average ability to earn the prevailing wage.

a. (2) On the basis of prior authorization from the Mexican Government salaries lower than those established in the previous clause may be paid those emigrants admitted into the United States as members of the family of the worker under contract and who, when they are in the field, are able also to become agricultural laborers but who, by their condition of age or sex, cannot carry out the average amount of ordinary work.

b. The worker shall be exclusively employed as an agricultural laborer for which he has been engaged; any change from such type of employment shall be made with the express approval of the worker and with the authority of the Mexican Government.

c. There shall be considered illegal any collection by reason of commission or for any other concept demanded of the worker.

d. Work for minors under 14 years shall be strictly prohibited, and they shall have the same schooling opportunities as those enjoyed by children of other agricultural laborers.

e. Workers domiciled in the migratory labor camps or at any other place of employment under this understanding shall be free to obtain articles for their personal consumption, or that of their families, wherever it is most convenient for them.

f. Housing conditions, sanitary and medical services enjoyed by workers admitted under this understanding shall be identical to those enjoyed by the other agricultural workers in the same localities.

g. Workers admitted under this understanding shall enjoy as regards occupational diseases and accidents the same guarantees enjoyed by other agricultural workers under United States legislation.

h. Groups of workers admitted under this understanding shall elect their own representatives to deal with the employer, but it is understood that all such representatives shall be working members of the group. The Mexican consuls in their respective jurisdiction shall make every effort to extend all possible protection to all these workers on any questions affecting them.

i. For such time as they are unemployed under a period equal to 75% of the period (exclusive of Sundays) for which the workers have been contracted they shall receive a subsistence allowance at the rate of $3:00 per day. For the remaining 25% of the period for which the workers have been contracted during which the workers may be unemployed they shall receive subsistence on the same bases that are established for farm laborers in the United States.

Should the cost of living rise this will be a matter for reconsideration. The master contracts for workers submitted to the Mexican Government shall contain definite provisions for computation of subsistence and payments under this understanding.

j. The term of the contract shall be made in accordance with the authorities of the respective countries.

k. At the expiration of the contract under this understanding, and if the same is not renewed, the authorities of the United States shall consider illegal from an immigration point of view, the continued stay of the worker in the territory of the United States, exception made of cases of physical impossibility.

SAVINGS FUND

a) The respective agency of the Government of the United States shall be responsible for the safekeeping of the sums contributed by the Mexican workers toward the formation of their Rural Savings Fund, until such sums are transferred to the Mexican Agricultural Credit Bank which shall assume responsibilities for the deposit, for their safekeeping and for their application, or, in the absence of these, for their return.

b) The Mexican Government through the Banco de Credito Agricola will take care of the security of the savings of the workers to be used for payment of the agricultural implements, which may be made available to the Banco de Credito Agricola in accordance with exportation permits for shipment to Mexico with the understanding that the Farm Security Administration will recommend priority treatment for such implements.

NUMBERS

As it is impossible to determine at this time the number of workers who may be needed in the United States for agricultural labor employment, the employer shall advise the Mexican Government from time to time as to the number needed. The Government of Mexico shall determine in each case the number of workers who may leave the country without detriment to its national economy.

GENERAL PROVISIONS

It is understood that, with reference to the departure from Mexico of Mexican workers, who are not farm laborers, there shall govern in understandings reached by agencies of the respective Governments the same fundamental principles which have been applied here to the departure of farm labor.

It is understood that the employers will co-operate with such other agencies of the Government of the United States in carrying this understanding into effect whose authority under the laws of the United States are such as to contribute to the effectuation of the understanding.

Either government shall have the right to renounce this understanding, giving appropriate notification to the other Government 90 days in advance.

MIGRATORY WORKERS – AUGUST 4, 1942

This understanding may be formalized by an exchange of notes between the Ministry of Foreign Affairs of the Republic of Mexico and the Embassy of the United States of America in Mexico.

MEXICO CITY, the 23rd of July 1942.

(Source: Charles I. Bevans, "Treaties and other international agreements of the United States of America, 1776–1949." Department of State, U.S. Government Printing Office, 1968, 1069–75.)

Document 3: Immigration Reform and Control Act of 1986

When: November 6, 1986

Significance: Offered a path to legalization for millions of undocumented workers during the Reagan era.

An Act to amend the Immigration and Nationality Act to revise and reform the immigration laws, and for other purposes.

Be it enacted by the Senate and House of Representatives of the United States of America in Congress assembled,

SECTION 1. SHORT TITLE; REFERENCES IN ACT.

(a) SHORT TITLE. – This Act may be cited as the "Immigration Reform and Control Act of 1986". "8 USC 1101 note"

TITLE II – LEGALIZATION

SEC. 201. LEGALIZATION OF STATUS.

Immigrants line up at the Mexican Consulate in Chicago to obtain a matrícula card, an identification card issued by the Mexican government to its immigrants to the United States since the 1870s but not until recently used for interactions with U.S. institutions. The City of Chicago in June 2002 voted to recognize the matrícula, allowing its holders to open bank accounts, get library cards, and otherwise participate more fully in U.S. civic life. Undocumented immigrants who carry the matrícula remain prohibited from working and still risk deportation. AP Photo/Stephen J. Carrera.

(a) PROVIDING FOR LEGALIZATION PROGRAM.—(1) Chapter 5 of title II is amended by inserting after section 245 (8 U.S.C. 1255) the following new section:

"ADJUSTMENT OF STATUS OF CERTAIN ENTRANTS BEFORE JANUARY 1, 1982, TO THAT OF PERSON ADMITTED FOR LAWFUL RESIDENCE

"SEC. 245A. "8 USC 1255a" (a) TEMPORARY RESIDENT STATUS.—The Attorney General shall adjust the status of an alien to that of an alien lawfully admitted for temporary residence if the alien meets the following requirements:

"(1) TIMELY APPLICATION.—

"(A) DURING APPLICATION PERIOD.—Except as provided in subparagraph (B), the alien must apply for such adjustment during the 12-month period beginning on a date (not later than 180 days after the date of enactment of this section) designated by the Attorney General.

"(B) APPLICATION WITHIN 30 DAYS OF SHOW-CAUSE ORDER.—An alien who, at any time during the first 11 months of the 12-month period described in subparagraph (A), is the subject of an order to show cause issued under section 242, "8 USC 1252" must make application under this section not later than the end of the 30-day period beginning either on the first day of such 18-month period or on the date of the issuance of such order, whichever day is later.

"(C) INFORMATION INCLUDED IN APPLICATION.—Each application under this subsection shall contain such information as the Attorney General may require, including information on living relatives of the applicant with respect to whom a petition for preference or other status may be filed by the applicant at any later date under section 204(a). "8 USC 1154"

"(2) CONTINUOUS UNLAWFUL RESIDENCE SINCE 1982.—

"(A) IN GENERAL.—The alien must establish that he entered the United States before January 1, 1982, and that he has resided continuously in the United States in an unlawful status since such date and through the date the application is filed under this subsection.

"(B) NONIMMIGRANTS.—In the case of an alien who entered the United States as a nonimmigrant before January 1, 1982, the alien must establish that the alien's period of authorized stay as a nonimmigrant expired before such date through the passage of time or the alien's unlawful status was known to the Government as of such date.

"(C) EXCHANGE VISITORS.—If the alien was at any time a nonimmigrant exchange alien (as defined in section 101(a)(15)(J)), "8 USC 1101" the alien must establish that the alien was not subject to the two-year foreign residence requirement of section 212(e) "8 USC 1182" or has fulfilled that requirement or received a waiver thereof.

"(3) CONTINUOUS PHYSICAL PRESENCE SINCE ENACTMENT.—

"(A) IN GENERAL.—The alien must establish that the alien has been continuously physically present in the United States since the date of the enactment of this section.

"(B) TREATMENT OF BRIEF, CASUAL, AND INNOCENT ABSENCES.—An alien shall not be considered to have failed to maintain continuous physical presence in the United States for purposes of subparagraph (A) by virtue of brief, casual, and innocent absences from the United States.

"(C) ADMISSIONS.—Nothing in this section shall be construed as authorizing an alien to apply for admission to, or to be admitted to, the United States in order to apply for adjustment of status under this subsection.

"(4) ADMISSIBLE AS IMMIGRANT.—The alien must establish that he—

"(A) is admissible to the United States as an immigrant, except as otherwise provided under subsection (d)(2),

"(B) has not been convicted of any felony or of three or more misdemeanors committed in the United States,

"(C) has not assisted in the persecution of any person or persons on account of race, religion, nationality, membership in a particular social group, or political opinion, and

"(D) is registered or registering under the Military Selective Service Act, "50 USC app. 451" if the alien is required to be so registered under that Act.

For purposes of this subsection, an alien in the status of a Cuban and Haitian entrant described in paragraph (1) or (2)(A) of section 501(e) of Public Law 96-422 "8 USC 1522 note" shall be considered to have entered the United States and to be in an unlawful status in the United States.

"(b) SUBSEQUENT ADJUSTMENT TO PERMANENT RESIDENCE AND NATURE OF TEMPORARY RESIDENT STATUS.—

"(1) ADJUSTMENT TO PERMANENT RESIDENCE.—The Attorney General shall adjust the status of any alien provided lawful temporary resident status under subsection (a) to that of an alien lawfully admitted for permanent residence if the alien meets the following requirements:

"(A) TIMELY APPLICATION AFTER ONE YEAR'S RESIDENCE.—The alien must apply for such adjustment during the one-year period beginning with the nineteenth month that begins after the date the alien was granted such temporary resident status.

"(B) CONTINUOUS RESIDENCE.—

"(i) IN GENERAL.—The alien must establish that he has continuously resided in the United States since the date the alien was granted such temporary resident status.

"(ii) TREATMENT OF CERTAIN ABSENCES.—An alien shall not be considered to have lost the continuous residence referred to in clause (i) by reason of an absence from the United States permitted under paragraph (3)(A).

"(C) ADMISSIBLE AS IMMIGRANT.—The alien must establish that he—

"(i) is admissible to the United States as an immigrant, except as otherwise provided under subsection (d)(2), and

"(ii) has not been convicted of any felony or three or more misdemeanors committed in the United States.

"(D) BASIC CITIZENSHIP SKILLS.—

"(i) IN GENERAL.—The alien must demonstrate that he either—

"(I) meets the requirements of section 312 "8 USC 1423" (relating to minimal understanding of ordinary English and a knowledge and understanding of the history and government of the United States), or

"(II) is satisfactorily pursuing a course of study (recognized by the Attorney General) to achieve such an understanding of English and such a knowledge and understanding of the history and government of the United States.

"(ii) EXCEPTION FOR ELDERLY INDIVIDUALS.—The Attorney General may, in his discretion, waive all or part of the requirements of clause (i) in the case of an alien who is 65 years of age or older.

"(iii) RELATION TO NATURALIZATION EXAMINATION.—In accordance with regulations of the Attorney General, an alien who has demonstrated under clause (i)(I) that the alien meets the requirements of section 312 may be considered to have satisfied the requirements of that section "8 USC 1401" for purposes of becoming naturalized as a citizen of the United States under title III.

"(2) TERMINATION OF TEMPORARY RESIDENCE.—The Attorney General shall provide for termination of temporary resident status granted an alien under subsection (a)—

"(A) if it appears to the Attorney General that the alien was in fact not eligible for such status; v(B) if the alien commits an act that (i) makes the alien inadmissible to the United States as an immigrant, except as otherwise provided under subsection (d)(2), or (ii) is convicted of any felony or three or more misdemeanors committed in the United States; or

"(C) at the end of the thirty-first month beginning after the date the alien is granted such status, unless the alien has filed an application for adjustment of such status pursuant to paragraph (1) and such application has not been denied.

"(3) AUTHORIZED TRAVEL AND EMPLOYMENT DURING TEMPORARY RESIDENCE.—During the period an alien is in lawful temporary resident status granted under subsection (a)—

"(A) AUTHORIZATION OF TRAVEL ABROAD.—The Attorney General shall, in accordance with regulations, permit the alien to return to the United States after such brief and casual trips abroad as reflect an intention on the part of the alien to adjust to lawful permanent resident status under paragraph (1) and after brief temporary trips abroad occasioned by a family obligation involving an occurrence such as the illness or death of a close relative or other family need.

"(B) AUTHORIZATION OF EMPLOYMENT.—The Attorney General shall grant the alien authorization to engage in employment in the United States and provide to that alien an 'employment authorized" endorsement or other appropriate work permit.

"(c) APPLICATIONS FOR ADJUSTMENT OF STATUS.—

"(1) TO WHOM MAY BE MADE.—The Attorney General shall provide that applications for adjustment of status under subsection (a) may be filed—

"(A) with the Attorney General, or

"(B) with a qualified designated entity, but only if the applicant consents to the forwarding of the application to the Attorney General.

As used in this section, the term "qualified designated entity" means an organization or person designated under paragraph (2).

"(2) DESIGNATION OF QUALIFIED ENTITIES TO RECEIVE APPLICATIONS.— For purposes of assisting in the program of legalization provided under this section, the Attorney General—

"(A) shall designate qualified voluntary organizations and other qualified State, local, and community organizations, and

"(B) may designate such other persons as the Attorney General determines are qualified and have substantial experience, demonstrated competence, and traditional long-term involvement in the preparation and submittal of applications for adjustment of status under section 209 or 245, "8 USC 1159, 1255" Public Law 89-732, or Public Law 95-145.

"(3) TREATMENT OF APPLICATIONS BY DESIGNATED ENTITIES.—"8 USC 1255 note" Each qualified designated entity must agree to forward to the Attorney General applications filed with it in accordance with paragraph (1)(B) but not to forward to the Attorney General applications filed with it unless the applicant has consented to such forwarding. No such entity may make a determination required by this section to be made by the Attorney General.

"(4) LIMITATION ON ACCESS TO INFORMATION.—Files and records of qualified designated entities relating to an alien's seeking assistance or information with respect to filing an application under this section are confidential and the Attorney General and the Service shall not have access to such files or records relating to an alien without the consent of the alien.

"(5) CONFIDENTIALITY OF INFORMATION.—Neither the Attorney General, nor any other official or employee of the Department of Justice, or bureau or agency thereof, may—

"(A) use the information furnished pursuant to an application filed under this section for any purpose other than to make a determination on the application or for enforcement of paragraph (6),

"(B) make any publication whereby the information furnished by any particular individual can be identified, or

"(C) permit anyone other than the sworn officers and employees of the Department or bureau or agency or, with respect to applications filed with a designated entity, that designated entity, to examine individual applications.

Anyone who uses, publishes, or permits information to be examined in violation of this paragraph shall be fined in accordance with title 18, United States Code, or imprisoned not more than five years, or both.

"(6) PENALTIES FOR FALSE STATEMENTS IN APPLICATIONS.—Whoever files an application for adjustment of status under this section and knowingly and willfully falsifies, misrepresents, conceals, or covers up a material fact or makes any false, fictitious, or fraudulent statements or representations, or makes or uses any false writing or document knowing the same to contain any false, fictitious, or fraudulent statement or entry, shall be fined in accordance with title 18, United States Code, or imprisoned not more than five years, or both.

"(7) APPLICATION FEES.—

"(A) FEE SCHEDULE.—The Attorney General shall provide for a schedule of fees to be charged for the filing of applications for adjustment under subsection (a) or (b)(1).

"(B) USE OF FEES.—The Attorney General shall deposit payments received under this paragraph in a separate account and amounts in such account shall be available, without fiscal year limitation, to cover administrative and other expenses incurred in connection with the review of applications filed under this section.

"(d) WAIVER OF NUMERICAL LIMITATIONS AND CERTAIN GROUNDS FOR EXCLUSION.—

"(1) NUMERICAL LIMITATIONS DO NOT APPLY.—The numerical limitations of sections 201 and 202 "8 USC 1151, 1152" shall not apply to the adjustment of aliens to lawful permanent resident status under this section.

"(2) WAIVER OF GROUNDS FOR EXCLUSION.—In the determination of an alien's admissibility under subsections (a)(4)(A), (b)(1)(C)(i), and (b)(2)(B)—

"(A) GROUNDS OF EXCLUSION NOT APPLICABLE.—The provisions of paragraphs (14), (20), (21), (25), and (32) of section 212(a) "8 USC 1182" shall not apply.

"(B) WAIVER OF OTHER GROUNDS.—

"(i) IN GENERAL.—Except as provided in clause (ii), the Attorney General may waive any other provision of section 212(a) in the case of individual aliens for humanitarian purposes, to assure family unity, or when it is otherwise in the public interest.

"(ii) GROUNDS THAT MAY NOT BE WAIVED.—The following provisions of section 212(a) may not be waived by the Attorney General under clause (i):

"(I) Paragraphs (9) and (10) (relating to criminals).

"(II) Paragraph (15) (relating to aliens likely to become public charges) insofar as it relates to an application for adjustment to permanent residence by an alien other than an alien who is eligible for "42 USC 1381" benefits under title XVI of the Social Security Act or section 212 "42 USC 1382 note" of Public Law 93-66 for the month in which such alien is granted lawful temporary residence status under subsection (a).

"(III) Paragraph (23) relating to drug offenses), except for so much of such paragraph as relates to a single offense of simple possession of 30 grams or less of marihuana.

"(IV) Paragraphs (27), (28), and (29) (relating to national security and members of certain organizations).

"(V) Paragraph (33) (relating to those who assisted in the Nazi persecutions).

"(iii) SPECIAL RULE FOR DETERMINATION OF PUBLIC CHARGE.—An alien is not ineligible for adjustment of status under this section due to being inadmissible under section 212(a)(15) "8 USC 1182" if the alien demonstrates a history of employment in the United States evidencing self-support without receipt of public cash assistance.

"(C) MEDICAL EXAMINATION.—The alien shall be required, at the alien's expense, to undergo such a medical examination (including a determination of immunization status) as is appropriate and conforms to generally accepted professional standards of medical practice.

"(e) TEMPORARY STAY OF DEPORTATION AND WORK AUTHORIZATION FOR CERTAIN APPLICANTS.—

"(1) BEFORE APPLICATION PERIOD.—The Attorney General shall provide that in the case of an alien who is apprehended before the beginning of the application period described in subsection (a)(1)(A) and who can establish a prima facie case of eligibility to have his status adjusted under subsection (a) (but for the fact that he may not apply for such adjustment until the beginning of such period), until the alien has had the opportunity during the first 30 days of the application period to complete the filing of an application for adjustement, the alien—

"(A) may not be deported, and

"(B) shall be granted authorization to engage in employment in the United States and be provided an 'employment authorized' endorsement or other appropriate work permit.

"(2) DURING APPLICATION PERIOD.—The Attorney General shall provide that in the case of an alien who presents a prima facie application for adjustment of status under subsection (a) during the application period, and until a final determination on the application has been made in accordance with this section, the alien—

"(A) may not be deported, and

"(B) shall be granted authorization to engage in employment in the United States and be provided an 'employment authorized' endorsement or other appropriate work permit.

"(f) ADMINISTRATIVE AND JUDICIAL REVIEW.—

"(1) ADMINISTRATIVE AND JUDICIAL REVIEW.—There shall be no administrative or judicial review of a determination respecting an application for adjustment of status under this section except in accordance with this subsection.

"(2) NO REVIEW FOR LATE FILINGS.—No denial of adjustment of status under this section based on a late filing of an application for such adjustment may be reviewed by a court of the United States or of any State or reviewed in any administrative proceeding of the United States Government.

"(3) ADMINISTRATIVE REVIEW.—

"(A) SINGLE LEVEL OF ADMINISTRATIVE APPELLATE REVIEW.—The Attorney General shall establish an appellate authority to provide for a single level of administrative appellate review of a determination described in paragraph (1).

"(B) STANDARD FOR REVIEW.—Such administrative appellate review shall be based solely upon the administrative record established at the time of the determination on the application and upon such additional or newly discovered evidence as may not have been available at the time of the determination.

"(4) JUDICIAL REVIEW.—

"(A) LIMITATION TO REVIEW OF DEPORTATION.—There shall be judicial review of such a denial only in the judicial review of an order of deportation under section 106. "8 USC 1105a"

"(B) STANDARD FOR JUDICIAL REVIEW.—Such judicial review shall be based solely upon the administrative record established at the time of the review by the appellate authority and the findings of fact and determinations contained in such record shall be conclusive unless the applicant can establish abuse of discretion or that the findings are directly contrary to clear and convincing facts contained in the record considered as a whole.

"(g) IMPLEMENTATION OF SECTION.—

"(1) REGULATIONS.—The Attorney General, after consultation with the Committees on the Judiciary of the House of Representatives and of the Senate, shall prescribe—

"(A) regulations establishing a definition of the term 'resided continuously,' as used in this section, and the evidence needed to establish that an alien has resided continuously in the United States for purposes of this section, and

"(B) such other regulations as may be necessary to carry out this section.

"(2) CONSIDERATIONS.—In prescribing regulations described in paragraph (1)(A)—

"(A) PERIODS of CONTINUOUS RESIDENCE.—The Attorney General shall specify individual periods, and aggregate periods, of absence from the United States which will be considered to break a period of continuous residence in the United States and shall take into account absences due merely to brief and casual trips abroad.

"(B) ABSENCES CAUSED BY DEPORTATION OR ADVANCED PAROLE.—The Attorney General shall provide that—

"(i) an alien shall not be considered to have resided continuously in the United States, if, during any period for which continuous residence is required, the alien was outside the United States as a result of a departure under an order of deportation, and

"(ii) any period of time during which an alien is outside the United States pursuant to the advance parole procedures of the Service shall not be considered as part of the period of time during which an alien is outside the United States for purposes of this section.

"(C) WAIVERS OF CERTAIN ABSENCES.—The Attorney General may provide for a waiver, in the discretion of the Attorney General, of the periods specified under subparagraph (A) in the case of an absence from the United States due merely to a brief temporary trip abroad required by emergency or extenuating circumstances outside the control of the alien.

"(D) USE OF CERTAIN DOCUMENTATION.—The Attorney General shall require that—

"(i) continuous residence and physical presence in the United States must be established through documents, together with independent corroboration of the information contained in such documents, and

"(ii) the documents provided under clause (i) be employment-related if employment-related documents with respect to the alien are available to the applicant.

"(3) INTERIM FINAL REGULATIONS.—Regulations prescribed under this section may be prescribed to take effect on an interim final basis if the Attorney General determines that this is necessary in order to implement this section in a timely manner.

"(h) TEMPORARY DISQUALIFICATION OF NEWLY LEGALIZED ALIENS FROM RECEIVING CERTAIN PUBLIC WELFARE ASSISTANCE.—

"(1) IN GENERAL.—During the five-year period beginning on the date an alien was granted lawful temporary resident status under subsection (a), and notwithstanding any other provision of law—

"(A) except as provided in paragraphs (2) and (3), the alien is not eligible for—

"(i) any program of financial assistance furnished under Federal law (whether through grant, loan, guarantee, or otherwise) on the basis of financial need, as such programs are identified by the Attorney General in consultation with other appropriate heads of the various departments and agencies of Government (but in any event including the program of aid to families with dependent children under part A of title IV of the Social Security Act), "42 USC 601"

"(ii) medical assistance under a State plan approved under title XIX of the Social Security Act, "42 USC 1396" and

"(iii) assistance under the Food Stamp Act "7 USC 2026" of 1977; and

"(B) a State or political subdivision therein may, to the extent consistent with subparagraph (A) and paragraphs (2) and (3), provide that the alien is not eligible for the programs of financial assistance or for medical assistance described in subparagraph (A)(ii) furnished under the law of that State or political subdivision.

Unless otherwise specifically provided by this section or other law, an alien in temporary lawful residence status granted under subsection (a) shall not be considered (for purposes of any law of a State or political subdivision providing for a program of financial assistance) to be permanently residing in the United States under color of law.

"(2) EXCEPTIONS.—Paragraph (1) shall not apply—

"(A) to a Cuban and Haitian entrant (as defined in paragraph (1) or (2)(A) of section 501(e) "8 USC 1255 note" of Public Law 96-422, as in effect on April 1, 1983), or

"(B) in the case of assistance (other than aid to families with dependent children) which is furnished to an alien who is an aged, blind, or disabled individual as defined in section 1614(a)(1) of the Social Security Act).

"(3) RESTRICTED MEDICAID BENEFITS.—

"(A) CLARIFICATION OF ENTITLEMENT.—Subject to the restrictions under subparagraph (B), for the purpose of providing aliens with eligibility to receive medical assistance—

"(i) paragraph (1) shall not apply,

"(ii) aliens who would be eligible for medical assistance but for the provisions of paragraph (1) shall be deemed, for purposes of title XIX of the Social Security Act, "42 USC 1396" to be so eligible, and

"(iii) aliens lawfully admitted for temporary residence under this section, such status not having changed, shall be considered to be permanently residing in the United States under color of law.

"(B) RESTRICTION OF BENEFITS.—

"(i) LIMITATION TO EMERGENCY SERVICES AND SERVICES FOR PREGNANT WOMEN.—Notwithstanding any provision of title XIX of the Social Security Act (including subparagraphs (B) and (C) of section 1902(a)(10) of such Act), aliens who, but for subparagraph (A), would be ineligible for medical assistance under paragraph (1), are only eligible for such assistance with respect to—

"(I) emergency services (as defined for purposes of section 1916(a)(2)(D) of the Social Security Act), and

"(II) services described in section 1916(a)(2)(B) of such Act (relating to service for pregnant women).

"(ii) NO RESTRICTION FOR EXEMPT ALIENS AND CHILDREN.—The restrictions of clause (i) shall not apply to aliens who are described in paragraph (2) or who are under 18 years of age.

"(C) DEFINITION OF MEDICAL ASSISTANCE.—In this paragraph, the term 'medical assistance' refers to medical assistance under a State plan approved under title XIX of the Social Security Act. "42 USC 1396"

"(4) TREATMENT OF CERTAIN PROGRAMS.—Assistance furnished under any of the following provisions of law shall not be construed to be financial assistance described in paragraph (1)(A)(i):

"(A) The National School Lunch Act. "42 USC 1751 note"

"(B) The Child Nutrition Act of 1966.

"(C) The Vocational Education Act of 1963. "42 USC 1771 note"

"(D) Chapter 1 of the Education Consolidation and Improvement Act of 1981. "20 USC 2301 note"

"(E) The Headstart-Follow Through Act. "20 USC 3801 et seq"

"(F) The Job Training Partnership Act. "42 USC 2921"

"(G) Title IV of the Higher Education Act of 1965. "29 USC 1501 note"

"(H) The Public Health Service Act. "20 USC 1070"

"(I) Titles V, XVI, and XX, and parts B, D, and E of title IV, of the Social Security Act "42 USC 201 note" (and titles I, X, XIV, and XVI of such Act "42 USC 701, 1381, 1397, 620, 651, 670" as in effect without regard to the amendment made by section 301 of the Social Security Amendments of 1972). "42 USC 301, 1201, 1351, 1381"

"(5) ADJUSTMENT NOT AFFECTING FASCELL-STONE BENEFITS.—For the purpose of section 501 "42 USC 1381-1383e" of the Refugee Education Assistance Act of 1980 "8 USC 1522 note" (Public Law 96-122), assistance shall be continued under such section with respect to an alien without regard to the alien's adjustment of status under this section.

"(i) DISSEMINATION OF INFORMATION ON LEGALIZATION PROGRAM.— Beginning not later than the date designated by the Attorney General under subsection (a)(1)(A), the Attorney General, in cooperation with qualified designated entities, shall broadly disseminate information respecting the benefits which aliens may receive under this section and the requirements to obtain such benefits."

(2) The table of contents for chapter 5 of title II is amended by inserting after the item relating to section 245 the following new item:

"Sec. 245A. Adjustment of status of certain entrants before January 1, 1982, to that of person admitted for lawful residence."

(b) CONFORMING AMENDMENTS.—(1) Section 402 of the Social Security Act is amended by adding at the end thereof the following new subsection: "42 USC 602"

"(f)(1) For temporary disqualification of certain newly legalized aliens from receiving aid to families with dependent children, see subsection (h) of section 245A of the Immigration and Nationality Act.

"(2) In any case where an alien disqualified from receiving aid under such subsection (h) is the parent of a child who is not so disqualified and who (without any adjustment of status under such section 245A) is considered a dependent child under subsection (a)(33), or is the brother or sister of such a child, subsection (a)(38) shall not apply, and the needs of such alien shall not be taken into account in making the determination under subsection (a)(7) with respect to such child, but the income of such alien (if he or she is the parent of such child) shall be included in making such determination to the same extent that income of a stepparent is included under subsection (a)(31)."

(2)(A) Section 472(a) of such Act "42 USC 672" is amended by adding at the end thereof (after and below paragraph (4)) the following new sentence: "In any case where the child is an alien disqualified under section 245A(h) of the Immigration and Nationality Act from receiving aid under the State plan approved under section 402 in or for the month in which such agreement was entered into or court proceedings leading to the removal of the child from the home were instituted, such child shall be considered to satisfy the requirements of paragraph (4) (and the corresponding requirements of section 473(a)(1)(B)), with respect to that month, if he or she would have satisfied such requirements but for such disqualification."

(B) Section 473(a)(1) of such Act "42 USC 673" is amended by adding at the end thereof (after and below subparagraph (C)) the following new sentence: "The last sentence of section 472(a) shall apply, for purposes of subparagraph (B), in any case where the child is an alien described in that sentence."

(c) MISCELLANEOUS PROVISIONS.—

(1) PROCEDURES FOR PROPERTY ACQUISITION OR LEASING.—"8 USC 1255a note"—Notwithstanding the Federal Property and Administrative Services Act of 1949 (40 U.S.C. 471 et seq.), the Attorney General is authorized to expend from the appropriation provided for the administration and enforcement of the Immigration and Nationality Act, "8 USC 1101 note" such amounts as may be necessary for the leasing or acquisition of property in the fulfillment of this section. This authority shall end two years after the effective date of the legalization program.

(2) USE OF RETIRED FEDERAL EMPLOYEES.—Notwithstanding any other provision of law, the retired or retainer pay of a member or former member of the Armed Forces of the United States or the annuity of a retired employee of the Federal Government who retired on or before January 1, 1986, shall not be reduced while such individual is temporarily employed by the Immigration and Naturalization Service for a period of not to exceed 18 months to perform duties in connection with the adjustment of status of aliens under this section. The Service shall not temporarily employ more than 300 individuals under this paragraph. Notwithstanding any other provision of law, the annuity of a retired employee of the Federal Government shall not be increased or redetermined under chapter 83 or 84 of title 5, "5 USC 8301" United States Code, as a result of a period of temporary employment under this paragraph.

(Source: http://www.oig.lsc.gov/legis/irca86.htm)

Document 4: Proposition 187 of 1994—Arguments in Favor and Against

Significance: Divided Californians. While approved by voters, it was overturned by the courts as infringement on federal government powers.

Official Title and Summary Prepared by the Attorney General

ILLEGAL ALIENS. INELIGIBILITY FOR PUBLIC SEEVICES. VERIFICATION AND REPORTING. INITIATIVE STATUTE.

Makes illegal aliens ineligible for public social services, public health care services (unless emergency under federal law), and public school education at elementary, secondary, and post-secondary levels.

Requires various state and local agencies to report persons who are suspected illegal aliens to the California Attorney General and the United States Immigration and Naturalization Service. Mandates California Attorney General to transmit reports to Immigration and Naturalization Service and maintain records of such reports. Makes it a felony to manufacture, distribute, sell, or use false citizenship or residence documents.

Argument in Favor of Proposition 187

California can strike a blow for the taxpayer that will be heard across America; in Arizona, in Texas and in Florida in the same way Proposition 13 was heard across the land.

Proposition 187 will go down in history as the voice of the people against arrogant bureaucracy.

WE CAN STOP ILLEGAL ALIENS,

If the citizens and the taxpayers of our state wait for the politicians in Washington and Sacramento to stop the incredible flow of ILLEGAL ALIENS, California will be in economic and social bankruptcy.

We have to act and ACT NOW! On our ballot, Proposition 187 will be the first giant stride in ultimately ending the ILLEGAL ALIEN invasion.

It has been estimated that ILLEGAL ALIENS are costing taxpayers in excess of 6 billion dollars a year,

While our own citizens and legal residents go wanting, those who choose to enter our country ILLEGALLY get royal treatment at the expense of the California taxpayer.

IT IS TIME THIS STOPS!

Welfare, medical and educational benefits are the magnets that draw these ILLEGAL ALIENS aeross our borders.

Senator Robert Byrd (D-West Virginia), who voted against federal reimbursement for state funds spent on ILLEGAL ALIENS, said "states must do what they can for themselves".

PROPOSITION 187 IS CALIFORNIA's WAY.

Should those ILLEGALLY here receive taxpayer subsidized education including college?

Should our children's classrooms be over-crowded by those who are ILLEGALLY in our country?

Should our Senior Citizens be denied full service under Medi-Gal to subsidize the cost of ILLEGAL ALIENS?

Should those ILLEGALLY here be able to buy and sell forged documents without penalty?

Should tax paid bureaucrats be able to give sanctuary to those ILLEGALLY in our country?

If your answer to these questions is NO, then you should support Proposition 187.

The federal government and the state government have been derelict in their duty to control our borders. It is the role of our government to end the benefits that draw people from around the world who ILLEGALLY enter our country. Our government actually entices them.

Passage of Proposition 18? will send a strong message that California will no longer tolerate the dereliction of the duty by our politicians.

Vote YES on Proposition 187.

The Save Our State Coalition is comprised of Democrats, Republicans and Independents. It includes all races, colors and creeds with the same common denominator. We are American, by birth or naturalization; we are Americans!

We were outraged when our State Legislature voted on July 5th to remove dental care as a medical option and force the increase of the cost of prescription drugs for Senior Citizens.

Then, as a final slap in the face, they voted to continue **free** pre-natal care for ILLEGAL ALIENS!

Vote YES ON PROPOSITION 187. ENOUGH IS ENOUGH!

ASSEMBLYMAN DICK MOUNTJOY *Author of Proposition 187*

RONALD PRINCE
Chairman of the "'Save Our State" Committee

MAYOR BARBARA KILEY
Co-Chair of the "Save Our State" Committee

Rebuttal to Argument in Favor of Proposition 187

Proposition 187 promoters claim their initiative would go down in history. We agree.

PROPOSITION 187 IS ONE OF THE MOST POORLY DRAFTED INITIATIVES IN CALIFORNIA's HISTORY.

"The initiative is filled with provisions that collide with state and federal laws, state and U.S. constitutional protections and with state and federal court rulings."

California Senate Office of Research

PROPOSITION 187 ALSO MAY SET A RECORD FOR COSTING TAXPAYERS $10 BILLION!

"Because the requirements of the: S.O,S, initiative (187) violate federal Medi-Cal law, the state's entire Medi-Cal program would be in jeopardy of losing all regular Medicaid funding..."

"To make up for the upwards of $7 billion in lost federal funds, state spending on Medi-Cal would have to double."

National Health Law Program

"...... school districts will most likely be required to disclose information from education records in violation of FERPA (Family Ed.ucational Rights and Privacy Act) in order to comply with the prepared State law (Proposition 187)."

As a result, *"schools would no longer be able to receive Federal education funds."*

U.S. Secretary of Education Richard Riley

California's Senate Office of Research estimates the loss to our public schools and colleges could exceed $3 billion.

Proposition 187 would go down in history, all right. If approved, 187 would be long remembered as the initiative that TOOK A BAD SITUATION AND MADE IT MUCH WORSE—$10 BILLION WORSE!

Meanwhile, PROPOSITION 187 DOES ABSOLUTELY NOTHING TO BEEF UP ENFORCEMENT AT THE BORDER or CRACK DOWN on EMPLOYERS WHO HIRE UNDOCUMENTED WORKERS.

VOTE NO on PROPOSITION 187!

PAT DINGSDALE
President, California State PTA

MICHAEL B. HILL, M.D.
President, American College of Emergency Physicians, California Chapter

HOWARD L. OWENS
Legislative Director, Congress of California Senior

Argument Against Proposition 187

Something must be done to stop the flow of illegal immigrants coming across the border.

Unfortunately, PROPOSITION 187 DOESN'T DO A THING TO BEEF UP ENFORCE-MENT AT THE BORDER. It doesn't even, crack down on employers who hire illegal immigrants.

illegal immigration is a REAL problem, but Proposition 187 is NOT A REAL SOLUTION. It's not even a start in the right direction.

Proposition 187 would only COMPOUND EXISTING PROBLEMS and cause a host of new ones—EXPENSIVE ones!

PROPOSITION 187 COULD END UP COSTING TAXPAYERS $1.0 BILLION.

Education, health care and legal analysts all come to the same conclusion. Because Proposition 187 is POORLY DRAFTED, it directly conflicts with several important federal laws. As a result, CALIFORNIA COULD LOSE BILLIONS in FEDERAL FUNDING.

Even the U.S. Secretary of Education has concluded Proposition 187 could cause California schools to lose federal funds. Our schools could lose more than $3 BILLION.

Health care experts have further determined Proposition 187 could cost California $7 BILLION in lost federal funding for Medi-Cal for seniors and other legal residents.

PROPOSITION 187 WOULD TURN OUR SCHOOLS INTO IMMIGRATION OFFICES,

It requires public school officials to thoroughly verify the citizenship of EVERY child and EVERY parent—more than 10 MILLION people.

The costs and time involved in undertaking this PAPERWORK NIGHTMARE is impossible to calculate. Schools already are hurting from budget cuts. Proposition 187 would divert even more funds away from classrooms.

PROPOSITION 187 WOULD KICK 400,000 KIDS OUT OF SCHOOL AND ONTO THE STREETS.

An estimated 400,000 KIDS would be kicked out of school» but Proposition 187 WONT result in their deportation. Just what we need—400,000 kids hanging out on street corners. We all know what happens to kids who don't finish school.

Is this supposed to reduce CRIME and GRAFFITI?

PROPOSITION 187 CREATES A POLICE STATE MENTALITY.

It forces public officials to deny vital services to anyone they SUSPECT might not be a legal resident. But Proposition 187 doesn't define the basis for such suspicion. Is it the way you speak? The sound of your last name? The shade of your skin?

PROPOSITION 187 THREATENS THE HEALTH OF ALL CALIFORNIANS.

It would forbid doctors and nurses from giving immunizations or basic medical care to anyone SUSPECTED of being an illegal immigrant.

Every day, hundreds of thousands of undocumented workers HANDLE OUR FOOD SUPPLY in the fields and restaurants. Denying them basic health care would only SPREAD COMMUNICABLE DISEASES THROUGHOUT OUR COMMUNITIES and place us ALL at risk.

PROPOSITION 187 COULD COST TAXPAYERS $10 BILLION, BUT IT WONT STOP THE FLOW OF ILLEGAL IMMIGRANTS OVER THE BORDER.

Illegal immigration is ILLEGAL. Isn't it time we enforce the law?

Proposition 187 doesn't beef up enforcement at the border or crack down on the employers who continue to hire illegal immigrants.

Send the politicians a message. Tell them to start enforcing the law. VOTE NO on PROPOSITION 187.

SHERMAN BLOCK
Sheriff, Lot Angeles County
D. A. ("DEL") WEBER
President, California Teachers Association
RALPH R. OCAMPO, M.D.
President, California Medical Association

Rebuttal to Argument Against Proposition 187

The argument against Proposition 187 is emotional, thoughtless and pure mindless babble.

The real opponents of Proposition 187, the special interests who have pledged millions of dollars to defeat our initiative, have a deep financial interest in continuing the present policy. Remember: Illegal aliens are a big business for public unions and well connected medical clinics. You pay the bills, they reap the benefits,

These monied interests have the unmitigated gall to tell the California voter that by ending illegal immigration the cost to the taxpayer will skyrocket! Are they out of their minds?

Their argument states that passage of Proposition 187:

"Doesn't crack down on employers."

FEDERAL LAW ALREADY PROHIBITS HIRING ILLEGALS.

"187 could end up costing taxpayers $10 billion.

NONSENSE, HOW CAN GETTING RID OF THE PRESENT COSTS END UP COSTING MORE?

They say, "187 is badly written." NONSENSE.

THE SPECIAL INTERESTS ATTACKING PROPOSITION 187 INCLUDE THE CALIFORNIA TEACHERS ASSOCIATION AND THE CALIFORNIA MEDICAL ASSOCIATION. BOTH CONSTITUTE THE STATE'S BIGGEST LOBBYING GROUPS WHO OPPOSE US, THEY PROTECT THEIR OWN INTERESTS—NOT YOURS.

Don't be deceived by greedy, special interests that benefit from the failures in our immigration policies.

Why should we give more comfort and consideration to illegal aliens than to *our* needy American citizens? Many aged and mentally impaired Americans go without government largesse. Isn't it time to consider our citizens?

The groups spending millions to maintain the failures of the status quo only do so for their own selfishness. VOTE YES ON PROPOSITION 187.

ASSEMBLYMAN DICK MOUNTJOY
Author, Proposition 187/S.O.S.
CONGRESSMAN JAY KIM
Advisor, Proposition 187/S.O.S.
JESSE LAGUNA
Chairman, Border Solution Task Force

Document 5: Congressional Research Service Document

When: 2001

Significance: Commitment by Presidents Bush and Fox to work together on immigration issues in the pre-9/11 period.

Order Code RL32735
Congressional Research Service-Library of Congress,
Report for Congress—Received through CRS Web
Mexico-United States Dialogue on Migration and Border Issues, 2001-2005

"President Bush's February 2001 Visit to Guanajuato, Mexico Launches Bilateral Migration Talks. When President Bush met with President Fox in mid-February 2001, migration issues were among the main topics, with Mexican officials expressing concern about the number of migrants who die each year while seeking entry into the United States. President Fox has been pressing proposals for legalizing undocumented Mexican workers in the United States through amnesty or guest worker arrangements as a way of protecting their human rights. In the Joint Communique following the Bush-Fox meeting, the two presidents agreed to instruct appropriate officials "to engage, at the earliest opportunity, in formal high level negotiations aimed at achieving short and long-term agreements that will allow us to constructively address migration and labor issues between our two countries." During the joint press conference, President Bush indicated that there was a movement in Congress to review the drug certification requirements, and he expressed confidence in President Fox's efforts to combat drug trafficking.

Several months later, on May 25, 2001, President Bush telephoned President Fox to express condolences for the recent deaths of 14 Mexican migrants in the Arizona desert, and both leaders reaffirmed their commitment to enhance safety along the border and to continue to make progress on migration issues. Press reports suggested that proposals to regularize the status of Mexican workers in the United States were being considered by the Administration and by Congress, but President Bush indicated that blanket amnesty would not be proposed.

President Fox's Early September 2001 Official Visit to Washington, D.C. Advances Migration Talks and Launches Partnership for Prosperity. During the opening day of President Fox's official visit to Washington, D.C. in early September 2001, he recognized that the anticipated migration agreements had not been reached, but he called for the two governments to reach agreement on migration proposals by the end of the year.

At the end of the meetings, the Joint Statement of September 6, 2001, summarized the meeting as follows:

"The Presidents reviewed the progress made by our joint working group on migration chaired by Secretaries Powell, Castaneda, and Creel and Attorney General Ashcroft and noted this represented the most fruitful and frank dialogue we have ever had on a subject so important to both nations. They praised implementation of the border safety initiative, and recognized that migration related issues are deeply felt by our publics and vital to our prosperity, wellbeing, and the kind of societies we want to build. They renewed their commitment to forging new and realistic approaches to migration to ensure it is safe, orderly, legal and dignified, and agreed on the framework within which this ongoing effort is based. This includes matching willing workers with willing employers; serving the social and economic needs of both countries; respecting the human dignity of all migrants, regardless of their status; recognizing the contribution migrants make to enriching both societies; shared responsibility for ensuring migration takes place through safe and legal channels. Both stressed their commitment to continue our discussions, instructing the high-level working group to reach mutually satisfactory results on border safety, a temporary worker program and the status of undocumented Mexicans in the United States. They requested that the working group provide them proposals with respect to these issues as soon as possible. The Presidents recognized that this is an extraordinarily challenging area of public policy, and that it is critical to address the issue in a timely manner and with appropriate thoroughness and depth."

(Source: California Ballot pamphlet, November 1994.)

Document 6: Development, Relief, and Education for Alien Minors Act of 2005 (US DREAM Act), S. 2075

When: November 18, 2005

Significance: The act would legalize undocumented immigrants who came to the United States as children. The bill failed to gain approval in Congress.
IN THE SENATE OF THE UNITED STATES, November 18, 2005

A BILL;
To amend the Illegal Immigration Reform and Immigrant Responsibility Act of 1996 to permit States to determine State residency for higher education purposes and to authorize the cancellation of removal and adjustment of status of certain alien students who are long-term United States residents and who entered the United States as children, and for other purposes.

Be it enacted by the Senate and House of Representatives of the United States of America in Congress assembled,

SECTION 1. SHORT TITLE.
This Act may be cited as the "Development, Relief, and Education for Alien Minors Act of 2005" or the "DREAM Act of 2005."

SECTION 2. DEFINITIONS.

In this Act:

(1) INSTITUTION OF HIGHER EDUCATION- The term "institution of higher education" has the meaning given that term in section 101 of the Higher Education Act of 1965 (20 U.S.C. 1001).

(2) UNIFORMED SERVICES- The term "uniformed services" has the meaning given that term in section 101(a) of title 10, United States Code.

SECTION 3. RESTORATION OF STATE OPTION TO DETERMINE RESIDENCY FOR PURPOSES OF HIGHER EDUCATION BENEFITS.

(a) In General- Section 505 of the Illegal Immigration Reform and Immigrant Responsibility Act of 1996 (8 U.S.C. 1623) is repealed.

(b) Effective Date- The repeal under subsection (a) shall take effect as if included in the enactment of the Illegal Immigration Reform and Immigrant Responsibility Act of 1996.

SECTION 4. CANCELLATION OF REMOVAL AND ADJUSTMENT OF STATUS OF CERTAIN LONG-TERM RESIDENTS WHO ENTERED THE UNITED STATES AS CHILDREN.

(a) Special Rule for Certain Long-Term Residents Who Entered the United States as Children-4

(1) IN GENERAL- Notwithstanding any other provision of law and except as otherwise provided in this Act, the Secretary of Homeland Security may cancel removal of, and adjust to the status of an alien lawfully admitted for permanent residence, subject to the conditional basis described in section 5, an alien who is inadmissible or deportable from the United States, if the alien demonstrates that–

(A) the alien has been physically present in the United States for a continuous period of not less than 5 years immediately preceding the date of enactment of this Act, and had not yet reached the age of 16 years at the time of initial entry;

(B) the alien has been a person of good moral character since the time of application;

(C) the alien–

(i) is not inadmissible under paragraph (2), (3), (6)(B), (6)(C), (6)(E), (6)(F), or (6)(G) of section 212(a) of the Immigration and Nationality Act (8 U.S.C. 1182(a)), or, if inadmissible solely under subparagraph (C) or (F) of paragraph (6) of such subsection, the alien was under the age of 16 years at the time the violation was committed; and

(ii) is not deportable under paragraph (1)(E), (1)(G), (2), (3)(B), (3)(C), (3)(D), (4), or (6) of section 237(a) of the Immigration and Nationality Act (8 U.S.C. 1227(a)), or, if deportable solely under subparagraphs (C) or (D) of paragraph (3) of such subsection, the alien was under the age of 16 years at the time the violation was committed;

(D) the alien, at the time of application, has been admitted to an institution of higher education in the United States, or has earned a high school diploma or obtained a general education development certificate in the United States; and

(E) the alien has never been under a final administrative or judicial order of exclusion, deportation, or removal, unless the alien has remained in the United States under color of law or received the order before attaining the age of 16 years.

(2) WAIVER- The Secretary of Homeland Security may waive the grounds of ineligibility under section 212(a)(6) of the Immigration and Nationality Act and the grounds of deportability under paragraphs (1), (3), and (6) of section 237(a) of that Act for humanitarian purposes or family unity or when it is otherwise in the public interest.

(3) PROCEDURES- The Secretary of Homeland Security shall provide a procedure by regulation allowing eligible individuals to apply affirmatively for the relief available under this subsection without being placed in removal proceedings.

(b) Termination of Continuous Period- For purposes of this section, any period of continuous residence or continuous physical presence in the United States of an alien who applies for cancellation of removal under this section shall not terminate when the alien is served a notice to appear under section 239(a) of the Immigration and Nationality Act (8 U.S.C. 1229(a)).

(c) Treatment of Certain Breaks in Presence-

(1) IN GENERAL- An alien shall be considered to have failed to maintain continuous physical presence in the United States under subsection (a) if the alien has departed from the United States for any period in excess of 90 days or for any periods in the aggregate exceeding 180 days.

(2) EXTENSIONS FOR EXCEPTIONAL CIRCUMSTANCES- The Secretary of Homeland Security may extend the time periods described in paragraph (1) if the alien demonstrates that the failure to timely return to the United States was due to exceptional circumstances. The exceptional circumstances determined sufficient to justify an extension should be no less compelling than serious illness of the alien, or death or serious illness of a parent, grandparent, sibling, or child.

(d) Exemption From Numerical Limitations- Nothing in this section may be construed to apply a numerical limitation on the number of aliens who may be eligible for cancellation of removal or adjustment of status under this section.

(e) Regulations-

(1) PROPOSED REGULATIONS- Not later than 180 days after the date of enactment of this Act, the Secretary of Homeland Security shall publish proposed regulations implementing this section. Such regulations shall be effective immediately on an interim basis, but are subject to change and revision after public notice and opportunity for a period for public comment.

(2) INTERIM, FINAL REGULATIONS- Within a reasonable time after publication of the interim regulations in accordance with paragraph (1), the Secretary of Homeland Security shall publish final regulations implementing this section.

(f) Removal of Alien- The Secretary of Homeland Security may not remove any alien who has a pending application for conditional status under this Act.

SECTION 5. CONDITIONAL PERMANENT RESIDENT STATUS.

(a) In General-

(1) CONDITIONAL BASIS FOR STATUS- Notwithstanding any other provision of law, and except as provided in section 6, an alien whose status has been adjusted under section 4 to that of an alien lawfully admitted for permanent residence shall be considered to have obtained such status on a conditional basis subject to the provisions of this section. Such conditional permanent resident status shall be valid for a period of 6 years, subject to termination under subsection (b).

(2) NOTICE OF REQUIREMENTS-

(A) AT TIME OF OBTAINING PERMANENT RESIDENCE- At the time an alien obtains permanent resident status on a conditional basis under paragraph (1), the Secretary of Homeland Security shall provide for notice to the alien regarding the provisions of this section and the requirements of subsection (c) to have the conditional basis of such status removed.

(B) EFFECT OF FAILURE TO PROVIDE NOTICE- The failure of the Secretary of Homeland Security to provide a notice under this paragraph—

(i) shall not affect the enforcement of the provisions of this Act with respect to the alien; and

(ii) shall not give rise to any private right of action by the alien.

(b) Termination of Status-

(1) IN GENERAL- The Secretary of Homeland Security shall terminate the conditional permanent resident status of any alien who obtained such status under this Act, if the Secretary determines that the alien—

(A) ceases to meet the requirements of subparagraph (B) or (C) of section 4(a)(1);

(B) has become a public charge; or

(C) has received a dishonorable or other than honorable discharge from the uniformed services.

(2) RETURN TO PREVIOUS IMMIGRATION STATUS- Any alien whose conditional permanent resident status is terminated under paragraph (1) shall return to the immigration

status the alien had immediately prior to receiving conditional permanent resident status under this Act.

(c) Requirements of Timely Petition for Removal of Condition-

(1) IN GENERAL- In order for the conditional basis of permanent resident status obtained by an alien under subsection (a) to be removed, the alien must file with the Secretary of Homeland Security, in accordance with paragraph (3), a petition which requests the removal of such conditional basis and which provides, under penalty of perjury, the facts and information so that the Secretary may make the determination described in paragraph (2)(A).

(2) ADJUDICATION OF PETITION TO REMOVE CONDITION-

(A) IN GENERAL- If a petition is filed in accordance with paragraph (1) for an alien, the Secretary of Homeland Security shall make a determination as to whether the alien meets the requirements set out in subparagraphs (A) through (E) of subsection (d)(1).

(B) REMOVAL OF CONDITIONAL BASIS IF FAVORABLE DETERMINATION- If the Secretary determines that the alien meets such requirements, the Secretary shall notify the alien of such determination and immediately remove the conditional basis of the status of the alien.

(C) TERMINATION IF ADVERSE DETERMINATION- If the Secretary determines that the alien does not meet such requirements, the Secretary shall notify the alien of such determination and terminate the conditional permanent resident status of the alien as of the date of the determination.

(3) TIME TO FILE PETITION- An alien may petition to remove the conditional basis to lawful resident status during the period beginning 180 days before and ending 2 years after either the date that is 6 years after the date of the granting of conditional permanent resident status or any other expiration date of the conditional permanent resident status as extended by the Secretary of Homeland Security in accordance with this Act. The alien shall be deemed in conditional permanent resident status in the United States during the period in which the petition is pending.

(d) Details of Petition-

(1) CONTENTS OF PETITION- Each petition for an alien under subsection (c)(1) shall contain information to permit the Secretary of Homeland Security to determine whether each of the following requirements is met:

(A) The alien has demonstrated good moral character during the entire period the alien has been a conditional permanent resident.

(B) The alien is in compliance with section 4(a)(1)(C).

(C) The alien has not abandoned the alien's residence in the United States. The Secretary shall presume that the alien has abandoned such residence if the alien is absent from the United States for more than 365 days, in the aggregate, during the period of conditional residence, unless the alien demonstrates that alien has not abandoned the alien's residence. An alien who is absent from the United States due to active service in the uniformed services has not abandoned the alien's residence in the United States during the period of such service.

(D) The alien has completed at least 1 of the following:

(i) The alien has acquired a degree from an institution of higher education in the United States or has completed at least 2 years, in good standing, in a program for a bachelor's degree or higher degree in the United States.

(ii) The alien has served in the uniformed services for at least 2 years and, if discharged, has received an honorable discharge.

(E) The alien has provided a list of all of the secondary educational institutions that the alien attended in the United States.

(2) HARDSHIP EXCEPTION-

(A) IN GENERAL- The Secretary of Homeland Security may, in the Secretary's discretion, remove the conditional status of an alien if the alien—

(i) satisfies the requirements of subparagraphs (A), (B), and (C) of paragraph (1);

(ii) demonstrates compelling circumstances for the inability to complete the requirements described in paragraph (1)(D); and

(iii) demonstrates that the alien's removal from the United States would result in exceptional and extremely unusual hardship to the alien or the alien's spouse, parent, or child who is a citizen or a lawful permanent resident of the United States.

(B) EXTENSION- Upon a showing of good cause, the Secretary of Homeland Security may extend the period of the conditional resident status for the purpose of completing the requirements described in paragraph (1)(D).

(e) Treatment of Period for Purposes of Naturalization- For purposes of title III of the Immigration and Nationality Act (8 U.S.C. 1401 et seq.), in the case of an alien who is in the United States as a lawful permanent resident on a conditional basis under this section, the alien shall be considered to have been admitted as an alien lawfully admitted for permanent residence and to be in the United States as an alien lawfully admitted to the United States for permanent residence. However, the conditional basis must be removed before the alien may apply for naturalization.

SECTION 6. RETROACTIVE BENEFITS UNDER THIS ACT.

If, on the date of enactment of this Act, an alien has satisfied all the requirements of subparagraphs (A) through (E) of section 4(a)(1) and section 5(d)(1)(D), the Secretary of Homeland Security may adjust the status of the alien to that of a conditional resident in accordance with section 4. The alien may petition for removal of such condition at the end of the conditional residence period in accordance with section 5(c) if the alien has met the requirements of subparagraphs (A), (B), and (C) of section 5(d)(1) during the entire period of conditional residence.

SECTION 7. EXCLUSIVE JURISDICTION.

(a) In General- The Secretary of Homeland Security shall have exclusive jurisdiction to determine eligibility for relief under this Act, except where the alien has been placed into deportation, exclusion, or removal proceedings either prior to or after filing an application for relief under this Act, in which case the Attorney General shall have exclusive jurisdiction and shall assume all the powers and duties of the Secretary until proceedings are terminated, or if a final order of deportation, exclusion, or removal is entered the Secretary shall resume all powers and duties delegated to the Secretary under this Act.

(b) Stay of Removal of Certain Aliens Enrolled in Primary or Secondary School- The Attorney General shall stay the removal proceedings of any alien who-

(1) meets all the requirements of subparagraphs (A), (B), (C), and (E) of section 4(a)(1);

(2) is at least 12 years of age; and

(3) is enrolled full time in a primary or secondary school.

(c) Employment- An alien whose removal is stayed pursuant to subsection (b) may be engaged in employment in the United States, consistent with the Fair Labor Standards Act (29 U.S.C. 201 et seq.), and State and local laws governing minimum age for employment.

(d) Lift of Stay- The Attorney General shall lift the stay granted pursuant to subsection (b) if the alien-

(1) is no longer enrolled in a primary or secondary school; or

(2) ceases to meet the requirements of subsection (b)(1).

SECTION 8. PENALTIES FOR FALSE STATEMENTS IN APPLICATION.

Whoever files an application for relief under this Act and willfully and knowingly falsifies, misrepresents, or conceals a material fact or makes any false or fraudulent statement or representation, or makes or uses any false writing or document knowing the same to contain any false or fraudulent statement or entry, shall be fined in accordance with title 18, United States Code, or imprisoned not more than 5 years, or both.

SECTION 9. CONFIDENTIALITY OF INFORMATION.

(a) Prohibition- No officer or employee of the United States may-

(1) use the information furnished by the applicant pursuant to an application filed under this Act to initiate removal proceedings against any persons identified in the application;

(2) make any publication whereby the information furnished by any particular individual pursuant to an application under this Act can be identified; or

(3) permit anyone other than an officer or employee of the United States Government or, in the case of applications filed under this Act with a designated entity, that designated entity, to examine applications filed under this Act.

(b) Required Disclosure- The Attorney General or the Secretary of Homeland Security shall provide the information furnished under this section, and any other information derived from such furnished information, to–

(1) a duly recognized law enforcement entity in connection with an investigation or prosecution of an offense described in paragraph (2) or (3) of section 212(a) of the Immigration and Nationality Act (8 U.S.C. 1182(a)), when such information is requested in writing by such entity; or

(2) an official coroner for purposes of affirmatively identifying a deceased individual (whether or not such individual is deceased as a result of a crime).

(c) Penalty- Whoever knowingly uses, publishes, or permits information to be examined in violation of this section shall be fined not more than $10,000.

SECTION 10. EXPEDITED PROCESSING OF APPLICATIONS; PROHIBITION ON FEES.

Regulations promulgated under this Act shall provide that applications under this Act will be considered on an expedited basis and without a requirement for the payment by the applicant of any additional fee for such expedited processing.

SECTION 11. HIGHER EDUCATION ASSISTANCE.

Notwithstanding any provision of the Higher Education Act of 1965 (20 U.S.C. 1001 et seq.), with respect to assistance provided under title IV of the Higher Education Act of 1965 (20 U.S.C. 1070 et seq.), an alien who adjusts status to that of a lawful permanent resident under this Act shall be eligible only for the following assistance under such title:

(1) Student loans under parts B, D, and E of such title IV (20 U.S.C. 1071 et seq., 1087a et seq., 1087aa et seq.), subject to the requirements of such parts.

(2) Federal work-study programs under part C of such title IV (42 U.S.C. 2751 et seq.), subject to the requirements of such part.

(3) Services under such title IV (20 U.S.C. 1070 et seq.), subject to the requirements for such services.

SECTION 12. GAO REPORT.

Seven years after the date of enactment of this Act, the Comptroller General of the United States shall submit a report to the Committees on the Judiciary of the Senate and the House of Representatives setting forth–

(1) the number of aliens who were eligible for cancellation of removal and adjustment of status under section 4(a);

(2) the number of aliens who applied for adjustment of status under section 4(a);

(3) the number of aliens who were granted adjustment of status under section 4(a); and

(4) the number of aliens whose conditional permanent resident status was removed under section 5.

(Source: http://dreamact.info/index.php?option=com_fulltext&bill=S.2075&Itemid=53)

FURTHER READINGS

Borjas, George, ed. *Mexican Immigration to the United States*. Chicago: University of Chicago Press, 2007.

Calavita, Kitty. *Inside the State: The Bracero Program, Immigration, and the INS*. New York: Routledge, 1992.

Chavez, Leo R. *Shadowed Lives: Undocumented Immigrants in American Society*. New York: Harcourt Brace Jovanovich, 1992.

Durand, Jorge, and Douglas Massey, eds. *Crossing the Border: Research from the Mexican Migration Project*. New York: Russell Sage Foundation, 2004.

Guskin, Jane, and David Wilson. *The Politics of Immigration: Questions and Answers*. New York: Monthly Review Press, 2007.

LeMay, Michael. *Guarding the Gates: Immigration and National Security*. Westport, Conn.: Praeger Security International, 2006.

Martinez, Oscar. *Troublesome Border*. Tucson: University of Arizona Press, 2006.

Payan, Tony. *The Three US-Mexico Border Wars: Drugs, Immigration, and Homeland Security*. Westport, Conn.: Praeger Security International, 2006.

Romero, Fernando. *Hyper-Border: The Contemporary US-Mexico Border and Its Future*. New York: Princeton Architectural Press, 2007.

CHAPTER 10

The Security Debate and Immigration

Thomas Cieslik

By the summer of 2001 the U.S. government was close to coming to an agreement with the new Mexican President, Vicente Fox, over a temporary work visa program for Mexicans. However, after the terror attacks on the World Trade Center in New York City and the Pentagon in Washington, D.C., on September 11, 2001, security became the number one priority in U.S. foreign policy, effectively halting negotiations. Since then, public debate has inevitably linked national security to immigration, especially as the terrorists were foreigners in U.S. territory. The debate was joined by numerous anti-immigrant groups (Krikorian 2004). Prominent among them were supporters of the Minutemen project, which is criticized because of its self-styled justice. The Minutemen and other nativists believe that Mexicans have started a "reconquista." They assert that Mexicans want to reconquer territories like California, Arizona, New Mexico, and Texas—territories Mexico lost in its war against the United States 1846–1848.

According to data from the Department of Homeland Security and the Pew Hispanic Center, some 1 million migrants cross the border every year illegally. Around 60 percent are caught and expelled while the rest remain in the United States. Today an estimated 12 million people reside in this country without legal documentation. In 2006, U.S. President George W. Bush recognized that the immigration issue required reform, in part because he was seeking the Hispanic vote. In a speech on January 7, 2004, the president proposed a new, temporary worker program. After his reelection, he urged Congress in his State of the Union address on February 2, 2005, to fix the immigration problem: "America's immigration system is also outdated—unsuited to the needs of our economy and to the values of our country. We should not be content with laws that punish hardworking people who want only to provide for their families, and deny businesses willing workers, and invite chaos at our border. It is time for an immigration policy that permits temporary guest workers to fill jobs Americans will not take, that rejects amnesty, that tells us who is entering and leaving our country, and that closes the border to drug dealers and terrorists." Although his proposal did not include specific plans about how temporary worker visas would be implemented, it set various initiatives and bills in Congress in motion.

In 2006 the immigration debate essentially became a security debate. Reform bills were stalled in Congress because both Republicans and Democrats could not agree about what the government should do about the estimated 12 million illegal immigrants in the United States; meanwhile, tension on the border began rising. For example, a border patrol agent shot a migrant who was crossing illegally into the United States through a drainage tunnel near El Paso, Texas, in July 2007. Numerous books and articles have recently emerged in the debate between supporters of the border vigilantes and anti-immigration movements on the one hand and liberal organizations supporting immigration on the other. A few include:

1. Buchanan, Patrick. *State of Emergency—The Third World Invasion and Conquest of America.* New York: St. Martin's Press, 2006.
2. Gilchrist, Jim and Jerome Corsi. *Minutemen—The Battle to Secure America's Borders.* Los Angeles: World Ahead Publishing, 2006.
3. Huntington, Samuel. *Who We Are: The Challenge to America's National Identity.* New York: Simon & Schuster, 2004.
4. Swain, Carol. *The New White Nationalism in America.* Cambridge: Cambridge University Press, 1992.
5. Zeskind, Leonard. "The New Nativism—The Alarming Overlap between White Nationalists and Mainstream Anti-immigrant Forces." *The American Prospect*, Vol. 16 (November 2005).

Border patrol spokesman Doug Mosier said, "We are seeing more aggressive behavior. The frustration level of some of these smuggling organizations is really starting to manifest. [...] Shootings are connected to a 30 percent increase in assaults against agents so far [in 2007]" (*New York Times*, July 3, 2007).

A large part of the problem is that there are a number of street gangs from Central America among the smuggling organizations, locally known as "maras." The routes for smuggling migrants overlap with those used for drugs, turning the border region into a major operation field for the main Mexican drug cartels. The pressure for more border security, therefore, is not only to deal with illegal aliens but also to stop spillover from Mexico's "Cartel War" on drug trafficking. The drug and gang-related violence escalated in 2000, particularly along the Arizona and Texas borders. With the Merida Agreement of 2007, the United States made a commitment to support the Mexican government in its antidrug efforts by allocating money for new intelligence equipment, modern communication systems, and police training programs within the framework of a future, regional security partnership.

Amidst the national security debate, many states affected by immigration took swift action against undocumented migration. In the state of Arizona, for example, 56 percent of the population voted for Proposition 200 on November 2, 2004. This state initiative requires individuals to prove their citizenship before they can register to vote or apply for public benefits. Moreover, it also requires public officials to report anyone who is unable to show his or her citizenship documentation. Consequently, it denies illegal migrants access to Arizona public services, but it cannot deny them federally mandated public benefits, such as K-12 public education, or entitlements, such as food stamps or subsidized school lunches.

The new law has created fear among immigrants, and many afraid to search for federally funded services. The sponsors of Proposition 200, such as Protect Arizona NOW, which is supported by the Federation for American Immigration Reform (FAIR), set an example of how civil organizations can put pressure on both government and public opinion in the country. This has inspired other local organizations to prepare similar referendum initiatives in Hasleton, PA, for example. "As of August 2006, more than half of the states of the United States had passed anti-immigrant measures. The state measures were sponsored by both Republicans and Democrats and range from stiffening penalties for employers who hire undocumented migrants to ensuring that undocumented migrants do not receive public benefits.

In July 2006, the city of Hazelton, Pennsylvania, passed one of the nation's harshest measures, approving $1,000 fines to landlords who rent to undocumented migrants and denying business permits to employers who give them jobs" (Lynn-Doty 2007, 126).

The American Civil Liberties Union took the legislation to court. Town officials couldn't prove in a trial that undocumented immigrants were somehow responsible for an increase in crime, and a federal court declared the landmark decision unconstitutional. Nevertheless, Hazelton's initiative is part of a nationwide trend in which extreme anti-immigrant proposals are becoming popular. A bill proposed by U.S. Senator John Shadegg (R-Arizona), which would have denied citizenship to the children of illegal migrants, is another case in point. Although his bill was defeated in December 2005, his idea remained popular.

In another instance, the state of Arizona put a law into effect in August 2005 that gave prosecutors the power to prosecute "coyotes" (the Mexican word for human traffickers) at the border. In another example of how local laws have had an impact on national legislation, we can observe the government's reaction to a statement made by the leader of the Minutemen project, Chris Simcox, on April 20, 2006. Since he declared that the American people would "exercise their rights to protect their lives and property by initiating construction of fencing along the border on private land unless President Bush immediately deployed the National Guard ... (before Memorial Day)." The threat to begin this kind of vigilantism could be understood as an action to undermine the federal authority. President Bush quickly announced, on May 15, the deployment of 6,000 troops to support the border patrol, paid for by the federal government and placed under the supervision of state governors.

In 2006, the government also announced the end of the "catch and release" practice at the border through the creation of detention facilities. To beef up the funding for border security, the U.S. government raised the budget from $4.6 billion in fiscal year 2001 to $10.4 billion in fiscal year 2006. It also increased the number of border patrol agents from about 9,000 to more than 12,000—2008 would mark a doubling in the number of border patrol agents since U.S. President George W. Bush took office.

Despite federal actions, individual states introduced faster rules and decisions on immigration. According to the National Conference of State Legislatures, more than 570 bills dealing with immigration, employment, and trafficking were introduced in state legislatures in 2006, with 84 of these enacted throughout 32 states. Moreover, the number of immigration bills has consistently increased over the last few years. In 2005, for example, 300 bills were introduced and 38 enacted. In only the first seven months of 2007, more than 1,400 immigration-related bills were introduced in fifty states. Out of these, some 170 were enacted. This number reflects the sense of urgency and the political will of states to decide and act on a phenomenon U.S. citizens widely consider to be a major political problem.

At the federal level the immigration debate wavered between the House of Representatives and the Senate. The following legislation (all failed) are examples of how the debate focused more on enhancing security at the border than on regulating migration:

- S. 1823 Illegal Immigration Enforcement and Empowerment Act
- S. 2049 Border Security and Modernization Act of 2005
- H.R.3704 Protecting America Together Act of 2005
- H.R.3622 Border Protection Corps Act
- H.R.4099 Homeland Security Volunteerism Enhancement Act of 2005

On December 17, 2005, the House of Representatives passed the H.R. 4437 Border Protection, Antiterrorism, and Illegal Immigration Control Act of 2005. The so-called Sensenbrenner Bill, named after its sponsor House Republican James Sensenbrenner, passed by a vote of 239 to 182. Immigrant and civil rights groups considered this bill to be very harsh. It would have required all employers to use an electronic database for the verification of the employees' eligibility; it would have authorized building a fence along the U.S.-Mexican border; it would have authorized local authorities to enforce federal immigration laws; and it would have made supporting undocumented migrants whose life is in danger a criminal act. Moreover, the bill would have transferred $1 billion to the state Criminal Alien Assistance Program.

Undocumented migrants would have also been barred from basic public services. As a consequence, rallies started in the spring of 2006 against these measures, culminating in nationwide manifestation marches on May 1, dubbed "A Day without Immigrants."

The Senate discussed several bills before they considered the S. 2611 Comprehensive Immigration Reform Act of 2006 by a vote of 62 to 36. Like the H.R. 4437, it sought to improve border security, regulate immigration, and enforce employment regulations at the worksite. Unlike the House bill, however, the Senate's established a temporary worker program and created a path toward legalization and eventual citizenship. Yet the two approaches proved irreconcilable. On September 14, 2006, the U.S. House of Representatives passed the H.R. 6061 Secure Fence Act with 238 (among them 64 Democrats) to 138 votes, which was then signed by President Bush on October 26. It authorized the construction of 700 miles of double-layered fencing that would cover one-third of the 2,100-mile border, mainly from California to Arizona. The virtual fence, equipped with sensors, cameras, and aerial surveillance, was scheduled for completion by the end of 2008.

In his speeches, President Bush continued to state his support of comprehensive immigration reform that doesn't automatically allow amnesty but does look for legal ways to obtain U.S. citizenship, especially when migrants have roots in the United States. He also supported having them pay a fine for breaking the law when they entered the country illegally, pay taxes, learn English, and assimilate into U.S. society.

The Senate looked for a compromise bill that would include basic elements from two previously failed bills, namely, the S. 1033 Secure America and Orderly Immigration Act proposed by Senators Ted Kennedy and John McCain in May 2005 and the S. 1438 Comprehensive Enforcement and Immigration Reform Act of 2005 proposed by Senators

The Secure Fence Act of 2006 authorized the construction of 700 miles of double-layered fencing equipped with sensors and cameras and patrolled by aerial surveillance drones. Department of Defense/Sgt. Dan Heaton.

John Cornyn and John Kyl in July 2005. They also added sections on enforcement provisions of the 2005 REAL ID Act and the 2006 Secure Fence Act.

In short, the Senate's proposed Comprehensive Immigration Reform Act of 2007 sought to provide opportunities for undocumented aliens to obtain legal status. The proposed visa would have given its holder the right to stay in the United States and access to a Social Security number. After eight years, it would have turned into a United States Permanent Resident Card (green card). But this act would have also furthered the militarization of the U.S.-Mexican border with the funding of 300 miles of vehicle barriers, 105 cameras and radar towers, and 20,000 more border patrol agents. Moreover, it planned to restructure visa criteria for highly skilled workers according to a point system and increase employer penalties for hiring illegal aliens up to $75,000—to verify the legal status of employees electronically. Finally, it would have implemented a guest worker program for some 200,000 migrants (the original plan was 400,000) with the opportunity to enjoy multiple extended stays after an interim year out of the country for each.

The Senate bill received criticism from both Republicans and Democrats. The former called the proposal an amnesty, whereas the latter criticized the restrictions placed on family reunifications as unfair. Human rights groups and Hispanic organizations claimed that the guest worker program would create an underclass of workers without benefits. As a fragile compromise, the Senate's bill failed. It couldn't achieve a balance between security interests and the legalization of undocumented migrants. The bill also included parts of the Development, Relief, and Education for Alien Minors Act, the so-called DREAM Act. Introduced various times unsuccessfully into both houses, the proposal was to grant citizenship to minors who immigrated illegally in the past into the United States. In the end, supporters haven't given up promoting reform in the immigration debate. At the same time, the security business in the United States is booming. By the end of 2007 Michael Chertoff, secretary of the U.S. Department for Homeland Security, spoke of progress in building the security fence and in apprehending an increasing number of aliens violating U.S. immigration laws.

DOCUMENTS

Document 1: Speech of President Bush Concerning New Temporary Worker Program

When: January 7, 2004

Significance: This speech characterizes a change in the Bush administration. After new security priorities in the wake of September 11, 2001, interrupted and eventually derailed any comprehensive immigration agreement with the Mexican government, the president asked Congress to develop a new, temporary worker program that would fit American interests and reflect the new reality that the United States is facing. The presidential proposal initiated a new public debate about migration.

DID YOU KNOW?

Maras

"Maras" refers to criminal gangs from Central America, mostly from Guatemala, El Salvador, and Honduras. Originally, people from Central America escaped from civil wars and dictatorships in the 1980s to the United States. Their descendents formed gangs in the Latino ghettos of Los Angeles, and they named themselves *mara*, which is a Spanish slang for a group of people or gang. But it is also the name of a deadly ant in Central America. After the end of dictatorship in El Salvador in 1992, the United States expelled and deported many Salvadorans back to their country. Many of them continued to stay in the gangs because they had neither professional prospects nor families. They are active in drug trafficking, prostitution, smuggling, assaults, and burglaries. Many of them tried to reenter the United States illegally by crossing Mexico. Maras members display tattoos on their bodies to show their affiliation to one of the gangs. The most important and influential gangs are the Mara Salvatrucha, the Mara 18, and the Sombra Negra. All live in brutal rivalry. The killing of innocents (mostly undocumented migrants) is part of the test of courage to become part of the gang.

DID YOU KNOW?

Coyotes

"Coyote" is the Mexican word for human trafficker or smuggler. It is originally from Nahuatl, an indigenous language, and name of the once widely common prairie wolf in North and Central America. Sometimes human traffickers are also named "polleros," which literally means poulterer. Their goods are human beings, mainly from Mexico and Central America, who want to cross the U.S.-Mexican border illegally. According to data from the U.S. border patrol, between 1998 and 2004 around 2,000 people died at the border. Over the last few years the number has increased to an estimated 500 per year. Many of them die in the deserts at the common border of Sonora, Arizona, or Chihuahua, New Mexico/Texas due to heat strokes, dehydration, or hypothermia. Others are raped and murdered, even by the coyotes themselves. The Mexican border city Ciudad Juárez, for example, gained notoriety for hundreds of unsolved murders of young women. Analysts also blamed the complicity of local police and government officials. Nevertheless, the coyotes' services are still highly demanded by immigrants leaving their homes in the hope of gaining work and a better life in the United States. They are willing to pay up to 5,000 USD for their accompaniment through the deserts across the border.

President Bush Proposes New Temporary Worker Program

Remarks by the President on Immigration Policy

THE PRESIDENT: (…) Many of you here today are Americans by choice, and you have followed in the path of millions. And over the generations we have received energetic, ambitious, optimistic people from every part of the world. By tradition and conviction, our country is a welcoming society. America is a stronger and better nation because of the hard work and the faith and entrepreneurial spirit of immigrants.

Every generation of immigrants has reaffirmed the wisdom of remaining open to the talents and dreams of the world. And every generation of immigrants has reaffirmed our ability to assimilate newcomers—which is one of the defining strengths of our country. (…)

The contributions of immigrants to America continue. About 14 percent of our nation's civilian workforce is foreign-born. Most begin their working lives in America by taking hard jobs and clocking long hours in important industries. Many immigrants also start businesses, taking the familiar path from hired labor to ownership.

As a Texan, I have known many immigrant families, mainly from Mexico, and I have seen what they add to our country. They bring to America the values of faith in God, love of family, hard work and self reliance—the values that made us a great nation to begin with. We've all seen those values in action, through the service and sacrifice of more than 35,000 foreign-born men and women currently on active duty in the United States military. One of them is Master Gunnery Sergeant Guadalupe Denogean, an immigrant from Mexico who has served in the Marine Corps for 25 years and counting. Last year, I was honored and proud to witness Sergeant Denogean take the oath of citizenship in a hospital where he was recovering from wounds he received in Iraq. I'm honored to be his Commander-in-Chief, I'm proud to call him a fellow American. (Applause.)

As a nation that values immigration, and depends on immigration, we should have immigration laws that work and make us proud. Yet today we do not. Instead, we see many employers turning to the illegal labor market. We see millions of hard-working men and women condemned to fear and insecurity in a massive, undocumented economy. Illegal entry across our borders makes more difficult the urgent task of securing the homeland. The system is not working. Our nation needs an immigration system that serves the American economy, and reflects the American Dream.

Reform must begin by confronting a basic fact of life and economics: some of the jobs being generated in America's growing economy are jobs American citizens are not filling. Yet these jobs represent a tremendous opportunity for workers from abroad who want to work and fulfill their duties as a husband or a wife, a son or a daughter.

Their search for a better life is one of the most basic desires of human beings. Many undocumented workers have walked mile after mile, through the heat of the day and the cold of the night. Some have risked their lives in dangerous desert border crossings, or entrusted their lives to the brutal rings of heartless human smugglers. Workers who seek only to earn a living end up in the shadows of American life—fearful, often abused and exploited. When they are victimized by crime, they are afraid to call the police, or seek recourse in the legal system. They are cut off from their families far away, fearing if they leave our country to visit relatives back home, they might never be able to return to their jobs.

The situation I described is wrong. It is not the American way. Out of common sense and fairness, our laws should allow willing workers to enter our country and fill jobs that Americans have are not filling. (Applause.) We must make our immigration laws more rational, and more humane. And I believe we can do so without jeopardizing the livelihoods of American citizens.

Our reforms should be guided by a few basic principles. First, America must control its borders. Following the attacks of September the 11th, 2001, this duty of the federal government has become even more urgent. And we're fulfilling that duty.

For the first time in our history, we have consolidated all border agencies under one roof to make sure they share information and the work is more effective. We're matching all visa applicants against an expanded screening list to identify terrorists and criminals and immigration violators. This month, we have begun using advanced technology to better record and track aliens who enter our country—and to make sure they leave as scheduled. We have deployed new gamma and x-ray systems to scan cargo and containers and shipments at ports of entry to America. We have significantly expanded the Border Patrol—with more than a thousand new agents on the borders, and 40 percent greater funding over the last two years. We're working closely with the Canadian and Mexican governments to increase border security. America is acting on a basic belief: our borders should be open to legal travel and honest trade; our borders should be shut and barred tight to criminals, to drug traders, to drug traffickers and to criminals, and to terrorists.

> ## DID YOU KNOW?
>
> ### Vicente Fox
>
> In 2000 the former manager of the Coca Cola Company in Mexico, Vicente Fox, was elected as the first Mexican president from the Christian Democratic "National Action Party" after a 71-year authoritarian rule by the PRI (Institutional Revolutionary Party). It was also the first election since 1920 that a candidate from the opposition had been elected in democratic and fair elections. Fox won the election with the simple majority of 43 percent against Francisco Labastida (PRI) who had 36 percent. Cuauhtémoc Cárdenas of the left wing Party of the Democratic Revolution (PRD) won 17 percent. The newly elected president initiated a number of reforms to strengthen democracy and rule of law. However, fundamental change, such as reforming the economy, the tax system, and the structure of the state oil company PEMEX, have so far failed because of the resistance of the Mexican Congress. In international politics he has wavered between advocating closer ties to the United States to open criticism on the U.S. war in Iraq. His main objective—signing an agreement on immigration reform or at least a guest worker plan—failed because of developments after the terror attacks of September 11, 2001, in the United States. Throughout his presidency the net migration rate continually increased. He supported the right of Mexicans abroad to vote because their remittances directly contribute to economic growth and the livelihood of the people in the country.

Second, new immigration laws should serve the economic needs of our country. If an American employer is offering a job that American citizens are not willing to take, we ought to welcome into our country a person who will fill that job.

Third, we should not give unfair rewards to illegal immigrants in the citizenship process or disadvantage those who came here lawfully, or hope to do so.

Fourth, new laws should provide incentives for temporary, foreign workers to return permanently to their home countries after their period of work in the United States has expired.

Today, I ask the Congress to join me in passing new immigration laws that reflect these principles, that meet America's economic needs, and live up to our highest ideals. (Applause.)

I propose a new temporary worker program that will match willing foreign workers with willing American employers, when no Americans can be found to fill the jobs. This program will offer legal status, as temporary workers, to the millions of undocumented men and women now employed in the United States, and to those in foreign countries who seek to participate in the program and have been offered employment here. This new system should be clear and efficient, so employers are able to find workers quickly and simply. (...)

Some temporary workers will make the decision to pursue American citizenship. Those who make this choice will be allowed to apply in the normal way. They will not be given unfair advantage over people who have followed legal procedures from the start. I oppose amnesty, placing undocumented workers on the automatic path to citizenship. Granting amnesty encourages the violation of our laws, and perpetuates illegal immigration. America is a welcoming country, but citizenship must not be the automatic reward for violating the laws of America. (Applause.)

The citizenship line, however, is too long, and our current limits on legal immigration are too low. My administration will work with the Congress to increase the annual number of green cards that can lead to citizenship. Those willing to take the difficult path of citizenship—the path of work, and patience, and assimilation—should be welcome in America, like generations of immigrants before them. (Applause.)

In the process of immigration reform, we must also set high expectations for what new citizens should know. An understanding of what it means to be an American is not a formality in the naturalization process, it is essential to full participation in our democracy. My administration will examine the standard of knowledge in the current citizenship test. We must ensure that new citizens know not only the facts of our history, but the ideals that have shaped our history. Every citizen of America has an obligation to learn the values that make us one nation: liberty and civic responsibility, equality under God, and tolerance for others.

This new temporary worker program will bring more than economic benefits to America. Our homeland will be more secure when we can better account for those who enter our country, instead of the current situation in which millions of people are unknown, unknown to the law. Law enforcement will face fewer problems with undocumented workers, and will be better able to focus on the true threats to our nation from criminals and terrorists. And when temporary workers can travel legally and freely, there will be more efficient management of our borders and more effective enforcement against those who pose a danger to our country. (Applause.)

This new system will be more compassionate. Decent, hard-working people will now be protected by labor laws, with the right to change jobs, earn fair wages, and enjoy the same working conditions that the law requires for American workers. Temporary workers will be able to establish their identities by obtaining the legal documents we all take for granted. And they will be able to talk openly to authorities, to report crimes when they are harmed, without the fear of being deported. (Applause.)

The best way, in the long run, to reduce the pressures that create illegal immigration in the first place is to expand economic opportunity among the countries in our neighborhood. In a few days I will go to Mexico for the Special Summit of the Americas, where we will discuss ways to advance free trade, and to fight corruption, and encourage the reforms that lead to prosperity. Real growth and real hope in the nations of our hemisphere will lessen the flow of new immigrants to America when more citizens of other countries are able to achieve their dreams at their own home. (Applause.) (...)

(Source: Internet-URL: http://www.whitehouse.gov/news/releases/2004/01/20040107-3.html)

Document 2: Chris Simcox, Minutemen to Build Arizona-Mexico Border Fence

When: April 20, 2006

Significance: This statement warned the government to secure the border against illegal immigrants. It gave the government a deadline; otherwise, the Minutemen would build a fence on their own land to protect the U.S. frontier. The Minutemen argued that the government is responsible for the nation's security because Americans pay taxes for it.

Minutemen to Build Arizona-Mexico Border Fence

Chris Simcox, president of the Minuteman Civil Defense Corps ("MCDC"), today announced plans by the MCDC to work with local Arizona land owners to build border security fencing on private land along the border with Mexico.

At present, six private land owners have partnered with the Minutemen for the commencement of construction of border fencing on their land. Surveillance cameras on the fencing will be monitored via computer by registered Minutemen across the country. We have chosen a fence design that is based on the Israeli fences in Gaza and on the West Bank that have cut terrorist attacks there by 95% or more. In order to be effective, a fence should not be easy to compromise by climbing over it with a ladder, cutting through it with wire cutters, ramming it with a vehicle, or tunneling under it undetected. No fence can be a 100% impenetrable barrier—but a good design will be time-consuming enough to get through that Border Patrol agents can be alerted to get to a point of attempted intrusion before the intrusion can be completed. Our design does this. You can see it at www.WeNeedAFence.com.

Two construction companies to date have offered to inaugurate groundbreaking, coordinate volunteer construction crews and donate the use of the necessary heavy construction equipment.

The groundbreaking will begin in Arizona on Memorial Day weekend, unless in the interim President Bush deploys National Guard and reserve troops to immediately secure the out-of-control southern border.

The fencing will be built with privately donated funds, engineering and labor and will be used as an example to educate the public about the feasibility and efficacy of fencing to secure America's borders from illegal incursion by aliens and international criminal cartels. A non-profit organization dedicated specifically to this purpose will facilitate and administer donations for construction of the fence. Monetary and in-kind contributions for this effort will go directly into building materials for this private, volunteer fencing project. (...)

"President Bush and Congress have taxed the wages of the American people to pay for the protection of our country, and expended those dollars to subsidize millions of low-wage illegal workers with housing, education, medical care, and welfare benefits. Yet even the most basic level of national territorial integrity requires that our elected representatives secure the border. Should they continue to refuse to do their Constitutional duty, the Minutemen will again step into the breach and commence building the required border barriers on private land and with private donations.

"Should President Bush and Congress fail to fulfill their oaths of office, and meet their Constitutional obligation to protect these United States from invasion, we, the sovereign people of the United States, having suffered a long train of abuses at the hand of a willfully insolent government, do hereby declare that these States ought, should and will be protected by American Minutemen."

(Source: Internet-URL: The Minutemen National Blog: http://minutemanhq.com/b2/index.php/national/2006/04)

Document 3: Secure Fence Act of 2006, Bill H.R. 6061

When: September 13, 2006

Significance: Republican Peter T. King introduced this bill, which passed the House of Representatives and the Senate and became a law on October 26, 2006. It authorizes the construction of additional fencing along the U.S.-Mexican border, the installation of more checkpoints, and the Department of Homeland Security to increase the usage of advanced technology at the border.

Title: To Establish Operational Control over the International Land and Maritime Borders of the United States. Short title: Secure Fence Act of 2006.

An Act: To establish operational control over the international land and maritime borders of the United States

Be it enacted by the Senate and House of Representatives of the United States of America in Congress assembled,

SECTION 1. SHORT TITLE.

This Act may be cited as the "Secure Fence Act of 2006".

SEC. 2. ACHIEVING OPERATIONAL CONTROL ON THE BORDER.

(a) IN GENERAL.—Not later than 18 months after the date of the enactment of this Act, the Secretary of Homeland Security shall take all actions the Secretary determines necessary and appropriate to achieve and maintain operational control over the entire international land and maritime borders of the United States, to include the following—

(1) systematic surveillance of the international land and maritime borders of the United States through more effective use of personnel and technology, such as unmanned aerial vehicles, ground-based sensors, satellites, radar coverage, and cameras; and

(2) physical infrastructure enhancements to prevent unlawful entry by aliens into the United States and facilitate access to the international land and maritime borders by United States Customs and Border Protection, such as additional checkpoints, all weather access roads, and vehicle barriers.

(b) OPERATIONAL CONTROL DEFINED.—In this section, the term "operational control" means the prevention of all unlawful entries into the United States, including entries by terrorists, other unlawful aliens, instruments of terrorism, narcotics, and other contraband.

(c) REPORT.—Not later than one year after the date of the enactment of this Act and annually thereafter, the Secretary shall submit to Congress a report on the progress made toward achieving and maintaining operational control over the entire international land and maritime borders of the United States in accordance with this section.

[...]

PUBLIC LAW 109–367—OCT. 26, 2006 120 STAT. 2639

(1) in the subsection heading by striking "NEAR SAN DIEGO, CALIFORNIA"; and

(2) by amending paragraph (1) to read as follows:

"(1) SECURITY FEATURES.—

"(A) REINFORCED FENCING.—In carrying out subsection

(a), the Secretary of Homeland Security shall provide for at least 2 layers of reinforced fencing, the installation of additional physical barriers, roads, lighting, cameras, and sensors—

"(i) extending from 10 miles west of the Tecate, California, port of entry to 10 miles east of the Tecate, California, port of entry;

"(ii) extending from 10 miles west of the Calexico, California, port of entry to 5 miles east of the Douglas, Arizona, port of entry;

"(iii) extending from 5 miles west of the Columbus, New Mexico, port of entry to 10 miles east of El Paso, Texas;

"(iv) extending from 5 miles northwest of the Del Rio, Texas, port of entry to 5 miles southeast of the Eagle Pass, Texas, port of entry; and

"(v) extending 15 miles northwest of the Laredo, Texas, port of entry to the Brownsville, Texas, port of entry.

"(B) PRIORITY AREAS.—With respect to the border described—

"(i) in subparagraph (A)(ii), the Secretary shall ensure that an interlocking surveillance camera system is installed along such area by May 30, 2007, and that fence construction is completed by May 30, 2008; and

"(ii) in subparagraph (A)(v), the Secretary shall ensure that fence construction from 15 miles northwest of the Laredo, Texas, port of entry to 15 southeast of the Laredo, Texas, port of entry is completed by December 31, 2008.

"(C) EXCEPTION.—If the topography of a specific area has an elevation grade that exceeds 10 percent, the Secretary may use other means to secure such area, including the use of surveillance and barrier tools."

[...]

(Source: Internet-URL: http://frwebgate.access.gpo.gov/cgi-bin/getdoc.cgi?dbname=109_cong_public_laws&docid=f:publ367.109.pdf)

Document 4: Bill to Amend the Immigration and Nationality Act, H.R. 4437

When: June 12, 2005

Significance: This bill sponsored by Republican James Sensenbrenner sought to enhance border security and strengthen the enforcement of immigration laws. Although the House of Representatives passed it on December 16, 2005, by a vote of 239 to 182, the Senate rejected it on July 28, 2007.

Border Protection, Antiterrorism, and Illegal Immigration Control Act of 2005

Title I: Securing United States Borders - (Sec. 101) Directs the Secretary of Homeland Security (Secretary) to take all appropriate actions to maintain operational control over the U.S. international land and maritime borders, including: (1) systematic surveillance using unmanned aerial vehicles (UAVs), ground-based sensors, satellites, radar coverage, and cameras; (2) physical infrastructure enhancements to prevent unlawful U.S. entry and facilitate United States Customs and Border Protection border access; (3) hiring and training additional Border Patrol agents; and (4) increasing deployment of United States Customs and Border Protection personnel to border areas with high levels of unlawful entry.

Requires the Secretary to annually report to Congress respecting border control progress.

(Sec. 102) Directs the Secretary to report to the appropriate congressional committees respecting: (1) a comprehensive border surveillance plan; and (2) a National Strategy for Border Security to achieve operational control over all U.S. borders and ports of entry.

(Sec. 103) Directs the Secretary to report to the appropriate congressional committees respecting implementation of the cross-border security agreements signed by the United States with Mexico and Canada.

(Sec. 104) Directs the Secretary to: (1) enhance connectivity between the Automated Biometric Identification System (IDENT) and the Automated Fingerprint Identification System (IAFIS) fingerprint databases; and (2) collect all fingerprints from each alien required to provide fingerprints during the alien's initial enrollment in the integrated entry and exit data system.

(Sec. 105) Directs the Secretary to report to Congress respecting the "One Face at the Border" inspection initiative at U.S. ports of entry.

(Sec. 106) Directs the Secretary to implement a plan to ensure clear and secure two-way communication capabilities: (1) among all Border Patrol agents conducting operations between ports of entry; (2) between Border Patrol agents and their respective Border Patrol stations; (3) between Border Patrol agents and residents in remote areas along the international land border who do not have mobile communications; and (4) between all appropriate Department of Homeland Security (DHS) border security agencies and state, local, and tribal law enforcement agencies.

(Sec. 107) Directs the Secretary, subject to appropriations, to increase full-time port of entry inspectors by at least 250 for each of FY2007-FY2010. Authorizes appropriations for related training and support.

(Sec. 108) Directs the Secretary, subject to appropriations, to increase border and port canine detection teams by at least 25% for each of FY2007-FY2011.

(Sec. 109) Directs: (1) the Inspector General of DHS to review the compliance of each Secure Border Initiative contract above $20 million with applicable cost requirements, performance objectives, program milestones, inclusion of small, minority, and women-owned businesses, and timelines; and (2) the Secretary to report to the appropriate congressional committees respecting each review.

Authorizes additional FY2007-FY2009 appropriations for the Inspector General.

(Sec. 110) Directs the Comptroller General of the United States to review DHS Border Patrol agent training.

(Sec. 111) Directs the Secretary to report to the appropriate congressional committees respecting the National Capital Region (NCR) airspace security mission's impact on border security, including: (1) resources and resource sources devoted or planned to be devoted to NCR airspace security; and (2) an assessment of such resources' impact upon traditional border missions.

(Sec. 112) Directs the Secretary to reimburse (up to prior-to-damage value) property owners for costs associated with repairing damages to the property owners' private infrastructure constructed on a U.S. government right-of-way delineating the international land border when such damages are: (1) the result of unlawful entry of aliens; and (2) confirmed by the appropriate DHS personnel and submitted to the Secretary.

[...]

Title II: Combatting Alien Smuggling and Illegal Entry and Presence

(Sec. 201) Amends INA to revise the definition of "aggravated felony" to include all smuggling offenses, and illegal entry and reentry crimes where the sentence is a year or more.

(Sec. 202) Revises alien smuggling and related offense provisions to: (1) provide mandatory minimum sentences for smuggling convictions; (2) revise criminal offense and criminal penalty provisions; (3) expand seizure and forfeiture authority; and (4) provide extraterritorial jurisdiction over such offenses.

(Sec. 203) Makes illegal U.S. presence a crime.

Increases prison penalties for first-time improper U.S. entry. Expands: (1) penalties for marriage and immigration-related entrepreneurship fraud; and (2) criminal penalties imposed upon aliens who illegally enter the United States or who are present illegally following convictions of certain crimes.

(Sec. 204) Provides mandatory minimum sentences, with a specified affirmative defense exception, for aliens convicted of reentry after removal.

(Sec. 205) Subjects an individual who knowingly aids or conspires to allow, procure, or permit a removed alien to reenter the United States to criminal penalty, the same imprisonment term as applies to the alien so aided, or both.

(Sec. 206) Includes among smuggling crimes the carrying or use of a firearm during such activity.

(Sec. 207) States that: (1) the provision barring entry to aliens who have made false claims to U.S. citizenship also applies to aliens who have made false claims to U.S. nationality; and (2) the Secretary shall have access to any information kept by any federal agency regarding persons seeking immigration benefits or privileges.

(Sec. 208) Revises voluntary departure provisions to: (1) reduce the maximum period of voluntary departure that can be granted before the conclusion of removal proceedings from 120 to 60 days, and reduce such period from 60 to 45 days after the conclusion of removal proceedings; (2) require (currently, authorizes that such bond be provided) an alien receiving voluntary departure prior to conclusion of removal proceedings to post a bond or show that a bond would create a financial hardship or is unnecessary to guarantee departure; (3) require as part of a voluntary departure agreement that the alien waive all rights to any further motion, appeal, application, petition, or petition for review relating to removal or relief or protection from removal; (4) provide that a subsequent appeal would invalidate the voluntary departure grant, as would the alien's failure to depart; (5) provide that failure to depart in violation of such an agreement would subject the alien to a $3,000 fine, make the alien ineligible for various immigration benefits for ten years after departure, and prohibit the reopening of removal proceedings, except to apply for withholding of removal or restriction on removal to a country where the alien's life or freedom would be threatened or to seek protection against torture; (6) authorize the Secretary to reduce the period of inadmissibility for certain aliens previously removed or unlawfully present; and (7) preclude courts from reinstating, enjoining, delaying, or tolling the period of voluntary departure.

(Sec. 209) Makes aliens ordered removed from the United States who fail to depart ineligible for discretionary relief from removal pursuant to a motion to reopen during the time they remain in the United States and for a period of ten years after their departure, with the exception of motions to reopen to seek withholding of removal to a country where the alien's life or freedom would be threatened or to seek protection against torture.

Subjects aliens who improperly enter the United States after voluntarily departing to improper entry fine and/or imprisonment provisions.

(Sec. 210) Directs the Secretary to establish a Fraudulent Documents Center (Forensic Document Laboratory) to: (1) collect information on fraudulent documents intended for U.S. use from federal, state, and local law enforcement agencies, and foreign governments; (2) maintain a database of such information for ongoing distribution to law enforcement agencies.

[...]

Title III: Border Security Cooperation and Enforcement - (Sec. 301) Directs the Secretary and the Secretary of Defense to: (1) develop a joint strategic plan to increase Department of Defense (DOD) surveillance equipment use, including UAVs, at or near U.S. international land and maritime borders; and (2) report to the appropriate congressional committees.

States that nothing in this section amends the prohibition on posse comitatus use of the Army or the Air Force.

(Sec. 302) Directs the Secretary to: (1) assess border security vulnerabilities on Department of the Interior land directly adjacent to the U.S. land border; and (2) provide additional border security assistance as necessary.

(Sec. 303) Directs the Secretary to design and carry out a national border security exercise for the purposes of: (1) involving officials from federal, state, territorial, local, tribal, and international governments and private sector representatives; (2) testing and evaluating U.S. capacity to detect and disrupt border threats; and (3) testing and evaluating information sharing capability among federal, state, territorial, local, tribal, and international governments.

(Sec. 304) Directs the Secretary to establish the Border Security Advisory Committee.

(Sec. 305) Authorizes the Secretary to permit a state, local government, or Indian tribe to use federal funds received under the State Homeland Security Grant Program, the Urban Area Security Initiative, or the Law Enforcement Terrorism Prevention Program for border security activities usually performed by a federal agency but which, pursuant to an agreement, are being performed by state, local, or tribal government.

(Sec. 306) Directs the Secretary to establish a university-based Center for Excellence for Border Security, which shall address the most significant threats, vulnerabilities, and consequences posed by U.S. borders and border control systems.

[...]

Title IV: Detention and Removal - (Sec. 401) Requires mandatory detention of an alien apprehended illegally seeking to enter the United States at a U.S. port of entry or land or maritime border as of October 1, 2006, unless such alien is: (1) paroled into the United States for humanitarian or public benefit reasons; or (2) is permitted to withdraw an application for admission and immediately departs from the United States. Provides that during the period 60 days after enactment of this Act and prior to October 1, 2006, an apprehended alien may be released with notice to appear only if: (1) the Secretary determines that the alien is not a national security risk; and (2) the alien provides a bond of not less than $5,000.

Exempts from mandatory detention an alien who is a native or citizen of a Western Hemisphere country with whose government the United States does not have full diplomatic relations (currently, Cuba).

States that nothing in such provision shall be construed as limiting: (1) an alien's right to apply for asylum or for relief or deferral of removal based on a fear of persecution; and (2) the Secretary's authority to determine whether an alien claiming asylum shall be detained or released after a finding of a credible fear of persecution.

[...]

Title VI: Terrorist and Criminal Aliens - (Sec. 601) Prohibits an alien deportable on grounds of terrorism from being granted withholding of removal.

Expands specified terrorism-related grounds for refusal of amnesty.

Makes such amendments retroactive to all aliens in removal, deportation, or exclusion proceedings and to all applications pending on or filed after the date of enactment of this Act.

(Sec. 602) Permits indefinite detention of specified dangerous aliens under orders of removal who cannot be removed, subject to review every six months. States that habeas corpus review of such provisions shall be available only in the U.S. District Court for the District of Columbia after exhaustion of administrative remedies.

(Sec. 603) Increases penalties and sets mandatory minimum sentences for an alien who fails to depart when ordered removed, hampers removal, or fails to present himself or herself for removal.

(Sec. 604) Makes ineligible for admission, and bars from seeking waiver of inadmissibility, an alien who has: (1) been convicted of misuse of Social Security numbers and cards, or identification document-related fraud; (2) been convicted of an aggravated felony; (3) procured citizenship unlawfully; or (4) been convicted of a crime of domestic violence, stalking, child abuse, child neglect, or child abandonment, or has violated a protective order.

(Sec. 605) Makes an asylee or refugee convicted of an aggravated felony ineligible for permanent resident status adjustment. Applies such provision retroactively.

[...]

Title VII: Employment Eligibility Verification - (Sec. 701) Amends INA to direct the Secretary to establish and maintain a telephone- or electronic media-based employment eligibility verification system.

Requires such system to: (1) provide verification or tentative non-verification of an individual?s identity and employment eligibility within three days of an inquiry; and (2) provide, in the case of tentative non-verification, a secondary process for final verification or non-verification within ten days.

Provides that: (1) the Commissioner of Social Security shall develop a process for comparing names and social security numbers against appropriate databases to ensure timely and accurate responses to employer inquiries; and (2) the Secretary shall develop a process for comparing names and alien identification or authorization numbers, and shall investigate multiple uses of the same social security number that suggest fraud.

Limits federal use of the verification system, and states that such provision does not authorize issuance of a national identity card.

Limits verification system-related individual relief to procedures under the Federal Tort Claims Act. Prohibits class actions. Immunizes from civil or criminal liability a person or entity who takes action in good faith reliance on verification system information.

Repeals provisions respecting evaluation of and changes to the current employment verification system.

(Sec. 702) Sets forth employer verification requirements with respect to an affirmative defense to liability for employment of unauthorized workers, including revision of attestation and retention of verification form provisions.

[...]

(Source: Internet-URL: http://thomas.loc.gov/cgi-bin/bdquery/z?d109:HR04437:@@@D&summ2=m&)

Document 5: Proposed Bill: Comprehensive Immigration Reform Act of 2006, S. 2611

When: April 7, 2006

Significance: This bill sponsored by Senator Arlen Specter sought to provide a comprehensive immigration reform that reflected security enforcement on the one hand and the political will and necessity to legalize undocumented aliens and to offer them temporary work permits on the other. It passed the Senate by a vote of 62 to 36 on May 25, 2006, and was in principle fundamentally in opposition to H.R. 4437.

Comprehensive Immigration Reform Act of 2006

Title I: Border Enforcement - Subtitle A: Assets for Controlling United States Borders - (Sec. 101) Directs the Secretary of Homeland Security (Secretary), for each of FY2007-FY2011, to: (1) increase by not less than 500 the number of full-time active duty port of entry inspectors and provide related training, equipment, and support (authorizes FY2007-FY2011 appropriations); and (2) increase by not less than 200 the number of Department of Homeland Security (DHS) positions assigned to investigate alien smuggling.

[...]

(Sec. 102) Directs the Secretary to procure additional technological assets, including unmanned aerial vehicles (UAVs), to achieve operational U.S. border control and to establish a border security perimeter (virtual fence) to provide a barrier to illegal immigration.

Directs the Secretary and the Secretary of Defense to: (1) develop a plan to increase the use of Department of Defense (DOD) surveillance equipment to prevent illegal immigration along the U.S. international land borders; and (2) report to Congress.

[...]

(Sec. 104) Authorizes the Secretary to maintain temporary or permanent checkpoints on roadways in border patrol sectors located near the U.S.-Mexico border.

(Sec. 105) Authorizes the Secretary to: (1) construct additional ports of entry along the U.S. international land borders; and (2) improve existing ports of entry.

(Sec. 106) Directs the Secretary to provide for: (1) fencing, vehicle barrier, and road construction and improvements in the Yuma and Tucson, Arizona, sectors; and (2) fencing and vehicle barrier construction in other high trafficked areas along the southern border. Requires: (1) construction completion within two years; and (2) a report to the Committees. Authorizes appropriations.

Subtitle B: Border Security Plans, Strategies, and Reports - (Sec. 111) Directs the Secretary to: (1) develop a systematic surveillance plan for the U.S. international land and maritime borders; and (2) report to Congress.

(Sec. 112) Directs the Secretary to: (1) develop a National Strategy for Border Security that describes actions to achieve operational control over all U.S. ports of entry and the U.S. land and maritime borders; (2) consult with appropriate state, local, tribal, and private entities; and (3) submit such Strategy to Congress within one year of enactment of this Act.

[...]

Subtitle C: Other Border Initiatives - (Sec. 121) Directs the Secretary, by October 1, 2007, to: (1) enhance connectivity between DHS' Automated Biometric Fingerprint Identification System (IDENT) and the Federal Bureau of Investigation's (FBI) Integrated Automated Fingerprint

Identification System (IAFIS); and (2) collect all fingerprints from each alien required to provide fingerprints during the alien's initial enrollment in the integrated entry and exit data system.

[...]

(Sec. 131) Requires mandatory detention of an alien apprehended illegally seeking to enter the United States at a U.S. port of entry or land or maritime border as of October 1, 2007, unless such alien is: (1) paroled into the United States for humanitarian or public benefit reasons; or (2) permitted to withdraw an admission application and immediately departs from the United States. Provides that during the period 60 days after enactment of this Act and prior to October 1, 2007, an apprehended alien may be released with notice to appear only if: (1) the Secretary determines that the alien is not a national security risk; and (2) the alien provides a bond of not less than $5,000.

Exempts from mandatory detention an alien who is a native or citizen of a Western Hemisphere country with whose government the United States does not have full diplomatic relations (currently, Cuba).

States that nothing in such provision shall be construed as limiting: (1) an alien's right to apply for asylum or for relief or deferral of removal based on a fear of persecution; and (2) the Secretary's authority to determine whether an alien claiming asylum shall be detained or released after a finding of a credible fear of persecution.

(Sec. 132) Amends federal criminal law to make it unlawful for a person to elude customs, immigration, or agriculture inspection or fail to stop at the command of a U.S. enforcement officer or employee at a port of entry or customs or immigration checkpoint.

States that a person who commits such an offense shall be: (1) fined; (2) imprisoned for not more than three years, or both; (3) imprisoned for not more than ten years, or both, if he or she attempts to inflict or inflicts bodily injury; (4) imprisoned for any term of years or for life, or both, if death results, and may be sentenced to death; or (5) both fined and imprisoned.

States that: (1) if two or more persons conspire to commit such offense, and one or more of such persons do any act to effect the conspiracy, each shall be punishable as a principal, except that the sentence of death may not be imposed; and (2) for the purposes of seizure and forfeiture of a vehicle or other conveyance in the commission of such offense, or in the case of disregarding the lawful authority or command of any U.S. officer or employee, such conduct shall constitute prima facie evidence of smuggling aliens or merchandise.

Subjects a person who fails to obey the lawful orders of a border enforcement officer to fine and/or up to five years' imprisonment.

[...]

Subtitle D: Border Tunnel Prevention Act - Border Tunnel Prevention Act - (Sec. 142) Amends federal criminal law to prohibit the construction or financing of an unauthorized tunnel or subterranean passage that crosses an international border between the United States and another country. Imposes a 20-year prison term for such offense. Doubles penalties for persons who use such a tunnel or passage to unlawfully smuggle an alien, illegal goods, controlled substances, weapons of mass destruction, or members of a terrorist organization.

Imposes a ten-year prison term on any person who recklessly permits the construction or use of such a tunnel or passage on land that such person owns or controls.

Subjects to forfeiture any property involved in, or traceable to, the construction or financing of such a tunnel or passage.

[...]

Subtitle E: Border Law Enforcement Relief Act - Border Law Enforcement Relief Act of 2006 - (Sec. 153) Authorizes the Secretary to award FY2007-FY2011 grants to a tribal, state, or local law enforcement agency located in a county within 100 miles of a U.S. border with Canada or Mexico, or in a county beyond 100 miles that has been certified by the Secretary as a high impact area (as defined by this Act), to provide assistance in addressing: (1) criminal activity that occurs by virtue of proximity to the border; and (2) the impact of any lack of border security.

[...]

Subtitle F: Rapid Response Measures - (Sec. 161) Authorizes the Secretary, if the governor of a border state declares an international border security emergency and requests additional Border Patrol agents, to provide such state with up to 1,000 additional agents. Directs the Secretary to ensure that agents are not precluded from performing patrol duties and apprehending violators of law, except in unusual circumstances if the temporary use of fixed deployment positions is necessary.

[...]

Title II: Interior Enforcement - (Sec. 201) Amends INA to expand the scope of terrorist and security-related activities for which asylum, cancellation of removal, voluntary departure, permanent residence registry for certain aliens entering the United States before 1972, and exceptions to restrictions on removal will be denied.

Applies such provisions to any act or condition constituting a ground for inadmissibility, excludability, or removal occurring or existing on or after the date of enactment of this Act.

(Sec. 202) Revises provisions respecting detention and removal of aliens under order of removal.

Permits extension of the 90-day detention period for an alien under order of removal if the alien fails to: (1) make all reasonable efforts to comply with the removal order; or (2) cooperate with DHS efforts to establish the alien's identity and carry out the removal order, including failing to make timely application for travel or departure documents, or acting to prevent such removal.

States that the removal period shall: (1) not begin until the alien is in DHS custody; and (2) if the alien is transferred to another federal or state agency, be tolled until return to DHS custody.

Authorizes the Secretary to detain an alien subject to an administrative final order of removal who has been granted a stay of removal during the pendency of such stay.

Authorizes the Secretary to parole an alien ordered removed and provide that such alien not be detained unless: (1) the alien violates parole conditions; or (2) removal becomes reasonably foreseeable.

Requires that a detention review process be established for aliens under order of removal who have effected an entry and are cooperating with removal. Sets forth evidence provisions.

Authorizes the Secretary to detain an alien for 90 days beyond the original removal (and extension) period. Authorizes the Secretary to detain an alien beyond such 90-day period until removal if the Secretary certifies in writing that: (1) it is likely that the alien will be removed in the foreseeable future; or (2) the alien has a highly contagious disease that poses a public safety threat, release of the alien would have serious adverse foreign policy consequences or would threaten U.S. national security, or the alien's release would threaten the community or an individual because of the alien's criminal history.

Authorizes the Secretary to: (1) renew detention by certification every six months (provides that the alien shall be released from detention if certification is not renewed); (2) condition an alien's release; and (3) re-detain persons on supervised release.

Directs the Secretary to detain an alien who has effected an entry and is not cooperating with removal or if the Secretary has certified the detention.

Restricts judicial review of detention to habeas corpus petitions in U.S. district court after exhaustion of all administrative remedies.

Amends federal criminal law to permit a judicial officer to consider a person's immigration (and removal) status or whether such person has committed specified felonies in bail determinations.

(Sec. 203) Revises the definition of "aggravated felony" to: (1) provide that sexual abuse of a minor will be considered an aggravated felony whether or not the victim's minority is established by evidence contained in the record of conviction or by extrinsic evidence; (2) include all smuggling offenses, and illegal entry and reentry crimes where the sentence is a year or more; and (3) include certain accessory roles.

Makes the provisions of this section effective on the date of enactment of this Act, and applicable to acts occurring on or after such date.

States that specified amendments made by of the Illegal Immigration Reform and Immigrant Responsibility Act of 1996 to the definition of aggravated felony shall continue to apply whether the conviction was entered before, on, or after September 30, 1996.

[...]

Title III: Unlawful Employment of Aliens - (Sec. 301) Amends INA to revise unlawful employment of alien provisions.

Makes it unlawful for an employer to hire or to recruit or refer for a fee for U.S. employment: (1) knowing, or with reckless disregard, that the alien is an unauthorized alien with respect to such employment; or (2) an individual unless such employer meets document certification and Electronic Employment Verification System requirements.

Makes it unlawful for an employer, after lawfully hiring an alien, to continue to employ the alien knowing that the alien is (or has become) an unauthorized alien with respect to such employment.

Makes it unlawful for an employer who uses a contract, subcontract, or exchange to obtain the labor of an alien in the United States knowing, or with reckless disregard that: (1) the alien is an unauthorized alien with respect to such labor; or (2) the person hiring such alien failed to comply with document certification and Electronic Employment Verification System requirements. Provides that: (1) the person hiring the alien shall provide the employer with his or her employer identification number; and (2) failure to do so shall be a recordkeeping violation.

Makes good faith compliance by an employer with document certification and Electronic Employment Verification System (upon mandatory or discretionary participation) requirements an affirmative defense.

Authorizes the Secretary, upon reasonable cause to believe that an employer has failed to comply with this section, to require that the employer certify within 60 days (with a discretionary extension) that the employer is in compliance or has instituted a compliance program.

Requires that an employer hiring or recruiting or referring for a fee verify a person's employment eligibility by: (1) employer attestation that the employer has verified the identity and eligibility for employment of the individual by examining specified documents (U.S. passport, state drivers license, permanent resident or employment authorization card, or alternative identifying document); (2) employee attestation of U.S. work eligibility ($5,000 fine and/or three years' imprisonment for false representation of employability); and (3) employer retention of such attestations for five years for recruiting and referrals, and for hiring the later of five years or one year after termination of employment.

Sets forth additional employer document and recordkeeping requirements. Subjects an employer to civil penalties for recordkeeping violations.

States that nothing in this section authorizes the issuance or use of a national identification card.

[...]

(Source: Internet-URL: http://thomas.loc.gov/cgi-bin/bdquery/z?d109:SN02611:@@@D&summ2=m&)

Document 6: Proposed Bill: Comprehensive Immigration Reform Act of 2007, S. 1348

When: May 9, 2007

Significance: This bill was characterized as a compromise between the Republicans and the Democrats in the 110th U.S. Congress. On the one hand, it would have provided a path to legal status and citizenship for undocumented migrants. On the other hand, it would have continued the militarization of the border. The sponsor of the bill was Harry Reid, but it included the cooperation of Senators Kennedy, McCain, Kyl, Lindsey Graham and input from President George W. Bush, who supported it. On June 7 three votes on cloture for the bill failed. Nevertheless, it was brought back for discussion on June 25 because of the pressure of President Bush, who urged for this comprehensive reform. Although a series of votes on amendments and cloture took place, it finally failed on June 28 with the last vote on cloture by a vote of 46 to 53.

Title: Secure Borders, Economic Opportunity and Immigration Reform Act of 2007; Short title: Comprehensive Immigration Reform Act of 2007

A Bill

To provide for comprehensive immigration reform and for other purposes.

Be it enacted by the Senate and House of Representatives of the United States of America in Congress assembled,

TITLE I—BORDER ENFORCEMENT
Subtitle A—Assets for Controlling United States Borders
Subtitle B—Border Security Plans, Strategies, and Reports

SEC. 111. SURVEILLANCE PLAN.
SEC. 112. NATIONAL STRATEGY FOR BORDER SECURITY.

(a) Requirement for Strategy- The Secretary, in consultation with the heads of other appropriate Federal agencies, shall develop a National Strategy for Border Security that describes actions to be carried out to achieve operational control over all ports of entry into the United States and the international land and maritime borders of the United States.

(b) Content- The National Strategy for Border Security shall include the following:

(1) The implementation schedule for the comprehensive plan for systematic surveillance described in section 111.

(2) An assessment of the threat posed by terrorists and terrorist groups that may try to infiltrate the United States at locations along the international land and maritime borders of the United States.

(3) A risk assessment for all United States ports of entry and all portions of the international land and maritime borders of the United States that includes a description of activities being undertaken–

(A) to prevent the entry of terrorists, other unlawful aliens, instruments of terrorism, narcotics, and other contraband into the United States; and

(B) to protect critical infrastructure at or near such ports of entry or borders.

(4) An assessment of the legal requirements that prevent achieving and maintaining operational control over the entire international land and maritime borders of the United States.

(5) An assessment of the most appropriate, practical, and cost-effective means of defending the international land and maritime borders of the United States against threats to security and illegal transit, including intelligence capacities, technology, equipment, personnel, and training needed to address security vulnerabilities.

(6) An assessment of staffing needs for all border security functions, taking into account threat and vulnerability information pertaining to the borders and the impact of new security programs, policies, and technologies.

(7) A description of the border security roles and missions of Federal, State, regional, local, and tribal authorities, and recommendations regarding actions the Secretary can carry out to improve coordination with such authorities to enable border security and enforcement activities to be carried out in a more efficient and effective manner.

(8) An assessment of existing efforts and technologies used for border security and the effect of the use of such efforts and technologies on civil rights, personal property rights, privacy rights, and civil liberties, including an assessment of efforts to take into account asylum seekers, trafficking victims, unaccompanied minor aliens, and other vulnerable populations.

(9) A prioritized list of research and development objectives to enhance the security of the international land and maritime borders of the United States.

(10) A description of ways to ensure that the free flow of travel and commerce is not diminished by efforts, activities, and programs aimed at securing the international land and maritime borders of the United States.

(11) An assessment of additional detention facilities and beds that are needed to detain unlawful aliens apprehended at United States ports of entry or along the international land borders of the United States.

(12) A description of the performance metrics to be used to ensure accountability by the bureaus of the Department in implementing such Strategy.

(13) A schedule for the implementation of the security measures described in such Strategy, including a prioritization of security measures, realistic deadlines for addressing the security and enforcement needs, an estimate of the resources needed to carry out such measures, and a description of how such resources should be allocated.

(c) Consultation- In developing the National Strategy for Border Security, the Secretary shall consult with representatives of—

(1) State, local, and tribal authorities with responsibility for locations along the international land and maritime borders of the United States; and

(2) appropriate private sector entities, nongovernmental organizations, and affected communities that have expertise in areas related to border security.

(d) Coordination- The National Strategy for Border Security shall be consistent with the National Strategy for Maritime Security developed pursuant to Homeland Security Presidential Directive 13, dated December 21, 2004.

(e) Submission to Congress-

(1) STRATEGY- Not later than 1 year after the date of the enactment of this Act, the Secretary shall submit to Congress the National Strategy for Border Security.

(2) UPDATES- The Secretary shall submit to Congress any update of such Strategy that the Secretary determines is necessary, not later than 30 days after such update is developed.

(f) Immediate Action- Nothing in this section or section 111 may be construed to relieve the Secretary of the responsibility to take all actions necessary and appropriate to achieve and maintain operational control over the entire international land and maritime borders of the United States.

SEC. 113. REPORTS ON IMPROVING THE EXCHANGE OF INFORMATION ON NORTH AMERICAN SECURITY.
SEC. 114. IMPROVING THE SECURITY OF MEXICO'S SOUTHERN BORDER.
SEC. 115. COMBATING HUMAN SMUGGLING.
SEC. 116. DEATHS AT UNITED STATES-MEXICO BORDER.
SEC. 117. COOPERATION WITH THE GOVERNMENT OF MEXICO.

(a) Cooperation Regarding Border Security- The Secretary of State, in cooperation with the Secretary and representatives of Federal, State, and local law enforcement agencies that are involved in border security and immigration enforcement efforts, shall work with the appropriate officials from the Government of Mexico to improve coordination between the United States and Mexico regarding—

(1) improved border security along the international border between the United States and Mexico;

(2) the reduction of human trafficking and smuggling between the United States and Mexico;

(3) the reduction of drug trafficking and smuggling between the United States and Mexico;

(4) the reduction of gang membership in the United States and Mexico;

(5) the reduction of violence against women in the United States and Mexico; and

(6) the reduction of other violence and criminal activity.

(b) Cooperation Regarding Education on Immigration Laws- The Secretary of State, in cooperation with other appropriate Federal officials, shall work with the appropriate officials from the Government of Mexico to carry out activities to educate citizens and nationals of Mexico regarding eligibility for status as a nonimmigrant under Federal law to ensure that the citizens and nationals are not exploited while working in the United States.

(c) Cooperation Regarding Circular Migration- The Secretary of State, in cooperation with the Secretary of Labor and other appropriate Federal officials, shall work with the appropriate officials from the Government of Mexico to improve coordination between the United States and Mexico to encourage circular migration, including assisting in the development of economic opportunities and providing job training for citizens and nationals in Mexico.

(d) Consultation Requirement- Federal, State, and local representatives in the United States shall consult with their counterparts in Mexico concerning the construction of additional fencing and related border security structures along the international border between the United States and Mexico, as authorized by this title, before the commencement of any such construction in order to–

(1) solicit the views of affected communities;

(2) lessen tensions; and

(3) foster greater understanding and stronger cooperation on this and other important security issues of mutual concern.

(e) Annual Report- Not later than 180 days after the date of enactment of this Act, and annually thereafter, the Secretary of State shall submit to Congress a report on the actions taken by the United States and Mexico under this section.

Subtitle C–Other Border Security Initiatives

SEC. 121. BIOMETRIC DATA ENHANCEMENTS.
SEC. 122. SECURE COMMUNICATION.
SEC. 123. BORDER PATROL TRAINING CAPACITY REVIEW.
SEC. 124. US-VISIT SYSTEM.
SEC. 125. DOCUMENT FRAUD DETECTION.
SEC. 126. IMPROVED DOCUMENT INTEGRITY.
SEC. 127. CANCELLATION OF VISAS.
SEC. 128. BIOMETRIC ENTRY-EXIT SYSTEM.
SEC. 129. BORDER STUDY.

(Source: Internet-URL: http://frwebgate.access.gpo.gov/cgi-bin/getdoc.cgi?dbname=110_cong_bills&docid=f:s1348pcs.txt.pdf)

Document 7: Proposed DREAM Act of 2007, S. 2205

When: October 18, 2007

Significance: Senators Durbin, Hagel, and Lugar introduced this bill, even though the former DREAM acts had been introduced several times in both the House and the Senate since November 2005 without success. The bill provides a fast track to citizenship for illegal immigrant minors to either serve in the U.S. military or go to college. The bill reflects in particular the political desire to regulate the status quo of those (Hispanic) minors already living in the United States. It also authorizes the cancellation of removal and adjustment of status of certain alien students who are long-term United States residents and who entered the United States as children. For more information see http://www.dreamact.info/.

Title: Development, Relief, and Education for Alien Minors Act of 2007; Short title: DREAM Act of 2007

A Bill

To authorize the cancellation of removal and adjustment of status of certain alien students who are long-term United States residents and who entered the United States as children, and for other purposes.

Be it enacted by the Senate and House of Representatives of the United States of America in Congress assembled,

[...]

SEC. 3. CANCELLATION OF REMOVAL AND ADJUSTMENT OF STATUS OF CERTAIN LONG-TERM RESIDENTS WHO ENTERED THE UNITED STATES AS CHILDREN.

(a) Special Rule for Certain Long-Term Residents Who Entered the United States as Children-

(1) IN GENERAL- Notwithstanding any other provision of law and except as otherwise provided in this Act, the Secretary may cancel removal of, and adjust to the status of an alien lawfully admitted for permanent residence, subject to the conditional basis described in section 4, an alien who is inadmissible or deportable from the United States, if the alien demonstrates that—

(A) the alien has been physically present in the United States for a continuous period of not less than 5 years immediately preceding the date of enactment of this Act, and had not yet reached the age of 16 years at the time of initial entry;

(B) the alien has been a person of good moral character since the date of enactment of this Act;

(C) the alien–

(i) is not inadmissible under paragraph (2), paragraph (3), subparagraph (B), (C), (E), (F), or (G) of paragraph (6), or subsection (C) of paragraph (10) of section 212(a) of the Immigration and Nationality Act (8 U.S.C. 1182(a)), except that if the alien is inadmissible solely under subparagraph (C) or (F) of paragraph (6) of such section, the alien had not yet reached the age of 16 years at the time the violation was committed; and

(ii) is not deportable under subparagraph (E) or (G) of paragraph (1), paragraph (2), subparagraph (B), (C), or (D) of paragraph (3), paragraph (4), or paragraph (6) of section 237(a) of the Immigration and Nationality Act (8 U.S.C. 1227(a)), except that if the alien is deportable solely under subparagraph (C) or (D) of paragraph (3) of such section, the alien had not yet reached the age of 16 years at the time the violation was committed;

(D) the alien, at the time of application, has been admitted to an institution of higher education in the United States, or has earned a high school diploma or obtained a general education development certificate in the United States;

(E) the alien has never been under a final administrative or judicial order of exclusion, deportation, or removal, unless the alien—

(i) has remained in the United States under color of law after such order was issued; or

(ii) received the order before attaining the age of 16 years; and

(F) the alien was had not yet reached the age of 30 years on the date of enactment of this Act.

(2) WAIVER- Notwithstanding paragraph (1), the Secretary of Homeland Security may waive the ground of ineligibility under section 212(a)(6) of the Immigration and Nationality Act and the ground of deportability under paragraphs (1), (3), and (6) of section 237(a) of that Act for humanitarian purposes or family unity or when it is otherwise in the public interest.

(3) PROCEDURES- The Secretary shall provide a procedure by regulation allowing eligible individuals to apply affirmatively for the relief available under this subsection without being placed in removal proceedings.

(b) Termination of Continuous Period- For purposes of this section, any period of continuous residence or continuous physical presence in the United States of an alien who applies for cancellation of removal under this section shall not terminate when the alien is served a notice to appear under section 239(a) of the Immigration and Nationality Act (8 U.S.C. 1229(a)).

(c) Treatment of Certain Breaks in Presence-

(1) IN GENERAL- An alien shall be considered to have failed to maintain continuous physical presence in the United States under subsection (a) if the alien has departed from the United States for any period in excess of 90 days or for any periods in the aggregate exceeding 180 days.

(2) EXTENSIONS FOR EXCEPTIONAL CIRCUMSTANCES- The Secretary may extend the time periods described in paragraph (1) if the alien demonstrates that the failure to timely return to the United States was due to

exceptional circumstances. The exceptional circumstances determined sufficient to justify such an extension shall be no less compelling than serious illness of the alien, or death or serious illness of a parent, grandparent, sibling, or child of the alien.

(d) Exemption From Numerical Limitations- Nothing in this section may be construed to apply a numerical limitation on the number of aliens who may be eligible for cancellation of removal or adjustment of status under this section.

(e) Regulations-

(1) PROPOSED REGULATIONS- Not later than 180 days after the date of enactment of this Act, the Secretary shall publish proposed regulations implementing this section. Such regulations shall be effective immediately on an interim basis, but are subject to change and revision after public notice and opportunity for a period for public comment.

(2) INTERIM, FINAL REGULATIONS- Within a reasonable time after publication of the interim regulations in accordance with paragraph (1), the Secretary shall publish final regulations implementing this section.

SEC. 4. CONDITIONAL PERMANENT RESIDENT STATUS.

(a) In General-

(1) CONDITIONAL BASIS FOR STATUS- Notwithstanding any other provision of law, and except as provided in section 5, an alien whose status has been adjusted under section 3 to that of an alien lawfully admitted for permanent residence shall be considered to have obtained such status on a conditional basis subject to the provisions of this section. Such conditional permanent resident status shall be valid for a period of 6 years, subject to termination under subsection (b).

(2) NOTICE OF REQUIREMENTS-

(A) AT TIME OF OBTAINING PERMANENT RESIDENCE- At the time an alien obtains permanent resident status on a conditional basis under paragraph (1), the Secretary shall provide for notice to the alien regarding the provisions of this section and the requirements of subsection (c) to have the conditional basis of such status removed.

(B) EFFECT OF FAILURE TO PROVIDE NOTICE- The failure of the Secretary to provide a notice under this paragraph—

(i) shall not affect the enforcement of the provisions of this Act with respect to the alien; and

(ii) shall not give rise to any private right of action by the alien.

(3) LIMITATION ON REMOVAL- The Secretary may not remove an alien who has a pending application for conditional permanent resident status under this section.

(b) Termination of Status-

(1) IN GENERAL- The Secretary shall terminate the conditional permanent resident status of any alien who obtained such status under this Act, if the Secretary determines that the alien—

(A) ceases to meet the requirements of subparagraph (B) or (C) of section 3(a)(1);

(B) has become a public charge; or

(C) has received a dishonorable or other than honorable discharge from the uniformed services.

(2) RETURN TO PREVIOUS IMMIGRATION STATUS- Any alien whose conditional permanent resident status is terminated under paragraph (1) shall return to the immigration status the alien had immediately prior to receiving conditional permanent resident status under this Act.

(c) Requirements of Timely Petition for Removal of Condition-

(1) IN GENERAL- In order for the conditional basis of permanent resident status obtained by an alien under subsection (a) to be removed, the alien must file with the Secretary, in accordance with paragraph (3), a petition which requests the removal of such conditional basis and which provides, under penalty of perjury, the facts and information so that the Secretary may make the determination described in paragraph (2)(A).

(2) ADJUDICATION OF PETITION TO REMOVE CONDITION-

(A) IN GENERAL- If a petition is filed in accordance with paragraph (1) for an alien, the Secretary shall make a determination as to whether the alien meets the requirements set out in subparagraphs (A) through (E) of subsection (d)(1).

(B) REMOVAL OF CONDITIONAL BASIS IF FAVORABLE DETERMI-NATION- If the Secretary determines that the alien meets such requirements, the Secretary shall notify the alien of such determination and immediately remove the conditional basis of the status of the alien.

(C) TERMINATION IF ADVERSE DETERMINATION- If the Secretary determines that the alien does not meet such requirements, the Secretary shall notify the alien of such determination and terminate the conditional perma-nent resident status of the alien as of the date of the determination.

(3) TIME TO FILE PETITION- An alien may petition to remove the condi-tional basis to lawful resident status during the period beginning 180 days before and ending 2 years after either the date that is 6 years after the date of the granting of conditional permanent resident status or any other expiration date of the conditional permanent resident status as extended by the Secretary in accordance with this Act. The alien shall be deemed in conditional permanent resident status in the United States during the period in which the petition is pending.

(d) Details of Petition-

(1) CONTENTS OF PETITION- Each petition for an alien under subsection (c)(1) shall contain information to permit the Secretary to determine whether each of the following requirements is met:

(A) The alien has demonstrated good moral character during the entire period the alien has been a conditional permanent resident.

(B) The alien is in compliance with section 3(a)(1)(C).

(C) The alien has not abandoned the alien's residence in the United States. The Secretary shall presume that the alien has abandoned such residence if the alien is absent from the United States for more than 365 days, in the aggregate, during the period of conditional residence, unless the alien demon-strates that alien has not abandoned the alien's residence. An alien who is absent from the United States due to active service in the uniformed services has not abandoned the alien's residence in the United States during the period of such service.

(D) The alien has completed at least 1 of the following:

(i) The alien has acquired a degree from an institution of higher education in the United States or has completed at least 2 years, in good standing, in a program for a bachelor's degree or higher degree in the United States.
(ii) The alien has served in the uniformed services for at least 2 years and, if discharged, has received an honorable discharge.

(E) The alien has provided a list of each secondary school (as that term is defined in section 9101 of the Elementary and Secondary Education Act of 1965 (20 U.S.C. 7801)) that the alien attended in the United States.

(2) HARDSHIP EXCEPTION-

(A) IN GENERAL- The Secretary may, in the Secretary's discretion, remove the conditional status of an alien if the alien—

(i) satisfies the requirements of subparagraphs (A), (B), and (C) of paragraph (1);
(ii) demonstrates compelling circumstances for the inability to complete the requirements described in subparagraph (D) of such paragraph; and
(iii) demonstrates that the alien's removal from the United States would result in exceptional and extremely unusual hardship to the alien or the alien's spouse, parent, or child who is a citizen or a lawful permanent resident of the United States.

(B) EXTENSION- Upon a showing of good cause, the Secretary may extend the period of conditional resident status for the purpose of completing the requirements described in subparagraph (D) of paragraph (1).

(e) Treatment of Period for Purposes of Naturalization- For purposes of title III of the Immigration and Nationality Act (8 U.S.C. 1401 et seq.), in the case of an alien who is in the United States as a lawful permanent resident on a conditional basis under this section, the alien shall be considered to have been admitted as an alien lawfully admitted for permanent residence and to be in the United States as an alien lawfully admitted to the United States for permanent residence. However, the conditional basis must be removed before the alien may apply for naturalization.

[...]

(Source: Internet-URL: http://thomas.loc.gov)

Document 8: Homeland Security Secretary Michael Chertoff, Remarks on the State of Immigration

When: November 6, 2007

Significance: This report gives a detailed overview about the activities of the U.S. Department of Homeland Security. It promotes the construction of the security fence due to the fact that smuggling continues. The message to the public is clear: Although Congress failed to pass comprehensive migration reform, the government is doing its part to protect the border.

Secretary Chertoff:

(...) I think you'll remember that this past August, after Congress failed to pass the proposed immigration reform bill, we announced that we were going to use the tools that we

In a continuing effort to demonstrate the federal government's commitment to enforcing border security, President George W. Bush and Department of Homeland Security Secretary Michael Chertoff spoke at the Federal Law Enforcement Training Center in Artesia, N.M., on June 6, 2006. AP Photo/Charles Dharapak.

have, such as they are, sharpen them up and go about the business of getting control of the border. And to that end, this past August the administration announced a series of reforms to strengthen immigration enforcement and to meet our nation's workforce needs to the extent the law permits so that we could try to fill the gap left open by Congress's failure to act to address the challenges comprehensively.

Among the 26 items that we put forward in our proposal, one was a commitment to provide periodic "State of Immigration" reports to the American people. Today, about a month after the close of the fiscal year, is the first of what I anticipate will be a number of briefings over the next year. (…)

From the standpoint of the Border Patrol, what we need to do is lengthen the amount of time we have to intercept illegal migrants between the time they cross the border and the time they reach the vanishing point. When you go to a place like San Diego, for example, you see that there are urban areas in very close proximity to the border. What that means and what that meant prior to the San Diego fence was that it was quite easy for people to literally run across the border and within a matter of moments, they were either in an urban area or on a highway or some place where they could vanish into the interior. What the fencing does is it slows up that process to give the Border Patrol an opportunity to get there.

Now the fence obviously doesn't do the same work in the middle of the wilderness, where there is no vanishing point within a matter of minutes or even a matter of hours, and that's why the need for fencing depends a great deal on the landscape and the topography of the particular part of the border.

But what I will tell you is, if we get the 670 miles of pedestrian and vehicle fencing done—that is to say, if Congress gives us the money to do the job properly—then by the end of 2008, we will have barriers from the Pacific Ocean to the New Mexico/Texas border, except in those areas where the landscape itself creates a natural barrier. And I think that's going to be a major step forward for the Border Patrol.

Another question I sometimes get asked is: why does it take so long to build a fence? And there was a chart we displayed a little bit earlier that showed that in the last fiscal year, we began going very slowly with building fencing, and then it all of a sudden escalated and ramped up right at the end of the fiscal year. There's a reason for that. You don't build fence a mile at a time. (...)

Worse yet, some proportion of the people who come in illegally don't come in to do legitimate work; they come in to commit crimes. And our first priority should be to identify anybody who is in this country illegally that is a criminal or a gang member, arrest them, lock them up, and then kick them out when they serve their time.

So what have we done to pursue these objectives? Again, some dramatic increases in effort and results. In fiscal year 2007, as part of Operation Community Shield, we arrested over 3,500 gang members and their associates; 1,489 of these arrests included criminal charges. That means, since we began the program a couple years ago, we've had 7,600 arrests, and members of 700 different gangs have been removed from the streets because of Operation Community Shield.

Over a three-month period this past summer, ICE arrested more than 1,300 violent street gang members and associates in 23 cities in 19 states. To give you two examples of the kinds of people we're picking up, there was one individual, a member of the notorious MS-13 gang, who was arrested in Boston in August of this year. His rap sheet includes assault and battery with a dangerous weapon, breaking and entering, and larceny, among other charges. Another MS-13 gang member who we picked up over the summer has a criminal history, including armed assault with intent to murder, assault and battery, and breaking and entering. We don't want to import these people to our country; we want to export them. We want to make them serve their jail time if they've committed a crime and we want to kick them out of the country. And that's exactly what Operation Community Shield does.

Now, related to this effort, ICE has also very substantially increased its program to locate, arrest and remove fugitives from justice who have defied court orders to leave the United States. When people are arrested, and they go through the immigration removal process, and they appear before an immigration judge and they litigate their case, and then they lose their case, and the judge says, "You must leave," and those people flee—what they are doing is not only remaining in the country illegally, they are defying a court order. That makes them a fugitive. In order to address the flagrant violation of law that is engaged in by people who defy orders to be removed, we have expanded the fugitive operations teams from 15 to 75, including adding 23 teams just in fiscal year 2007. This has reduced our case backlog on fugitives by more than 35,000 individuals this year.

The third element of interior enforcement has to do with worksite enforcement. If you go back to fiscal year 2002, we had only 25 arrests and 485 administrative arrests for worksite enforcement. But in fiscal year 2006, which was the first full year after we inaugurated our new comprehensive strategy to secure the border, we had 716 criminal cases and over 3,600 administrative arrests. And this past fiscal year, we went up to 863 criminal cases, and over 4,000 administrative arrests.

That is a real increase in the size and the potency of the sanctions and the number of sanctions we're bringing against people who are deliberately violating our laws against employing illegal aliens. In October of just this past year, last month, Richard Rosenbaum, the former president of a nationwide cleaning service, pled guilty to harboring illegal aliens and conspiring to defraud the United States. He will pay restitution to the United States in an amount expected to exceed $16 million. And he will also agree to forfeit bank accounts and currency totaling more than $1.1 million for knowingly hiring illegal aliens. Bottom line: the days of treating employers who violate these laws by giving them the equivalent of a corporate parking ticket—those days are gone. It's now felonies, jail time, fines and forfeitures.

Now, I want to be clear: I don't think most employers want to violate the law. I think the vast majority of employers really do want to comply with the law. But we've got to give them the tools to do the job and to make sure that they are in compliance. This is not all about sticks. There have got to be some carrots as well that help people do the right thing. And that means a couple of things: facilitating legal immigration by finding ways to improve that process, and also facilitating the process of determining that you have a legal workforce by giving employers easy-to-use and accurate tools that will allow them to verify that when they hire someone, that person has a lawful right to work in the United States.

One major element of our strategy is E-Verify. E-Verify, formerly known as Basic Pilot, is a web-based system administered by U.S. Citizenship and Immigration Services. It allows employers to electronically check whether a worker is authorized to work in our country. The basic version of this is to compare the name and the Social Security number to make sure they're accurate and that they match. An enhanced version we're currently putting online allows you to actually compare a picture of the person online, based on something we have in our federal files—and hopefully, eventually, pictures in driver's license files—to compare that picture with the person who's actually standing before you as the applicant. That would allow us to take E-Verify from simply a name-checking system to actually an identity-checking system.

E-Verify's popularity is growing. More than 24,000 companies were enrolled at the end of the fiscal year, but today that number is over 30,000. In terms of usage, more than 3.2 million new hires have been processed through E-Verify, and usage is growing by about 83 percent annually. Why? Because it's an easy tool to use. In more than 90 percent of cases, you get a response within seconds that clears a person. And even when there are discrepancies, most of them can be resolved within a very short period of time. (...)

At the same time, illegal immigration poses not only a challenge to the rule of law, but at least in some cases a challenge to our security and our public safety. And there, we are committed to making continued progress, recognizing it's not—Rome wasn't built in a day, and we're not going to turn this problem around in a day, but we're committed to continuing to make substantial, measurable progress to strengthen the border and make sure that the law against illegal immigration is enforced.

In the end, I ask Congress to come back to the table and talk about a way we might resolve this problem comprehensively and in an enduring fashion, so that we can leave our children a legacy of a well-regulated border and a sound economy. In the meantime, my commitment is this: we will enforce the laws as they are on the books, we will not close our eyes to law-breaking, and we will continue to devote all of the energy of the Department of Homeland Security to overcoming any obstacles that prevent us from making sure that the rule of law remains our lodestar in the area of immigration. (...)

(Source: Internet-URL: http://www.dhs.gov/xnews/releases/pr_1194447755019.shtm)

FURTHER READINGS

Internet Resources

ACLU: www.aclu.org/immigrants/
Department of Homeland Security: www.dhs.gov
Federation for American Immigration Reform: www.fairus.org
League of United Latin American Citizens: www.lulac.org
Migration Policy Institute (think tank): www.migrationpolicy.org
Minuteman Project: www.minutemanproject.com
National Conference of State Legislatures: www.ncsl.org
National Immigration Law Center: www.nilc.org
Pew Hispanic Center: www.pewhispanic.org
White House Speeches and New Releases on Immigration: www.whitehouse.gov/infocus/immigration/

Books

Cornelius, Wayne A., and Jessa M. Lewis, eds. *Impacts of Border Enforcement on Mexican Migration: The View from Sending Communities*. Boulder, Colo.: Lynne Rieder, 2007.

Loucky, James, Jeanne Armstrong, and Larry Estrada. *Immigration in America Today*. Westport, Conn.: Greenwood Press, 2006.

Toro-Morn, Maura I., and Marixsa Alicea. *Migration and Immigration A Global View*. Westport, Conn.: Greenwood Press, 2004.

U.S. Department of Homeland Security. *2006 Yearbook of Immigration Statistics*. Washington, D.C.: U.S. Department of Homeland Security, 2007.

Articles

Arizona's Proposition 200. http://www.azsos.gov/election/2004/info/PubPamphlet/english/prop200.pdf.

Bush, George W. "The State of the Union Address" (February 2, 2005). http://www.whitehouse.gov/news/releases/2005/02/20050202-11.html.

Hoefer, Michael, Nancy Rytina, and Christopher Campbell. "Estimates of the Unauthorized Immigrant Population Residing in the United States: January 2006." U.S. Department of Homeland Security, Office of Immigration Statistics (August 2007). http://www.dhs.gov/xlibrary/assets/statistics/publications/ill_pe_2006.pdf

Johnson, Kevin R., and Bernard Trujillo. "Immigration Reform, National Security after September 11, and the Future of North American Integration." *Minnesota Law Review* (Vol. 91). http://ssrn.com/abstract=962963.

Krikorian, Mark. "Keeping Terror Out: Immigration and Asymmetric Warfare." *The National Interest*, No. 75 (2004). http://www.findarticles.com/p/articles/mi_m2751/is_75/ai_n6077654/print.

Lynn-Doty, Roxanne. "Status of Exception on the Mexico-U.S. Border: Security, 'Decisions,' and Civilian Border Patrols." *International Political Sociology*, Vol. 1, Issue 2 (June 2007), 113–137.

Missey, Douglas. "Backfire at the Border. Why Enforcement without Legalization Cannot Stop Illegal Immigration." Trade Policy Analysis, Center for Trade Policy Studies, Cato Institute, No. 25 (June 13, 2005). http://www.freetrade.org/pubs/pas/tpa-029.pdf, access: October 30, 2007.

Morse, Ann, "Immigration Reform in 2006." National Conference of State Legislatures, *Legisbrief*, Vol. 15, No. 8 (February 2007).

Orrenius, Pia M., and Roberto Coronado, "The Effect of Illegal Immigration and Border Enforcement on Crime Rates along the U.S. Mexico Border." Working Paper 0303 (December 2005), Research Department, Federal Reserve Bank of Dallas. http://www.dallasfed.org/research/papers/2003/wp0303.pdf.

Pew Research Center for the People & the Press, Pew Hispanic Center, ed. "No Consensus on Immigration Problem or Proposed Fixes: America's Immigration Quandry" (March 30, 2006). http://people-press.org/reports/pdf/274.pdf.

Rosas, Gilberto. "The Managed Violences of the Borderlands: Treacherous Geographies, Policeability, and the Politics of Race." *Latino Studies*, No. 4 (2006), 401–418.

Skerry, Peter. "How Not to Build a Fence." *Foreign Policy*, Issue 156 (September/October 2006), 64–67.

CHAPTER 11

The Judiciary and U.S. Immigration Policy

Thomas Cieslik

Increased immigration into the United States over the last couple of decades has caused the Supreme Court to become more involved in legal matters concerning immigrants. This chapter presents some of the Court's decisions to underline the importance of judicial opinions in the political debate and the political process in the United States.

In 1982, the Supreme Court made a fundamental decision about the question of whether the state could deny public benefits to undocumented immigrants in the case *Plyler v. Doe*, 457 U.S. 202 (1982). The Court ruled that immigrants have the right to go to public schools and receive public benefits despite their status because they are residents of a state and reside therefore within the jurisdiction of the state.

Although this case did not specifically address the issue of children already born in the United States, it implied that children born to undocumented aliens in the United States would have citizenship by birthright as guaranteed by the Fourteenth Amendment. This interpretation is now again becoming a topic of debate, as can be seen in discussions surrounding the so-called DREAM Act.

In recent years the Court has dealt with the problem of deporting immigrants who commit a crime in the United States. In this context the term "aggravated felony" is significant. It was first used in 1988 to refer to very serious crimes such as murder. Over the years the U.S. Congress has expanded the definition and included a number of other criminal acts, such as drug trafficking, violence, and theft offenses that carry a prison sentence of a year or more, and even fraud or deceit. Moreover, some laws that are classified as misdemeanors under state law are classified as aggravated felonies under federal law. In general, non-citizens convicted of aggravated felony are subject to deportation and thus are also subject to mandatory detention and the loss of any rights to judicial review and to immigration relief such as asylum or voluntary departure.

On December 6, 2006, Justice Breyer stopped the deportation of a Pakistani native, Haroon Rashid, pending the Supreme Court's decision on his petition or certiorari. On February 20, 2007, the Supreme Court denied Rashid's petition on the basis of aggravated felony. The

Tenth Circuit Court with which the Supreme Court concurred had decided that Rashid, who had been a legal, permanent resident with his family since 1997, could be deported because he was sentenced to 401 days to jail for an assault conviction. In another case, a native Peruvian citizen, Duenas-Alvarez, who had been a permanent resident of the United States since 1998, was convicted of a theft offense. In 2002 he pleaded guilty to the charge of unlawful driving or taking of a vehicle according to the California Vehicle Code § 10851(a) and was sentenced to three years in prison.

In February 2004, the U.S. Department of Homeland Security started the process to deport him from the United States according to Section 237(a)(2)(A)(iii) of the Immigration and Naturalization Act, 8 U.S.C. § 1227(a)(2)(A)(iii), for having been convicted of an offense whose term of imprisonment is at least one year, 8 U.S.C. § 1101(a)(43)(G). The Board of Immigration Appeals also dismissed his appeal. After reviewing several cases cited by Duenas-Alvarez's lawyers, Justice Breyer wrote in the Supreme Court's decision on January 17, 2007, that the California statute did not differ from other jurisdictions in its generic definition of a theft offense. The Court thus rejected Duenas-Alvarez's claims and held that the legal immigrant could be deported.

Hiring undocumented immigrants is used to save money on wages. Recently, the Supreme Court considered such a case. In 2006 employees of Mohawk Industries of Georgia, the worldwide leading producer and distributor of carpet and laminated flooring, accused their employer of violating the RICO Act, an act usually applied to organized crime. The employees claimed that the employer had conspired and worked with third-party recruiters of unauthorized workers and then concealed this fact to reduce the wages of legitimate workers. RICO stands for the Racketeer Influenced and Corrupt Organizations Act. It is a U.S. federal law, enacted in 1970, precisely directed at criminal organizations.

In recent years the U.S. Supreme Court has taken a more active role in the immigration debate by accepting cases in which the legality of deporting immigrants convicted of felonies is at issue. U.S. Supreme Court.

Under the RICO Act, for example, conducting illegal business, also known as racketeering, can earn a fine of up to $25,000 and/or a prison sentence of up to twenty years. In 1996, an amendment to the RICO Act allowed parties concerned about foreign labor and inefficient governmental enforcement of immigration laws to sue businesses that hire undocumented workers. This amendment was used by Mohawk Industries employees in 2006. These factories, mainly in the electronics, textile, or machinery industry, import material on a tariff-free basis to assemble and manufacture for re-export.

Mohawk defended its position and argued that it couldn't be found liable for violating RICO because it was not an enterprise like organized crime, as was commonly understood under RICO. In *Mohawk v. Williams* the Supreme Court thus had to decide whether Mohawk violated RICO and whether it constituted an enterprise that could be prosecuted under this act.

The Mohawk case was not the first case of its kind, it was the first one to be brought before the Supreme Court. However, in recent years, more and more plaintiffs have sought claims against companies suspected of hiring undocumented workers. These lawsuits have become a new threat against companies and corporate officers because in some cases responsible managers have been convicted and served prison penalties. On April 26, 2006, the Supreme Court heard the Mohawk case in order to resolve the growing number of conflicts in the lower courts. On June 5, 2006, the Court dismissed the case, noting in a one-paragraph opinion that the case was remanded to the United States Court of Appeals for the Eleventh Circuit to be reviewed in light of the Court's decision in the similar case *Anza v. Ideal Steel Supply* Corp., issued on the same day. Though the Supreme Court did not resolve the question, it took the opportunity to emphasize that civil RICO claims are limited and can only survive if the plaintiff alleges that its injuries have been proximately caused by the alleged RICO violation. "The Court's rulings highlight a potential opportunity for companies and businesses defending against civil RICO claims" (Ryan, Kramer 2006).

Another case that directly impacts immigrants is *Fernandez-Vargas v. Gonzales*. Many immigrants cross the border illegally to find a job, and after a certain time they return to their own countries and try to enter the United States illegally again later. Fernandez-Vargas did this numerous times after being deported once in 1981. In 2001 he married a U.S. citizen. He was arrested while applying for permanent resident status. He appealed this arrest, and the decision to deport him. He argued that a decision should be made first on his application for permanent residency status because the law that allowed the reinstatement of his deportation was passed in 1997, sixteen years after he had been deported. Furthermore, the Immigration and Nationality Act Section 1255(i) permits foreigners who entered the United States without inspection to apply for legal resident status. However, at the same time the reinstatement statute in Section 1231(a)(5) allows a prior deportation order to be reinstated if an alien reenters the United States. Therefore, the Supreme Court denied his petition with the consequence that many undocumented workers will not be able to apply for legal status.

Drug possession is a serious crime in the United States. In the case *Lopez v. Gonzales* the Supreme Court considered the question of whether drug offenses are aggravated felonies with the consequence that the perpetrator faces mandatory deportation without the possibility of a waiver. In its decision on December 5, 2006, the Supreme Court argued that drug possession convictions are state felonies and that they would not be punished as felonies under federal law due to the fact that they are not classified as aggravated felonies in the Immigration and Nationality Act as defined in INA § 101 (a)(43)(B). The *Lopez v. Gonzales* case carried certain ramifications for both U.S. Supreme Court decisions and U.S. law. On June 29, 2005, the Seventh Circuit Court decided in *Gattem v. Gonzales*, 412 F. 3d 758 (7th Cir. 2005), that solicitation of a minor to engage in a sexual act is classified as sexual abuse of a minor. Although it is considered a lesser crime under Illinois law, it is constituted federally as an aggravated felony and therefore subject to immigration law. In the case *Lopez v. Gonzales* reflected, however, the opposite situation. His crime was a felony under state law but not an aggravated felony under federal law. In another case, Jòse Antonio Lopez, who crossed into the United States in 1986, was convicted of a drug felony in South Dakota in 1992.

Consequently, the immigration agency began his removal because immigration law included drug trafficking crimes as aggravated felonies [INA § 101 (a)(43), 8 U.S.C. § 1101 (a)(43)] both under federal and state law. Although immigration law does not exactly define "illicit trafficking," the definition of a drug-trafficking crime as "any felony punishable under the Controlled Substance Act" according to 18 U.S.C. § 924 (c) was sufficient to order the deportation of Jòse Antonio Lopez. This would mean that a conviction for possession of illicit drugs is, according to this interpretation, defined as a drug trafficking offense and constitutes an aggravated felony. The Supreme Court rejected the actions of the Board of Immigration Appeals and the Eighth Circuit of the U.S. Court of Appeals. The Supreme Court argued that deportation depends not on a judgment concerning the seriousness of an offense but "on varying state criminal classifications." Possession does not mean trafficking, argued Justice Souter. "Thus, the government can no longer deem a state felony possession offense to be an aggravated felony unless it would be a felony under federal law" (Vargas and Yang 2006:3). This Supreme Court decision had an impact on future drug possession cases. First-time drug possession does not mean mandatory deportation. However, a second offense could be deemed as an aggravated felony, thereby implying deportation.

DOCUMENTS

Document 1: *Rashid v. Gonzales*

When: Petition denied, February 20, 2007

Significance: In this case the Supreme Court took up the question of whether an offense is a "felony" under certain circumstances despite the fact that it is classified as a "misdemeanor" under state law. The decision had an enormous impact on the legal status of immigrants. Despite their legal and permanent residency in the United States, immigrants would be deported even if a court decides an offense as a misdemeanor but sets a sentence to jail of more than one year. Therefore, these convictions are considered as aggravated felony under federal law.

No. 06-930

In the Supreme Court of the United States

HAROON RASHID, PETITIONER

v.

ALBERTO R. GONZALES, ATTORNEY GENERAL

ON PETITION FOR A WRIT OF CERTIORARI TO THE UNITED STATES COURT OF APPEALS FOR THE TENTH CIRCUIT

BRIEF FOR THE RESPONDENT IN OPPOSITION

PAUL D. CLEMENT
Solicitor General
Counsel of Record
PETER D. KEISLER
Assistant
Attorney General
DONALD E. KEENER
Attorney
Department of Justice

DID YOU KNOW?

Felony

The term "felony" is used in common law systems for very serious crimes. In the United States legal system the federal government classifies a crime punishable by more than one year in prison as a felony. In comparison, a misdemeanor is a criminal act punishable of between five days and one year, whereas less than five days in prison is an infraction. Crimes that can be considered felonies are burglary, treason, murder, rape, kidnapping, espionage, and aggravated assault. Some states classify felonies according to their seriousness. In the worst case a felony conviction can result in the death penalty. According to U.S. law, felons who are not U.S. citizens may be deported after they have served their sentences.

Washington, D.C. 20530-0001
(202) 514-2217

QUESTION PRESENTED

Under 18 U.S.C. 16(b), an offense is a "crime of violence" if it "is a felony" and "by its nature, involves a substantial risk that physical force against the person or property of another may be used in the course of committing the offense." The question presented is whether an offense is a "felony" under that provision if, although it is punishable by more than one year of imprisonment, it is classified as a "misdemeanor" under state law.

In the Supreme Court of the United States
No. 06-930
HAROON RASHID, PETITIONER
v.
ALBERTO R. GONZALES, ATTORNEY GENERAL

ON PETITION FOR A WRIT OF CERTIORARI
TO THE UNITED STATES COURT OF APPEALS
FOR THE TENTH CIRCUIT

BRIEF FOR THE RESPONDENT IN OPPOSITION

OPINIONS BELOW

The opinion of the court of appeals (Pet. App. A) is not published in the Federal Reporter but is reprinted in 190 Fed. Appx. 676. The decisions of the Board of Immigration Appeals (Pet. App. B) and the immigration judge (Pet. App. D) are unreported. The prior decision of the Board of Immigration Appeals (Mot. to Vacate Stay App. C)1 is not published in the Administrative Decisions Under Immigration & Nationality Laws but is available at 2004 WL 2943549. The prior decision of the immigration judge (Mot. to Vacate Stay App. B) is unreported.

JURISDICTION

The judgment of the court of appeals was entered on August 3, 2006. The petition for a writ of certiorari was filed on November 1, 2006, and was placed on the Court's docket on January 9, 2007. The jurisdiction of this Court is invoked under 28 U.S.C. 1254(1).

STATEMENT

1. Petitioner is a native and citizen of Pakistan who entered the United States as a legal permanent resident in 1997. Gov't C.A. Br. 4. In March 2004, he was convicted, after a jury trial, of assault in the third degree, in violation of Section 18-3-204 of the Colorado Revised Statutes. Id. at 5; Mot. to Vacate Stay App. B at 1. Third-degree assault in Colorado is a "class 1 misdemeanor," Colo. Rev. Stat. § 18-3-204 (2004), which is punishable by a maximum of 18 months of imprisonment, id. § 18-1.3-501(1). Petitioner was sentenced to 401 days in jail, 366 of which were suspended. Gov't C.A. Br. 5.

In April 2004, the Department of Homeland Security (DHS) commenced removal proceedings against petitioner. Gov't C.A. Br. 4. It alleged that he was removable pursuant to 8

DID YOU KNOW?

Certiorari

Certiorari is a legal term, originally a jurisprudential expression in Latin. "Certiorem facere" means literally "to make certain," but translated it means "to search." It comes from the works of the Roman jurist Domitius Ulpianus. He was the chief advisor (praefectus praetorio) to the Roman Emperor Marcus Aurelius Severus Alexander (208–235). Among his works is *Ad Sabinum*. He published various collections of responses, disputations, rules, and criminal laws. In Roman law an action of certiorari allows a case to be heard, reviewed, and finally continued in court if evidence exists. In the United States, the term "certiorari is the writ" means that an appellate court will pass a formal written order to a lower court to allow the higher court to review the lower court's judgment where no appeal is possible as a matter of right. The "writ," which can be a warrant, for example, is issued by a public body of jurisdiction.

Since the Judiciary Act of 1925, most cases cannot be appealed to the U.S. Supreme Court. Chief Justice and former President William H. Taft initiated this act to lessen the Supreme Court's workload by removing the possibility of direct appeal to the court in most circumstances. Consequently, a party who wants the Supreme Court to review a decision of a state court files a "petition for writ of certiorari" in the Supreme Court. If the Court accepts the petition, the case could go for oral argument. Approximately 7,500 petitions are presented annually, but only around 80 to 150 cases are granted. The Supreme Court selects the cases very carefully according to the "Cert pool" mechanism, which was implemented in 1973 by Chief Justice Warren Burger. Each petition goes to a pool of clerks where memos are prepared for all members of the Justice. Finally, four out of the nine judges (the rule of four) must vote in favor of a writ of certiorari. However, a favorable vote does not mean that the Supreme Court will intervene in a lower court's decision. It only reflects the position of at least four judges that the circumstances explained in the petition would be sufficient to seek out or "search" the full Court in order to have the case and the lower court's decision reviewed. A denial of certiorari means only that the lower court decision is authoritative within its area of jurisdiction.

U.S.C. 1227(a)(2)(A)(iii), because the assault of which he was convicted was a "crime of violence" under 18 U.S.C. 16 for which the term of imprisonment was at least one year, and the offense was therefore an "aggravated felony" under 8 U.S.C. 1101(a)(43)(F). Gov't C.A. Br. 4. The term "crime of violence" is defined in 18 U.S.C. 16(b), the subsection relevant here, as "any * * * offense that is a felony and that, by its nature, involves a substantial risk that physical force against the person or property of another may be used in the course of committing the offense."

2. In his brief submitted to the immigration judge (IJ), petitioner conceded that the assault of which he was convicted is a "felony" within the meaning of 18 U.S.C. 16(b). Specifically, petitioner stated:

The federal definition of "felony" includes an offense if it is one for which the maximum term of imprisonment authorized is, at a minimum, "more than 1 year." 18 U.S.C. Section 3559(a)(5) (1994). In Colorado, the maximum sentence for a class 1 misdemeanor is 18 months imprisonment. Section 18-1.3-501 C.R.S. Therefore, the state misdemeanor offense of assault in the third degree meets the federal definition of "felony."

Mot. to Vacate Stay App. A at 3. Petitioner argued, however, that the Colorado offense of third-degree assault is not a "crime of violence" under Section 16(b) because the state statute does not "require[] the government to prove that force was used in causing injury, or that intentional use of force was used in causing injury." Ibid.

The IJ agreed with petitioner that he had been convicted of a "felony," noting that, although third-degree assault is designated as a class 1 misdemeanor under state law, "the punishment available is 18 months" and the offense therefore "is considered a felony under [federal] standards." Mot. to Vacate Stay App. B at 2. The IJ nevertheless concluded that the assault was not a "crime of violence," because it did not satisfy the other requirements of Section 16(b). Id. at 2-3. The IJ therefore ruled that the charge of removability had not been sustained. Mot. to Vacate Stay App. B.

DHS appealed, and the Board of Immigration Appeals (BIA) reversed. Mot. to Vacate Stay App. C. The BIA noted in its decision that the IJ had apparently found petitioner's offense "to be a felony under federal law since it carried a possible sentence of 18 months." Id. at 2. Relying on the record of conviction, however, the BIA held that the IJ had erred in concluding that the assault did not otherwise satisfy the requirements of Section 16(b). Id. at 2-3. […]

3. Petitioner filed a petition for review in the court of appeals, claiming that the assault of which he was convicted was not a "crime of violence." He made a number of arguments in support of that claim, but, consistent with his position before the agency, he did not argue that the offense was not a "felony" under 18 U.S.C. 16(b). Pet. C.A. Br. 19-31; Pet. C.A. Reply Br. 10-25.

The court of appeals rejected petitioner's claim, and denied the petition for review, in an unpublished per curiam opinion. Pet. App. A. In holding that the assault was a "crime of violence" under Section 16(b), the court reasoned that the jury instructions in the criminal case were such that the guilty verdict necessarily reflected a finding that the crime involved a substantial risk that petitioner would use physical force against the victim. Id. at 5-6. In a footnote, the court observed that the BIA had "characterized the [assault] conviction as a felony under federal law" and that petitioner "does not challenge this ruling." Id. at 3 n.2.2

ARGUMENT

Petitioner contends (Pet. 3-8) that the assault of which he was convicted is not a "felony" under 18 U.S.C. 16(b) because, even though it is punishable by a maximum of 18 months of imprisonment, it is classified as a misdemeanor under state law. That contention was not administratively exhausted; it was not pressed or passed upon in the court of appeals; it is without merit; and it is not the basis of a circuit conflict. Further review is therefore unwarranted.

1. Under 8 U.S.C. 1252(d)(1), "[a] court may review a final order of removal only if * * * the alien has exhausted all administrative remedies available to the alien as of right." The

courts of appeals have uniformly held that an alien challenging an order of removal is required to exhaust particular issues in the administrative process. That is, an alien must not only appeal to the BIA before seeking judicial review, he must raise before the BIA every claim that he wishes to be considered by the reviewing court. Indeed, with the exception of the Second Circuit, see *Zhong v. United States Dep't of Justice*, 461 F.3d 101, 131-132 (2006) (Kearse, J., dissenting), the courts of appeals have uniformly treated the requirement of issue exhaustion in removal cases as not only mandatory but jurisdictional.

Far from having raised before the agency the claim that he raises in his certiorari petition, petitioner affirmatively conceded both before the IJ and before the BIA that the Colorado offense of which he was convicted "meets the * * * definition of 'felony'" in 18 U.S.C. 16(b). Mot. to Vacate Stay App. A at 3; id. App. D at 1. He has therefore failed to exhaust administrative remedies, and there is accordingly a statutory bar to judicial review of the claim. For that reason alone, certiorari should be denied.

2. Quite apart from the failure to satisfy the requirement of 8 U.S.C. 1252(d)(1) by raising the issue before the BIA, petitioner did not raise in the court of appeals the claim that he raises in his certiorari petition, see Pet. C.A. Br. 19-31; Pet. C.A. Reply Br. 10-25, and the court of appeals did not decide that claim. The court merely noted that the BIA had "characterized the [assault] conviction as a felony under federal law" and that petitioner "does not challenge this ruling." Pet. App. A at 3 n.2. This Court's "traditional rule * * * precludes a grant of certiorari," absent exceptional circumstances, "when 'the question presented was not pressed or passed upon below.'" *United States v. Williams*, 504 U.S. 36, 41 (1992) (quoting id. at 58 (Stevens, J., dissenting)); see, e.g., *Evans v. Chavis*, 126 S. Ct. 846, 854 (2006); *Clingman v. Beaver*, 544 U.S. 581, 598 (2005); *South Fla. Water Mgmt. Dist. v. Miccosukee Tribe of Indians*, 541 U.S. 95, 109 (2004). And petitioner points to no "exceptional circumstances," *Cooper Indus., Inc. v. Aviall Servs., Inc.*, 543 U.S. 157, 169 (2004), that would justify a deviation from that traditional rule in this case.

3. The contention raised in the certiorari petition is in any event without merit. As explained below, an offense punishable by more than one year of imprisonment is a "felony" under 18 U.S.C. 16(b), even if it is classified as a "misdemeanor" under state law.

a. Title 18 of the United States Code contains no specific definition of "felony." When a word is not defined by statute, however, courts "normally construe it in accord with its ordinary or natural meaning." *Smith v. United States*, 508 U.S. 223, 228 (1993). Long-standing usage of the term "felony" in Title 18 focuses, not on the label placed on the crime, but on the "severity of the punishment" imposed by the convicting jurisdiction. *Jerome v. United States*, 318 U.S. 101, 108 n.6 (1943). Throughout Title 18, unless otherwise indicated, the term "felony" has been understood to refer to a crime punishable by death or imprisonment for more than one year. *Adams v. United States* ex rel. McCann, 317 U.S. 269, 272 n.2 (1942).5 Indeed, until 1984, Congress specifically defined "felony" in Title 18 as "[a]ny offense punishable by death or imprisonment for a term exceeding one year." 18 U.S.C. 1(1) (1982). In 1984, Congress replaced that provision with 18 U.S.C. 3559, which, while lacking a specific definition, continues to classify all federal criminal offenses for sentencing purposes based on the length of the "maximum term of imprisonment authorized" and to make any offense for which the authorized penalty is more than one year of imprisonment a felony. 18 U.S.C. 3559(a); see also Sentencing Guidelines § 2L1.2, comment. (n.2) (defining "felony" as "any federal, state, or local offense punishable by imprisonment for a term exceeding one year"). The longstanding definition of "felony" is repeated, either in terms or in substance, throughout the United States Code.

Courts are thus properly "reluctant to infer, absent a clear indication to the contrary, that Congress intended to abandon its long-established practice of using the term 'felony' to describe offenses punishable by more than one year's imprisonment." *United States v. Robles-Rodriguez*, 281 F.3d 900, 904 (9th Cir. 2002). There is no such indication to the contrary, much less a clear indication to the contrary, in 18 U.S.C. 16(b). Instead, all indications are that Congress did not intend that the determination of whether a person has been convicted of a "crime of violence" under Section 16(b) would turn on whether a crime punishable by more than one year in prison happened to be called a "felony" or a "misdemeanor" by the convicting jurisdiction.

First, defining "felony" by reference to the maximum punishment authorized for an offense under the law of the convicting jurisdiction provides a level of uniformity by preventing the federal consequences of a state-law conviction from turning upon varying nomenclature. See *Small v. United States*, 544 U.S. 385, 393 (2005); cf. *Lopez v. Gonzales*, 127 S. Ct. 625, 633 (2006) (rejecting interpretation of 8 U.S.C. 1101(a)(43)(B) that would result in "state-by-state disparity"). Second, by identifying the offenses covered by Section 16(b) as felonies, Congress obviously wanted to ensure that crimes of a particular degree of seriousness were included, and the maximum term of imprisonment is a far more reliable indicator of a crime's seriousness than whether it happens to be labeled a "felony" or a "misdemeanor" by the State. Third, inasmuch as two States eschew the felony-misdemeanor distinction altogether, see N.J. Stat. Ann. § 2C:1-4 (West 2005); Me. Rev. Stat. Ann. tit. 17-A, § 1252 (West 2006), mere labels would not always suffice for categorizing an offense as a "crime of violence" under 18 U.S.C. 16(b). Fourth, reliance on the felony/ misdemeanor label would be particularly unsuitable under the aggravated-felony provision, because that provision attaches consequences to foreign as well as to state (and federal) crimes. 8 U.S.C. 1101(a)(43) (final paragraph).

b. Petitioner relies heavily (Pet. 6-7) on the Third Circuit's decision in *Francis v. Reno*, 269 F.3d 162, 166-171 (2001), which held that the label employed by the convicting jurisdiction determines whether a person has been convicted of a "felony" for purposes of 18 U.S.C. 16(b), regardless of the maximum term of imprisonment. The principal justification for the decision in Francis was that interpreting "felony" in 18 U.S.C. 16(b) to mean an offense punishable by a prison term of more than one year would render redundant the language in 8 U.S.C. 1101(a)(43)(F) providing that a "crime of violence" (as defined in 18 U.S.C. 16) is an "aggravated felony" only if "the term of imprisonment [is] at least one year." 269 F.3d at 170; see Pet. 7. That reasoning is flawed, for three fundamental reasons.

First, the "felony" limitation in 18 U.S.C. 16 appears only in subsection (b) of that provision. Under subsection (a), any offense that "has as an element the use, attempted use, or threatened use of physical force against the person or property of another" is a "crime of violence," 18 U.S.C. 16(a), whether it is "a felony or a misdemeanor," S. Rep. No. 225, 98th Cong., 1st Sess. 307 (1983). The at-least-one-year-of-imprisonment language in 8 U.S.C. 1101(a)(43)(F) therefore imposes an important limitation on the "crimes of violence" under 18 U.S.C. 16(a) that qualify as "aggravated felonies."

Second, classifying an offense as a "crime of violence" under either subsection of 18 U.S.C. 16 has a variety of consequences outside the immigration context. For example, Congress has criminalized certain conduct undertaken in the course of committing a crime of violence; it has criminalized certain conduct undertaken by someone who has been convicted of a crime of violence; and it has criminalized certain conduct that has as an element the commission, attempted commission, or intended commission of a crime of violence. In those contexts, 8 U.S.C. 1101(a)(43)(F) has no application at all, and thus the language in that provision on which the Third Circuit relied could not render the term "felony" redundant even when 18 U.S.C. 16(b) is applied in those contexts.

Third, the "felony" limitation in 18 U.S.C. 16(b) refers to the sentence that was authorized by law, whereas the condition in 8 U.S.C. 1101(a)(43)(F) that "the term of imprisonment [is] at least one year" refers to the sentence that was actually imposed, see *United States v. Pacheco*, 225 F.3d 148, 153-154 (2d Cir. 2000), cert. denied, 533 U.S. 904 (2001); *Alberto-Gonzalez v. INS*, 215 F.3d 906, 909-910 (9th Cir. 2000); *United States v. Graham*, 169 F.3d 787, 789-791 (3d Cir.), cert. denied, 528 U.S. 845 (1999). The two limitations thus have independent functions. Nor are all the crimes covered by each limitation necessarily subsumed in the category of those covered by the other. As explained above, a "felony" under federal law is an offense for which the authorized term of imprisonment is more than one year, whereas the condition in 8 U.S.C. 1101(a)(43)(F) is that the term actually imposed is "at least" one year. The latter condition would be satisfied, but the former would not, if the alien was convicted of an offense that carried a maximum sentence of one year of imprisonment and was sentenced to the one-year statutory maximum. Conversely, the former condition would be satisfied, but the latter would not, if the alien was convicted of an offense that carried a maximum sentence of more than one year and was sentenced to a term of less than one year.

4. Petitioner asserts (Pet. 6) that the Fifth, Seventh, and Ninth Circuits have also addressed the question presented in the petition and have come to the same conclusion as the Third Circuit in Francis. That assertion is mistaken. The Fifth and Ninth Circuits have expressly declined to address the question presented here, on the ground that the crime at issue was not a "felony" under any conceivable definition of the term. See *United States v. Villegas-Hernandez*, 468 F.3d 874, 883-885 (5th Cir. 2006); *Ortega-Mendez v. Gonzales*, 450 F.3d 1010, 1015 (9th Cir. 2006). The Seventh Circuit decision on which petitioner relies, *Flores v. Ashcroft*, 350 F.3d 666 (2003), likewise had no occasion to address the question, because the crime at issue there—a Class A misdemeanor—was not punishable by more than one year in prison, see Ind. Code § 35-50-3-2 (2004).

Petitioner also asserts (Pet. 5-6) that the Second, Fourth, Sixth, Tenth, and Eleventh Circuits have addressed the question presented in the petition and have reached a different conclusion than the Third Circuit in Francis. That assertion is also mistaken. The cases on which petitioner relies addressed an entirely distinct question: whether a misdemeanor can be an "aggravated felony" under the immigration laws if it otherwise satisfies the applicable definition. (Each case holds that it can.) See Pacheco, 225 F.3d at 154-155; *Wireko v. Reno*, 211 F.3d 833, 835-836 (4th Cir. 2000); *United States v. Gonzales-Vela*, 276 F.3d 763, 766-768 (6th Cir. 2001); *United States v. Saenz-Mendoza*, 287 F.3d 1011, 1013-1015 (10th Cir.), cert. denied, 537 U.S. 923 (2002); *United States v. Christopher*, 239 F.3d 1191, 1193-1194 (11th Cir.), cert. denied, 534 U.S. 877 (2001).

Francis, therefore, is the only court of appeals decision cited by petitioner (and the only one of which we are aware) that has addressed the question whether a crime punishable by more than one year of imprisonment is a "felony" under 18 U.S.C. 16(b) if it is classified as a "misdemeanor" under state law. See also note 11, supra (noting that Third Circuit followed Francis in Singh). And although Francis incorrectly answered that question no, the decision below (which in any event is unpublished) does not conflict with Francis, because the Tenth Circuit was not asked to, and did not, decide that question in this case.

4. CONCLUSION

The petition for a writ of certiorari should be denied.
Respectfully submitted.
PAUL D. CLEMENT
Solicitor General
PETER D. KEISLER
Assistant Attorney General
DONALD E. KEENER
Attorney
(Source: Internet-URL: http://www.usdoj.gov/osg/briefs/2006/0responses/2006-0930.resp.html)

Document 2: *Gonzales v. Duenas-Alvarez*

Title: 549 U.S._(2007);

No. 04-74471, 2006 U.S. App. LEXIS 9904 (9th Cir. 2006), *cert. granted*, 75 U.S.L.W. 3162 (U.S. Sept. 26, 2006) (No. 05-1629)

When: Argued December 5, 2006; decided January 17, 2007

Significance: The Supreme Court supports the deportation of immigrants who are sentenced to jail, even in the case of a person who aids and abets, as aiders and abettors are not treated differently from principals, neither under state nor under federal criminal law.

No. 05-1629

In the Supreme Court of the United States

ALBERTO R. GONZALES, ATTORNEY GENERAL, PETITIONER

v.

LUIS ALEXANDER DUENAS-ALVAREZ

ON PETITION FOR A WRIT OF CERTIORARI
TO THE UNITED STATES COURT OF APPEALS
FOR THE NINTH CIRCUIT

REPLY BRIEF FOR THE PETITIONER

PAUL D. CLEMENT
Solicitor General
Counsel of Record
Department of Justice
Washington, D.C. 20530-0001
(202) 514-2217

REPLY BRIEF FOR THE PETITIONER

In the decision below, the Ninth Circuit applied its holding in *Penuliar v. Gonzales*, 435 F.3d 961, 970 n.6 (2006), petition for cert. pending, No. 05-1630 (filed June 22, 2006), that "aiding and abetting liability is [not] included in the generic definition of a 'theft offense'" under the "aggravated felony" provision of the Immigration and Nationality Act (INA), 8 U.S.C. 1101(a)(43)(G). As the petition demonstrates (at 6-25), that holding is incorrect; it conflicts with decisions of other courts of appeals; and, if left unreviewed, it will have a substantial effect on the administration of the immigration laws. Respondent does not seriously dispute any of those propositions. Instead, he contends (Br. in Opp. 8-17) that the issue raised in the petition is not presented in this case, because the decision below did not rest on the ground that "theft offense" excludes aiding and abetting; he contends (id. at 17-26) that, even if the decision did rest on that ground, a ruling in the government's favor would not change the outcome, because California Vehicle Code § 10851(a) (West 2000) imposes liability on accessories after the fact, who are not covered by the generic definition of "theft offense"; and he contends (Br. in Opp. 28-29) that it would in any event be premature for the Court to grant certiorari, because the Ninth Circuit recently granted rehearing en banc in *United States v. Vidal*, 426 F.3d 1011 (2005), rehearing granted, 453 F.3d 1114 (2006), which presents the question whether a violation of Section 10851(a) is a "theft offense" under the Sentencing Guidelines. Each of those contentions is without merit.

A. The Question Presented In The Petition Is Squarely Presented In This Case

Relying on the fact that California Vehicle Code § 10851(a) includes the term "accessory" and that "accessory" as used in California Penal Code § 32 (West 1999) is an accessory after the fact (which is distinct from an aider and abettor), respondent interprets Penuliar as holding that Section 10851(a) is broader than the generic definition of "theft offense," not because "aiding and abetting liability is not included in the generic definition," but because Section 10851(a) "reaches accessories after the fact." Br. in Opp. 6-7. As a consequence, according to respondent, the question presented in the petition "does not * * * pertain to the holding in Penuliar." Id. at 14. Respondent is mistaken, because his description of the rationale for Penuliar's holding is inaccurate. The decision in that case (and therefore in this one) rested squarely on the ground that Section 10851(a) covers aiding and abetting.

In holding that a violation of Section 10851(a) is not categorically a "theft offense" in Penuliar, the Ninth Circuit explained that it had held in *United States v. Corona-Sanchez*, 291 F.3d 1201 (2002) (en banc), that "a conviction under California's general theft statute, California Penal Code § 484(a), was not a categorical 'theft offense'" in part because "a defendant can be convicted of the substantive offense for aiding and abetting a theft."

Penuliar, 435 F.3d at 969. The court went on to say that it had "recently applied this same reasoning" in *Martinez-Perez v. Gonzales*, 417 F.3d 1022 (2005), which held that "a grand theft conviction under California Penal Code § 487(c) did not categorically constitute a theft offense" because "a defendant can be convicted of a substantive violation of § 487(c) based on an aiding and abetting theory alone." Penuliar, 435 F.3d at 969 (quoting Martinez-Perez, 417 F.3d at 1028). The court then held that "[a] conviction under California's vehicle theft statute is broader than the generic definition of a 'theft offense' * * * for the same reason," and quoted a California decision for the proposition that Section 10851(a) permits a conviction if the defendant "aided or assisted" in the driving with the requisite state of mind. Id. at 969-970 (emphasis added) (quoting *People v. Clark*, 251 Cal. App. 2d 868, 874 (1967)). In so holding, the court rejected the contention raised in the government's rehearing petition that "aiding and abetting liability is included in the generic definition of a 'theft offense,'" finding it foreclosed by Martinez-Perez. Id. at 970 n.6. Nowhere in its decision in Penuliar did the Ninth Circuit rely upon, address, or even mention the theory advanced in respondent's brief in opposition.

B. Resolving The Question Presented In The Government's Favor Would Change The Outcome Of The Case

In the alternative, respondent contends that certiorari should be denied even if Penuliar did rely on the fact that Section 10851(a) reaches aiding and abetting, because the Ninth Circuit's ultimate decision—that a violation of the statute is not categorically a "theft offense"—is still correct. Br. in Opp. 7, 17-26. That is so, according to respondent, because Section 10851(a) includes the term "accessory," an "accessory" under California Penal Code § 32 is an accessory after the fact, and an accessory after the fact to a theft has not committed a generic "theft offense." Ibid. As a consequence, respondent argues, there is "an alternate ground for affirmance" even if the government's reading of Penuliar is correct. Id. at 7, 17. Respondent did not make that argument in his briefs to the Board of Immigration Appeals and the court of appeals, and it is therefore not properly before this Court. In any event, the argument is mistaken.

1. As an initial matter, while it is true that "accessory" as used in California Penal Code § 32 is an accessory after the fact, it is not clear that Section 10851(a) reaches accessories after the fact. California Penal Code § 32 appears to set forth an offense (i.e., a proscription of certain conduct), rather than defining a term ("accessory") for purposes of giving meaning to that term where it appears elsewhere in California statutes. Support for that view is found both in the language of Section 32 itself and in the fact that the very next section of the Penal Code describes the penalties for the offense of being an accessory, see Cal. Penal Code § 33 (West 1999).

Even if Section 32 defines a term, however, respondent cites no case holding that "accessory" in Section 10851(a) of the Vehicle Code has the same meaning it has in Section 32 of the Penal Code. That conclusion is in fact undermined by a comparison of the texts of the two provisions. Section 32 of the Penal Code describes conduct after completion of the felony that is intended to conceal the crime or enable the principal to avoid punishment (...), while Section 10851(a) of the Vehicle Code describes conduct involved in the commission of the offense itself (being "a party or an accessory to or an accomplice in the driving or unauthorized taking or stealing" of a vehicle). Indeed, the very California decision on which the Ninth Circuit relied in Penuliar for the proposition that Section 10851(a) reaches aiders and abettors, see 435 F.3d at 970, suggests that it does not reach accessories after the fact. Instead, that case suggests that the statutory phrase "any person who is a party or an accessory to or an accomplice in the driving or unauthorized taking or stealing" is merely shorthand for aider and abettor. See Clark, 251 Cal. App. 2d at 874 (to convict a defendant on the theory that he was "a party or [an] accessory to or an accomplice in the driving," it must be shown that the defendant "aided or assisted" in the driving with the requisite state of mind).

2. Even if Section 10851(a) reaches accessories after the fact, and even if the statute is therefore broader than the generic definition of "theft offense" in the INA, a holding by this Court that the generic definition includes aiding and abetting will still change the outcome of the case. If this Court were to hold that the California statute covers accessories after the

fact, all that would follow is that a violation of the statute is not a "theft offense" as a "categorical" matter. It would not follow that respondent's offense is not a "theft offense" under the "modified categorical" approach.

In Penuliar, as in this case, the alien was charged with violating Section 10851 as a principal. Applying the "modified categorical" approach, the Ninth Circuit held that the charging instruments were nevertheless "insufficient to unequivocally demonstrate that [the alien] actually pled guilty to activity of a principal," because "under California law an accusatory pleading against an aider or abettor may be drafted in an identical form as an accusatory pleading against a principal." Penuliar, 435 F.3d at 971 (emphasis added). The same is not true, however, of an accusatory pleading against an accessory after the fact. "[W]hile it is now generally accepted that a defendant may be charged as if a principal and convicted on proof that he aided another, a conviction as an accessory after the fact cannot be sustained upon an indictment charging the principal crime." 2 Wayne R. LaFave, Substantive Criminal Law § 13.6, at 405 (2d ed. 2003) (footnote omitted). The reason for the distinction is that, as respondent recognizes, accessories after the fact "are not liable, as aiders and abettors are, for the underlying offense of the principal." Br. in Opp. 12; see id. at 20 n.17 (citing cases).

Accordingly, even if Section 10851(a) covers accessories after the fact, a defendant charged with violating the statute as a principal has necessarily not been convicted as an accessory after the fact, and therefore has been convicted of a "theft offense" under the "modified categorical" approach—unless the generic definition excludes aiding and abetting. Because Penuliar holds that the generic definition of "theft offense" does exclude aiding and abetting, a contrary holding by this Court on that issue will change the outcome of this case, as well as that of the many others in which the alien was charged with violating Section 10851(a) as a principal. Indeed, if the generic definition of "theft offense" includes aiding and abetting, it makes little practical difference whether the government is required to meet its burden under the "categorical" or the "modified categorical" approach, because, in the vast majority of cases of this type, the same documents that establish the fact of conviction-the charging instrument and corresponding judgment—also establish that the alien was convicted as a principal or an aider and abettor.

3. In any event, the rule challenged by the government—that the generic definition of "theft offense" excludes aiding and abetting—is not limited to cases involving a violation of Section 10851(a). The Ninth Circuit has applied the rule to California theft statutes that do not include the term "accessory." See Corona-Sanchez, 291 F.3d at 1207-1208 (general theft under California Penal Code § 484(a) (West 1999)); Martinez-Perez, 417 F.3d at 1027-1028 (grand theft under California Penal Code § 487(c) (West 1999)). Accordingly, even if respondent is correct about the significance of that term in Section 10851(a), the exclusion of accessory-after-the-fact liability from the generic definition of "theft offense" could not provide an alternative basis for holding that an alien charged with violating a different theft statute in California (or any other State) has not been convicted of a "theft offense" under either the "modified categorical" or the "categorical" approach.

C. The Question Presented Is Ripe For This Court's Review

Respondent contends that it would in any event be premature for this Court to grant certiorari, because the Ninth Circuit recently granted rehearing en banc in Vidal, supra. Respondent is again mistaken.

Contrary to respondent's contention, the Ninth Circuit does not "appear[] ready" in Vidal "to address the question presented by the Government" in this case. Br. in Opp. 29. Vidal involves the question whether a violation of Section 10851(a) is a "theft offense" under Section 2L1.2 of the Sentencing Guidelines. That guideline, unlike the INA provision at issue here, explicitly includes aiding and abetting in the definition. See Sentencing Guidelines § 2L1.2, comment. (n.5). The three-judge panel in Vidal unanimously distinguished Penuliar on that ground, see 426 F.3d at 1015; id. at 1018 (Browning, J., concurring in part), and the question presented in this case is not one of the questions presented in the petition for rehearing en banc in Vidal, see 04-50185 Pet. for Reh'g & Suggestion for Reh'g En Banc at 2-17. The Ninth Circuit has already denied rehearing en banc on that question, moreover, in Penuliar itself. 435 F.3d at 964.

Respondent correctly points out (Br. in Opp. 8, 29) that the Ninth Circuit may decide in Vidal whether a violation of Section 10851(a) is not categorically a "theft offense" under the Guide lines because the statute includes the term "accessory" and the Guidelines do not explicitly cover accessory-after-the-fact liability. See 04-50185 Pet. for Reh'g & Suggestion for Reh'g En Banc at 2, 5-7. A decision in favor of the defendant on that issue, however, would have no effect on the issue in this case. As explained above (at 5-8), even if the inclusion of "accessory" in Section 10851(a) means that a violation of that statute is not categorically a "theft offense," an alien charged as a principal has been convicted of a "theft offense" under the "modified categorical" approach if "theft offense" includes aiding and abetting and, in any event, the Ninth Circuit has applied the rule challenged here to statutes that do not include the term "accessory."

There are a number of other issues raised in the rehearing petition in Vidal. But it is not clear which, if any, of those issues the en banc court will address. Moreover, none of the other issues affects the question presented in this case—whether "theft offense" under the INA includes aiding and abetting—and it is not clear how, if at all, the Ninth Circuit's decision on any of them would affect the ultimate disposition of this case in any other respect. Those other issues, therefore, provide no basis for postponing resolution of the question presented in this case. Further delay would be particularly unwarranted because of the large number of immigration cases affected by the Ninth Circuit's rule that "theft offense" in 8 U.S.C. 1101(a)(43)(G) altogether excludes aiding and abetting, see Pet. 15-21; because that rule is clearly erroneous and conflicts with the rule applied in other circuits; and because there is likely to come a point in the near future at which the issue no longer reaches the Ninth Circuit, inasmuch as the Board of Immigration Appeals is bound by that court's decisions in cases arising there, see, e.g., In re Anselmo, 20 I. & N. Dec. 25, 31-32 (B.I.A. 1989).

* * * * *

For the foregoing reasons and those stated in the petition for a writ of certiorari, the petition for a writ of certiorari should be granted.

Respectfully submitted.

PAUL D. CLEMENT

Solicitor General

SEPTEMBER 2006

(Source: Internet-URL: http://www.usdoj.gov/osg/briefs/2006/2pet/7pet/2005-1629.pet.rep.html)

Document 3: *Mohawk Indus v. Williams*

Title: 126 S. Ct. 2016 (U.S. 2006)

When: June 5, 2006

Significance: On June 5, 2006, the Supreme Court argued that under the RICO Act an employer who hires illegal aliens with the help of outside recruiters can indeed be considered a RICO enterprise and can thus be prosecuted.

No. 05-465

In the Supreme Court of the United States

MOHAWK INDUSTRIES, INC., PETITIONER

v.

SHIRLEY WILLIAMS, ET AL.

ON WRIT OF CERTIORARI
TO THE UNITED STATES COURT OF APPEALS
FOR THE ELEVENTH CIRCUIT

BRIEF FOR THE UNITED STATES
AS AMICUS CURIAE SUPPORTING RESPONDENTS

PAUL D. CLEMENT
Solicitor General
Counsel of Record
ALICE S. FISHER
Assistant Attorney General
MICHAEL R. DREEBEN
Deputy Solicitor General
MALCOLM L. STEWART
Assistant to the Solicitor
General
SANGITA K. RAO
Attorney
Department of Justice
Washington, D.C. 20530-0001
(202) 514-2217

QUESTION PRESENTED

Whether an association between (a) a corporation that is alleged to have engaged in the systematic hiring and employment of illegal workers and (b) outside recruiters who are alleged to have assisted in those practices can constitute an "enterprise" within the meaning of the Racketeer Influenced and Corrupt Organizations Act (RICO), 18 U.S.C. 1961 et seq.

In the Supreme Court of the United States

No. 05-465

MOHAWK INDUSTRIES, INC., PETITIONER
v.
SHIRLEY WILLIAMS, ET AL.

ON WRIT OF CERTIORARI
TO THE UNITED STATES COURT OF APPEALS
FOR THE ELEVENTH CIRCUIT

BRIEF FOR THE UNITED STATES
AS AMICUS CURIAE SUPPORTING RESPONDENTS

INTEREST OF THE UNITED STATES

The Racketeer Influenced and Corrupt Organizations Act (RICO), 18 U.S.C. 1961 et seq., imposes criminal and civil liability for specified forms of racketeering activity committed by a "person" in connection with an "enterprise." The United States frequently brings criminal and civil enforcement actions under RICO. This case presents the question whether and under what circumstances a corporation, together with outside recruiters who are alleged to have facilitated the corporation's unlawful employment practices, can form a RICO "enterprise." Because the United States frequently initiates suits in which a corporation is alleged to be a constituent member of a RICO "enterprise," the United States has a substantial interest in the Court's resolution of this case.

STATEMENT

1. RICO makes it "unlawful for any person employed by or associated with any enterprise engaged in, or the activities of which affect, interstate or foreign commerce, to conduct or participate, directly or indirectly, in the conduct of such enterprise's affairs through a pattern of racketeering activity or collection of unlawful debt." 18 U.S.C. 1962(c). RICO's definitional section states that the term "'enterprise' includes any individual, partnership,

corporation, association, or other legal entity, and any union or group of individuals associated in fact although not a legal entity." 18 U.S.C. 1961(4). The term "racketeering activity" is defined to encompass acts that are indictable under, inter alia, 18 U.S.C. 1546 or Section 274 of the Immigration and Nationality Act. See 18 U.S.C. 1961(1)(A) and (F) (2000 & Supp. II 2002). A person who violates RICO is subject to criminal penalties, see 18 U.S.C. 1963, and to civil liability, see 18 U.S.C. 1964(c).

2. On January 6, 2004, respondents filed suit against petitioner on behalf of a putative class of petitioner's current or former hourly employees who are legally authorized to work in the United States. See J.A. 7-31 (Complaint). The complaint alleged that petitioner had "engaged in the widespread employment of illegal workers, i.e., workers who are not authorized to be employed in the United States," J.A. 8, and that petitioner's employment practices constituted a "pattern of racketeering activity" within the meaning of 18 U.S.C. 1961(5) because petitioner "ha[d] committed hundreds, and probably thousands, of violations of 8 U.S.C. § 1324(a) and 18 U.S.C. § 1546," J.A. 22; see J.A. 18-23. The complaint further alleged that petitioner had committed those violations through "an association-in-fact enterprise with third party employment agencies and other recruiters * * * that supply [petitioner] with illegal workers." J.A. 23. The complaint explained that recruiters are paid a fee for workers supplied to petitioner; that recruiters provide a pool of employees for petitioner's work needs; that some recruiters locate workers in Texas and transport them to Georgia; that other recruiters employ illegal workers themselves and then transport them to petitioner for a fee; and that "[t]hese recruiters are sometimes assisted by [petitioner's] employees who carry a supply of social security cards for use when a prospective or existing employee needs to assume a new identity." Ibid. The complaint further alleged that "[t]he recruiters and [petitioner] share the common purpose of obtaining illegal workers for employment by [petitioner]"; that "[t]he enterprise has worked in this fashion continuously over at least the last five years"; and that petitioner "participates in the operation and management of the affairs of the enterprise." Ibid.

3. The district court denied petitioner's motion to dismiss respondents' RICO claims. Pet. App. 24a-61a. Petitioner contended, inter alia, that respondents had not adequately alleged the existence of a RICO "enterprise." The district court rejected that contention, see id. at 40a-48a, and certified its ruling for interlocutory appeal, see id. at 68a-72a.

4. The court of appeals granted petitioner's request for permission to appeal under 28 U.S.C. 1292(b), see Pet. App. 67a, and affirmed in relevant part, id. at 1a-23a.

The court of appeals held that the numerous and ongoing violations of federal immigration law alleged in respondents' complaint would constitute a "pattern of racketeering activity" for purposes of RICO. See Pet. App. 5a-6a. The court further held that respondents had "sufficiently alleged an 'enterprise' under RICO; that is an association-in-fact between [petitioner] and third-party recruiters." Id. at 7a. The court explained that "[petitioner] and the third-party recruiters are distinct entities that, at least according to the complaint, are engaged in a conspiracy to bring illegal workers into this country for [petitioner's] benefit. As such, the complaint sufficiently alleges an 'enterprise' under RICO." Id. at 7a-8a. The court also held that the complaint had adequately alleged a common purpose among the members of the enterprise, in light of the allegations that "the members of the enterprise stand to gain sufficient financial benefits from [petitioner's] widespread employment and harboring of illegal workers." Id. at 8a. Finally, the court of appeals stated that respondents had "sufficiently alleged that [petitioner] is engaged in the operation or management of the enterprise." Id. at 8a-9a.

The court of appeals acknowledged (Pet. App. 9a-10a) that in Baker v. IBP, Inc., 357 F.3d 685, 690-691, cert. denied, 543 U.S. 956 (2004), the Seventh Circuit had held that substantially similar allegations did not state a claim under RICO because those allegations suggested the existence of divergent goals among the members of the purported "enterprise." The court of appeals declined to adopt the Baker court's approach, however, explaining that in the Eleventh Circuit "there has never been any requirement that the 'common purpose' of the enterprise be the sole purpose of each and every member of the enterprise." Pet. App. 10a. The court concluded: "In this case, the complaint alleges that [petitioner] and the recruiters, under [petitioner's] direction, worked together to recruit illegal workers to come to Georgia and that they had the common purpose of providing illegal workers to [petitioner] so that [petitioner] could reduce its labor costs and the recruiters could get paid. This commonality is all that this circuit's case law requires." Ibid.

SUMMARY OF ARGUMENT

I. As used in RICO, the term "enterprise" encompasses a de facto alliance among corporations or similar artificial legal entities. Although such associations are not specifically mentioned in 18 U.S.C. 1961(4), Section 1961(4) is introduced by the word "includes" and is intended to provide an illustrative rather than an exhaustive roster of RICO "enterprise[s]." That construction of the statutory term accords with common usage and established legal principles: the word "enterprise" is often used to refer to collaborative ventures that do not involve the creation of a discrete legal entity, and corporations are generally deemed capable of entering into agreements (including illicit agreements) on the same terms as natural persons. Petitioner's reliance on the rule of lenity is misplaced, both because Congress has directed that RICO is to be liberally construed, and because no serious ambiguity exists as to whether a de facto association of corporations can constitute a RICO "enterprise." The government's criminal and civil enforcement efforts under RICO would be significantly impaired if the only associations in fact that could be treated as RICO enterprises were those composed exclusively of individuals.

II. Respondents' complaint adequately alleged that petitioner and outside recruiters had entered into a de facto alliance having the essential attributes—a common purpose and a continuing organizational presence—of a RICO associated-in-fact enterprise. More is alleged here than a contract between legally distinct entities. Rather, the complaint alleged that distinct business entities entered into a longstanding arrangement designed to facilitate the repeated commission of racketeering crimes. Such an alliance is properly regarded as an associated-in-fact RICO enterprise, even if the terms of the arrangement are determined through arms-length negotiations between the parties. The fact that a corporation's liability under 18 U.S.C. 1962(c) may turn on whether it commits racketeering crimes through its own employees or in combination with others is a natural consequence of the judgment, which has long been reflected in the law of conspiracy and which informs the application of RICO, that collaborative criminal endeavors pose distinct threats to the public welfare.

ARGUMENT

I. THE RICO TERM "ENTERPRISE" ENCOMPASSES AN ASSOCIATION IN FACT THAT INCLUDES A CORPORATION AS A CONSTITUENT MEMBER

RICO's definitional section states that, as used in the statute, the term "'enterprise' includes any individual, partnership, corporation, association, or other legal entity, and any union or group of individuals associated in fact although not a legal entity." 18 U.S.C. 1961(4). Section 1961(4) thus describes two "type[s] of enterprise to be covered by the statute—those that are recognized as legal entities and those that are not." *United States v. Turkette*, 452 U.S. 576, 582 (1981). The latter type of enterprise is "a group of persons associated together for a common purpose of engaging in a course of conduct," and its existence "is proved by evidence of an ongoing organization, formal or informal, and by evidence that the various associates function as a continuing unit." Id. at 583.

Petitioner contends (Br. 12-26) that, because a corporation is not an "individual" within the meaning of Section 1961(4), an association in fact of which a corporation is a constituent member cannot be a RICO "enterprise." Although petitioner's premise is correct, its suggested conclusion does not follow. Section 1961(4), which is introduced by the word "includes," neither provides an exhaustive roster of the "enterprise[s]" covered by RICO nor excludes a de facto alliance that would constitute an "enterprise" under the usual understanding of that term. Petitioner's proposed categorical rule that a corporation cannot be a constituent part of an associated-in-fact RICO enterprise is thus unsupported by the statutory text, and it would hinder the effective implementation of the law in both the criminal and civil contexts.

A. Section 1961(4) Of Title 18 Contains An Illustrative, Rather Than Exclusive, List Of RICO "Enterprises"

1. Section 1961(4) of Title 18 states that the term "enterprise" "includes" the various entities enumerated in that provision. 18 U.S.C. 1961(4). "In [definitional] provisions of statutes and other writings, 'include' is frequently, if not generally, used as a word of extension or enlargement rather than as one of limitation or enumeration." *American Surety Co. v. Marotta*, 287 U.S. 513, 517 (1933); see *Webster's Third New International Dictionary* 1143 (1993) (defining "include" to mean, inter alia, "to place, list, or rate as a part or component of a whole or of a larger group, class, or aggregate"). When 18 U.S.C. 1961 (2000 & Supp. II 2002) is read as a whole, it is clear that the verb "includes" in Section 1961(4) should be interpreted in that manner, and that the list that follows should be treated as illustrative rather than exclusive.

As petitioner explains (Br. 16-17 & n.7), "the term 'includes' may sometimes be taken as synonymous with 'means,'" and thus as introducing a comprehensive list. *Helvering v. Morgan's, Inc.*, 293 U.S. 121, 125 (1934). Read as a whole, however, the definitional section of RICO (18 U.S.C. 1961 (2000 & Supp. II 2002)) makes clear that Congress did not intend for the word "includes" to have that effect in 18 U.S.C. 1961(4). That definitional section contains four subsections that use the word "includes" (18 U.S.C. 1961(3), (4), (9), and (10)), and five that use the word "means" (18 U.S.C. 1961(1), (2), (6), (7), and (8)). In interpreting similarly structured provisions, in which some definitions are introduced by "means" and others by "includes," this Court has consistently declined to treat the two words as synonymous, and has construed the word "includes" to introduce an illustrative rather than an exclusive list. As the Court explained in Helvering, "[t]he natural distinction would be that where 'means' is employed, the term and its definition are to be interchangeable equivalents, and that the verb 'includes' imports a general class, some of whose particular instances are those specified in the definition." 293 U.S. at 125 n.1; accord Marotta, 287 U.S. at 517 ("When the section as a whole is regarded, it is evident that these verbs are not used synonymously or loosely but with discrimination and a purpose to give each a meaning not attributable to the other."); *United States v. New York Tel. Co.*, 434 U.S. 159, 169 & n.15 (1977) (holding that the definition of "property" contained in former Federal Rule of Criminal Procedure 41(h) "does not restrict or purport to exhaustively enumerate all the items which may be seized pursuant to Rule 41," and explaining that, "[w]here the definition of a term in Rule 41(h) was intended to be all inclusive, it is introduced by the phrase 'to mean' rather than 'to include'"); cf. *Phelps Dodge Corp. v. NLRB*, 313 U.S. 177, 189 (1941) ("To attribute… a [limiting] function to the participial phrase introduced by 'including' is to shrivel a versatile principle to an illustrative application."); U.S. Amicus Br. at 12-13, S.D. *Warren Co. v. Maine Bd. of Envtl. Protection*, No. 04-1527 (argued Feb. 21, 2006).

The definition of "pattern of racketeering activity" contained in 18 U.S.C. 1961(5), and this Court's construction of that provision, reinforce the conclusion that the verb "includes" in Section 1961(4) should not be treated as synonymous with "means." Section 1961(5) states that the term "'pattern of racketeering activity' requires at least two acts of racketeering activity." 18 U.S.C. 1961(5) (emphasis added). This Court has attached significance to Congress's choice of verbs, explaining that "the definition of a 'pattern of racketeering activity' differs from the other provisions in § 1961 in that it states that a pattern 'requires at least two acts of racketeering activity,' not that it 'means' two such acts. The implication is that while two acts are necessary, they may not be sufficient." *Sedima, S.P.R.L. v. Imrex Co.*, 473 U.S. 479, 496 n.14 (1985) (citation omitted). The Court has focused on the verb "requires" to give the phrase "pattern of racketeering activity" a narrower construction than would have been warranted if Section 1961(5) were introduced by the word "means." See *H.J. Inc. v. Northwestern Bell Tel. Co.*, 492 U.S. 229, 237-243 (1989). Congress's use in Section 1961(4) of the introductory verb "includes" should likewise be viewed as denoting broader coverage than would the word "means."

2. Petitioner contends that Congress's express reference in Section 1961(4) to "group[s] of individuals associated in fact" suggests an intent not to cover associations in fact composed

in part of artificial legal entities such as corporations. See Pet. Br. 14-15 (citing, inter alia, *Chevron U.S.A. Inc. v. Echazabal*, 536 U.S. 73, 81 (2002)).2 But while the maxim *expressio unius est exclusio alterius* is often a useful aid to statutory construction, it is not properly applied where, as here, Congress has used the verb "includes" to introduce a non-exhaustive list of examples. By introducing Section 1961(4) with the word "includes," within a provision in which other definitions are introduced by the word "means," Congress signaled that the omission of particular types of enterprises from the list that follows should not be read to imply a deliberate exclusion. Compare *Echazabal*, 536 U.S. at 80 (explaining that "the expansive phrasing of 'may include' points directly away from the sort of exclusive specification" that the *expressio unius* maxim might otherwise suggest).

The legislative history confirms that understanding. Both the Senate and House Reports accompanying RICO stated that the term "enterprise" was defined "to include associations in fact, as well as legally recognized associative entities. Thus, infiltration of any associative group by any individual or group capable of holding a property interest can be reached." S. Rep. No. 617, 91st Cong., 1st Sess. 158 (1969) (emphasis added); see H.R. Rep. No. 1549, 91st Cong., 2d Sess. 56 (1970) (using identical language). The Committees' description of the statutory definition as encompassing "any associative group" substantially undermines petitioner's contention (Br. 14-15) that Congress used the phrase "union or group of individuals associated in fact" (18 U.S.C. 1961(4)) specifically to exclude such associations. Cf. *Turkette*, 452 U.S. at 580 ("There is no restriction upon the associations embraced by the definition [of 'enterprise'].").

In *New York Telephone*, this Court rejected a proposed inference very similar to the one advocated by petitioner here. The Court in *New York Telephone* construed former Federal Rule of Criminal Procedure 41(h), which provided that "[t]he term 'property' is used in this rule to include documents, books, papers and any other tangible objects." 18 U.S.C. App. at 1465 (1976); see *New York Tel.*, 434 U.S. at 169. Relying in particular on the fact that other definitions in Rule 41(h) were "introduced by the phrase 'to mean'" (id. at 169 n.15), this Court stated that, "[a]lthough Rule 41(h) defines property 'to include documents, books, papers and any other tangible objects,' it does not restrict or purport to exhaustively enumerate all the items which may be seized pursuant to Rule 41." Id at 169. Notwithstanding Rule 41(h)'s express reference to "tangible objects," this Court concluded that "Rule 41 is sufficiently broad to include seizures of intangible items such as dial impulses recorded by pen registers as well as tangible items." Id. at 170. Similarly here, in the context of 18 U.S.C. 1961 taken as a whole, Section 1961(4)'s reference to "group[s] of individuals associated in fact" does not preclude the possibility that other associative groups could qualify as RICO "enterprises."

B. Petitioner's Construction Of The RICO Term "Enterprise" Is Inconsistent With The Usual Understanding Of That Term And Would Hinder The Effective Implementation Of The Statute

1. Congress's use of the word "includes" to introduce 18 U.S.C. 1961(4) does not give courts unfettered discretion to decide whether a de facto alliance between a corporation and other actors should be treated as a RICO "enterprise." Cf. Pet. Br. 16 (citing *Willheim v. Murchison*, 342 F.2d 33, 42 (2d Cir.), cert. denied, 382 U.S. 840 (1965)). Rather, it simply means that, if the term "enterprise" would otherwise be understood to encompass such an alliance, it should be treated as covered, notwithstanding its omission from the list of illustrative examples contained in Section 1961(4).

At the time of RICO's enactment in 1970, the term "enterprise" would naturally have been understood to encompass not only discrete legal entities, but also de facto alliances formed for the purpose of achieving a common objective. This Court's opinions in the years preceding RICO's enactment used the term in that manner.4 In addition, the Travel Act, which was enacted in 1961 and prohibited interstate travel or the use of interstate commercial facilities in connection with "any business enterprise involving" specified crimes (18 U.S.C. 1952(b) (1964)), had repeatedly been applied to collaborative criminal endeavors that did not involve the creation of any distinct legal entity. See, e.g., *United States v.*

Brennan, 394 F.2d 151, 153 (2d Cir.), cert. denied, 393 U.S. 839 (1968); *United States v. Zizzo*, 338 F.2d 577, 580 (7th Cir. 1964), cert. denied, 381 U.S. 915 (1965). Indeed, petitioner does not contend that such de facto alliances fall outside the usual understanding of the word "enterprise."

Once that general principle has been established, neither common English usage nor background legal principles suggest that the term "enterprise" should be understood to exclude alliances composed in whole or in part of corporations. "After all, incorporation's basic purpose is to create a distinct legal entity," *Cedric Kushner Promotions, Ltd. v. King*, 533 U.S. 158, 163 (2001), that is treated at law as a "person." A corporation is generally capable of entering into contractual agreements on the same terms as natural persons, and the rights and obligations established by such contracts are those of the corporation alone. See, e.g., *Domino's Pizza, Inc. v. McDonald*, 126 S. Ct. 1246, 1250 (2006) ("[I]t is fundamental corporation and agency law… that the shareholder and contracting officer of a corporation has no rights and is exposed to no liability under the corporation's contracts."). A corporation is also deemed capable of joining a conspiracy and is subject to potential civil and criminal liability therefore. See 10 Fletcher Cyclopedia of the Law of Private Corporations §§ 4884, 4951.50, at 330-331, 668-669 (2001 rev. ed.). There is no sound reason to treat corporations as incapable of entering into the sort of de facto alliance that would constitute a RICO "enterprise" if it were formed solely by natural persons. The Seventh Circuit has explained:

The statute says "'enterprise' includes"—not "'enterprise' means." The point of the definition is to make clear that it need not be a formal enterprise; "associated in fact" will do. Surely if three individuals can constitute a RICO enterprise, as no one doubts, then the larger association that consists of them plus entities that they control can be a RICO enterprise too. Otherwise while three criminal gangs would each be a RICO enterprise, a loose-knit merger of the three, in which each retained its separate identity, would not be, because it would not be an association of individuals. That would make no sense.

United States v. Masters, 924 F.2d 1362, 1366 (7th Cir.), cert. denied, 500 U.S. 919 and 502 U.S. 823 (1991).

2. Petitioner's reliance (Br. 19-20) on the rule of lenity is misplaced. The rule of lenity is not a restriction on congressional power, but a canon of statutory construction. See, e.g., *Liparota v. United States*, 471 U.S. 419, 427 (1985) (characterizing the rule of lenity as "a time-honored interpretive guideline when the congressional purpose is unclear"); *Busic v. United States*, 446 U.S. 398, 407 (1980). The rule "is not to be applied where to do so would conflict with the implied or expressed intent of Congress." Liparota, 471 U.S. at 427.

Here, application of the rule of lenity would contravene Congress's intent. RICO expressly provides that the statute should be "liberally construed to effectuate its remedial purposes." Pub. L. No. 91-452, § 904(a), 84 Stat. 947; see Sedima, 473 U.S. at 497-498 (inferring principle that "RICO is to be read broadly" both from "Congress' self-consciously expansive language and overall approach" and from the statute's liberal-construction clause). The presumption that statutes having criminal applications should be construed narrowly cannot be controlling where, as here, Congress has directed courts to employ a different interpretive methodology.

In any event, the rule of lenity "is not applicable unless there is a grievous ambiguity or uncertainty in the language and structure of the Act, such that even after a court has seized everything from which aid can be derived, it is still left with an ambiguous statute." *Chapman v. United States*, 500 U.S. 453, 463 (1991) (citations, brackets, and internal quotation marks omitted). In light of the structure of 18 U.S.C. 1961 as a whole and this Court's decisions construing comparable definitional provisions (see pp. 7-8, supra), no "grievous ambiguity" exists as to whether a de facto alliance of corporations can constitute a RICO "enterprise." Far from establishing such ambiguity, petitioner merely seeks to avoid the natural reach of the term "enterprise."

3. The United States frequently brings criminal or civil enforcement actions alleging that the defendants have violated 18 U.S.C. 1962(c) by conducting or participating in the conduct of the affairs of an associated-in-fact RICO "enterprise" that consists in part of a

corporation or other artificial legal entity. The categorical rule advocated by petitioner, under which the only associations in fact that could be treated as RICO "enterprises" would be those composed exclusively of individuals, would significantly impair the government's ability to enforce the statute's substantive provisions and to obtain effective remedies.

a. Criminal and civil RICO defendants often conduct both racketeering and other activities through multiple legal entities. See, e.g., *United States v. Goldin Indus., Inc.*, 219 F.3d 1271, 1273 (11th Cir.), cert. denied, 531 U.S. 1015 (2000); *United States v. Feldman*, 853 F.2d 648, 651-656 (9th Cir. 1988), cert. denied, 489 U.S. 1030 (1989). In some instances, the defendant's control over multiple legal entities that are nominally distinct from each other may be essential to the achievement of his criminal goals. In such cases, treatment of the corporations or similar entities as components of a single RICO "enterprise" reflects the essential character of the defendant's unlawful scheme.

b. In order to establish a violation of 18 U.S.C. 1962(c), the government must prove that the defendant "conduct[ed] or participate[d], directly or indirectly, in the conduct of [an] enterprise's affairs through a pattern of racketeering activity or collection of unlawful debt." Although a "'pattern of racketeering activity' requires at least two acts of racketeering," 18 U.S.C. 1961(5), two such acts are not always sufficient to establish the requisite "pattern," see H.J. Inc., 492 U.S. at 237-238; p. 9, supra. "To establish a RICO pattern it must also be shown that the predicates themselves amount to, or that they otherwise constitute a threat of, continuing racketeering activity." 492 U.S. at 240; see id. at 242 ("Predicate acts extending over a few weeks or months and threatening no future criminal conduct do not satisfy this requirement: Congress was concerned in RICO with long-term criminal conduct.").

When a defendant perpetrates criminal conduct through the coordinated activities of nominally distinct corporations, it may be difficult for the government to prove the requisite "pattern of racketeering activity" with respect to any single corporation, even though such a pattern is evident when the activities of all such corporations are viewed together. Under petitioner's theory, however, the government would be precluded from relying upon the cumulative activities of different corporations (or similar artificial entities) to demonstrate that the defendant conducted the affairs of an "enterprise" through a "pattern of racketeering activity." That rule "would perversely insulate the most sophisticated racketeering combinations from RICO's sanctions, the precise opposite of Congress' intentions." *United States v. Huber*, 603 F.2d 387, 394 (2d Cir. 1979), cert. denied, 445 U.S. 927 (1980).

c. Even when acceptance of petitioner's legal theory would not altogether preclude a RICO criminal or civil action from going forward, it might hinder the effective implementation of the statute's remedial provisions. Petitioner contends (Br. 41) that its interpretive approach will not "impair RICO's usefulness as a tool to attack corporate wrongdoing" because "the officers and managers who direct a corporation to engage in racketeering activity will always be appropriate § 1962(c) defendants when they conduct the affairs of that corporation through a pattern of racketeering activity." A prosecution of the blameworthy corporate officers, however, would not enable the government to obtain forfeiture of the corporation's own assets, including profits the corporation may have realized as a direct result of its racketeering. See 18 U.S.C. 1963(a); *Russello v. United States*, 464 U.S. 16, 20-29 (1983) (profits and proceeds derived from racketeering in violation of 18 U.S.C. 1962(c) are forfeitable under Section 1963(a)). Because "the Government is entitled to seek forfeiture of only the defendant's interest in property that was derived from, or was used to commit, the criminal offense," *United States v. BCCI Holdings, Luxembourg, S.A.*, 69 F. Supp. 2d 36, 51 (D.D.C. 1999) (emphasis added), the United States can obtain RICO forfeitures of corporate assets only by bringing a prosecution against the corporation itself. And because liability under 18 U.S.C. 1962(c) requires proof "of two distinct entities: (1) a 'person'; and (2) an 'enterprise' that is not simply the same 'person' referred to by a different name," Cedric Kushner, 533 U.S. at 161, the government's ability to prosecute the corporation will often depend upon its ability to allege and prove the existence of a larger RICO enterprise.

The prohibitions of 18 U.S.C. 1962(c) apply to "any person," with the term "person" defined to include "any individual or entity capable of holding a legal or beneficial interest in property." 18 U.S.C. 1961(3). That definition clearly encompasses a corporation, and the text of Section 1962(c) provides no basis for exempting corporations from RICO liability in situations where natural persons would be covered. Cf. H.J. Inc., 492 U.S. at 249 ("Legitimate businesses 'enjoy neither an inherent capacity for criminal activity nor immunity from its consequences.'") (quoting Sedima, 473 U.S. at 499). As this Court's decision in Cedric Kushner makes clear, a corporation (like a natural person) that unilaterally commits RICO predicate acts cannot be held liable under Section 1962(c) on the theory that it conducted its own affairs through a pattern of racketeering activity. See 533 U.S. at 162-163. In that circumstance, the individual corporate officers who oversaw the unlawful conduct may be the only available RICO defendants. But when a corporation enters into a de facto alliance that would constitute a Section 1961(4) association in fact if it were formed by individuals, a rule that would insulate the corporation from RICO liability is unsupported by RICO's text, and it would disserve the statute's purposes.

Acceptance of petitioner's position would also substantially impair the government's ability to obtain effective relief in cases involving the corruption of labor unions. The civil RICO remedies available to the United States under 18 U.S.C. 1964 were intended in significant part to address the corrupt control and influence of organized crime over labor unions and related legal entities. See, e.g., S. Rep. No. 617, supra, at 77-83; H.R. Rep. No. 1574, 90th Cong., 2d Sess. 5-9 (1968). To address that problem, the United States has brought numerous civil RICO lawsuits, which typically allege the existence of an associated-in-fact RICO enterprise consisting of a labor union, related benefit plans, other related legal entities, and corrupt union officials and organized crime figures. In such cases, the United States has obtained injunctive relief against the union-defendants, including appointment of court officers to monitor union operations and to enforce union election-reform and ethical-practices requirements on an ongoing basis. Under petitioner's construction of 18 U.S.C. 1961(4), however, the government would be precluded from naming as a defendant (and obtaining equitable relief against) the union itself. Although the government could proceed against corrupt individuals under Section 1962(c) (since the union would constitute a RICO "enterprise"), the relief available against individual defendants would not adequately address systemic problems of union corruption.

II. RESPONDENTS' COMPLAINT ADEQUATELY ALLEGED A VIOLATION OF 18 U.S.C. 1962(c)

Petitioner contends that, if the allegations of respondents' complaint are deemed sufficient to state a claim under 18 U.S.C. 1962(c), every contract between a corporation and persons outside the corporate structure will result in the formation of a RICO associated-in-fact "enterprise." See, e.g., Pet. Br. 40 (asserting that the Eleventh Circuit's approach "recognizes an 'enterprise' whenever a corporation contracts with another entity"). That argument is misconceived. The government or a private plaintiff obviously cannot establish the existence of a RICO "enterprise" simply by proving a contractual agreement between legally distinct actors. Other well-established legal principles prevent such an overbroad application of RICO by defining the characteristics—chiefly, a shared purpose among the members and a continuing organizational presence—that an associated-in-fact enterprise must be shown to possess. Petitioner's proposed categorical rule, to the effect that business entities engaged in "arms-length dealings" (Br. i) can never combine to form a RICO associated-in-fact enterprise, is both unnecessary and unsound.

A. Respondents' Complaint Adequately Alleged That Petitioner Has Participated In The Operation Of A RICO Enterprise

This Court in Turkette described the basic attributes of a RICO associated-in-fact enterprise. The Court explained that such an enterprise is "a group of persons associated together for a common purpose of engaging in a course of conduct," and that its existence "is proved by evidence of an ongoing organization, formal or informal, and by evidence that the various associates function as a continuing unit." 452 U.S. at 583; see, e.g., *United States v. Rogers*, 89 F.3d 1326, 1335-1338 (7th Cir.), cert. denied, 519 U.S. 999 (1996); *United States v. Blinder*, 10 F.3d 1468, 1473-1475 (9th Cir. 1993); *United States v. Church*, 955 F.2d 688,

697-699 (11th Cir.), cert. denied, 506 U.S. 881 (1992). The instant case comes to this Court on a motion to dismiss under Federal Rule of Civil Procedure 12(b)(6), and it is well settled that "a complaint should not be dismissed for failure to state a claim unless it appears beyond doubt that the plaintiff can prove no set of facts in support of his claim which would entitle him to relief." *Conley v. Gibson*, 355 U.S. 41, 45-46 (1957). Respondents' complaint adequately alleged that an enterprise having the characteristics set forth in Turkette existed, and that petitioner participated in the conduct of the enterprise's affairs.

1. Respondents alleged that "[t]he recruiters and [petitioner] share the common purpose of obtaining illegal workers for employment by [petitioner]." J.A. 23. Proof of that allegation at trial would satisfy the "common purpose" requirement articulated in Turkette. In *Baker v. IBP, Inc.*, 357 F.3d 685, 691, cert. denied, 543 U.S. 956 (2004), the Seventh Circuit found similar allegations to be inadequate to establish the requisite "common purpose," based in part on the fact that "the recruiters want to be paid more for services rendered" while the employer "would like to pay them less." That holding is erroneous because, as the court of appeals in this case recognized, there is no "requirement that the 'common purpose" of the enterprise be the sole purpose of each and every member of the enterprise." Pet. App. 10a.

Indeed, in few if any associated-in-fact enterprises is there complete unity of purpose among the group's members. In the paradigmatic criminal syndicate, some members may receive specified sums for particular acts, while others may receive an agreed-upon percentage of the proceeds; and it can safely be assumed that each member of the enterprise will be principally concerned with maximizing his own "take." Cf. Russello, 464 U.S. at 19-20 (describing associated-in-fact enterprise in which the owner of a commercial building paid a flat fee to an arsonist and collected insurance proceeds after the building was destroyed). When two individuals enter into a continuing arrangement in which the first sells wholesale quantities of narcotics to the second, who then resells to users, the desire of the first individual to maximize the wholesale price and of the second individual to minimize it does not prevent the formation of an associated-in-fact enterprise. Rather, the shared objective of facilitating narcotics trafficking satisfies the "common purpose" requirement. The same principle applies here.

2. Respondents also adequately alleged the existence of an "ongoing organization" whose "various associates function as a continuing unit." Turkette, 452 U.S. at 583. Respondents alleged that petitioner had "engaged in an open and ongoing pattern of" immigration-law violations during a five-year period, assisted by recruiters who "work closely with [petitioner] to meet its employment needs by offering a pool of illegal workers who can be dispatched to a particular [petitioner] facility on short notice as the need arises." J.A. 23. The complaint further alleged that some recruiters "have relatively formal relationships with [petitioner] in which they employ illegal workers and then loan or otherwise provide them to [petitioner] for a fee," and that such "recruiters are sometimes assisted by [petitioner's] employees who carry a supply of social security cards for use when a prospective or existing employee needs to assume a new identity." Ibid. Respondents thus alleged that a de facto alliance between petitioner and the recruiters, in which each member of the enterprise performed a defined function, had operated continuously during an extended period of time to provide petitioner a steady stream of unlawful workers.

3. To prevail in this case, respondents must ultimately demonstrate that petitioner "conduct[ed] or participate[d], directly or indirectly, in the conduct of [the] enterprise's affairs through a pattern of racketeering activity." 18 U.S.C. 1962(c). Respondents' generalized averment that petitioner "participates in the operation and management of the affairs of the enterprise" (J.A. 23) would likely have been sufficient to survive a motion to dismiss. See Fed. R. Civ. P. 8(a)(2) (complaint must contain "a short and plain statement of the claim showing that the pleader is entitled to relief"); cf. *Hamling v. United States*, 418 U.S. 87, 117 (1974) (so long as a criminal defendant is fairly apprised of the charge against him, "[i]t is generally sufficient that an indictment set forth the offense in the words of the statute itself"). Any doubt on that point is eliminated by respondents' more specific allegations that the recruiters "work closely with [petitioner] to meet its employment needs by offering a pool

of illegal workers" and "are sometimes assisted by [petitioner's] employees who carry a supply of social security cards." J.A. 23.

B. No Exception To RICO's Prohibitions Exists For "Arms-Length Dealings" Between Distinct Business Entities

Petitioner frames the question presented (Br. i) as whether business entities "engaged in ordinary, arms-length dealings can constitute an 'enterprise' under [RICO]." Petitioner contends (Br. 27) that the Eleventh Circuit's approach "improperly allows plaintiffs to pursue [RICO] claims against a corporation by alleging that the corporation entered into routine business relationships to perform the activities of the corporation." Contrary to petitioner's contention, nothing in RICO precludes a finding that commercial actors engaged in an "arms-length business arrangement" (Br. 35) have formed an associated-in-fact "enterprise."

1. As explained above (see pp. 21-24, supra), the principles announced by this Court in Turkette, and subsequently applied in numerous court of appeals decisions, place meaningful limits on the ability of the government and private plaintiffs to allege and prove the existence of an associated-in-fact RICO enterprise. In particular, the requirements that the members of an associated-in-fact enterprise share a "common purpose" (Turkette, 452 U.S. at 583), and that "the various associates function as a continuing unit" (ibid.), ensure that business entities will not be deemed to have formed a RICO enterprise simply by entering into private contracts. Contrary to petitioner's suggestion (Br. 40), the adequacy of respondents' complaint therefore does not depend on the proposition that a RICO "enterprise" exists "whenever a corporation contracts with another entity."

2. Petitioner describes this case as involving "routine business relationships" (Br. 27) and observes (Br. 38) that "[h]iring employees is a core corporate function." The specific conduct alleged in respondents' complaint, however—i.e., petitioner's alleged knowing and systematic violations of federal immigration law during an extended period of time through an alliance with outside recruiters—cannot plausibly be characterized as a "routine" business practice. Petitioner is not immunized from RICO liability simply because its alleged racketeering activities fall within a more general category of corporate practices that are essential to the operation of a business.

By way of analogy, suppose that a seemingly legitimate pharmaceutical company diverted a portion of its manufacturing capacity to the illicit production of methamphetamine. If the company entered into an ongoing arrangement with another entity, which agreed to furnish the raw materials for methamphetamine production on a continuing basis in order to facilitate the company's unlawful practices, the government could properly charge the pharmaceutical company under 18 U.S.C. 1962(c), on the theory that the two entities were constituent members of a RICO associated-in-fact enterprise. The defendant in those circumstances could not avoid prosecution by arguing that the manufacture of drugs is a "core corporate function" of a pharmaceutical company, and that the government therefore had alleged nothing more than unlawful conduct of the company's "own business" (Pet. Br. 38).

With respect to the adequacy of respondents' complaint, moreover, it is crucial that the outside recruiters are alleged to have been knowing participants in petitioner's scheme to locate and employ illegal aliens. See J.A. 23. A quite different situation would be presented if an employment agency regularly located and referred legal workers to a business corporation, which then utilized the workers in the performance of racketeering acts. If the employment agency was unaware of the corporation's unlawful conduct, the two entities would lack the requisite "common purpose" and therefore could not be regarded as constituent members of an associated-in-fact enterprise, even if the agency's referrals were essential as a practical matter to the corporation's illicit endeavors. The "common purpose" requirement thus helps to ensure that a corporation is not held liable under 18 U.S.C. 1962(c) for what is in substance unilateral misconduct.

3. Petitioner contends (Br. 30-32) that, because the courts of appeals have consistently refused to treat a corporation together with its officers and employees as an associated-in-fact enterprise, this Court should hold that such an enterprise cannot consist of a business corporation and its contracting partner. That is a non sequitur. Because the recruiters who are

alleged to have assisted in petitioner's unlawful practices stand in a fundamentally different relation to the corporation than do petitioner's employees, treatment of petitioner and the outside recruiters as members of an associated-in-fact enterprise is (if respondents' allegations are taken as true) fully consistent with the text and purposes of RICO.

a. Because 18 U.S.C. 1962(c) "require[s] some distinctness between the RICO defendant and the RICO enterprise," a RICO defendant (whether a natural person or an artificial entity) cannot be held liable under Section 1962(c) based solely on proof that it conducted its own affairs through a pattern of racketeering activity. Cedric Kushner, 533 U.S. at 162. The necessary distinctness exists where, as here, the Section 1962(c) defendant is one member of an alleged associated-in-fact enterprise. See, e.g., *United States v. Perholtz*, 842 F.2d 343, 353-354 (D.C. Cir.), cert. denied, 488 U.S. 821 (1988); *Haroco, Inc. v. American Nat'l Bank & Trust Co.*, 747 F.2d 384, 401 (7th Cir. 1984), aff'd, 473 U.S. 606 (1985). Proof that an alleged association in fact is an "ongoing organization" whose members join to "function as a continuing unit," Turkette, 452 U.S. at 583, by its nature implies that the group should be regarded for purposes of RICO as an entity distinct from any single member. In virtually every case in which the United States alleges the existence of a RICO association in fact, the defendant is alleged to be a member of that enterprise. See, e.g., Russello, 464 U.S. at 19; Turkette, 452 U.S. at 578-579. And Congress's determination that an association in fact should be treated as a RICO "enterprise" would be largely negated if the persons who form such an association were immune from liability for the illicit conduct of its affairs.

b. As petitioner observes (Br. 30-31), the courts of appeals have agreed that a corporation cannot be held liable under 18 U.S.C. 1962(c) for conducting the affairs of a purported association in fact consisting of the corporation and its own employees. See, e.g., *Riverwoods Chappaqua Corp. v. Marine Midland Bank, N.A.*, 30 F.3d 339, 344 (2d Cir. 1994) (Riverwoods). Contrary to petitioner's suggestion (Br. 39), however, that rule does not rest on the mere fact that a corporation contracts with its employees for the performance of tasks that benefit the corporation. Rather, because an employee is part of the corporation, the two are not naturally characterized as forming a combination that can meaningfully be distinguished from the corporation itself. The recruiters who are alleged to have assisted petitioner in its unlawful employment practices, by contrast, have no place within petitioner's corporate structure. Indeed, petitioner repeatedly characterizes the dealings between itself and the recruiters as being conducted at "arms-length" (e.g., Pet. Br. i). The rationale for the rule announced in Riverwoods and like cases is therefore inapplicable here.

As the government's brief in Cedric Kushner explained, the Riverwoods holding also serves to prevent circumvention through artful pleading of 18 U.S.C. 1962(c)'s requirement that the alleged violator must be distinct from the RICO enterprise. See U.S. Amicus Br. at 16, Cedric Kushner (No. 00-549). A corporation together with its employees will necessarily satisfy the requirements set forth in Turkette—i.e., that the government or private plaintiff prove the existence of an "ongoing organization" whose members share a "common purpose" and "function as a continuing unit." 452 U.S. at 583. Thus, if a corporation and its personnel could be treated as fellow members of an associated-in-fact enterprise, "the prohibition on naming the same corporation as both the defendant and the RICO enterprise could be routinely evaded by listing corporate officers and employees as part of the enterprise, without affecting the gravamen of the complaint." U.S. Amicus Br. at 16, Cedric Kushner (No. 00-549). No comparable danger of circumvention exists here, since a corporation and outside entities may be treated as constituent members of an associated-in-fact enterprise only if the plaintiff alleges and proves that the group members were not merely contractually linked, but also shared a "common purpose" and "function[ed] as a continuing unit." Turkette, 452 U.S. at 583.

c. Petitioner suggests (e.g., Br. 35) that it is somehow anomalous to distinguish, for purposes of Section 1962(c)'s coverage, between cases in which a corporation undertakes a pattern of racketeering activity through its own employees, and cases in which it receives the assistance of persons outside the corporate structure. That distinction, however, follows directly from the fact that Section 1962(c) prohibits, not the commission of racketeering crimes per se, but the use of racketeering activity to operate or manage an enterprise that is distinct from the violator itself. See *Reves v. Ernst & Young*, 507 U.S. 170, 177-185 (1993); Cedric Kushner, 533 U.S. at 160-163.12 The necessary consequence of that limitation on Section 1962(c)'s coverage is that criminal conduct undertaken in collaboration with others may trigger distinct legal sanctions that do not apply in cases of wholly unilateral wrongdoing. That feature of RICO is scarcely novel: the law of conspiracy has long reflected the judgment that "collective criminal agreement—partnership in crime—presents a greater potential threat to the public than individual delicts." *Callanan v. United States*, 364 U.S. 587, 593 (1961).

9. CONCLUSION
The judgment of the court of appeals should be affirmed.
Respectfully submitted.
PAUL D. CLEMENT
Solicitor General
ALICE S. FISHER
Assistant Attorney General
MICHAEL R. DREEBEN
Deputy Solicitor General
MALCOLM L. STEWART
Assistant to the Solicitor
General
SANGITA K. RAO
Attorney
MARCH 2006
(Source: Internet-URL: http://www.usdoj.gov/osg/briefs/2005/3mer/1ami/2005-0465.mer.ami.pdf)

Document 4: *Fernandez-Vargas v. Gonzales*

Title: 548 U.S._(2006), (No. 04-1376) 394 F. 3d 881, affirmed.

When: Argued March 22, 2006; decided June 22, 2006

Significance: Undocumented aliens who have entered the United States several times and have been deported at least once cannot apply for legal permanent resident status and will be again subject to deportation on the basis of the reinstatement statute, Section 1231(a)(5) of the Immigration and Nationality Act, regardless of whether or not this law was enacted after his or her first deportation.

No. 04-1376

In the Supreme Court of the United States

Humberto Fernandez-Vargas, petitioner

v.

Alberto R. Gonzales, Attorney General

ON PETITION FOR A WRIT OF CERTIORARI
TO THE UNITED STATES COURT OF APPEALS
FOR THE TENTH CIRCUIT

BRIEF FOR THE RESPONDENT

Paul D. Clement
Solicitor General
Counsel of Record
Peter D. Keisler
Assistant Attorney General

Donald E. Keener
Alison Marie Igoe
Attorneys
Department of Justice
Washington, D.C. 20530-0001
(202) 514-2217

QUESTION PRESENTED

Whether 8 U.S.C. 1231(a)(5), which provides for the reinstatement of a previous order of removal against an alien who has illegally re-entered the United States, applies to an alien whose illegal re-entry predated the effective date of the provision.

In the Supreme Court of the United States

No. 04-1376

Humberto Fernandez-Vargas, petitioner

v.

Alberto R. Gonzales, Attorney General

ON PETITION FOR A WRIT OF CERTIORARI
TO THE UNITED STATES COURT OF APPEALS
FOR THE TENTH CIRCUIT

BRIEF FOR THE RESPONDENT

OPINION BELOW

The opinion of the court of appeals (Pet. App. 1a-18a) is reported at 394 F.3d 881.

JURISDICTION

The judgment of the court of appeals was entered on January 12, 2005. The petition for a writ of certiorari was filed on April 12, 2005. The jurisdiction of this Court is invoked under 28 U.S.C. 1254(1).

STATEMENT

1. This case involves the reinstatement of a previous order of deportation pursuant to 8 U.S.C. 1231(a)(5), which was enacted as part of the Illegal Immigration Reform and Immigrant Responsibility Act of 1996 (IIRIRA), Pub. L. No. 104-208, Div. C, § 305(a)(3), 110 Stat. 3009-599. Before IIRIRA was enacted, former 8 U.S.C. 1252(f) (1994) governed the reinstatement of a previous deportation order. That provision stated:

Should the Attorney General find that any alien has unlawfully reentered the United States after having previously departed or been deported pursuant to an order of deportation, whether before or after June 27, 1952, on any ground described in any of the paragraphs enumerated in subsection (e) of this section, the previous order of deportation shall be deemed to be reinstated from its original date and such alien shall be deported under such previous order at any time subsequent to such reentry. For the purposes of subsection (e) of this section the date on which the finding is made that such reinstatement is appropriate shall be deemed the date of the final order of deportation.

8 U.S.C. 1252(f) (1994).

IIRIRA repealed that provision and replaced it with 8 U.S.C. 1231(a)(5). The current provision states:

If the Attorney General finds that an alien has reentered the United States illegally after having been removed or having departed voluntarily, under an order of removal, the prior order of removal is reinstated from its original date and is not subject to being reopened or reviewed, the alien is not eligible and may not apply for any relief under this chapter, and the alien shall be removed under the prior order at any time after the reentry.

8 U.S.C. 1231(a)(5). Because the current provision prescribes that an alien who illegally re-enters the United States after having been removed is "not eligible and may not apply for

Following a July 2006 operation in Oklahoma City, Immigration and Customs Enforcement ("Police ICE") officers fingerprint detainees suspected of having defied final deportation orders. AP Photo/Ty Russell.

any relief," such an alien is ineligible and may not apply for, inter alia, adjustment of status to that of lawful permanent resident. See 8 U.S.C. 1255(i). Under the previous reinstatement provision, by contrast, an alien who illegally re-entered the United States after having been removed was permitted to petition for discretionary relief from removal, including an application for adjustment of status. See Pet. App. 10a-11a; Lattab v. Ashcroft, 384 F.3d 8, 12-13 (1st Cir. 2004).1

2. Petitioner, a citizen of Mexico, was deported from the United States on several occasions, including in October 1981. In January 1982, petitioner re-entered the United States without inspection. On April 1, 1997, the new reinstatement provision enacted by IIRIRA, 8 U.S.C. 1231(a)(5), became effective. Pet. App. 3a, 19a; Gov't C.A. Br. 6; see IIRIRA § 309(a), 110 Stat. 3009-625.

On March 30, 2001, nearly four years after IIRIRA's effective date, petitioner married a United States citizen. On May 30, 2001, petitioner filed an Application for Permission to Reapply for Admission Into the United States After Deportation or Removal (Form I-212). Petitioner also filed an application to adjust his status to that of lawful permanent resident based on a relative visa petition filed on his behalf by his wife. See 8 U.S.C. 1255(i). On November 7, 2003, the Department of Homeland Security (DHS) issued a notice of its intent to reinstate petitioner's previous deportation order pursuant to 8 U.S.C. 1231(a)(5) on the basis that petitioner illegally re-entered the United States after having been removed. On November 17, 2003, DHS issued an order reinstating petitioner's previous deportation order pursuant to Section 1231(a)(5), and also issued a warrant for petitioner's arrest and removal. Pet. App. 3a-4a, 19a-28a; Gov't C.A. Br. 6-7.

3. Petitioner sought review in the court of appeals of the reinstatement of his previous deportation order. He argued that, because he had illegally re-entered the country before IIRIRA's effective date, the application against him of the current reinstatement provision, 8 U.S.C. 1231(a)(5), would be impermissibly retroactive. Petitioner contended that he therefore was subject to the previous reinstatement provision, 8 U.S.C. 1252(f) (1994), and that he retains eligibility under that provision to apply for adjustment of status. The government

argued in response that application of the current reinstatement provision to petitioner does not have a retroactive effect, and that the current provision renders petitioner ineligible to apply for adjustment of status. Pet. App. 4a-5a; Gov't C.A. Br. 10-16.2

The court of appeals denied the petition for review, holding that application of Section 1231(a)(5) to petitioner does not produce a retroactive effect. Pet. App. 1a-18a.3 The court explained that the threshold question was whether Congress had prescribed the temporal reach of Section 1231(a)(5). See Landgraf v. USI Film Prods., 511 U.S. 244, 280 (1994). The court observed that the courts of appeals had reached conflicting conclusions on the issue. Pet. App. 12a-13a. While two courts of appeals had concluded that Congress made clear in the statute that Section 1231(a)(5) applies only to aliens who illegally re-enter the United States after IIRIRA's effective date, id. at 12a (citing Bejjani v. INS, 271 F.3d 670 (6th Cir. 2001); Castro-Cortez v. INS, 239 F.3d 1037, 1050-1053 (9th Cir. 2001)), six courts of appeals had concluded that the statute contains no clear indication concerning its temporal reach, id. at 12a-13a (citing Sarmiento Cisneros v. United States Att'y Gen., 381 F.3d 1277, 1283-1285 (11th Cir. 2004); Arevalo v. Ashcroft, 344 F.3d 1, 12-13 (1st Cir. 2003); Avila-Macias v. Ashcroft, 328 F.3d 108, 114 (3d Cir. 2003); Ojeda-Terrazas v. Ashcroft, 290 F.3d 292, 299 (5th Cir. 2002); Alvarez-Portillo v. Ashcroft, 280 F.3d 858, 865 (8th Cir. 2002); Velasquez-Gabriel v. Crocetti, 263 F.3d 102, 108 (4th Cir. 2001)). The court of appeals agreed with the majority of courts of appeals and held that Congress did not evince an unambiguous intent concerning the temporal scope of Section 1231(a)(5). Pet. App. 14a-16a.

The court then turned to the second step of the inquiry under this Court's retroactivity decisions, and addressed whether application of Section 1231(a)(5) would have a "retroactive effect, i.e., whether it would impair rights a party possessed when he acted, increase a party's liability for past conduct, or impose new duties with respect to transactions already completed." Landgraf, 511 U.S. at 280. The court concluded that Section 1231(a)(5) worked no retroactive effect in this case. The court recognized that certain courts of appeals had found that Section 1231(a)(5) would have a retroactive effect in the case of an alien who had applied for adjustment of status before IIRIRA's effective date or at least had become married to a United States citizen before that date. Pet. App. 16a-17a & n.12. The court explained, however, that petitioner had neither applied for adjustment of status nor become married by IIRIRA's effective date. Id. at 17a.

The court concluded that, in those circumstances, petitioner "had no protectable expectation of being able to adjust his status." Pet. App. 17a. The court reasoned that it "would be a step too far to hold that simply by re-entering the country, [he] created a settled expectation that if he did marry a U.S. citizen, he might then be able to adjust his status and defend against removal." Ibid. Because petitioner had not applied for (and was not eligible for) adjustment of status by the time of IIRIRA's effective date, the court of appeals held that application of Section 1231(a)(5) in this case did not have a retroactive effect. Id. at 17a-18a. The court therefore ruled that petitioner was subject to Section 1231(a)(5).

DISCUSSION

The courts of appeals disagree on the applicability of the current reinstatement provision, 8 U.S.C. 1231(a)(5), to an alien who had illegally re-entered the United States before IIRIRA's effective date of April 1, 1997. In light of that disagreement, and because the issue is an important and recurring one, the government does not oppose the granting of the petition for a writ of certiorari.

1. This Court's decisions prescribe a two-step framework for addressing whether a statute should be applied to factual circumstances that predate the statute's enactment. The first question is whether Congress has prescribed the temporal reach of the statute by mandating that the statute should apply (or not apply) to particular conduct before a specified date. See Martin v. Hadix, 527 U.S. 343, 352 (1999); Landgraf, 511 U.S. at 280. If the threshold inquiry reveals that "there is no congressional directive on the temporal reach of [the] statute," the inquiry turns to the second step, which entails a determination "whether the

application of the statute to the conduct at issue would result in a retroactive effect." Martin, 527 U.S. at 352; see Landgraf, 511 U.S. at 280.

The analysis at the second step of "whether a statute operates retroactively demands a commonsense, functional judgment about 'whether the new provision attaches new legal consequences to events completed before its enactment.'" Martin, 527 U.S. at 357-358 (quoting Landgraf, 511 U.S. at 270); see INS v. St. Cyr, 533 U.S. 289, 321-324 (2001). That determination turns on "familiar considerations of fair notice, reasonable reliance, and settled expectations." Martin, 527 U.S. at 358. If application of the statute in the circumstances at issue would produce a "retroactive effect," the Court "presume[s] that the statute does not apply" in those circumstances, in "keeping with [its] 'traditional presumption' against retroactivity." Id. at 343 (quoting Landgraf, 511 U.S. at 280).

a. The courts of appeals disagree on whether, under the first step of the retroactivity inquiry, Congress prescribed the applicability of Section 1231(a)(5) to an alien whose illegal re-entry predated the provision's effective date. The Sixth and Ninth Circuits have concluded that Congress mandated with requisite clarity that Section 1231(a)(5) does not apply to an alien who illegally re-entered the United States before IIRIRA's effective date. Bejjani, 271 F.3d at 676-687 (6th Cir.); Castro-Cortez, 239 F.3d at 1050-1053 (9th Cir.). Those two courts therefore have had no occasion to proceed to the second step of the inquiry to assess whether application of Section 1231(a)(5) to an alien who illegally re-entered the United States before IIRIRA's effective date would entail a retroactive effect. Eight courts of appeals (including the court below) have disagreed with the Sixth and Ninth Circuits on that initial question, and have held that Congress did not prescribe the temporal reach of Section 1231(a)(5). See Pet. App. 12a-13a (citing decisions from the First, Third, Fourth, Fifth, Eighth, and Eleventh Circuits); Faiz-Mohammad v. Ashcroft, 395 F.3d 799, 804 (7th Cir. 2005). Those courts therefore have proceeded to an assessment whether the application of Section 1231(a)(5) in the particular circumstances would have a retroactive effect.

b. Petitioner argues (Pet. 13-18) that Congress prescribed the temporal reach of Section 1231(a)(5) and mandated that the provision have no application to aliens whose illegal re-entry predated IIRIRA's effective date. The court of appeals below, consistent with the majority of the courts of appeals, correctly rejected that argument.

The text of Section 1231(a)(5) contains no indication of an intent to foreclose its application to aliens who had illegally re-entered the United States before IIRIRA's effective date. To the contrary, Section 1231(a)(5) provides by its terms for reinstatement of a previous removal order whenever "the Attorney General finds that an alien has reentered the United States illegally after having been removed or having departed voluntarily." 8 U.S.C. 1231(a)(5). The triggering event under the provision thus is not the illegal re-entry itself, but a finding by the Attorney General that the alien has illegally re-entered the country after having been removed; and the purpose of the provision is to streamline the process for dealing with the consequence of that finding (viz., removing the alien by reinstating the previous removal order in the event of such a finding).

Section 1231(a)(5) therefore governs the reinstatement of a previous removal order in the case of an alien who is found to have illegally re-entered the country, and its aim is thus to expedite the removal of the alien. See Martin, 527 U.S. at 363 (Scalia, J., concurring in part and concurring in the judgment) (observing that identification of relevant "reference point[] for the retroactivity determination" should "turn upon which activity the statute was intended to regulate"). See also Republic of Austria v. Altmann, 541 U.S. 677, 697 (2004) (finding that Foreign Sovereign Immunities Act applies to actions arising from pre-enactment conduct because relevant conduct regulated by Act is present assertion of immunity rather than past conduct giving rise to action). Section 1231(a)(5) does not centrally aim to regulate the illegal re-entry itself. Compare 8 U.S.C. 1326 (establishing crime of illegal re-entry following previous removal). Section 1231(a)(5) contains no suggestion that the applicability of its rules for reinstatement of a previous removal order might turn on the timing of the re-entry. Rather, it provides generally for reinstatement of a previous removal order upon a finding "that an alien has reentered the United States illegally," without indicating any distinction based on when that re-entry occurred. 8 U.S.C. 1231(a)(5) (emphasis added).

Petitioner does not focus on what Section 1231(a)(5) affirmatively says. He instead argues that Congress prescribed Section 1231(a)(5)'s temporal reach by negative implication. See Pet. 14-15. Petitioner relies on the language of the former reinstatement provision, 8 U.S.C. 1252(f) (1994), which was enacted in 1952 as part of the Immigration and Nationality Act (INA), ch. 477, 66 Stat. 163. Petitioner notes that the former provision allowed for reinstatement of a previous deportation order if the Attorney General should "find that any alien has unlawfully reentered the United States after having previously departed or been deported pursuant to an order of deportation, whether before or after June 27, 1952 [the date of the INA's enactment], on any ground described in any of the paragraphs enumerated in subsection (e)." 8 U.S.C. 1252(f) (1994) (emphasis added). In petitioner's view, by excluding comparable "before or after" language from Section 1231(a)(5), Congress indicated by negative implication its intention that the provision should not apply to an alien whose illegal re-entry predated the provision's effective date. As explained by the court below and other courts of appeals, however, "the silence that replaced [the 'before or after" language] cannot be considered a clear statement of congressional intent." Pet. App. 14a; see Faiz-Mohammad, 395 F.3d at 803-804; Sarmiento Cisneros, 381 F.3d at 1282; Avila-Macias, 328 F.3d at 113.

That is especially true because petitioner's argument rests on the flawed assumption (Pet. 14) that the phrase, "before or after June 27, 1952," in the previous reinstatement provision concerned the date of the alien's illegal re-entry rather than the date of the alien's previous "order of deportation" or the date that the alien "previously departed or [was] deported" pursuant to that order. 8 U.S.C. 1252(f) (1994). Because the "before or after" language immediately followed the reference to the alien's "having previously departed or been deported pursuant to an order of deportation," the most natural reading is that the "before or after" language pertained to the date that the alien departed or was deported or to the date of the previous deportation order. That conclusion is reinforced by the fact that the language that immediately followed the "before or after" language addressed the grounds for the previous deportation, i.e., "on any ground described in any of the paragraphs enumerated in subsection (e) of this section." Because the "before or after" language in the previous reinstatement provision concerned the date of the alien's deportation or departure or the date of the previous deportation order—rather than the date of the alien's illegal re—entry-the absence of parallel language in Section 1231(a)(5) scarcely suggests that Congress intended to draw a distinction based on the timing of an illegal re-entry.

Petitioner also contends (Pet. 15) that, when considered in light of the presumption against retroactivity, Congress's failure to state explicitly that Section 1231(a)(5) applies to aliens whose illegal re-entry predated the statute's effective date itself indicates an in tent that the provision should not apply in those circumstances. That argument rests on a fundamental misconception about the presumption against retroactivity.

The presumption by nature assumes significance only if the statute's application in the circumstances would produce a "retroactive effect." See, e.g., Martin, 527 U.S. at 352. As this Court has made clear, a "statute does not operate 'retrospectively' merely because it is applied in a case arising from conduct antedating the statute's enactment or upsets expectations based in prior law." Landgraf, 511 U.S. at 269 (citation omitted). Rather, the "conclusion that a particular rule operates 'retroactively' comes at the end of a process of judgment concerning the nature and extent of the change in the law and the degree of connection between the operation of the new rule and a relevant past event." Id. at 270. Petitioner, by contrast, would invoke the presumption against retroactivity at the outset as a reason to construe Section 1231(a)(5) as implicitly specifying its temporal reach, regardless of whether the application of Section 1231(a)(5) in that situation would have a "retroactive effect." However, in the absence of such an effect, application of the statute would not be "retroactive" in the first place, and no presumption would apply. See Pet. App. 14a ("[A]lthough Congress is deemed to act with the Landgraf 'default rule' in mind, an equally valid conclusion is that Congress remained silent in expectation that the courts would proceed to determine, on a case-by-case basis, whether the statute would have an impermissibly retroactive effect."); Alvarez-Portillo, 280 F.3d at 864-865.

2. Because the court of appeals disagreed with the conclusion of the Sixth and Ninth Circuits and determined instead that Congress did not clearly prescribe the temporal reach of Section 1231(a)(5), the court proceeded to assess whether application of Section 1231(a)(5) to petitioner would entail a "retroactive effect." The court concluded that application of Section 1231(a)(5) to petitioner would not produce a retroactive effect, emphasizing that petitioner had neither applied for adjustment of status nor become married before IIRIRA's effective date. Pet. App. 17a-18a. In those circumstances, the court reasoned, petitioner "had no protectable expectation of being able to adjust his status." Id. at 17a.

a. Petitioner argues (Pet. 19-22) that applying Section 1231(a)(5) to any alien whose illegal re-entry predated IIRIRA's effective date would entail a retroactive effect. He reasons that, because Section 1231(a)(5) renders all such aliens ineligible for discretionary relief from removal, the provision increases liability for past conduct in a manner that results in a retroactive effect. In support of that argument, petitioner relies (Pet. 20) on this Court's observation in *INS v. St. Cyr*, supra, that "[t]here is a clear difference, for the purposes of retro activity analysis, between facing possible deportation and facing certain deportation." 533 U.S. at 325. Petitioner's argument lacks merit.

The Court has explained that "a statute is not made retroactive merely because it draws upon antecedent facts for its operation." Landgraf, 511 U.S. at 270 n.24 (internal quotation marks omitted). Indeed, "[e]ven uncontroversially prospective statutes may unsettle expectations and impose burdens on past conduct," such as a "new property tax or zoning regulation" that "upset[s] the reasonable expectations that prompted those affected to acquire property," or a "new law banning gambling" that "harms the person who had begun to construct a casino before the law's enactment." Id. at 269 n.24 (emphasis added). Section 1231(a)(5) is "uncontroversially prospective" in the same sense. Just as a new property tax is applied on a going forward basis, Section 1231(a)(5) reflects Congress's intention to apply new rules for the reinstatement of removal orders on a going forward basis. Because the provision aims to streamline the process for removing aliens who are found to have illegally re-entered the country, its application to reinstatement proceedings that take place after IIRIRA's effective date is inherently prospective. Petitioner's retroactivity argument erroneously focuses on the past re-entry rather than on the reinstatement procedure, while the statute focuses on the latter.

Furthermore, whether the application of a statute qualifies as "retroactive" turns on "familiar considerations of fair notice, reasonable reliance, and settled expectations." Landgraf, 511 U.S. at 270; see Martin, 527 U.S. at 357-358. Judged by those standards, the application of Section 1231(a)(5) does not produce a "retroactive effect." As an initial matter, Section 1231(a)(5) did not have the effect of converting conduct that was lawful when it took place into unlawful conduct. Rather, the immigration laws have long proscribed—and made criminal—an illegal re-entry by an alien who was previously ordered removed. See, e.g., 8 U.S.C. 1326. Because an alien who illegally re-entered the country before Section 1231(a)(5)'s effective date was engaging in an unlawful and criminal act, there is minimal force to any claim that applying the provision's elimination of discretionary relief from removal to such an alien would be unfair, affect primary conduct, or interfere with legitimate expectations. See Landgraf, 511 U.S. at 282 n.35 ("[C]oncerns of unfair surprise and upsetting expectations are attenuated in the case of intentional employment discrimination, which has been unlawful for more than a generation."). See also id. at 281-282.

Although Section 1231(a)(5) eliminates the availability of discretionary relief from removal to an alien who re-entered the country illegally and whose previous removal order is reinstated, that feature does not have a "retroactive effect" within the meaning of this Court's decisions. The Court's analysis in St. Cyr is instructive. The Court held that IIRIRA's elimination of discretionary relief from removal under former 8 U.S.C. 1182(c) (1994) for aliens who are convicted of an aggravated felony resulted in a "retroactive effect" in the case of an alien who had pleaded guilty to an aggravated felony before IIRIRA's effective date. 533 U.S. at 321-325. The Court explained that aliens consider the immigration consequences of a conviction when deciding whether to enter a guilty plea, and that preserving the possibility of discretionary "relief would have been one of the principal benefits sought by defendants deciding whether to accept a plea offer or instead to proceed to trial." Id. at 323. Because aliens relied upon the availability of discretionary relief in deciding to enter into a guilty plea, the Court reasoned, "it would surely be contrary to 'familiar considerations of fair notice, reasonable reliance, and settled expectations' to hold that IIRIRA's subsequent restrictions deprive them of any possibility of such relief." Id. at 323-324 (quoting Landgraf, 511 U.S. at 270) (citation omitted).

The application of Section 1231(a)(5) to an alien whose illegal re-entry predated IIRIRA's effective date does not implicate the concerns of detrimental reliance or unfair notice that gave rise to the Court's finding of a "retroactive effect" in St. Cyr. While the Court reasoned in St. Cyr that an alien might have made a different decision concerning whether to enter a guilty plea if discretionary relief from removal were unavailable to him, an alien whose unlawful re-entry predated IIRIRA's effective date could make no comparable claim. An alien who illegally re-entered notwithstanding the prospect of criminal prosecution and punishment could make no persuasive claim that he nonetheless may have elected to forgo an illegal re-entry if he were ineligible to seek discretionary relief from removal.

Moreover, in the context of the present case, an alien who unlawfully re-enters the United States generally is not qualified at that time to obtain an adjustment of status that would enable him to remain here lawfully. See 8 U.S.C. 1255(i)(2) (requiring that alien be "eligible to receive an immigrant visa" and be "admissible" for permanent residence in order to qualify for adjustment of status). An alien therefore could have no reasonable expectation of obtaining an adjustment of status at the time of his illegal re-entry. As the court of appeals explained, "[i]t would be a step too far to hold that simply by re-entering the country, [petitioner] created a settled expectation that if he did marry a U.S. citizen, he might then be able to adjust his status and defend against removal." Pet. App. 17a. In its opinion in St. Cyr, the Second Circuit similarly distinguished between an alien's decision whether to commit a crime that renders him removable and an alien's later decision whether to plead guilty to such a crime. St. Cyr v. INS, 229 F.3d 406, 418-419 (2d Cir. 2000), aff'd, 533 U.S. 289 (2001). With respect to the decision whether to commit the crime in the first place, the court explained that it "would border on the absurd to argue that * * * aliens might have decided not to commit drug crimes * * * had they known that if they were not only imprisoned but also, when their prison term ended, ordered deported, they could not ask for a discretionary waiver of deportation." Id. at 418. This Court affirmed the Second Circuit's decision in St. Cyr, and gave no indication that it disagreed with that aspect of the court of appeals' analysis.

Finally, although application of Section 1231(a)(5)'s bar against discretionary relief from removal to petitioner has the effect of rendering him ineligible to apply for an adjustment of status, an "adjustment of status is merely a procedural mechanism by which an alien [who is already in the United States] is assimilated to the position of one seeking to enter the United States." In re Rainford, 20 I. & N. Dec. 598, 601 (Bd. of Immigr. Appeals 1992). Before Congress created the mechanism of an adjustment of status in 1952, "aliens in the United States who were not immigrants had to leave the country and apply for an immigrant visa at a consulate abroad." Elkins v. Moreno, 435 U.S. 647, 667 (1978). Under the adjustment-of-status procedure, an alien already within the United States is treated as if he were seeking admission from abroad but is permitted to remain here while the application is pending. See ibid.; Tibke v. INS, 335 F.2d 42, 44-45 (2d Cir. 1964); In re S-, 9 I. & N. Dec. 548, 553-554 (Att'y Gen. 1962). An adjustment of status thus is a "wholly procedural" mechanism, under which "the alien must still satisfy applicable substantive standards and persuade the Attorney General to exercise his discretion favorably." Tibke, 335 F.2d at 45. This understanding of the adjustment-of-status process underscores the lack of any retroactive effect. Because Section 1231(a)(5)'s application to petitioner ultimately affects the procedures by which, and the location from which, he may seek discretionary admission into the country, the provision's application is not retroactive in effect. Compare Landgraf, 511 U.S. at 274 (explaining that statutes "conferring or ousting jurisdiction" apply in pending cases because "[a]pplication of a new jurisdictional rule usually takes away no substantive right but simply changes the tribunal that is to hear the case") (internal quotation marks omitted); id. at 275 ("Changes in procedural rules may often be applied in suits arising before their enactment without raising concerns about retroactivity."). For all of those reasons, the court of appeals was correct in concluding that the mere fact that an alien's illegal re-entry predated IIRIRA's effective date, without more, does not mean that application of Section 1231(a)(5) to the alien would entail a "retroactive effect."

b. Among the majority of courts of appeals that have held that Congress did not prescribe Section 1231(a)(5)'s temporal reach and that therefore have proceeded to the second step of the retroactivity inquiry, no court of appeals has held that the mere fact that an alien's illegal re-entry predated IIRIRA's effective date, without more, establishes that application of Section 1231(a)(5) would have a "retroactive effect." The First, Seventh, and Eleventh Circuits have held that, where an alien not only had illegally re-entered the United States before IIRIRA's effective date but also had applied for adjustment of status by that date, application of Section 1231(a)(5) would result in a retroactive effect. See Faiz-Mohammad, 395 F.3d at 809-810; Sarmiento Cisneros, 381 F.3d at 1284; Arevalo, 344 F.3d at 14. The courts of appeals disagree on whether Section 1231(a)(5) also produces a retroactive effect when applied to an alien who had not filed an application for adjustment of status by IIRIRA's effective date but had become married to a United States citizen by that date. The Eighth Circuit has held that Section 1231(a) gives rise to a retroactive effect in that situation, see Alvarez-Portillo, 280 F.3d at 867, but the Fourth Circuit has reached the contrary conclusion, see Velasquez-Gabriel, 263 F.3d at 108-110.

This case does not raise any issues of that type because petitioner neither became married nor applied for adjustment of status before IIRIRA's effective date. Accordingly, if this Court were to agree with the government and the majority of courts of appeals and conclude that Congress did not prescribe the temporal reach of Section 1231(a)(5), the facts of this case would not present an opportunity to address whether Section 1231(a)(5) would have a retroactive effect when applied to an alien who had applied for adjustment of status before IIRIRA's effective date (or to an alien who had become married by that date). Instead, this case would raise only the question whether the mere fact that an alien's illegal re-entry predated IIRIRA's effective date, without more, renders application of Section 1231(a)(5) unfairly retroactive.

Although the Court could consider awaiting a vehicle that might present certain of the other retroactivity issues potentially raised by Section 1231(a)(5)—such as whether the provision would be retroactive in the case of an alien who had applied for adjustment of status before IIRIRA's effective date—the government believes that review is warranted in this case. There is a square circuit conflict on whether Section 1231(a)(5) applies to an alien whose illegal re-entry predated IIRIRA's effective date. The provision does not apply in that situation in the Sixth and Ninth Circuits, see p.8, supra, but it does apply in the Tenth Circuit under the decision below as well as in other courts of appeals, see Labojewski v. Gonzales, 407 F.3d 814, 821-822 (7th Cir. 2005); Velasquez-Gabriel, 263 F.3d at 108-110. If this Court agrees with the government and concludes that Congress did not prescribe Section 1231(a)(5)'s temporal reach and that application of the provision to petitioner does not have a retroactive effect, the Court's analysis will substantially inform the proper resolution of the various other retroactivity questions potentially raised by Section 1231(a)(5). Conversely, if this Court were to agree with petitioner and conclude either that Congress prescribed that Section 1231(a)(5) does not apply to any alien whose illegal re-entry predated IIRIRA's effective date or that application of the provision to any such alien would entail a retroactive effect, the Court's resolution would obviate the need to address any of the other retroactivity issues raised by Section 1231(a)(5) that have been considered by the courts of appeals.

Finally, the issue presented by the facts of this case is of substantial practical significance. Although it is difficult to formulate a reliable estimate of the number of aliens who unlawfully re-entered the country before IIRIRA's effective date and remain in the country, the government believes that the number is substantial and is likely to remain so for some time. The question whether Section 1231(a)(5)'s reinstatement provisions may be applied to such aliens when they are found within the country is of significant practical importance to the effective and efficient enforcement of the Nation's immigration laws. The importance of the issue is underscored by the fact that, according to statistics retained by the Department of Justice, the Ninth Circuit—one of the two courts of appeals that has adopted the sweeping rule that Section 1231(a)(5) may not be applied to any aliens who re-entered before its enactment—is currently responsible for roughly 45% of the immigration docket in the courts of appeals.

CONCLUSION

The petition for a writ of certiorari should be granted.

Respectfully submitted.

Paul D. Clement
Solicitor General
Peter D. Keisler
Assistant Attorney General
Donald E. Keener
Alison Marie Igoe
Attorneys

SEPTEMBER 2005

(Source: Internet-URL: http://www.usdoj.gov/osg/briefs/2005/0responses/2004-1376.resp.html)

Document 5: *Lopez v. Gonzales*

Title: No. 05-547, 549 U.S._, 2006 U.S. LEXIS 9442 (Dec. 5, 2006)

When: Argued October 3, 2006; decided December 5, 2006

Significance: The Supreme Court's decision in the case *Lopez v. Gonzales* has an impact on the question of whether the possession of drugs is a felony, as it would be in the case of drug trafficking—that is an aggravated felony—with the consequence of mandatory deportation for non-U.S. citizens. The Supreme Court's decision also reflects the necessity of an exact use of the English language in order to avoid incorrect interpretations of laws. The Court rejected the governmental argument that state drug offense would indicate that a convicted person had to have committed a prior drug offense and should thus be treated as the equivalent of a federal recidivist, which would then be classified as an aggravated felony.

No. 05-547

In the Supreme Court of the United States

JOSE ANTONIO LOPEZ, PETITIONER

v.

ALBERTO R. GONZALES, ATTORNEY GENERAL

ON PETITION FOR A WRIT OF CERTIORARI
TO THE UNITED STATES COURT OF APPEALS
FOR THE EIGHTH CIRCUIT

BRIEF FOR THE RESPONDENT

PAUL D. CLEMENT
Solicitor General

Counsel of Record
PETER D. KEISLER
Assistant Attorney General
DONALD E. KEENER
JOHN ANDRE
Attorneys
Department of Justice
Washington, D.C. 20530-0001
(202) 514-2217

QUESTION PRESENTED

The Immigration and Nationality Act attaches a variety of immigration consequences to an alien's commission of an "aggravated felony," 8 U.S.C. 1101(a)(43). The Act defines "aggravated felony" to include "any felony punishable under the Controlled Substances Act." 18 U.S.C. 924(c)(2) (as incorporated into 8 U.S.C. 1101(a)(43)(B)). That term applies to offense conduct "whether in violation of Federal or State law." 8 U.S.C. 1101(a)(43) (final paragraph). The question presented is:

Whether the commission of a controlled substance offense that is a felony under state law, but that is generally punishable under the Controlled Substances Act only as a misdemeanor, constitutes an "aggravated felony," where the alien was sentenced under State law to more than one year of imprisonment.

In the Supreme Court of the United States

No. 05-547

JOSE ANTONIO LOPEZ, PETITIONER

v.

ALBERTO R. GONZALES, ATTORNEY GENERAL

ON PETITION FOR A WRIT OF CERTIORARI
TO THE UNITED STATES COURT OF APPEALS
FOR THE EIGHTH CIRCUIT

BRIEF FOR THE RESPONDENT

OPINIONS BELOW

The opinion of the court of appeals (Pet. App. 1a-7a) is reported at 417 F.3d 934. The decisions of the Board of Immigration Appeals (Pet. App. 8a-9a) and of the immigration judge (Pet. App. 10a-20a) are unreported.

JURISDICTION

The court of appeals entered its judgment on August 9, 2005. The petition for a writ of certiorari was filed on October 31, 2005. The jurisdiction of this Court is invoked under 28 U.S.C. 1254(1).

STATEMENT

1. Under the Immigration and Nationality Act (INA), an alien who commits an "aggravated felony," as defined in 8 U.S.C. 1101(a)(43), may be ordered removed from the United States, 8 U.S.C. 1227(a)(2)(A)(iii). The commission of an aggravated felony also limits the potential forms of relief from removal that are available to the alien, including, as relevant here, rendering the alien ineligible to apply for cancellation of removal, see 8 U.S.C. 1229b(a)(3) and (b)(1)(C).

The INA defines an "aggravated felony" by reference to a lengthy list of criminal offenses, one of which is "illicit trafficking in a controlled substance (as defined in section 802 of title 21), including a drug trafficking crime (as defined in section 924(c) of title 18)." 8 U.S.C. 1101(a)(43)(B). The term "aggravated felony" applies to such offenses "whether in violation of Federal or State law." 8 U.S.C. 1101(a)(43) (final paragraph).

Section 924(c) of Title 18, in turn, defines "drug trafficking crime" as "any felony punishable under the Controlled Substances Act (21 U.S.C. 801 et seq.), the Controlled Substances Import and Export Act (21 U.S.C. 951 et seq.), or the Maritime Drug Law Enforcement Act (46 U.S.C. App. 1901 et seq.)." Title 18 more generally defines a "felony" as an offense for which "the maximum term of imprisonment authorized" exceeds one year. 18 U.S.C. 3559. The Controlled Substances Act also defines "felony" generally as "any Federal or State offense classified by applicable Federal or State law as a felony." 21 U.S.C. 802(13). The Controlled Substances Act further defines a "felony drug offense" as "an offense that is punishable by imprisonment for more than one year under any law of the United States or of a State or foreign country that prohibits or restricts conduct relating to narcotic drugs, marijuana, anabolic steroids, or depressant or stimulant substances." 21 U.S.C. 802(44), as amended by the Anabolic Steroid Control Act of 2004, Pub. L. No. 108-358, § 2, 118 Stat. 1663.

2. Petitioner is a native and citizen of Mexico who entered the United States illegally in 1985 or 1986. In 1990, he adjusted his status to that of a lawful permanent resident. Pet. App. 1a-2a, 11a. In 1997, petitioner was indicted in South Dakota state court on one count of possessing cocaine, one count of distributing cocaine, and one count of conspiracy to distribute cocaine. Admin. Rec. (A.R.) 224-227. Petitioner ultimately pleaded guilty to aiding and abetting the possession of a controlled substance (cocaine). Pet. App. 13a; A.R. 399-402. Under South Dakota law at that time, the possession of cocaine was a felony punishable by up to five years of imprisonment. See S.D. Codified Laws §§ 22-42-5 (Michie 1988); id. § 22-6-1(7) (Michie 1988 & 1997 Supp.). Also under South Dakota law, a person found guilty of aiding and abetting an offense "is legally accountable[] as a principal to the crime." S.D. Codified Laws § 22-3-3 (West 2004); see S.D. Codified Laws § 22-3-3 (Michie 1988). Petitioner was sentenced to five years of imprisonment, of which he served 15 months. Pet. App. 14a. The Immigration and Naturalization Service subsequently charged petitioner with being subject to removal based on his conviction of a controlled substance violation and his conviction of an aggravated felony. Id. at 12a; A.R. 433; see 8 U.S.C. 1227(a)(2)(A)(iii) and (B)(i).

An immigration judge sustained both charges of removability. Pet. App. 10a-20a. The immigration judge ruled first (id. at 16a) that petitioner was removable based on the controlled substance violation, a charge that was "not disputed." Relying on controlling precedent from the Board of Immigration Appeals (Board), the immigration judge further ruled that petitioner's state felony controlled substance offense constituted an aggravated felony because it was a drug trafficking crime under 18 U.S.C. 924(c). Pet. App. 16a (citing In re Yanez-Garcia, 23 I. & N. Dec. 390 (BIA 2002)). Finally, the immigration judge ruled that petitioner's commission of an aggravated felony statutorily disqualified him from obtaining the discretionary relief of cancellation of removal. Pet. App. 20a (citing 8 U.S.C. 1229b(a)(3)).

The Board affirmed in a brief opinion. Pet. App. 8a-9a.

3. The court of appeals affirmed. Pet. App. 1a-7a. At the outset, the court held (Pet. App. 3a) that the REAL ID Act of 2005, Pub. L. No. 109-13, § 106(a)(1)(A)(iii), 119 Stat. 310, made clear the court's jurisdiction to review the question of law raised by petitioner concerning the proper definition of "aggravated felony" under 8 U.S.C. 1101(a)(43). While the INA contains a general prohibition on judicial review of denials of discretionary relief by the Attorney General, see 8 U.S.C. 1252(a)(2)(B), the REAL ID Act excepted questions of law from that jurisdictional bar, see Pub. L. No. 109-13, § 106(a)(1)(A)(iii).

The court of appeals then held (Pet. App. 4a) that petitioner's felony conviction constituted an "aggravated felony." Following its prior decision in *United States v. Briones-Mata*, 116 F.3d 308 (8th Cir. 1997) (per curiam), the court held that the "plain language" of Section 1101(a)(43) and the criminal law provisions it incorporates establish that "any felony punishable under the Controlled Substances Act," "under either state or federal law," is an aggravated felony. Pet. App. 4a. Because petitioner's conviction was for a felony offense and was for conduct that was independently punishable under the Controlled Substances Act, the court held that it qualified as an "aggravated felony" (Pet. App. 5a), which rendered petitioner ineligible for cancellation of removal (id. at 7a). In so holding, the court noted (id. at 4a-5a) that its decision accorded with the Fifth Circuit's decision in *United States v.*

Hernandez-Avalos, 251 F.3d 505, cert. denied, 534 U.S. 935 (2001), but was contrary to the Ninth Circuit's decision in *Cazarez-Gutierrez v. Ashcroft*, 382 F.3d 905 (9th Cir. 2004).

DISCUSSION

While the decision of the court of appeals is correct, the courts of appeals are divided on whether a state-law felony drug offense qualifies as an "aggravated felony" if it would be punishable only as a misdemeanor under federal law. That issue is a recurring one that arises in both the immigration context and in the federal criminal sentencing context. The courts of appeals are divided in both the immigration and sentencing areas, with some circuits classifying state-law felonies differently in the two contexts. The proper resolution of the issue has important implications for enforcement of the Nation's immigration and criminal laws, and thus merits this Court's review. This case appears to be an appropriate vehicle for resolution of that question.

1. a. Immigration Context. The courts of appeals have issued conflicting rulings on whether an "aggravated felony" under the INA, 8 U.S.C. 1101(a)(43), includes a state-law felony conviction for a drug offense that would be punishable only as a misdemeanor under the relevant federal controlled substances law. The Fifth Circuit, like the court of appeals here, Pet. App. 4a, has held that a state-law felony conviction constitutes an "aggravated felony" as long as the offense conduct would be punishable—either as a felony or a misdemeanor—under the statutorily designated federal controlled substances laws (i.e., the Controlled Substances Act, 21 U.S.C. 801 et seq., the Controlled Substances Import and Export Act, 21 U.S.C. 951 et seq., or the Maritime Drug Law Enforcement Act, 46 U.S.C. App. 1901 et seq.). See *United States v. Hernandez-Avalos*, 251 F.3d 505, 508 (5th Cir.), cert. denied, 534 U.S. 935 (2001); see also *Salazar-Regino v. Trominski*, 415 F.3d 436, 448 (5th Cir. 2005), petition for cert. pending, No. 05-830 (filed Dec. 22, 2005).

The Second, Third, and Ninth Circuits, by contrast, have held in immigration cases that a state-law offense will qualify as an "aggravated felony" only if the offense would also be punishable as a felony under federal law. See *Cazarez-Gutierrez v. Ashcroft*, 382 F.3d 905, 910-918 (9th Cir. 2004); *Gerbier v. Holmes*, 280 F.3d 297, 307-316 (3d Cir. 2002); *Aguirre v. INS*, 79 F.3d 315, 317-318 (2d Cir. 1996). The issue is currently pending in the Seventh and Tenth Circuits. See *Gonzales-Gomez v. Achim*, No. 05-2728 (7th Cir.) (argued Jan. 4, 2006); *Gonzalez-Gonzalez v. Weber*, No. 04-1181 (10th Cir.) (argued March 8, 2005).

b. Criminal Sentencing Context. The Sentencing Guidelines adopt the INA's definition of "aggravated felony" for purposes of authorizing an eight-level adjustment in the advisory sentencing range for illegal reentry convictions. See Sentencing Guidelines § 2L1.2(b)(1)(C) and comment (n.3(A)); see also 8 U.S.C. 1326(b)(2) (authorizing a sentence of up to 20 years for reentry by an alien whose prior removal "was subsequent to a conviction for commission of an aggravated felony"). In construing the phrase "aggravated felony" in 8 U.S.C. 1101(a)(43)(B) in the sentencing context, the courts of appeals have recently come into conflict.

Almost every court of appeals to consider the question in a sentencing case has held that state-law controlled substance felonies constitute aggravated felonies even if punishable only as a misdemeanor under federal law. See *United States v. Wilson*, 316 F.3d 506, 512-514 (4th Cir.), cert. denied, 538 U.S. 1025 (2003); *United States v. Pornes-Garcia*, 171 F.3d 142, 145-148 (2d Cir.), cert. denied, 528 U.S. 880 (1999); *United States v. Simon*, 168 F.3d 1271, 1272 (11th Cir.), cert. denied, 528 U.S. 844 (1999); *United States v. Hinojosa-Lopez*, 130 F.3d 691, 693-694 (5th Cir. 1997); *United States v. Briones-Mata*, 116 F.3d 308, 309-310 (8th Cir. 1997) (per curiam); *United States v. Cabrera-Sosa*, 81 F.3d 998, 1000-1001 (10th Cir.), cert. denied, 519 U.S. 885 (1996); *United States v. Restrepo-Aguilar*, 74 F.3d 361, 364-366 (1st Cir. 1996). The Ninth Circuit likewise has held that a state-law drug felony is sufficient, *United States v. Ibarra-Galindo*, 206 F.3d 1337, 1339-1340 (9th Cir. 2000), cert. denied, 531 U.S. 1102 (2001), at least where the maximum punishment authorized by state law exceeds one year of imprisonment, *United States v. Robles-Rodriguez*, 281 F.3d 900, 904-905 (9th Cir. 2002). See also *United States v. Cordoza-Estrada*, 385 F.3d 56, 58 (1st Cir. 2004) (same as Robles).

The Sixth Circuit, however, recently held in the sentencing context that the state-law offense must also be punishable as a felony under federal law before it will constitute an aggravated felony. See *United States v. Palacios-Suarez*, 418 F.3d 692, 697-700 (6th Cir. 2005). But that court has indicated that, even if the offense conduct ordinarily would be punishable only as a misdemeanor under federal law, the state offense will still qualify as an aggravated felony if the defendant's recidivist history would have rendered him eligible for a felony sentence had he been prosecuted under federal law. Id. at 700. See also *United States v. Simpson*, 319 F.3d 81, 85-86 & n.6 (2d Cir. 2002) (same); *United States v. Haggerty*, 85 F.3d 403, 406 (8th Cir. 1996) (same); *United States v. Forbes*, 16 F.3d 1294, 1301 (1st Cir. 1994) (same).

The fact that the Second and Ninth Circuits have adopted different readings of the same statutory language in 8 U.S.C. 1101(a)(43)(B), depending on whether that immigration law provision is implicated in an immigration case or a sentencing case, further compounds the confusion. Compare Cazarez-Gutierrez, supra, and Aguirre, supra, with Ibarra-Galindo, supra, and Pornes-Garcia, supra; contrast Palacios-Suarez, 418 F.3d at 697 (refusing to adopt differing constructions of the statutory text for immigration and sentencing cases); Hernandez-Avalos, 251 F.3d at 509 (same); cf. *Leocal v. Ashcroft*, 543 U.S. 1, 12 n.8 (2004) (courts "must interpret [a] statute consistently, whether we encounter its application in a criminal or noncriminal context").

Accordingly, the question presented has been broadly considered by the courts of appeals and the conflict is entrenched and multi-dimensional. Further consideration of the question by other courts of appeals will simply exacerbate, rather than ameliorate, the conflict. An exercise of this Court's certiorari jurisdiction to resolve the question is warranted.

2. The question of when state felony drug offenses constitute aggravated felonies under the INA is a frequently recurring issue of significant importance. The Department of Homeland Security has informed this Office that, in Fiscal Year 2005, more than 77,000 aliens with criminal records were ordered removed from the United States, and that approximately 9.5% of those aliens had arrests for drug possession offenses. While it is difficult to calculate precisely how many of those removals turned upon denominating the crime an "aggravated felony," because statistics are not kept at that level of detail, the large number of removals that arise annually involving aliens convicted of controlled substance offenses confirms what the case law and the federal government's experience in administering the immigration laws indicate: the characterization of a state controlled substance felony as an aggravated felony is a frequently recurring issue, and continued confusion about the proper interpretation of that term consumes significant governmental and private resources and complicates and delays the proper enforcement of the immigration laws.

Indeed, the lack of uniformity in circuit precedent has prompted the Board of Immigration Appeals to eschew administration of a consistent definition of "aggravated felony" in immigration cases. Initially, in In re K-V-D-, 22 I. & N. Dec. 1163 (1999), the Board held that a state felony drug possession conviction would qualify as an aggravated felony only if it also was punishable as a felony under the applicable federal drug laws. But, because it came to recognize "[t]he analytical difficulties inherent in the hypothetical felony approach," and be cause contrary federal circuit rulings had overriden the Board's K-V-D- decision in a number of circuits, the Board subsequently abandoned K-V-D- as precedent. In re Yanez-Garcia, 23 I. & N. Dec. 390, 393 (BIA 2002). The Board held in Yanez-Garcia, instead, that it would follow the rule adopted by the circuit court of appeals in which the immigration case arose concerning when a state drug offense qualifies as an aggravated felony. Id. at 393-398. In the circuits that had not decided the issue, the Board determined that it would apply the rule that a state felony possession offense is an aggravated felony as long as it is punishable under federal law as either a felony or a misdemeanor, because that approach "bears considerable logical force and flows coherently and intuitively from the relevant statutory language," while avoiding the "often-convoluted hypothetical analysis that can be difficult to apply in practice," id. at 397-398. Granting the petition in this case thus would promote stability and a consistent approach to the definition of aggravated felony in immigration cases.

CONCLUSION
The petition for a writ of certiorari should be granted.
Respectfully submitted.
PAUL D. CLEMENT
Solicitor General
PETER D. KEISLER
Assistant Attorney General
DONALD E. KEENER
JOHN ANDRE Attorneys
(Source: Internet-URL: http://www.usdoj.gov/osg/briefs/2005/0responses/2005-0547.resp.html)

FURTHER READINGS

The United States Department of Justice files a number of briefs and other pleadings with the Supreme Court: http://www.usdoj.gov/osg/briefs/brieftype.htm

The Supreme Court of the United States: http://www.supremecourtus.gov

The American Immigration Law Foundation dedicates to the public understanding of both immigration law and immigration policy and its values to American society: http://www.ailf.org

The Legal Information Institute from the Law School of Cornell University offers an archive of decisions of the Supreme Court of the United States: http://www.law.cornell.edu/supct/index.html

The immigration portal from a leading immigration law publisher: http://www.ilw.com

The volunteer association of attorneys, researchers and legislators, the Friends of Immigration Law Enforcement (FILE), works on behalf of Americans to ensure that immigration laws are being enforced: http://fileus.org/about_file.html

The Immigrant Defense Project of the New York Defenders Association: http://www.nysda.org/idp/index.htm

ARTICLES

Legomsky, Stephen "The New Path of Immigration Law: Asymmetric Incorporation of Criminal Justice Norms." *Washington and Lee Law Review*, Vol. 64, Issue 2 (2007), 469.

Mailman, Stanley, and Stephen Yale-Loehr/ "Supreme Court Shortens Reach of 'Aggravated Felonies.'" *New York Law Journal* (December 13, 2006). http://www.millermayer.com/site/new/aggrav_felonies.html.

Ryan, David M., and Kelly B. Kramer. "Two Recent Supreme Court Decisions Reaffirm that RICO Claims Must Satisfy Strict Proximate Cause Standard" (June 21, 2006). http://www.nixonpeabody.com/services_pubdetail.asp?ID=1582&SID=59.

Vargas, Manuel D., and Marianne C. Yang. "Practice Advisory: Criminal Defense of Immigrants in State Drug Cases—The impact of Lopez v. Gonzales." New York State Defenders Association, Immigrant Defense Project (December 14, 2006). http://www.nysda.org/idp/docs/06_PostLopezAdvisoryforStateCriminalDefense%2012%2014%2006.pdf.

CHAPTER 12

The Immigration Debate and the U.S. Economy

Thomas Cieslik

The marches for immigrant rights on May 1, 2006, highlighted the current tensions about undocumented immigrants in the country. In many U.S. cities, predominantly Hispanics protested peacefully against the proposed laws and tighter restrictions on immigration. The organizers of the nationwide "A Day Without Immigrants" indicated that immigrants were here to help the U.S. people and economy. By carrying American flags they showed their support for U.S. society.

In Chicago, 300,000 demonstrators participated in the march. Despite their generally positive attitude toward immigrants, several politicians criticized the protest actions. One of them was Bill Richardson, the governor of New Mexico. He implied, for example, that the immigrants' message was quite confusing: "Come to America to work, yet they're not working. I'd rather see the individuals, all these demonstrations, going to congressional offices, pushing the Congress to act on immigration reform."

This chapter provides a closer look at the impact of immigration on the U.S. economy and on U.S. society with a focus on interest groups at home and abroad involved in the issue.

Apart from the statements made by political party candidates and representatives' positions on U.S. immigration (see chapter 13), a variety of international, national, and local organizations have also made policy recommendations for comprehensive immigration reform in the United States. I present a brief selection of positions on immigration to the United States that reflect the wide span of opinion in the public debate.

According to a study by the Pew Hispanic Center in Washington, D.C., about 7.2 million undocumented workers had entered the United States, making up 4.9 percent of the overall labor force. Among farm workers, up to 24 percent are undocumented, while 14 percent are undocumented in the construction business. The unemployment rate for undocumented workers in the second quarter of 2006 was 5.2 percent (Kochhar 2006). Over half of these are from Mexico. According to data from the U.S. Census Bureau from 2006, more than 28 million people with Mexican roots live and work in the United States, an estimated 11 million of them born in Mexico. Out of the population over sixteen years of age, 69 percent are economically active, and their unemployment rate is 8.3 percent. Almost one quarter of this population offer services, primarily in households, while 21.1 percent work in production sites or transport materials. Another 20.4 percent work in offices or in sales. The construction business employs 17.6 percent, and 14 percent have jobs as professionals or hold some kind of administrative position. Only 2.6 percent work as farmers.

Immigrants demonstrate the entrepreneurial spirit for which the United States is famous. The Kauffmann Foundation's index shows that entrepreneurial activity is nearly 40 percent higher for immigrants than for native-born U.S. citizens (Wadhwa 2007). Moreover, a new study by Carole Keeton Strayhorn (2006) argues that in the long run the impact of immigration on public budgets is positive (Griswold 2007b). Strayhorn's research rejects a very often quoted, study conducted by the National Research Council in 1997 entitled *The New Americans: Economic, Demographic, and Fiscal Effects of Immigration*. The Council calculated that a typical immigrant without a high school education would have a negative net present value of $89,000. However, Keeton Strayhorn's study developed a prognosis about the contribution of immigrants' descendants for public services. It found that immigrants' children would pay around $76,000 more in taxes than they would receive in public benefits. Keeton Strayhorn projected that, in Texas in 2005, the estimated 1.4 million undocumented aliens had a positive impact on the state budget by paying 504 million USD taxes, and to the economy by contributing approximately $17.7 billion.

Immigration worldwide is too often met by xenophobia and racism, especially in nations that suffer economic slowdowns and fear foreign overpopulation. Although America is a nation of immigrants, it was historically characterized by Anglo-Saxon culture and protestant religion and has been susceptible to xenophobia. A common argument against immigration is that foreigners take away jobs and commit crime. These claims are not verifiable. While unemployment can be higher in areas with large immigrant populations if the immigrants are badly educated and are not willing to integrate into society, it is also true that there is no direct linkage to crime. More than 130 of the U.S. nation's top experts on immigration and crime wrote an open letter to federal and state policymakers stating that immigration does not lead to higher crime rates and argued for an immigration policy based on facts rather than myth.

Liberal organizations, such as the Atlas Economic Research Foundation or the Hispanic American Center for Economic Research (HACER), argue in favor of letting the free market regulate the supply and demand of workers. Influential pressure groups such as the Western Governors' Association, the National Conference of State Legislatures, or the Council on Foreign Relations advocate strict law enforcement on the one hand, but on the other hand also argue that the political and economical conditions in Latin America, especially in Mexico and Central America, have to be improved toward good governance and market reforms to create more jobs and diminish the migration flow. Furthermore, migration numbers are lower today than they were at the peak of the Great Migration one hundred years ago (5.1 immigrants per 1,000 U.S. citizens today compared to an average of 10.4 immigrants between 1901 and 1910; Griswold 2007a).

International and religious groups have also reacted in the debate. The Mexican government under President Vicente Fox created a representative office "Instituto de los Mexicanos en el Exterior" for Mexicans abroad to put pressure on Hispanic voters in elections. Religious organizations such as the American Jewish Committee or the U.S. Conference of Catholic Bishops' Committee also advocated a more humane policy on immigration. They defend the rights of migrants and want legislation that offers them opportunities to work in the United States. The farmer lobby associations in particular argue that restrictive immigration laws could lead to delayed harvests, crop losses, and also poorer quality products. One of the most important associations is the American Farm Bureau Federation. It demands a workable program that permits the recruitment of temporary agricultural workers and at the same time eventually opens the path to permanent residency in the United States. U.S. farmers have problems filling open jobs, and the farmers associations would like to see more reform along the lines of the Agricultural Job Opportunities, Benefits, and Security Act of 2006, or the AgJOBS Act, which is vital to agriculture.

This act established a pilot program, the so-called blue card, that moves qualified agricultural workers who worked in the United States for a two-year period until December 31, 2005, to permanent resident status. The current H-2a temporary guest worker program is too expensive for employers due to the fact that they have to provide free housing for the workers. Labor organizations are more critical of immigration and fear a downward pressure on salaries, especially when firms contract workers below the minimum wage.

Finally, the U.S. Chamber of Commerce, which represents more than 3 million enterprises and is thus the world's largest business federation, wants a "reliable, efficient, accurate and workable employment eligibility confirmation system that is easy to use so that businesses can decipher federal immigration laws without expensive lawyers." At the same time it staunchly defends the interests of U.S. workers, particularly that they should not be displaced by foreign workers. The U.S. Chamber of Commerce is thus in favor of strict law enforcement in the fight against employers who hire undocumented workers to exploit them but more immigration flexibility.

DOCUMENTS

Document 1: Council on Foreign Relations, Recommendations: Increase Labor Mobility within North America

When: May 2005

Significance: Under the chairs of John P. Manley, Pedro Aspe, and William F. Weld an independent task force of widely recognized academics and decision-makers from the United States, Canada, and Mexico developed several steps and recommendations on how to deepen the NAFTA process into a real North American integration process. Among their recommendations, such as establishing common security perimeters, expanding border infrastructure, coordinating intelligence services, expanding military cooperation, and developing a North American Border Pass, the Task Force suggested laying the groundwork for the freer flow of people within North America by 2010, along with joint screening of travelers from third-world countries. This recommendation in particular is very reminiscent of the European Union's Schengen model. Furthermore, the authors put forth the analysis that a large gap in wages is behind Mexican migration. They thus advocate the creation of better economic opportunities in Mexico, including sustainable reforms in tax, economic, and energy policies to support economic development by expanding investment and productivity in the energy sector, enhancing governmental transparency, deepening judicial reforms, improving the education system, supporting small and medium-sized producers in their efforts to take advantage of the NAFTA process, and increasing the federal tax base as a percentage of the gross domestic product. At around 15 percent, Mexico has one of lowest tax incomes among the OECD countries. Finally, the document includes the recommendation to increase labor mobility within North America.

DID YOU KNOW?

E-Verify

The U.S. Department of Homeland Security in cooperation with the Social Security Administration operates the Employment Eligibility Verification Program and its database, which permits employers to check whether a newly hired employee is allowed to work in the United States electronically. E-Verify is free and voluntary, and currently more than 30,000 companies are enrolled in this system. According to information from Homeland Security, 3.2 million new hires have been processed as of November 2007, and the system can manage up to 25 million inquiries annually. Furthermore, the system also offers a Photo Screening Tool that permits biometric verification and is intended to prevent identity theft.

This particular document, because it is elaborated by prominent personalities, could seriously influence current decision-makers. At least U.S. President George W. Bush is convinced that labor regulation that expands labor mobility, such as the agreement reached in March 2005 in Waco, Texas between Bush, Canadian Prime Minister Paul Martin, and Mexican President Vicente Fox, would commit all three countries to greater cooperation and joint action in order to build a Security and Prosperity Partnership for North America. This political framework underlined the political will of the three North American nations to emphasize democracy, the market economy, and security in the shadow of terrorist attacks and threats. The Task Force also developed the proposal to strengthen both governmental tri-national relations and the building of an effectively working North American inter-parliamentary group. With that policy recommendation, the North Atlantic Free Trade Agreement is on the way to being transformed eventually into a type of political union, similar to the European Union.

Increase Labor Mobility within North America

People are North America's greatest asset. Goods and services cross borders easily; ensuring the legal transit of North American workers has been more difficult. Experience with the NAFTA visa system suggests that its procedures need to be simplified, and such visas should be made available to a wider range of occupations and to additional categories of individuals such as students, professors, bona fide frequent visitors, and retirees.

To make the most of the impressive pool of skill and talent within North America, the three countries should look beyond the NAFTA visa system. The large volume of undocumented migrants from Mexico within the United States is an urgent matter for those two countries to address. A long-term goal should be to create a "North American preference"—new rules that would make it much easier for employees to move and for employers to recruit across national boundaries within the continent. This would enhance North American competitiveness, increase productivity, contribute to Mexico's development, and address one of the main outstanding issues on the Mexican-U.S. bilateral agenda. Canada and the United States should consider eliminating restrictions on labor mobility altogether and work toward solutions that, in the long run, could enable the extension of full labor mobility to Mexico as well.

WHAT WE SHOULD DO NOW

• **Expand temporary migrant worker programs.**

Canada and the United States should expand programs for temporary labor migration from Mexico. For instance, Canada's successful model for managing seasonal migration in the agricultural sector should be expanded to other sectors where Canadian producers face a shortage of workers and Mexico may have a surplus of workers with appropriate skills. Canadian and U.S. retirees living in Mexico should be granted working permits in certain fields, for instance as English teachers.

• **Implement the Social Security Totalization Agreement negotiated between the United States and Mexico.**

This agreement would recognize payroll contributions to each other's systems, thus preventing double taxation.

WHAT WE SHOULD DO BY 2010

• **Create a "North American preference."**

Canada, the United States, and Mexico should agree on streamlined immigration and labor mobility rules that enable citizens of all three countries to work elsewhere in North America with far fewer restrictions than immigrants from other countries. This new system should be both broader and simpler than the current system of NAFTA visas. Special immigration status should be given to teachers, faculty, and students in the region.

• **Move to full labor mobility between Canada and the United States.**

To make companies based in North America as competitive as possible in the global economy, Canada and the United States should consider eliminating all remaining barriers to the ability of their citizens to live and work in the other country. This free flow of people would offer an important advantage to employers in both countries by giving them rapid access to a larger pool of skilled labor, and would enhance the well-being of individuals in both countries by enabling them to move quickly to where their skills are needed. In the long term, the two countries should work to extend this policy to Mexico as well, though doing so will not be practical until wage differentials between Mexico and its two North American neighbors have diminished considerably.

• Mutual recognition of professional standards and degrees.

Professional associations in each of the three countries make decisions on the standards to accept professionals from other countries. But despite the fact that NAFTA already encourages the mutual recognition of professional degrees, little has actually been done. The three governments should devote more resources to leading and creating incentives that would encourage the professional associations of each of the three countries to develop shared standards that would facilitate short-term professional labor mobility within North America.

Source: Council on Foreign Relations with the Canadian Council of Chief Executives and the Consejo Mexicano de Asuntos Internacionales, eds. "Building a North American Community, Report of an Independent Task Force," No. 53 (New York: Council on Foreign Relations), 26–28.

Document 2: Western Governors Urge Senate to Pass Comprehensive Bill on Illegal Immigration

When: March 27, 2006

Significance: The Western Governor's Association (WGA) promotes a conservative approach toward the immigration issue. It represents nineteen states, serves as a leadership forum, and advances regional interests. The following text is a press statement released by Paul Orbuch about the need to implement a comprehensive migration reform that also fits states' interests. The WGA demands a policy that protects and preserves the safety of the United States and its citizens, but recognizes also that industries need a legal supply of workers from abroad when they are otherwise not available. The WGA, however, is against a blanket amnesty of undocumented persons and advocates levering sanctions against them. Moreover, they also insist that border security and enforcement must be improved through better coordination among the federal agencies with their Mexican counterparts, especially against the flow of illegal migrants and human and drug trafficking organizations. The WGA also proposes an aggressive fight against the root causes of illegal migration, which would require better political and economical conditions in Latin America. Progress should be acknowledged in foreign aid to the governments which are willing and able to improve the standard of living in their countries. Furthermore, the WGA is in favor of sanctions for employers that knowingly hire undocumented workers.

Border Security, employment-based visas, guest worker program and state reimbursement critical pieces

DENVER—Western governors today urged the Senate Judiciary Committee to pass a comprehensive bill on illegal immigration that would improve border security and enforcement, increase employment-based visas, create a temporary guest worker program and ensure states are reimbursed for the enormous amounts they must spend to apprehend and incarcerate illegal immigrants.

Govs. Janet Napolitano (Ariz.), Chair of the Western Governors' Association, and Jon Huntsman, Jr. (Utah), serve as lead governors for immigration issues. In a letter to the Judiciary

Committee's leadership – Sens. Arlen Specter and Patrick Leahy – the governors thanked them for shepherding a comprehensive reform bill through their committee, which met again today.

"As you know, the illegal immigration problem is greatly affecting many of our states. We all share the desire to alleviate the burdens it has placed on our state and local governments, our business and our citizens," the letter stated. "We cannot overstate either the importance of this problem to our States or our desire to see Congress act on this pressing problem."

The letter summarized key provisions supported by Western governors:

Border Security and Enforcement – *We support your efforts to substantially increase the number of border patrol personnel and to enhance border security and surveillance through technological innovations. We ask you to also consider adding language to authorize the completion of a comprehensive database that will interface with state, national and international criminal and terrorist databases, and includes state-of-the-art privacy safeguards. In addition, we believe that the construction of Western regional federal correctional facilities to house criminal aliens who have been apprehended and convicted in state criminal justice systems should be authorized. To the maximum extent possible, families that are detained should be kept together and kept separate from the general population in detention facilities.*

Reimbursement of Costs Incurred by States – *States and localities have incurred enormous costs as a result of the failure to control illegal entries along our international borders. We support your efforts to require the Department of Homeland Security to either assume responsibility for detained individuals or to compensate States for these costs.*

Labor Pool and Visa Issues – *We support your efforts to more than double the number of employment-based visas, and particularly your efforts to increase them for the high-tech and bio-tech industries as well as for seasonal hospitality workers.*

Enactment of a Guest Worker Program is Essential – *A national temporary guest worker program should be established to supplement areas where there are documented shortages of U.S. workers. We heartily support your efforts to include a temporary guest worker program in the bill. We agree that the sanctions that have been under discussion for undocumented individuals already residing in the U.S. such as fines, payment of back taxes, background checks, and demonstrating proficiency in learning English are appropriate and necessary. We would oppose granting blanket amnesty to these individuals.*

The complete WGA policy resolution on U.S. Mexico Border Security and Immigration Reform: www.westgov.org/wga/policy/06/immigration.pdf

(Source: Internet-URL: http://www.westgov.org/wga/press/immigration3-24-06.htm)

Document 3: National Conference of State Legislatures, Policy on Immigration Reform

When: Adopted at the NCSL Executive Meeting on May 6, 2006

Significance: The National Conference of State Legislatures (NCSL) is a bipartisan organization that serves the legislators and staffs of the nation's fifty states. The NCSL understands itself as an advocate for the interests of the states before federal agencies and the Congress. Due to the fact that the states' parliaments have passed many bills to regulate migration, the NCSL promotes a balance between border security, law enforcement, and a temporary worker program for immigrants to legalize their status.

NCSL Policy on Immigration Reform

The National Conference of State Legislatures (NCSL) recognizes the challenges facing our country in matters related to immigration. Federal immigration policy must strike a balance among core principles of our democracy: preserving the safety and security of our nation, encouraging the economic strength of our states and communities, and recognizing our history as a nation of immigrants. The Constitution sets out the parameters of the federal government's jurisdiction over immigration policy. This traditionally has included admissions and terms and conditions for work and residence. However, the impact of the federal government's immigration policy decisions are directly felt by the states. States and localities implement programs required by federal law, provide services mandated by the courts, and initiate programs and policies to address the specialized needs of immigrants and encourage their integration into the economic, social and civic life of their adopted communities. States often bear the costs of immigration, especially in our education, health and law enforcement systems, with limited federal reimbursement.

State legislators call on Congress and the Administration to pursue comprehensive immigration reform that enhances our border security and addresses the inequities in the current system. Immigration reform and implementation requires true collaboration between state and federal leaders. Our nation's immigration laws must not contain unfunded mandates nor preempt areas of existing state authority. Federal immigration reform will not be comprehensive unless it addresses the impact of immigration on the states.

Border Security & Enforcement

Securing all of America's borders, ports, and airports is essential to preserving our national security and maintaining the safety of all Americans. NCSL urges the federal government to fulfill its responsibilities with regard to border security and encourages a renewed state-federal cooperation in countering human trafficking and drug smuggling.

NCSL supports full, appropriate and necessary federal funding for increases in Department of Homeland Security border enforcement personnel and for improvements in technology and infrastructure. Investments in technology and infrastructure can effectively leverage manpower and maximize the capacity of federal border enforcement agents in securing the borders. Related to efforts against human trafficking and drug smuggling, states have been leaders in addressing these concerns. We encourage the federal government to increase its enforcement of these crimes. The federal government should plan and fully fund the required services and facilities related to these crimes.

State lawmakers are also concerned about interior enforcement. Employment verification is a critical component of enforcement requiring federal reforms. NCSL reaffirms that states have the right to provide incentives and sanctions to encourage compliance. State governments are also employers, and we oppose efforts to treat state governments differently from the private sector in meeting federal employment verification requirements.

The Role of State and Local Law Enforcement

NCSL has long-standing policy ("Immigration Law Enforcement") related to the role of state and local law enforcement in immigration law. State legislators believe that enforcement of federal immigration laws is a federal responsibility. State involvement in enforcement of our nation's immigration law should be at state option under the current Memorandum of Understanding (MOU) process provided for in the Illegal Immigration Reform and Immigrant Responsibility Act of 1996 (IIRIRA).

NCSL holds firmly that states do not have "inherent authority" to enforce federal civil immigration law. We also oppose efforts to perpetuate this myth of "inherent authority" indirectly by shifting federal responsibility of immigration enforcement to state and local law officers through the criminalization of *any* violation of federal immigration law. State and local government law enforcement and public safety personnel are already asked, without the benefit of adequate federal assistance, to incarcerate, detain and transport illegal immigrants who have committed crimes. Making unlawful presence a crime would force state and local law enforcement agencies to educate themselves in the vast complexities of civil immigration law and regulation without the benefit of federal training and expertise, and with little, if any, likelihood of adequate federal funding. NCSL is strongly opposed to any efforts to shift enforcement of civil immigration laws to state and local law enforcement agencies.

State lawmakers do support the existing MOU process that gives states and localities the option to enter into a voluntary formal agreement with the U.S. Department of Justice and the U.S. Department of Homeland Security. When training under the MOU process is fully funded by the federal government, this is a viable way to give communities the choice of whether local enforcement of federal immigration laws is appropriate for them. NCSL supports efforts to provide adequate federal funding for training of law enforcement personnel in states who choose to enter MOUs.

NCSL strongly supports full reimbursement to states for the State Criminal Alien Assistance Program (SCAAP). The current SCAAP program only provides 25% reimbursement of current costs, according to a recent General Accountability Office study. NCSL also opposes any effort to coerce state participation in enforcement of federal immigration law by withholding SCAAP program funds.

Unfunded Mandates and Cost-Shifts to States

CBO has estimated significant costs to the states in education and health care systems. The 1996 federal welfare law established a five-year bar on SCHIP/Medicaid, food stamps, TANF and SSI for legal immigrants. Yet, state governments are still the providers of last resort, particularly in protecting public health and public safety and providing emergency health care. State governments also fund and provide critical English-language instruction and public education to newcomers that is essential for promoting public safety, reducing community tensions and integrating newcomers into our communities, including those who might be here on a temporary basis. Most immigration reform proposals in Congress would impose significant cost-shifts to state and local government. NCSL urges Congress to include in immigration reform a funding stream to address the entire fiscal impacts on state governments of any guest worker program, earned legalization and/or increases in the number of immigrants. Such funding should be subject to appropriation by state legislatures so that it can be best targeted to the state's individual needs including government, faith-based or non-profit institutions, most in need of the support.

Temporary Worker Program

NCSL supports the creation of a temporary worker program. It is our view that a temporary worker program goes hand-in-hand with achieving true border security. Providing a legal channel for those that want to come to our country for work will reduce illegal border crossings and enable our federal law enforcement agents to focus their efforts on individuals attempting to enter or already in the country for the purpose of doing our nation harm. A temporary worker program will also strengthen many sectors of our economy by providing a legal workforce.

With the creation of a temporary worker program, concerns arise about the provision of health and education services to the temporary workers. The idea of requiring sending countries to subsidize some of these costs should be further investigated. We encourage Congress to consider such ideas on a demonstration project level. We look forward to working with Congress and with the U.S. Department of Homeland Security to determine the best way to prevent cost-shifts to state government for these costs.

Earned Legalization

NCSL affirms the right and responsibility of the federal government to determine federal immigration policy, including the existence and form of any earned legalization program. NCSL reiterates our existing policy supporting the promotion of citizenship as a national priority. Efforts should be made and sufficient resources should be allocated to facilitate the naturalization process in a timely manner. NCSL supports the creation of an earned legalization program for illegal immigrants currently in the country. Illegal immigrants are living and working in our communities. They are our neighbors and as both workers and entrepreneurs they contribute to the economic vitality of our nation. Our schools are making investments in children from "mixed-status" households where the parents are illegal immigrants, yet the children are citizens. A mass deportation or crackdown on illegal immigrants currently in the country would have detrimental impacts on our communities.

An earned legalization program should not offer amnesty. Rather, it should offer a punishment that is proportional to the offense. Those immigrants who accept punishment and indicate their willingness to become full members of our society should have the opportunity to do so. Encouraging immigrants to come out of the shadows will lead to safer and more secure communities, by allowing law enforcement officials to focus their efforts on those who wish to do the community harm.

(Source: Internet-URL: http://www.ncsl.org/programs/press/2006/immpolicy.htm)

Document 4: Atlas Economic Research Foundation, Immigration, the Latino Community, and the Bush Agenda

When: 2007

Significance: The Atlas Economic Research Foundation is an influential and classical liberal, nongovernmental organization that promotes a free society, respect for private property rights, the market order, and limited government under the rule of law. Here the group argues that Hispanics should be able to easily become part of American society. This stance is based on the Foundation's conservative values and positive attitude toward a free enterprise system.

Immigration, the Latino Community, and the Bush Agenda

By Alejandro A. Chafuen
Presented to the Institute for Political Science of the Catholic University of Portugal
"Our future connection with Spain renders that, the most necessary of the modern languages ... Spanish. Bestow great attention on this and endeavor to acquire an accurate knowledge of it. Our future connections with Spain and Spanish America will render that language a valuable acquisition." Thomas Jefferson

Americans of Hispanic or Latino decent are the fastest growing component of the U.S. economy. With estimates ranging between 40 and 45 million U.S. residents, the Hispanic-American economic sector produces more than Brazil, the largest economy in South America. Those who have worked across the U.S. and the Americas have witnessed the great diversity that exists between Hispanics, and also recognize the community's enormous potential to contribute and become part of the American dream. Hispanic roots in the United States are very deep and continue to expand as Hispanic Americans are becoming an increasingly influential political and economic force. Their progress will ultimately depend on the incentives they will face or help create through their involvement in civil society. (...)

Macroeconomic policies

Are low interest rates having a special positive effect on the Hispanic immigrant population? A large part of growth in the employment of Hispanic immigrants has taken place in the construction industry. In analyzing interest rates, rather than speaking of Bush's policies, one should speak of Greenspan's policies, yet there is merit in maintaining good policies. Interest rates are determined by several components, time preference (pure interest), risk factors, and inflationary premiums and expectations. So far, the large deficits during 2001-2005 have not caused a sharp spike in rates, but the more they continue the more they will affect interest rates.

In the short run, deficit spending might be generating higher rates of growth while keep-ing the interest rates low, maintaining the economy on the expansionary side of the cycle. This impacts the entire economy, and continues to make the United States an attractive destination for immigrants.

There is some worry that the policy of the Fed to avoid falling into a depression after Sep-tember 11, 2001, may have created a real-estate bubble, especially in major cities around the USA. At under 6%, Hispanic Americans, even recent immigrants in the United States, have an unemployment rate which is lower than any other Central or South American country. That would be the envy of Europeans including Spain, the Hispanic motherland.

So far, given the dismal track record of paper money, the country has faced low price inflation. Hispanic Americans have low savings, and many keep their savings in cash. Many would suffer more from an increase of inflation which affects the poor in a disproportionate way. When one compares the collection plate at Sunday Spanish and English religious serv-ices, one can't help but be struck by seeing the large amount of dollar bills overflowing from the collection plates at Spanish Masses.

Hispanics should have the same fear as the rest of the population. The large expansion of government spending during President Bush's term will eventually have to be paid. One way of paying for government spending is with increased debt. This will likely lead to higher interest rates, with the potential of halting the expansion of the construction sector, which is a major employer of recent Latino immigrants. Rather, if the Federal Reserve chooses to inflate, immigrants will also suffer from seeing their cash savings eroded.

The impact of a slowing economy on Hispanic Americans working in construction busi-nesses might encourage them to seek new areas of the country in which to offer their serv-ices. The largest growth in their population already has been taking place in Georgia and the Carolinas. Unlike their competitors who tend to be unionized and have inflexible attitudes, immigrant workers are willing to take almost any job. Yet, during the next economic down turn, we might see an increase in societal conflict, and some will use immigrants as scape-goats. Others will try to use the opportunity to mobilize them and encourage them to accuse the free-enterprise system and American institutions for their plight.

Facilitating trade with Hispanic America positively affects Hispanic Americans living in the United States, especially those who are more entrepreneurial and can take advantage of easier regulations and lower costs to engage in trade of goods and services with people from their country of origin. Free trade agreements, even when they fall far short from ideal liberal trade pacts, help bring people together.

In addition, it is likely that Hispanic Americans working in areas which receive greater benefits by free trade agreements will increase the amount of Latino immigrants they hire in comparison with other groups.

I see the Bush administration paying stronger attention than Democrats to furthering free trade in the Americas. Nevertheless many in his party are putting-up stumbling blocks. The debate, however, is too nuanced to have an effect on Hispanic American attitudes, or their gratitude to our country.

Free trade agreements will increase the well-being at home and therefore the income dif-ferences will tend to disappear.

What I learned about Hispanic Americans encourages me to redouble the efforts to work for creating a better framework for an ownership society: Promoting education, health and social security reform which gives a bigger say to individuals, parents and the private sector; enhancing, or at least not putting barriers to economic and social solutions arising from the private sector (from remittances to faith-based solutions); and promote a vibrant economy based on private property, free trade, within a framework of sound money and low taxation. Economic and social policy as the above increase their chances of learning the American way of freedom, responsibility and working for the common good.

Immigrants, like capital, are attracted by a variety of factors, but the rule of law is the most valuable treasure the United States of America has to offer. Protecting the rule of law from the all-invading "rule of regulations" is particularly important for those who need just and affordable rules of entry into a market. Immigrants are such those people. The over-regulated economy of Europe is driving the large majority of immigrants, even those who are legal, to informality.

Two-thirds of the "problem" is a Mexican-American issue. We should therefore redouble our efforts to promote solutions south of the border. Mexico might soon have a left leaning populist as its leader amidst a neighboring Central America full of Cuban agents fueled by Venezuelan oil money. Encouraging policies that strengthen Mexico's political and economic scene is essential to prevent an even worse explosion of illegal immigration.

Independently of what happens to future immigration policy, Hispanic Americans will play an increasingly important role in the future of the United States. But integration with our culture will be more difficult. Unlike what happened in other periods of heavy immigration, those who come to the United States today are tied to their native communities financially and culturally. This is especially the case with Mexicans and Central Americans. Thanks to globalization and increased productivity, immigrants today can afford to call their native countries for less than 10 cents a minute, choose among several TV channels in Spanish, have access to multiple radio stations and attend Spanish religious services at the church of their choice.

Almost all for-profit companies have special marketing departments and strategies to reach Hispanic Americans with products with a message they understand. Anyone trying to reach them will have to do the same. Some Republican and conservative leaders will still be able to get elected with messages that neglect or confront Hispanic Americans, but in general, Democrats and Republicans will pay increasing attention and develop special lines of communication.

At least during the next decade Republicans will have a tough time competing with Democrats in trying to lure Hispanic Americans with paternalistic "affirmative action" policies, and Democrats will also find it difficult to compete with the Republicans in offering a conservative values agenda. Leaders of both parties will try, but they will risk alienating their base. The more Hispanic Americans continue to prosper, the less appealing paternalistic policies will be for them, and the more their values will mimic those of non-Hispanic whites. When that moment comes, it will make less sense in studying or crafting policies to reach the Latino community.

Polls show that Hispanic Americans favor an ownership society agenda in the area of education, social security, and health care. This agenda will be helpful for legal Hispanic Americans, but might not be such a good idea for informals. As Hernando de Soto, the world-renowned ownership society champion has shown, ownership also enables identification. Participation in private, but legal, educational, health care, or pension schemes would put in danger those who are "illegally" or informally in the United States. But as most Hispanic Americans are legal residents, the Bush administration "ownership society" proposals or even their promotion should have a positive effect on their attitudes toward becoming part of an American dream built on conservative values and the free enterprise system.

Source: Alejandro Chafuen, CEO and President of the Atlas Economic Research Foundation.

Document 5: American Jewish Committee, Perspectives on U.S. Immigration Policy

When: March 2007

Significance: The American Jewish Committee (AJC), established in 1906, is the nation's oldest human relations group, dedicated to the promotion of pluralistic and democratic societies. Steeped in the Jewish tradition of "welcoming the stranger," AJC has been a strong voice on immigration and refugee issues since its founding, advocating for a fair, generous, and effective immigration policy.

Perspectives on U.S. Immigration Policy

More than a million activists took to America's streets in May 2006 to highlight the contributions of immigrants throughout the country. The snapshot of faces spanned all corners of American society—blue collar workers struggling below minimum wage, religious leaders reciting biblical teachings, parents, children, students, teachers, and average American citizens supporting their friends and neighbors. The diverse group was bound together by a desire to fix the nation's broken immigration system that has created an illegal underclass of society, exposed vulnerabilities in U.S. security, and profoundly impacted the lives of millions. The faith-based community, including the American Jewish Committee, has long been at the forefront of the national discourse on immigration, speaking on behalf of congregants, immigrants and social service providers alike. Faith-based organizations have joined civil rights groups, organized business and labor, and many others to support a comprehensive approach to immigration reform.

The problem of illegal immigration is not new—more than two decades ago, Congress passed The Immigration Reform and Control Act of 1986; comprehensive legislation aimed at stemming the flow of undocumented immigrants by pairing enhanced enforcement with legalization programs for those already in the country. Unfortunately, the IRCA failed to address the future flow of immigrants to the U.S. and had far-reaching negative implications for the estimated 3.1 million immigrants in the country—families were divided and hundreds of thousands were left in limbo.

The nearly 2 million immigrants who did not qualify for the legalization program developed into an undocumented underclass that persists today. Over the last two decades, this community has swelled to colossal levels, peaking at 10 to 12 million immigrants living illegally throughout the United States today.

The issue moved to center stage during the 109th Congress and the 2006 election cycle, as immigrants became a favorite political pawn of conservative restrictionists. Headlines splashed across the pages of newspapers around the country, warning America of the danger posed by illegal immigrants. The vigilante "Minutemen" inflamed tensions when armed civilians began patrolling the Southern border in an effort to stop unauthorized entry into the United States.

The Minutemen share one common belief with the activists who took to the streets in May: America's immigration system is broken. Tattered from years of abuse and mired by horrendous backlogs and outdated technology, the process designed as a gateway to a better life in America has proven to be just the opposite—a barrier to progress and a threat to our national security.

From the United States Congress to many town councils, political bodies have engaged in the national debate and drafted countless resolutions aimed at finding a solution to the ever-growing problem. Some have showed promise while others have seemed punitive, onerous, and even spiteful.

As a nation of laws, America must bolster enforcement in an effort to enhance our homeland security. However, these efforts alone will not stem the tide of illegal immigration. The demand for low-wage immigrant workers far outweighs the supply—according to a Pew Hispanic Center study, the current U.S. economy requires about 500,000 new full-time workers each year, and the current system provides 5,000 worker visas for these positions. Until these numbers are brought into equilibrium, the promise of work will continue to draw immigrants to cross the U.S. border illegally.

A piecemeal approach to the immigration problem will not be successful. Spending on enforcement increased from $1 billion in 1985 to $4.9 billion in 2002, and yet we now have an estimated 11 million immigrants in this country illegally, with as many as 300,000 more joining our population each year.

Instead, any reform must be comprehensive, addressing our economic needs, human rights values, and homeland security interests. Four basic principles should guide future legislative efforts.

America's immigration system should incorporate:

1. Fair and effective enforcement policies consistent with core American values.

   Enhanced border security and effective enforcement measures should help prevent further illegal immigration while allowing law enforcement to focus on identifying and preventing entry of those who seek to do us harm.

2. A path to legal status for hard-working immigrants in the United States.

   Millions of immigrants currently in the United States must be given the opportunity to become lawful permanent residents by meeting a rigorous set of criteria. Mass deportations or detentions will not provide an incentive for individuals to come out of the shadows.

3. Reforms to America's family-based immigration system.

   Under the current system, women find themselves unable to support their families as they wait for their husbands' paperwork to be processed. Parents and children are often separated for extended periods of time due to the enormous backlog in immigration applications. These waiting-times must be reduced and families attempting to reunite through legal avenues should be assured that the system is workable and efficient.

4. The creation of legal avenues for workers to enter the United States.

   The U.S. economy demands immigrant labor, and many workers are eager to pursue a better life in America. Yet immigrant workers are often subjected to inhumane work conditions, wages far below the legal minimum, and no opportunities for advancement or mobility. Employers are able to pay migrant workers rates far below the legal minimum, thereby subjecting U.S. workers to impossible competition. Proposals to develop a visa system that fluctuates with the economy would allow for the creativity and flexibility necessary to protect U.S. and immigrant workers alike while providing a viable solution for employers.

Some 800 immigrants from 88 countries of origin recited the Pledge of Allegiance during their citizenship ceremony in Columbus, Ohio, in April 2005. Despite such massive ceremonies, many immigrants continue to experience lengthy processing delays in their quest for citizenship. AP Photo/Kiichiro Sato.

The 110th Congress faces a steep challenge: To conceive and execute a thoughtful package of legislative reforms that will address America's social and political realities. America must find a sensible way to honor and continue a proud tradition of a liberal immigration system while addressing future economic and social needs.

Source: Brooke Menschel, Assistant Legislative Director of the American Jewish Committee. The document was prepared for the conference "Perspectives and Proposals on Migration" in San Diego, organized by the Washington, D.C. and Mexico City offices of the Friedrich Naumann Stiftung für die Freiheit.

Document 6: Friedrich Naumann Stiftung für die Freiheit, Six Proposals for Regulating Migration in North America

When: April 2007

Significance: This document was presented at the 175th Executive Committee Meeting of the *Liberal International* in Cancun with its convention theme "Migration, analyzing the challenges it poses for the 21st century," alongside Red Liberal de America Latina and the Mexican party Nueva Alianza. The document has had an impact on policy formation of liberal, free democratic and libertarian parties around the world.

Concluding Policy-Recommendations

First: Improving the dialogue among policy makers from the USA, Mexico and Central America.

The fact that the negotiations for a comprehensive migration reform have been failed so far is a result of both the lack of communication and misinterpretation. According to Latin American political tradition, the President is the main decision maker in foreign policy. However, neglecting the U.S. Congress is the main failure of Latin American policy makers, because the Senate and the House of Representatives are the key players in the legislation of a migration reform.

Furthermore, until today Latin American politicians have not understood that there is no natural right of immigration toward the United States. The security issue and the fear for terrorist infiltration through the border is a serious concern within the U.S. In the protection of national security, human rights issues are sometimes pushed into the background. This leads to the question what Mexico and Central America contribute to enhance security measures in North America against global terrorism, human and drug trafficking?

Second: Latin America needs to speak with one voice.

There can be no doubt that Washington D.C. is the world's political center. Thousands of (non-)governmental institutions and organizations, think tanks, embassies and enterprises have representation there. It is obvious that connecting constituents with lawmakers is the necessary tool for successful public policy promotion. The Latin American institutions and embassies should speak together for their interests with one loud voice. In order to be heard by US lawmakers. They should act like lobbyists do.

Third: Respecting the human rights of the migrants.

The violation of human rights of migrants by gangs, international organized crime groups like the Mara Salvatrucha, police, border patrol or private vigilant groups like the Minutemen in Arizona is a very serious problem. In order to improve the guarantee of the migrants' rights, National Human Rights Commission and NGOs should work together and sue everyone who violates these rights. But, in general, national governments in Latin America have to improve the human rights conditions and the treatment of aliens. A high number of violations are happening at the Guatemalan-Mexican border or in the Northern Mexican border cities like the femicides in Ciudad Juarez for example. It is not convincing to blame always

U.S. authorities for human rights' violation when the same government has not the political will or the force to guarantee security in its own country.

Fourth: Contributing to regional security.

Mexico and Central America have high crime rates. It is obvious that especially crime like drug and human trafficking spreads out to North America. Among the undocumented immigrants are not only Hispanics; according to the statistics of the Border Patrol foreigners from Asia, Middle East or Africa have tried to cross the border illegally. The U.S. public fears that passing Mexico is a possible way for international terrorists to enter the U.S. Therefore, Mexico and the Central American States need to enhance their own immigration system and border security. They should offer participation in international peace operations against global terrorism in order to proof credibility. Furthermore, they need to extend the cooperation with U.S. security agencies. Wrong pride or national egoism under the shield of national sovereignty won't improve the regional security.

Fifth: Enhancing regional development and social cohesion.

Remittances will play a more decisive role in developing regions than they currently do. But an intelligent macroeconomic policy framework and comprehensive economic reforms may support more innovative intergovernmental cooperation. The reduction of economic dependence supports political independence, sovereignty and credibility. The development of a coherent strategy in the use of remittances for investment in infrastructure and education could decrease migration pressure. Additionally, political and economic concepts of social and regional cohesion could be applied in less developed regions. The integrative transformation of the Plan Puebla-Panama into a real development concept like a Plan Phoenix-Puebla-Panama might be a step forward toward a Free Customs Zone from Alaska to Panama. The United States could enlarge its commerce zones seriously when the legislature permits a real liberal market that includes new forms of mobility, but at least a variety of opportunities: from temporary worker migrants, nationalization to legalization initiatives. Eventually, the US could re-win confidence in Latin America that the government has lost due to an ignorant hegemonic behavior and the negligence of social conditions.

Sixth: Implementing concepts for the political and economic transformation in Mexico and Central America.

It is necessary to start with a real fight on the reasons of migration. None prefers to leave his hometown, family and friends when working conditions would not be so miserably. The lack of true liberal market reforms, that create competition and job opportunities, the arrogance of elites and family clans for the poor, the missing understanding of the creation of a middle class, the missing valuing for democracy, anti-corruption and rule of laws are obstacles for this process in Latin America. The United States are so attractive to migrants because of liberty and job opportunities that facilitate the economic and social ascent. Consequently, the U.S. should convince Latin American politicians and publicity in a positive way that democracy, capitalism, competition and a free (social) market is the best answer to misery and oppression. The U.S. lost its good image in the past because of unilateral decisions in foreign politics. Anti-democratic elites, most of them left populist, are blaming the U.S. for failure in neo-mercantilists experiences as a scapegoat. However, their concepts remind on the dictatorship of communist utopias of the 20th century. Again, the U.S. needs to work on credibility and confidence-building in Latin America as a responsible actor with soft power.

Source: Cieslik, Thomas (compiler). "Beyond the Wall: Perspectives and Proposals on Migration," Working Paper (Mexico City: Friedrich Naumann Stiftung für die Freiheit), 29–31.

Document 7: American Immigration Law Foundation, Open Letter on Immigrants and Crime

When: July 2, 2007

Significance: The Immigration Policy Center (IPC) sent an open letter on immigration and crime to the decision makers in the executive and legislative arms of the United States. The IPC is the research unit of the American Immigration Law Foundation in Washington, D.C. The letter was signed by 136 experts and academics in immigration issues. They state that violent crime in the United States is not principally committed by undocumented aliens.

Open Letter on Immigrants and Crime

Dear Mr. President, Members of Congress, and Governors:

Immigration has enriched the economy and culture of the United States since the founding of the nation. Yet immigrants long have been scapegoats for many social problems that afflict the nation. As a result, myths and stereotypes about immigrants, rather than established facts, far too often serve as the basis for public perceptions that drive misguided immigration policies.

One of the most pervasive misperceptions about immigrants is that they are more likely to commit predatory crimes than are the native-born. Popular movies, television series, and a sensationalizing news media propagate the enduring image of immigrant communities permeated by crime and violence. But this widespread belief is simply wrong.

Numerous studies by independent researchers and government commissions over the past 100 years repeatedly and consistently have found that, in fact, immigrants are less likely to commit crimes or to be behind bars than are the native-born. This is true for the nation as a whole, as well as for cities with large immigrant populations such as Los Angeles, New York, Chicago, and Miami, and cities along the U.S.-Mexico border such as San Diego and El Paso.

That immigration does not automatically lead to higher crime rates is evident in the fact that crime rates have fallen in the United States at the same time immigration has increased. Since the early 1990s, immigration to the United States—both legal and undocumented—has reached historic highs. Yet rates of violent crime and property crime have declined sharply over the same period, and the violent crime rate has reached historic lows. Moreover, among men age 18–39 (who comprise the vast majority of the prison population), the incarceration rate of the native-born is much higher than the incarceration rate of the foreign-born.

Immigrants in every ethnic group in the United States have lower rates of crime and imprisonment than do the native born. This is true for all immigrant groups—including the Mexicans, Salvadorans, and Guatemalans who comprise most of the undocumented immigrants in the country. Even though immigrants from these countries are far more likely than natives to have less than a high-school education and to live in poverty, they are far less likely to be behind bars or to commit crimes. Moreover, teenage immigrants are much less likely than native-born adolescents to engage in risk behaviors such as delinquency, violence, and substance abuse that often lead to imprisonment.

The problem of violent crime in the United States is not caused by immigrants, regardless of their legal status. To be sure, the large-scale undocumented immigration of the past 10 years has caused significant fiscal and administrative problems for state and local governments, and has placed unexpected burdens on overcrowded schools in areas where immigrants are concentrated. But it has not raised rates for violent crimes or crimes against property, and immigrants should not be subject to selective laws and practices based on false claims to the contrary. Immigration is a national issue that requires uniform federal policies based on accurate assessments of U.S. economic and demographic needs.

There are real dangers inherent in the myth that immigrants are more prone to criminality than are the native-born. This inaccurate assumption has flourished in a post-9/11 climate of fear in which terrorism and undocumented immigration often are mentioned in the same breath. It was a key rationalization for provisions in the 2001 USA PATRIOT Act that authorized the arrest, imprisonment, and deportation of non-citizens without judicial review—practices that harken back to the Alien and Sedition Acts of 1798.

Immigrants and natives alike deserve a reasoned public debate on immigration that addresses the many complexities of the issue. We, as sociologists, criminologists, legal scholars and other social scientists, both academics and practitioners in the criminal justice system, including prosecutors, police officers, and criminal attorneys, strongly urge state and national policymakers who are drafting laws that affect immigrants to base these laws on demonstrated facts rather than on false assumptions.

(Source: Internet-URL: http://www.ailf.org/ipc/ipc_openletter0507.shtml, access: July 3, 2007 (currently no longer available).)

FURTHER READINGS

Internet Sources

U.S. Department of Commerce: http://www.commerce.gov/

U.S. Department of Labor: http://www.dol.gov/
>Has a special section about the Immigration and Nationality Act (INA) with an extensive part about the different visa programs: http://www.dol.gov/compliance/laws/comp-ina.htm

U.S. Census Bureau: http://www.census.gov/

U.S. Chamber of Commerce on immigration issues: http://www.uschamber.com/issues/index/immigration/default

The American Federation of Labor and Congress of Industrial Organizations (AFL-CIO) is a voluntary federation of fifty-five national and international labor unions: http://www.aflcio.org/issues/civilrights/immigration/

The statements of the American Jewish Committee on immigration: http://www.ajc.org/site/c.ijITI2PHKoG/b.838517/k.37FD/Immigration.htm

The American Farm Bureau Federation: http://www.fb.org/

Arguments for immigration: http://www.fb.org/issues/docs/immigration07.pdf

Atlas Economic Research Foundation: http://www.atlasusa.org

The California Immigrant Policy Center addresses the public debate with information on the economic impact of immigration to its state: http://caimmigrant.org/index.php

U.S. Conference of Catholic Bishops' Committee on migration and refugees: http://www.usccb.org/mrs

Cato Institute Center for Trade Policy Studies with a list of essays on immigration: http://www.freetrade.org/issues/immigration.html

Numerous articles and analysis about immigrants and economy from the Century Foundation: http://www.immigrationline.org/feature.asp

The Farm Labor Organization Committee: http://www.floc.com

The Hispanic American Center for Economic Research (HACER): http://www.hacer.org/

The online-edition of the *Wall Street Journal* has an "econoblog," in which the two academics Gordon Hanson and Philip Martin discuss the pro and contra of immigration: http://online.wsj.com/public/article/SB115100948305787940-tA5PP0Ya_9U0AlXBQQhnaDyMIYc_20060725.html?mod=tff_main_tff_top

Books and Articles

Anderson, Stuart. "The Debate over Immigration's Impact on U.S. Workers and the Economy." Arlington, Va.: National Foundation for American Policy, 2006. http://www.nfap.com/researchactivities/studies/EDO0706.pdf.

Fitzgerald, David. "State and Emigration: A Century of Emigration Policy in Mexico," Working Paper 123 (September 2005). University of California, San Diego: Center for Comparative Immigration Studies. http://www.ccis-ucsd.org/Publications/wrkg123.pdf.

Griswold, Daniel. "Comprehensive Immigration Reform: Finally Getting It Right." *Free Trade Bulletin*, Center for Trade Policy Studies, 29 (May 16, 2007), 2007a. http://www.freetrade.org/pubs/FTBs/FTB-029.pdf.

Griswold, Daniel. "The Fiscal Impact of Immigration Reform: The Real Story." *Free Trade Bulletin*, Center for Trade Policy Studies, 30 (May 21, 2007), 2007b. http://www.freetrade.org/pubs/FTBs/FTB-030.pdf.

Keeton Strayhorn, Carole. "Undocumented Immigrants in Texas: A Financial Analysis of the Impact to the State Budget and Economy." Office of the Texas Comptroller, Special Report (December 2006). http://caimmigrant.org/repository/wp-content/uploads/2007/01/undocumented.pdf.

Kochhar, Rakesh. "Latino Labor Report 2006: Strong Gains in Employment." Washington, D.C.: Pew Hispanic Center (September 27, 2006). http://pewhispanic.org/reports/report.php?ReportID=70.

Smith, James P., and Barry Edmonston, eds. *The New Americans: Economic, Demographic, and Fiscal Effects of Immigration.* Washington, D.C.: National Academies Press, 1997.

Wadhwa, Vivek et. al. "America's New Immigrant Entrepreneurs," Master of Engineering Management Program, Duke University; School of Information, U.C. Berkeley, first part (January 4, 2007): http://www.kauffman.org/pdf/entrep_immigrants_1_61207.pdf, second part (June 11) Education, Entrepreneurship and Immigration: http://www.kauffman.org/pdf/entrep_immigrants_2_61207.pdf.

CHAPTER 13

Immigration and Electoral Campaign Politics

Thomas Cieslik

By the summer of 2007, efforts to reach a comprehensive immigration reform law had failed. The setback was of concern to many within the American electorate, as Americans wanted a solution to the situation of 12 million illegal immigrants living in the United States. Despite efforts to tighten security at the U.S.-Mexican border, it seemed that the flow of immigrants continued unabated. The immigration issue became a key concern in the 2008 U.S. presidential election campaign.

At both the state and the federal level, public officials—most notably the White House and Congress—had difficulty coming together on immigration, reflecting tensions in balancing security concerns against the country's historical tendency to welcome immigrants. On the one hand, America welcomed European immigrants over much of its history, as well as in the twentieth century, other immigrants from around the world. On the other hand, current security concerns following the events of September 11, 2001, have influenced Americans to prioritize their own personal safety.

The immigration debate, particularly as it impacted Hispanics, seeped into the electoral campaign in different ways. First, both Democratic and Republican candidates were involved in debates in Spanish and broadcasted political advertisements in Spanish, thus recognizing the importance of Hispanics, now, at 46 percent, the largest ethnic group in the United States, approximately 14 percent of the population. Because many Hispanics are ineligible to vote due to age or status, the voting Hispanics account for just 9 percent of the electorate.

At first, Hispanic voters leaned heavily toward one candidate in particular. In December 2007 a Pew Hispanic Center poll showed that support among Hispanic Democrats for Hillary Clinton was 59 percent, with 15 percent for Barack Obama. The Pew Foundation also found that 57 percent of Hispanics identified themselves as Democrats and 23 percent as Republicans and that Hispanics felt that Democrats would show more concern for issues such as immigration than Republicans. Taylor and Fry, authors of the Pew survey, felt that Hispanics would be a swing vote in the presidential race because of their sizeable presence in four of the six states that President Bush carried by only a small margin in 2004: New Mexico

Transportation Safety Administration (TSA) agents screen passengers and baggage at the busy main terminal of the Denver International Airport. Fraudulent travel documents account for many of the arrests made by the TSA, which is a branch of the Department of Homeland Security. AP Photo/Jack Dempsey.

(37 percent Hispanic voters), Florida (14 percent), Nevada (12 percent Hispanic), and Colorado (12 percent Hispanic).

Impre-Media, the largest Hispanic news agency in the United States, conducted a poll in the states with the largest Hispanic populations: California, New York, Florida, Illinois, and Texas. The survey found that Clinton had the support of 55 percent of Hispanics to Obama's 6 percent. It is interesting that New Mexico Governor Bill Richardson, who is part Mexican, hardly registered in the Impre-Media poll.

In the 2008 Iowa caucuses, immigration was the top issue discussed by voters, at 33 percent, according to a poll by the Cable News Network (CNN), surpassing the economy, at 26 percent; the war on terror, at 21 percent; and the Iraq War, at 17 percent. This result surprised observers, because Iowa does not have a large Latino population and is not a border state. The number of immigrants here has increased dramatically, from 23,000 in 1990 to 113,000 in 2007 according to the conservative-learning *Washington Times* (*Washington Times*, Jan. 8, 2008).

The most predictably anti-immigrant candidate among the Republicans was Rep. Tom Tancredo (R-Colo.), who had made the issue his major work in Congress. He proposed a fence and the denial to an illegal immigrant of any chance to apply for legal residency and citizenship. Former Arkansas Governor Mike Huckabee said that he supported the Minute-man project to protect the border. Sen. John McCain (R-Ariz.), a previous proponent of immigration reform, had to position himself to look tough on immigration, as did former New York City Mayor Rudolph Giuliani, who was accused of being soft on illegal immigrants in multiethnic and multicultural New York City. Rival Fred Thompson, former senator from Tennessee, called New York a "sanctuary city" and—like Giuliani—talked up security and border issues, trying to make himself look serious about immigration. In all, the candidates did their best in the primaries to outdo their opponents with the toughest language on immigration, while at the same time doing their best to find elements of "softness" in their opponents' positions (Associated Press, October 24, 2007).

Immigration positions of the candidates hardened to such an extent that as one journalist noted, "Looking at the Republicans at this point, it is often hard to find much difference among most of the leading contenders. They sound just as tough as the candidate who has been the angriest on immigration, Representative Tom Tancredo" (Luo 2007).

On the Democratic side, there was no great eagerness to address the issue. Neither Barack Obama nor Hillary Clinton wanted to propose ambitious approaches to encourage a path to legalization of undocumented workers. Democrats did support security measures along the U.S.-Mexican border, fearing a perceived weakness on border security would cost them victory. The only strong contrarian voice among Democrats was Gov. Bill Richardson of New Mexico, who, as the first serious Hispanic candidate for the Democrats and a "border governor" of vast experience, understood better than his colleagues the complexity of the issue. As Richard Benedetto observed, immigration has been a tricky electoral issue for both parties: "It's a tricky issue for both Republicans and Democrats because it's an emotional issue that can be sloganeered very easily. The public has a general feel for that issue on a gut level" (Sammon 2007).

In short, the public and politicians are divided on the immigration issue, and the candidates' positions reflect the deeply divided views on immigration among Americans at large. As the following selection of documents shows, Republicans remained generally against making any concessions on the issue, this despite their effort to court the Latino vote through advertisements and Spanish-language televised presidential debates. Democrats see the issue as more complicated. Democrats do prefer comprehensive immigration reform, but the Democratic candidates felt compelled to refrain from addressing it as a central issue in their respective campaigns. For their part, Americans remain sensitive to what they regard as immigration issues, namely, the economy, job losses, border security, and the "War on Terror." At the time of this writing, both contenders—Barack Obama and John McCain—have been careful to avoid missteps; the candidates shy away from making any strongly sympathetic statements about the immigration issue. Only in 2009 will we see any movement on the issue.

DOCUMENTS

Document 1: U.S. Senator Hillary Rodham Clinton, D-N.Y., Reforming Our Immigration System

When: 2007

Significance: Hillary Clinton supported the Comprehensive Immigration Reform Act of 2006 (which passed the Senate but died in the House of Represntatives), which included border security and a guest worker program. She agrees with finding a solution to legalize the 12 million undocumented aliens through the process of paying fines, taxes, learning English, and applying for permanent resident status. She writes on her senatorial homepage that she strongly believes in the American immigration heritage, but she underlines the rule of law. Finally, she strongly supports the DREAM Act to give the children of illegal immigrants born in the United States U.S. citizenship.

Reforming our immigration system

Our immigration system is in crisis. The laws we currently have on the books are inadequate and no longer serve our best interests. As a nation, we place a premium on compassion, respect, and policies that help families, but our immigration laws don't reflect that.

Hillary has consistently called for comprehensive immigration reform that respects our immigrant heritage and honors the rule of law. She believes comprehensive reform must have as essential ingredients a strengthening of our borders, greater cross-cooperation with our neighbors, strict but fair enforcement of our laws, federal assistance to our state and local governments, strict penalties for those who exploit undocumented workers, and a path to earned legal status for those who are here, working hard, paying taxes, respecting the law, and willing to meet a high bar.

Hillary strongly believes we need to do more to know who is in our country by securing our borders and ensuring that employers comply with the law against hiring and exploiting undocumented workers. She supports deploying new technology that can help stop the flow of undocumented immigrants into the country and an employer verification system that is universal, accurate, timely, and does not lead to discrimination and abuse by employers.

Along with these changes, Hillary believes we need to repair those broken portions of our immigration system that irrevocably damage families and force citizens and lawful immigrants to choose between their newly adopted country and living with their spouse or children. We have a national interest in fostering strong families. This is why she introduced an amendment during consideration of the immigration reform bill that would have taken steps to protect the sanctity of families. Our American values demand no less.

And Hillary understands that our immigration policies have a direct impact on American workers. She opposes a guest worker program that exploits workers and creates a supply of cheap labor that undermines the wages of U.S. workers. Hillary believes all workers deserve safe conditions and decent wages. She supports an Ag Jobs program, which will keep our agricultural industry vibrant while enabling agricultural workers to receive the fair wages and labor protections they ought to receive.

When Hillary is president, comprehensive immigration reform will be a top priority.

Ready to Lead

Hillary has advocated for policies to help smooth the transition of legal immigrants once they arrive in the U.S. so that they can add to our economy and culture.

- She championed the Legal Immigrant Children's Health Improvement Act, which would give states the option to provide federally funded Medicaid and SCHIP benefits to low-income legal immigrant children and pregnant women.
- She wrote the Access to Employment and English Acquisition Act to meet the growing demand for English language courses and other job skills.
- She strongly supports the DREAM Act, which provides a path to citizenship through military service or higher education for children who were brought to the U.S. by their parents.
- She offered an amendment to make family reunification the guiding principle of our immigration system.

Document 2: U.S. Senator Christopher Dodd, D-Connecticut, Statement of Senator Dodd on Immigration Reform Act

When: June 28, 2007

Significance: On his candidate website, Dodd promoted "new strength" for America, calling for the restoration of its Constitution and its leadership in the world. His official Senate website presented only a few comments on immigration. As a senator he called for stronger penalties for those employers that knowingly give undocumented aliens jobs. At the same time he was in favor of the motion to invoke cloture of the bill S. 1639, the Secure Borders, Economic

Opportunity and Immigration Reform Act of 2007. In a press statement, he blamed President Bush for the failure of this act because the president was unable to convince the Republican members of Congress of the necessity to pass this immigration reform.

Statement of Senator Dodd on Immigration Reform Act

"I am deeply disappointed that the Senate voted against the motion to invoke cloture on S. 1639. With over 12 million undocumented workers in America, a dysfunctional immigration system, and broken borders, our country is facing an immigration crisis that undermines the rule of law, divides families and threatens our national security. The American people expected this Congress to find a workable and comprehensive solution to resolve this crisis. This bill was far from perfect, especially in terms of the guest worker program and family unification. But it offered us an opportunity to move beyond the status quo and fix some of these problems including by investing billions of dollars in border security and practically dealing with the undocumented population. Moreover, by proceeding with the bill and potentially going to conference with the House, we would have had a further opportunity to address some of its shortcomings. Instead, with the bill's defeat, our nation is less secure, our immigration crisis will only fester and deepen, and we have reverted to a silent form of amnesty by doing absolutely nothing. The President has spoken time and again of the importance of achieving comprehensive immigration reform. This was meant to be his signature domestic issue. As this vote made crystal clear today, he failed to deliver as did his party. The President's inability to lead on this issue, as on Iraq, has once again come at an enormous cost to this nation."

(Source: Internet-URL: http://dodd.senate.gov/index.php?q=node/3963/print)

Document 3: Former Senator John Edwards, D-N.C., Latinos for Edwards

When: August 24, 2007

Significance: Edwards promotes a very practical vision of immigration. On the one hand, he wants to stop illegal immigration; on the other hand, he favors the idea of integrating aliens into American society by having them pay a fine and learn English.

Comprehensive Immigration Reform

Our immigration system needs a fundamental overhaul. Our economy is harmed by an underground economy that features a large and unprotected labor force. And our values are violated by a system that keeps families apart and forces people to live in the shadows, vulnerable to abuse. The first step is to control our borders and stop illegal trafficking. At the same time, it is unrealistic to think that we can deport more than 12 million people. Edwards believes we need to give people here the opportunity to pay a fine and learn English to earn American citizenship.

Edwards will end the backlog of background checks for people who are already in this country and are applying to become lawful permanent residents and, eventually, citizens. Our immigration policies should bring families together, not keep them apart. Edwards believes family reunification is an important value that should be preserved in our immigration laws.

Internet-URL: http://johnedwards.com/issues/latinos/

Document 4: Rep. Dennis Kucinich, D-Ohio, Immigration

When: 2007

Significance: Kucinich outlines his immigration policy on his page on the House of Representatives website. He takes a very liberal position toward immigration. For example, he voted against the construction of the security fence along the U.S.-Mexico border, and he supports creating a pathway for the legalization of undocumented immigrants.

Immigration Refugees

Congressman Kucinich is a strong advocate on behalf of refugees, who flee their homelands because they fear persecution on account of their race, religion, membership in a social group, political opinion or national origin. He has sponsored several bills to make it easier for refugees, who make up 6% of all immigrants, to come to the United States. Congressman Kucinich believes that if refugees can demonstrate that they have a well-founded fear of persecution, then the United States has a moral responsibility to assist them.

Defending the Rights of Legal Immigrants

Congressman Kucinich was an original cosponsor of legislation that would prohibit the use of "secret evidence" in trials conducted by the Immigration and Naturalization Service. He believes that the cornerstone of our judicial system is that evidence cannot be used against someone unless he or she has the chance to confront it. Congressman Kucinich strives to ensure the rights of all citizens regardless of race, religion, creed, ethnic orientation, sexual orientation, disabilities or age.

In the 107th Congress, during welfare reauthorization legislation, Congressman Kucinich led efforts to restore basic benefits to legal immigrants withdrawn by the 1996 welfare reform legislation. The Congressman believes that all tax-paying, productive members of our society should be treated equally.

Border Control

In the 105th Congress, Congressman Kucinich supported a bill to assign up to 10,000 military personnel to assist in border control activities. There was a need for more Border Patrol agents to monitor the United States' borders with Mexico and Canada. More agents would help prevent the unlawful entry of persons into this country, especially for persons who pose a security risk. This bill further allowed for military personnel to assist U.S. Customs in the inspection of cargo, vehicles, and aircraft at points of entry into the United States.

Congressman Kucinich also supported changes to the immigration bill regarding better enforcement of employer sanctions against firms that hire undocumented aliens. Many immigrants cross the border illegally or remain in the country illegally after their visas expire. Firms who illegally hire undocumented workers only encourage the practice of illegal border crossing. The bill passed in Congress and was signed into law by President Clinton.

Internet-URL: http://kucinich.house.gov/Issues/Issue/?IssueID=1562

Document 5: U.S. Senator Barack Obama, D-Ill., Immigration and the Border

When: 2007

Significance: Obama proposes a point system to obtain citizenship after five years. Furthermore, he favors legislation that creates a new employment eligibility system with which companies could verify that their employees are legal residents. He also supports more personnel and better infrastructure on the border to halt illegal immigration.

Immigration and the Border

"In approaching immigration reform, I believe that we must enact tough, practical reforms.... We need stronger enforcement on the border and at the workplace.... But for reform to work, we also must respond to what pulls people to America.... Where we can reunite families, we should. Where we can bring in more foreign-born workers with the skills our economy needs, we should.... The time to fix our broken immigration system is now. It is critical that as we embark on this enormous venture to update our immigration system, it is fully reflective of the powerful tradition of immigration in this country and fully reflective of our values and ideals."

Barack Obama has played a leading role in crafting comprehensive immigration reform. Obama believes the immigration issue has been exploited by politicians to divide the nation rather than find real solutions. This divisiveness has allowed the illegal immigration problem to worsen, with borders that are less secure than ever and an economy that depends on millions of workers living in the shadows. Obama believes that our broken immigration system can only be fixed by putting politics aside and offering a complete solution that secures our border, enforces our laws and reaffirms our heritage as a nation of immigrants.

Creating Secure Borders

Barack Obama wants to preserve the integrity of our borders. He supports additional personnel, infrastructure, and technology on the border and at our ports of entry. Obama believes we need additional Customs and Border Protection agents equipped with better technology and real-time intelligence.

Improve Our Immigration System

The overwhelming majority of immigrants, both legal and undocumented, come to this country with the hope that hard work and sacrifice will secure a better life for their children. Every year, a million people enter the country legally and another 500,000-800,000 people come illegally or illegally overstay their visas. Barack Obama believes we must fix the broken system to meet the needs of the U.S. economy. Obama believes immigrant workers should have legal protections to avoid abuse and downward pressure on American wages and working conditions. He also realizes the need to increase the number of people we allow into the country legally to a level that keeps families together and meets the demand for jobs that employers cannot fill.

Obama joined Rep. Luis Gutierrez (D-IL) to introduce the Citizenship Promotion Act to ensure that immigration application fees are both reasonable and fair. The U.S. Citizenship and Immigration Services decided to raise fees on applications to as much as $2,400 for a family of four. Obama's bill reverses large fee increases for legal immigrants seeking to become citizens and provides grants to states to help promote citizenship. Another key choke point in the process to becoming a legal permanent resident or a U.S. citizen is the F.B.I. name/security check. Many law-abiding legal immigrants see their immigration applications delayed by months and often years as the overwhelmed F.B.I. completes their background checks. Obama introduced legislation that passed the Senate to improve the speed and accuracy of these background checks.

In the most recent immigration debate on the U.S. Senate floor, Obama fought to improve and pass a comprehensive bill. Obama introduced amendments to put greater emphasis on keeping immigrant families together and to revisit a controversial new points system that never received a proper public hearing. Obama will continue to work for a comprehensive bill that fixes our broken immigration system.

Bring People out of the Shadows

There are millions of people living in the shadows who would like to fully embrace our values and become full members of our democracy. For the millions living here illegally but otherwise playing by the rules, we must encourage them to come out of hiding and get right with the law. Barack Obama supports a system that allows undocumented immigrants who are in good standing to pay a fine, learn English, not violate the law, and go to the back of the line for the opportunity to become citizens.

Remove Incentives to Enter Illegally

To remove incentives to enter the country illegally, we need to crack down on employers that hire undocumented immigrants. Barack Obama has championed a proposal with Senators Charles Grassley (R-IA), Ted Kennedy (D-MA), and Max Baucus (D-MT) to create a new employment eligibility verification system so employers can verify that their employees are legally eligible to work in the U.S.

Reform H-1B Visas

Immigrants have helped create wealth in America's economy. Barack Obama supports improvements in our visa programs, including the H-1B program, to attract some of the world's most talented people to America. However, Barack Obama would like to see immigrant workers less dependent on their employers for their right to stay in the country and would hold accountable employers who abuse the system and their workers.

Honor Our Immigrant Troops

About 69,300 foreign-born men and women serve in the U.S. armed forces; roughly 5 percent of the total active-duty force. Of those, 43 percent (29,800) are not U.S. citizens. The Pentagon says that more than 100 immigrant soldiers have died in combat in Iraq and Afghanistan. Barack Obama believes that legal immigrants who have fought for us overseas should have expedited procedures towards citizenship.

Document 6: Gov. Bill Richardson of New Mexico, Realistic Immigration Reform

When: 2007

Significance: In 2005, Governor Richardson declared a state of emergency along the border with Mexico. With this declaration he protested against the government in Washington, D.C., which he insisted was ignoring growing lawlessness, violent crime, and drug trafficking at the border. After his declaration he made $1.75 million available to local law enforcement agencies along the border in order to reduce crime. Furthermore, he was the first governor to send National Guard troops to the border. In spite of his measures against the flow of undocumented workers, he also wants to give them opportunities. Those who pass a security background check, pay back taxes and fines, and demonstrate the will to learn English should eventually be granted legal status. Others must leave. He looks also forward to establishing a strong partnership with the Mexican government to support President Calderon in undertaking his economic reforms, which could in turn lead to more job opportunities there.

Realistic Immigration Reform

I am committed to implementing comprehensive reforms that secure our borders and our ports and provide for an effective and humane immigration policy

As the governor of a border state I deal with the effects of immigration, legal and illegal, every day. The federal government has not done enough to solve the problem. In 2005 violent crime, drugs, and crime were out of control along New Mexico's border with Mexico. I took action, declaring a state of emergency along the border, making $1.75 million available to local law enforcement agencies to increase patrols and add personnel. As a result, arrests are up, crime is down, and the flow of undocumented immigrants has slowed. The New Mexico border town of Village of Columbus, for example, saw an 80 percent reduction in crime.

Building a fence will not increase security, just as attempting to deport 12 million illegal immigrants is not feasible or reasonable. I believe a realistic immigration reform plan must address the problem from all sides—securing the border, penalizing employers for knowingly hiring illegal workers, offering a tough but reasonable path to legalization, engaging Mexico in the reform process, and improving our current immigration quota system.

Secure the Border by Hiring and Training Enough Patrol Guards to Cover the Entire Border

We must more than double the number of guards, and provide them with the best surveillance technology available.

Establish a *Reasonable* Path to Legalization for Many of Those Who Are Already Here

This is not amnesty, but is a tough but fair opportunity for legalization and the possibility of citizenship. Most of the illegal workers in the country are hard-working, law-abiding people simply pursuing the American Dream. Those who pass a background check, learn English, pay back taxes and fines for being here illegally get the opportunity for legal status. Those that don't must leave.

Crack Down on Immigration Fraud and Illegal Workers

We should offer informant visas and cash rewards for aliens who provide law enforcement with credible information on human traffickers and document forgers. As President, I would establish a fraudulent documents task force to constantly update law enforcement and border officials on the latest fraudulent documents being marketed for entry into the United States. In addition, I believe we must improve identification documentation of immigrant workers.

Eliminate One of the Prime Attractions for Illegal Workers

We must crack down on employers who knowingly hire undocumented immigrants and enforce the laws already on the books. After establishing a national ID system, employers will have no excuses.

Work in Partnership with the Mexican Government and Nations throughout Latin America

Mexico is our friend and a major trading partner but they must take action to help reduce the northward flow of illegal immigrants and illegal drugs. We must improve border infrastructure to streamline the movement of goods through the free-trade zones along the border, revitalizing communities on both sides of the border and creating much-needed jobs. The

Secretary General of the Organization of American States appointed me as a special envoy to Latin American to promote initiatives that focus on economic development and immigration. Through intensive diplomacy and face-to-face dialogue we must demonstrate to OAS member states that they have an equal responsibility to help solve the immigration problem.

Throughout my career I have worked closely and effectively with Mexico on issues such as border security, trade, and education. As Governor I convinced the Mexican government to bulldoze a section of the border town of Las Chepas, where abandoned buildings had become staging points for bringing illegal immigrants and drugs into the U.S. I also met with President Calderon to discuss how the United States and Mexico can work together to solve the problems associated with illegal immigration. I don't need to learn about the problems or to figure out how to get things done. I've done it.

Increase the Number of Legal Immigrants Allowed into the United States Each Year

The number of guest workers allowed at any one time must be based upon the needs of the U.S. economy. Our goal must be to meet demand for jobs that go unfilled by American citizens, and no more.

I Was the First Governor in the Nation to Send National Guard Troops to the Border

In 2006 President Bush called for the deployment of National Guard troops to fortify the nation's borders and stem the flow of undocumented immigrants. I was the first Governor to honor that request and send National Guard support to the existing border patrol forces, with the condition that the assignment was temporary until the administration could recruit and train a large number of new Border Patrol agents.

(Source: Internet-URL: http://www.richardsonforpresident.com/issues/immigration)

Document 7: U.S. Senator John McCain, R-Ariz., Border Security and Immigration Reform

When: 2007

Significance: For McCain border security is very important in times of terrorism. But also he views the new left populism in Latin America, à la that stemming from Venezuelan President Chavez, as a challenge to immigration. Economic and democratic reforms in Latin American countries, therefore, are necessary to reduce emigration. In general, he also supports the plan that immigrants need to learn English, American history, and civics in order to integrate successfully into society.

Border Security and Immigration Reform

Immigration is one of those challenging issues that touch on many aspects of American life.

I have always believed that our border must be secure and that the federal government has utterly failed in its responsibility to ensure that it is secure. If we have learned anything from the recent immigration debate, it is that Americans have little trust that their government will honor a pledge to do the things necessary to make the border secure.

As president, I will secure the border. I will restore the trust Americans should have in the basic competency of their government. A secure border is an essential element of our national security. Tight border security includes not just the entry and exit of people, but also the effective screening of cargo at our ports and other points of entry.

But a secure border will contribute to addressing our immigration problem most effectively if we also:

Recognize the importance of building strong allies in Mexico and Latin America who reject the siren call of authoritarians like Hugo Chavez, support freedom and democracy, and seek strong domestic economies with abundant economic opportunities for their citizens.

Recognize the importance of pro-growth policies—keeping government spending in check, holding down taxes, and cutting unnecessary regulatory burdens—so American businesses can hire and pay the best.

Recognize the importance of a flexible labor market to keep employers in business and our economy on top. It should provide skilled Americans and immigrants with opportunity. Our education system should ensure skills for our younger workers, and our retraining and assistance programs for displaced workers must be modernized so they can pursue those opportunities

Recognize the importance of assimilation of our immigrant population, which includes learning English, American history and civics, and respecting the values of a democratic society.

Recognize that America will always be that "shining city upon a hill," a beacon of hope and opportunity for those seeking a better life built on hard work and optimism.

Border security and our failed immigration system are more examples of an ailing Washington culture in need of reform to regain the trust of Americans. In too many areas—from immigration and pork barrel spending to Social Security, health care, energy security and tax relief—business-as-usual politics prevents addressing the important challenges facing our nation.

(Source: Internet-URL: http://www.johnmccain.com/Informing/Issues/68db8157-d301-4e22-baf7-a70dd8416efa.htm)

Document 8: Former Mayor Rudolph Giuliani of New York City, Commitment: I Will End Illegal Immigration, Secure Our Borders, and Identify Every Non-Citizen in Our Nation

When: August 13, 2007

Significance: Giuliani opposed bill S. 1348—the Comprehensive Immigration Reform Act of 2007—which eventually failed. Instead of focusing on the need to regulate immigration first, he emphasizes border security and strong rule of law to protect the American people. Unlike other candidates he strongly advocates immediate deportation for illegal aliens who commit a felony. In his opinion, immigrants must learn English before becoming U.S. citizens. He also finds it essential to establish a national identification system to verify immigrants' legal status.

Commitment: I will end illegal immigration, secure our borders, and identify every non-citizen in our nation.

"Real immigration reform must put security first because border security and homeland security are inseparable in the terrorists' war on us. The first responsibility of the federal government is to protect our citizens by controlling America's borders, while ending illegal immigration and identifying every non-citizen in our nation. We must restore integrity, accountability and the rule of law to our immigration system to regain the faith of the American people."

Control Our Nation's Borders

Bring Order To The Border: Congress authorized the construction of 700 miles of border fence in 2006 and then appropriated over $1.1 billion for border security. However, Washington has only built a few dozen miles of fence. Rudy will commit to building the fence - both physical and high-tech—now, while deploying and maintaining 20,000 Border Patrol agents and measuring their progress toward ending illegal immigration. It is important to accomplish this goal in order to preserve and expand legal immigration.

Implement BorderStat: Rudy will propose BorderStat to bring accountability to measuring the progress in securing our borders. BorderStat is modeled after the Mayor's successful New York City program CompStat which helped reduce the city's crime by imposing accountability. It will use key indicators to identify both effective enforcement strategies that demonstrate tangible results and areas of the border where we are failing so the failures can be immediately corrected.

Identify All Non-Citizens Entering and Exiting America

Issue a Single, Tamper-Proof Biometric ID Card: Rudy will propose the Secure Authorized Foreign Entry Card (SAFE Card) to be uniform for all non-citizen workers and students, utilizing tamper-proof and biometric features for secure identification.

Create a Single National Database of Foreigners: It is critical to America's security to have one national database of non-citizens in our country. Rudy will propose consolidating all existing databases into one so a foreigner's legal status can be quickly checked.

Identify Those Who Have Left the Country with Biometric Check-out System: Forty-five percent of illegal immigrants in America came into our country legally but overstayed their visas. Rudy believes we need a biometric check-out system so we know who has left America and can focus enforcement on those who remain.

Deport Criminal Aliens

Deport All Illegal Aliens Who Commit a Felony: America currently only deports 14% of the roughly 300,000 foreigners who commit crimes in our country. Rudy will commit to deporting all foreign individuals who have abused their privilege of staying in the United States.

Americanize Immigrants

Require All Immigrants to Truly Read, Write and Speak English: Rudy believes immigration and Americanization go hand-in-hand. As President, he will propose that all immigrants who want to become citizens must truly read, write, and speak English and learn American civics. For the American experiment to succeed, we need a common language.

Document 9: Former Governor Mike Huckabee of Arkansas, Immigration

When: 2007

Significance: Huckabee presents a hard-line position on the immigration issue. Securing the borders is top priority. Immigration is a threat because of potential terrorism. He is against amnesty for illegal immigrants and clearly states that he wants to discourage further economic integration because it would lead to more immigration from Latin America. Support for the arrest and deportation of illegal and criminal immigrants represents another consequence of his strict law-and-order policy.

Immigration

Securing our borders must be our top priority and has reached the level of a national emergency.

The Governor supports the $3 billion the Senate has voted for border security. This money will train and deploy 23,000 more agents, add four drone planes, build 700 miles of fence and 300 miles of vehicle barriers, and put up 105 radar and camera towers. This money will turn "catch and release" into "catch and detain" of those entering illegally, and crack down on those who overstay their visas.

In this age of terror, immigration is not only an economic issue, but also a national security issue. Those caught trying to enter illegally must be detained, processed, and deported.

The Governor opposes and will never allow amnesty. He opposed the amnesty President Bush and Senator McCain tried to ram through Congress this summer, and opposed the misnamed DREAM Act, which would have put us on the slippery slope to amnesty for all.

The Governor opposes and will not tolerate sanctuaries for illegals. The federal government must crack down on rogue cities that willfully undermine our economy and national security.

The Governor opposes giving driver's licenses to illegals and supports legislation to prevent states from doing so.

The Governor will stop punishing cities which try to enforce our laws and protect the economic well-being, physical safety, and quality of life of their citizens.

The Governor opposes and will not tolerate employers who hire illegals. They must be punished with fines and penalties so large that they will see it is not worth the risk.

The Governor opposes the economic integration of North America that would create open borders among the United States, Canada, and Mexico. He will never yield one iota or one inch of our sovereignty.

The Governor will take our country back for those who belong here. No open borders, no amnesty, no sanctuary, no false Social Security numbers, no driver's licenses for illegals.

Governor Huckabee knows that securing our borders must be our top priority and has reached the level of a national emergency. He is as sick and tired as you are that it is harder for us to get on an airplane in our hometown than it is for all these illegals to cross our international border unchallenged.

We cannot stem the tide of illegals until we turn the tide. Before you fix the damage to your house caused by a leaking roof, you have to stop the leak, which the Governor is determined to do.

The Governor supported the $3 billion Congress passed this summer for border security. This desperately needed money will train and deploy 23,000 more agents, add four drone planes, build 700 miles of fence and 300 miles of vehicle barriers, and put up 105 radar and camera towers. This money will turn "catch and release" into "catch and detain" of those entering illegally and crack down on those who overstay their visas.

But where is this $3 billion? The President threatened to veto the bill it was part of! Now the Senate has again voted for this money as part of the Defense Bill. The Governor will continue to fight until we get these funds.

In this age of terror, immigration is not only an economic issue, but also a national security issue. We must know who is coming into our country, where they are going, and why they are here. All those who are caught trying to enter illegally must be detained, processed, and deported. As Governor, he ordered his state troopers to work with the Department of Homeland Security to arrest illegals and enforce federal immigration law.

The Governor opposes and will never allow amnesty. He passionately rejected the amnesty bill that President Bush and Sen. McCain tried to ram through Congress this summer after secret meetings of an under-the-radar cabal of amnesty-loving senators.

The Governor opposed the misnamed DREAM Act, which was a nightmare because it would have put us on the slippery slope to amnesty for all. Because once we open that door even a crack, we'll never get it closed again.

The Governor opposes and will not tolerate sanctuaries for illegals. The federal government must enforce our existing laws by cracking down on rogue cities and towns that willfully undermine our economy and our homeland security by giving benefits and protection to illegals. The consequences for illegal entry must be swift, certain, and uniform throughout our country.

The Governor opposes giving driver's licenses to illegals, such as Governor Spitzer is trying to do in New York. The Governor supports legislation that would prevent the states from granting this privilege to illegals. In 2005, he signed legislation that prevents illegals in Arkansas from getting driver's licenses.

The Governor will stop punishing cities which are trying to enforce our laws. He will appoint judges who will uphold the law, not side with the ACLU against cities like Hazelton, Pennsylvania, which are trying to protect the economic well-being, physical safety, and quality of life of their citizens.

The Governor will not tolerate employers who hire illegals – they must be punished by fines and penalties so large that they will understand it is not worth the risk. Once again, as with Hazelton, liberal judges are gumming up the works. Right now, a court in San Francisco—Pelosiland—has delayed enforcement of the "no match" letters for Social Security numbers that the Department of Homeland Security will use to crack down on those who hire illegals. If illegals cannot find work, they will go back where they belong. The Governor will do everything he can to hasten their trip home by denying them employment. The Governor strongly opposes the economic integration of North America that would have open borders among the United States, Canada, and Mexico. He knows we must have closed and secure borders. He will never yield either one inch or one iota of our sovereignty. He will recognize no authority but our Constitution.

Governor Huckabee will take our country back for those who belong here and those who are willing to play by the rules for the privilege to come here. No open borders, no amnesty, no sanctuary, no false Social Security numbers, no driver's licenses for illegals.

(Source: Internet-URL: http://www.mikehuckabee.com)

Document 10: Rep. Ron Paul, R-Texas, Border Security and Immigration Reform

When: 2007

Significance: Ron Paul presents a six-point plan for immigration and border security on his website that includes the deportation of those who overstay their visas. Paul also calls for the elimination of the birthright citizenship granted to children born in the United States when their parents are undocumented foreigners.

Border Security and Immigration Reform

The talk must stop. We must secure our borders now. A nation without secure borders is no nation at all. It makes no sense to fight terrorists abroad when our own front door is left unlocked. This is my six-point plan:

- Physically secure our borders and coastlines. We must do whatever it takes to control entry into our country before we undertake complicated immigration reform proposals.
- Enforce visa rules. Immigration officials must track visa holders and deport anyone who overstays their visa or otherwise violates U.S. law. This is especially important when we recall that a number of 9/11 terrorists had expired visas.
- No amnesty. Estimates suggest that 10 to 20 million people are in our country illegally. That's a lot of people to reward for breaking our laws.
- No welfare for illegal aliens. Americans have welcomed immigrants who seek opportunity, work hard, and play by the rules. But taxpayers should not pay for illegal immigrants who use hospitals, clinics, schools, roads, and social services.
- End birthright citizenship. As long as illegal immigrants know their children born here will be citizens, the incentive to enter the U.S. illegally will remain strong.
- Pass true immigration reform. The current system is incoherent and unfair. But current reform proposals would allow up to 60 *million* more immigrants into our country,

according to the Heritage Foundation. This is insanity. Legal immigrants from all countries should face the same rules and waiting periods.

(Source: Internet-URL: http://www.ronpaul2008.com)

Document 11: Rep. Tom Tancredo, R-Colo., Immigration

When: 2007

Significance: Tancredo opposes amnesty for undocumented aliens. He wants to reduce the flow by cutting social benefits for them. Moreover, he proposes that the number of legal migrants should be cut to a maximum of a quarter million per year. By quoting former President Theodore Roosevelt (1901–1909) he underlines his position on immigration: respect the American way of life, the rule of law, and the will to assimilate into this society.

Immigration

There is no doubt that America is facing an illegal immigration crisis. Currently, there are at least 12 million illegal aliens living in America. I am absolutely opposed to amnesty. In addition to rewarding those who broke our laws, amnesties simply do not solve the problem of illegal immigration. The only realistic solution to the problem of illegal immigration is a strategy of attrition, which seeks to reduce the flow of the illegal alien population over time by cutting off the incentives for coming to and staying in America – most importantly by eliminating the jobs magnet. America must also reexamine its legal immigration policies.

Since 1990, that number has been roughly one million yearly—and that doesn't count illegal aliens. America should reduce legal immigration to 250,000 people a year, which will allow the newcomers to assimilate.

"In the first place, we should insist that if the immigrant who comes here in good faith becomes an American and assimilates himself to us, he shall be treated on an exact equality with everyone else, for it is an outrage to discriminate against any such man because of creed, or birthplace, or origin. But this is predicated upon the person's becoming in every facet an American, and nothing but an American. There can be no divided allegiance here. Any man who says he is an American, but something else also, isn't an American at all. We have room for but one flag, the American flag. We have room for but one language here, and that is the English language. And we have room for but one sole loyalty and that is a loyalty to the American people" (Theodore Roosevelt 1907).

Document 12: Former Senator Fred Thompson, R-Tenn., Border Security and Immigration Reform Plan

When: 2007

Significance: Like most Republican candidates, Thompson rejects amnesty for illegal immigrants. He classifies immigration as a national security issue and depicts an immigration plan that focuses on border security, law enforcement, and a new immigration law that relates immigration to the interests of the United States.

Border Security and Immigration Reform Plan

In the post-9/11 world, immigration is much more of a national security issue. A government that cannot secure its borders and determine who may enter and who may not, fails in a fundamental responsibility. As we take steps to secure our borders and enforce our laws, we must also ensure that our immigration laws and policies advance our national interests in a variety of areas, and that the immigration process itself is as fair, efficient, and effective as possible.

Securing the Border and Enforcing the Law

A fundamental responsibility of the federal government is to secure the nation's borders and enforce the law. The following policies and initiatives will put the nation on a path to success:

1. *No Amnesty.* Do not provide legal status to illegal aliens. Amnesty undermines U.S. law and policy, rewards bad behavior, and is unfair to the millions of immigrants who follow the law and are awaiting legal entry into the United States. In some cases, those law-abiding and aspiring immigrants have been waiting for several years.

2. *Attrition through Enforcement.* Reduce the number of illegal aliens through increased enforcement against unauthorized alien workers and their employers. Without illegal employment opportunities available, fewer illegal aliens will attempt to enter the country, and many of those illegally in the country now likely will return home. Self-deportation can also be maximized by stepping up the enforcement levels of other existing immigration laws. This course of action offers a reasonable alternative to the false choices currently proposed to deal with the 12 million or more aliens already in the U.S. illegally: either arrest and deport them all, or give them all amnesty. Attrition through enforcement is a more reasonable and achievable solution, but this approach requires additional resources for enforcement and border security:

   A. Doubling ICE agents handling interior enforcement, increasing the Border Patrol to at least 25,000 agents, and increasing detention space to incarcerate illegal aliens we arrest rather than letting them go with a promise to show up later for legal proceedings against them.

   B. Adding resources for the Department of Justice to prosecute alien smugglers, people involved in trafficking in false identification documents, and previously deported felons.

   C. Maximizing efforts to prosecute and convict members of criminal alien gangs, such as MS-13 and affiliated gangs. These gangs have brought unusual levels of violence to more than 30 U.S. states and have also become very active in drug-smuggling, gun-smuggling, and alien-smuggling.

   D. Implementing fully and making greater use of the expedited removal process already allowed under federal law.

   E. Enabling the Social Security Administration to share relevant information with immigration and law enforcement personnel in a manner that will support effective interior enforcement efforts.

3. *Enforce Existing Federal Laws.* Enforce the laws Congress has already enacted to prevent illegal aliens from unlawfully benefiting from their presence in the country:

   A. End Sanctuary Cities by cutting off discretionary federal grant funds as appropriate to any community that, by law, ordinance, executive order, or other formal policy, directs its public officials not to comply with the provisions of 8 USC 1373 and 8 USC 1644, which prohibit any state or local government from restricting in any way communications with the Department of Homeland Security "regarding the immigration status, lawful or unlawful, of an alien in the United States."

   B. Deny discretionary Federal education grants as appropriate to public universities that violate federal law by offering in-state tuition rates to illegal aliens without also offering identical benefits to United States citizens, regardless of whether or not they live in the state, as required by 8 USC 1623.

    C. Deny discretionary Federal grants as appropriate to states and local governments that violate federal law by offering public benefits to illegal aliens, as prohibited by 8 USC 1621(a).

4. *Reduce the Jobs Incentive.* Ensure employee verification by requiring that all U.S. employers use the Department of Homeland Security's electronic database (the E-Verify system) to confirm that a prospective employee is authorized to work in the U.S. Now that the technology is proven, provide sufficient resources to make the system as thorough, fast, accurate, and easy-to-use as possible.

5. *Add to the Cost of Hiring Illegal Aliens.* Deny a tax deduction to employers for the wages they pay to illegal aliens, thereby dramatically increasing the real cost of employing illegal aliens. Businesses that do not play by the rules should not be rewarded under our tax system.

6. *Bolster Border Security.* Finish building the 854-mile wall along the border by 2010 as required by 8 USC 1103. Extend the wall beyond that as appropriate and deploy new technologies and additional resources to enhance detection and rapid apprehension along our borders by 2012.

7. *Increased Prosecution.* Deploy the additional assets outlined above to prosecute alien smugglers ("coyotes"), alien gang members, previously deported felons, and aliens who have repeatedly violated our immigration laws much more vigorously.

8. *Rigorous Entry/Exit Tracking.* Complete the implementation of a system to track visa entrants and exits, as has been required by federal law for more than ten years, and connect it to the FBI's National Crime Information Center (NCIC), in order to curb visa overstays and permit more effective enforcement.

Improving the Legal Immigration Process. The United States is a nation of immigrants. We must continue to welcome immigrants and foreign workers who come to our country legally, giving priority to those who can advance the nation's interests and common good. Immigrants and foreign workers who play by the rules need to be rewarded with faster and less burdensome service, not delays that last years. Advancing the following initiatives will require close cooperation between all levels of government, the business community, and concerned citizens:

1. *Maximize Program Efficiency.* Reduce the backlogs and streamline the process for immigrants and employers who seek to follow the law. Also, simplify and expedite the application processes for temporary visas. This can be accomplished by hiring more personnel at Citizenship and Immigration Services and the FBI. Caps for any category of temporary work visa would be increased as appropriate, if it could be demonstrated that there are no Americans capable and willing to do the jobs.

2. *Enhanced Reporting.* Improve reporting to the government by businesses that rely on temporary workers so that the government can track whether the visa holder remains employed.

3. *Modernize Immigration Law/Policy.* Change the nature of our legal immigration system to welcome immigrants who can be economic contributors to our country, are willing to learn the English language, and want to assimilate.

    A. Reduce the scope of chain migration by giving family preference in the allocation of lawful permanent resident status only to spouses and minor children of U.S. citizens, and no one else (no siblings, no parents, no adult children, etc.).

    B. Eliminate the diversity visa lottery.

1. *English as Official Language.* Make English the official language of the United States to promote assimilation and legal immigrants' success, and require English proficiency in order for any foreign person to be granted lawful permanent resident status.

2. *Freedom from Political Oppression.* Preserve U.S. laws and policies to ensure that the United States remains a beacon and a haven for persons fleeing political oppression, while assuring appropriate admission standards are maintained.

3. *Service to Country.* Place those foreign persons who are lawfully present in the country and who serve honorably in the Armed Forces of the United States on a faster, surer track to U.S. citizenship.

(Source: Internet-URL: http://www.fred08.com/virtual/Immigration.aspx)

FURTHER READINGS

Internet Sources

The U.S. Department of State information: http://usinfo.state.gov/politics/elections/issues.html

The *New York Times* on the immigration positions of the main presidential candidates: http://politics.nytimes.com/electionguide/2008/issues/immigration/index.html#republicans; http://politics.nytimes.com/election-guide/2008/issues/immigration/index.html#democrats

"OnTheIssue" puts together the opinions of every political leader on every issue: http://ontheissues.org/default.htm

Conservative website "NumbersUSA" warns of an overpopulation threat and evaluates critically the votes of U.S. decision makers on the immigration issue: http://www.numbersusa.com/index

The Vernon K. Krieble Foundation: http://www.krieble.org/

Books

Aleinikoff, Thomas Alexander, David A. Martin, and Hiroshi Motomura. *Immigration and Nationality Laws of the United States: Selected Statutes, Regulations and Forms.* Eagan, Minn.: Thomson West, 2007.

Buchanan, Patrick J. *State of Emergency: The Third World Invasion and Conquest of America.* New York: Thomas Dunne Books/St. Martin's Press, 2006.

Dougherty, Jon E. *Illegals: The Imminent Threat Posed by Our Unsecured U.S.-Mexico Border.* Nashville: WND-Books, 2004.

Gania, Edwin. *U.S. Immigration Step by Step* (Legal Survival Guides), 3rd ed. Naperville, Ill.: Sphinx Publishing, 2006.

Gilchrist, Jim, and Jerome R. Corsi. *Minutemen: The Battle to Secure America's Borders.* Los Angeles: World Ahead Publishing, 2006.

Hayworth, J. D. *Whatever It Takes: Illegal Immigration, Border Security and the War on Terror.* Washington, D.C.: Regnery Publishing, 2006.

Holbrook, Ames. *The Deporter: One Agent's Struggle against the U.S. Government's Refusal to Expel Criminal Aliens.* New York: Sentinel HC, 2007.

Mac Donald, Heather, Victor Davis Hanson, and Steven Malanga. *The Immigration Solution: A Better Plan Than Today's.* Chicago: Ivan R. Dee, 2007.

Swain, Carol. *Debating Immigration.* New York: Cambridge University Press, 2007.

Tancredo, Tom. *In Mortal Danger: The Battle for America's Border and Security.* Nashville: WND-Books, 2006.

Weissbrodt, David S., and Laura Danielson. *Immigration Law and Procedure in a Nutshell,* 5th ed. Eagan, Minn.: West Group Publishing, 2005.

Wooldridge, Frosty. *Immigration's Unarmed Invasion: Deadly Consequences.* Bloomington, Ind.: AuthorHouse, 2004.

Articles

Judis, John. "Hillary Clinton's Firewall: Will Barack Obama's Anemic Standing Among Latinos Be His Undoing?" *The New Republic* (December 18, 2007). Originally published: http://www.tnr.com/politics/story.html?id=314e8fae-3fd3-4af2-bfde-f0f8e069c1fe, also published at Carnegie Endowment for International Peace: http://www.carnegieendowment.org/publications/index.cfm?fa=view&id=19818&prog=zpg&proj=zusr.

Labastida-Tovar, Elena. "The Impact of NAFTA on the Mexican-U.S. Border Region." In *The Politics, Economics and Culture of Mexican-US Migration: Both Sides of the Border*, edited by Edward Ashbee, Helene Balslev Clausen, and Carl Pedersen. New York: Palgrave-Macmillan, 2007, 107–132.

Luo, Michael. "Border Issues Divide U.S. Hopefuls." *International Herald Tribune* (November 18, 2007).

Sammon, Bill. "Illegal Immigration Hurts Dems." *The Examiner* (November 17, 2007).

Taylor, Paul, and Richard Fry. "Hispanics and the 2008 Election: A Swing Vote?" (December 6, 2007). http://pewhispanic.org/reports/report.php?ReportID=83.

Conclusion

The immigration debate likely will remain a front-and-center issue in U.S. politics for years to come since it remains an important economic and security issue. Although it is almost certain that any immigration reform will be linked to measures to secure American borders, a new president and Congress should find fewer constraints in working toward a comprehensive measure that includes both a temporary worker program and a path for undocumented workers toward citizenship. The prospect for comprehensive reform is all the more probable because the Republican contender, John McCain, was himself a sponsor of a previous attempt at comprehensive reform. It seems that consensus is more possible in 2009 than it was during the Bush years. American business leaders are also likely to become more vocal about the need to increase the pool of qualified workers during the next congress.

However, outright opposition to any sort of loosening of immigration policy for security, cultural, and economic reasons will continue to manifest itself in the years to come. How legislators will address the controversial nature of the issue will determine how much Congress is able to move reform forward in 2009 and beyond. The immigration debate clearly will also be shaped by the health of the American economy in the coming years and by the confidence that Americans have in their economy.

In the final analysis, it must be remembered that, historically, the cyclical ebb and flow of the immigration debate is nothing new. As the documents presented in these chapters illustrate, the American immigration debate has moved through many phases. The most significant anti-immigrant movements in the early years of the Republic were directed against Catholics—most notably German and Irish Catholics during the mid-1800s—then against Chinese migrants from the mid-1800s until well into the twentieth century. The Dillingham Report of the pre-World War I era made a clear distinction between more "desirable" and less "desirable" immigrants, reflecting the strong prejudices of that time and a bias in favor of white Anglo-Saxon immigrants and against Southern European immigrants from Italy and the Slavic and Jewish immigrants from Central and Eastern Europe.

Today, after many years of a relatively open immigration policy, the United States at the start of the twenty-first century is once again having to evaluate its immigration policies and the role that immigration will play in the years ahead. This is no small policy matter and will help shape the country's future. Immigration is not simply an issue that can be resolved by one sweeping legislative reform approved in haste. The future debate over immigration will be difficult, hopefully lively and constructive, and in the end, very necessary for the country.

APPENDIX A

Key Immigration Legislation in U.S. History

1790

Naturalization Act of 1790

Granted naturalization to any 'free white person' living in the country for two years

1795

Naturalization Act of 1795

Naturalization granted only after fourteen years of residence

1798

Naturalization Act of 1798

Naturalization period reduced to five years; part of Alien and Sedition Acts, which gave the president power to expel any alien deemed dangerous

1882

Chinese Exclusion Act

Banned Chinese national laborers from immigrating to the United States (finally repealed in 1943)

1917

Immigration Act of 1917

Required a literacy test for the first time; expanded the category of foreigners to be excluded from the United States

1921

Emergency Quota Act of 1921

Established national quotas

1924

National Origins Act (Immigration and Nationality Act) of 1924

Reduced quota numbers established in 1921, with immigration from the Soviet Union and Italy being most severely cut back in order to control inflow of post-World War I immigration

1942

Bracero Program (Emergency Labor Program)

Allowed entry of Mexican laborers to make up for domestic labor shortfall during World War II

1952

Immigration and Nationality Act

Revised quotas to eliminate racial distinctions for the first time to allow people from any country the chance to enter the United States and at the same time ended the ban on Asian immigrants

1965

Immigration and Nationality Act Amendments

Abolished all the remaining national origin quotas and caps for immigration from the Western and Eastern Hemispheres were established

1980

Refugee Act of 1980

Increased overall quota for refugee entry to the United States, largely in response to refugees of Vietnam War

1986

Immigration Reform and Control Act (IRCA)

Created penalties for employers who knowingly hire unauthorized immigrants, but also contained an amnesty for 3,000,000 long-residing undocumented immigrants.

1990

Immigration Act of 1990

Established categories of employment-based immigration and placed a cap on non-immigrant workers

1994

Proposition 187 of California

Aimed at excluding undocumented workers from all social services; signed into law in 1994, but a judge ruled the proposition unconstitutional in 1998

1996

Illegal Immigration Reform and Immigrant Responsibility Act (IIRIRA)

Imposed more strict penalties on illegal immigration and increased the categories under which both legal 'green card' holders and illegal immigrants can be deported

APPENDIX B

Resources on the Immigration Issue

The issue of immigration remains controversial and divisive. It attracts the attention of lawmakers and citizens alike. Below are some of the many websites of government agencies, think tanks, research centers, and advocacy groups that are involved in various ways with this contentious issue. There is also a list of international agencies and organizations involved in dealing with migration matters.

FEDERAL GOVERNMENT AGENCY AND DEPARTMENT WEBSITES

Department of Homeland Security

http://www.dhs.gov

It is a cabinet department of the United States government. It is responsible for protecting America's borders and preventing terrorist attacks against the country. Among the duties is the prevention of the illegal entry of individuals into the United States.

U.S. Citizenship and Immigration Services (formerly U.S. Immigration and Naturalization Service)

http://www.uscis.gov

After the creation of the Department of Homeland Security (DHS), it has assumed the functions of the Immigration and Naturalization Service (INS) within DHS. USCIS promotes national security and addresses U.S. immigration cases, processes immigrant visa petitions, adjudicates naturalization petitions, and hears asylum and refugee applications.

Department of Labor

http://www.dol.gov

This agency is responsible for certifying immigrant petitions to work inside the United States and setting out regulations for hiring foreign workers. Employers must prove to the Department of Labor in most circumstances that a search for an American worker was conducted prior to employing a foreign national to do the specified job.

U.S. Immigration and Customs Enforcement (ICE)

http://www.ice.gov

ICE is an investigative arm of DHS. It is responsible for investigating vulnerabilities at U.S. borders, including such matters as illegal trafficking of persons, and is important in guaranteeing and strengthening border security.

Department of State

www.state.gov

The State Department represents the United States abroad. It also provides information to Americans traveling abroad. It offers assistance regarding visas to enter the United States. One key service is its monthly bulletin showing available family-based and employment-based visas (http://travel.state.gov/visa/frvi/bulletin/bulletin_1770.html).

U.S. Census Bureau/Immigration Data

http://www.census.gov/population/www/socdemo/immigration.html

The U.S. Census Bureau collects data on a wide variety of social, political, economic, demographic, and cultural indicators. It is also involved with the collection of data on immigration to the United States.

Federal Bureau of Investigation

www.fbi.gov

It is a branch of the Department of Justice (www.doj.gov). The FBI is the key federal agency responsible for investigating threats to the United States on its own soil, including the presence of foreign nationals that may pose a threat to the nation's security.

Drug Enforcement Agency

www.usdoj.gov/dea

It is a branch of the Department of Justice. The DEA is responsible for America's anti-drug efforts and is also involved in breaking up smuggling rings, including immigrant smuggling rings.

Coast Guard

http://www.uscg.mil

It is responsible for maintaining vigilance over America's coastlines and preventing entry by unwarranted vessels. It is involved in intercepting boats carrying illegal cargo, including unauthorized persons, into the United States.

Government Accountability Office

www.gao.gov

This office monitors federal government spending and government programs. It also audits federal expenditures and issues opinions on federal expenditure. The GAO has produced reports evaluating border security measures, such as spending on the border fence between the United States and Mexico.

Library of Congress

http://lcweb2.loc.gov/learn/features/immig/introduction.html
The Library of Congress is the nation's library and includes accessible online collections on a wide variety of subjects. It has useful online information on U.S. immigration and immigration history.

National Archives and Records Administration

www.archives.gov
It holds the records of the U.S. federal government with online access to many different topics, including legal manuscripts, the federal register, and census data for educators, researchers, and the general public.

National Museum of American History

http://americanhistory.si.edu
Part of the U.S. government's Smithsonian Institutes, the National Museum documents American history with a lot of information and many documents are accessible online.

RESEARCH CENTERS AND THINK TANKS

Immigration Policy Center

http://www.immigrationpolicy.org
The Immigration Policy Center (IPC) is the research arm of the American Immigrant Law Foundation. Its mission is to provide policymakers, academics, the media, and the public with accurate information of the impact of immigration on U.S. society and its economy. Its policy briefs and reports tend to focus on the importance of immigration for the United States.

Center for Immigration Studies

http://www.cis.org
The Center for Immigration Studies (CIS) is a nonprofit research think tank that analyzes the social, fiscal, economic, demographic, and other impacts of immigration on the United States. In its stated mission, it seeks to reduce immigration numbers but to offer immigrants admitted "a warmer welcome."

Pew Hispanic Center

www.pewhispanic.org
The Pew Hispanic Center is a nonpartisan research center funded by the Pew Charitable Trusts. Its mission is to improve understanding of the Latino community in the United States and its growing impact on the country. It does not take a position on immigration, but it conducts opinion surveys and focuses on such subjects as demography, economics, education, identity, immigration, labor, politics, and remittances.

Pew Research Center

www.pewresearch.org

The Pew Research Center is an independent opinion research center that studies attitudes toward the press, politics, and public policies. It is sponsored by the Pew Charitable Trusts. It conducts surveys on many issues that confront Americans, including the immigration issue.

Immigration History Research Center—University of Minnesota

www.ihrc.umn.edu

It is an interdisciplinary research center that is part of the College of Liberal Arts of the University of Minnesota. It conducts research on international migration with a particular emphasis on immigrant and refugee life inside the United States. It seeks to enrich the contemporary debate about international migration from historical and scholarly perspectives.

Center for Research on Immigration Policy (CRIP)—RAND

www.rand.org/education/projects/crip.html

RAND's Center for Research on Immigration Policy (CRIP) was founded in 1988 to conduct analytical research and policy analysis on immigration and immigrant policies. It works with decision makers at the federal, state, local, and international levels, as well as other groups, through seminars, briefings, conferences, and publications.

Center for Research on Immigration, Population, and Public Policy—University of California, Irvine

http://www.cri.uci.edu

UCI's Center conducts policy-relevant research on international migration and population processes. Its main focus is U.S. immigration. It encourages multidisciplinary research projects and focuses on multigenerational incorporation experiences of immigrant groups in the United States.

The Heritage Foundation

www.heritage.org/research/immigration

The Heritage Foundation is a think tank that seeks to create and promote conservative public policies based on the principle of free enterprise, limited government, individual freedom, strong national defense, and traditional American values. The Immigration Project works on policies that would help welcome newcomers but at the same time ensure that newcomers embrace America's civic culture and democratic institutions.

FAIR: The Federation for American Immigration Reform

http://www.fairus.org

FAIR is a national, public-interest, nonprofit organization of citizens who are concerned that the nation's immigration policies must be reformed in the national interest. FAIR seeks to improve border security, stop illegal immigration, and to promote immigration levels consistent with national interest. Its publications and research are used by academics and government officials.

Center for Comparative Immigration Studies—University of California at San Diego

www.ccis-ucsd.org

CCIS is an organized research unit of the University of California at San Diego. It is an interdisciplinary and international research and training program devoted to comparative work on international migration and refugee movements. Its primary focus is cross-national policy-oriented research and to disseminate its conducted research to academics, policy-makers, and NGOs through conferences, seminars, and publications.

Russell Sage Foundation

www.russellsage.org

The Foundation is involved in the conduct and publication of social science research. Its program on U.S. immigration focuses on the entry of immigrants into political and civic life in the United States and the immigrant experience outside of traditional gateway cities.

CATO Institute

www.cato.org

The CATO Institute is a nonprofit, free-market, libertarian-oriented research think tank that seeks to promote the values of limited government, individual liberty, free markets, and peace into public policy. Its Center for Trade Policy Studies conducts studies on immigration and supports the greater free movement of peoples.

Migration Policy Institute

http://www.migrationpolicy.org

The MPI is an influential Washington, D.C.-based independent nonprofit and nonpartisan institute dedicated to the study of the international movement of people worldwide. It provides research and analysis that is used by academics and legislators alike to help make informed public policy decisions about immigration.

International Migration Institute

http://www.imi.ox.ac.uk

This Oxford University Institute is committed to developing a long-term and comprehensive perspective on global migration dynamics, including to developing new theoretical and methodological approaches and strengthening global capacity for ongoing research to adapt to changing patterns and processes of migration.

Center for International and European Law on Immigration and Asylum

http://migration.uni-konstanz.de/content/index.php?lang=en

Based at the University of Konstanz, in Germany, this research center aims to help develop a common framework for migration and asylum law through its various research projects and conferences.

Population Studies Center—University of Michigan

http://www.psc.isr.umich.edu/
The center engages in research and training on a number of population-related issues including urbanization and cities as well as immigration and internal migration in the United States.

International Center for Migration, Ethnicity and Citizenship—New School University

http://www.newschool.edu/icmec
The center carries out research on issues of international migration, ethnic groups, and citizenship, and emphasizes a cross-disciplinary approach. The research projects focus on refugee flows internationally and policy responses, incorporation and citizenship issues, and the impact of immigration on U.S. cities

Institute for the Study of International Migration—Georgetown University

http://www.isim.georgetown.edu
The institute focuses on all forms of international migration, including the causes of international migration and the possible policy responses, immigration and refugee laws and policies, and the comparative analysis of migration policies, the impact of international migration on social policy, economic policy, foreign policy, and demographics.

Centre for Refugee Studies—York University, Canada

http://www.yorku.ca/crs
Canada's York University's Centre for Refugee Studies fosters interdisciplinary research in migration studies, human rights, refugee rights, poverty and gender studies, and their relationships with development, globalization, the environment, and conflict.

Centre of Excellence for Research on Immigration and Diversity—University of British Columbia, Canada

http://www.riim.metropolis.net
This institute focuses on the impact of Canadian immigrants on local economies, families, educational systems and physical infrastructures in urban areas. Current research looks at immigrant integration into schools, ethnic identity, language, labor market, and gender issues.

Centre for the Study of Migration—University College London

http://www.politics.qmul.ac.uk/migration/index.html
The centre's research focuses on all aspects of migration, including emigration and immigration processes, ethnic identity, and racial discrimination.

Migration Research Unit—University of London

http://www.geog.ucl.ac.uk/mru
The center carries out research on migration at the national, European, and international levels and focuses on the relationships between public policy and patterns of migration. It

pays particular attention to asylum, refugees, brain drains and gains, return migration, and labor migration.

Sussex Centre for Migration Research—University of Sussex

http://www.sussex.ac.uk/migration
The center focuses on migration issues, diasporas, transnational communities, and development and migration policies.

Centre on Migration, Policy and Society—University of Oxford

http://www.compas.ox.ac.uk
The center undertakes interdisciplinary research on key themes of global migration and seeks to understand the relationships between international relations and global political economy and migrants' perceptions.

European Association for Population Studies

http://www.eaps.nl
The institute is primarily concerned with migration studies in Europe, including internal migration in Europe, international migration to Europe, and demographic transitions in Europe.

European Research Center on Migration and Ethnic Relations

http://www.ercomer.org
The center promotes comparative research on migration, interethnic relations, discrimination, ethnic conflicts, minorities, and social exclusion, with a specific focus on the region of Europe.

IMMIGRATION AND HUMAN RIGHTS

American Civil Liberties Union (ACLU)—Immigrant's Rights Section

http://www.aclu.org/immigrants/index.html
The ACLU is committed to protecting Americans' First Amendment rights, the right to equal protection under the law, the right to due process, and the right to privacy. The ACLU takes up cases where there is perceived infringement against the freedoms and rights of both documented and undocumented immigrants in the country.

Amnesty International U.S.A.

http://www.amnestyusa.org
AI is a Nobel Prize-winning grassroots international organization that monitors and reports on abuses of human rights across the globe. It has over 1.8 million members worldwide. It undertakes research and action to improve rights and freedoms of individuals around the world. It gives attention to women's human rights, issues of torture and disappearances, extrajudicial executions, peacekeeping, and internal displacements. It also addresses migration within the above contexts.

Human Rights Watch

http://www.hrw.org

Human Rights Watch is an international organization that seeks to protect human rights of people around the world. They support activists in preventing discrimination, upholding freedom, and protecting people from crimes during wartime, and investigate human rights violations. HRW also documents abuses against migrants crossing borders, including labor exploitation, discrimination, physical and sexual abuse, forced labor, arbitrary imprisonment, and denial of asylum issues.

U.S. Committee for Refugees and Immigrants

www.refugees.org

The U.S. Committee for Refugees and Immigrants addresses the needs and rights of people in forced or voluntary migration around the world by advancing fair and humane public policy, facilitating direct professional services, and promoting the full participation of migrants in community life.

National Immigrant Justice Center

http://www.immigrantjustice.org

The NIJC is dedicated to ensuring human rights protection and access to justice for all immigrants, refugees, and asylum seekers. It provides direct legal services to these groups and advocates on behalf of these groups through education, policy reform proposals, and impact litigation.

American Friends Service Committee

http://www.afsc.org/ImmigrantsRights

The American Friends Service Committee is a Quaker-based organization committed to nonviolence and justice and is dedicated to development, social justice, and world peace. It does international work that also involves improving the conditions of social justice for migrants.

National Network for Immigrant and Refugee Rights

http://www.nnirr.org

The National Network for Immigrant and Refugee Rights is a national organization that is made up of local immigrant, refugee, community, religious and civil society, and labor groups to educate communities and the general public on immigration-related issues.

American Immigration Law Foundation

http://www.ailf.org

The American Immigration Law Foundation works to increase understanding in the United States of immigration law and policy and the value of immigration to U.S. society and advocates fairness under the law. It offers support for litigation in this area.

International Rescue Committee

http://www.theirc.org

The IRC is a global network of first responders, humanitarian relief workers, educators, health care providers, community leaders, activists, and volunteers committed to providing safety, sanctuary, and sustainable change to millions of people around the world whose lives are destroyed by violence and oppression.

International Committee of the Red Cross

http://www.icrc.org
The Red Cross is mandated by the Geneva Conventions to provide assistance and humanitarian relief to victims of conflict and internal violence.

NEWS SOURCES AND WEBLOGS ON IMMIGRATION

FOX News on Immigration

http://www.foxnews.com/specialsections/immigration

CNN News on Immigration

http://edition.cnn.com/ELECTION/2008/issues/issues.immigration.html

Lou Dobbs of CNN on Immigration

http://Loudobbs.tv.cnn.com

Immigration News Blog—Institute for Research on Labor and Employment Library

http://iirl-immigration-news.blogspot.com
The blog provides information on immigrants and employment and the contribution of immigrants to the economy

The Immigration Blog by Michelle Malkin

http://michellemalkin.com/immigration
The blog provides a more conservative and skeptical view of immigration and immigrants.

Immigration Prof Blog—A Member of the Law Professors Blog Network

http://lawprofessors.typepad.com/immigration
The blog provides information about immigration and law.

Immigration Blog of the Houston Chronicle

http://blogs.chron.com/immigration
The Houston Chronicle blog covers the immigration issue.

National Immigrant Justice Center Blog

http://www.immigrantjustice.org/blog
The blog of NIJC.

Immigration Law Reform Blog

http://immigrationlawreformblog.blogspot.com
The blog discusses immigration reform proposals.

Immigration Blog of the Orange County (California) Register

http://immigration.freedomblogging.com/
Blog of the OC Register.

Blogs for Borders

http://blogs4borders.blogspot.com
The blog is concerned with border security issues.

FILMS ON IMMIGRATION

The immigration debate has received a great deal of attention in the print, television, radio, and Internet media. There have also been a growing number of popular films and documentaries that address immigration. Below is a sample of some that touch upon the immigration theme.

Documentaries

Island of Hope—Island of Tears: The Story of Ellis Island: The American Immigration Experience (Produced by Charles Guggenheim, presented by National Park Service, U.S. Department of the Interior; 2004)

Wetback: The Undocumented Documentary (Produced by Heather Haynes, Act Now Productions; 2005)

The Ties that Bind: Immigration in the United States (Directed by Jose Roberto Guttierez, produced by Maryknoll World Productions; 1996)

Immigration by the Numbers (Produced by Roy Howard Beck, The Social Contract Press; 1997)

Border War: The Battle over Illegal Immigration (Directed by Kevin Knoblock, Genius Entertainment; 2006)

La ciudad / The City (Directed by David Riker, North Star Films, New Yorker Video; 1998, 2000)

Cochise County, USA: Cries from the Border (Directed by Mercedes Maharis, Genius Products; 2005)

Death on a Friendly Border (Directed by Rachel Antell, Filmakers Library; 2001)

The Other Side / El otro lado (Directed by Christopher Walker, BBC, Bullfrog Films; 2001)

The Other Side of the Border (PBS; 1988)

Destination America: U.S. Immigration (PBS; 2005)

Popular Films

Under the Same Moon (Director: Patricia Riggen; 2007)
Crossing Arizona (Director: Josephy Mathew; 2005)
Maria Full of Grace (Director: Joshua Marston; 2004)

The Terminal (Director: Steven Spielberg; 2004)

Lost Boys of Sudan (Directors: Megan Mylan and Jon Shenk; 2003)

Gangs of New York (Director: Martin Scorsese; 2002)

Bend It Like Beckham (Director: Gurinder Chadha; 2002)

Monsoon Wedding (Director: Mira Nair; 2000)

Tortilla Soup (Director: Maria Ripoll; 2000)

The Perez Family (Director: Mira Nair; 1995)

Moscow on the Hudson (Director: Paul Mazursky; 1984)

El Norte (Director: Gregory Nava; 1983)

Bibliography

Abrams, Jim. "Congress Looks to Boost U.S. Tourism." *Washington Post*. July 5, 2007.

Ackerman, Kenneth. *Boss Tweed: The Rise and Fall of the Corrupt Pol Who Conceived the Soul of Modern New York*. New York: Carroll and Graf, 2005.

Adams, John. *Bordering the Future: The Impact of Mexico on the United States*. Westport, CT: Praeger, 2006.

Alba, Richard. *Remaking the American Mainstream: Assimilation and Contemporary Immigration*. Cambridge: Harvard University Press, 2003.

Andreas, Peter, and Timothy Snyder, eds. *The Wall Around the West: State Borders and Immigration Controls in North America and Europe*. Lanham, MD: Rowman and Littlefield, 2000.

Anrig, Greg, Jr., and Tova Andrea Wang. *Immigration's New Frontiers: Experiences from the Emerging Gateway States*. Century Foundation Press, 2006.

Ashbee, Edward, Helene Balsley Clausen, and Carl Pedersen. *The Politics, Economics and Culture of Mexican-U.S. Migration: Both Sides of the Border*. New York: Palgrave, 2007.

Bean, Frank, and Stephanie Bell-Rose, eds. *Immigration and Opportunity: Race, Ethnicity And Employment in the United States*. New York: Russell Sage, 1999.

Bean, Frank, et al. eds. *At the Crossroads: Mexico and U.S. Immigration Policy*. Lanham, MD: Rowman and Littlefield, 1997.

Bennett, David, *The Party of Fear: From Nativist Movements to the New Right in American History*, Chapel Hill: University of North Carolina Press, 1988.

Bischoff, Henry. *Immigration Issues*. Westport, CT: Greenwood Press, 2002.

Borjas, George. *Heaven's Door: Immigration Policy and the American Economy*. Princeton: Princeton University Press, 2001.

Borjas, George J., ed. *Issues in the Economics of Immigration*, Chicago: University of Chicago Press, 2000.

Borjas, George J., ed. *Mexican Immigration to the United States*, Chicago: University of Chicago Press, 2007.

Briggs, Vernon. *Mass Immigration and the National Interest: Policy Directions for the New Century*. 3rd edition. Armonk, New York: M.E. Sharpe, 2003.

Brown, Mary Elizabeth. *Shapers of the Great Debate on Immigration: A Biographical Dictionary*. Westport, CT: Greenwood Press, 1999.

Brownstone, David, and Irene Franck. *Facts about American Immigration*. New York: H.M. Wilson, 2001.

Burns, Vincent, and Kate Dempsey Peterson. *Terrorism: A Documentary and Reference Guide*. Westport, CT: Greenwood, 2005.

Camarota, Steven. *Immigration from Mexico: Assessing the Impact of the United States*. Washington, DC: Center for Immigration Studies, 2001.

Carless, Will. "Hate Crime Spikes, According to Latest Figures." *Voice of San Diego*, Jan 21, 2008.

Chang, Gordon. *Asian Americans and Politics: Perspectives, Experiences, Prospects*. Palo Alto: Stanford University Press, 2001.

Chomsky, Aviva. *"They Take Our Jobs!" and 20 Other Myths about Immigration*. Boston: Beacon Press, 2007.

Ciment, James, ed. *Encyclopedia of American Immigration*. Armonk: M.E. Sharpe, 2001.

Ciongoli, Kenneth, and Jay Parini. *Passage to Liberty: The Story of Italian Immigration and the Rebirth of America*. New York: Regan Books, 2002.

Clarke, Duncan. *A New World: The History of Immigration into the United States*. San Diego, CA: Thunder Bay Press, 2000.

Cornelius, Wayne, et al., eds. *Controlling Immigration: A Global Perspective*. Stanford: Stanford University Press, 2004.

Croddy, Marshall. *The Immigration Debate: Historical and Current Issues of Immigration*. 2nd edition. Los Angeles: Constitutional Rights Foundation, 2003.

Daniels, Roger. *Coming to America: A History of Immigration and Ethnicity in American Life*. 2nd edition. New York: Harper Collins, 2002.

Daniels, Roger. *Guarding the Golden Door: American Immigration Policy and Immigrants since 1882*. New York: Hill and Wang, 2004.

Daniels, Roger, and Harry Kitano. *Debating American Immigration, 1882-Present*. Lanham, MD: Rowman and Littlefield, 2003.

DeLaet, Debra. *U.S. Immigration Policy in an Age of Rights*. Westport, CT: Praeger, 2000.

Dinnerstein, Leonard, and David Reimers. *Ethnic Americans*. 4th Edition. New York: Columbia University Press, 1999.

Duignan, Peter, and L.H. Gann, eds. *The Debate in the United States over Immigration*. Stanford: Hoover Institution, 1998.

Dummett, Michael, *On Immigration and Refugees*. New York: Routledge, 2001.

Edmonston, Barry, ed. *Statistics on U.S. Immigration: An Assessment of Data Needs for Future Research*. National Academy Press, 1996.

Eldredge, Dirk Chase. *Crowded Land of Liberty: Solving America's Immigration Crisis*. Bridgehampton, New York: Bridge Works Publications, 2001.

Farnam, Julie. *U.S. Immigration Laws Under the Threat of Terrorism*. New York: Algora, 2005.

Fernandes, Deepa. *Targeted: Homeland Security and the Business of Immigration*. New York: Seven Stories Press, 2007.

Fischer, Claude, and Michael Hout. *Century of Difference: How America Changed in the Last One Hundred Years*. Russell Sage Foundation, 2006.

Florida, Richard. "America's Looming Creativity Crisis." *Harvard Business Review*. October 2004.

Foner, Nancy. *From Ellis Island to JFK: New York's Two Great Waves of Immigration*. New Haven: Yale University Press, 2000.

Gabaccia, Donna. *Immigration and American Diversity. A Social and Cultural History*. Malden, MA: Blackwell, 2002.

Gerdes, Louise I., ed. *Immigration*. San Diego, CA: Greenhaven Press, 2005.

Gerstle, Gary, and John Mollenkopf, eds. *E Pluribus Unum? Contemporary and Historical Perspectives on Immigrant Political Incorporation*. New York: Russell Sage, 2001.

Gibney, Matthew, and Randall Hansen, eds. *Immigration and Asylum: From 1900 to The Present*. Santa Barbara: ABC-CLIO, 2005.

Gimpel, James, and James Edwards. *The Congressional Politics of Immigration Reform*. Boston: Allyn and Bacon, 1999.

Graham, Otis. *Unguarded Gates: A History of America's Immigration Crisis*. Lanham, MD: Rowman and Littlefield, 2004.

Haerens, Margaret, ed. *Illegal Immigration*. Detroit : Greenhaven Press, 2006.

Haines, David, and Karen Rosenblum, eds. *Illegal Immigration in America: A Reference Handbook*. Westport, CT: Greenwood, 1999.

Harris, Nigel. *Thinking the Unthinkable: The Immigration Myth Exposed*. London: I.B. Taurus, 2002.

Hayes, Helene. *U.S. Immigration Policy and the Undocumented: Ambivalent Lives, Furtive Lives*. Westport, CT: Praeger, 2001.

Hayter, Teresa. *Open Borders: The Case Against Immigration Controls*. 2nd Ed. London: Pluto Press, 2004.

Hayworth, John D., and Joseph Eule. *Whatever It Takes: Illegal Immigration, Border Security, and the War on Terror*. Washington, DC: Regnery, 2006.

Hing, Bill Ong. *Deporting our Souls: Values, Morality and Immigration Policy*. Cambridge: Cambridge University Press, 2006.

Hing, Bill Ong, *Defining America through Immigration Policy*. Philadelphia: Temple University Press, 2004.

Hing, Bill Ong. *Immigration and the Law: A Dictionary*. Santa Barbara, CA: ABC-CLIO, 1999.

Hirschman, Charles, Philip Kasinitz, and Josh DeWind, eds. *The Handbook of International Migration: The American Experience*. New York: Russell Sage, 1999.

Huntington, Samuel. *Who Are We? The Challenges to America's National Identity*. New York: Simon and Schuster, 2004.

Jacobson, David, ed. *The Immigration Reader: America in a Multidisciplinary Perspective*. Malden, MA: Blackwell, 1998.

Jaynes, Gerald. *Immigration and Race: New Challenges for American Democracy*. New Haven: Yale University Press, 2000.

Johnson, Kevin. *Opening the Floodgates: Why America Needs to Rethink its Borders and Immigration Laws*. New York: NYU Press, 2007.

Johnson, Paul. *A History of the American People*. New York: Harper Collins, 1997.

Jones, Maldwyn A. *The Limits of Liberty: American History, 1607–1992*. Second edition. Oxford: Oxford University Press, 1995.

Kanstroom, Daniel. *Deportation Nation: Outsiders in American History*. Cambridge, MA: Harvard University Press, 2007.

King, Desmond. *Making Americans: Immigration, Race, and the Origins of the Diverse Democracy*. Cambridge, MA: Harvard University Press, 2000.

King, Richard, ed. *Postcolonial America*. Urbana, IL: University of Illinois Press, 2000.

Knowles, Valerie. *Strangers at our Gates: Canadian Immigration and Immigration Policy, 1540-2006*. Toronto and Tonawanda, New York: Dundurn, 2007.

Lee, Erika. *At America's Gates: Chinese Immigration during the Exclusion Era, 1882-1943*. Chapel Hill: University of North Carolina Press, 2003.

Lemay, Michael. *Illegal Immigration: A Reference Handbook*. Santa Barbara, CA: ABC-CLIO, 2007.

Lemay, Michael. *Guarding the Gates: Immigration and National Security*. Westport, CT: Praeger, 2006.

Lemay, Michael. *U.S. Immigration: A Reference Handbook*. Santa Barbara, CA: ABC-CLIO, 2004.

Lin, Ann Chih, and Nicole Green, eds. *Immigration*. Washington, DC: CQ Press, 2002.

Loucky, James, Jeanne Armstrong, and Larry Estrada, eds. *Immigration in America Today: An Encyclopedia*. Westport, CT: Greenwood, 2006.

Lynch, James, and Rita Simon. *Immigration the World Over: Statutes, Policies, and Practices.* Lanham, MD: Rowman and Littlefield, 2003.

MacDonald, Heather, Victor Davis Hanson, and Steven Malanga, *The Immigration Solution: A Better Plan than Today's.* Chicago: Ivan R. Dee, 2007.

Magana, Lisa. *Straddling the Border: Immigration Policy and the INS.* Austin: University of Texas Press, 2003.

Martin, Philip, and Peter Duignan. *Making and Remaking America: Immigration into the United States.* Stanford: Hoover Institution, 2003.

Martinez, Jr., Ramiro, and Abel Valenzuela, Jr. *Immigration and Crime: Race, Ethnicity, and Violence.* New York: New York University Press, 2006.

Massey, Douglas, Jorge Durand, and Nolan Malone. *Beyond Smoke and Mirrors: Mexican Immigration in an Era of Economic Integration.* New York: Russell Sage, 2002.

McCaffrey Paul, ed. *Hispanic Americans.* New York: H.H. Wilson Co, 2007.

McPherson, James M. *Battle Cry of Freedom: The Civil War Era.* New York: Ballantine Books, 1988.

Mendoza, Louis, and S. Shankar, eds. *Crossing into America: The New Literature of Immigration.* New York: W.W. Norton, 2003.

Miller, Debra A., ed. *Illegal Immigration.* Detroit: Greenhaven, 2007.

Min, Pyong Gap, ed. *Mass Migration to the United States: Classical and Contemporary Periods.* Walnut Creek, CA: Altamira Press, 2002.

Morison, Samuel Eliot. *The Oxford History of the American People. Volume II: 1789 through Reconstruction.* London: Meridian, 1994.

Muller, Thomas. *Immigrants and the American City.* New York: NYU Press, 1993.

Myers, Ernest, ed. *Challenges of a Changing America: Perspectives on Immigration and Multiculturalism in the United States.* San Francisco: Caddo Gap, 2001.

Navarrette, Ruben, Jr. "English-Only Laws Serve to Divide." *San Diego Union-Tribune,* December 6, 2007.

Newton, Lina. *Illegal, Alien or Immigrant: The Politics of Immigration Reform.* New York: NYU Press, 2007.

Ngai, Mae M. *Impossible Subjects: Immigration and the Making of Modern America.* Princeton: Princeton University Press, 2004.

Ono, Kent, and John Sloop. *Shifting Borders: Rhetoric, Immigration, and California's Proposition 187.* Philadelphia: Temple University Press, 2002.

Park, John. *Elusive Citizenship: Immigration, Asia Americans, and the Paradox of Civil Rights.* New York: NYU Press, 2004.

Parry, Wayne. "Report Says Bias Against Muslims Up in 2004." *Seattle Times,* May 11, 2005.

Passel, Jeffrey. *The Size and Characteristics of the Unauthorized Migrant Population in the US: Estimates Based on the March 2005 Current Population Survey.* Pew Hispanic Center, March 7, 2006.

Portes, Alejandro, and Ruben Rumbaut. *Immigrant America: A Portrait.* Third edition. Berkeley: University of California Press, 2006.

Proper, Emberson Edward. *Colonial Immigration Laws: A Study of the Regulation of Immigration by the English Colonies in America.* New York: Columbia University Press, 1900.

Ramer, Holly. "Immigration a Big Issue to NH, Iowa GOP." Associated Press, Dec. 17 2007.

Reimers, David. *Unwelcome Strangers: American Identity and the Turn Against Immigration.* New York: Columbia University Press, 1998.

Renshon, Stanley. *The 50% American: Immigration and National Identity in the Age of Terror.* Washington, DC: Georgetown, 2005.

Robbins, Albert. *Coming to America: Immigrants from Northern Europe.* New York: Delacort Press, 1981.

Robertson, Gary. "Easley: Community Colleges Should Admit Illegal Immigrants." *Charlotte Observer*, May 8, 2008.

Rodriguez, Gregory. *Mongrels, Bastards, Orphans, and Vagabonds: Mexican Immigration and the Future of Race in America*. New York: Pantheon, 2007.

Roleff, Tamara, ed. *Immigration*. San Diego: Greenhaven, 2004.

Romano, Benjamin. "Mr. Gates Goes to Washington as Microsoft Gets More H-1Bs than Any U.S. Tech." *Seattle Times*, March 11, 2008.

Romero, Victor. *Alienated: Immigrant Rights, the Constitution, and Equality in America*. New York: NYU Press, 2005.

Rosenblum, Marc. *The Transnational Politics of U.S. Immigration Policy*. La Jolla, CA: Center for Comparative Immigration Studies-UCSD, 2004.

Rutenberg, Jim. "Karl Rove, Top Bush Aid, to Step Down." *International Herald Tribune*, August 13, 2007.

Schlesinger, Arthur Meier. "The Rise of the City, 1878-1898." In *The Historians' History of the United States*. Volume 2, edited by Andrew Bersky and James Shenton. New York: G.P. Putnam and Sons, 1966.

Shanks, Cheryl. *Immigration and the Politics of American Sovereignty, 1890-1990*. Ann Arbor: University of Michigan Press, 2001.

Shea, Therese. *Immigration to America: Identifying Different Points of View about an Issue*. New York: Rosen Publishing Group, 2006.

Shulman, Steven, ed. *The Impact of Immigration on African Americans*. New Brunswick, NJ: Transaction, 2004.

Spagat, Elliot. "Judge Temporarily Blocks SoCal City's Anti-Illegal Immigrant Law." *San Francisco Chronicle*, November 16, 2006.

Spencer, Sarah, ed. *The Politics of Migration*. Oxford: Blackwell, 2003.

Spickard, Paul. *Almost All Aliens: Immigration, Race, and Colonialism in American History and Identity*. New York: Routledge, 2007.

Suarez-Orozco, Marcelo, Carola Suarez-Orozco, and Desiree Baolian Qin, eds. *The New Immigration: An Interdisciplinary Reader*. New York: Routledge, 2005.

Suro, Roberto. *Strangers Among Us: How Latino Immigration Is Transforming America*. New York: Alfred Knopf, 1998.

Swain, Carol, ed. *Debating Immigration*. New York: Cambridge University Press, 2007.

Tichenor, Daniel. *Dividing Lines: The Politics of Immigration Control in America*. Princeton: Princeton University Press, 2002.

Tong, Benson. *The Chinese Americans*. Boulder: University of Colorado Press, 2003.

Trueba, Enrique. *The New Americans: Immigrants and Transnationals at Work*. Lanham: Rowman and Littlefield, 2004.

Ueda, Reed, ed. *A Companion to American Immigration*. Oxford: Blackwell, 2006.

Waters, Mary C., and Reed Ueta (with Helen Marrow). *The New Americans: A Guide To Immigration since 1965*. Cambridge, MA: Harvard, 2007.

Williams, Mary E., ed. *Immigration: Opposing Viewpoints*. San Diego, CA: Greenhaven Press, 2004.

Wucker, Michelle. *Lockout: Why America Keeps Getting Immigration Wrong When Our Prosperity Depends on Getting It Right*. New York: Public Affairs, 2006.

Yoshida, Chisato. *The Economics of Illegal Immigration*. New York: Palgrave, 2005.

Zinn, Howard. *A People's History of the United States, 1492-Present*. New York: Harper Collins, 1999.

Zolberg, Aristide. *A Nation by Design: Immigration Policy in the Fashioning of America*. New York: Russell Sage, 2006.

Zuniga, Victor, and Ruben Hernandez-Leon. *New Destinations: Mexican Immigration in the United States*. New York: Russell Sage, 2005.

Index

About the Authors

THOMAS CIESLIK is Assistant Professor of International Relations at the University of Wurtzburg, Germany.

DAVID FELSEN is Assistant Professor of International Relations at the Marshall Goldsmith School of Management, Alliant International University, San Diego, CA.

AKIS KALAITZIDIS is Assistant Professor of Political Science at the University of Central Missouri.